Second Workshop on Language Technologies for Historical and Ancient Languages (LT4HALA 2022)

Held at LREC 2022

Marseille, France
25 June 2022

Editors:

Rachele Sprugnoli
Marco Passarotti

ISBN: 978-1-7138-6127-0

Printed from e-media with permission by:

Curran Associates, Inc.
57 Morehouse Lane
Red Hook, NY 12571

Some format issues inherent in the e-media version may also appear in this print version.

Association for Computational Linguistics
209 N. Eighth Street
Stroudsburg, Pennsylvania 18360

Phone: 1-570-476-8006
Fax: 1-570-476-0860

acl@aclweb.org

Additional copies of this publication are available from:

Curran Associates, Inc.
57 Morehouse Lane
Red Hook, NY 12571 USA
Phone: 845-758-0400
Fax: 845-758-2633
Email: curran@proceedings.com
Web: www.proceedings.com

LREC 2022 Workshop
Language Resources and Evaluation Conference
20-25 June 2022

Second Workshop on Language Technologies for Historical and Ancient Languages (LT4HALA 2022)

PROCEEDINGS

Editors: Rachele Sprugnoli and Marco Passarotti

Proceedings of the LREC 2022 Second Workshop on Language Technologies for Historical and Ancient Languages LT4HALA 2022

Edited by: Rachele Sprugnoli and Marco Passarotti

For more information:
European Language Resources Association (ELRA)
9 rue des Cordelières
75013, Paris
France
http://www.elra.info
Email: lrec@elda.org

Preface

These proceedings include the papers accepted for presentation at the Second Workshop on Language Technologies for Historical and Ancient Languages (LT4HALA 2022).[1] The workshop was held on June 25th 2022 in Marseille, France, co-located with the 13th Edition of the Language Resources and Evaluation Conference (LREC).[2]

The workshop wants to provide a venue to discuss research works on a wide range of topics concerning the building, analysis, exploitation and distribution of collections of digitized texts written in historical and ancient languages, with a specific focus on the development and application of Language Technologies (LTs) for such purposes.

The topics of the workshop are strictly bound to the peculiar characteristics of textual data for historical and ancient languages, which set them apart from modern languages, with a significant impact on LTs. Among the topics covered by the workshop are issues about the digitization process of textual sources, like handling spelling variation, and detecting and correcting OCR errors. Also concerned are questions about the automatic processing of various layers of metalinguistic annotation, which are made complex by the sparsity and inconsistency of texts that present considerable orthographic variation, are sometimes incomplete and belong to a large spectrum of literary genres. Such issues raise problems of adaptation of Natural Language Processing (NLP) tools to address diachronic/diatopic/diastratic variation in texts, which requires to be properly evaluated.

The various LTs tasks related to the topics of LT4HALA require a strict collaboration between scholars from different disciplinary areas. In such respect, the objective of the LT4HALA workshop series is to foster cross-fertilization between the Computational Linguistics community and the areas in the Humanities dealing with historical linguistic data, e.g. historians, philologists, linguists, archaeologists and literary scholars. Such a wide and diverse range of disciplines and scholars involved in the development and use of LTs for historical and ancient languages is mirrored by the large set of topics covered by the papers published in these proceedings, including the creation of annotated corpora and advanced computational lexical resources for historical languages, the development of models for performing various NLP tasks, the application of machine translation and linguistic analyses based on the empirical evidence provided by textual resources.

As large as the number of topics discussed in the papers is that of the either ancient/dead languages or the historical varieties of modern/living ones concerned. In total, the languages tackled in the proceedings are the following: Latin, Italian, Japanese, Chinese, Hungarian, French, Spanish, German, Portuguese, Dutch, Vedic Sanskrit, Ancient Greek (and Cypro-Greek), Ancient Hebrew, Maya, Umbrian and a set of languages of ancient Italy, namely Oscan, Faliscan, Celtic and Venetic.

In the call for papers, we invited to submit proposals of different types, such as experimental papers, reproduction papers, resource papers, position papers and survey papers. We asked both for long and short papers describing original and unpublished work. We defined as suitable long papers (up to 8 pages, plus references) those that describe substantial completed research and/or report on the development of new methodologies. Short papers (up to 4 pages, plus references) were instead more appropriate for reporting on works in progress or for describing a singular tool or project. We encouraged the authors of papers reporting experimental results to make their results reproducible and the entire process of analysis replicable, by distributing the data and the tools they used. Like for LREC, the submission process was single-blind. Each paper was reviewed but three independent reviewers from a program committee made of 24 scholars (12 women and 12 men) from 16 countries. In total, we received 24 submissions from 56 authors from institutions located in 10 countries: Italy (24 authors), Japan (7 authors), Switzerland (6 authors), Germany (5 authors), United States (4 authors), Belgium (3 authors), France (3 authors), Sweden (3 authors), Denmark (1 author), Spain (1 author). After the reviewing process, we accepted 18 submissions, leading to an acceptance rate of 75%.

[1] https://circse.github.io/LT4HALA/2022/

[2] https://lrec2022.lrec-conf.org/en/

LT4HALA 2022 was also the venue of the second edition of EvaLatin, the campaign devoted to the evaluation of NLP tools for Latin.[3] EvaLatin was started in 2020 (co-located with the first edition of LT4HALA) considering the important role played by textual data and linguistic metadata in the study of historical and ancient languages, with a special focus on Latin due to its prominence among such languages, both for the size and for the degree of diversity of its texts. Running evaluation campaigns in such a scenario is essential to understand the level of accuracy of the NLP tools used to build and analyze resources featuring texts that show those peculiar characteristics mentioned above. The second edition of EvaLatin focussed on three shared tasks (i.e. Lemmatization, PoS Tagging, Morphological Features Tagging), each featuring three sub-tasks (i.e. Classical, Cross-Genre, Cross-Time). These sub-tasks were designed to measure the impact of genre and diachrony on NLP tools performances, a relevant aspect to keep in mind when dealing with the diachronic and diatopic diversity of Latin texts, which are spread across a time span of two millennia all over Europe. Participants were provided with shared data in the CoNLL-U format and all the necessary evaluation scripts. They were required to submit a technical report for each task (with all the related sub-tasks) they took part in. The maximum length of the reports was 4 pages (plus references). In total, 2 technical reports of EvaLatin, corresponding to as many participants, are included in these proceedings. All reports received a light review by the organizers to check the correctness of the format, the exactness of the results and ranking reported, as well as the overall exposition. The proceedings also feature a paper detailing some specific aspects of the second edition of EvaLatin, like dataset, annotation criteria and results of the shared tasks.

Besides EvaLatin, LT4HALA 2022 hosted also the first edition of EvaHan, an evaluation campaign of NLP tools for the Ancient Chinese language, organized by a team of scholars directed by Bin Li (School of Chinese Language and Literature, Nanjing Normal University), which includes Yiguo Yuan (Nanjing Normal University), Minxuan Feng (Nanjing Normal University), Chao Xu (Nanjing Normal University) and Dongbo Wang (Nanjing Agricultural University).[4] EvaHan focussed on one joint task of Word Segmentation and PoS Tagging. Test data of Ancient Chinese, which is dated back around 1000BC-221BC, were provided in raw format, featuring only Chinese characters and punctuation. The participants were provided with two sets of test data, to evaluate the accuracy rates of the systems respectively on data excerpted from the same work (the Zuozhuan book) included in the training set, without overlapping, and on data from another, yet similar, text. A pretrained model consisting in word embeddings built over a large corpus of traditional Chinese was provided as well. In total, 9 technical reports of EvaHan, corresponding to as many participants, are included in these proceedings. Like for Evalatin, all reports received a light review by the organizers of EvaHan and the proceedings include a short paper with the details of the campaign.

We are grateful to the organizers of EvaHan, who contributed to extend the range of historical and ancient languages of the LT4HALA workshop and showed how some NLP-related issues concern ancient and historical languages per se, despite their typological differences.

Rachele Sprugnoli
Marco Passarotti

[3] `https://circse.github.io/LT4HALA/2022/EvaLatin`

[4] `https://circse.github.io/LT4HALA/2022/EvaHan`

Organizers:

Rachele Sprugnoli, Università degli Studi di Parma (Italy)
Marco Passarotti, Università Cattolica del Sacro Cuore (Italy)

Program Committee:

Marcel Bollmann, University of Copenhagen (Denmark)
Gerlof Bouma, University of Gothenburg (Sweden)
Harry Diakoff, Alpheios Project (USA)
Stefanie Dipper, Ruhr-Universität Bochum (Germany)
Hanne Eckhoff, Oxford University (UK)
Margherita Fantoli, University of Leuven (Belgium)
Heidi Jauhiainen, University of Helsinki (Finland)
Neven Jovanovic, University of Zagreb (Croatia)
Timo Korkiakangas, University of Helsinki (Finland)
Bin Li, Nanjing Normal University (P.R. China)
Eleonora Litta, Università Cattolica del Sacro Cuore (Italy)
Chao-Lin Liu, National Chengchi University (Taiwan)
Barbara McGillivray, Turing Institute (UK)
Beáta Megyesi, Uppsala University (Sweden)
Giulia Pedonese, Università Cattolica del Sacro Cuore (Italy)
Saskia Peels, University of Groningen (The Netherlands)
Matteo Pellegrini, Università Cattolica del Sacro Cuore (Italy)
Eva Pettersson, Uppsala University (Sweden)
Sophie Prévost, Laboratoire Lattice (France)
Philippe Roelli, University of Zurich (Switzerland)
Matteo Romanello, Université de Lausanne (Switzerland)
Halim Sayoud, USTHB University (Algeria)
Dongbo Wang, Nanjing Agricultural University (P.R. China)

EvaLatin 2022 Organizers:

Rachele Sprugnoli, Università degli Studi di Parma (Italy)
Margherita Fantoli, KU Leuven (Belgium)
Flavio M. Cecchini, Università Cattolica del Sacro Cuore, Milan (Italy)
Marco Passarotti, Università Cattolica del Sacro Cuore, Milan (Italy)

EvaHan 2022 Organizers:

Bin Li, Nanjing Normal University (P.R. China)
Yiguo Yuan, Nanjing Normal University (P.R. China)
Minxuan Feng, Nanjing Normal University (P.R. China)
Chao Xu, Nanjing Normal University (P.R. China)
Dongbo Wang, Nanjing Agricultural University (P.R. China)

Table of Contents

Identifying Cleartext in Historical Ciphers
Maria-Elena Gambardella, Beata Megyesi and Eva Pettersson 1

Detecting Diachronic Syntactic Developments in Presence of Bias Terms
Oliver Hellwig and Sven Sellmer 10

Accurate Dependency Parsing and Tagging of Latin
Sebastian Nehrdich and Oliver Hellwig 20

Annotating "Absolute" Preverbs in the Homeric and Vedic Treebanks
Luca Brigada Villa, Erica Biagetti and Chiara Zanchi 26

CHJ-WLSP: Annotation of 'Word List by Semantic Principles' Labels for the Corpus of Historical Japanese
Masayuki Asahara, Nao Ikegami, Tai Suzuki, Taro Ichimura, Asuko Kondo, Sachi Kato and Makoto Yamazaki 31

The IKUVINA Treebank
Mathieu Dehouck 38

Machine Translation of 16Th Century Letters from Latin to German
Lukas Fischer, Patricia Scheurer, Raphael Schwitter and Martin Volk 43

A Treebank-based Approach to the Suprema Constructio in Dante's Latin Works
Flavio Massimiliano Cecchini and Giulia Pedonese 51

From Inscriptions to Lexica and Back: A Platform for Editing and Linking the Languages of Ancient Italy
Valeria Quochi, Andrea Bellandi, Fahad Khan, Michele Mallia, Francesca Murano, Silvia Piccini, Luca Rigobianco, Alessandro Tommasi and Cesare Zavattari 59

BERToldo, the Historical BERT for Italian
Alessio Palmero Aprosio, Stefano Menini and Sara Tonelli 68

In Search of the Flocks: How to Perform Onomasiological Queries in an Ancient Greek Corpus?
Alek Keersmaekers and Toon Van Hal 73

Contextual Unsupervised Clustering of Signs for Ancient Writing Systems
Michele Corazza, Fabio Tamburini, Miguel Valério and Silvia Ferrara 84

Towards the Creation of a Diachronic Corpus for Italian: A Case Study on the GDLI Quotations
Manuel Favaro, Elisa Guadagnini, Eva Sassolini, Marco Biffi and Simonetta Montemagni 94

Automatic Translation Alignment for Ancient Greek and Latin
Tariq Yousef, Chiara Palladino, David J. Wright and Monica Berti 101

Handling Stress in Finite-State Morphological Analyzers for Ancient Greek and Ancient Hebrew
Daniel Swanson and Francis Tyers 108

From Inscription to Semi-automatic Annotation of Maya Hieroglyphic Texts
Cristina Vertan and Christian Prager 114

Multilingual Named Entity Recognition for Medieval Charters Using Stacked Embeddings and Bert-based Models.
Sergio Torres Aguilar 119

Linguistic Annotation of Neo-Latin Mathematical Texts: A Pilot-Study to Improve the Automatic Parsing of the Archimedes Latinus
Margherita Fantoli and Miryam de Lhoneux 129

The First International Ancient Chinese Word Segmentation and POS Tagging Bakeoff: Overview of the EvaHan 2022 Evaluation Campaign
Bin Li, Yiguo Yuan, Jingya Lu, Minxuan Feng, Chao Xu, Weiguang QU and Dongbo Wang . . 135

Automatic Word Segmentation and Part-of-Speech Tagging of Ancient Chinese Based on BERT Model
Yu Chang, Peng Zhu, Chaoping Wang and Chaofan Wang 141

Ancient Chinese Word Segmentation and Part-of-Speech Tagging Using Data Augmentation
Yanzhi Tian and Yuhang Guo 146

BERT 4EVER@EvaHan 2022: Ancient Chinese Word Segmentation and Part-of-Speech Tagging Based on Adversarial Learning and Continual Pre-training
Hailin Zhang, Ziyu Yang, Yingwen Fu and Ruoyao Ding 150

Construction of Segmentation and Part of Speech Annotation Model in Ancient Chinese
Longjie Jiang, Qinyu C. Chang, Huyin H. Xie and Zhuying Z. Xia 155

Simple Tagging System with RoBERTa for Ancient Chinese
Binghao Tang, Boda Lin and Si Li 159

The Uncertainty-based Retrieval Framework for Ancient Chinese CWS and POS
Pengyu Wang and Zhichen Ren 164

Data Augmentation for Low-resource Word Segmentation and POS Tagging of Ancient Chinese Texts
Yutong Shen, Jiahuan Li, Shujian Huang, Yi Zhou, Xiaopeng Xie and Qinxin Zhao 169

A Joint Framework for Ancient Chinese WS and POS Tagging Based on Adversarial Ensemble Learning
Shuxun Yang 174

Glyph Features Matter: A Multimodal Solution for EvaHan in LT4HALA2022
Wei Xinyuan, liu Weihao, Qing Zong, zhang shao qing and Baotian Hu 178

Overview of the EvaLatin 2022 Evaluation Campaign
Rachele Sprugnoli, Marco Passarotti, Flavio Massimiliano Cecchini, Margherita Fantoli and Giovanni Moretti 183

An ELECTRA Model for Latin Token Tagging Tasks
Wouter Mercelis and Alek Keersmaekers 189

Transformer-based Part-of-Speech Tagging and Lemmatization for Latin
Krzysztof Wróbel and Krzysztof Nowak 193

Conference Program

Saturday, June 25, 2022

Long and Short Papers

Identifying Cleartext in Historical Ciphers
Maria-Elena Gambardella, Beata Megyesi and Eva Pettersson

Detecting Diachronic Syntactic Developments in Presence of Bias Terms
Oliver Hellwig and Sven Sellmer

Accurate Dependency Parsing and Tagging of Latin
Sebastian Nehrdich and Oliver Hellwig

Annotating "Absolute" Preverbs in the Homeric and Vedic Treebanks
Luca Brigada Villa, Erica Biagetti and Chiara Zanchi

CHJ-WLSP: Annotation of 'Word List by Semantic Principles' Labels for the Corpus of Historical Japanese
Masayuki Asahara, Nao Ikegami, Tai Suzuki, Taro Ichimura, Asuko Kondo, Sachi Kato and Makoto Yamazaki

The IKUVINA Treebank
Mathieu Dehouck

Machine Translation of 16Th Century Letters from Latin to German
Lukas Fischer, Patricia Scheurer, Raphael Schwitter and Martin Volk

A Treebank-based Approach to the Supprema Constructio in Dante's Latin Works
Flavio Massimiliano Cecchini and Giulia Pedonese

From Inscriptions to Lexica and Back: A Platform for Editing and Linking the Languages of Ancient Italy
Valeria Quochi, Andrea Bellandi, Fahad Khan, Michele Mallia, Francesca Murano, Silvia Piccini, Luca Rigobianco, Alessandro Tommasi and Cesare Zavattari

BERToldo, the Historical BERT for Italian
Alessio Palmero Aprosio, Stefano Menini and Sara Tonelli

Saturday, June 25, 2022 (continued)

In Search of the Flocks: How to Perform Onomasiological Queries in an Ancient Greek Corpus?
Alek Keersmaekers and Toon Van Hal

Contextual Unsupervised Clustering of Signs for Ancient Writing Systems
Michele Corazza, Fabio Tamburini, Miguel ValÃ©rio and Silvia Ferrara

Towards the Creation of a Diachronic Corpus for Italian: A Case Study on the GDLI Quotations
Manuel Favaro, Elisa Guadagnini, Eva Sassolini, Marco Biffi and Simonetta Montemagni

Automatic Translation Alignment for Ancient Greek and Latin
Tariq Yousef, Chiara Palladino, David J. Wright and Monica Berti

Handling Stress in Finite-State Morphological Analyzers for Ancient Greek and Ancient Hebrew
Daniel Swanson and Francis Tyers

From Inscription to Semi-automatic Annotation of Maya Hieroglyphic Texts
Cristina Vertan and Christian Prager

Multilingual Named Entity Recognition for Medieval Charters Using Stacked Embeddings and Bert-based Models.
Sergio Torres Aguilar

Linguistic Annotation of Neo-Latin Mathematical Texts: A Pilot-Study to Improve the Automatic Parsing of the Archimedes Latinus
Margherita Fantoli and Miryam de Lhoneux

Saturday, June 25, 2022 (continued)

EvaHan Technical Reports

The First International Ancient Chinese Word Segmentation and POS Tagging Bake-off: Overview of the EvaHan 2022 Evaluation Campaign
Bin Li, Yiguo Yuan, Jingya Lu, Minxuan Feng, Chao Xu, Weiguang QU and Dongbo Wang

Automatic Word Segmentation and Part-of-Speech Tagging of Ancient Chinese Based on BERT Model
Yu Chang, Peng Zhu, Chaoping Wang and Chaofan Wang

Ancient Chinese Word Segmentation and Part-of-Speech Tagging Using Data Augmentation
Yanzhi Tian and Yuhang Guo

BERT 4EVER@EvaHan 2022: Ancient Chinese Word Segmentation and Part-of-Speech Tagging Based on Adversarial Learning and Continual Pre-training
Hailin Zhang, Ziyu Yang, Yingwen Fu and Ruoyao Ding

Construction of Segmentation and Part of Speech Annotation Model in Ancient Chinese
Longjie Jiang, Qinyu C. Chang, Huyin H. Xie and Zhuying Z. Xia

Simple Tagging System with RoBERTa for Ancient Chinese
Binghao Tang, Boda Lin and Si Li

The Uncertainty-based Retrieval Framework for Ancient Chinese CWS and POS
Pengyu Wang and Zhichen Ren

Data Augmentation for Low-resource Word Segmentation and POS Tagging of Ancient Chinese Texts
Yutong Shen, Jiahuan Li, Shujian Huang, Yi Zhou, Xiaopeng Xie and Qinxin Zhao

A Joint Framework for Ancient Chinese WS and POS Tagging Based on Adversarial Ensemble Learning
Shuxun Yang

Glyph Features Matter: A Multimodal Solution for EvaHan in LT4HALA2022
Wei Xinyuan, Liu Weihao, Qing Zong , Zhang Shao Qing and Baotian Hu

EvaLatin Technical Reports

Overview of the EvaLatin 2022 Evaluation Campaign
Rachele Sprugnoli, Marco Passarotti, Flavio Massimiliano Cecchini, Margherita Fantoli and Giovanni Moretti

An ELECTRA Model for Latin Token Tagging Tasks
Wouter Mercelis and Alek Keersmaekers

Transformer-based Part-of-Speech Tagging and Lemmatization for Latin
Krzysztof WrÃ³bel and Krzysztof Nowak

Proceedings of the Second Workshop on Language Technologies for Historical and Ancient Languages (LT4HALA 2022), pages 1–9
Language Resources and Evaluation Conference (LREC 2022), Marseille, 25 June 2022

Identifying Cleartext in Historical Ciphers

Maria-Elena Gambardella, Beáta Megyesi, Eva Pettersson
Dept. of Linguistics and Philology, Uppsala University
mariaelena.gambardella@gmail.com, {beata.megyesi, eva.pettersson@lingfil.uu.se}

Abstract

In historical encrypted sources we can find encrypted text sequences, also called *ciphertext*, as well as non-encrypted cleartexts written in a known language. While most of the cryptanalysis focuses on the decryption of ciphertext, cleartext is often overlooked although it can give us important clues about the historical interpretation and contextualisation of the manuscript. In this paper, we investigate to what extent we can automatically distinguish cleartext from ciphertext in historical ciphers and to what extent we are able to identify its language. The problem is challenging as cleartext sequences in ciphers are often short, up to a few words, in different languages due to historical code-switching. To identify the sequences and the language(s), we chose a rule-based approach and run 7 different models using historical language models on various ciphertexts.

1. Introduction

Since humankind created written language there has been a need to send messages to each other in a safe way, without the interference of a third party.

Historical ciphers are encoded, hand-written manuscripts aiming at hiding the content of the message. Historical ciphers usually contain encoded sequences of various symbols, so called ciphertexts, as well as cleartexts, i.e. non-encrypted text written in a known language. All text sequences that have not been encrypted, but are left in its original form are called cleartext.

During the decryption process, the ability to distinguish cleartext from ciphertext is essential, since cleartext can give clues to the underlying language of the cipher and help us in the historical interpretation and contextualisation of the manuscript. By analyzing the cleartext of the cipher we can make educated guesses about the topic and the context of the document, which can lead to the decryption of important keywords, or the encoded named entities, such as locations or names of persons (Megyesi et al., 2019).

Cleartext might be a longer text, or short sequences of words making language identification more challenging. The scribe might use one or several languages in the same cipher, as code-switching was common in our history. And while ciphertexts are often represented by a specific symbol system designed for the particular cipher, such as digits, alphabets, graphic signs or a combination of them, cleartext consists of the alphabet of the language(s) involved. An example of cleartext and ciphertext sequences following each other in a historical cipher from 1625 is illustrated in Figure 1.

The goal of our study is to automatically identify the cleartext sequences in ciphers, and their language(s). We use historical language corpora for which we create word-based and character-based language models of various orders from unigrams to fivegrams. We build models for 16 European languages: Czech, Dutch, English, French, German, Greek, Hungarian, Icelandic, Italian, Latin, Polish, Portuguese, Russian, Slovene, Spanish and Swedish.

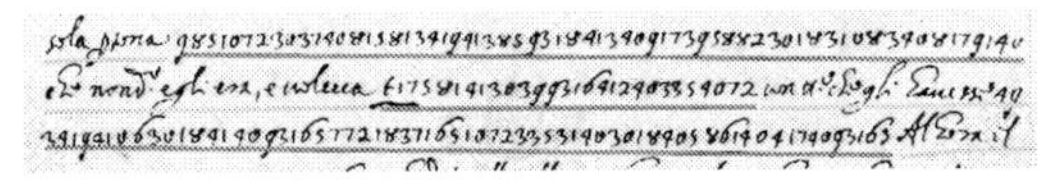

Figure 1: Excerpt of a cipher with ciphertext (in red) and cleartext (in green). Record 69 in the DECODE database (ASV, 2016b).

The work has been carried out within the DECRYPT project (Megyesi et al., 2020) aiming at the development of a research infrastructure for the study of historical cryptology. More specifically, the purpose of the project is to create resources and tools for (semi-)automatic transcription, cryptanalysis and decryption of historical encrypted documents.

In the remaining part of the paper, we give an overview of language identification in historical text followed by attempts made with regard to language identification in ciphers. In Section 3, we present the method to automatically segment cleartext and ciphertext in ciphers, and identify the language of the cleartext. In Section 4, we describe the results and in Section 5, we conclude our findings.

2. Background

Automatic language identification of a text is claimed to be a solved problem in natural language processing. When we browse or translate text using Google, the system identifies the language of the text with high accuracy. This applies especially to longer and modern text. However, when only a few words are typed in and/or when we are dealing with historical text, identifying the language becomes harder with less reliable results. In this section, we give an overview of language identification in general, and then we describe previous studies on attempts made for language identification in historical ciphers in particular.

2.1. Language Identification

Language identification is the task of recognizing the language a text is written in. The aim is to create systems that are able to recognize any human language, being it in the form of speech, sign language or handwritten text. The methods used are many, ranging from decision rules to neural networks, and the task can be applied to many areas. In the field of translation the use of language identification can be dated back to the 80s when (Beesley, 1988) created a prototype system for language identification for online texts. Another use of language identification we can find is in multilingual document storage and retrieval where one of the challenges is to disambiguate the so called "false friends", i.e. a word that holds different meanings in two languages, but is written in the same way in both languages (e.g. *gift* meaning "present" in English, but "married" in Swedish).

Texts in which several languages are present and also alternated, a phenomenon called code-switching, are commonly occurring, both in modern and in historical texts. Within the NLP community, several studies have been carried out to identify where code-switching occurs and which languages are involved. The First and Second Workshops on Computational Approaches to Code Switching organized in 2014 (Diab et al., 2014) and 2016 (Diab et al., 2016) were the first workshops dedicated to the topic. They organized shared tasks to identify languages in code-switched data. The most popular and successful approaches were based on machine learning algorithms. In (Shirvani et al., 2016), they performed token-level identification using a Logistic Regression model with L2-regularization to generate language labels on the tokens. The results outperformed the other participants, ranking the system at first place for the language pair Spanish-English.

There have been attempts in using deep learning algorithms to perform code-switching identification, with very good results. In (Samih et al., 2016), the authors present a long short-term memory (LSTM) approach relying on word and character representations, where the output is fine-tuned using a conditional random field (CRF) classifier to capture contextual meaning. They did not use any linguistic resources, making the model language independent. The results outperformed the other participants ranking the system at first place for the language pair Modern Standard Arabic-Dialectal Arabic and second for the language pair Spanish-English at the Second workshop.

Despite the highly rising interest in the use of deep learning ones, there are still researchers interested in using rule-based methods. In (Chanda et al., 2016), the authors tag their dataset of Spanish-English tweets at a word level and use three different dictionaries to recognize the language of each word. If the word is tagged as both languages, it is given to a Predictor-Corrector algorithm, which checks the tag given to the previous and next word; if they are the same it will give the same tag to the mixed word, otherwise it will tag it as ambiguous. Although the results achieved in the second workshop in 2016 do not outperform the other participants' systems, they outperformed the baseline.

2.2. Language Identification in Ciphers

When it comes to language identification in ciphers, like research on detecting cleartext in a cipher and identifying its language, this task presents a noticeable lack of literature. To the best of our knowledge, the only attempt in language identification in this field has been carried out in (Pettersson and Megyesi, 2019), where the authors present an approach to automatically mapping ciphertext sequences to keys in order to return the plaintext from the ciphertext by using homophonic substitution. Historical language models are consulted to guess the language used to write the decrypted plaintext. They use three ciphertexts from the DECODE database (Megyesi et al., 2019) for training and one for evaluation.

The first step for the cipher-key mapping algorithm consists of storing code-value pairs and the length of the longest code processed from the key file. In the second step, the transcribed text is matched against the code-value pairs. The search method is a non-greedy search-and-replace mechanism, which consists in checking the length of each word with the longest code in the cipher. Different approaches to matching are applied depending on the length of the given word: 1) if it is shorter than or equal to the longest word, it is checked whether the word can be matched with a code and if so, the word is replaced with the value attached to that code; 2) if the word cannot be matched with a code or if its length is longer than the longest word, then the algorithm iterates over the word, character by character, and try to match these characters with a code: if the approach is successful, the current character is merged with the succeeding character, and the algorithm tries to match the longer sequence with a code until its length is equal to the longest word's length. If there is no match when the word reaches the longest word's length, the sequence is replaced by a question mark. The third step is to identify the language of the decrypted text that was generated in the previous steps. This is done based on word-based language models from the HistCorp webpage,[1] where the plaintext words are compared to the words in the language model for each language. The model outputs a ranked list of these languages showing the percentage of words in the plaintext file that are found in the model for each language.

Next we turn to the description of our work.

3. Method

In this section, we will describe our approach to detect cleartext and identify its language. We start by describing the data, both the ciphers used and the historical corpora for the creation of the language models.

[1]https://cl.lingfil.uu.se/histcorp/langmodels.html

3.1. Ciphers and Transcriptions

To detect cleartext in ciphers, we need transcribed manuscripts with ciphertext and cleartext sequences marked along with their language ID. The DECODE database[2] contains a collection of almost 3000 ciphertexts and keys from Early Modern times in Europe (Megyesi et al., 2019). Over 400 ciphers are available with their transcriptions. All transcribed manuscripts follow the same guideline for consistency (Megyesi, 2020). An example of an original cipher with cleartext followed by ciphertext is exemplified in Figure 2 and its corresponding transcription is shown in Figure 3.

First, the transcription begins with comment lines (starting with "#") which provide information about the file. Then, the content of the cipher is transcribed, symbol by symbol and row by row. Digits are transcribed as numerals in ASCII (1 is transcribed as "1", 2 as "2", 0 as "0"), along with the Latin alphabet including capitalized letters (a is transcribed as "a", capital B as "B"), and punctuation marks (".","!",). For other symbols, we use the Unicode names. Each symbol is transcribed separately, and we add a space between each symbol. In case of spacing in the original, multiple spaces are introduced as these might mark word boundaries in the underlying plaintext. Uncertain symbols are transcribed with added question mark "?" immediately following the uncertain element. To be able to distinguish between ciphertext and cleartext, cleartext sequences are marked in brackets as:

< CLEARTEXT LANG Symbol sequence >.

If the manuscript contains several lines of cleartext, each new line is represented by a new CLEARTEXT tag. LANG denotes the language the cleartext is written in, marked by a language ID as defined by ISO 639-12 two-letter codes for languages (e.g. ES for Spanish). If there is some doubt about the cleartext language, the language ID is defined as unidentified (UN).

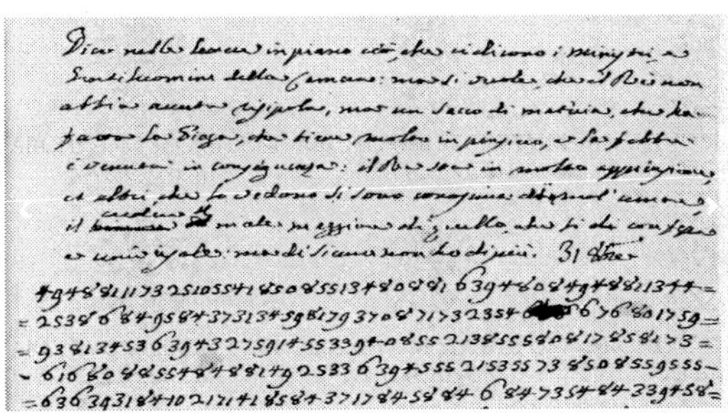

Figure 2: Excerpt of a cipher with ciphertext and cleartext. Record 198 in the DECODE database (ASV, 2016a).

The transcriptions were preprocessed to make computation easier. We removed all question marks representing uncertainty (e.g. 8? is returned as 8) and kept the first alternative in case of multiple interpretations (e.g. 6/8? is returned as 6). We then converted all Unicode names into symbols (by using the `lookup` function in the `unicodedata` module). We removed all spaces between the codes as well as the cleartext and plaintext tags. Finally, we corrected remaining errors caused by the manual transcritpion, such as missing brackets and wrong unicode names. The result is a collection of texts which looked exactly as their original historical manuscripts without any annotation.

```
#CATALOG NAME: Segr. di Stato/Portogallo 117/5
#IMAGE NAME: 104r.jpg
#TRANSCRIBER NAME: Midas
#DATE OF TRANSCRIPTION: May 5, 2017
#TRANSCRIPTION TIME: 20 min.

#IMAGE NAME: 104r.jpg
<CLEARTEXT IT Dice nella lettera in piano ciò che ci dicono i ministri, e>
<CLEARTEXT IT Gentilhuomini della Camera: ma si vuole che il Re non abbia>
<CLEARTEXT IT avuto risipola,  ma un sacco di materia che ha>
<CLEARTEXT IT fatto la Piaga, che tiene molto in pensiero, e la febbre>
<CLEARTEXT IT è venuta in conseguenza: il Re sta in molta apprensione,>
<CLEARTEXT IT et altri che lo vedono si sono conosciuti ???? umore,>
<CLEARTEXT IT il credere il male peggiore di quello che si confessa>
<CLEARTEXT IT è universale: ma di sicuro non ho di più. 31 8bre>
4 9 4 8 8 1 1 1 7 3 2 6 1 0 6 5 4 1 8 6 0 8 6 6 1 3 4 8 0 8 8 1 6 3 9 4 8 0 8 4 9 4 8 8 1 1 3 4 4 ~
~ 2 5 3 8 6 8 4 9 5 8 4 3 7 3 1 3 4 5 9 8 1 7 9 3 7 0 8 7 1 7 3 2 3 5 4 67 6 7 6 8 0 1 7 5 9 ^
~ 9 3 8 1 3 4 5 3 6 3 9 4 3 2 7 5 9 1 4 5 5 3 3 9 4 0 8 5 5 2 1 3 8 5 5 5 8 0 8 1 7 8 5 8 1 7 3 ×
- 6 1 6 8 0 8 8 5 5 4 8 4 8 8 1 4 9 2 5 3 3 6 3 9 4 5 5 5 2 1 5 3 5 5 7 3 8 5 9 8 5 5 9 5 5 5 -
~ 6 3 6 3 9 3 1 8 4 1 0 2 1 7 1 4 1 8 5 8 4 3 7 1 7 8 4 5 8 9 4 6 8 4 7 3 5 4 8 4 3 3 9 4 5 8 ~
```

Figure 3: Excerpt of a cipher transcription with ciphertext and cleartext. Record 198 in the DECODE database (ASV, 2016a).

The dataset used in our study consists of 214 documents in 8 different languages. Transcriptions of two longer enciphered manuscripts are also present: the Borg (Aldarrab et al., 2017) and the Copiale(Cop, 2011 2020) ciphers, dated back to the 18th and the 17th centuries, respectively. To test if the models overgenerate we also included some texts without any cleartext.

As we can see in Table 1, the language with the most documents is Hungarian, followed by French, Italian, Spanish, Latin. In the sample, we can also find documents with multiple languages such as a combination of Latin and French, where the cleartext was written in Latin and the ciphertext was decoded into French. Some languages occur in one document only, such as Dutch and Portuguese. We could not create a balanced sample, we took simply what we could get.

In the manuscripts, we find a large variation of symbols used to encode the text. In Table 2, we show the distribution of symbols across the training and test sets. The most frequent symbol set used in the ciphers are digits, representing around 78% of our data. The second most used symbol set is a combination of digits and Latin letters (around 15% of the dataset), followed by a combination of digits, Latin letters and graphic signs (around 6% of the dataset). The least used symbol set is the combination of graphic signs and Latin letters representing around 1% of the dataset.

The dataset was partitioned into 60% for training and 40% for test, with no development set. The motivation behind this choice is that we were not planning to use machine learning, so the training set does not necessarily need to have a lot more data compared to the test set and the same applies for the absence of a development set. The transcriptions of the long ciphers, the Borg

[2] https://de-crypt.org/decode

Language	Num of doc for training set	Num of doc for test set
Hungarian	32	22
French	29	20
Italian	29	20
Spanish	25	17
Latin	5	3
Latin/French	4	2
Portuguese	0	1
Dutch	0	1
Unknown	0	1
No cleartext	1	2

Table 1: Language distribution in the dataset.

and the Copiale, both with non-standard symbols, were divided into 50% for training and 50% for testing.

3.2. Language Models

Inspired by the work of (Pettersson and Megyesi, 2019), we decided to include 16 European languages, all with freely available historical corpora through the HistCorp platform (Pettersson and Megyesi, 2018). The included languages are: Czech, Dutch, English, French, German, Greek, Hungarian, Icelandic, Italian, Latin, Polish, Portuguese, Russian, Slovene, Spanish and Swedish. Historical corpora with diplomatic editions are available for all, along with pre-trained language models which are perfectly suitable and adaptable for our purposes; both for cleartext detection and language identification.

The language models are built using the IRSTLM open source toolkit (Federico et al., 2008). Every language has word-based models, including up to 3-grams, and character-based models, including up to 5-grams. The models are text files with the token in the first column and their absolute frequency in the second column. In order to use these models for both language identification and cleartext detection, we created two dictionaries: one collecting all items in the word-based language models and one collecting all items in the character-based language models (see Table 3 for size of each language model).

The motivation behind using historical language models rather than larger modern models is related to the nature of the texts analyzed. Because historical ciphers contain historical language with different spelling and vocabulary used at the time, language models built on historical texts seemed to be appropriate for our purposes.

In order to use the language models, we build two dictionaries: one collecting word-based language models and one collecting character-based language models. The motivation behind choosing a dictionary as our data structure is because of the relative speed with which items can be retrieved. Being a hash table, when we search for an item we look directly at the "slot" that holds the name of the item we are looking for and retrieve its value. This search is equal to *O(1)*, meaning that the size of the dictionary has no effect on the search, since it is constant (Miller and Ranum, 2006).

For the word-based dictionary, unigrams and bigrams were used (3-grams turned out to be computationally too heavy to be useful for our task). For the character-based dictionary, 3-grams, 4-grams and 5-grams were used. The motivation for not using unigrams and bigrams in the character-based setting, is that these short segments are more likely to be part of several different language models. For example, *ia* can be a common suffix in both Spanish and Italian, but for longer *n*-grams we can get more unique combinations for certain languages. The dictionaries have words or characters as keys and a list of tuples in the form `(language, frequency)` ranked by the second item with the first one being the one with the highest relative frequency as values.

3.3. Cleartext Detection

To distinguish cleartext sequences from ciphertexts, we were inspired by the the work of (Chanda et al., 2016), as explained in Section 2.1. In particular, we were interested to see how the approach of analyzing modern social media (Twitter) data on word level could be applied to and how well it could perform on historical texts.

We decided to experiment with various types of models. For our baseline model we chose unigrams only on a word-based level. In addition to the baseline, we tried six different n-gram combinations:

1) For the first model (Word 1gram Threshold on FRequency, W1_TFR), we considered only unigrams, but not the least frequent ones. We set a threshold of 1 on the absolute frequency of all unigrams when creating the word-based dictionary from the language models. The motivation for this is to see how removing the least frequent words could affect the results of cleartext detection.

2) For the second model (Word 1gram Threshold on Letters, W1_TL), we also considered unigrams, but only those which presented letters. In order to achieve this goal, we set a threshold where unigrams which presented digits were not considered (e.g. '23gf' or '65.'). The motivation behind this is that words containing numbers seem to be less likely to be text than code and therefore should possibly be ignored.

3) For the third model (Word 1gram Threshold on Letters + Word 2gram, W1_TL + W2), we considered a combination of bigrams and unigrams with the same threshold as in the second model (1L). The model will first check if the bigram is present in the dictionary and if not, it will split the bigram into unigrams and check if each of these is present in the dictionary. The motivation behind this combination is the fact that

Set	Digits	Graphic Signs + Latin letters	Digits + Latin letters	Digits + Latin letters + Graphic Signs
Training	96	2	20	7
Test	70	2	8	9

Table 2: Symbol set distribution in the dataset.

Language	Words	Chars
Czech	4,364,685	25,359,937
Dutch	14,549,599	87,206,041
English	90,983,314	451,860,888
French	366,437	1,964,634
German	256,039,161	1,748,530,003
Greek	11,179,688	135,546,052
Hungarian	2,169,442	13,567,260
Icelandic	983,517	5,478,104
Italian	7,635,969	48,277,101
Latin	95,181,455	663,451,162
Polish	3,203,330	16,980,174
Portuguese	3,178,447	17,342,279
Russian	25,822	283,024
Slovene	18,081,602	92,197,951
Spanish	7,381,647	41,052,708
Swedish	17,606,410	104,409,451

Table 3: Size of language models.

some words can be difficult to identify when taken individually, but when we consider their neighbouring word the process could be easier. For example, in the case of dates, such as *August 1697*, it could be easier to identify *1697* as part of a date if it is considered together with *August* than if it would be considered alone.

4) For the fourth model (Word 1gram Threshold on Letters + Word 2grams + CHaracters 2-, 3-, 4-grams, W1_TL + W2 + CH345), we considered a combination of bigrams and unigrams from the third model and added 3-grams, 4-grams and 5-grams on a character level. The model will first check if the bigram is present in the dictionary and if not, it will split the bigram into unigrams and check if each of these is present in the dictionary. If the unigram is not in the dictionary, the model will check the combination of characters in the character-based dictionary. The motivation behind adding characters to the model is the fact that in the past, words could be spelled in different ways and using character-based language models could help us capture these words, even if the word as a whole is not recognised in a dictionary.

5) For the fifth model (Word 1gram Threshold on Letters + Word 2grams + CHaracters 2-, 3-, 4-grams Threshold on Letters, W1_TL + W2 + CH345_TL), we considered a combination of bigrams, unigrams and characters as in the fourth model, but we also added the same threshold that we have on the unigrams to the characters, that is n-grams which presented digits were not considered (e.g. '23gf' or '65.' are not considered).

6) For the sixth model (Word 1gram Threshold on Letters + Word 2grams Threshold on Letters + CHaracters 2-, 3-, 4-grams Threshold on Letters, W1_TL + W2_TL + CH345_TL), we considered the same combination of bigrams, unigrams and characters as in the fifth model, but we also added a threshold to the bigrams, where bigrams which presented only digits were ignored (e.g. '23 45' is not considered, but '23 Agoust' is). The motivation behind having such a threshold for the bigrams is to increase our chances to capture text. Our intuition is that a combination of two numbers is more likely to be code than a combination of a number and a word and should therefore be ignored.

```
Given line
Au Camp devant Anclam le 3__1__

Cleartext detection
[['Au', 'text'], ['Camp', 'text'], ['devant', 'text'], ['Anclam',
'text'], ['le', 'text'], ['3__1__', 'code']]

Detection of cleartext boundaries
[['<CLEARTEXT Au', 'text'], ['Camp', 'text'], ['devant', 'text'],
['Anclam', 'text'], ['le >', 'text'], ['3__1__', 'code']]

Language identification in the best performing model
[['<CLEARTEXT Au', 'french'], ['Camp', 'french'], ['devant',
'french'], ['Anclam', 'latin'], ['le >', 'italian'], ['3__1__',
'code']]

Result
<CLEARTEXT FR Au Camp devant Anclam le > 3__1__
```

Figure 4: Example of how the algorithm works with models using unigrams.

Our algorithm analyzes each file in our data set line by line, as they are transcribed. For the baseline model and models 1 and 2, it splits each line into unigrams and we forward each unigram to a function that assigns a 'text' tag if the word is found in the word-based dictionary or a 'code' tag in the event that the n-gram is not found. For model 3 to model 6, we split each line in bigrams and we search for these n-grams in a slightly different manner: we first search for the bigram in the word-based dictionary, and if the bigram is not found we split it into its unigrams and search for each of them in the word-based dictionary again. If the unigram is not found, we search for the combination of characters: if the unigram is shorter than or equal to five, we search for the entire unigram in the character-based dictionary. And because the dictionary contains only 3-grams, 4-grams and 5-grams, combinations that are shorter than three will be automatically identified as 'code'. If the unigram is longer than five we first search for the first five characters, and if those are not found we search for the last five. If no match is found the tag 'code' is given to the unigram. The motivation behind checking the first and last five characters is to try and check certain parts of the word with the character-based language models. The first five characters could be checked as the stem of a word, and the last five as common inflectional suffixes.

As a result, every n-gram in the line receives a tag and we then give this line to another function to perform cleartext detection. This is done by checking if the n-grams which have the 'text' tag are preceded or followed by the 'code' tag or another 'text' tag: if the n-gram is preceded by a n-gram with the tag 'code', the current n-gram is the beginning of the cleartext and we attach the opening cleartext tag to that word ('<CLEARTEXT'). If it is followed by a n-gram with the tag 'code' or if we reach the end of the line, the current n-gram is the end of the cleartext and we attach the closing cleartext tag to that word ('>'). As the next step, we identify the language of the cleartext sequences.

3.4. Language Identification

In order to perform language identification, we choose the best performing model for cleartext detection and change the tag assignment function slightly: instead of just giving a generic 'text' tag, the function would look for the word in the dictionaries and if it is found it will retrieve the language with the highest relative frequency and assign it to the n-gram. Next, the tagged line is given to another function to decide the language for the whole line, by counting the occurrences for each language in the line. Because bigrams are more relevant than unigrams, we multiply each bigram score by 1 and each unigram score by 0.5. Finally, we output a ranked list of languages with the one with the highest frequency being the first.

4. Results and Discussion

Before we present and discuss the results, we describe the evaluation to measure model performance.

4.1. Evaluation

In order to evaluate our models, we decided to use different measurements. The first measure is to calculate the total line match, where we check for each text output by our models how many of its lines are totally matched with the respective gold standard text. This measure gives us an idea about how well the model is performing overall, without considering specifically the language identification and cleartext detection part. It also gives us an idea of how well the model performs automatic annotation in general.

The second measure is for the calculation of partial line match, where we check if some parts of the cleartext were detected in the line. This measure gives us an idea about how well the model is performing cleartext detection, although partially. Partial performance can be relevant for annotation tasks to detect cleartext quicker.

The third measure is to calculate the standard measures of accuracy, precision, recall and F1-score. These measures give us an idea of how well the model performs cleartext detection and if the models overgeneralize or undergeneralize the detection.

The fourth measure calculates the accuracy in the language identification task, by comparing the tags in each text output by our model with the tags in the gold standard. This measure gives us an idea of how well our models perform in the language identification task.

In order to evaluate language identification accuracy, we iterate through the gold standard file line by line and retrieve the same line in the output file. We first count all the language tags in the gold standard file and then we retrieve all the lines where a language was identified in both the gold standard and our model output files: if the tag in the gold standard text is the same as the one in the output text, we add 1 to the count of the matched tags. We then divide the matched tags by the total number of language tags and multiply by 100 to get the percentage.

4.2. Results of Cleartext Detection

The results from the six models measured on the test set along with the baseline is presented in Table 4. All models with the exception of model 1 outperformed the baseline. Model 4 is the next worst, generating a low partial match, and low precision, but compensate for high a recall. The best performing model is model 6 with F1-Score of 92.46% and the next best is model 5 with F1 score of 91.47%. The results confirm our initial hypothesis that combining character-based bigrams and unigrams can help improving the performance of cleartext detection. It also confirms our hypothesis that having a certain threshold is necessary to avoid overgeneralization, since recall and precision gets better with the introduction of these thresholds.

4.3. The Impact of Symbols

Since ciphers might consists of symbols that co-occur with the plaintext alphabet, we measure model performance on ciphers with various symbol sets. Figure 5 illustrated the model performance measures as F1 on documents with various symbol sets: digits (D), graphic signs (G), letters (L), and various combinations that occur in the test set.

The easiest documents with cleartext to identify turn out to be the ciphers that use graphic signs only. This is not surprising since the cleartexts in the Latin alphabet are clearly distinguishable from the ciphertext with

Model	Total line	Partial line	Accuracy	Precision	Recall	F1
baseline	44.34	80.83	72.12	74.29	84.11	78.90
model 1: W1_TFR	42.72	80.76	71.52	74.32	82.90	78.38
model 2: W1_TL	56.05	93.76	89.75	92.92	82.63	87.47
model 3: W1_TL+W2	51.74	88.99	88.42	90.20	83.33	86.63
model 4: W1_TL+W2+CH345	41.75	67.88	77.36	70.74	93.00	80.36
model 5: W1_TL+W2+CH345_TL	63.16	89.09	93.64	90.48	92.49	91.47
model 6: W1_TL+W2_TL+CH345_TL	67.98	93.85	94.77	92.64	92.28	**92.46**

Table 4: Results (%) for each model on the test set.

graphic symbols and therefore easy to model, as indicated by the high F1 scores of over 90% for almost all models.

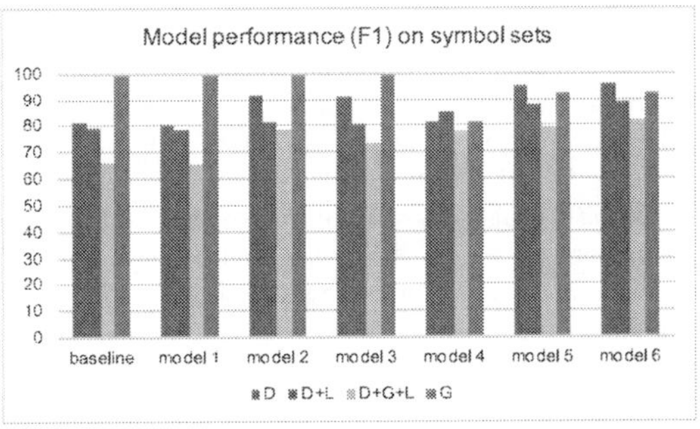

Figure 5: Model performance (F1) on symbol sets: D-digits, G-graphic signs, L-Letters.

The best performing model in general is model 6, scoring 96.03% for ciphertexts using digits, 88.87% for ciphertexts using a combination of digits and letters and 82.17% for ciphertexts using a combination of digits, letters and graphic signs. This model was able to detect the cleartext in the document which presented Unknown cleartext and able to see that no cleartext was present in the document which had none. It is clear that the more combination of symbol sets are used for encryption, the more difficult the identification of cleartext and ciphertext sequences become.

In general, model 6 achieves highest performance for all symbol sets with the exception of graphic signs only. Ciphertexts using a symbol set made of digits were the ones which performed best with model 6. This could be due to the fact that it is easier to detect text in a ciphertext where only numerals are used for code and only letters are used for text. Ciphertexts using a symbol set made of digits and letters and ciphertexts using a symbol set made of digits, letters and graphic signs benefit from model 6 as well, but because it is more difficult to decide if letters are text or code the model performs slightly worse than expected, but reaching a high score nevertheless.

4.4. Results of Language Identification

As the last part of the evaluation, we measure the accuracy of language identification on the line level to account for code-switching in cleartexts with different languages in different lines. The best performing model — model 6 — achieves 44.68% accuracy for the identification of the correct cleartext language.

The models perform differently depending on the languages of the cleartext, as shown in Table 5. The language with the highest accuracy obtained is Dutch with a score of 88.89% followed by Portuguese with a score of 85.29%, although these appear in one document only as part of the test set. If we look at the languages with most data, we can see that Spanish is the best performing language reaching a score of 64.69%.

Because these scores were lower than expected albeit less surprising given that it is hard to automatically guess a language based on such a small context as a few words even for humans, we decided to run the same task on the document level taking into account all cleartext sequences in the document. The reason why we chose this approach is the fact that most ciphertexts in our dataset contain one cleartext language only. Therefore, we chose the most frequent language tag for all cleartext segments in that document and assigned it to the given file. The accuracy for language identification on a document level for the best performing model (model 6) was 70.40%.

Given the results we can conclude that language identification on a document level seems to reach better scores than on a line level. The language with the highest score in language identification accuracy on the document level is Dutch and Portuguese with a score of 100.0%, see Table 5. If we look at the languages with most data, French is the best performing language during testing reaching a score of 100.0%.

When it comes to languages we need to keep in mind certain factors: although Dutch and Portuguese have the best performing results, it is worth mentioning that we had available only one ciphertext for each language. The same goes for Latin and a combination of Latin and French where we had 8 and 6 ciphertexts available, respectively. If we consider the languages that had a bigger amount of data, Spanish is the best performing language. This could be due to the fact that the language model was fairly big, counting around 2.4 million n-grams, and there were fewer annotation doubts in the transcriptions, making it easier to detect words. It can be argued that Latin has a bigger language model, counting 20.3 million n-grams, and therefore more n-

Language	Number of texts	Accuracy-Line	Accuracy-Document
Hungarian	22	16.24	18.18
French	20	57.32	100.0
Italian	20	49.38	75.0
Spanish	17	64.69	94.12
Latin	3	18.45	33.33
Latin/French	2	55.38	50.0
Dutch	1	88.89	100.0
Portuguese	1	85.29	100.0

Table 5: Results (%) for LI for each language on the line and document levels on the test set.

grams useful for the detection of cleartext. Although this is true, we need to remember that Latin texts presented more annotation doubts compared to other languages, making it more difficult to detect words. At the same time, we can find Latin words in other language models as well, since Latin was widely used also in texts mainly written in another language. Hungarian presented similar characteristics as Latin, with more annotation doubts in its transcriptions than other languages, but at the same time it also had a smaller language model, counting 1.6 million n-grams. French and Italian follow Spanish and this can be due to the size of data and low amount of annotation doubts.

5. Conclusion

In this paper, we addressed the problem of detecting cleartext in a ciphertext and identifying its language. In order to perform this task we used the language models available on the HistCorp platform, and created two dictionaries: one containing unigrams and bigrams on a word level and one containing 3-grams, 4-grams and 5-grams on a character level. We then built our baseline model using unigrams only and compared it against 6 models which used unigrams only, or a combination of unigrams and bigrams, or a combination of unigrams and bigrams on word-level and 3-grams, 4-grams and 5-grams on character-level. We experimented with different thresholds for all order n-grams both on a word level and on a character level. Our intuition was that by combining unigrams, bigrams and characters while having a threshold on each of them, the model would perform better. Our idea was that the threshold could filter out items which could have been misunderstood as cleartext when they were code, or vice versa. In order to perform the cleartext detection task we checked the text line by line. If the n-grams analyzed were present in the dictionaries and depending on the model, we gave a 'text' tag or a 'code' tag for each text sequence. In order to evaluate the models, we used different measurements such as total line match, partial line match, accuracy, precision, recall and F1 to have a complete overview and understanding of how the models were performing.

Our results confirmed our hypothesis with the model using a combination of unigrams, bigrams on a word level and 3-grams, 4-grams and 5-grams on a character level, reaching the highest F1-score of 92.06%. A threshold was used on all n-grams: unigrams on a word level and all n-grams on a character level had a threshold on items that presented at least one digit, whereas bigrams on a word level had a threshold on items that presented only digits.

For the language identification task, the results for each language were quite diverse, probably due to the differences in the size of the language models. We noticed that on a line level Spanish reached good results among the languages which had a more balanced ratio of training and test set (64.69%).

Future research should consider using a combination of the best performing model in this paper with 3-grams on a word level and see if a threshold could further improve the performance of the model. We believe that including higher order n-grams can help the model to detect more difficult combinations of words such as *27th August 1679*, where with a lower order n-gram *27* and *1679* could be detected as code.

It would be of interest that future research investigates how to deal with doubts in the transcriptions in a deeper way. A suggestion could be to take the words that the annotators were unsure about and try to find the most similar one in the language models. This approach could improve both cleartext detection and language identification since it will reduce the chances of these words being tagged as code.

Future research might also apply machine learning algorithms to this task, but only in the event that more data would be available. Regarding the language identification task, a research suggestion could be to create equally sized language models for all languages, so that words have a lower chance to be assigned to the wrong language because of lower relative frequencies due to lack of data.

All in all, we find the results promising, especially the cleartext identification task while language identification of a couple of words remains challenging.

6. Bibliographical References

Aldarrab, N., Knight, K., and Megyesi, B. (2017). The borg cipher. `https://cl.lingfil.uu.se/~bea/borg`. Accessed: 2020-01-31.

ASV. (2016a). Reproduced excerpt from the Vatican Secret Archive, i. 1025, Segretario di Stato, Francia, doss. 117, DECODE link: https://de-crypt.org/decode Record ID 198.

ASV. (2016b). Reproduced excerpt from the Vatican Secret Archive, i. 1025, Segretario di Stato, Francia, doss. 64-8, DECODE link: https://de-crypt.org/decode Record ID 69.

Beesley, K. R. (1988). Language identifier: A computer program for automatic natural-language identification of on-line text. In *Proceedings of the 29th annual conference of the American Translators Association*, volume 47, page 54.

Chanda, A., Das, D., and Mazumdar, C. (2016). Columbia-jadavpur submission for emnlp 2016 code-switching workshop shared task: System description. In *Proceedings of the Second Workshop on Computational Approaches to Code Switching*, pages 112–115.

(2011–2020). The Copiale Cipher. `https://cl.lingfil.uu.se/~bea/copiale`. Accessed: 2020-01-31.

Mona Diab, et al., editors. (2014). *Proceedings of the First Workshop on Computational Approaches to Code Switching*, Doha, Qatar. Association for Computational Linguistics.

Mona Diab, et al., editors. (2016). *Proceedings of the Second Workshop on Computational Approaches to Code Switching*, Austin, Texas, November. Association for Computational Linguistics.

Federico, M., Bertoldi, N., and Cettolo, M. (2008). Irstlm: an open source toolkit for handling large scale language models. In *Ninth Annual Conference of the International Speech Communication Association*.

Megyesi, B., Blomqvist, N., and Pettersson, E. (2019). The decode database: Collection of historical ciphers and keys. In *The 2nd International Conference on Historical Cryptology, HistoCrypt 2019, June 23-26 2019, Mons, Belgium*, pages 69–78.

Megyesi, B., Esslinger, B., Fornés, A., Kopal, N., Láng, B., Lasry, G., Leeuw, K. d., Pettersson, E., Wacker, A., and Waldispühl, M. (2020). Decryption of historical manuscripts: the decrypt project. *Cryptologia*, pages 1–15.

Megyesi, B. (2020). Transcription of historical ciphers and keys. In *the 3rd International Conference on Historical Cryptology*. Linköping University Electronic Press.

Miller, B. N. and Ranum, D. L. (2006). *Problem Solving with Algorithms and Data Structures Using Python*. Franklin, Beedle and Associates.

Pettersson, E. and Megyesi, B. (2018). The HistCorp Collection of Historical Corpora and Resources. In *Proceedings of the Digital Humanities in the Nordic Countries 3rd Conference*, Helsinki, Finland, March.

Pettersson, E. and Megyesi, B. (2019). Matching keys and encrypted manuscripts. In *The 22nd Nordic Conference on Computational Linguistics (NoDaLiDa'19)*. Linköping University Electronic Press.

Samih, Y., Maharjan, S., Attia, M., Kallmeyer, L., and Solorio, T. (2016). Multilingual code-switching identification via lstm recurrent neural networks. In *Proceedings of the Second Workshop on Computational Approaches to Code Switching*, pages 50–59.

Shirvani, R., Piergallini, M., Gautam, G. S., and Chouikha, M. (2016). The howard university system submission for the shared task in language identification in spanish-english codeswitching. In *Proceedings of the second workshop on computational approaches to code switching*, pages 116–120.

Proceedings of the Second Workshop on Language Technologies for Historical and Ancient Languages (LT4HALA 2022), pages 10–19
Language Resources and Evaluation Conference (LREC 2022), Marseille, 25 June 2022

Detecting Diachronic Syntactic Developments in Presence of Bias Terms

Oliver Hellwig, Sven Sellmer
Heinrich Heine Universität Düsseldorf
Institute for Language and Information
{Oliver.Hellwig, sellmer}@uni-duesseldorf.de

Abstract

Corpus-based studies of diachronic syntactic changes are typically guided by the results of previous qualitative research. When such results are missing or, as is the case for Vedic Sanskrit, are restricted to small parts of a transmitted corpus, an exploratory framework that detects such changes in a data-driven fashion can support the research process. In this paper, we introduce an infinite relational model (Kemp et al., 2006) that groups syntactic constituents based on their structural similarities and their diachronic distributions. We propose a simple way to control for register and intellectual affiliation, and discuss our findings for four syntactic structures in Vedic texts.

Keywords: Historical syntax, Vedic Sanskrit, infinite relational model

1. Introduction

When studying diachronic linguistic change from a corpus-based perspective, it is – often silently – assumed that the linguistic phenomena of interest are known from previous qualitative studies (Hilpert and Gries, 2016, 44ff.). Such an assumption may not hold for under-resourced premodern languages with a limited history of research. In such cases, it can be useful to have an exploratory framework that draws attention to phenomena that change in time, while simultaneously controlling for other influence variables such as intellectual affiliation or register. We propose such a framework for detecting diachronic trends in the syntax of Vedic Sanskrit (or Vedic), a premodern Indo-Aryan language with a large corpus of religious and ritualistic texts composed in the second and first millenia BCE (Renou, 1956). Most previous research on Vedic syntax has concentrated on the oldest Vedic texts and a limited number of research questions (see Sec. 2 of this paper), and only few studies have tried to quantify the phenomena they describe, especially from a diachronic perspective. Given that a syntactic treebank of Vedic is now available (see Sec. 3), this research situation thus leaves ample space for quantitative approaches.

Studying diachronic syntactic changes is challenging because the number of interacting units grows nonlinearly with the size of the dependency tree and interesting phenomena may not be directly read off the joint surface representation. In this paper, we therefore focus on individual syntactic constituents which are composed of the morpho-syntactic representation of a word and its relation to its syntactic head. Consider, as an example, the solid dependency arc in Fig. 1a. This left-branching arc of length one marks the nominative singular noun *udumbaraḥ* 'fig-tree' as the subject of the finite verb *ajāyata* 'grew'. While the joint representation of this arc (*udumbara-* acting as a subject and placed directly to the left of its head) is rare and therefore offers only limited linguistic insights, combinations of its subfeatures are better suited to highlight linguistically interesting and especially interpretable phenomena (see Fig. 1b; details in Sec. 4.1). We therefore extract the subfeatures of the noun *udumbaraḥ*, i.e. part-of-speech, morpho-syntax and details about the syntactic relation, and form their Cartesian product. This step generates new, more abstract representations of the constituent such as nsubj:+1 → NOUN (a nominal subject is found directly to the left of its head), or ∅:left → NOUN (an unspecified [∅: wildcard] nominal dependent is found anywhere to the left of its head). In this way we abstract from the syntactic surface as, for instance, nsubj:∅ → Nom. (a word in nominative case serves as subject) may apply to a verbal clause as in Fig. 1b or to a nominal identity state-

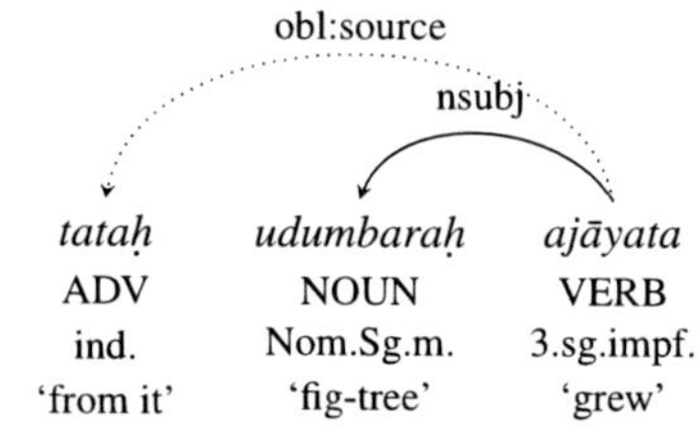

(a) A sample sentence with morpho-syntax: 'A fig-tree grew from it.'

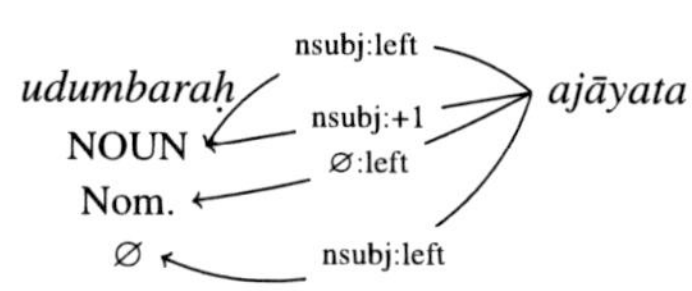

(b) Constructing abstract representations of the constituent *udumbaraḥ* in Fig. 1a

Figure 1: A sample sentence (Kaṭha-Saṃhitā 6.1.6) and some constituents generated from its subject *udumbaraḥ*

ment such as *yajñaḥ prajāpatiḥ* '[the god] Prajāpati [is the] sacrifice' where the subject *prajāpatiḥ* is found to the right of the predicate *yajñaḥ*. We expect that such abstract constituents ('constituents' in the following) reveal syntactic patterns that are easier to interpret and more frequent than the joint surface representations and therefore more useful for exploratory linguistic studies.

We now want to determine which constituents show diachronic variation while controlling for the Vedic school of each text (see Sec. 3) and for register, two variables that influence the linguistic form of Vedic texts (Witzel, 1989; Hock, 1997; Cohen, 2008). While, for instance, Cochran–Mantel–Haenszel tests (Agresti, 2007) could be applied here, the large number of factor combinations results in sparse count tensors which do not allow for a meaningful statistical interpretation. Moreover, many constituents differ from each other only in minor aspects (e.g. a noun placed to the left of its head vs. a noun placed directly to the left of its head), and it is not clear a priori which of such variants should be studied in greater detail. We hypothesize, however, that similar constituents have similar chronological distributions. Aggregating similar constituents may therefore produce more stable results. Starting from these ideas, we interpret the constituents as nodes in a similarity graph G. G has an edge between two constituents if they occur in the analysis of the same surface form. From the sentence in Fig. 1 we can, for instance, deduce that the constituents NOUN/Nom/∅/+1 and ∅/∅/nsub/left are connected in G because they are both analyses of the same surface form *udumbaraḥ*. The graph-based approach has the advantage that abstract representations of a surface form have good chances to occur in diverse syntactic constructions and thereby connect constructions that differ strongly at first view.

As the resulting graph is large and therefore difficult to interpret, we partition its nodes (i.e. the constituents) using a variant of the infinite relation model (IRM; Kemp et al. (2006)). The IRM is a Bayesian model that groups objects from multiple domains based on their n-ary relations. In our case, all objects (constituents) come from the same domain, and a binary relation between two objects is present if both represent the same surface form at least twice in the treebank. We extend this model by constituent specific normal distributions that record how much the chronological distribution of a constituent deviates from the maximum likelihood estimate of the corpus distribution. This chronological information is represented in the form of unary attributes attached to each node of the IRM. The aim of the IRM is therefore to find partitions containing constituents that are both similar with regard to their morpho-syntactic information and their chronological distributions. Constituents in the partitions produced by the IRM are finally ranked using an information-theoretic criterion that takes the bias terms (school, register) into account.

Section 2 of this paper gives a short overview of related work. The data is described in Sec. 3, and the model is defined in Sec. 4. Section 5 reviews four syntactic phenomena detected by the model and discusses possible limitations of the approach. Section 6 summarizes the paper. Code and data are available at `https://github.com/OliverHellwig/sanskrit/tree/master/papers/2022-lt4hala-syntax`.

2. Related research

Much of the work on Sanskrit syntax has been devoted to Vedic (Hock, 2015b; Hock, 2015a). Issues of morpho-syntax such as case syntax, verbal nouns and converbs form the bulk of this research, whereas only few studies deal with word and constituency order. Apart from overviews like Gonda (1971), diachronic approaches are rarely found. Changes in word order are sometimes investigated in the context of the Indo-European background and the influence of substrate languages (Lehmann, 1974; Hock, 1984). There are also studies that trace the development of certain syntactic phenomena over time (Renou, 1937), or study temporal stratification (Wüst, 1928), but all in all the amount of research helpful for our task is limited. One major problem is that the youngest stratum of Vedic has largely been neglected in research (Wezler, 2001).

While diachronic semantics have recently received much attention in linguistics and NLP (see e.g. Haase et al. (2021) and Frermann and Lapata (2016)), the question how to detect syntactic changes is only rarely addressed. Closest to what we aim at in this paper is the exploratory tool described by Schätzle et al. (2019) which visualizes the relationship between multiple linguistic features and can thus be used for detecting previously unnoticed diachronic syntactic changes. Further data-driven approaches to historical syntax are discussed in Hilpert and Gries (2016).

3. Data

The syntactic data are taken from the Vedic Treebank (VTB).[1] Compared to previous versions of the VTB (Hellwig et al., 2020; Biagetti et al., 2021; Hellwig and Sellmer, 2021) its current version has been extended substantially. It now contains 18,061 sentences from 37 texts, including texts from the White Yajurveda as well as extracts from the Śrauta Sūtras, the manuals of the solemn ritual. Table 1 describes the composition of the VTB in terms of the influence variables considered in this paper. As the treebank is biased towards late prose texts and the schools of the Rig- and Yajurveda, controlling these variables is even more important.

Most Vedic texts contain a large number of mantras, i.e. verbatim citations from the old metrical Saṃhitās. Mantras are cited at virtually every step of a sacrifice in

[1] `https://github.com/OliverHellwig/sanskrit/tree/master/papers/2020lrec/treebank`

Layer				
RV	MA	PO	PL	SU
9,817	28,989	25,211	40,618	31,636
School				
AV	Black YV	RV	SV	White YV
16,053	31,536	51,732	19,910	17,040
Register				
metrical	prose			
38,806	97,465			

Table 1: Number of words in the Vedic Treebank grouped by the influence variables considered in this paper. The layers (first compartment) are sorted in ascending chronological order (*Rigveda* proper, Mantra language, old prose, late prose, Sūtra language).

order to guarantee its success (Patton, 2006) and therefore account for about 6% of all words in the VTB. Because mantras contain archaic linguistic material they impede the chronological analysis of Vedic syntax. We therefore completely remove mantras from the data.

Each Vedic text can be assigned to one of five Vedic schools. These schools differ in which role their main priests assume in the solemn sacrifice, and their texts therefore focus on different aspects of this sacrifice (Renou, 1947). We also know the register of each text. The most problematic part is chronological information. There have been numerous attempts to date the Vedic corpus as a whole or parts thereof, none of which has found unanimous support in the scholarly community (Hellwig, 2020). As a consequence, all we have is a vague relative order of Vedic texts which is disputed in many details. Given this state of research, each text is assigned to one of five consecutive diachronic layers whose arrangement is based on ideas proposed by Witzel (1989) and Kümmel (2000):

1. Early Vedic [= RV]: *Rigveda* 2-7, 9
2. Old Vedic [= MA]: *Rigveda* 1, 8, 10; metrical portions of the *Atharvaveda-* and *Yajurveda-Saṃhitās* ('Mantra language')
3. Middle Vedic [= PO]: prose portions of the Saṃhitās, the older parts of Brāhmaṇas, Āraṇyakas, and Upaniṣads
4. Young Vedic [= PL]: younger parts of Brāhmaṇas, Āraṇyakas (both prose), and Upaniṣads (partly prose, partly verse)
5. Late Vedic [= SU]: ancillary texts (Sūtras), mostly prose

4. Model

4.1. Creating the constituents and their distributions

Starting from the intuition that part-of-speech, morpho-syntax, the Universal Dependencies (UD; Nivre et al. (2016)) label and the placement of a word with regard to its syntactic head are relevant features when studying syntactic change, we create constituents by forming all possible combinations of these four features. We include a wildcard option (∅) for each of them; this means that the respective feature can take any value in a given constituent. In the following, a semicolon separates options, and a number in square brackets indicates the number of options for each feature:

POS: the actual POS tag; ∅ [2]

Morpho-syntax: the case for words with nominal inflection, ind(eclinable), fin(ite) or inf(inite) for verbal forms; ∅[2]

UD label: the actual label; ∅ [2]

Placement: the signed distance between the position of the head and the dependent, cut off at a distance of 4; the absolute value of this distance; dependent to the left or to the right of its head; ∅ [4]

There are $2 \cdot 2 \cdot 2 \cdot 4 = 32$ constituent representations of each surface form. We denote a constituent by the quadruple of its values; NOUN/Gen/nmod/-1, for example, is a noun in genitive case that acts as a nominal modifier and stands directly to the left of its head.

We calculate the empirical distribution $\mathbf{o}_i^f \in \mathbb{R}_+^5, \sum_j o_{ij}^f = 1$ of one of the three influence variables f (time, school, register) for a given constituent i by counting the frequency of the constituent in each factor level of the variable and normalizing these counts. The respective expected distribution $\mathbf{e}_i^f \in \mathbb{R}_+^5, \sum_j e_{ij}^f = 1$ is obtained by subtracting the counts for i from the respective corpus counts and normalizing. The differences $\mathbf{d}_i^t \in \mathbb{R}^5$ between the expected and observed distributions for the chronological variable describe to which degree the distribution of constituent i deviates from the global estimate calculated without knowledge about i. These differences are used as input for the unary relations in our model ($\mathbf{n} \in \mathbb{Z}_{\geq 0}^5$: vector of global corpus counts for the five chronological slots; $N = \sum_i^5 n_i$; $\mathbf{m}_i \in \mathbb{Z}_{\geq 0}^5$: counts for constituent i):

$$\mathbf{d}_i^t = \mathbf{o}_i^t - \mathbf{e}_i^t = \frac{\mathbf{m}_i}{\sum_{j=1}^5 m_{ij}} - \frac{\mathbf{n} - \mathbf{m}_i}{N - \sum_{j=1}^5 m_{ij}} \quad (1)$$

While pre-processing the data, we use a G-test (Agresti, 2007) that assesses if the distribution of $\mathbf{o}_i^t$ differs significantly from $\mathbf{e}_i^t$ at an error level of 0.01. If it does not, the respective constituent is discarded from the data set because its chronological distribution cannot be said to differ from the corpus distribution at the given error level. This step reduces the number of constituents from 5,153 to 3,605 and thus helps to concentrate on chronologically relevant phenomena.

4.2. Constructing and partitioning the graph

We are interested in grouping constituents that describe related syntactic surface phenomena and that have similar diachronic distributions (see Sec. 1). To achieve the first aim, we construct an undirected graph G each vertex of which is one constituent. G has an edge e_{ij} between vertices i, j if the constituents i, j occur at least once as analyses of the same surface form (see

N number of distinct constituents
K current number of partitions inferred by the model
$\mathbf{z} \in \mathbb{Z}_+^N$ partition assignments of the N constituents
n_k number of constituents assigned to partition k
$\mathbf{g} \in \mathbb{Z}_2^{N(N-1)/2}$ binary edges in G
$\mathbf{\Theta} \in \mathbb{R}_{[0,1]}^{K(K-1)/2}$ parameters of Bernoulli distributions that model the presence of edges $\mathbf{e}$ in G
$\mathbf{A}_{kl}$ number of edges in G that connect constituents assigned to groups k and l
$\mathbf{B}_{kl}$ number of cases in which two constituents assigned to groups k and l are not connected by an edge in G
$\mathbf{a}_l^i$ number of cases in which G has a connection between constituent i and another constituent which is assigned to partition l
$\mathbf{b}_l^i$ number of cases in which G does not have a connection between constituent i and another constituent assigned to partition l
$\boldsymbol{\mu} \in \mathbb{R}^{K \times 5}, \boldsymbol{\sigma} \in \mathbb{R}_+^{K \times 5}$ parameters of the partition specific chronological Normal distributions
$\boldsymbol{\alpha}, \boldsymbol{\beta}, \boldsymbol{\sigma}, \boldsymbol{\mu}_0, \boldsymbol{\sigma}_0$ parameters of the prior distributions of the Dirichlet process, the edge Betas and the Normals on the partitions

Figure 2: Notation for the Gibbs sampler (eqs. 3 and 4)

Sec. 4.1). Edges are unweighted, because the selection of texts in the VTB as well as the Vedic corpus as a whole are biased samples from the Vedic language, and absolute counts may rather represent scholarly and ritualistic preferences. – Using the notation from Fig. 2, the generative process of our model can be described as follows:

$$\begin{aligned} z_i &\sim \mathrm{DP}(\boldsymbol{\alpha}) \\ \Theta_{ab} &\sim \mathrm{Beta}(\boldsymbol{\beta}),\ g_{ij} \sim \mathrm{Bern}(\Theta_{z_i z_j}) \\ d_{ik} &\sim \mathcal{N}(\mu_{z_i k}, \sigma^2_{z_i k}) \end{aligned} \tag{2}$$

The model draws the latent assignment z_i of constituent i from a Dirichlet process with concentration parameter α. The value of the edge g_{ij} between constituents i and j is drawn from a Bernoulli distribution whose parameter depends on the partitions assigned to i and j. Finally, the univariate Normal distributions determine how well the chronological profile of constituent i fits that of the partition to which i is assigned. It should be noted that we use five univariate Normals instead of one five-dimensional Normal because we have no a priori intuition about how the covariance matrix between the five diachronic layers defined in Sec. 3 should be structured. While we could infer the posterior of the covariance from the data using an inverse Wishart distribution, we choose the comparatively easier univariate approach for this exploratory model. For the same reason, we set the univariate precision values to constant small values (0.1) in order to obtain clear chronological profiles.
To obtain a collapsed Gibbs sampler, we remove all information about constituent i from the data (counts $\mathbf{A}_*^{-i}, \mathbf{B}_*^{-i}$) and calculate the product of the posterior (for $k \leq K$) and prior predictives (for $k = K + 1$) of the Dirichlet process, the actual IRM (on which see e.g. Ishiguro et al. (2014)) and the univariate Normal distributions. A histogram of the difference values calculated using eq. 1 shows that the values of $\mathbf{d}$ are normally distributed around zero. Setting $\mu_0 = 0$, the posterior predictive of a Normal distribution for layer v given all constituents assigned to group k therefore has the following parameters (see e.g. Bishop (2006, 98); $\mathbb{I}[\ldots]$ is the indicator function):

$$m_{kv} = \frac{\sigma_0^2 \sum_{j=1}^N (\mathbb{I}[z_j = k] d_{jv}^t)}{n_k \sigma_0^2 + \sigma^2},\ s_{kv}^2 = \frac{\sigma_0^2 \sigma^2}{\sigma^2 + n_k \sigma_0^2} + \sigma_0^2 \tag{3}$$

For the respective prior predictive we obtain $m'_{kv} = 0$, $s'^2_{kv} = \sigma^2 + \sigma_0^2$. – In the following update equation the upper row gives the posterior, the lower one the prior predictive, and $\mathrm{B}(x, y)$ is the Beta function:

$$\begin{aligned} & p(z_i = k | \mathbf{z}^{-i}, \mathbf{e}^{-}, \mathbf{\Theta}, \boldsymbol{\mu}, \boldsymbol{\sigma}, \alpha, \beta, \mu_0, \sigma_0) \\ & \quad \propto \left. \begin{matrix} n_k \\ \alpha \end{matrix} \right\} \cdot \prod_l \frac{\mathrm{B}(A_{kl}^{-i} + a_l^i + \beta, B_{kl}^{-i} + b_l^i + \beta)}{\mathrm{B}(A_{kl}^i + \beta, B_{kl}^i + \beta)} \\ & \quad \cdot \left\{ \begin{matrix} \prod_{v=1}^5 \mathcal{N}(d_{iv} | m_{kv}, s_{kv}^2) \\ \prod_{v=1}^5 \mathcal{N}(d_{iv} | m'_{kv}, s'^2_{kv}) \end{matrix} \right. \end{aligned} \tag{4}$$

4.3. Weighting the members of the inferred partitions

In the last step, we order the members of each partition. Our aim is to find constituents whose chronological distributions deviate clearly from their expected ones as estimated from the corpus, while their distributions over schools and registers conform to the respective expected values as closely as possible. A natural way for formalizing this notion of closeness is provided by the Hellinger distance between the expected and observed distributions for each of the three factors. The Hellinger distance is confined to $[0, 1]$, with zero meaning no difference between $\mathbf{e}$ and $\mathbf{o}$ and one meaning maximum dissimilarity. We calculate the Hellinger distances for time (h_i^t), school (h_i^s) and register (h_i^r) and use the following expression for weighting constituent i:

$$w_i = (h_i^s + h_i^r) - h_i^t \tag{5}$$

w_i becomes less than zero if the observed chronological distribution differs strongly from the expected one, but the observed distributions over schools and registers conform to their expected values.

5. Evaluation

This section provides a qualitative evaluation of some salient trends detected by the proposed model after it was trained for 100 epochs with hyper-parameters $\alpha = 1$, $\beta = 0.5$, $\sigma = \sigma_0 = 0.1$.[2] Due to lack of

[2]The results are not really sensitive to the choice of α and β which is probably due to the fact that the constituents generate strongly connected components in G.

space, we concentrate on selected partitions detected by the model. Those not discussed here either have high weights (eq. 5) and are therefore correlated with the bias terms, or capture well known diachronic trends such as an increasing preference for elliptic constructions (UD label orphan) in the Sūtra literature.

5.1. Compounds

Some of the strongest chronological signals h^t come from partition #11 which contains constituents found in predominantly long nominal compounds. Nominal composition is one of the few areas in which the annotation scheme of the VTB extends the UD standard (Hellwig and Sellmer, 2021) because nominal compounds in late Vedic and especially in classical Sanskrit can encode a wide range of syntactic functions that would be expressed with verbal sentences in other languages (Lowe, 2015). Vedic linguistics have early noticed the chronologically increasing preference for complex compounds (Wackernagel, 1905, 24-26), and our model thus discovered a known diachronic trend.

Partition 11 represents three major aspects of compounding. First, coordinative compounds (UD label compound with sublabel coord) correspond to the class of dvandva ('pair') compounds in traditional Sanskrit grammar which enumerate concepts by juxtaposing their stems. The usage of such compounds is especially widespread in the Gṛhya- and Dharmasūtras and becomes the preferred mode of coordination in classical Sanskrit.

Second, compounds involving nominal (nmod) modifiers of nouns also get more prominent towards the end of the Vedic period. Many of these compounds express a possessive relation as in *sūkta-anta*, lit. "hymn-end", i.e. "end of the hymn", and thus belong to the class of tatpuruṣa compounds in indigenous terminology. Figure 3 plots the ratios of individual levels of the two influencing variables time and register for the constituent NOUN/Cpd/nmod/∅. Each point in the left part of the plot gives the ratio e^t_j/o^t_j for layer j (see eq. 1), and the whiskers indicate the 95% confidence interval of this ratio. The dashed horizontal line indicates equal proportions, i.e. $e^t_j = o^t_j$; if the whiskers intersect with this horizontal line, the ratio cannot be said to differ from 1 at an error level of 5%. The plot shows that the proportion of this constituent increases monotonically over the five layers of the VTB and additionally makes a large jump in the last one. However, other influence variables must be considered as well. In this case, the distribution over the registers (Fig. 3, right) replicates the chronological trend because such compounds are underrepresented in the early metrical texts and over-represented in prose. As the ratio of compounded nominal modifiers already increases slightly from the first to the second metrical layer (RV → MA) and clearly between the older and younger prose layers (PO → PL), it seems plausible that the register is not the central influencing variable and a real chronological trend is discernible here.

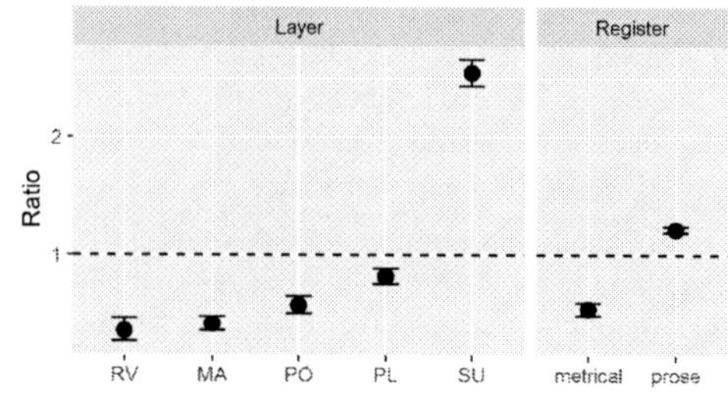

Figure 3: Ratio plots (see p. 5) for the constituent NOUN/Cpd/nmod/∅; see the listing in Sec. 3 for the chronological labels (RV etc.).

Third, closely connected with the two preceding categories are long compounds in general. Their presence can be deduced from members of partition 11 that represent long syntactic arcs in compounds such as ∅/Cpd/∅/4.

Partition 11 also demonstrates how endeavors to control for bias variables are hampered in corpora with a limited coverage. Apart from a strong chronological signal h^t, the top entries in this partition have a strong signal h^s indicating an uneven distribution over the Vedic schools. Mainly responsible for the strength of h^s are texts belonging to the school of the Rigveda. Closer inspection of the data reveals that the predominance of Rigvedic material is due to long compounds found in the Gautama-Dharmasūtra, a late Rigvedic. Other Vedic schools have composed such Dharmasūtras as well, and we are currently working on including samples from them in the VTB. An apparent school-related skew therefore can be explained with selection bias in this case.

Another interesting type of compounds is part of partition 90 which contains clauses modifying nouns (acl) and verbs (advcl). Constituents of the type VERB/Cpd/acl/∅ typically involve verbal nouns in their stem forms compounded with a governing noun as in the phrase *jaritāraḥ suta-somāḥ* 'singers who have pressed Soma' (Rigveda 1.2.2bc) where the head *soma-* is modified by the past participle *suta-* (from *sav* 'press'). As Fig. 4 shows, such constructions are well attested in the oldest metrical levels of Vedic (RV, MA), but lose popularity in the two subsequent layers of Vedic prose (PO, PL), a trend already mentioned by Wackernagel (1905, 315-321). The preference for these constructions increases strongly in the last layer of the Vedic corpus where we find complex, sometimes irregular compound formations as at Āśvalāyana-Gṛhyasūtra 1.17.2: ... *vrīhi-yava-māṣa-tilānām* ... *pūrṇa-śarāvāni nidadhāti* 'he puts down vessels filled with rice, wheat, beans and sesame'. Here the noun *śarāva* 'vessel' is modified by the verbal noun *pūrṇa* (from *par*^{i}*/prā* 'to fill') which is in turn modified by a dvandva compound enumerating different types of

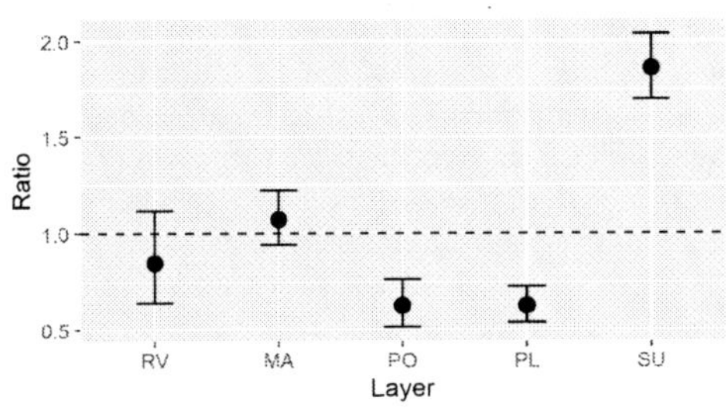

Figure 4: Ratio plot of verbal nouns functioning as clausal modifiers in compounds

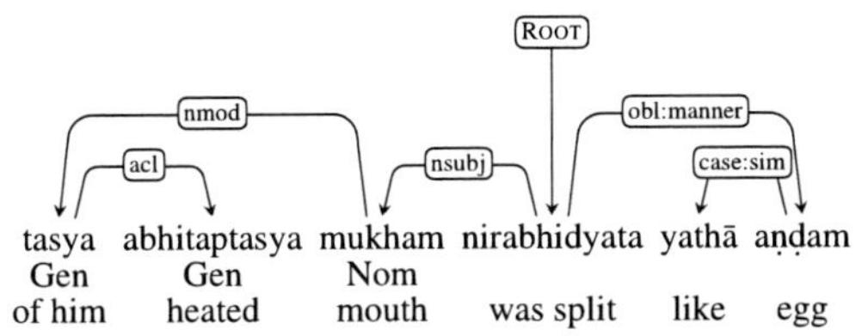

Figure 5: Proto-*genitivus absolutus* at Aitareya-Upaniṣad 1.1.4: "When he was heated, his mouth was split like an egg."

food.

5.2. Precursors of the *genitivus absolutus*

Partition 108 consists almost exclusively of clauses (acl) that modify nouns in nominative, accusative and genitive case in any relative placement. The highest coefficients w (see eq. 5) in this partition are reported for verbal nouns in genitive case that are preferably found to the right of their congruent heads. An example of this construction is displayed in Fig. 5. Here, the past participle *abhitaptasya* (from *abhi tap* 'heat') modifies the pronoun *tasya* which in turn expresses the possessor of the subject *mukham* 'mouth'. While the past participle is preferred in the Vedic prose, analogous constructions with a present participle are found in early metrical texts as well (see e.g. Rigveda 10.38.2c).

Both types of constructions have in common that the modified noun stands in a possessive relation to another word in the sentence, typically its subject (*mukham* in Fig. 5). Oertel (1926, 101ff.) interpreted such cases as precursors of the *genitivus absolutus*. This idea is supported by the fact that these acl constructions are especially frequent in the two oldest layers (Fig. 6) whereas possible replacements such as the *locativus absolutus* and regular adverbial clauses become more popular in prose (see the left half of Fig. 7). It should, however, be noted that the corresponding ratio plots of the register (Fig. 7, right) point to pronounced differences between metrical and prose texts which is why the model does not mention them among the top rated constituents according to eq. 5. We may therefore just face a register split in the proper Vedic corpus (layers RV–PL) and early echoes of classical Sanskrit in the last layer.

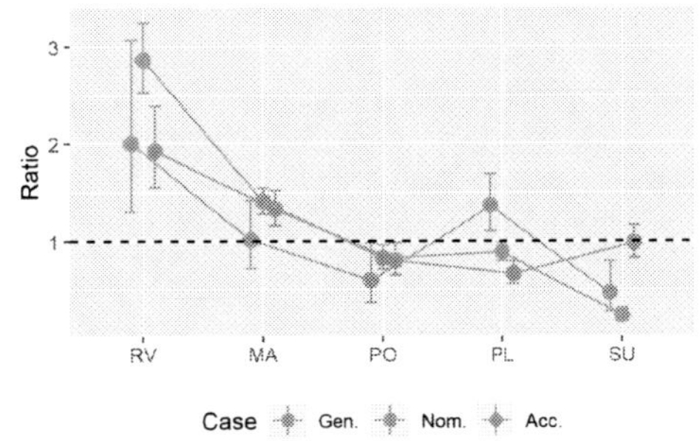

Figure 6: Ratio plots for the proto-*genitivus absolutus* (VERB/Gen/acl/∅) and related adnominal constructions of participles

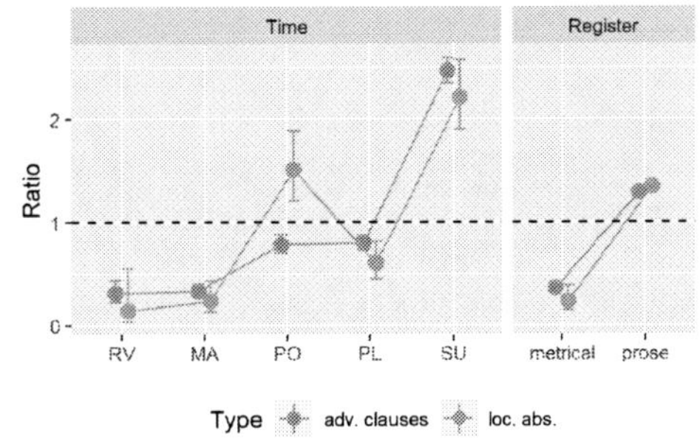

Figure 7: Ratio plots for the *locativus absolutus* (VERB/Loc/advcl/∅) and adverbial clauses in general (VERB/IV/advcl/∅)

As was mentioned above, partition 108 also contains clausal modifiers in nominative and accusative case. The structural link that connects these constituents with those in genitive case are more abstract representations such as VERB/∅/acl/|1| also found in this partition. The data in Fig. 6 shows that the frequency ratios of these two types decrease over the first three layers of the VTB in a similar way as those of the genitive. While, however, the construction in the nominative case becomes dispreferred in the last layer, constructions in the accusative become more popular again towards the end of the Vedic period. This trend is mainly due to accusative participles placed directly in front of their heads as at *Śāṅkhāyana-Gṛhyasūtra* 3.3.10: *abhyaktam aśmānam … nikhanet* 'he may bury an anointed stone' where the accusative noun *aśmānam* 'stone' is modified by the past participle of *abhi añj* 'anoint'. Note that Delbrück (1878, 41) interprets such prenominal placement of verbal nouns as indicating that they had assumed an adjectival function.

5.3. Clausal subjects

Partition 22 combines two types of constituents that are structurally and functionally unrelated at first view. The highest values of w are reported for verbal nouns

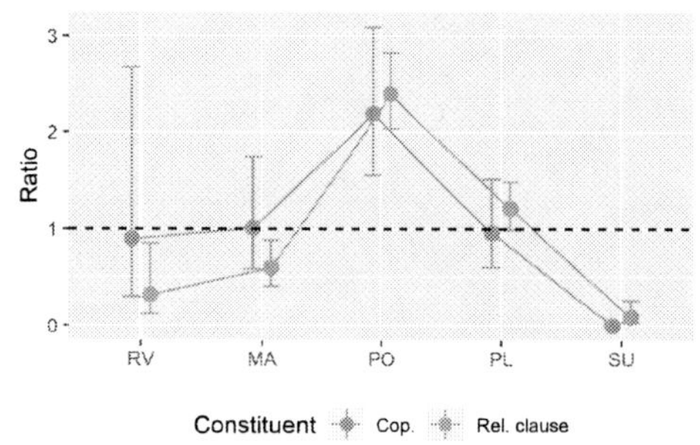

Figure 8: Ratio plots for verbal nouns derived from copulae (VERB/Nom/cop/∅) and relative clauses functioning as subjects (VERB/∅/csubj/∅; see Sec. 5.3)

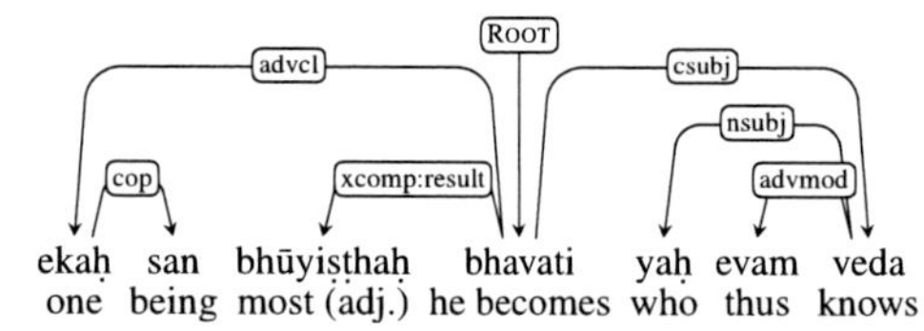

Figure 9: Combination of a clausal subject and the participle of a copula at *Maitrāyaṇī-Saṃhitā* 1.9.5: "He who knows thus obtains most although he is only one."

of copulae in nominative case that function as clausal components (acl) of a noun, directly followed by clausal subjects (csubj) placed (far) to the right of their – mostly verbal – heads. Most of the clausal subjects occur in stereotyped expressions of the form *yaḥ evam veda* 'who knows thus' and variants thereof which describe what a sacrificer must know in order to make a ritual successful (see e.g. Freedman (2012)). The copulae functioning as acl have a similar distribution over the chronological layers (see Fig. 8), and they are occasionally part of the same sentence as the clausal subjects. The example in Fig. 9 shows that both constructions functionally resemble adverbial clauses: While the copula construction has a concessive sense, the clausal subject gives the condition, i.e. the right knowledge of the ritual, for achieving the intended aim. Amano (2009, 121-125) explains the zero subject in such statements by the fact that these exegetical texts assume the sacrificer as the agent if not stated otherwise. The clear chronological distribution in Fig. 8 may therefore be caused by changes in style and content rather than by chronological changes although clausal subjects that have an adverbial sense can already be found in the *Rigveda* (Hettrich, 1988, 575,615) and are therefore not ad hoc formations in the Vedic prose.

Because the csubj constructions preferably occur in stereotyped phrases that can be detected by string search, they also allow to estimate how well the distribution of this constituent in the VTB approximates its distribution in the digitized parts of the Vedic corpus. We form the ratios of csubj constructions and syntactically annotated words per text (r_1) and compare them with the ratios of the string *ya evaṃ veda* and the number of characters per text (r_2).[3] Kendall's rank correlation of r_1 and r_2 yields $\tau = 0.245$ ($Z = 1.4062$, $p = 0.16$) and thus a weak correlation that is not statistically significant at an error level of 10%. The distribution found in the VTB obviously does not fully reflect the corpus distribution, a caveat one should keep in mind when using treebanks of limited coverage for diachronic studies.

5.4. The rise and fall of oblique pronominal arguments

In the last case study, we consider partition 114 which assembles pronouns in any relative placement that function as oblique arguments of verbs. At first view, the ratio plots in Fig. 10 suggest that the members of this partition show clear diachronic developments while register seems to play no role. As pronouns are a closed class of words and have received much scholarly attention in the past (Gotō, 2013), a more detailed inspection of this partition appears worthwhile. After discarding quantifiers with pronominal inflection, we are left with four classes of pronouns for which Fig. 11 gives chronological ratio plots.

Apparently, the four classes have very different diachronic distributions, and the chronological profile in Fig. 10 is a superimposition of them. The profile of the personal pronouns (Skt. *mad-* 'I', *tvad-* 'you') in Fig. 11 is due to register differences: The earliest metrical texts directly address deities and thus make use of pronouns of the second and first person. More interesting is the distribution of the relative pronoun (*ya-*) the ratios of which decrease slowly, but constantly. It may well be the case that we observe a genre-specific phenomenon here that Hock (1992) explains with greater restrictions that didactic Vedic prose imposes on the use of apposite relative clauses: Vedic prose texts focus on imparting knowledge about the ritual in the most effective way and therefore refrain from giving elaborate side information which could be encoded in relative clauses. Although the amount of data is limited (there are only 125 relative pronouns used as oblique arguments in the VTB), such a conclusion receives further support from the fact that almost half of the occurrences in the latest layer come from the *Śvetāśvatara-Upaniṣad*, a speculative text in verses that represents a completely different genre than the Sūtra texts typical for this layer. Genre-related mechanisms may also explain the unexpected distribution of the oblique forms of interrogative pronouns. The peak in Fig. 11 is caused by stereotyped pairs of questions and answers that deal with aspects of the sacrifice and are at least

[3]Note that Sandhi, i.e. phonetic merging of words, prevents a straightforward word count in Vedic texts stored in plain text format.

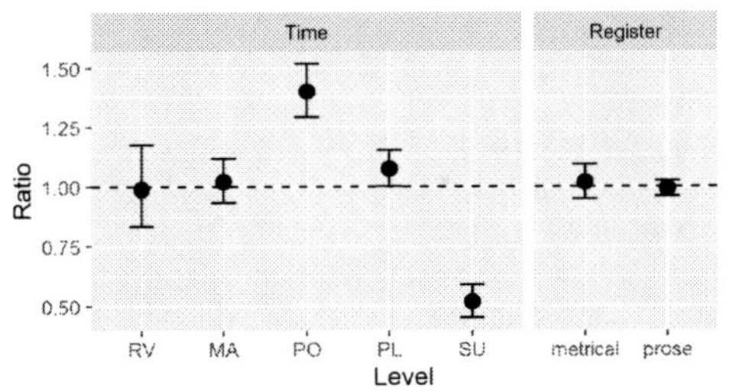

Figure 10: Ratio plots for pronouns functioning as oblique arguments (PRON/∅/obl/∅)

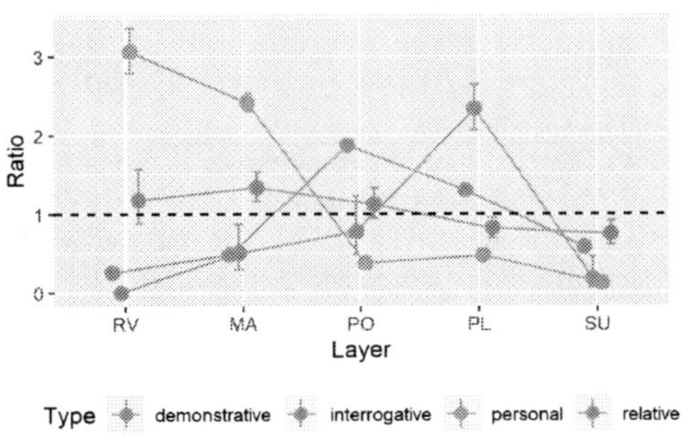

Figure 11: Chronological plot from Fig. 10 (left), split by four classes of pronouns

structurally related to ritualized question-answer contests called *brahmodya* (Thompson, 1997).

The largest class of oblique pronominal arguments consists of impersonal pronouns (labelled 'demonstrative' in Fig. 11). Only four of them occur more than ten times as oblique arguments in the VTB: *sa-/ta-* (anaphoric; see Amano (2009, 55ff.)),[4] *eṣa-/eta-* (discourse deixis, points to something known to hearer and speaker; see Kümmel (2014)) and the enclitic anaphora *a-/ena-* (Amano, 2009, 64ff.). In addition there are instances of the proximal deictic pronoun *ayam-*. Most of the oblique forms of this pronoun are identical with the respective forms of *a-/ena-* in unaccented texts and for this reason not differentiated from this paradigm in the VTB. These cases are subsumed under the class 'unassigned' in Fig. 12. The four types of pronouns show a similar diachronic distribution in Fig. 12: While instances in the two oldest, metrical layers are rare, they occur most frequently in the oldest prose (PO) just to slowly disappear again. The few occurrences of *eṣa-/eta* in the Sūtra layer, for example, are mostly confined to stereotyped uses of the instrumental feminine which refers to mantras accompanying ritual acts.

[4]The frequent use of the accusative singular neuter of this pronoun as a local or temporal adverb is not recorded in Fig. 12 because these instances are syntactically labelled with advmod.

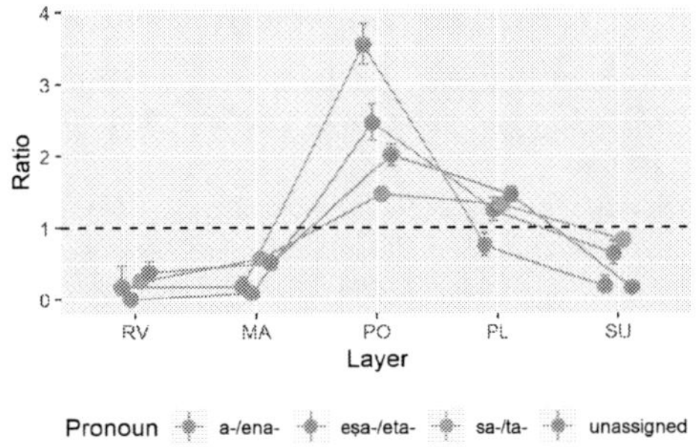

Figure 12: Details for the demonstrative pronouns from Fig. 11

6. Summary

Studying diachronic syntactic changes typically takes its way from qualitative to quantitative research because richly annotated treebanks make it possible to follow the chronological trajectories of syntactic structures marked as noteworthy in qualitative studies. In this paper we have taken the opposite direction because the qualitative work available for Vedic syntax is limited. We have developed a framework that proposes, in a purely data-driven fashion, abstract syntactic structures whose frequencies probably change with time while controlling for influence variables such as register and intellectual affiliation. One obvious way to extend this framework is to allow for combinations of multiple constituents; and another one to account for the content of the source passages as derived, for instance, from contextualized word embeddings.

The method developed here also serves as an intermediate step towards a better understanding of the chronology of Vedic: We aim at finding constituents with a clear chronological profile that can help in clarifying the dates of chronologically disputed Middle and Late Vedic texts. The four case studies in Sec. 5 have shown that some diachronic variation can be explained with differences in style and content after a closer inspection. Such an outcome would not be *per se* problematic for studying the chronology of Vedic – a stylistic change is as good for determining the age of a text as a syntactic one. The central challenge is, however, that the preliminary chronology of the Vedic corpus (see Sec. 3) is ultimately grounded on style and content so that such an approach runs the risk of circularity. Controlling for the content of text passages and above all a careful qualitative scrutiny of possible chronological signals are therefore indispensable for obtaining a clearer picture of this important historical corpus.

Acknowledgments

Oliver Hellwig and Sven Sellmer were funded by the German Federal Ministry of Education and Research, FKZ 01UG2121, when doing research for this paper.

7. Bibliographical References

Agresti, A. (2007). *An Introduction to Categorical Data Analysis*. John Wiley and Sons, Hoboken, New Jersey.

Amano, K. (2009). *Maitrāyaṇī Saṃhitā I–II. Übersetzung der Prosapartien mit Kommentar zur Lexik und Syntax der älteren vedischen Prosa*. Hempen, Bremen.

Biagetti, E., Hellwig, O., Ackermann, E., Widmer, P., and Scarlata, S. (2021). Evaluating syntactic annotation of ancient languages. Lessons from the Vedic Treebank. *Old World*.

Bishop, C. M. (2006). *Pattern Recognition and Machine Learning*. Springer.

Cohen, S. (2008). *Text and Authority in the Older Upaniṣads*. Brill, Leiden.

Delbrück, B. (1878). *Die altindische Wortfolge aus dem Śatapathabrāhmaṇa*. Verlag der Buchhandlung des Waisenhauses, Halle.

Freedman, Y. (2012). Altar of words: Text and ritual in Taittirīya Upaniṣad 2. *Numen*, 59(4):322–343.

Frermann, L. and Lapata, M. (2016). A Bayesian model of diachronic meaning change. *Transactions of the Association for Computational Linguistics*, 4:31–45.

Gonda, J. (1971). *Old Indian*. Handbuch der Orientalistik, Zweite Abteilung, Erster Band, Erster Abschnitt. E.J. Brill, Leiden.

Gotō, T. (2013). Pronouns. In Toshifumi Gotō, et al., editors, *Old Indo-Aryan Morphology and its Indo-Iranian Background*, pages 66–78. Verlag der Österreichischen Akademie der Wissenschaften.

Haase, C., Anwar, S., Yimam, S. M., Friedrich, A., and Biemann, C. (2021). SCoT: Sense clustering over time: A tool for the analysis of lexical change. In *Proceedings of the 16th Conference of the European Chapter of the Association for Computational Linguistics: System Demonstrations*, pages 198–204.

Hellwig, O. and Sellmer, S. (2021). The Vedic treebank. In Erica Biagetti, et al., editors, *Building New Resources for Historical Linguistics*, pages 31–40. Pavia University Press.

Hellwig, O., Scarlata, S., Ackermann, E., and Widmer, P. (2020). The treebank of Vedic Sanskrit. In Nicoletta Calzolari, et al., editors, *Proceedings of the LREC*, pages 5139–5148.

Hellwig, O. (2020). Dating and stratifying a historical corpus with a Bayesian mixture model. In *Proceedings of LT4HALA*, pages 1–9.

Hettrich, H. (1988). *Untersuchungen zur Hypotaxe im Vedischen*. de Gruyter, Berlin.

Hilpert, M. and Gries, S. T. (2016). Quantitative approaches to diachronic corpus linguistics. In Merja Kytö et al., editors, *The Cambridge Handbook of English Historical Linguistics*, pages 36–53. Cambridge University Press.

Hock, H. H. (1984). (Pre-)Rig-Vedic convergence of Indo-Aryan with Dravidian? Another look at the evidence. *Studies in the Linguistic Sciences*, 14(1):89–108.

Hock, H. H. (1992). Some peculiarities of Vedic-prose relative clauses. *Wiener Zeitschrift für die Kunde Südasiens*, 36:19–29.

Hock, H. H. (1997). Chronology or Genre? Problems in Vedic Syntax. In Michael Witzel, editor, *Inside the Texts – Beyond the Texts: New Approaches to the Study of the Vedas*, pages 103–126. Harvard University, Cambridge, MA.

Hock, H. H. (2015a). A bibliography of Sanskrit syntax. In Peter M. Scharf, editor, *Sanskrit syntax. Selected papers presented at the seminar on Sanskrit syntax and discourse structures, 13-15 June, 2013, Université Paris Diderot*, pages 399–470. The Sanskrit Library.

Hock, H. H. (2015b). Some issues in Sanskrit syntax. In Peter M. Scharf, editor, *Sanskrit syntax. Selected papers presented at the seminar on Sanskrit syntax and discourse structures, 13-15 June, 2013, Université Paris Diderot*, pages 1–52.

Ishiguro, K., Sato, I., and Ueda, N. (2014). Collapsed variational Bayes inference of infinite relational model. *arXiv preprint arXiv:1409.4757*.

Kemp, C., Tenenbaum, J. B., Griffiths, T. L., Yamada, T., and Ueda, N. (2006). Learning systems of concepts with an infinite relational model. In *Proceedings of the AAAI*, volume 3, pages 381–388.

Kümmel, M. J. (2014). Pāṇini 5.3.5 and the function of sanskrit etád. In Hans Henrich Hock, editor, *Vedic Studies: Language, Texts, Culture, and Philosophy*, pages 39–56. Rashtriya Sanskrit Sansthan and D.K. Printworld, New Delhi.

Kümmel, M. J. (2000). *Das Perfekt im Indoiranischen. Eine Untersuchung der Form und Funktion einer ererbten Kategorie des Verbums und ihrer Entwicklung in den altindoiranischen Sprachen*. Reichert, Wiesbaden.

Lehmann, W. P. (1974). *Proto-Indo-European syntax*. University of Texas Press, Austin.

Lowe, J. J. (2015). The syntax of Sanskrit compounds. *Language*, 91(3):71–115.

Nivre, J., De Marneffe, M.-C., Ginter, F., Goldberg, Y., Hajic, J., Manning, C. D., McDonald, R., Petrov, S., Pyysalo, S., Silveira, N., et al. (2016). Universal dependencies v1: A multilingual treebank collection. In *Proceedings of the Tenth International Conference on Language Resources and Evaluation (LREC'16)*, pages 1659–1666.

Oertel, H. (1926). *The Syntax of Cases in the Narrative and Descriptive Prose of the Brāhmaṇas. I. The Disjunct Use of Cases*. Carl Winter's Universitätsbuchhandlung, Heidelberg.

Patton, L. L. (2006). *Bringing the Gods to Mind: Mantra and Ritual in Early Indian Sacrifice*. University of California Press, Berkeley.

Renou, L. (1937). *La décadence et la disparition du*

subjonctif. Number 1 in Monographies sanskrites. Adrien-Maisonneuve, Paris.

Renou, L. (1947). *Les écoles védiques et la formation du Véda.* Imprimerie Nationale, Paris.

Renou, L. (1956). *Histoire de la Langue Sanskrite.* Edition IAC, Lyon.

Schätzle, C., Dennig, F. L., Blumenschein, M., Keim, D. A., and Butt, M. (2019). Visualizing linguistic change as dimension interactions. In *Proceedings of the 1st International Workshop on Computational Approaches to Historical Language Change*, pages 272–278.

Thompson, G. (1997). The brahmodya and Vedic discourse. *Journal of the American Oriental Society*, 117(1):13–37.

Wackernagel, J. (1905). *Altindische Grammatik. Band II, 1: Einleitung zur Wortlehre. Nominalkomposition.* Vandenhoeck & Ruprecht, Göttingen.

Wezler, A. (2001). Zu der Frage des 'Strebens nach äußerster Kürze' in den Śrautasūtras. *Zeitschrift der Deutschen Morgenländischen Gesellschaft*, 151:351–366.

Witzel, M. (1989). Tracing the Vedic dialects. In Colette Caillat, editor, *Dialectes dans les littératures indoaryennes*, pages 97–265. Collège de France, Paris.

Wüst, W. (1928). *Stilgeschichte und Chronologie des Ṛgveda*, volume XVII of *Abhandlungen für die Kunde des Morgenlandes.* Deutsche Morgenländische Gesellschaft, Leipzig.

Proceedings of the Second Workshop on Language Technologies for Historical and Ancient Languages (LT4HALA 2022), pages 20–25
Language Resources and Evaluation Conference (LREC 2022), Marseille, 25 June 2022

Accurate Dependency Parsing and Tagging of Latin

Sebastian Nehrdich[1,2], Oliver Hellwig[1,3]
[1]Institute for Language and Information, Heinrich-Heine-Universität Düsseldorf.
[2]Khyentse Center for Tibetan Buddhist Textual Scholarship, Universität Hamburg.
[3]Department of Comparative Language Science, University of Zürich.
nehrdich@uni-duesseldorf.de, Oliver.Hellwig@uni-duesseldorf.de

Abstract

Having access to high-quality grammatical annotations is important for downstream tasks in NLP as well as for corpus-based research. In this paper, we describe experiments with the Latin BERT word embeddings that were recently be made available by Bamman and Burns (2020). We show that these embeddings produce competitive results in the low-level task of morpho-syntactic tagging. In addition, we describe a graph-based dependency parser that is trained with these embeddings and clearly outperforms various baselines.

Keywords: Latin, biaffine parser, Universal Dependencies, morpho-syntax

1. Introduction

Among the ancient languages in the Universal Dependency (UD) collection of treebanks, Latin has the largest amount of data, and its individual treebanks cover a substantial range of the language including Classical Latin (Crane et al., 2001), Christian authors (Haug and Jøhndal, 2008), a treebank dedicated to the work of Thomas Aquinas (ITTB, Cecchini et al. (2018)) and samples from Late Latin written in the Tuscany (Cecchini et al., 2020). In spite of these resources, large parts of the Latin literature have remained syntactically unanalyzed so far. Developing a reliable morpho-syntactic tagger as well as a syntactic parser for Latin is therefore a desideratum, and several publications have addressed this problem.

While the parser described in the early publication by Koch (1994) works with feature unification, most subsequent models use transition- or graph-based approaches. Bamman and Crane (2008) use the MST parser (McDonald et al., 2005) and obtain labeled attachment scores (LAS) of 54% using gold and 50% using automatically annotated morpho-syntactic information on Perseus data. The authors show that the accuracy is strongly correlated with the amount of non-projective constructions. McGillivray and Passarotti (2009) report experiments with the best parsers available at that time, reaching unlabeled attachment score (UAS) of about 79% and LAS of about 71% on the ITTB. Lee et al. (2011) propose an undirected graphical model that performs joint morpho-syntactic and dependency analysis and that improves over a pipelined approach in the UAS. The authors emphasize the importance of morpho-syntax for successfully parsing morphologically rich languages such as Latin. Ponti and Passarotti (2016) apply a neural parser with feature templates to the ITTB, achieving 90.97% UAS and 86.5% LAS. Slightly better scores are reported by Straka et al. (2019) who use a pipelined model (see Sec. 3 of this paper). Their work will serve as a baseline for model comparison in this paper. Most recently, Gamba et al. (2021) further developed the architecture proposed in Ponti and Passarotti (2016) and achieved 92.85% UAS and 89.44% LAS on the ITTB.

One problem noted by many authors is domain adaptation: Parsers trained on one Latin treebank perform suboptimally when applied to another (see e.g. Passarotti and Ruffolo (2010) and McGillivray and Passarotti (2009), Table 5), a fact that is due to the heterogeneous nature of the corpora and the marked linguistic changes in Christian and medieval Latin (on which see e.g. Dinkova-Bruun (2011) and Vincent (2016)). Another problem is the rich morpho-syntax of Latin and the resulting non-configurationality and freedom of word order, esp. for some classical authors. Andor et al. (2016) have shown that from among the two parsing architectures widely used nowadays, graph-based and transition-based, graph-based parsers are better suited for morphologically rich languages with a high degree of non-projectivity. In this paper, we therefore describe a graph-based parsing architecture that improves over previously reported results by considerable margins. Our architecture is a modified version of the biaffine parser proposed by Dozat and Manning (2017), and uses the contextualized BERT embeddings (Devlin et al., 2019) recently made available for Latin (Latin BERT; Bamman and Burns (2020)). With the help of these contextualized BERT embeddings, our parser is able to outperform the current state of the art by a clear margin. It is especially efficient when no grammatical annotation is available or the training corpus is comparatively small. In addition, we augment the space of the input features by morpho-syntactic information, which further increases the performance.

We make the code of this parser available at: `https://github.com/sebastian-nehrdich/latin-parser`

Section 2 of this paper describes the architectures of two taggers and the dependency parser, and Sec. 3

specifies the experimental settings and discusses the results of our experiments. Section 4 summarizes this paper.

2. Model specification

For morpho-syntactic tagging we use a linear transformation followed by a softmax operation on top of the pre-trained Latin BERT model (Bamman and Burns, 2020), a contextual word embedding model that uses the BERT architecture. It has 12 layers, a hidden dimensionality of 768 and was trained on a total number of 642.7M tokens taken from a large variety of digitized Latin texts ranging from 200 BCE to 1922 CE. We allow all parameters of the model to be fine-tuned during training.

For our dependency parsing experiments we use the biaffine architecture of Dozat and Manning (2017) to which a character based convolutional neural network (CharCNN) was added. This CNN uses the individual characters of each inflected form as input (Rotman and Reichart, 2019; Zhang et al., 2015). Our implementation of the parser is based on the DCST by Rotman and Reichart (2019). However, we decided not to apply the pretraining steps used in the DCST model because a series of experiments (details not reported) shows that these steps do not improve the accuracy of the parser, which is probably due to the comparatively large size of the training corpus and the expressiveness of the input features used here.

The main extension of our parser is that we integrate a contextual word embedding model and a larger number of categorical linguistic input features. In the same way as in the biaffine model, these features are represented as continuous, randomly initialized embeddings. We use embedding dimensions of 100 for all features whose values are set to the gold values provided by the UD data sets. We consider the following input features for the parser:

Morpho-syntax: Case, number and gender of each word, as provided by the UD conllu files. These features are fully specified for nouns, adjectives, non-personal pronouns and verbal nouns with a nominal inflection (e.g. participles of various tenses). Personal pronouns have case and number information. We make use of both atomic features (e.g. 'Acc', 'Sing' and 'Neut' each taken as a separate input feature) and their joint representations (e.g. 'Acc Sing Neut').

Verbal nouns: Verbal nouns convey syntactic information. We therefore evaluate a joint combination of the tense and the type of verbal nouns.

Word representations: We perform experiments with three types of word representations. First we use the character representation of each inflected word form as input for the CharCNN, following Rotman and Reichart (2019). Second we use the fastText Latin model made available by Grave et al. (2018) as static embedding model of complete words. This model has a dimensionality of 300 and has been trained on Latin Common Crawl and Wikipedia data. We decided to use fastText since it was shown in Sprugnoli et al. (2019) that its ability to model model morphology by taking subword units into account is beneficial for synonym-selection tasks. Third we evaluate how the parser performs with Latin BERT as embedding model. In this setting the representation of each inflected form is generated by taking the average of its subword embeddings produced by the Latin BERT model.

3. Experiments

We run experiments on the following tasks: POS tagging, linguistic feature tagging and dependency parsing. For POS tagging, the current state of the art is given in Bamman and Burns (2020). For linguistic feature tagging and dependency parsing it is set by UDPipe 2.0 (Straka et al., 2019). UDPipe 2.0 is a multitask model that jointly predicts POS tags, linguistic features, lemmas and dependency trees. The model is described in detail in Straka (2018). In Straka et al. (2019), UDPipe 2.0 was evaluated with two different settings: One initialized with static word embeddings and one with contextual ones. The contextual word embedding model used by these authors is BERT Multilingual Uncased (Devlin et al., 2019), a model trained on the Wikipedia dumps of the 100 languages with the largest Wikipedias, including Latin.

We use the following three treebanks from the UD framework for all our experiments: The Index Thomisticus Treebank (Cecchini et al. (2018), ITTB), containing works by Thomas Aquinas (390,785 training tokens); the PROIEL treebank (Haug and Jøhndal, 2008), containing both classical and medieval works (172,133 training tokens); and the Perseus Latin Treebank (Bamman and Crane, 2006), containing works from the Classical period (18,184 training tokens). We also create a merged dataset where the training data from all three corpora is joined and duplicates are removed from the training data. We use this merged dataset in all our experiments to evaluate how it affects the respective performance. The following abbreviations are used in the tables reporting the results of our experiments:

UDP2: UDPipe 2.0

Biaffine: the biaffine parser that we adapted for our experiments

WE: static word embeddings (see Straka (2018))

FT: Latin fastText static word embeddings

CLE: character-level embeddings

MBERT: Multilingual Bert Uncased

Feats: morpho-syntactic features; joint representation for UDPipe 2.0, jointly and atomic repr. for biaffine

Merged: Merged training corpora

Model	ITTB	PROIEL	Perseus
UDP2 WE+CLE	96.97	91.53	79.20
UDP2 WE+CLE+MBERT	97.05	91.54	80.43
Latin BERT individual	97.1	94.0	**90.8**
Latin BERT merged	**97.3**	**94.2**	86.7

Table 1: Accuracy of the morpho-syntactic tagger on the UD treebanks for Latin.

3.1. POS Tagging and Morpho-Syntax

Our experiments on POS Tagging mirror the results in Bamman and Burns (2020). We evaluated how merging the training data of the three corpora affects the performance, but could not achieve a consistent performance increase with this method. We report the results for predicting morpho-syntactic features in Tab. 1. The results show that there is a clear increase in accuracy for all three corpora when using the Latin BERT model, while the MBERT model used by UDPipe 2.0 only gives a slight increase in performance (see the first two rows of Tab. 1). With over 10% the increase is most pronounced for the Perseus corpus. We assume that this is due to the comparatively small size of this corpus, a scenario in which pretraining is especially effective. While merging the training data brings a further increase in accuracy in the case of ITTB and PROIEL, this step leads to a clear decrease for Perseus, possibly to be explained by domain effects. Another possible reason could be the different annotation guidelines of these corpora.

3.2. Dependency Parsing

We show the results of the dependency parsing task in Tab. 2. UDPipe 2.0 has been evaluated with static word embeddings (WE) as well as MBERT, adding character level embeddings (CLE) in both cases. The results in the second row of Tab. 2 show that adding the MBERT embedding to UDPipe 2.0 results in slight improvements in UAS and LAS for ITTB, an improvement in LAS for PROIEL and a clear improvement in UAS and LAS for Perseus.

The biaffine model with morpho-syntactic features (`Biaffine WE+CLE+POS+Feats`) shows a clear improvement over UDPipe 2.0 for all three corpora. Merging the training data of the three corpora (setting `Biaffine WE+CLE+POS+Feats+Merged`) leads to a lower UAS for ITTB, while for PROIEL it increases UAS and decreases LAS, and for Perseus it clearly improves both UAS and LAS.

The biaffine model based on the Latin BERT without WE/CLE/POS and linguistic features (`Biaffine Latin BERT`) produces a higher UAS than `Biaffine WE+CLE+POS+Feats` on all three corpora. For LAS, the performance only increases in the case of PROIEL. Adding WE, CLE and POS (`Biaffine Latin BERT+WE+CLE+POS`) to Latin BERT increases the performance of the biaffine parser for all corpora in both UAS and LAS. Finally, the combination of Latin BERT with fastText, CLE, POS and all available linguistic features (`Biaffine LatinBERT+FT+CLE+POS+Feats`) gives the best performance for all three corpora in terms of both UAS and LAS. Similar to the experiments with UDPipe 2.0 (see above) merging the training corpora does not produce a clear-cut outcome (setting `Biaffine Latin BERT+FT+CLE+POS+Feats+Merged`).

While this strategy does not improve the scores for ITTB and PROIEL, it leads to a notable improvement in the case of Perseus.

These results allow for three major observations. First, Latin BERT is a powerful embedding model that significantly boosts performance when compared with non-contextual embedding models and MBERT. We hypothesize that the nature of the textual data used for pretraining is decisive for the performance of the contextual models. The New Latin material of the Wikipedia used for training the MBERT model covers only a small domain compared to the large amount of data which was used for the training of Latin BERT, and which spans a variety of domains from the classical era to the 21st century. In fact, our results show that even a biaffine parser initialized with Latin BERT without any other linguistic features (`Biaffine Latin BERT`) is able to outperform the UAS of a non-contextual model with full POS and linguistic feature information. This shows that BERT models, when trained on a sufficient amount of data from appropriate domains, are able to successfully capture syntactic information.

The second important observation is that adding gold annotated POS information, static word embeddings and character level embeddings on top of the Latin BERT model gives the biaffine parser another notable boost in performance. The best scores are reached when morpho-syntactic features are used as well. This leads us to the conclusion that providing the parser with linguistic features clearly improves its performance, as was already observed by Lee et al. (2011), even if these features are added on top of an already expressive contextual embedding model.

Third, merging the training data only leads to a better performance for the relatively small Perseus corpus, while the larger ITTB and PROIEL show a slight but consistent decrease in UAS and LAS. For the ITTB, one possible explanation of this contradictory behavior (more data, but worse performance) resembles the one brought forward for the case of MBERT embeddings above: The additional data mostly come from the Latin literature of the classical period and late Antiquity and may therefore differ from Thomas' Latin in terms of their vocabulary and the degree of configurationality. If this is the case, it can be seen as a warning against a simple "more is better" strategy when augmenting the training set for NLP tasks.

To better understand the differences between static and contextual embeddings, we calculate label-

Model	ITTB		PROIEL		Perseus	
	UAS	LAS	UAS	LAS	UAS	LAS
UDP2 WE+CLE	91.06	88.8	83.34	78.66	71.20	61.28
UDP2 WE+CLE+MBERT	91.25	89.10	83.34	78.70	74.39	64.68
Gamba et al. (2021)	92.85	89.44				
Biaffine WE+CLE+POS+Feats	92.74	91.52	84.66	81.58	75.43	69.48
Biaffine WE+CLE+POS+Feats+Merged	92.58	91.52	85.73	80.39	81.28	75.73
Biaffine Latin BERT	92.84	90.91	87.81	83.98	81.54	73.33
Biaffine Latin BERT+WE+CLE+POS	93.55	92.56	88.82	85,82	82.38	75.42
Biaffine Latin BERT+FT+CLE+POS+Feats	**94.04**	**92.99**	**89.21**	**86.34**	83.57	77.63
Biaffine Latin BERT+FT+CLE+POS+Feats+Merged	93.59	92.47	88.90	86.18	**85.37**	**80.16**

Table 2: Performance of the parser on the different UD treebanks for Latin.

wise accuracy scores for three models from Tab. 2, counting those cases as correct in which the label and the head of a syntactic relation are predicted correctly. We order the labels by label-wise differences between the best (`Biaffine LatinBERT+FT+CLE+POS+Feats`) and the worst of our models (`Biaffine WE+CLE+POS+Feats`). Results for the five labels with the highest and the lowest of these differences are displayed in Fig. 1. Judging from the first four labels in the upper compartment of Fig. 1, the best model performs especially well for complex syntactic structures, whose analysis needs access to sentence-level information. Somehow unexpectedly, all models have problems with coordinating conjunctions (cc) although they belong to a closed class of words; in several cases, this is due to wrong attachment. Cases with low differences between `Biaffine LatinBERT+FT+CLE+POS+Feats` and `Biaffine WE+CLE+POS+Feats` include labels which typically have short dependency lengths as well as the three labels advmod, amod and case. The poor performance that all models show for vocatives may be due to issues in the gold data, as many interjections such as *mehercules* or *heu* are labelled syntactically as vocatives on the dependency level, but as `INTJ` on the POS level.

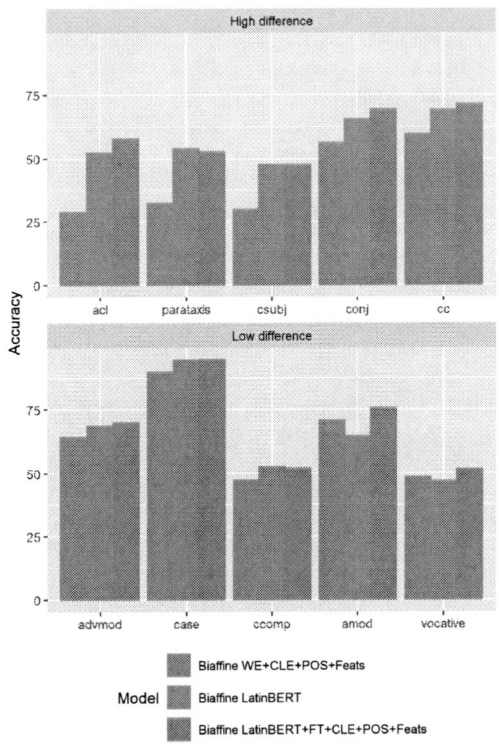

Figure 1: Comparison of label-wise accuracy scores for selected models from Tab. 2. The plot gives the labels with the highest (top) and lowest (bottom) differences between `Biaffine LatinBERT+FT+CLE+POS+Feats` and `Biaffine WE+CLE+POS+Feats`

4. Summary

This paper has shown that even a syntactically challenging language such as Latin can be analyzed with high accuracy scores when appropriate off-the-shelf components are combined in the right way. The decisive element for all three tasks discussed in this paper are contextualized word embeddings, whose application improves scores especially clearly for the small Perseus corpus. Another important result is that adding gold morpho-syntax and static word embeddings further improves the quality of a parser working with contextualized embeddings. Morpho-syntax may seem problematic when it comes to analyzing Latin texts for which this information is not yet available. As, however, the morpho-syntactic and especially the POS tagger come close to human performance for some corpora studied here, one may consider to use a pipelined approach that first runs these taggers on unannotated texts and subsequently applies the dependency parser to the enhanced representations. This is exactly the road we are planning to take when re-analyzing the LatinISE corpus (McGillivray, 2012). We hope that such an enhanced resource can yield better insights in the historical development of the Latin language.

Acknowledgments

Sebastian Nehrdich and Oliver Hellwig were funded by the German Federal Ministry of Education and Research, FKZ 01UG2121, when doing research for this paper.

5. Bibliographical References

Andor, D., Alberti, C., Weiss, D., Severyn, A., Presta, A., Ganchev, K., Petrov, S., and Collins, M. (2016). Globally normalized transition-based neural networks. In *Proceedings of the 54th Annual Meeting of the Association for Computational Linguistics (Volume 1: Long Papers)*, pages 2442–2452, Berlin, Germany, August. Association for Computational Linguistics.

Bamman, D. and Burns, P. J. (2020). Latin BERT: A contextual language model for classical philology. arXiv:2009.10053 [cs.CL].

Bamman, D. and Crane, G. (2006). The design and use of a Latin dependency treebank. pages 67–78.

Bamman, D. and Crane, G. (2008). Building a dynamic lexicon from a digital library. In *Proceedings of the 8th ACM/IEEE-CS joint conference on Digital libraries*, pages 11–20.

Cecchini, F. M., Passarotti, M., Marongiu, P., and Zeman, D. (2018). Challenges in converting the *Index Thomisticus* treebank into universal dependencies. Brussels, Belgium.

Cecchini, F. M., Korkiakangas, T., Passarotti, M., et al. (2020). A new Latin treebank for Universal Dependencies: Charters between ancient Latin and Romance languages. In *Proceedings of the LREC*, pages 933–942.

Crane, G., Chavez, R. F., Mahoney, A., Milbank, T. L., Rydberg-Cox, J. A., Smith, D. A., and Wulfman, C. E. (2001). Drudgery and deep thought. *Communications of the ACM*, 44(5):34–40.

Devlin, J., Chang, M.-W., Lee, K., and Toutanova, K. (2019). BERT: Pre-training of Deep Bidirectional Transformers for language understanding. In *Proceedings of the 2019 Conference of the North American Chapter of the Association for Computational Linguistics: Human Language Technologies, Volume 1 (Long and Short Papers)*, pages 4171–4186, June.

Dinkova-Bruun, G. (2011). Medieval Latin. In James Clackson, editor, *A Companion to the Latin Language*, pages 284–302. Blackwell Publishing.

Dozat, T. and Manning, C. D. (2017). Deep biaffine attention for neural dependency parsing. In *5th International Conference on Learning Representations*, pages 1–8.

Gamba, F., Passarotti, M., and Ruffolo, P. (2021). More data and new tools. Advances in parsing the Index Thomisticus Treebank. In *Proceedings of the CHR*, pages 108–122.

Grave, E., Bojanowski, P., Gupta, P., Joulin, A., and Mikolov, T. (2018). Learning word vectors for 157 languages. In *Proceedings of the International Conference on Language Resources and Evaluation (LREC 2018)*.

Haug, D. T. T. and Jøhndal, M. L. (2008). Creating a parallel treebank of the old indo-european bible translations. pages 27–34.

Koch, U. (1994). The enhancement of a dependency parser for Latin. Technical report, Athens, Georgia.

Lee, J. S., Naradowsky, J., and Smith, D. A. (2011). A discriminative model for joint morphological disambiguation and dependency parsing. In *Proceedings of the 49th Annual Meeting of the Association for Computational Linguistics: Human Language Technologies*, pages 885–894.

McDonald, R., Pereira, F., Ribarov, K., and Hajic, J. (2005). Non-projective dependency parsing using spanning tree algorithms. In *Proceedings of the EMNLP*, pages 523–530.

McGillivray, B. and Passarotti, M. (2009). The development of the "Index Thomisticus" treebank valency lexicon. In *Proceedings of the EACL 2009 Workshop on Language Technology and Resources for Cultural Heritage, Social Sciences, Humanities, and Education (LaTeCH–SHELT&R 2009)*, pages 43–50.

McGillivray, B. (2012). LatinISE corpus. LINDAT/CLARIAH-CZ digital library at the Institute of Formal and Applied Linguistics (ÚFAL), Faculty of Mathematics and Physics, Charles University.

Passarotti, M. C. and Ruffolo, P. (2010). Parsing the Index Thomisticus Treebank. Some preliminary results. In *15th International Colloquium on Latin Linguistics*, pages 714–725. Innsbrucker Beiträge zur Sprachwissenschaft.

Ponti, E. M. and Passarotti, M. (2016). Differentia compositionem facit. A slower-paced and reliable parser for Latin. In *Proceedings of the Tenth International Conference on Language Resources and Evaluation (LREC'16)*, pages 683–688.

Rotman, G. and Reichart, R. (2019). Deep contextualized self-training for low resource dependency parsing. *Transactions of the Association for Computational Linguistics*, 7:695–713.

Sprugnoli, R., Passarotti, M., and Moretti, G. (2019). Vir is to moderatus as mulier is to intemperans - lemma embeddings for latin. pages 1–7, 11.

Straka, M., Straková, J., and Hajič, J. (2019). Evaluating contextualized embeddings on 54 languages in POS tagging, lemmatization and dependency parsing. arXiv:1908.07448 [cs.CL].

Straka, M. (2018). UDPipe 2.0 prototype at CoNLL 2018 UD shared task. In *Proceedings of the CoNLL 2018 Shared Task: Multilingual Parsing from Raw Text to Universal Dependencies*, pages 197–207, Brussels, Belgium, October. Association for Computational Linguistics.

Vincent, N. (2016). Continuity and change from Latin to Romance. In James Adams et al., editors, *Early and Late Latin. Continuity or Change?*, pages 1–13. Cambridge University Press, Cambridge.

Zhang, X., Zhao, J., and LeCun, Y. (2015). Character-level convolutional networks for text classification. In C. Cortes, et al., editors, *Advances in Neural Information Processing Systems*, volume 28, pages 649–657. Curran Associates, Inc.

Proceedings of the Second Workshop on Language Technologies for Historical and Ancient Languages (LT4HALA 2022), pages 26–30
Language Resources and Evaluation Conference (LREC 2022), Marseille, 25 June 2022

Annotating "Absolute" Preverbs in the Homeric and Vedic Treebanks

Luca Brigada Villa,[1] Erica Biagetti,[2] Chiara Zanchi[2]
[1]University of Bergamo/University of Pavia, [2]University of Pavia
luca.brigadavilla@unibg.it, {erica.biagetti, chiara.zanchi01}@unipv.it

Abstract

Indo-European preverbs are uninflected morphemes attaching to verbs and modifying their meaning. In Early Vedic and Homeric Greek, these morphemes held ambiguous morphosyntactic status raising issues for syntactic annotation. This paper focuses on the annotation of preverbs in so-called "absolute" position in two Universal Dependencies treebanks. This issue is related to the broader topic of how to annotate ellipsis in Universal Dependencies. After discussing some of the current annotations, we propose a new scheme that better accounts for the variety of absolute constructions.

Keywords: Universal Dependencies, preverbs, Ancient Greek and Sanskrit linguistics

1. Introduction

In this paper, we discuss the current annotation scheme of Early Vedic and Homeric Greek preverbs (PVs) and propose a new one. Our data is extracted from the R̥gvedic portion of the Vedic TreeBank (VTB, Hellwig et al., 2020)[1] and from a rule-based Universal Dependencies (UD) conversion of the Iliad and Odyssey (Homeric TreeBank; HTB)[2] treebanked at the *Perseus Project*.[3] This paper documents the first step toward the larger goal of systematizing the annotation of PVs occupying other syntactic positions through semiautomatic methods. In particular, we deal with ancient Indo-European PVs in the so-called "absolute position", virtually replacing a verbal form. This issue relates to the larger question of how elliptical structure should be annotated in UD.

Section 2 familiarizes the readers with Indo-European PVs and their UD annotation. Section 3 focuses on absolute usages. Section 4 describes data extraction. Section 5 discusses their current annotation in the VTB and HTB. Finally, section 6 contains the annotation proposal.

2. PVs in Early Vedic and Homeric Greek

Indo-European PVs are uninflected morphemes attaching to verbs and modifying verbal meaning (e.g., Homeric Greek *baínō* 'walk' vs. *ana-baínō* 'upward-walk'). In Proto-Indo-European, PVs were free positioning spatial adverbs, which later underwent functional bifurcation into univerbated prefixes proper and adpositions.

In both Early Vedic and Homeric Greek, this diachronic development was still ongoing: the same uninflected morphemes held an ambiguous morphosyntactic status, functioning as adverbs, nominal or verbal modifiers, adpositions, and PVs proper (for discussion and examples, see Zanchi, 2019: 65-116, 173-183 with references). In early Indo-European languages, PVs could semantically modify verbs without morphological univerbation. Take for instance examples (1) and (2) from Early Vedic and Homeric Greek, in which the preverbs *prá* 'forward' and *en* 'in' are separated from the verbs *vocam* 'say' and *ebḗsamen* 'stepped' that they modify (Zanchi 2019: 98; 181).

(1) R̥V 1.59.6a

prá	***nū́***	*mahitvám̐*
forward	now	greatness(F).ACC
vr̥ṣabhásya	***vocam̐***	
bull.GEN	say.INJ.AOR.1SG	

'Now I proclaim the greatness of the bull [=Indra].'

(2) *Od.* 11.4

en	*dè*	*tà*	*mêla*
in	PTC	DEM.ACC.PL.N	sheep(N).ACC.PL
labóntes			***ebḗsamen***
take.PTCP.AOR.NOM.PL			walk.AOR.3PL

'As we have taken the sheep, we stepped into (the ships).'

The original syntactic freedom of PVs, shown by examples (1) and (2), emerges even more clearly when they occur in the so-called "absolute" position, virtually "substituting" a verbal form (cf. section 3).

2.1 PVs Current Annotation in UD

PVs' ambiguous categorial status raises issues for annotation: disambiguating PVs' function is a non-trivial task, even for human annotators. Ideally, the *deprel advmod* should be used for adverbs, *compound:prt* for PVs (even if "detached" from verbs), and *case* for adpositions. Practically, it is often very difficult to distinguish adverbial from preverbal usages in both languages (in the VTB, *advmod* is exclusively used, whereas the HTB employs *compound:prt*). Furthermore, especially in Early Vedic, adpositional usages can be difficult to sort out, and the *case* label is sometimes used in unclear cases. The syntactic annotation of absolute PVs is thoroughly discussed in section 5.

Ambiguities encountered at the syntactic level are mirrored in the assignation of part-of-speech tags. In the HTB, the part-of-speech tag ADV is given to adverbs and preverbs, whereas adpositions are tagged as ADP; the occurrences in which PVs hold an ambiguous status are not annotated in a consistent way. For example, in (3) the PV *ek* '(lit.) out of' occurring in tmesis initial position is annotated as ADP taking the genitive plural *astragálōn*.

[1] https://github.com/OliverHellwig/sanskrit/tree/master/papers/2020lrec/treebank.

[2] https://github.com/francescomambrini/katholou/tree/main/ud_treebanks/agdt/data.

[3] https://perseusdl.github.io/treebank_data/.

(3) *Od.* 11.64-65
ek *dé* *moi* *aukhḕn*
out_of PTC 3SG.DAT neck.NOM
astragálōn *eágē*
neck_vertebra.GEN.PL break.AOR.PASS.3SG
'My neck broke from the vertebrae.'

In the quasi-identical passage in *Od.* 10.559-560, the same preverb is annotated as ADV.[4]
In the VTB, ADV is employed in all cases.

3. Preverbs in Absolute Position

PVs in absolute position seem to function as "proxies" for the verb (Chantraine, 1953: 82). The "omitted" verbal form can be recovered either from the previous linguistic material or from the extralinguistic context. For example, in (4) the verb *bhare* 'I bring' can be recovered from the hymn's opening verse *prá vaḥ ... suṣṭutím ... bhare* 'I bring forth to you my good praise'. In (5), instead, a motion verb such as √*gam-* 'go' or *sám* √*car-* 'converge' can be recovered based on similar comparative constructions involving cows moving towards (*abhí*) their calves that occur elsewhere in the RV.

(4) R̥V 2.16.7
prá *te* *nā́vaṁ* *ná*
forward 2SG.DAT boat.ACC like
sámane *vacasyúvam*
assembly.LOC eloquent.ACC
'Within the assembly, (I bring) forth to you my eloquent (formulation), like a boat.'

(5) R̥V 9.86.2
dhenúr *ná* *vatsám* *páyasā*
milk-cow.NOM like calf.ACC milk.INST
abhí *vajríṇam* *índram*
towards with_mace.ACC Indra.ACC
índavo
drop.NOM.PL
'As a milk-cow (goes) to her calf with milk, the drops [...] (go) to Indra, possessor of the mace.'

Absolute uses of PVs are found both in independent clauses, such as (4) and (5), and in dependent ones, such as (6); in the latter case, the preverb *epí* "substitutes" for the compound verb *épeimi* 'be there'. Absolute PVs are also frequently found in coordinated clauses: in (7), the first conjunct contains the compound verb *pàr ... etíthei* '(he) placed beside', whereas in the second conjunct the PV alone is repeated (on PV repetition see Dunkel, 1979; Klein, 2007).

(6) *Il.* 1.514
nēmertès *mèn* *dḗ* *moi*
infallible.ACC PTC PTC 1SG.DAT
hypóscheo ... *epeì*
give.IMPV.AOR.2SG.MID CONJ
oú *toi* ***épi*** *déos.*
NEG 2SG.DAT upon fear.NOM
'Give me your infallible promise [...] for there (is) nothing to make you afraid.'

(7) *Od.* 8.70
pàr *d'* ***etíthei*** *káneon*
beside PTC place.IMPF.3SG basket.ACC
kalḗn *te* *trápezan,*
beautiful.ACC PTC table.ACC
pàr *dè* *dépas* *oínoio.*
beside PTC cup.ACC wine.GEN
'And beside him he placed a basket and a beautiful table, and a cup of wine.'

4. Data Extraction

In order to analyze the annotations for PVs occurring in absolute position in Homeric Greek and Early Vedic (see Section 5), we implemented two queries to extract from the HTB and the VTB all sentences in which such elements occur. First, we identified the patterns that may involve such lemmas (as discussed in section 3), then, we wrote a Python script[5] to get all the matching sentences from the treebanks. All the functions used to design the queries rely on the Python conllu module.[6]
The target elements of the queries were tokens whose lemmas are included in the list of PVs (see Appendix) and another token, from which the former depended. In the HTB, we looked for tokens whose part-of-speech is NOUN or PRON and that have *advcl* or *conj* as dependency relation. Furthermore, the PV's *deprel* has to be *compound:prt*. In the VTB, we looked for tokens that govern a PV via the relation *orphan*. The token can have any part-of-speech but cannot be a finite verb. As finite verbs lack VerbForm in the conllu *feats* field, if the head of the PV was a verb, we restricted the selection to those for which the VerbForm feature was specified. If it had any other part-of-speech, we included the pattern in the results without checking anything else.

5. Current Annotation of Absolute PVs

UD marks all kinds of ellipses by promoting a member of the elliptical clause to the head position on the base of a "coreness" hierarchy:

(8) *nsubj* > *obj* > *iobj* > *obl* > *advmod* > *csubj* > *xcomp* > *ccomp* > *advcl* > *dislocated* > *vocative*

The promoted member takes the syntactic relation that the elided element would bear; to signal that the dependency structure is incomplete, all non-promoted dependents of the elided elements receive the relation *orphan* (Figure 1; see also Schuster, Lamm, and Manning, 2017 with references).[7]

[4] The passage in *Od.* 10.559-560 is quasi-identical to that in *Od.* 11.64-65 in that it includes the dative *hoi* of the third person pronoun instead of *moi*. This difference is not relevant for the purposes of our analysis.

[5] The analyzed data and the Python (Van Rossum and Drake, 2009) script employed for this study are available at: https://github.com/unipv-larl/preverbs. The scripts were only used to extract the patterns and analyze their annotation. They can be used to extract data from other portions of the VTB and can easily implemented to fix the annotation automatically with the correction proposed in this paper.

[6] https://pypi.org/project/conllu/#description

[7] https://universaldependencies.org/u/overview/specific-syntax.html#ellipsis

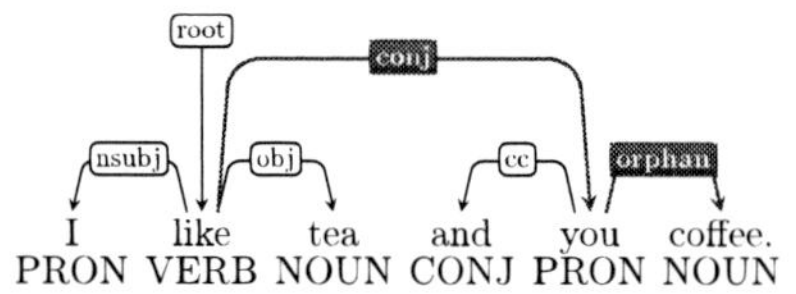

Figure 1: Annotation scheme for verb ellipsis.

In the VTB and HTB, PVs' absolute uses are annotated following the basic ellipsis representation: one argument of the "omitted" verb is promoted to the head position and governs the PV. However, the two treebanks differ as to the relation holding between the PV and the promoted element: in the VTB, the PV takes the *orphan* relation, whereas in the HTB it depends on the promoted noun via the *compound:prt* relation. Compare Figures 2 and 3:

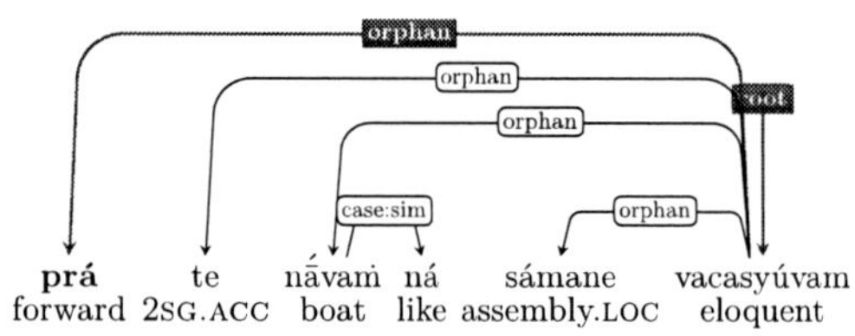

Figure 2: Dependency tree for (1) in the VTB.

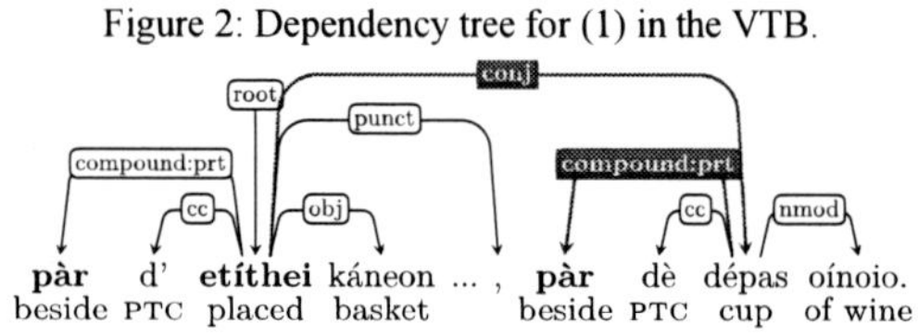

Figure 3: Dependency tree for (4) in the HTB.

In the case of Early Vedic, this annotation scheme derives from the fact that verbal arguments and adjuncts precede adverbial modifiers in the UD promotion hierarchy in (8): since PVs are always annotated as *advmod*, they cannot be promoted to the head position if other verbal arguments or adjuncts are available, given that the latter occupy a higher position in the hierarchy. However, this results in a linguistically unrealistic annotation, since in such constructions it is the PV, and not a verbal argument/adjunct, that "substitutes" for the verb. Furthermore, the variety of constructions in which absolute PVs can occur is lost in the annotation, as the scheme always treats PVs as *orphans*.

Issues related to the promotion hierarchy especially arise when the clause contains an explicit subject: in (9), the coordinated subjects *díphros* 'chariot' and *híppoi* 'horses' are promoted to head position, instead of the PV *pára*, which stands for the compound verb *páreimi* 'be present, or the adjunct *toi* 'for you'.

(9) *Od.* 3.325

ei *d'* *ethéleis* *pezós,* ***pára***
CONJ PTC will.2SG by_land.NOM beside
toi *díphros* *te* *kaì* *híppoi*
2SG.DAT chariot.NOM PTC CONJ horse.NOM.PL
'If you will go by land, here (are) a chariot and horses at hand for you.'

Besides the same problematic head promotion, the HTB shows the additional issue of employing *compound:prt* to tag the relation between the PV and the promoted element: this relation should exclusively be used for idiomatic syntagmatic verbs and not for PVs depending on nouns.[8]

Differently from the VTB, the HTB is enriched with enhanced dependencies which allow for adding empty nodes to represent verb ellipsis. In the case of absolute PVs, the enhanced graph contains an empty node for the "omitted" verb, on which the PV depends via the *compound:prt* relation, as in Figure 4.

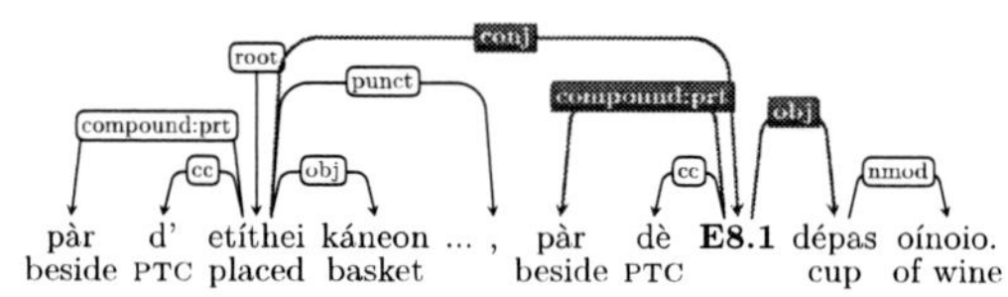

Figure 4: Enhanced graph for (4) in the HTB.

At first sight, the enhanced representation is satisfying, for it allows for representing the different constructions in which absolute PVs can occur (the empty node may be *root*, *advcl*, *acl*, *conj*, among others). However, while in the case of ellipsis in coordination there is general agreement on the need to recover a verbal form, it is not clear that the same holds for non-coordinative contexts. In some languages such as spoken Russian, the overt expression of motion via a motion verb is unnecessary in many contexts, as shown in (10) (Zanchi, 2019: 106). Similarly, in German, the combination of a modal verb such as *müssen* and a prepositional phrase such *as in die Stadt* 'into town', shown in (11), can express motion without any motion verb; example (11) is taken from the UD version of the Hamburg Dependency Treebank (HDT),[9] where the modal verb is promoted to head position (Figure 5).

(10) a. *Ty* ***kuda****?*[10]
'Where (are) you (going)?'
b. *V metro*[11]
'To the subway.'

(11) *Was tut die Kleinfamilie, wenn sie ... nicht mehr* ***in die Stadt muss****?*
'What does the small family do when [...] they no longer have to (go) into town?'

[8] https://universaldependencies.org/u/dep/compound-prt.html

[9] https://github.com/UniversalDependencies/UD_German-HDT/blob/master/README.md

[10] Vasin, Ivan Švedov, Muž, 37, 1969, http://www.ruscorpora.ru/en/

[11] Sergej, Sergej Puskepalis, Muž, 40, 1966, http://www.ruscorpora.ru/en/

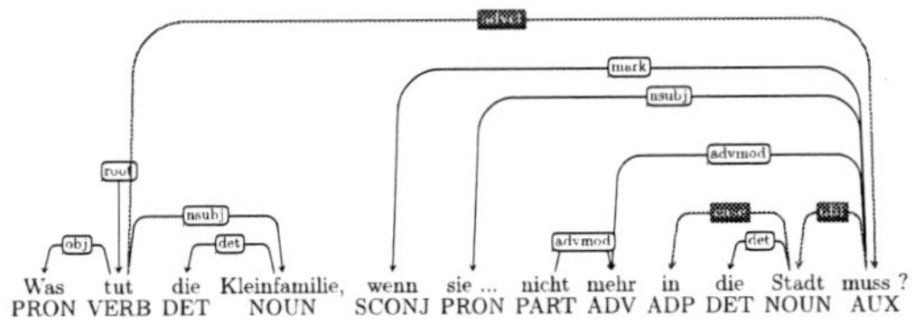

Figure 5: Dependency tree for (11) in the HDT.

The same argument can be used for cases such as (5), in which the Vedic PV *abhí* alone might express directed motion without necessarily assuming a verbal form. Finally, in copular sentences, such as (6) and (9), the need to recover a verbal form is even less straightforward. While overt copulas are optional in Homeric Greek and Early Vedic, in many languages the relation between a subject and a nominal predicate systematically lacks overt marking (Stassen, 2013).

6. Annotation Proposal

Considering the above discussion, we suggest the following annotation scheme for absolute uses of PVs in the HTB and VTB:

a) Verb ellipsis in coordinative contexts:

If the treebank is enriched with enhanced dependencies, empty nodes should be substituted for the elided verb. The PV should depend on the empty node via *compound:prt* (cf. the annotation shown in Figure 4).

If enhanced dependencies are not employed, as in the VTB, PVs should be promoted to the role of head, instead of verbal arguments. Note that *compound(:prt)* is not included in the coreness hierarchy presented in Section 5 and thus preverbs taking this relation are not considered possible candidates for promotion to the head position. However, since absolute PVs convey most information on the kind of motion event expressed in the sentence, they would be better substitutes for elided verbs than subjects or other dependents in the hierarchy.

Accordingly, all verb arguments should depend on the promoted PV via the *orphan* relation. In order to retain syntactic information on the type of argument of each orphaned element, we suggest adding sub-relations such as *:subj*, *:obj*, or *:obl*.[12] See Figure 6, based on example (7):

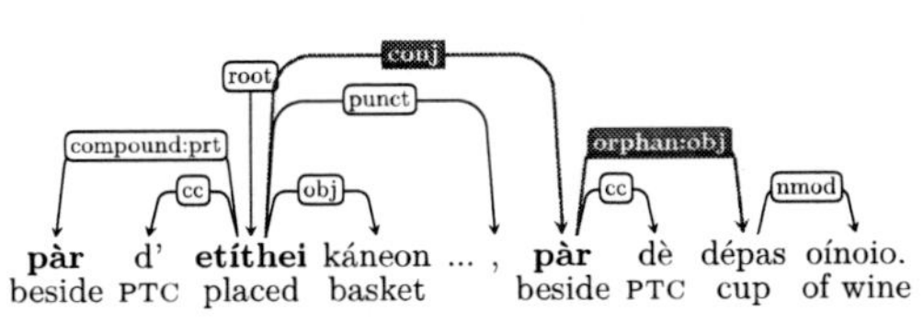

Figure 6: Suggested basic graph for ellipsis in coordination.

b) Verb ellipsis in non-coordinative contexts:

Regardless of whether the treebank contains enhanced dependencies or not, we suggest promoting the PV to the head position (*root*, *advcl*, *xcomp*, etc.), without the mediation of empty nodes. Other elements should depend on the promoted PV via *orphan* specified by the relevant sub-relation. See Figure 7, based on example (4):

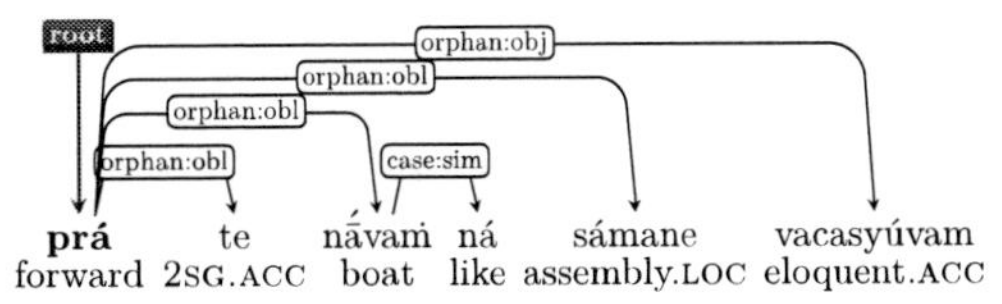

Figure 7: Suggested graph for ellipsis outside of coordination.

c) Zero copula for predicate nominals:

Finally, PVs in zero copula constructions should also be treated as the heads of the construction. In this case, however, the subject depends on the PV via *subj*, as in ordinary copula constructions. Compare Figure 8, where the PV *pàra* functions as *root* (see ex. (9)), with Figure 9, where the adjective *hatró(os)* is the *root*.

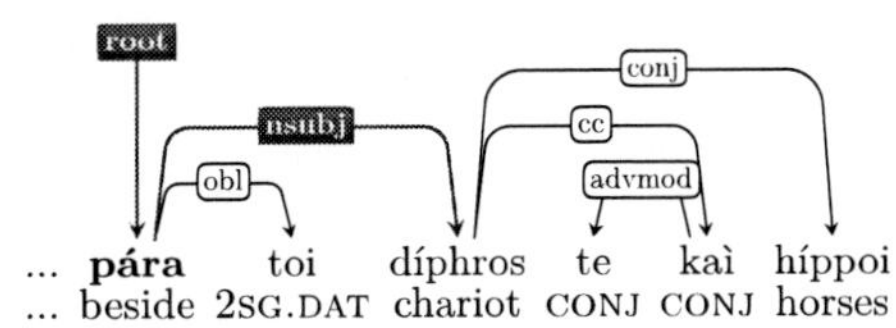

Figure 8: Suggested annotation for zero copula constructions with PV = *root*.

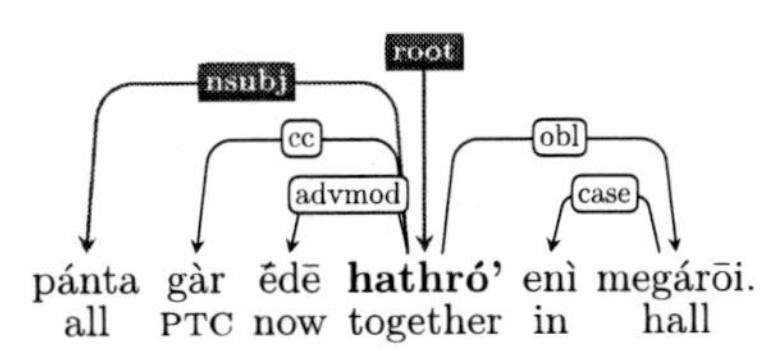

'For all are now gathered together in the hall.' (*Od.* 2.410)

Figure 9: UD annotation scheme for zero copula constructions with Adj = *root*.

7. Conclusion and future perspectives

After discussing the current syntactic annotation of Early Vedic and Homeric Greek PVs in absolute position, in this paper we proposed a new annotation scheme for these constructions.

The proposed annotation has multiple advantages:

- it does not level out the variety of constructions in which absolute PVs occur;
- it uses annotation practices that are already part of UD guidelines;

[12] This proposal resembles the one developed by Joakim Nivre and Daniel Zeman as part of the discussion of the second version of the UD guidelines (see Schuster, Lamm, and Manning, 2017: 130-131). To retain syntactic information on each remnant, Nivre and Zeman suggested employing composite relations of the type `conj>subj`, `conj>obj`, etc. Our proposal is moved by the same intention but exploits UD extensions to ordinary dependency relations. This allows users to decide whether to include sub-relations or not when querying the treebanks. Note that sub-relations would be especially useful for Homeric Greek where the same case form can fulfill different syntactic relations.

- it does not add empty nodes where unnecessary, thus making the subsequent evaluation of the data easier;
- it keeps all the syntactic information in the annotation thanks to the addition of sub-relations;
- it can easily be extended to similar constructions of other ancient and modern languages.

This paper documents the first step toward the larger goal of systematizing the annotation of PVs occupying other syntactic positions through semiautomatic methods. Such systematization would represent a major improvement for the UD treebanks of ancient Indo-European languages: it would coherently account for the variety of constructions in which these uninflected items occur, thus facilitating (cross-linguistic) research upon them. The interest in PVs goes beyond Indo-European studies, crosscutting grammaticalization studies and lexical typological studies in the expression of motion events.

Acknowledgments

We wish to thank Oliver Hellwig and the three anonymous reviewers who provided insightful feedback for a substantial improvement of the final version of this paper. Final responsibility remains our own.

8. Bibliographical References

Chantraine, P. 1953. *Grammaire homérique*. Tome 2: Syntaxe. Paris: Klincksieck.

Dunkel, G.E. 1979. Preverb repetition. *Münchener Studien zur Sprachwissenschaft* 38: pages 41–82.

Hellwig, O., Scarlata, S., Ackermann, E., and Widmer, P. 2020. The Treebank of Vedic Sanskrit. In *Proceedings of The 12th Language Resources and Evaluation Conference* (LREC 2020), pages 5137–146. http://www.lrec-conf.org/proceedings/lrec2020/index.html.

Klein, J.S. 2007. On the Nature and Function of Preverb Repetition in the Rigveda. *Studien zur Indologie und Iranistik* 24: pages 91-103.

Schuster, S., Lamm, M., and Manning, C.D. 2017. Gapping constructions in universal dependencies v2. *In Proceedings of the NoDaLiDa 2017 Workshop on Universal Dependencies* (UDW 2017), pages 123–132.

Stassen, L. 2013. Zero Copula for Predicate Nominals. In *The World Atlas of Language Structures Online*, Dryer, Matthew S. and Haspelmath, Martin (eds.), Leipzig: Max Planck Institute for Evolutionary Anthropology. http://wals.info/chapter/120, Accessed on 2021-11-12.

Van Rossum, G. and Drake, F.L. 2009. *Python 3 Reference Manual*. Scotts Valley, CA: CreateSpace.

Zanchi, C. 2019. *Multiple preverbs in ancient Indo-European languages*. Tübingen: Narr.

Appendix: List of PV lemmas

Early Vedic: *apa, ava, ā, ud, ni, nis, parā, puras, pra, sam, vi, achā, ati, adhi, anu, antar, api, abhi, upa, tiras, paras, pari, puras, purā, prati.*[13]

Homeric Greek: *amphí, aná, antí, apó, diá, en, eis, ek, epí, hypér, hypó, katá, metá, pará, perí, pró, prós, sýn.*

[13] Note that, differently from later Vedic and Classical Sanskrit, Early Vedic texts contain word accents (*ápa, áva, ā́,* etc.). However, in order to lemmatize words attested in Early Vedic text together with those attested in later Vedic or Classical Sanskrit, the digitized text of the *Ṛgveda* employed by the VTB does not contain word accents.

Proceedings of the Second Workshop on Language Technologies for Historical and Ancient Languages (LT4HALA 2022), pages 31–37
Language Resources and Evaluation Conference (LREC 2022), Marseille, 25 June 2022

CHJ-WLSP: Annotation of 'Word List by Semantic Principles' Labels for the Corpus of Historical Japanese

Masayuki Asahara♣♮†, Nao Ikegami♢, Tai Suzuki♠‡, Taro Ichimura◯, Asuko Kondo♠, Sachi Kato♡, Makoto Yamazaki♣
♣National Institute for Japanese Language and Linguistics, ♮Tokyo University of Foreign Studies
♢Saitama University, ♠University of Tokyo, ◯ Kyoto Prefectural University, ♡ Mejiro University,
‡ Professor Emeritus at the University of Tokyo
† masayu-a@ninjal.ac.jp

Abstract

This article presents a word-sense annotation for the Corpus of Historical Japanese: a mashed-up Japanese lexicon based on the 'Word List by Semantic Principles' (WLSP). The WLSP is a large-scale Japanese thesaurus that includes 98,241 entries with syntactic and hierarchical semantic categories. The historical WLSP is also compiled for the words in ancient Japanese. We utilized a morpheme-word sense alignment table to extract all possible word sense candidates for each word appearing in the target corpus. Then, we manually disambiguated the word senses for 647,751 words in the texts from the 10th century to 1910.

Keywords: Historical Japanese, Word Sense Annotation

1. Introduction

The 'Corpus of Historical Japanese' (CHJ) (NINJAL, Japan, 2022) is a large-scale diachronic corpus based on the texts from the late 7th century to the early 20th century, which is a word-segmented and morphological information (POS) annotated corpus. The 'Word List by Semantic Principles' (WLSP) (NINJAL, Japan, 2004) is a large-scale Japanese thesaurus that includes 98,214 entries with syntactic and hiearchical semantic categories. The historical version of Word List by Semantic Principles (*Nihon Koten Taisho Bunrui Goihyo*, hWLSP) (Miyajima et al., 2014) is a thesaurus based on the old word senses of the vocabulary. These two language resources are compiled of the contemporary and historical words in the same word sense hierarchy.

This paper presents annotation of the WLSP/hWLSP sense labels for the Corpus of Historical Japanese. Annotating word senses (syntactic and semantic categories) for the historical corpus enables us to explore the historical changes in words. The distribution of syntactic and semantic categories shows the changes in writing styles and the difference in semantic contents. The word sense labels can also be used as the semantic index to search the texts. Furthermore, the word sense labels help the novice to read classical literature.

We present the annotation procedure and basic statistics. Section 2 presents the used language resources of WLSP and CHJ. Section 3 presents the annotation procedure with the goal. Section 4 presents the basic statistics of the label distributions. Section 5 is conclusions and our current issues.

2. Prerequisites

2.1. Word List by Semantic Principles

Word List by Semantic Principles (WLSP)[1] is one of the major thesauri for contemporary Japanese. The first version of the WLSP was released in 1964 by Kokuritsu Kokugo Kenkyusho, and a newer, expanded version was published in 2004 (NINJAL, Japan, 2004). Its comma-separated values (CSV) file of the expanded version can be used for research purposes.[2]

The data include more than 90,000 words with four syntactic categories (nominal words, verbal words, modifier words, and others) and several hierarchical semantic levels. The categories are indicated with one integer digit to the left of a radix point and four fractional digits to the right of the radix point. Table 1 shows an example of the word '昨年 (Last Year)', which is assigned a value of 1.1642. Here, the first '1. 体' presents the syntactic part **Class**, which is referred to as the 'Nominal Word', while '1642' presents the hierarchical semantic part, as follows: the first digit **Division**, '.1 関係', refers to the top-level semantic category 'Relation'; the two digits **Section** '.16 時間' refer to the second-level semantic category 'Time'; and the four digits **Article** '.1642 過去' refer to the finest-grained semantic category 'Past Time'. These five digits are therefore referred to as the **Article number**. The syntactic categories are 1. 体 Nominal Word, 2. 用 Verbal Word, 3. 相 Modifier Word, and 4. 他 Other (e.g., Conjunction, Interjection, Greeting). The semantic categories are .1 関係 Relation, .2 主体 Subject, .3 活動 Action, .4 生産物 Product, and 5. 自然 Nature. Though the thesaurus defines word senses for content words, the word senses for functional words and symbols are not defined in the WLSP. Furthermore, proper nouns

[1] `https://clrd.ninjal.ac.jp/goihyo.html`
[2] 200,000 yen (+ tax) for commercial use.

Table 1: Example Entry from the 'Word List by Semantic Principles'

「昨年」 'Last Year': 1.1642			
Syntactic Category	Semantic Category		
	Top Level	Second Level	Finest Level
Class	Division	Section	Article
体	関係	時間	過去
Nominal Word	Relation	Time	Past Time
1.	.1	.16	.1642

are not defined in the WLSP. Therefore, the functional words and proper nouns tend to be out-of-vocabulary. The historical version of WLSP defines the same word sense hierarchy as the contemporary version of WLSP for the ancient literature in Japan. Whereas the contemporary version of the article number is with a period (e.g., 1.1642), the historical version of the article number is without a period like (e.g., 11642).

2.2. Corpus of Historical Japanese

Corpus of Historical Japanese (CHJ) is a diachronic corpus from the Nara period to the Meiji and Taisho eras. This corpus enables advanced concordance search by annotating morpheme information to the sentences. It can be used online through the search system 'Chunagon'[3] free of charge.

We annotated WLSP/hWLSP word sense labels (Article numbers) for the subset of CHJ. Table 2 shows the annotation target samples. Samples are the identifier for the literature in CHJ. Descriptions are the title in Japanese and their (literal) English translation. Year is the year of the establishment of the literature. Words are the word count in the annotated samples[4]. At the moment, we annotated 647,751 words from 11 samples.

3. Annotation Procedures

3.1. Goal

We show the goal of the large-scale word sense annotation procedure. Table 3 an annotation example of Taketori Monogatari. The pSample and pStart columns are the offset information in the CHJ. The corpus is word segmented and morphological information annotated. The table shows orthToken (surface form) and the lemma of the original corpus. Though space in the table did not permit us to insert the POSs for the words, the annotator can also see the POS labels and annotate the word sense labels in the Article Num. column. '野山' (*hills*) is annotated the contemporary Article Number 1.5240. Class 1. is 体 (Nominal Word); Division .5 is 自然 (Nature); Section .52 is 天地 (Heaven and Earth); Article .5240 is 山野 (Hilly areas). 交じる (*goes into*) annotates the historical Article Number 21532[5]. Class 2 is 用 (Verbal Word); Division 1 is 関係 (Relation); Section 15 is 作用 (Interaction); Article 1532 is (Enter). Note that the functional words, symbols, and some of the proper nouns are not annotated.

3.2. Annotation Work Flow

Firstly, in order to establish the method of the large-scale word sense annotation on CHJ, we performed the word sense annotation on contemporary Japanese.

The BCCWJ and CHJ are word segmented and POS based on UniDic POS tagset[6]. We compiled the alignment table between WLSP and UniDic Lemma ID: WLSP2UniDic (Kondo and Tanaka, 2020) [7]. The WLSP2UniDic can be used as the word sense assigner with the morphological analyzer ChaMame (stand alone version) [8]. The word sense assigner annotates all possible word sense label candidates in WLSP for the UniDic lemmaID.

We performed the word sense annotation on the Balanced Corpus of Contemporary Written Japanese (BCCWJ) (Maekawa et al., 2014) with the word sense assigner. The annotators resolve word sense disambiguation for all possible word sense label candidates. If the word should be assigned other than the word sense label candidates, the annotators assign the most appropriate word sense label for the out-of-vocabulary sense. In this process, the annotator check the WLSP lookup tools of CradleExpress[9] in Section 7. As a result, we annotated 347,094 words and published as BCCWJ-WLSP (Kato et al., 2018)[10].

After finishing BCCWJ-WLSP, we performed the word sense annotation on the CHJ. Previously, Ikegami (Ikegami, 2017) annotated the WLSP labels for adjectives of the early middle Japanese based on hWLSP. We annotated 0900 竹取, 0934 土佐, 1212 方丈, 1336 徒然 samples by the same work flow of BCCWJ-WLSP. The

[3] https://chunagon.ninjal.ac.jp

[4] The annotation of 1642 虎明 is for not whole data.

[5] As we stated previously, the Article Number of hWLSP is without a period, whereas the one of WLSP is with a period.

[6] https://clrd.ninjal.ac.jp/unidic/en/

[7] https://github.com/masayu-a/WLSP2UniDic

[8] https://ja.osdn.net/projects/chaki/releases/p15635

[9] https://cradle.ninjal.ac.jp/wlsp

[10] https://github.com/masayu-a/BCCWJ-WLSP

Samples	Descriptions	Year	Words
0900 竹取	Taketori Monogatari (*lit. The Tale of the Bamboo Cutter*)	10th century	12,757
0934 土佐	Tosa Nikki (*lit. Tosa Diary*)	10th century	8,208
1100 今昔	Konjaku Monogatari-shu (*lit. Anthology of Tales from the Past*)	Heian period	175,598
1212 方丈	Hojoki (*lit. Square-jo Record*)	1212	5,402
1220 宇治	Uji Shui Monogatari (*lit. Gleanings from Uji Dainagon Monogatari*)	13th Century	120,705
1252 十訓	Jikkin-sho (*A Miscellany of Ten Maxims*)	1252	90,177
1336 徒然	Tsurezuregusa (*Essays in Idleness*)	ca. 1330	40,834
1642 虎明	Toraakira-bon Kyogen [a]	1642	5,448
1895 太陽	Taiyo *The Sun* (Magazine) [b]	1895	46,394
1904 小読	1st Jinjo Shogaku Tokuhon (Textbook) [c]	1904	45,334
1910 小読	2nd Jinjo Shogaku Tokuhon (Textbook)	1910	96,894
Total			647,751

[a] https://iss.ndl.go.jp/books/R100000002-I000008304623-00
[b] https://viaf.org/viaf/184683725/
[c] https://dglb01.ninjal.ac.jp/ninjaldl/bunken.php?title=kokutei1

Table 2: Annotation Targets

pSampleID	pStart	orthToken	lemma	Article Num.	Class	Class Label	Division	Division Label
20-竹取 0900_00001	250	野山	野山	1.5240	1	体	5	自然
20-竹取 0900_00001	270	に	に					
20-竹取 0900_00001	280	まじり	交じる	21532	2	用	1	関係
20-竹取 0900_00001	310	て	て					
20-竹取 0900_00001	320	竹	竹	1.5401	1	体	5	自然
20-竹取 0900_00001	330	を	を					
20-竹取 0900_00001	340	とり	取る	2.3811	2	用	3	活動
20-竹取 0900_00001	360	つつ	つつ					
20-竹取 0900_00001	380	、	、					

Translation: *While (the old man) goes into mountains and collects bamboos,*

Table 3: Annotation Example of Taketori Monogatari

annotator can see the translation from ancient Japanese to contemporary Japanese. Through the work, we compiled the alignment table between hWLSP and UniDic Lemma ID: WLSP2UniDic_historical [11].
Finally, we performed large-scale word sense annotation for the other samples in CHJ. The word sense candidates are extracted from both WLSP2UniDic and WLSP2UniDic_historical. The annotator resolved the polysemous words using the translation.

4. Statistics

4.1. Statistics: Syntactic Categories (Class)

Table 4 shows the basic statistics of syntactic categories (Class). We annotated 647,751 words in total. 353,890 words are 'Unlabelled', which are functional words, symbols, and proper nouns, since article numbers of these words are not defined in WLSP.
In order to explore the statistical biases of syntactic categories for the samples, we performed a chi-square test for the contingency table, excluding unlabelled word[12].

Table 5 shows the standardized residuals, which are measures of the strength of the difference between observed and expected values. The standardized residuals are standard and normal distribution (a mean of zero and a standard deviation of one). Therefore, when the absolute value of the statistics is over 1.96, the data shows the difference of the significance level 0.05[13].
Below, we confirm the statistical biases for syntactic categories. Concerning nominal words 1 . 体, the samples of 0900 竹取 and 1220 宇治 are small rates, and the samples of 1895 太陽 and 1910 小読 are large rates. Concerning verbal words 2. 用, the samples of 1895 太陽 and 1910 小読 are small rates, and the samples of 1100 今昔 and 1220 宇治 are large rates. The rates of nominal and verbal words are in complementary relation. Concerning modifier words 3. 相, the samples of 1252 十訓 and 1100 今昔 are small rates, and the sample of 1336 徒然 is large rates. Concerning other words 4. 他, the samples of 1100 今昔, 1220 方丈, and 1252 十訓 are small rates, and the samples of 1895 太陽 and

[11] https://github.com/masayu-a/WLSP2UniDic_historical

[12] We also performed a chi-square test for the data including labelled data. The tendencies of the statistical biases on the labelled word are nearly the same. However, the result with unlabelled data shows the tendencies of the statistical biases of functional words.

[13] However, we should consider p-value under multiple comparison correction.

	1. 体	2. 用	3. 相	4. 他	Unlabelled	Total
0900 竹取	2,318	2,252	706	72	7,409	12,757
0934 土佐	1,710	1,272	453	45	4,728	8,208
1100 今昔	40,687	29,498	8,518	1,189	95,706	175,598
1212 方丈	1,433	792	342	100	2,735	5,402
1220 宇治	24,214	21,336	6,290	716	68,149	120,705
1252 十訓	19,808	13,039	3,974	460	52,896	90,177
1336 徒然	8,876	6,138	2,688	213	22,919	40,834
1642 虎明	1,255	811	369	88	2,925	5,448
1895 太陽	13,256	6,131	3,116	853	23,038	46,394
1904 小読	10,846	5,312	2,620	794	25,762	45,334
1910 小読	28,915	12,833	6,388	1,135	47,623	96,894
Total	153,318	99,414	35,464	5,665	353,890	647,751

Table 4: Basic Statistics: Syntactic Categories (Class)

	1. 体	2. 用	3. 相	4. 他
0900 竹取	-13.05	12.91	2.57	-3.12
0934 土佐	-3.62	3.40	1.77	-2.74
1100 今昔	-8.26	21.65	-14.30	-10.59
1212 方丈	1.62	-4.53	1.20	6.87
1220 宇治	-30.90	36.19	-0.78	-10.40
1252 十訓	3.96	5.00	-8.94	-10.43
1336 徒然	-7.27	1.26	12.45	-7.42
1642 虎明	-2.45	-1.80	3.96	5.72
1895 太陽	14.61	-25.52	6.22	19.98
1904 小読	9.40	-20.47	5.86	22.42
1910 小読	31.72	-40.03	6.70	6.65

Table 5: Chi-square Test: Syntactic Categories Excluding Unlabelled Words

1904 小読 are large rates.

The appendix 8 includes the distances of syntactic categories evaluation. The figure 2 shows the distances among the samples. The result shows that the neighbouring sample pairs in chronological order are smaller distances than other pairs.

4.2. Statistics: Semantic Categories (Division)

Table 6 shows the basic statistics of semantic categories (Division). The division labels of .2 主体 and .4 生産物 are only defiled in the class 1. 体. So, these two labels are relatively small.

We explore the statistical biases of semantic categories for the samples by chi-square test for the contingency table excluding unlabelled word. Table 7 shows the standardized residuals of chi-squared test. Concerning .3 活動, the samples of 1252 十訓 and 1336 徒然 are large rates, and the samples of 1904 小読 and 1910 小読 are small rates. We regard it as the correlation of the rate 2. 用 in the syntactic category. Concerning .4 生産物, the samples of 1904 小読 and 1910 小読 are large rates, and the sample of 1895 太陽 is a small rate. Concerning .5 自然, the samples of 1904 小読 and 1910 小読 are large rates, and the samples of 1100 今昔 and 1895 太陽 are small rates.

The results of samples around 1900 (1895 太陽, 1904 小読, and 1910 小読) shows that the distributions of semantic category do not show synchronic similarities in the same era. The difference in genres (magazines vs. textbook) are observed in the difference in the distributions of semantic category. The appendix 8 includes the distances of semantic categories evaluation. The figure 3 shows the distances among the samples. The result shows that the neighbouring sample pairs in the chronological order are not smaller distances as the syntactic category distance.

5. Conclusions

This study presents large-scale word sense label annotation on the Corpus of Historical Japanese. We presented the annotation work flow and the basic statistics of the results. The data will publish via `https://github.com/masayu-a/CHJ-WLSP` as the stand-off annotation format [14], and also are shared for the applicant of NINJAL Joint Usage Projects (NINJAL language resources).

Below, we present the current issues of the CHJ-WLSP. **Word sense label granularity**: Though the word sense label design is based on WLSP/hWLSP, the granularity of the word sense is limited. For example, the word 'い

[14]Excluding the surface form and lemma from the Table 3.

	.1 関係	.2 主体	.3 活動	.4 生産物	.5 自然	Unlabelled	Total
0900 竹取	2,335	577	1,722	229	485	7,409	12,757
0934 土佐	1,540	360	1,002	167	411	4,728	8,208
1100 今昔	37,538	12,221	21,942	3,615	4,576	95,706	175,598
1212 方丈	1,335	255	637	147	293	2,735	5,402
1220 宇治	24,924	6,726	14,857	2,661	3,388	68,149	120,705
1252 十訓	16,323	5,461	11,789	1,540	2,168	52,896	90,177
1336 徒然	8,279	2,011	5,710	714	1,201	22,919	40,834
1642 虎明	1,122	389	667	113	232	2,925	5,448
1895 太陽	11,403	3,324	6,888	609	1,132	23,038	46,394
1904 小読	8,915	2,960	4,107	1,363	2,227	25,762	45,334
1910 小読	23,521	6,426	10,881	3,025	5,418	47,623	96,894
Total	137,235	40,710	80,202	14,183	21,531	353,890	647,751

Table 6: Basic Statistics: Semantic Categories (Division)

	.1 関係	.2 主体	.3 活動	.4 生産物	.5 自然
0900 竹取	-4.50	-6.55	8.13	-1.87	4.93
0934 土佐	-2.91	-6.03	2.00	-0.08	10.21
1100 今昔	1.89	13.84	1.28	-4.66	-20.33
1212 方丈	3.49	-6.45	-3.97	1.66	7.29
1220 宇治	3.67	-7.73	5.55	2.79	-8.55
1252 十訓	-12.08	4.75	20.08	-6.71	-11.99
1336 徒然	-1.35	-10.51	14.20	-5.42	-3.30
1642 虎明	-2.25	2.28	-0.97	-0.82	3.62
1895 太陽	6.77	1.74	7.86	-16.49	-15.16
1904 小読	-3.34	5.32	-20.51	14.44	22.51
1910 小読	5.06	-5.71	-28.45	14.91	34.26

Table 7: Chi-square Test: Semantic Categories Excluding Unlabelled Words

みじ (lemma: いみじい)' (*extreme*) is assigned the article number 31920 (相-関係-量-程度-程度: Modifier-Relation-Degree-Degree). The word can be used in both positive and negative contexts. The polarity of the word sense is not encoded in the WLSP article number. In order to explore more deep linguistic research, we need to introduce more fine-grained word sense labels. Contextual word embedding techniques might introduce the more fine-grained word sense definition. We need to perform the comparison between the vector spaces of word embeddings and human judgement.

Word unit in Japanese: This work is based on the word delimitation of Short Unit Word (SUD) by NINJAL. The other word delimitation is Long Unit Word (LUW) by NINJAL, which defines the base phrase (文節 Bunsetsu) in Japanese. In some cases, the compound word of LUW cannot be composed by their constituents of SUW word senses. We annotate the LUW word sense labels for 1100 今昔 and 1220 宇治 samples. However, we have not organised language resources.

Balanced Sampling: The word sense label annotation for the ancient languages is quite difficult task. The work should be done by an expert in the literature of that era. We select the target samples when we can hire an expert in the literature. Therefore, the sampling of CHJ-WLSP is not balanced.

All word WSD: We still have several issues with the manual annotation procedures. The work is very time-consuming. Nevertheless, the constructed historical language resource size is 647,751 words. Moreover, we constructed 347,094 words of word sense labelled data on the contemporary language resources. We can use around one million word sense labelled data. It might be enough for training all word WSD (word sense disambiguation) tools. The tools enable us to reduce the manual annotation cost.

6. Acknowledgments

This work is partially presented in poster session of Japanese domestic conference of The Society for Japanese Linguistics on May 2022. We thank Mr. Hara, Ms. Sogo, and Ms. Nagumo for their assistance with the annotation, and NINJAL colleagues for comments that greatly improved the manuscript. This research was supported by JSPS KAKENHI Grant Numbers JP17H00917(2017-2021), NINJAL Project of Center for Corpus Development (2016-2021), and NINJAL Project 'Evidence-based Computational Psycholinguistics Using Annotation Data' (2022-2027).

7. Appendix: CredleExpress

CredleExpress is a lexicon viewer for WLSP. Figure 1 shows the form. The left figure shows the query.

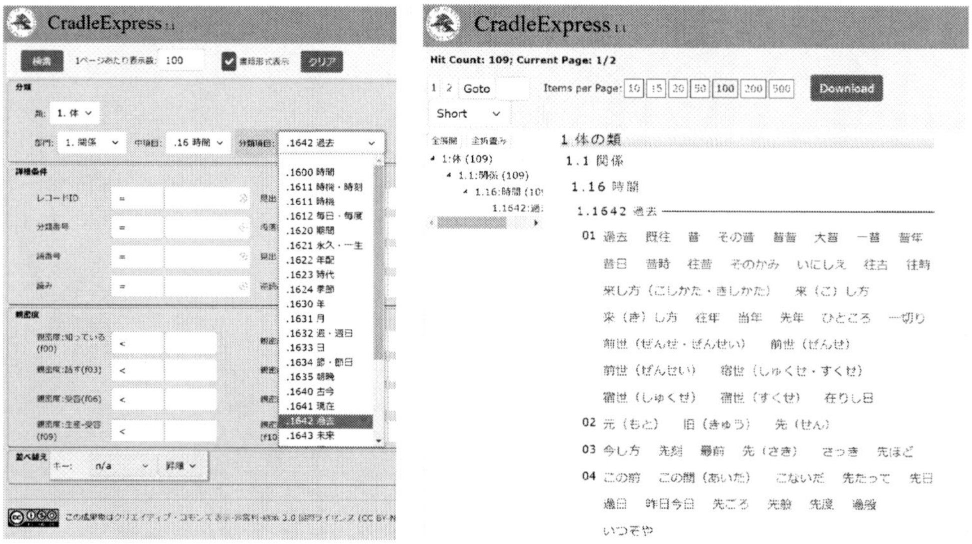

https://cradle.ninjal.ac.jp/wlsp/

Figure 1: CradleExpress

We can choose the syntactic and semantic categories. The right figure shows the query results. By clicking a word in the results, the viewer shows further information about the word.

8. Appendix: Similarities of Syntactic/Semantic Categories among samples

Figure 2 and 3 shows the distances of syntactic and semantic category distributions. The distances are evaluated by the R dist method with euclidean (2-norm) of the frequency vectors of samples. The figures are plotted by corrplot. The larger (blue) circles are longer distanced pairs.

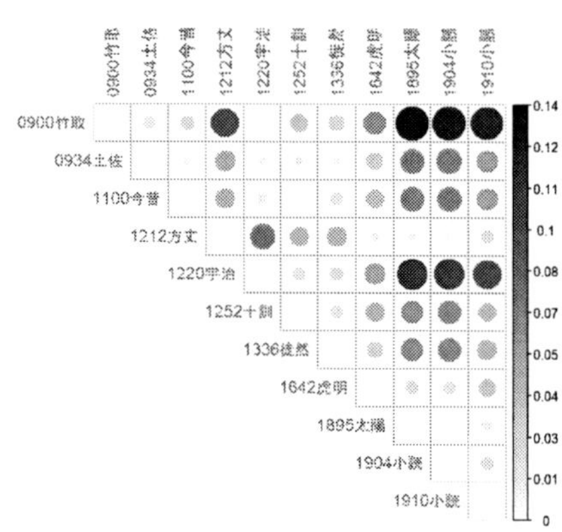

Figure 2: The Distances of Syntactic Category Distributions

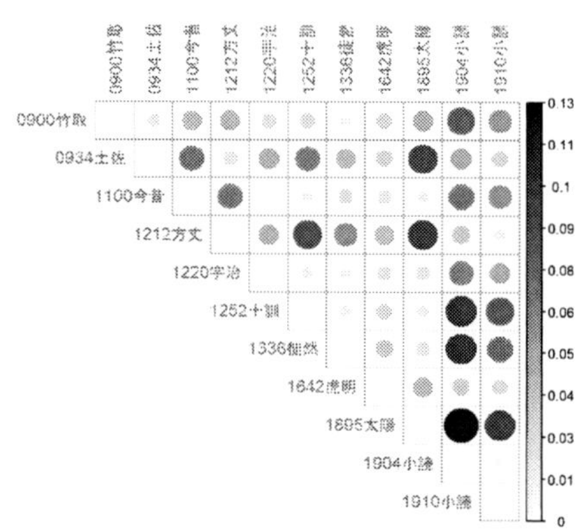

Figure 3: The Distances of Semantic Category Distributions

9. Bibliographical References

Ikegami, N. (2017). Nihongo Rekishi Kopasu Heian-jidai-hen Shutsugen Keiyoushi ni-taisuru Koten Bunruigoihyou Bango Anoteshon (in Japanese) (*lit. hWLSP article number annotations on adjectives in the Corpus of Historical Japanese Heian Period Edition*). In *The 23rd Annual Meeting of the Association for Natural Language Processing, Japan*, pages 310–313.

Kato, S., Asahara, M., and Yamazaki, M. (2018). Annotation of 'Word List by Semantic Principles' labels for the Balanced Corpus of Contemporary Written Japanese. In *Proceedings of the 32nd Pacific Asia Conference on Language, Information, and Computation*.

Kondo, A. and Tanaka, M. (2020). Construction of

an Alignment Table between 'Word List by Semantic Principles' and UniDic. *NINJAL Research Paper*, (18):77–91.

Maekawa, K., Yamazaki, M., Ogiso, T., Maruyama, T., Ogura, H., Kashino, W., Koiso, H., Yamaguchi, M., Tanaka, M., and Den, Y. (2014). Balanced Corpus of Contemporary Written Japanese. *Language Resources and Evaluation*, 48:345–371.

Miyajima, T., Ishii, H., Abe, S., and Suzuki, T. (2014). *Nihon Koten Taisho Bunrui Goihyo*. Kasama-shoin.

NINJAL, Japan, editor. (2004). *Word List by Semantic Principles, - Revised and Enlarged Edition*. Dainippon-tosho.

NINJAL, Japan. (2022). Corpus of Historical Japanese.

Proceedings of the Second Workshop on Language Technologies for Historical and Ancient Languages (LT4HALA 2022), pages 38–42
Language Resources and Evaluation Conference (LREC 2022), Marseille, 25 June 2022

The 𐌉𐌊𐌖𐌅𐌉𐌍𐌀 Treebank

Mathieu Dehouck
LATTICE, CNRS, ENS-PSL, Université Sorbonne Nouvelle
mathieu.dehouck@ens.psl.eu

Abstract

In this paper, we introduce the first dependency treebank for the Umbrian language (an extinct Indo-European language from the Italic family, once spoken in modern day Italy). We present the source of the corpus : a set of seven bronze tablets describing religious ceremonies, written using two different scripts, unearthed in Umbria in the XVth century. The corpus itself has already been studied extensively by specialists of old Italic and classical Indo-European languages. So we discuss a number of challenges that we encountered as we annotated the corpus following Universal Dependencies' guidelines from existing textual analyses.

Keywords: Umbrian, Universal Dependencies, Treebank

1. Introduction

The Umbrian language was an Indo-European language from the Italic branch spoken in modern day Umbria (Italy) before the rise of the Roman empire. It is known mostly from seven bronze tablets discovered during the late middle ages known as the Iguvine tablets (or Eugubian, Eugubine tablets). It is one of the best preserved Italic languages after Latin and as such it is of great interest for both the study of old Italic languages and the linguistic environment in Italy at the rise of the Roman empire but also for general Indo-European linguistics. Furthermore, its content sheds light on the religious practices of non Roman, Italic peoples during the last centuries B.C.

The Umbrian language, while being close to Latin, has a number of interesting properties that set it apart, one of them being its wide use of cliticised postpositions where Latin uses prepositions. This could make it useful for research in computational typology for example. There is no fixed orthography in Umbrian and the tablets even use two different scripts which makes it an interesting resource for research in normalisation and/or generalisation techniques to spelling variation. Likewise, the tablets represent various time periods of the language, and thus the various forms, when they are not purely free variations, also represent sound changes that occurred in Umbrian.

Our goal with the IKUVINA treebank is to make the Umbrian language easily accessible for NLP researchers and other interested people. Due to its peculiarities, this corpus can be used for typological, diachronic or normalisation research amongst other.

In this paper, we report on the process of turning an already analysed corpus into CoNLL-U format following Universal Dependencies (Zeman et al., 2022) guidelines. In section 2, we present the Umbrian language, its scripts and the Iguvine tablets. In section 3, we present a number of challenges we encountered as we started to annotate the corpus. In section 4, we discuss the expected output format. Then, we discuss the remaining work and conclude.

Figure 1: The word **ikuvina** as found in the eighth line of the recto of tablet I.

Figure 2: The word "iiovina" as found in the twenty-third line of the recto of tablet VI.

2. The Umbrian Language

The Umbrian language is an Indo-European language of the Italic branch (Hammarström et al., 2021). It was spoken in what is nowadays central Italy around the modern region of Umbria until around the first century B.C. The main Umbrian source is a collection of seven bronze tablets discovered in 1444 near the city of Scheggia (Prosdocimi, 1984). We describe the tablets themselves in section 2.2.

Typologically, Umbrian has a flexible SOV word order supported by a case system akin to the Latin one, with indirect objects often coming after the verb (but not always). It is also a pro-drop language, but the sheer number of imperative verb forms in the corpus (it contains long series of instructions) may not do justice to the actual structure of the language.

2.1. The Scripts

Umbrian was written in both its own Umbrian alphabet (an old Italic script based on the Etruscan alphabet) and in an adapted version of the Latin alphabet at a later stage. Earlier texts written in the original Umbrian alphabet are written from right to left while the ones written using the Latin alphabet are written from left to right. Figure 1 shows the word **ikuvina** written in the original Umbrian alphabet and figure 2 shows its Latin script version "iiovina". Both are forms of the adjective corresponding to the city of Iguvium (modern day Gubbio), from which the English "Iguvine" also derives.

In order to make the distinction clearer, unless stated otherwise, we follow the standard practice of using bold face to render transliterated Umbrian script and standard face with double quotes (when necessary) for Latin script.
One of the peculiarities of the Umbrian alphabet is its lack of dedicated letters for the voiced dental plosive [d] and the voiced velar plosive [g] which are thus rendered by the same characters as their unvoiced counterparts [t] (**t**) and [k] (**k**) respectively. In the later Latin script however, "d" and "g" are used for these voiced sounds, but old practices still occur, thus we find both "crabovie" and "grabovie" (the name of a god) in tablet VI. Note that some earlier [g] rendered as **k** in Umbrian had palatalised by the time of the Latin tablets and where rendered with a plain "i" (Ancillotti and Cerri, 1996), thus giving "iiovina" in figure 2 instead of an hypothetical "*igovina"
While the Umbrian alphabet has a character for the voiced bilabial plosive [b], it is also sometimes written **p** by analogy with the other two plosive series. Note that **p** can also be used to represent a fricative sound which also has its own character in the Umbrian alphabet giving pairs such as **kutef/kutep** (in secret). Thus, the Umbrian **p** can stand for any of the three Latin "b", "p", and "f".
Similarly, the original Umbrian alphabet lacks of an independent character to represent the sound [o] (or [ɔ]), which is usually rendered by the Umbrian character **u** but sometimes by the Umbrian **a**. Ultimately "o" is used in the later Latin script.
However, the Umbrian alphabet has a dedicated letter for [w] (**v**) which merges with [u] (**u**, "v") in Latin versions. And it also has two unique characters, one noting what seems to be a post-alveolar fricative (transliterated **ç**) rendered "s̀" in later Latin tablets, and one for a kind alveolar fricative trill (transliterated **ř**) rendered "rs" in later Latin tablets.

2.2. The Iguvine Tablets

The seven bronze tablets have sizes ranging from 40 cm × 28 cm for the smallest (tablets III and IV) up to 86 cm × 56.5 cm for the largest (tablets VI and VII) (Weiss, 2019). The seven tablets describe rites and religious ceremonies to be performed by an Umbrian brotherhood including animal sacrifices, purification rituals and food offerings to the gods.
Strong similarities between the Umbrian and the Latin sections of the text and a number of sound changes have led specialists to conclude that the Latin section is a rendering of the same ceremony already described in the Umbrian section but was written at a later stage of the language history (Poultney, 1959).
Table 1 reports on a number of statistics about the tablets broken down by face and scripts. Note that this is only relevant for the verso of tablet V which has inscriptions in both the earlier Umbrian script and the later Latin one.

Tab.	Face	Script	Lines	Chars	Words
I	recto	Umbrian	34	1268	231
I	verso	Umbrian	45	1852	331
II	recto	Umbrian	1+43	1988	323
II	verso	Umbrian	29	1164	198
III	recto	Umbrian	35	1076	177
IV	recto	Umbrian	33	1083	165
V	recto	Umbrian	29	856	154
V	verso	Umbrian	7	146	26
		Latin	11	474	96
VI	recto	Latin	59	4603	844
VI	verso	Latin	65	5800	1020
VII	recto	Latin	54	4443	736
VII	verso	Latin	4	254	43

Table 1: Basic statistics about the raw unannotated Iguvine tablets. The number of lines, characters and words are reported for each tablet broken down by faces and script used for writing. Note that on tablet II, there is a line written vertically in the bottom left corner.

We estimated the number of characters using a standard transcription available in (Poultney, 1959) and on the tablets website[1] ignoring word separators. Since there are a few corrections and what seems to be mistakes and/or omissions, the eventual character count in the annotated corpus will diverge slightly from the raw counts from the tables. Likewise, we report the number of "orthographic words". We rely on word separators and line breaks as much as possible, but we count obvious deviations from these principles as unique words (e.g. on tablet I recto, at line 26, the last letter of the word **pesnim/u** (pray) appears on the following line but we still count the word only once). This gives a bit more than 4300 words overall. However, since Universal Dependencies' format allows us to represent dependency at the syntactic word level (e.g. cliticised adpositions can be handle separately from their host) the eventual token count for the annotated corpus will be higher than the raw word count.
Photographs of the actual tablets, as well as facsimiles, transcriptions, a translation in Italian, an Umbrian vocabulary and a number of other resources can be found on a dedicated website[1].

3. Annotation Process

Due to the singularity of the corpus, we followed a different approach to annotation than for most corpora annotated with dependency trees. The corpus is rather short, yet long enough to teach us something meaningful about its language and long enough to make it worth annotating for NLP practitioners. It has been known for almost six centuries and its language is close from a well documented one (Latin), thus it has already been extensively analysed and many translations have been proposed (all along the same lines). See for example the

[1] `www.tavoleeugubine.it`

work of Bagnolo (1792), Bréal (1875), Poultney (1959), Ancillotti and Cerri (1996). The interested reader can find a much more complete bibliography on the tablets' website[1].

Therefore, the main challenge is not so much to analyse the text itself, but rather to gather the textual analyses that have been published for it and to render them into a machine readable format. In our case we have chosen UD's CoNLL-U format since it is an open format and is widely used and understood by the NLP community. In the following paragraphs, we present a number of challenges that appeared as we annotated the corpus. The proposed solutions are exemplified in table 3.

Note that, while the Umbrian language is fairly well understood, a few words are still obscure and different sources propose different interpretations (see for example (Weiss, 2009) for a discussion on the analysis of the word **erus** for which there is no satisfactory translation yet). For example, **puni** has been understood as mead in (Poultney, 1959) and as flour in (Ancillotti and Cerri, 1996). Therefore, the translations proposed in this paper are tentative and may turn out to be erroneous as we learn more about the ancient Umbrians and their language. The analyses come from (Poultney, 1959) or (Ancillotti and Cerri, 1996), and we rely more on the latter when they disagree since it incorporates more recent works.

3.1. Sentence Segmentation

The original text is segmented into paragraphs. In the sections written in the Umbrian script, vertical spaces and indentations are used, while in the sections using the Latin script, hanging indentation is used. But there is no clear sentence division since punctuation is used for word separation rather than sentence separation.

We thus had to settle on a way to segment the text into sentences. We set the following guiding rule : unless there are some clear indications of subordination, typically a subordinating conjunction (`SCONJ`) such as **pune** (when) or **sve-** (if) sometimes accompanied by an adverb, we try to keep one finite verb per sentence. There are a few exceptions though. On tablet I, for example, we find five almost parallel sentences, they are repeated in table 2, with the verb **fetu** (sacrifice) being repeated twice in the second sentence. We decided to keep it as a unique sentence nonetheless with the second verb coordinated to the first one in order to maintain the original parallelism. The careful reader would have noticed that these sentences seem to come in pairs, the first starting with **preveres** (before the gates) and the second with **pusveres** (after the gates). The missing sentence starting with **preveres treplanes** (before the Trebulian gates), is actually the second sentence of tablet I, but since it is shorter than the other five, and have a different structure, we have not included it in the table.

3.2. Tokenisation

The original text uses punctuation symbols (: in Umbrian, · in Latin) to indicate word boundary. Beside a few cases of missegmentation reported in the literature (e.g. Tablet II, verso, line 20 starts with **pesni:mu:puni:pesnimu** (pray, flour, pray) where the first word should be **pesnimu** without a separator), we followed the original segmentation.

However, many adpositions whose Latin counterparts appear as prepositions, appear as cliticised postpositions (more rarely prepositions) in Umbrian. Since the CoNLL-U format provides a mean to segment surface orthographic words into syntactic words, we have decided to separate cliticised adpositions from their host in the syntactic analysis. We thus analyse **preveres** as **pre veres** (before the gates), **pusveres** as **pust veres** (after the gates), and the common **ukriper** as **ukri per** (for the mount) and **tutaper** as **tuta per** (for the city/state) for example. See table 3 for an example.

We also decided to separate forms made from a subordinating conjunction fused with a pronoun into their original components (e.g. **svepis** as **sve pis** (if someone)).

3.3. Lemmatisation

The main problem regarding lemmatisation is due to the overall small amount of Umbrian data that have reached us. While, thanks to its similarity with other Italic and Indo-European languages, and especially with Latin, it is possible to have a good understanding of the general grammar of Umbrian, we lack many forms for most of the recorded vocabulary. It is therefore virtually impossible to choose a single form (e.g. nominative singular for noun) to be used as lemma for most parts-of-speech. Thus, we have decided to lemmatise closed class words for which we have a better coverage in a first time. After having discussed the question with some of UD's main contributors, we settled on using reconstructed lemma for open class words when necessary and marking such cases with a special `ReconstructedLemma=Yes` feature in the `MISC` column of the CoNLL-U files.

3.4. POS and Morphological Analysis

A few words are ambiguous with regard to their part-of-speech. For example, we find in tablet I the word **vitluf/vitlup** (calf) followed by **turuf/turup** (bull) which would suggest an adjectival use, however we also find a feminine **vitlaf** (heifer) in a very similar context but which is not followed by a noun. The second form could be a case of substantivisation as commonly seen in Latin and in the later Romance languages. Note however, that their Latin cognates "vitulus", "taurus" and "vitula" with the same meanings are usually seen as nouns, so we decided to analyse **vitluf** as an adjective and **vitlaf** as a noun.

Similarly, we find **pustru** (afterward) twice in tablet I ("postro" in tablet VII), which is formally analysed as an adjective in its accusative singular neutral form (Ancillotti and Cerri, 1996), but only appears four times in the whole corpus, each time with an adverbial use, so we decided to mark them as such (`ADV`).

pusveres	treplanes	tref	sif	kumiaf	feitu	trebe	iuvie		ukriper	fisiu	tutaper	ikuvina
preveres	tesenakes	tre	buf		fetu	marte	krapuvi	fetu	ukripe	fisiu	tutaper	ikuvina
pusveres	tesenakes	tref	sif	feliuf	fetu	fise	saçi		ukriper	fisiu	tutaper	ikuvina
preveres	vehiies	tref	buf	kaleřuf	fetu	vufiune	krapuvi		ukriper	fisiu	tutaper	ikuvina
pusveres	vehiies	tref	hapinaf		fetu	tefre	iuvie		ukriper	fisiu	tutaper	ikuvina

Table 2: Five parallel sentences occurring on tablet I. They describe sacrifices of animals (pig, cattle and sheep) to be performed around three gates (**preveres**, **pusveres**). The text is not rendered in bold face for readability reasons, but the original is in Umbrian. In the second sentence, the verb **fetu** appears twice, while it only appears once in the other sentences. The first line reads "After the Trebulian gates, sacrifice three pregnant sows to Trebus Jove, for the Fisian mount, for the city of Iguvium.", the other lines are parallels for gods at other gates.

ID	FORM	LEM	UPOS	X	FEATS	H	DREL	DEPS	MISC
1-2	ukriper	_	_	_	_	_	_	_	_
1	ukri	ocar	NOUN	_	Case=Abl|Number=Sing	7	obl	_	_
2	per	per	ADP	_	_	1	case	_	_
3	fisiu	_	ADJ	_	Case=Abl|Number=Sing	1	amod	_	_
4-5	tutaper	_	_	_	_	_	_	_	_
4	tuta	tota	NOUN	_	Case=Abl|Number=Sing	1	conj	_	_
5	per	per	ADP	_	_	4	case	_	_
6	ikuvina	_	ADJ	_	Case=Abl|Number=Sing	4	amod	_	_
7	feitu	fakiom	VERB	_	Mood=Imp|Number=Sing|Person=2 Tense=Fut|VerbForm=Finite	0	root	_	RL=Yes

Table 3: The CoNLL-U format for the sentence **ukriper:fisiu:tutaper:ikuvina:feitu** (Sacrifice for the Fisian mount and the Iguvine city) present on tablet I. X stands for XPOS, H for HEAD, DREL for DEPREL and RL for ReconstructedLemma. Note that we do not use the XPOS column (except for storing annotation during the process) since our corpus is native UD. Note also that not all words already have a lemma (LEM).

Another problem comes from the number of orthographic variants and the tendency for consonants to disappear in word final position. This is well shown in table 2, as there is hardly any doubt that **tre** (three) and **ukripe** (for the mount) in the second line stand for **tref** and **ukriper** respectively. But while the correction is supported by enough evidence in the previous example, for less frequent words, two slightly different forms in different contexts may be fortuitous spelling variants or actual intended different forms. In such case, we stick to the analysis of (Ancillotti and Cerri, 1996) as much as possible.

3.5. Dependency

There are only a few difficulties in the application of the Universal Dependencies' guidelines (Zeman et al., 2022) once we have settled on a morphological analysis. The main reason is likely the small number of complex sentences. The corpus has a number of subordinated clauses but very few relative clauses.

The few subtleties come from ellipsis and direct discourse. We have a case of ellipsis in an enumeration in tablet I as : **tuta:tařinate:trifu:tařinate:turskum:naharkum:numem:iapuzkum:numem** (the Tadinate city, the Tadinate tribe, the Etruscan (name), the Naharcan name (and) the Iapuscan name) where **numem** (name) is elided after **turskum** (Etruscan) and where we therefore attach it directly to the head of the enumeration to maintain symmetry as proposed in UD guidelines. Note that we find the Latin script counterpart of this enumeration in tablet VII and that the Latin version is elided even more as "tuscom·naharcom·iapusco·nome".

Tablet VI contains invocations dedicated to "dei·grabovie" (a tutelary god of Iguvium) with direct report of what ought to be said during the rituals. For example, there are a lot of second person pronouns directed to the god and not to the reader. But there is no specific punctuation distinguishing the direct discourse (directed to the god) from the plain narrative (directed to the reader) thus attachment can sometimes be ambiguous.

4. Output Format

As discussed in section 2, the original corpus has been written with two different scripts (Umbrian and Latin). There has long been a standard transliteration of the Umbrian script using "ç" to represent an assumed post-alveolar fricative (rendered "Ş" in later Latin versions) and "ř" for a unique character rendered "rs" in later Latin versions. Therefore we plan on releasing a version of the treebank using the standard transliteration. However, there exists also an Old Italic block in the Unicode, that is used to encode the Umbrian alphabet amongst other old scripts. Thus we also plan on releasing a version of the section written in Umbrian using the Old Italic block of Unicode to render the original Umbrian script.

Repetition is also an issue. There are a number of very common sentences, for example, **puni:fetu** (sacrifice with flour) and its orthographic variants appear 10 times on tablet I alone. However, we decided to keep each sentence in order to preserve the structure of the corpus and since it is already limited in size. Thus, we will need to address the repetition issue when producing a standard split for training/testing machine learning algorithms.

5. Ongoing and Future Work

Out of the seven tablets, we have annotated most of tablet I and the Umbrian part of tablet V and we are in the process of annotating tablets II, III and IV. The text of tablet I partially annotated, was released in May 2022 as part of the UD 2.10 release (Zeman et al., 2022). Tablets V, VI and VII will appear in following releases.
We also need to find a way to create an interesting standard split (a division in training, development and testing sentences). As we mentioned earlier, there are a few very common sentences and some almost parallel sentences in the Umbrian and Latin sections. This could easily make sentences occur in the various splits and thus make testing metrics artificially high.
As any corpus, the IKUVINA corpus will be subject to evolution if errors are detected or if new discoveries require the corpus analysis to be reevaluated.
When the corpus is completely annotated, a natural research direction will be to see how well models trained on Latin data transfer to Umbrian, and how much work is need to make Latin Umbrian enough to be usable.
Beside Latin and Umbrian, Oscan is another Italic language with a decent amount of materials which could be interesting to the NLP community.

6. Conclusion

In this paper, we have presented the first dependency treebank for Umbrian, an old Indo-European language of the Italic branch. We have presented the source of the corpus : the Iguvine tablets and the scripts they are written with. Eventually, we have discussed a number of challenges appearing when annotating an already analysed corpus from an under-resourced extinct language as well as some solutions we have proposed.

7. Bibliographical References

Ancillotti, A. and Cerri, R. (1996). *Le tavole di Gubbio e la civiltà degli Umbri*. Jama, Perugia.

Bagnolo, G. F. G. (1792). *Le tavole di Gubbio interpretate e commentate*. Torino.

Bréal, M. (1875). *Les Tables eugubines*. Paris.

Hammarström, H., Forkel, R., Haspelmath, M., and Bank, S. (2021). Glottolog 4.5.

Poultney, J. W. (1959). *The Bronze Tables of Iguvium*. American Philological Association, Baltimore.

Prosdocimi, A. (1984). *Le tavole iguvine vol. 1*. L.S. Olschki Firenze.

Weiss, M. (2009). Umbrian erus. *East and West, Papers in IndoEuropean Studies*, page 241–264.

Weiss, M. (2019). *tabulae Iguvinae*. Oxford University Press.

Zeman, D., Nivre, J., and al. (2022). Universal dependencies 2.10. LINDAT/CLARIAH-CZ digital library at the Institute of Formal and Applied Linguistics (ÚFAL), Faculty of Mathematics and Physics, Charles University.

Proceedings of the Second Workshop on Language Technologies for Historical and Ancient Languages (LT4HALA 2022), pages 43–50
Language Resources and Evaluation Conference (LREC 2022), Marseille, 25 June 2022

Machine Translation of 16th Century Letters from Latin to German

Lukas Fischer, Patricia Scheurer, Raphael Schwitter, Martin Volk
Department of Computational Linguistics, University of Zurich
fischerl@cl.uzh.ch

Abstract

This paper outlines our work in collecting training data for and developing a Latin–German Neural Machine Translation (NMT) system, for translating 16th century letters. While Latin–German is a low-resource language pair in terms of NMT, the domain of 16th century epistolary Latin is even more limited in this regard. Through our efforts in data collection and data generation, we are able to train a NMT model that provides good translations for short to medium sentences, and outperforms GoogleTranslate overall. We focus on the correspondence of the Swiss reformer Heinrich Bullinger, but our parallel corpus and our NMT system will be of use for many other texts of the time.

Keywords: machine translation, low-resource language, medieval Latin

1. Introduction

Heinrich Bullinger (1504-1575) was a Swiss reformer with an extensive correspondence network across Switzerland and Europe. Roughly 10,000 handwritten letters addressed to Bullinger, and 2000 letters penned by himself have been preserved, but only a quarter of them have been edited. The Bullinger Digital[1] project aims to bring Bullinger's complete correspondence into digital form and make it accessible to the general public and to scholars. This includes scanning the original letters, recognising the hand-writings of the many writers (Ströbel et al., 2022), and making the letters available online.

The letters deal with politics, everyday life and religious questions, and discuss anything from the plague to thunderstorms. Since the addressees and writers range from relatives and close friends to the King of England, the style varies from colloquial to formal. The letters are predominantly written in Latin (LA), the second most frequent language is Early New High German (ENHG), and a significant number of letters contain code-switching between the two languages (Volk et al., 2022).

We will provide a translation of all Latin sentences within these letters into modern German (DE), which will be generated by a customised Machine Translation system. Therefore, one of the project's goals is the development of a Machine Translation model that is optimized for 16th century Latin. In this paper, we outline our approach in collecting training data for our Machine Translation models, and discuss the strategies that improved the performance of our translation systems.

2. Sentence Alignment

As we collect the majority of our training data ourselves, a crucial step in our pipeline is sentence alignment, to extract sentence-based parallel segments for training. We use two strategies for this, which are outlined below.

2.1. Bitext Miner

The LASER (Language-Agnostic SEntence Representations) library (Schwenk et al., 2017) provides an encoder to create sentence embeddings that was trained on 93 languages, including Latin and German. The library also includes a script that utilizes these sentence embeddings to find similar sentences across languages. For instance, Schwenk et al. (2019) use this method to compile parallel corpora from Wikipedia articles.

The algorithm assigns each found sentence pair a margin score: the higher the score, the more likely are the two sentences close translations. Thus, by discarding sentence pairs with a score below a certain threshold, the quality of the remaining dataset will increase, at the expense of its size. Schwenk et al. test for the optimal threshold by training multiple NMT systems for four different language pairs. They find that translation systems trained on datasets cut off using a margin threshold of 1.04 yield the best translations across the tested language pairs, therefore we also use this threshold in our pipeline.

2.2. Vecalign

Thompson and Koehn (2019) also utilize the LASER sentence embeddings in their Vecalign algorithm. In contrast to the Bitext Miner, which is built to find similar sentences in large, unordered datasets, Vecalign aims to create sentence alignments in parallel documents, which includes one-to-many and one-to-zero sentence alignments, similar to Hunalign (Varga et al., 2007) or Bleualign (Sennrich and Volk, 2011). Thompson and Koehn demonstrate that Vecalign outperforms the former two aligners, which is why we also adopt it in our pipeline.

Vecalign is best used on documents that are close and complete translations. For example, a manual translation by a known expert would be a good fit, whereas web-crawled texts of different lengths will result in

[1] Bullinger Digital Project Website (German)

Testset	Segments	Token DE	Token LA
Bullinger	121	2,061	1,515
bible-uedin	200	5,571	3,575

Table 1: Number of segments, German and Latin tokens in the testsets.

poor alignments. In these situations, we use the Bitext Miner instead.

Vecalign reports an alignment cost for each found alignment, and we choose to drop alignments with an alignment cost above 1, to avoid including too much noise in our training data.

3. Collecting and Generating Parallel Data

Latin is a low resource language, especially in the context of Neural Machine Translation. While Latin has served as the language of Science and Church for centuries, only a limited number of texts are digitally available, and even fewer texts come with a close translation. For instance, the OPUS website (Tiedemann, 2016), which hosts large collections of parallel corpora, only includes 100,000 translated segments for the language pair LA–DE. This number does not change significantly for other language combinations with Latin. In contrast, the collection of English to German (EN–DE) training data that is available through OPUS includes 424 million segments.

Therefore, one of our main contributions is collecting and generating suitable training data for our NMT system. In this section, we describe our sources and techniques for the creation of our data set. We use two different approaches to automatically align translated sentences, as previously discussed in Section 2. Please refer to Table 2 for an overview of the training data collected, and Table 1 for the testsets that we set aside.

3.1. OPUS Corpora

As previously mentioned, a small number of parallel corpora is already available from the OPUS website (Tiedemann, 2016). We used the largest two of them in our training data.

Wikimatrix: This corpus was created by Facebook Research. It consists of automatically mined and aligned sentences from Wikipedia, using the Bitext Miner pipeline of Facebook's LASER framework (Schwenk et al., 2019). This way, 17,000 sentence pairs were automatically aligned. See section 2.1 for a detailed description of LASER. Latin Wikipedia articles are created by members of the Wikipedia community, and are available on a variety of predominantly modern topics. For example, the Latin and German sentences below are taken from an article on a video game.[2]

[2] https://la.wikipedia.org/wiki/Grand_Theft_Auto_III

la: *Unus enim ex anni 2001 venditissimis ludis factus est.*

de: *Ende 2001 war es das am zweithäufigsten verkaufte Spielzeug in den USA.*

en: *At the end of 2001, it was the second best-selling toy in the United States.*

Notably, the prepositional phrase *in den USA (in the United States)* is omitted in the Latin version. Indeed, as this is an automatically compiled corpus, sentence pairs are only quasi-parallel, therefore, some noise and rough translations are to be expected. Furthermore, sentences in this corpus tend to be short, with an average length of roughly 13 tokens per German sentence.

bible-uedin: As the most translated book in the world, the bible is an obvious choice for translations from Latin. We used the corpus collected by (Christodouloupoulos and Steedman, 2015). We shuffle the corpus and slice off 200 sentences to be used as a test set. This leaves 30,000 sentence pairs for training, with an average sentence length slightly above 20 German tokens.

3.2. Manual Translations

At the start of the project, a scholar of the Swiss Reformation Studies Institute manually translated a small number of the Bullinger collection. This serves as our primary test set (see Table 1).

In the meantime, we have periodically received additional manual translations by the Swiss Reformation Studies Institute, and we are adding them to our training data (Table 2). While 154 segments is a small number, these high quality translations of in-domain data are very valuable.

The example below (which stems from the test set) illustrates the epistolar language of our target domain:

la: *Diu nihil ad te scripsi, chare mi Myconi, sed modo copiosius tecum colloquar per librum, quem mitto.*

de: *Ich habe lange nicht an dich geschrieben mein lieber Myconius, aber nun möchte ich mich mit dir durch das Buch unterhalten, welches ich hier schicke.*

en: *I haven't written to you for a long time, my dear Myconius, but now I would like to talk to you through the book that I am sending here.*

3.3. Crawled Data

We collect a substantial part of our training data from the websites described in this section. For this we write customized scripts based on the Python library `scrapy`.

vatican.va: The official website of the Vatican is accessible in 10 languages, among them German and Latin. We crawl all sites of the Latin version and check whether they contain a hyperlink to a German translation. If so, we save both documents and automatically align sentences. We find that Vecalign performs well

Corpus	Segments	Token DE	Token LA
WikiMatrix	17,847	225,673	174,303
bible-uedin	30,288	685,293	523,050
Bullinger Translations	154	4,021	2,994
vatican.va	60,589	805,508	598,877
Nuntii Latini	6,139	105,799	98,401
BKV	21,573	1,045,300	812,786
Vulgate	35,620	810,524	610,769
Perseus (DeepL)	14,870	287,960	190,957
Zurich Letters (DeepL)	1,825	47,672	34,385
Blarer (backtranslation)	2,868	54,415	43,679
Regests (backtranslation)	24,188	544,765	370,998
TOTAL	**215,961**	**4,616,930**	**3,461,199**

Table 2: Number of segments, as well as German and Latin tokens for each corpus included in our training data. The German segments of the Perseus and Zurich Letters data sets were translated from English with DeepL. The Latin segments in the Blarer and Regests data sets are backtranslations from German using GoogleTranslate.

for most documents, if they are structured identically and contain close and complete translations. For documents with incomplete translations, we use the Bitext Miner pipeline instead, since this algorithm ignores the document structure and excels at finding sentence pairs in large datasets. Please refer to section 2 for more information on the two sentence alignment algorithms. This way, we extract 60,589 quasi-parallel sentence pairs with an average length of 13 tokens.

The translations consist of the constitutions, declarations and decrees of the Second Vatican Council, as well as scriptures from the Apostolic Constitutions, the Catholic Catechisms and papal encyclicals. The following example is taken from an open letter by Pope Benedict XVI:

la: *Haec omnia divisiones genuerunt sive apud clerum sive apud fideles.*

de: *Das alles hat Spaltungen sowohl im Klerus als auch unter den Gläubigen verursacht.*

en: *All this has caused divisions both in the clergy and among the faithful.*

While these texts use a register that is different from 16th century letters, their ecclesiastical vocabulary is a good match for our target domain.

Nuntii Latini: Since 2004, *Vatican News*[3] has been publishing a weekly news summary in Latin and German. A typical entry consists of three short paragraphs per language. Therefore, the alignment of the paragraphs is straightforward, and we are able to add another 6,139 sentences to our training data.

While current news in modern Latin are not a perfect fit to our target domain, *Vatican News* is a source of high-quality close translations and therefore suitable as training data. The following example was published earlier this year:[4]

la: *Ad Diem universalem Pacis, qui I die mensis Ianuarii celebratur, quod attinet, Franciscus Papa enixe ad pacem fortius in mundo fovendam admonuit.*

de: *Zum Weltfriedenstag am 1. Januar hat Papst Franziskus eindringlich zu mehr Frieden in der Welt gemahnt.*

en: *On the occasion of the World Day of Peace on 1 January, Pope Francis made an urgent appeal for more peace in the world.*

BKV[5]: The Library of the Church Fathers (German: *Bibliothek der Kirchenväter*) is a collection of ancient Christian literature and corresponding (mostly German or French) translations. Notable authors in this corpus are Ambrosius, Hieronymus, Augustinus and Saint Gregory the Great. The excerpt below is taken of the book *Pastoral Care*:

la: *Quod Moyses utrumque miro opere explevit, qui praeesse tantae multitudini et noluit et obedivit.*

de: *Beides hat Moses in bewunderungswürdiger Weise beobachtet, als er nicht Führer eines so großen Volkes werden wollte und doch gehorchte.*

en: *Moses observed both in an admirable way when he did not want to become the leader of such a large people and yet obeyed.*

We crawl all Latin source texts with a German translation, and extract 21,573 parallel segments from this source. Notably, the average sentence length in this corpus is over 40 German tokens. Since some of these translations were incomplete, we use the Bitext Miner instead of Vecalign.

Biblia Vulgata: The Vulgate is a Latin translation of the Bible, dating back to the 4th century. It has been translated into German by Joseph Franz von Allioli in the 1830s. Since the Vulgate is structured into numbered verses, aligning the translations was straightfor-

[3]`www.vaticannews.va`

[4]Nuntii Latini – Die IV mensis ianuarii MMXXII

[5]`https://bkv.unifr.ch/`

ward. We collected 35,620 parallel segments this way, providing some alternate translations to the verses contained in the **bible-uedin** corpus.

3.4. Perseus

While there is no large digital collection of German translations to classical Latin texts, the Perseus Digital Library (Clérice et al., 2022) includes a large number of English translations of canonical Latin literature. All texts are available for download via their git repository[6]. We use LASER to mine English-Latin sentence pairs, and then translate the English sentences into German using DeepL[7], to create a synthetic parallel corpus. As can be seen in table 2, this method yields 14,870 sentence pairs, with an average sentence length of 19 tokens in German. Below is a sample sentence, which originally stems from *The Epistles of Ovid.* The Latin and English sentences are collected from Perseus, the German is a translation by DeepL.

la: *Increpet usque licet - tua sum, tua dicar oportet; Penelope coniunx semper Ulixis ero.*

de: *Lass ihn schimpfen; ich bin dein und muss dein genannt werden; Penelope wird immer die Frau des Odysseus bleiben.*

en: *Let him chide on; I am yours, and must be called yours; Penelope will ever remain the wife of Ulysses.*

3.5. Scans and Backtranslations

Some letters of the Bullinger correspondence have already been transcribed and translated in other edition projects. Since they are available in print only, we scan these letters and use an OCR software[8] to extract the text.

Zurich Letters (Hastings, 1968): This edition consists of the correspondence between Bullinger and other Swiss reformers with English Bishops. The letters are available in Latin and English, which allows us to automatically align sentences using Vecalign. This way, we collect 1825 English-Latin sentence pairs, and we use DeepL once again to translate the English sentences into German. The average sentence length of 16 tokens is identical to the one found in the Bullinger translations described in section 3.2, which is unsurprising, as they are from the same domain.

Below is a sample sentence from the Zurich letters data set. The German translation is by DeepL, while the Latin and English sentences are taken from the edition.

la: *Superiori die accepimus literas ex Anglia, quibus mors Mariae, inauguratio Elisabeth, et obitus cardinalis Poli confirmatur.*

de: *Wir haben gestern einen Brief aus England erhalten, in dem der Tod von Maria, die Thronbesteigung von Elisabeth und das Ableben von Kardinal Pole bestätigt wird.*

en: *We yesterday received a letter from England, in which the death of Mary, the accession of Elizabeth, and the decease of cardinal Pole is confirmed.*

Blarer Correspondence (Schieß, 1908): This edition contains the correspondence of the Blarer brothers (Ambrosius and Thomas), who were both in frequent contact with Heinrich Bullinger. Unfortunately, the German translations that come with these letters are summaries. Therefore it is not possible to create a sentence alignment suitable for training an NMT model. However, as GoogleTranslate vastly improved the quality for translations from and to Latin (see Section 4.1), we exploit this to translate the German sentences of the Blarer letters into Latin, following the idea of backtranslation proposed by Sennrich et al. (2016b).

This results in 2,868 German segments with Latin translations as additional training data. Since back-translations are synthetically generated and likely erroneous, we follow Caswell et al. (2019) and tag these segments with a special symbol (<*bt*>), before adding them to our training data:

la: <*bt*> *Mantuae concilium in Septembris sive proximo anno dilatum erit.*

de: *Das Konzil von Mantua soll auf September oder nächstes Jahr verschoben sein.*

en: *The Council of Mantua is said to be postponed to September or next year.*

Regests: The already edited Bullinger letters are prefaced by a regest, a German summary of the letter's content. We also use GoogleTranslate to create back-translations of these letter summaries. Unfortunately, typical characteristics of letters, such as direct speech and the use of second person singular, are exchanged with third person statements in the summaries. Nevertheless, using these texts as training data ensures that the model encounters the names of most of Bullinger's correspondents, as well as other named entities and specific vocabulary. The summaries consist of 24,188 segments, with an average length of 23 German tokens. The example below highlights characteristics of the summaries, as well as the sometimes erroneous nature of the back-translations in the duplication of *officorum* in Latin.

la: <*bt*> *Bullinger, qui officiorum officiorum assidue intermittitur, iustam causam habet ut alios petat ut hoc exemplum faciant.*

de: *Bullinger, der andauernd von Amtspflichten unterbrochen wird, hätte guten Grund, andere mit dieser Abschrift zu beauftragen.*

en: *Bullinger, who is constantly interrupted by official duties, would have good reason to hire others to do this transcript.*

[6] `https://github.com/PerseusDL/canonical-latinLit`

[7] `https://www.deepl.com/`

[8] ABBYY FineReader

4. Machine Translation

We have continually added more data to our training set and thus gradually improved our NMT system. Therefore, we are going to present eight models to highlight the impact of additional training data, as well as crucial strategies that improved the translation quality. In addition, we also describe our baseline models in this Section.

4.1. GoogleTranslate Baseline

We choose GoogleTranslate as a baseline to compare our NMT systems against. We use the BLEU metric (Papineni et al., 2002) to compare the performance of our systems to the baseline.

When we started the project in early 2021, we created a set of translations of the testsets using GoogleTranslate. At this time, GoogleTranslate still used Statistical Machine Translation (SMT) for language pairs that include Latin (GoogleTranslate, 2021) and while the translation of the bible testset was of an acceptable quality, the translation of the Bullinger testset was mostly unintelligible, which was also reflected in the low BLEU score of only 7.36 (see Table 3, B1, GoogleTranslate SMT).

However, GoogleTranslate implemented an NMT model for translations from Latin (to all of the 100+ available languages of the online system) over the course of the last year, achieving a much higher BLEU score of 17.07 for German when we translated the test sets again in the fall 2021 (B2, GoogleTranslate NMT).

4.2. Transformer Architecture

In all experiments, we use the transformer architecture with the base configuration by Vaswani et al. (2017). More specifically, we use the sockeye framework (Hieber et al., 2017). While Araabi and Monz (2020) have shown that optimizing hyperparameters for low-resource NMT greatly improves translation quality, we plan to test this once we have completed data collection, as the optimal settings change with increasing training corpus size.

Table 3 shows the results of our experiments E1–E8. Each subsequent experiment incorporates all training data and adopted strategies of the previous experiments.

4.3. Impact of Training Corpora, E1–E3

In our first experiment (E1), we use the **wikimatrix**, **bible-uedin**, **vatican.va**, **Nuntii Latini** and **Vulgate** corpora as training data, which amounts to 150,000 sentence pairs, or roughly 2 million Latin tokens. With this setup, we achieve a BLEU score of 11.14 on our indomain testset, which is comparable to the results reported by Martínez Garcia and García Tejedor (2020). They compile a Latin–Spanish training corpus from Saint Augustine translations with a similar size (2,2 million Latin tokens) to train a NMT model, which reaches a BLEU score of 10.01 on their indomain testset.

The E1 model already outperforms the SMT baseline for both testsets by a great margin. However, the GoogleTranslate NMT baseline still has a lead of 6 BLEU points on the Bullinger testset. Our training data has significant overlaps with the bible testset, due to the inclusion of the **Vulgate** translations and the fact that the bible is often quoted on **vatican.va**. Therefore, a direct comparison with the baseline is not possible for this testset.

In experiment E2, we add the **Bullinger translations** and the **BKV** corpus to the previous training data, which increases the training data size by 21,000 segments and bumps the BLEU score up to 12.15.

In in E3, we further add the **regest** backtranslations, which is another 24,000 segments, and an increase of BLEU points to 13.72.

While adding training data gradually increases BLEU, we observe that all previous NMT models particularly struggle with longer sentences, and they often fail at easy tasks such as correctly copying digits or translating dates.

4.4. Pretraining, E4–E7

Following Zoph et al. (2016), we add a pretraining step to our pipeline to make our model more robust and especially to improve its ability to preserve numbers (e.g. denoting years or measurements). The idea is that the model learns fluent German from a larger training corpus. The source language of this pretraining model should be closely related to Latin (Zoph et al., 2016), which is why we use Italian. However, we expect that using a German–Spanish or German–French corpus for pretraining will yield a similar result.

In E4, we download the German–Italian parallel segments of the Europarl corpus (Koehn, 2005) and train an Italian to German NMT system on this data. We use the same parameters as for the previous experiment. After training converges, we replace the IT–DE training data with our Latin–German corpora (all corpora listed in experiments **E1–E3** in Table 3) and continue training until the model converges again. This results in an increase of over 1.2 BLEU. Moreover, pretraining has the desired impact of improving the model's capability of correctly translating dates and numbers.

In E5 and E6 we add the **perseus**, **Zurich letters** and **Blarer** datasets to the training data, while retaining the pretraining in the pipeline. Overall, we add 16,000 segments, which improves the BLEU score by 1.5.

In E7, we replace the Europarl corpus with the Paracrawl corpus (Bañón et al., 2020) for pretraining. Thus, we increase the size of the pretraining data from 1,2 million to 6 million segments, which results in a stronger IT–DE pretrain model. In addition, this also improves the quality of the LA–DE model by another 0.6 BLEU points, which means our NMT performs as well as the GoogleTranslate-NMT baseline.

Exp	Description	N Segments	Bullinger	bible-uedin
B1	GoogleTranslate SMT (Feb. 2021)	-	7.36	9.67
B2	GoogleTranslate NMT (Oct. 2021)	-	17.07	15.89
E1	vulgate, vatican.va, nuntii latini, wikimatrix, bible	150,483	11.14	27.89
E2	+ Bullinger translations, BKV	172,210	12.15	28.10
E3	+ regests	196,398	13.72	27.65
E4	+ pretraining (Europarl IT–DE)	196,398	14.92	28.00
E5	+ perseus, Zurich letters	213,093	16.05	28.47
E6	+ blarer	215,961	16.57	26.97
E7	+ pretraining (Paracrawl IT–DE)	215,961	17.15	28.74
E8	+ normalize	215,961	19.50	28.63

Table 3: BLEU values on the Bullinger and the Bible testset achieved by the two GoogleTranslate baselines (**B1** and **B2**) and our own experiments **E1–8**. Our experiments all build on each other, thus, **E8** incorporates all the data sets of the previous seven experiments. **N Segments** gives the total number of segments in the training set for each experiment.

4.5. Normalization, E8

We use the CLTK (Classical Language Toolkit) normalizer (Johnson et al., 2021) to preprocess the Latin segments of our training data. In particular, CLTK automatically replaces any letters that have accents or macrons with their base form (e.g. *à* is replaced with *a*) and splits ligatures into their base characters (e.g. *æ* to *ae*).

CLTK also includes the option to replace all instances of *j* with *i* and *v* with *u*, as Latin often does not distinguish between these letters. However, we find that this has a negative effect on the BLEU value and therefore do not implement this option.

In addition, we also remove the diacritics from all *e caudatae* (ę and Ę), which frequently occur in the Bullinger correspondence, but are used inconsistently. Similarly, Sennrich et al. (2016a) also remove diacritics in the source language for Romanian–English translation to great effect, improving their BLEU score by 1.4.

As shown in Table 3, E8, adding normalization to Latin source sentences in addition to pretraining greatly improves the translation quality, as we achieve a BLEU score of 19.5. This system produces good translations for shorter and mid-length sentences. For instance, find below this model's translation of the example sentence from section 3.2:

la: *Diu nihil ad te scripsi, chare mi Myconi, sed modo copiosius tecum colloquar per librum, quem mitto.*

de: *Lange Zeit habe ich dir nichts geschrieben, mein lieber Myconius, aber jetzt werde ich mich ausführlicher mit dir unterhalten durch das Buch, das ich sende.*

en: *For a long time I have written nothing to you, my dear Myconius, but now I shall converse with you more fully through the book I am sending.*

This is a good translation, and even the name *Myconius* is translated correctly. In the following example translation, however, the idiom *die Spreu vom Weizen trennen (separate the wheat from the chaff)* is translated too literally:

la: *Spero tamen dominum tanto magis nos liberaturum, quanto magis paleae hae a tritico segregantur.*

de: *Ich hoffe jedoch, dass der Herr uns um so mehr befreien wird, je mehr diese Stroh von dem Weizen getrennt werden.*

en: *However, I hope that the more these straws are separated from the wheat, the more the Lord will set us free.*

For longer, more complicated sentences, our best system still struggles to produce accurate translations. However, with this setup, we outperform GoogleTranslate by two BLEU points.

5. Conclusion and Future Work

We have shown that by using a combination of existing parallel corpora, manual translations, web crawls, digitized texts and synthetic training data, we surpass the translation quality of our baseline.

Additionally, we have shown that pretraining on a similar language pair and normalizing Latin diacritics greatly enhances translation quality. Since there is limited previous research on Machine Translation from or into Latin, our research fills in an important gap in Digital Humanities and will hopefully inspire similar projects in the future.

While we are currently ahead of the GoogleTranslate baseline by two BLEU points, we have yet to evaluate whether this difference is apparent to human evaluators, and we plan to carry out such a qualitative comparison.

Furthermore, we are still collecting more training data, for example the translations by Schwitter (2018). In addition, we plan to greatly increase the amount of backtranslations in our training corpus, and test different methods of data augmentation, for example the tasks

proposed by Sánchez- Cartagena et al. (2021).
Finally, once we are happy with the size of our training corpus, we will optimize the hyperparameters of the transformer architecture.

6. Bibliographical References

Araabi, A. and Monz, C. (2020). Optimizing Transformer for Low-Resource Neural Machine Translation. *arXiv:2011.02266 [cs]*, November. arXiv: 2011.02266.

Bañón, M., Chen, P., Haddow, B., Heafield, K., Hoang, H., Esplà-Gomis, M., Forcada, M. L., Kamran, A., Kirefu, F., Koehn, P., Ortiz Rojas, S., Pla Sempere, L., Ramírez-Sánchez, G., Sarrías, E., Strelec, M., Thompson, B., Waites, W., Wiggins, D., and Zaragoza, J. (2020). ParaCrawl: Web-scale acquisition of parallel corpora. In *Proceedings of the 58th Annual Meeting of the Association for Computational Linguistics*, pages 4555–4567, Online, July.

Caswell, I., Chelba, C., and Grangier, D. (2019). Tagged Back-Translation. *arXiv:1906.06442 [cs]*, June. arXiv: 1906.06442.

Christodouloupoulos, C. and Steedman, M. (2015). A massively parallel corpus: the Bible in 100 languages. *Language resources and evaluation*, 49(2):375–395.

Clérice, T., Cerrato, L., Babeu, A., Almas, B., Jovanović, N., annettegessner, Burns, P. J., Stella, mkonieczny9805, Munson, M., Jøhndal, M., maryam foradi, zachhimes, MMernitz, Seydi, M., Celano, G. G. A., Scott, S., Huskey, S. J., and TDBuck. (2022). Perseusdl/canonical-latinlit. `https://doi.org/10.5281/zenodo.6418631`, April.

GoogleTranslate. (2021). Google Languages. `https://translate.google.com/intl/en/about/languages/#!/la`. (Accessed on 02/11/2021).

Hastings, R. (1968). *The Zurich Letters: Comprising the Correspondence of Several English Bishops and Others, with Some of the Helvetian Reformers, During the Early Part of the Reign of Queen Elizabeth*. Cambridge. Original Publication: 1842-1845.

Hieber, F., Domhan, T., Denkowski, M. J., Vilar, D., Sokolov, A., Clifton, A., and Post, M. (2017). Sockeye: A toolkit for neural machine translation. *CoRR*, abs/1712.05690.

Johnson, K. P., Burns, P. J., Stewart, J., Cook, T., Besnier, C., and Mattingly, W. J. B. (2021). The Classical Language Toolkit: An NLP framework for pre-modern languages. In *Proceedings of the 59th Annual Meeting of the Association for Computational Linguistics and the 11th International Joint Conference on Natural Language Processing: System Demonstrations*, pages 20–29, Online, August. Association for Computational Linguistics.

Koehn, P. (2005). Europarl: A Parallel Corpus for Statistical Machine Translation. In *Proceedings of Machine Translation Summit X: Papers*, pages 79–86, Phuket, Thailand, September.

Martínez Garcia, E. and García Tejedor, Á. (2020). Latin-Spanish Neural Machine Translation: From the Bible to Saint Augustine. In *Proceedings of LT4HALA 2020 - 1st Workshop on Language Technologies for Historical and Ancient Languages*, pages 94–99, Marseille, France, May. European Language Resources Association (ELRA).

Papineni, K., Roukos, S., Ward, T., and Zhu, W.-J. (2002). BLEU: A method for automatic evaluation of machine translation. In *Proceedings of ACL*, pages 311–318, Philadelphia, PA, USA.

Sánchez-Cartagena, V. M., Esplà-Gomis, M., Pérez-Ortiz, J. A., and Sánchez-Martínez, F. (2021). Rethinking Data Augmentation for Low-Resource Neural Machine Translation: A Multi-Task Learning Approach. *CoRR*, abs/2109.03645.

Schieß, T. (1908). *Briefwechsel der Brüder Ambrosius und Thomas Blaurer*. Freiburg.

Schwenk, H., Tran, K. M., Firat, O., and Douze, M. (2017). Learning joint multilingual sentence representations with neural machine translation. *CoRR*, abs/1704.04154.

Schwenk, H., Chaudhary, V., Sun, S., Gong, H., and Guzmán, F. (2019). Wikimatrix: Mining 135m parallel sentences in 1620 language pairs from wikipedia.

Raphael Schwitter, editor. (2018). *Martin Le Franc, Agreste Otium – De Bono Mortis*. Wiesbaden.

Sennrich, R. and Volk, M. (2011). Iterative, MT-based Sentence Alignment of Parallel Texts. In *Proceedings of the 18th Nordic Conference of Computational Linguistics (NODALIDA 2011)*, pages 175–182, Riga, Latvia, May. Northern European Association for Language Technology (NEALT).

Sennrich, R., Haddow, B., and Birch, A. (2016a). Edinburgh Neural Machine Translation Systems for WMT 16. *arXiv:1606.02891 [cs]*, June.

Sennrich, R., Haddow, B., and Birch, A. (2016b). Improving Neural Machine Translation Models with Monolingual Data. In *Proceedings of the 54th Annual Meeting of the Association for Computational Linguistics (Volume 1: Long Papers)*, pages 86–96, Berlin, Germany, August. Association for Computational Linguistics.

Ströbel, P. B., Clematide, S., Volk, M., Schwitter, R., Hodel, T., and Schoch, D. (2022). Evaluation of HTR models without ground truth material. *CoRR*, abs/2201.06170.

Thompson, B. and Koehn, P. (2019). Vecalign: Improved sentence alignment in linear time and space. In *Proceedings of the 2019 Conference on Empirical Methods in Natural Language Processing and the 9th International Joint Conference on Natural Language Processing (EMNLP-IJCNLP)*, pages 1342–1348, Hong Kong, China, November. Association for Computational Linguistics.

Tiedemann, J. (2016). OPUS – parallel corpora for everyone. In *Proceedings of EAMT*, page 384, Riga, Latvia.

Varga, D., Halacsy, P., Kornai, A., Nagy, V., Nemeth, L., and Tron, V. (2007). Parallel corpora for medium density languages. page 7.

Vaswani, A., Shazeer, N., Parmar, N., Uszkoreit, J., Jones, L., Gomez, A. N., Kaiser, L., and Polosukhin, I. (2017). Attention is all you need. In *Proceedings of NIPS*, June.

Volk, M., Fischer, L., Scheurer, P., Schwitter, R., Ströbel, P., and Suter, B. (2022). Nunc profana tractemus. detecting code-switching in a large corpus of 16th century letters. In *Proceedings of LREC-2022*, Marseille.

Zoph, B., Yuret, D., May, J., and Knight, K. (2016). Transfer Learning for Low-Resource Neural Machine Translation. *arXiv:1604.02201 [cs]*, April.

Proceedings of the Second Workshop on Language Technologies for Historical and Ancient Languages (LT4HALA 2022), pages 51–58
Language Resources and Evaluation Conference (LREC 2022), Marseille, 25 June 2022

A Treebank-based Approach to the *Supprema Constructio* in Dante's Latin Works

Flavio Massimiliano Cecchini, Giulia Pedonese
Università Cattolica del Sacro Cuore di Milano
Largo Gemelli 1, 20123 Milano (MI), Italy
{flavio.cecchini,giulia.pedonese}@unicatt.it

Abstract

This paper aims to apply a corpus-driven approach to Dante Alighieri's Latin works using UDante, a treebank based on *Dante Search* and part of the Universal Dependencies project. We present a method based on the notion of barycentre applied to a dependency tree as a way to calculate the "syntactic balance" of a sentence. Its application to Dante's Latin works shows its potential in analysing the style of an author, and contributes to the interpretation of the *supprema constructio* mentioned in *DVE* II vi 7 as a well balanced syntactic pattern modeled on Latin literary writing.
Keywords: Dante, treebanks, stylometrics

1. Introduction and Motivation

Dante Alighieri (1265–1321) is known as the author of the *Divine Comedy*, a poem describing the author's journey in the afterlife. This is legitimately considered his masterpiece, and its immediate success contributed to the creation of the Italian language (De Mauro and Allasia, 2005).

However, Dante was also a bilingual author writing verse and prose in Italian (*Rhymes*, *Vita Nova*, *The Banquet*, *The Divine Comedy*) and in Latin (*De vulgari eloquentia*, *Monarchia*, *Epistles*, *Eclogues*, *Questio de aqua et terra*).[1] This was not uncommon in the 14th Century, when Latin was the standard language for official writing and Italian was used for specific literary traditions such as the Sicilian love poetry, practical documents and informal communication. In his works, Dante makes an effort to promote the Italian language to a higher level by modeling it on Latin. For this reason, studying Dante's Latin could shed light on this creative process.

However, the tradition of Dante Studies lacks a systematic analysis of this side of Dante's production. The gap has been pointed out as a major issue (Curtius, 1948; Paratore, 1965; Brugnoli, 1965; Basile and Brugnoli, 1971) and is complicated by problems of attribution like those persisting around the *Epistle* XIII and the *Questio*.[2]

So far, the majority of linguistic studies and language resources have been focusing on Dante's Italian works, but a pivotal role has been played by *Dante Search*, a corpus offering the complete grammatical annotation of Dante's works and a syntactic annotation limited to his Italian production (Tavoni, 2011). Sporadic studies on the lexicon of Dante's Latin works are available, but only to highlight Dante's linguistic peculiarities through new formations and *hapax legomena*, especially those of the *DVE*, collected in a glossary attached to Aristide Marigo's critical edition (Alighieri, 1938).

More recent efforts have been made by the new *Vocabolario Dantesco Latino* (Albanese et al., 2019), a dictionary whose goal is to provide the first systematic study of Dante's Latin lexicon through the extensive use of Classical and Medieval Latin corpora. However, the project has only just been started with the publication of 119 entries and its major concern, as a dictionary, is not Dante's Latin syntax, although this aspect is often taken into account when relevant from the lexicographic standpoint. So far, the only complete lexical resource available for Dante's Latin is UDante, a treebank based on *Dante Search* and developed according to Universal Dependencies' guidelines (Cecchini et al., 2020b) and recently linked to the LiLa Knowledge Base (Passarotti et al., 2021) (see §2).

However, no one has ever attempted a description of Dante's Latin syntax despite the importance of such analysis in the relationship between the author and his sources. This is particularly relevant since Dante shows a unique theory of syntax in DVE II *vi* 7: here he calls *supprema constructio* the perfect syntactic structure taken from both Latin poetry and prose in order to write poetry in Italian in the highest possible style. Given the lack of a formal theory of syntax in ancient and Medieval times, Dante did not have the tools to articulate his intuition any further, and the definition of this syntactic pattern is still unclear. However, the *supprema constructio*, as Dante describes it, is applicable to both Latin and Italian regardless of the distinction between poetry and prose, thus allowing an interlinguistic approach.

The first corpus-driven study applied to Dante's syntax (Tavoni and Chersoni, 2013) is an attempt to formally

[1] For which the abbreviations used in the following are respectively *Mon*, *DVE*, *Egl*, *Epi*, *Que*.

[2] To cite only the most recent studies, a new attempt to verify the attribution of the epistle through machine learning has been made by Corbara et al. (2020). As for the *Questio*, Fioravanti (2017) points out that one of the used arguments was not known until after 1320, the date of its discussion.

describe the *suprema constructio* by extending a simplified version of the syntactic annotation of Dante's Italian works included in *Dante Search*. The interpretation resulting from Tavoni and Chersoni's study is that this pattern is characterized by a relatively low depth and symmetry, linking Dante's definition of *suprema constructio* to the idea of balance. Although their study is mainly focused on romance languages, the authors also point out that the analysis should be extended to the Latin authors mentioned in DVE II *vi* 7 as examples of style (Vergil, Ovid's *Metamorphoses*, Statius, Lucan, Livy, Pliny,[3] Frontinus and Paulus Orosius), but to this day the available annotated language resources only allow to create a small portion of such a corpus, at least in the context of Universal Dependencies (see §2).
This paper's aim is to develop a topological method in order to ground the stylistic interpretation of texts into the linguistic and mathematical representation of the dependency tree, as detailed in §3. The paper also presents (§4) a first application of this corpus-driven method to the analysis of Dante's Latin syntax to assess if the notion of *suprema constructio* could have interfered with his Latin writing, before concluding (§5).
All data and some scripts used in this paper are made available at the GitHub repository of one of the authors.[4]

2. Data

Our investigation is primarily conducted on data from the latest (v2.10) version of UDante[5] (Tavoni, 2011; Cecchini et al., 2020b), itself a treebank part of the Universal Dependency (UD) project[6] (de Marneffe et al., 2021) and including all five Latin works by Dante, as mentioned in §1.
Unfortunately, a survey of the availability of the Classical works cited by Dante as examples of "good (Latin) style" (see §1) in the same UD framework leads to unsatisfactory results. Only the UD Perseus treebank[7] (Bamman and Crane, 2011) and UD PROIEL[8] (Eckhoff et al., 2018) contain Classical texts, and among these only the Metamorphoses by Ovid and the Aeneid by Vergil in Perseus are of interest to the current work, and then only respectively book I and book VI are present. Further, both UD Perseus and UD PROIEL have "neglected" status as of UD v2.10,[9], meaning that their annotation quality is problematic in UD terms;[10] further still, the aforementioned texts are incomplete, as many sentences are missing,[11] so that we are finally left with only 68 sentences for the Aeneid and 183 for the Metamorphoses, some of which are themselves only snippets of more complex periods.[12] In the end, their scarcity and problematic annotation quality mean that we have to refrain from using these data in our investigation.
An attempt to obtain a more ample data set by using the UDPipe POS-tagger (Straka et al., 2016) on complete raw texts has also not yielded any acceptable results. To test the potential of this approach, we sketch an evaluation of a UDPipe model trained on all UD Latin treebanks on the first ten sentences it identifies on the raw texts of respectively book I of the Metamorphoses and book VI of the Aeneid, as taken from the Perseus Digital Library.[13] The gold standard is created as the manual correction of the UDPipe output by the two authors, following the latest standards for the annotation of Latin in UD, as exemplified by the UDante treebank. This results in two test sets of 234 and 199 tokens each. Since we are mostly interested in the structure of dependency trees rather than in the specific labels of dependency relations (see §3.1), we compute the *unlabeled attachment score* (UAS),[14] which ends up being an extremely low 40.2% in both cases (labeled attachment score is at 33.3% and 31.7% respectively). Despite the very small test sets, these scores, corroborated by further manual inspection, are evidence for a still unreliable automated parsing on which we cannot reasonably base our study: therefore, we have to stick only to the existing active UD treebanks for Latin, which are, besides UDante, the IT-TB (Passarotti, 2019) and LLTC (Cecchini et al., 2020a). In fact, despite such a negative appraisal for our specific case (and observing that Clas-

[3]It is still unclear if Dante refers to Pliny the Elder or Pliny the Younger, see Tavoni's commentary in (Alighieri, 2011, pp. 1454–1455).

[4]`https://github.com/Stormur/DanteSupremaConstructio`

[5]`https://github.com/UniversalDependencies/UD_Latin-UDante`

[6]`https://universaldependencies.org/`

[7]`https://github.com/UniversalDependencies/UD_Latin-Perseus`

[8]`https://github.com/UniversalDependencies/UD_Latin-PROIEL`

[9]See UD validation page at `http://quest.ms.mff.cuni.cz/udvalidator/cgi-bin/unidep/validation-report.pl`.

[10]Especially for what concerns parts of speech, morpholexical features and dependency relation, while the overall tree structures can be considered mostly sound. In fact, the UD version of these treebanks derives from a structurally reliable automated conversion between the original, manually annotated format as described by Bamman et al. (2007); also refer to (Cecchini et al., 2020a, §2) for details about this conversion process.

[11]Compare for example book I of the Metamorphoses in the treebank (sentences beginning with `phi0959`) and the original at `http://www.perseus.tufts.edu/hopper/text?doc=Perseus:text:1999.02.0029:book=1`.

[12]In Perseus, sentences are split also at "weak" punctuation marks such as *:* and *;*, differently than in UDante. This means among other things that co-ordinating and paratactical constructions will be underrepresented; see §3.3 and §4.

[13]`https://www.perseus.tufts.edu`

[14]The employed software is MaltEval (Nilsson and Nivre, 2008). Some formal adjustments of the CoNLL-U files are needed to take into account different tokenisations between automated output and manual gold standard.

sical Latin is underrepresented in UD), the structures described in §3 and the discussion framework in §4 are general enough that they can be pursued for any other UD treebank, and, even more generally, can be adapted to any set of treebanks, provided that they share an annotation formalism, so as to obtain meaningful comparisons. A big part of the difficulties encountered by UDPipe is most probably due to the great differences in lexicon and style between poetry on the one side, and a prevalence of treatise prose in UD Latin treebanks on the other; see e. g. the discussion in (Ponti and Passarotti, 2016, §7).

3. Linguistico-mathematical Background

The syntactic representation of a sentence following a dependency paradigm such as in UD (as opposed to a constituency or phrase approach; see (Osborne, 2019, §2)) is usually called a **dependency tree**, and, at a mathematical level, is defined (Havelka, 2007, §1) as a graph possessing an ordering of the nodes (corresponding to the linear order of the words) and being a) **directed**, i. e. each edge has a fixed orientation from one end to the other, and b) **rooted**, i. e. each node has at most one parent and there is one and only one node, the **root**, from which all other nodes can be reached. The corresponding, and motivating, linguistic interpretation of the root node (represented by the homonymous relation `root` in UD) is that of the most dominant element in the clause: usually, in non-elliptic clauses, the predicate (most frequently expressed by a verb, i. e. an element with part of speech `VERB` in UD), which determines the syntactic (argumental) structure and lexical composition of the utterance. However, on more mathematical bases, also other kinds of *centrality* notions can be defined and exploited (§3.1). Moreover, the interplay between the two dimensions of linear word order on one part and underlying non-linear syntactic structure on the other defines the notion of *non projectivity* (§3.2), which supplies a further interpretation key to the stylistic analysis of a text (see §4).

3.1. Roots and Barycentres

While the specific mathematical structure of dependency trees is chosen to represent linguistic structure also, but not exclusively, in view of given theoretical-linguistic assumptions, we can try to reverse this perspective and apply purely mathematical instruments on it to help linguistic investigations. In this sense, to pursue the stylistic analysis of Dante's work, we introduce the notion of **barycentre** (or median) of an undirected graph. This is defined in general (West, 2001, §2.1.55) as the set of nodes $\mathcal{B} \subset N$ in a graph $G = (N, E)$ such that for any node $b \in \mathcal{B}$ its so-called **total distance** $t(b) = \sum_{n \in N} d(b, n)$, i. e. the sum of the distances[15] from b to each other node, is minimal in the graph G. To compute the barycentre on a dependency tree, we must first consider its underlying undirected graph; then, the properties of trees assure us that the barycentre will always consist of either a single node or an edge, i. e. two adjacent nodes (Koschützki et al., 2005, §3.3.4). Now, in a dependency tree the root does not necessarily lie in the barycentre: we illustrate this in Figure 1[16] with a short sentence from the UDante corpus. Here, the predicate, the finite verb form *videtur*, is the root and governs a clausal subject (`csubj`), headed by the verb form *exaltatum*, which is the barycentre: a quick computation yields indeed a total distance of 7 for *exaltatum*, while of 10 for *videtur*, of 15 for *autem* and of 11 for all other nodes (see §3.3 for the details).

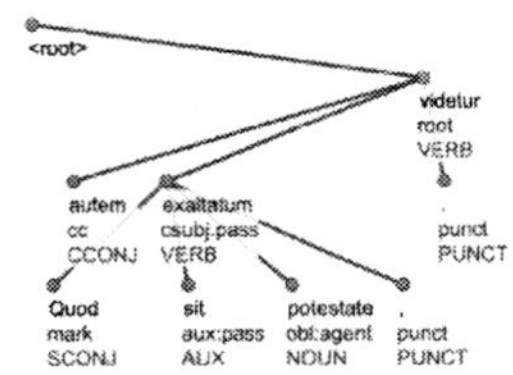

Figure 1: Sentence `DVE-186` with $\Delta = 1$.

The distance Δ between the root and the barycentre has only a lower bound depending on the **depth** of the dependency tree, i. e. the maximum distance from the root to any other node: in Figure 1 the depth is 2, so Δ can be at most 1 here. In general, if the depth is k, Δ can vary between 0 (i. e. root and barycentre coincide) and $k - 1$ (the barycentre cannot be a leaf node): for each of these values, it is possible to construct a dependency tree such that it attains that value,[17] so there are no other particular restrictions on Δ, apart those intrinsic in natural languages (cf. §4).

The linguistic interpretation that we associate to the barycentre and Δ is that of **syntactic balance**: the barycentre can be seen as the "main branching point" of the dependency tree, where the sentence is developed and expanded the most. A Δ of 0 implies that the arguments of the sentence are distributed (in a syntactic sense) "harmoniously", or symmetrically, with respect to the root, while greater values mean that the sentence "hinges" more heavily on a particular subordinated element and that it expands this more than others. This can be observed in Figure 1, where *videtur* 'it appears that' is seen to function just as a frame for the actual assertion *exaltatum sit potestate* 'it is exalted by power' (through the link *quod* 'that'). We propose this Δ as a more universally suited measure of syntactic balance

[15]The distance is defined as the number of edges on the shortest path(s) between two nodes; in a tree, given it is acyclical, the shortest path between two nodes is unique (West, 2001, §2.1.4). The distance $d(b, b)$ of a node from itself is zero.

[16]Produced by means of the CoNLL-U Viewer online tool at `https://universaldependencies.org/conllu_viewer.html`.

[17]The proof is rather trivial, but we unfortunately have no space to show it in this paper.

than the ASM ("asymmetry index") presented by Tavoni and Chersoni (2013, §5), by which it is ultimately inspired.

The problem of ASM is that of being based on a too literal notion of geometric, symmetric centrality with respect to the root: this might fit to a verb-medial order as found in Medieval Romance varieties, but is no longer applicable to a more variable word order with verb-final tendencies (at least in literary language) like that of Latin (cf. the diachronic perspective in (Ledgeway, 2012, §3.3)). In a typological perspective, we thus need to turn to a topological (i. e. based on the relative, not absolute, positions of the nodes) notion, like the barycentre, to take into account the syntactic structure of a sentence with no assumptions on its actual word order (which might vary between languages or even just in the same language according to different stylistical factors). To explore the interaction with the linear word order we make use of the concept of (non) projectivty instead (see §3.2).

The root-barycentre distance Δ also subsumes the DSM ("dishomogeneity") index described by Tavoni and Chersoni (2013, §5) in quantifying the imbalance represented by "heavier" (i. e. longer and with more nodes) branches of the dependency tree. The DSM is again based on the problematic definition of geometric "left" and "right" sides of the root. Both DSM and ASM are based on the distinction of "branches" and their lengths, but a) given the nested nature of clause subordination, it appears unclear if it is sensible to consider all subtrees of a child node of the root as different, individual branches with progressive lengths, instead of directly counting the maximal depth; and b) the expansion, i. e. the width (as opposed to the depth) of a subordination level is not considered. However, the barycentre (contrary e. g. to the simple eccentricity-based centre (West, 2001, §2.1.12)) is already sensitive to the distribution of nodes at given depths, as seen from the computation of total distance. So, the barycentre can be thought of as a typologically universal generalisation of DSM and ASM, with the benefit of being informative at the same time of both to depth and width of a dependency tree.

3.2. Non Projective Gaps and Nodes

There are many equivalent definitions of (non) projectivity (Havelka, 2007, §2.1). In the following, we are interested in the notion of **gaps of non projective edges** (Havelka, 2007, §2.2): in a dependency tree $G = (N, E)$, a node $n \in N$ lies in such a gap if, for any couple of nodes i and j surrounding it (i. e. $i < n < j$ in the linear ordering) and connected by an edge (i. e. (i, j) or $(j, i) \in E$), it does not belong to the subtree rooted in the head of that edge (i or j). It is these nodes that we call non projective, and on which we base our statistics in §4, while we do not consider as such the ends of the non projective edge. Linguistically speaking, non projective nodes in our sense are "displaced" words, in that they violate the expected contiguity of syntactic phrases, e. g. *eius* ***semper*** *populum defensantes* 'ever defending her people' (in `Epi-12`), where *semper* 'ever' intervenes inside the noun phrase *eius populum* 'her people'.

3.3. Computational Setting

To determine Δ on a dependency tree, we have first to take its undirected representation. These and other graph operations are implemented by means of the *NetworkX* module for Python[18] (Hagberg et al., 2008). We then consider only effective word nodes[19] and discard punctuation marks. Further, nodes in a "horizontal" relation (`conj`, `fixed`, `flat`, `parataxis`)[20] are collapsed onto one single node, to account for the fact that nodes in such a relation form a block wherein syntactic distances are null, and all must have the same distance from any other node in the tree.

We base our computation of non projective nodes (§3.2) on our own Python implementation of Algorithm 1 in (Havelka, 2007, p. 26). Incidentally, we note that this computation, and thus the occurrence of non projective dependency trees, is very sensitive (more so than Δ) to the chosen annotation formalism: the same sequence of nodes might or might not yield a non projective gap according to which node is selected as the head of a phrase, and this is seen e. g. in choices like considering a copula as the head of a copular construction, or not (as usual in UD).

4. Result Description

The following charts show the root-barycentre distance Δ in relation to the sentence depth in Thomas Aquinas' *Summa Contra Gentiles* (from the IT-TB; Figure 2) and in Dante's Latin works (from UDante; Figure 3).

The *Summa Contra Gentiles* is an example of extensive and high-quality data, and we use it as a reference in order to put the application of the method proposed in this paper into perspective: in both Figure 2 and Figure 3, the charts show a similar increase in Δ's value in proportion to sentence depth. As for Dante's Latin syntax, it can be observed that the majority of sentences has a depth range between 2 and 6 with a directly proportional Δ value between 0 and 2 with very few cases of $\Delta = 3$. This seems to be part of the various natural language phenomena of the family of "Zipf's laws",[21] and should be investigated further.

The same can be observed in each one of Dante's Latin works individually, with very slight differences

[18] https://www.python.org/

[19] Refer to `https://universaldependencies.org/format.html#words-tokens-and-empty-nodes` for technicalities.

[20] We point to `https://universaldependencies.org/u/dep/index.html` and also refer to (Osborne, 2019, §10.3).

[21] For a general reference, see (Manning and Schütze, 1999, §1.4.3).

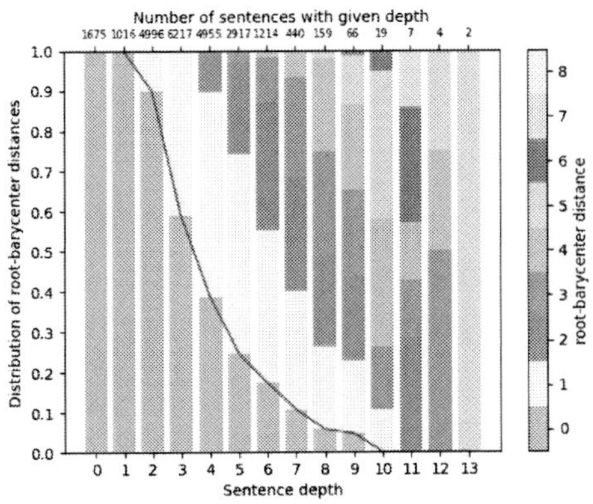

Figure 2: Δ chart of IT-TB, *Summa Contra Gentiles* (`ittb-scg`).

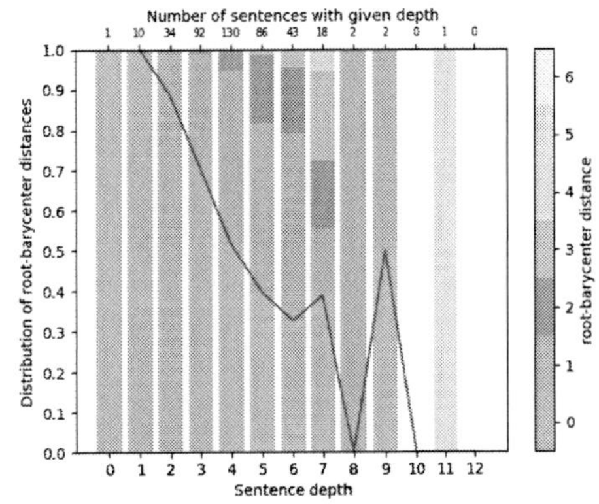

Figure 4: Δ chart of UDante, *De vulgari eloquentia* (`DVE`).

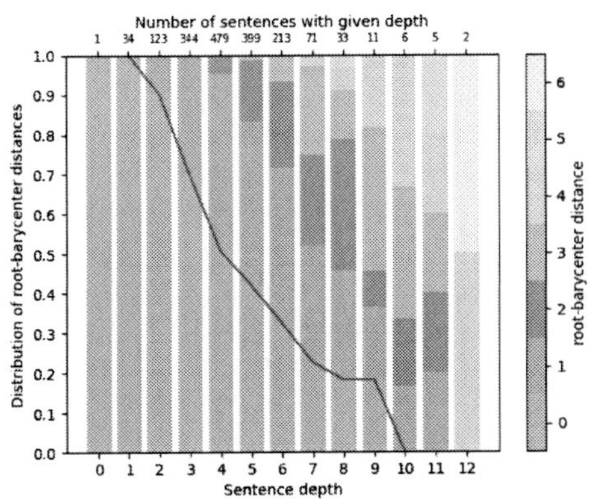

Figure 3: Δ chart over all UDante.

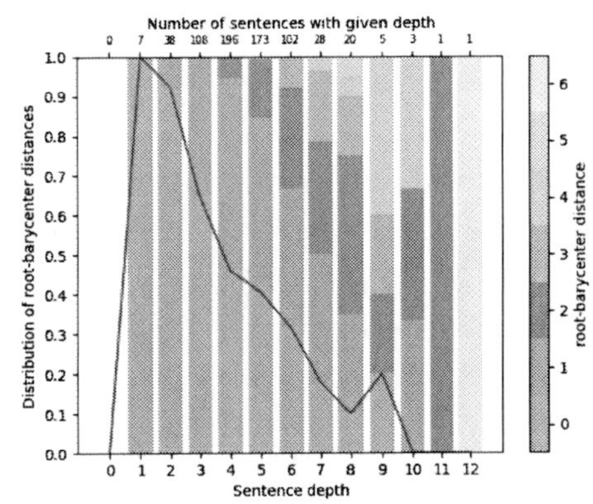

Figure 5: Δ chart of UDante, *Monarchia* (`Mon`).

which can nevertheless be brought into comparison. As shown in Figure 4, the *DVE* appears to be the most syntactically balanced work, even though it has the majority of non projective nodes, as defined in §3.2.

On the other hand, the prose of the *Mon*, in proportion, reaches higher values of Δ. This is shown in Figure 5, where the blue line highlighting the sentences with $\Delta = 0$ has a slightly steeper slope than that in Figure 4, and from the number of sentences where Δ's value is 2, 3 and above.

The difference in syntactic balance is highlighted considering two of the most complex sentences in *DVE* (depth 9, $\Delta = 0$) and *Mon* (depth 12, $\Delta = 6$). Although the two sentences have a remarkably above-average depth (and the same number of tokens, 41), their dependency trees show respectively a well balanced structure in *DVE* I *vi* 1, and a sentence whose branches plunge to the right in a sequence of relative clauses in *Mon* II *iii* 16; relative clauses (a subtype of adnominal clauses) are by definition one of the types of subordinate clauses which contribute the most to the expansion of a complex sentence, and their frequency is approximately the same in the *DVE* (2.7% of all dependency relations) and in the *Mon* (2.6%).

A similar trend is visible in the Δ chart of Dante's *Epistles* (Figure 6) and *Questio* (Figure 7), despite a significant decrease in the number of sentences, and an ensuing sparsity in the data.

The *Eclogues* (Figure 8) are the only example of Dante's Latin poetry and, although their trend is comparable to that observed for the works in prose, their syntactic depths, which are relatively low (and so their Δ value), clearly depend on the limits imposed by the verse.

5. Conclusions and future perspectives

In order to highlight the characteristics of Dante's Latin syntax, a more extensive comparison with Classical and Medieval treebanks is certainly to be called for. However, due to the lack of such resources at

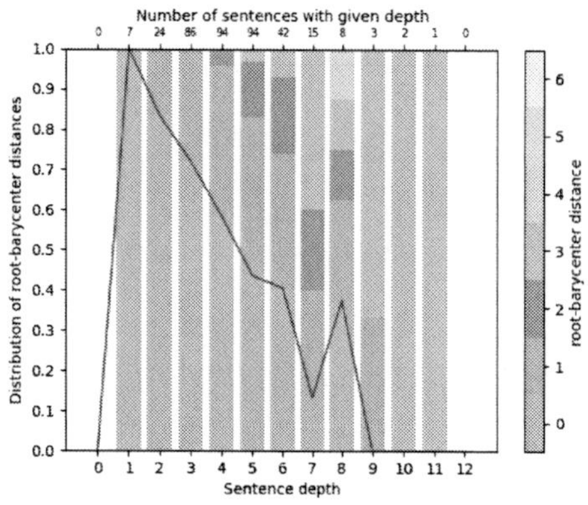

Figure 6: Δ chart of UDante, *Epistles* (Epi).

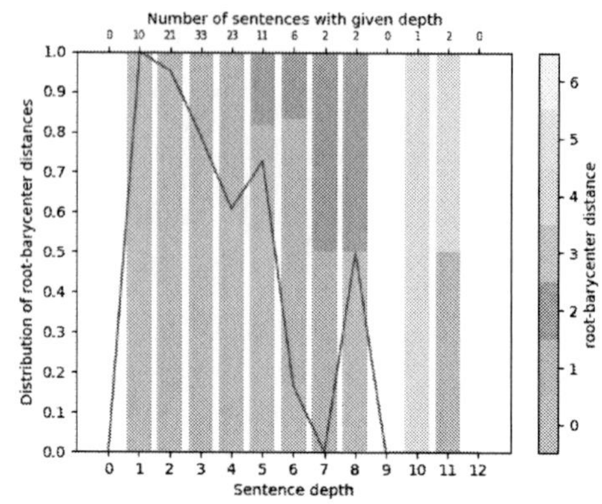

Figure 8: Δ chart of UDante, *Eclogues* (Eg).

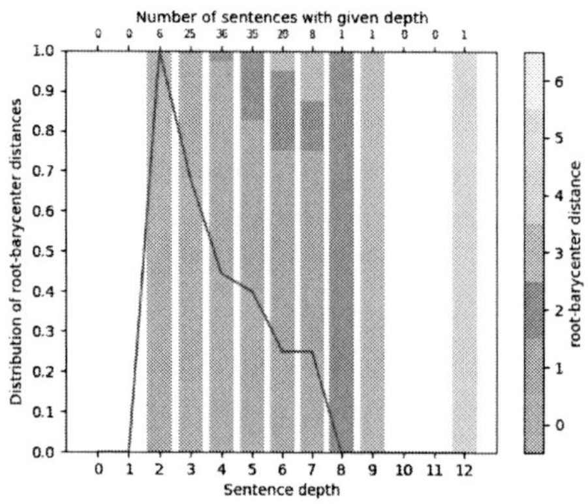

Figure 7: Δ chart of UDante, *Questio* (Que).

the current state of the art, especially within the UD framework, the method presented in this paper can be, at present, only reasonably applied to two resources: UDante and the IT-TB.

With regard to Dante, the starting point of the analysis is the study on the *supprema constructio* by Tavoni and Chersoni (2013). Even though its definition is still unclear (and will be until a treebank of all the Latin authors whom Dante quotes as examples of good Latin syntax is available), this paper translates Tavoni and Chersoni's indices of 'dishomogeneity' and 'asymmetry' (see §3.1) into a topological model based on the mathematical structure of dependency trees. This is achieved using the notions of barycentre and depth (§3.1) and projectivity (§3.2), and the application of this model to Dante's Latin syntax shows that it is entirely possible that Dante used the *supprema constructio* as an example of well balanced structure in his Latin writings.

Although still to be discussed within the frame of more general tendencies due to the nature of language which, in this case, is Latin (see §4), this is a robust and reproducible corpus-based method which allows to compare the development of syntactic balance in different works and in different authors, grounding the various stylistic interpretations to a computational approach.

6. Bibliographical References

Gabriella Albanese, et al., editors. (2019-). *Vocabolario Dantesco Latino*. Ongoing online publication at http://www.vocabolariodantescolatino.it.

Alighieri, D. (1938). *De vulgari eloquentia. Ridotto a miglior lezione e commentato da Aristide Marigo, con introduzione, analisi metrica della canzone, studio della lingua e glossario*, volume VI of *Opere di Dante*. Le Monnier, Florence, Italy.

Alighieri, D. (2011). *De vulgari eloquentia*, volume I of *Opere. Edizione diretta da Marco Santagata*. Mondadori, Milan, Italy.

Bamman, D. and Crane, G., (2011). *The ancient Greek and Latin dependency treebanks*, pages 79–98. Theory and Applications of Natural Language Processing. Springer, Berlin/Heidelberg, Germany.

Bamman, D., Crane, G., Passarotti, M., and Raynaud, S. (2007). Guidelines for the Syntactic Annotation of Latin Treebanks (v. 1.3). Tufts Published Scholarship. Tufts University's Digital Collections and Archives, Medford, MA, USA, February. Retrievable at http://hdl.handle.net/10427/42683.

Basile, B. and Brugnoli, G. (1971). Latino. In Umberto Bosco, editor, *Enciclopedia Dantesca*, volume 3, Rome, Italy. Istituto della Enciclopedia Italiana. Accessible online at https://www.treccani.it/enciclopedia/latino_(Enciclopedia-Dantesca)/.

Brugnoli, G. (1965). Il latino di Dante. In Casa di Dante, editor, *Dante e Roma. Atti del Convegno di studi, Roma 8-9-10 aprile 1965*, pages 51–71, Florence, Italy. Comitato nazionale per le celebrazioni del VII centenario della nascita di Dante, Le Monnier.

Cecchini, F. M., Korkiakangas, T., and Passarotti, M. (2020a). A New Latin Treebank for Universal Dependencies: Charters between Ancient Latin and Romance Languages. In Nicoletta Calzolari, et al., editors, *Proceedings of the Twelfth International Conference on Language Resources and Evaluation (LREC 2020)*, pages 933–942, Marseille, France, May. European Language Resources Association (ELRA).

Cecchini, F. M., Sprugnoli, R., Moretti, G., and Passarotti, M. (2020b). UDante: First Steps Towards the Universal Dependencies Treebank of Dante's Latin Works. In Johanna Monti, et al., editors, *Proceedings of the Seventh Italian Conference on Computational Linguistics (CLiC-it 2020, Bologna, Italy, March 1–3 2021)*, pages 99–105, Turin, Italy. Associazione italiana di linguistica computazionale (AILC), Accademia University Press. Retrievable at http://ceur-ws.org/Vol-2769/paper_14.pdf.

Corbara, S., Moreo, A., Sebastiani, F., and Tavoni, M. (2020). L'*Epistola a Cangrande* al vaglio della *Computational Authorship Verification*: risultati preliminari (con una postilla sulla cosiddetta ≪XIV Epistola di Dante Alighieri≫). In Alberto Casadei, et al., editors, *Nuove inchieste sull'epistola a Cangrande : atti della giornata di studi, Pisa 18 dicembre 2018*, number 2 in ILLA – Nuove Ricerche umanistiche, pages 153–187, Pisa, Italy. Pisa University Press. Retrievable at http://nmis.isti.cnr.it/sebastiani/Publications/Cangrande2020.pdf.

Curtius, E. R. (1948). *Europäische Literatur und lateinisches Mittelalter*. A. Francke Verlag, Bern, Switzerland.

de Marneffe, M.-C., Manning, C. D., Nivre, J., and Zeman, D. (2021). Universal Dependencies. *Computational Linguistics*, 47(2):255–308, July. Retrievable at https://direct.mit.edu/coli/article/47/2/255/98516/Universal-Dependencies.

De Mauro, T. and Allasia, C. (2005). *La fabbrica delle parole*. UTET, Turin, Italy.

Eckhoff, H. M., Bech, K., Bouma, G., Eide, K., Haug, D., Haugen, O. E., and Jøhndal, M. (2018). The PROIEL treebank family: a standard for early attestations of Indo-European languages. *Language Resources and Evaluation*, 52(1):29–65.

Fioravanti, G. (2017). Alberto di Sassonia, Biagio Pelacani e la *Questio de aqua et terra*. *Studi Danteschi*, LXXXII:81–97.

Hagberg, A. A., Schult, D. A., and Swart, P. J. (2008). Exploring Network Structure, Dynamics, and Function using NetworkX. In Gaël Varoquaux, et al., editors, *Proceedings of the 7th Python in Science Conference (SciPy2008)*, pages 11–15, Pasadena, CA, USA. Retrievable at http://conference.scipy.org/proceedings/SciPy2008/paper_2/. Software and documentation at https://networkx.org/.

Havelka, J. (2007). *Mathematical Properties of Dependency Trees and their Application to Natural Language Syntax*. Ph.D. thesis, Univerzita Karlova – Matematicko-fyzikální fakulta, Prague, Czech Republic, June. Retrievable at https://dspace.cuni.cz/handle/20.500.11956/12614?locale-attribute=en.

Koschützki, D., Lehmann, K. A., Peeters, L., Richter, S., Tenfelde-Podehl, D., and Zlotowski, O. (2005). Centrality Indices. In Ulrik Brandes et al., editors, *Network Analysis: Methodological Foundations*, number 3418 in Lecture Notes in Computer Science, pages 16–61, Berlin/Heidelberg, Germany. Springer.

Ledgeway, A. (2012). *From Latin to Romance*. Number 1 in Oxford studies in historical and diachronic linguistics. Oxford University Press, Oxford, UK.

Manning, C. and Schütze, H. (1999). *Foundations of Statistical Natural Language Processing*. MIT Press, Cambridge, MA, USA, May. Companion website: https://nlp.stanford.edu/fsnlp/.

Nilsson, J. and Nivre, J. (2008). MaltEval: an Evaluation and Visualization Tool for Dependency Parsing. In *Proceedings of the Sixth International Conference on Language Resources and Evaluation (LREC'08)*, Marrakech, Morocco, May. European Language Resources Association (ELRA). Retrievable at http://www.lrec-conf.org/proceedings/lrec2008/pdf/52_paper.pdf.

Osborne, T. (2019). *A Dependency Grammar of English*. John Benjamins, Amsterdam, Netherlands; Philadelphia, PA, USA.

Paratore, E. (1965). Il latino di Dante. *Cultura e scuola*, IV:94–124.

Passarotti, M., Pedonese, G., and Sprugnoli, R. (2021). Le opere di Dante tra annotazione linguistica e web semantico. *Linguistica e letteratura*, XLVI:45–71.

Passarotti, M., (2019). *The Project of the Index Thomisticus Treebank*, pages 299–320. Number 10 in Age of Access? Grundfragen der Informationsgesellschaft. De Gruyter Saur, Berlin, Germany; Boston, MA, USA. Retrievable at https://www.degruyter.com/view/book/9783110599572/10.1515/9783110599572-017.xml.

Ponti, E. M. and Passarotti, M. (2016). Differentia compositionem facit. A slower-paced and reliable parser for Latin. In *Proceedings of the Tenth International Conference on Language Resources and Evaluation (LREC'16)*, pages 683–688, Portorož, Slovenia, May. European Language Resources Association (ELRA).

Straka, M., Hajič, J., and Straková, J. (2016). UDPipe: Trainable pipeline for processing CoNLL-U files performing tokenization, morphological analysis, POS tagging and parsing. In *Proceedings of the Tenth International Conference on Language Resources and Evaluation (LREC'16)*, pages 4290–4297, Portorož, Slovenia, May. European Language Resources Association (ELRA).

Tavoni, M. and Chersoni, E. (2013). Ipotesi d'interpretazione della ≪supprema constructio≫ (*De vulgari eloquentia* II vi). *Studi di grammatica italiana*, XXXI–XXXII:131–158.

Tavoni, M. (2011). DanteSearch: il corpus delle opere volgari e latine di Dante lemmatizzate con marcatura grammaticale e sintattica. In Anna Cerbo, et al., editors, *Lectura Dantis 2002-2009. Omaggio a Vincenzo Placella per i suoi settanta anni*, volume 2 (2004–2005), pages 583–608, Naples, Italy. Il Torcoliere – Officine Grafico-Editoriali di Ateneo.

West, D. B. (2001). *Introduction to Graph Theory*. Prentice Hall, Englewood Cliffs, NJ, USA, second edition. Companion site at https://faculty.math.illinois.edu/~west/igt/.

Proceedings of the Second Workshop on Language Technologies for Historical and Ancient Languages (LT4HALA 2022), pages 59–67
Language Resources and Evaluation Conference (LREC 2022), Marseille, 25 June 2022

From Inscriptions to Lexicon and Back: A Platform for Editing and Linking the Languages of Ancient Italy

Valeria Quochi[1], Andrea Bellandi[1], Fahad Khan[1], Michele Mallia[1], Francesca Murano[2], Silvia Piccini[1], Luca Rigobianco[3], Alessandro Tommasi[4], Cesare Zavattari[1]
[1]Istituto di Linguistica Computazionale "A. Zampolli", Consiglio Nazionale delle Ricerche Italy, Pisa
[2]Dipartimento di Lettere e Filosofia, Università di Firenze
[3]Dipartimento di Studi Umanistici, Università di Venezia
[1]name.surname@ilc.cnr.it, [2]francesca.murano@unifi.it, [3]luca.rigobianco@unive.it
[4] Università di Pisa

Abstract

Available language technology is hardly applicable to scarcely attested ancient languages, yet their digital semantic representation, though challenging, is an asset for the purpose of sharing and preserving existing cultural knowledge. In the context of a project on the languages and cultures of ancient Italy, we took up this challenge. This paper thus describes the development of a user friendly web platform, EpiLexO, for the creation and editing of an integrated system of language resources for ancient fragmentary languages centered on the lexicon, in compliance with current digital humanities and Linked Open Data principles. EpiLexo allows for the editing of lexica with all relevant cross-references: for their linking to their testimonies, as well as to bibliographic information and other (external) resources and common vocabularies. The focus of the current implementation is on the languages of ancient Italy, in particular Oscan, Faliscan, Celtic and Venetic; however, the technological solutions are designed to be general enough to be potentially applicable to different contexts and scenarios.

Keywords: Digital Epigraphy, Restsprachen, Lexicon Editing and Linking

1. Introduction

Many languages spoken in antiquity have reached us through written testimonies that, in some cases, can be extremely limited both quantitatively and qualitatively. For these languages the denomination of *Restsprachen* 'languages of fragmentary attestation' is used, since their corpora can consist of a very small number of texts, even a few dozen, mostly typologically limited to the epigraphic form (inscriptions, stamps, coin legends). In terms of content, *Restsprachen* documentation is limited to the areas in which writing was selected by a given socio-cultural environment. The randomness of the findings amplifies the situation of fragmentation and precariousness of the knowledge we have of these linguistic systems, whose reconstruction is substantially partial, both in terms of grammar and lexicon, and limited in their sociolinguistic and diachronic complexity. It is often impossible to have a complete attestation of a declension or paradigm or to understand in depth the semantics of a form. This state of partiality has an impact, for example, on the lexicographic side, since lemmatization operations cannot take place appropriately, so it is necessary to resort to alternative forms of representation. Furthermore, the nature of the attestations makes an epigraphic approach to documentation indispensable.

Clearly, available language technology is hardly applicable without adjustments to this kind of languages because of both the high degree of uncertainty and data scarceness, which makes current machine learning and neural systems ineffective. Nevertheless, digital formalization and semantic representation of *Restsprachen* is an asset *per se* for the purpose of sharing and preserving existing knowledge. Setting up user-friendly digital tools that facilitate a full explicit encoding of available linguistic knowledge of these kind of languages according to up-do-date common models is certainly a challenge, but is, at the same time, important for bridging the digital gap and making the available knowledge and documentation widely accessible across disciplines.

This contribution takes up the challenge and describes the development of a user friendly web application, called EpiLexO, for the creation of lexica for fragmentary ancient languages with linking to the texts in which they are attested, as well as to bibliographic data and other (external) resources. The focus of the current implementation is on the languages of ancient Italy, as the platform comes to life within the project "Languages and Cultures of Ancient Italy. Historical Linguistics and Digital Models" (ItAnt hereafter)[1], which aims at investigating the cultures of ancient Italy on the basis of their relevant linguistic documentation bringing together methods and practices from traditional linguistics, philology, and digital technology. The technological solutions devised, however, are designed to be general enough to be potentially applicable to other contexts as well.

The paper is organized as follows. Section 2 sketches some background and related works; section 3 describes the platform design: the data encoding models and choices are described in §3.1 and §3.2, while the platform architecture is sketched in section 4. Section 5 describes the GUI by means of an exemplar use case.

[1]A project funded by the Italian Ministry of University and Research under the PRIN 2017 programme.

Finally, we conclude by sketching the scheduled future developments in section 6.

2. Background and Context

In the last decade, work on digital epigraphy was intense and, online platforms have flourished. It would be impossible in the limited space of a section to review all relevant experiences; therefore, we will briefly focus on the sources of inspiration for the present work.
The EAGLE project[2], part of Europeana, collects a massive amount of resources related to ancient world inscriptions, making them available for personal or research use. Its online platform allows for advanced searches over various databases such as the Epigraphic Database of Bari (EDB), the Epigraphic Database Heidelberg (EDH), and the Epigraphic Database Rome (EDR). It currently represents a reference within the digital epigraphy community, both in terms of quantity of materials made available and in terms of knowledge shared as open common vocabularies that, notwithstanding some limitations, are widely adopted.
Papiry.info[3] is a platform that contains a large collection of digital texts of Greek and Latin papyri and consists of two main components: a tool for searching and browsing the documents, and an editor which allows scholars to easily contribute to the collection by either creating new digital editions or proposing revisions of existing ones.
i.Sicily[4] offers a rich corpus of digital critical editions of inscriptions from ancient Sicily and an attractive web interface for the fruition of the digitized materials (Prag and Chartrand, 2019). The project has pushed the state of the art in digital epigraphy towards current language technology standards, such as the TEI EpiDoc XML format for digitizing inscriptions and partly towards the semantic web. Unlike most other similar initiatives, i.Sicily does not focus on texts only, rather these are enriched with bibliographic references and other metadata, such as person and geographic names from the Pleiades and Geonames vocabularies, and Trismegistos IDs.
Last but not least, the recent Cretan Institutional Inscriptions (CII) project delivers an EpiDoc XML database of inscriptions and offers an online search and consultation interface based on the EFES front-end service (Bodard and Yordanova, 2020). In addition to text encoding and the adoption of Linked Open Data (LOD) common vocabularies, the database includes cross-linked bibliography and various indices to allow for quick search on the contents (Vagionakis, 2021).
In most of the reviewed projects, language, i.e. the lexicon, is the great absentee. In ItAnt we therefore chose to focus on complementing the digital epigraphy landscape with tools for creating Semantic Web compliant ancient lexica and integrate them with texts and other online datasets.
The publication of language resources for ancient languages on the Semantic Web is still at a fairly early stage. One pioneering work on this topic is certainly the Linking Latin (LiLa) project[5], which created a knowledge base of linguistic resources for the Latin language, and publishes numerous such resources. One of the most innovative aspects of this knowledge base is that the different resources (lexica and corpora) are all linked together via lemmas (the core of the LiLa Lemma Bank). This, together with the use of standardized models for representing different resources (such as OntoLex-Lemon and its extensions for representing lexicons), ensures that the entirety of the knowledge base is interoperable both internally and externally.
One issue that arises frequently in the modeling of resources for ancient or historic languages is the necessity of representing etymological derivation. Although a consensus has not yet been reached within the linked data community, strategies for dealing with this have been proposed. Khan (2018) proposes an OntoLex-Lemon compatible vocabulary, *lemonEty*, for representing etymologies as hypothetical word histories; albeit not official, the *lemonEty* extension is the solutions adopted in LiLa (Mambrini and Passarotti, 2020).
Another issue very pertinent to humanities use cases is the linking together of lexicons with corpora, usually in order to represent the attestation of a lexical element in a corpus. From the lexical point of view this is the topic of a new set of specifications (currently in progress) designed to extend the OntoLex-Lemon guidelines with classes and properties for, among other things, representing such links; these are the Frequency Attestations and Corpus (FrAC) specifications (Chiarcos et al., 2020) [6].

3. The Platform

EpiLexO is a platform dedicated to the creation and editing of lexical resources for ancient fragmentary languages integrated, i.e. linked, to their 'testimonies' (i.e. transcriptions of epigraphic texts), to related bibliography, to contextual metadata, and to other relevant independent (LOD) resources, such as the LiLa Knowledge Base (Mambrini et al., 2020) and common vocabularies. Its implementation is based upon current standards in software design and relies on previous experiences within the Digital Humanities (DH) and Language Technology (LT) communities (cfr. §4 below). It is realized as a SOA system with strong frontend-backend separation of concerns in such a way that makes most services potentially reusable in different contexts. The web application is conceived to allow for a dual mode: (1) an 'edit mode' which allows for the editing of lexical data and its linking to the various external resources; and (2) a 'view mode', which will

[2] https://www.eagle-network.eu/

[3] https://papyri.info//

[4] http://sicily.classics.ox.ac.uk/

[5] https://lila-erc.eu/

[6] https://www.w3.org/community/ontolex/

allow users to search and study the digitized materials by cross querying on the different datasets. It shall also provide export functionalities to download data in LOD compliant formats.
In this contribution we describe its first implementation for dealing with the highly fragmentary attested languages of ancient Italy. Although still work-in-progress, the α version of the editing mode is complete. The intended users are historical linguists, expert in one of more ancient language(s).
In this platform, the lexicon is pivotal, as the focus of the whole system is language; text is here seen as instrumental for the construction and enrichment of the lexicon. Hence, the platform does not include text editing functionalities, rather it assumes the existence of a suitable corpus to be ingested. In practice, within the ItAnt project texts are encoded independently as described here below[7].

3.1. TEI EpiDoc

Within the ItAnt project, texts are encoded independently of the platform according to the TEI/EpiDoc guidelines[8], the de-facto standard for digital epigraphic projects, in order to create a digital edition of the ItAnt corpus by providing information concerning text both as a linguistic and a material object in a semantic format. Each inscription is described in its archeological, epigraphic and linguistic data; bibliographical references, commentaries and facsimiles are also provided. Concerning the identifiers section, we have chosen to include references to Trismegistos[9] and to the most important inscription collections, e.g. (Rix, 2002). The description of the support is enriched by reference to the Getty Vocabularies[10] in relation to the archeological object bearing text information (object type, material, execution tecniques), and to the EAGLE vocabularies[11] in relation to the inscription type. Finally, Pleiades[12] and Geonames[13] thesauri are used for respectively ancient and modern place-names. As an important innovation, every token in the inscriptions is marked as <w> and identified by the <xml:id> tag, to improve linkability. An example of the ItAnt text encoding can be seen if Fig.3.1 below, which contains a fragment of a Samnite instription.

Compared to texts concerning classical languages, ItAnt corpus requires a specific markup regarding some elements, for the presence of non-classical epigraphic uses which would otherwise remain inaccurately described[14]. For instance, an accurate information about the token separation is required especially for systems like the Venetic alphabets (which show an inter-syllabic separation). In such cases, we chose specific values for the @type of the <tei:rs> tag. Furthermore, important elements and specific linguistic problems are not always sufficiently taken into account by the EpiDoc guidelines: for example, EpiDoc does not offer the possibility to distinguish the identification of the writing system from the description of the language. This is an important conceptual distinction from a linguistic point of view, and is also relevant in the study of texts, since the documentation of a language can also be written using different scripts. For instance, the Oscan corpus is written using a national Etruscan-based and a modified Greek alphabets, and lately the Latin one. According to the EpiDoc recommendations, the @ident attribute of the <language> element describes the scripts as connected to a language. To discern these two aspects, we chose to describe the writing system within the <tei:scriptDesc> tag, using the @ref attribute to link the concepts of the vocabulary of ancient Italy scripts the ItAnt project is creating. The <language> tag is used only for the representation of the languages[15].

3.2. The EpiLexO Lexical Model

The modeling of *Restsprachen* constitutes the springboard to tackle a number of lexicographic issues raised by the adoption of models that have been mainly designed for widely attested living languages. Differently from other lexical resources, notably from the Lila knowledge base, the core of the Epilexo model, based on Ontolex-Lemon, is constituted by word forms. The fragmentary attestation of Italic languages, as mentioned in §1, often makes it impossible to identify the lemma, i.e. the conventional form chosen to represent the lexical entry and used for normalization purposes. Word forms in EpiLexo correspond to reconstructed orthographic representations and function as the hook for the linking to the textual elements, i.e. to the transcriptions of epigraphy texts, to bibliographic references and to external databases. Although word forms play a central role in the ItAnt lexicon, our knowledge of the morphology is often very limited and our analysis can be compromised by the fact that many of these forms are uncertain, as documented by inscriptions severely damaged by time. Thus, for example, in the inscription ItAnt_Osc_3 the form *legú* is expanded by some editors as *legú(m)*, which is to be interpreted as the

[7]This choice was also based on the consideration that work on TEI XML editors is presently quite advanced and that there might be opportunities in the future to integrate with them, rather then compete, see for instance Janssen (2016), Del Grosso and Nahli (2014) and Del Grosso (2015). In fact, an experiment within ItAnt is ongoing for encoding texts in TEI Epidoc with a Domain Specific Language based on the EUPORIA system (Boschetti and Del Grosso, 2018).

[8]https://epidoc.stoa.org/gl/latest/intro-intro.html//

[9]https://www.trismegistos.org//

[10]https://www.getty.edu/research/tools/vocabularies/aat///

[11]https://www.eagle-network.eu/resources/vocabularies/typeins//

[12]https://pleiades.stoa.org//

[13]http://www.geonames.org//

[14]Similar problems have also been addressed by the ILA project for the encoding of archaic Latin inscriptions (Sarullo, 2016)

[15]A paper focusing on the EpiDoc encoding of inscriptions by the ItAnt project is being prepared.

Figure 1: A fragment of the ItAnt_Oscan_3 edition of the Sa 2 inscription

```
<tei:div type="edition" subtype="interpretative" xml:space="preserve">
  <tei:div type="textpart" n="face_a" style="text-direction:r-to-l" rend="ductus:sinistrorse">
    <tei:ab>
      ....
        <tei:name type="patronymic" xml:id="Osc_3_1_1_w_6" ref="#p2"><tei:expan>
           <tei:abbr><tei:unclear>st</tei:unclear></tei:abbr><tei:ex>aatieís</tei:ex>
           </tei:expan>
        </tei:name>
        <tei:w xml:id="Osc_3_1_1_w_7">legú</tei:w>
        <tei:pc unit="word">.</tei:pc>
        <tei:w xml:id="Osc_3_1_1_w_8">tangi<tei:unclear>n</tei:unclear>úd</tei:w>
      <tei:lb n="2" xml:id="Osc_3_1_2"/>
        <tei:w xml:id="Osc_3_1_2_w_1">aam<tei:unclear>a</tei:unclear>n<tei:expan>
        <tei:ex>a</tei:ex></tei:expan>fed</tei:w>
        <tei:pc unit="word">.</tei:pc>
        <tei:w xml:id="Osc_3_1_2_w_2">e<tei:unclear>s</tei:unclear>í<tei:supplied
        reason="lost" evidence="previouseditor">dum</tei:supplied></tei:w>
        <tei:pc unit="word">.</tei:pc>
        <tei:w xml:id="Osc_3_1_2_w_3"><tei:supplied reason="lost"
        evidence="previouseditor">prúfat</tei:supplied><tei:unclear>e</tei:unclear>d</tei:w>
        <tei:pc unit="word">.</tei:pc>
        <tei:w xml:id="Osc_3_1_2_w_4"><tei:unclear>ú</tei:unclear>psed</tei:w>
        <tei:pc unit="word">.</tei:pc>
      ....
    </tei:ab>
  </tei:div>
</tei:div>
```

genitive plural of *leg-* 'law', while others expanded it as *legú(túm)*, which is to be interpreted as the genitive plural of a noun denoting a public institution. In order for the linguistic information to be reliable, it is therefore crucial to link lexical information with corpus evidence. To this end, we adopted some classes and properties, which are being developed as part of the FrAC extension to Ontolex, as mentioned in section 2 above. More specifically, each form of a lexical entry is associated to its exact occurrence(s) in the ItAnt digitized inscription(s) (if the epigraphy has been digitized and transcribed), or generically to the inscriptions it is attested in. The Attestation can then be further enriched with additional information, e.g. about whether the form reading is conjectural.

Etymological information is modeled with the *lemon-Ety* extension, mentioned in §2. For each lexical entry it is possible to specify either or both the Proto-Italic and Proto-Indo-European reconstructed forms (encoded as instances of the class *Etymon*, i.e. Lexical Entries with a special status) as well as the cognate words attested in sister languages (instances of the class *Cognate*). In order to specify the type of etymological derivation process, and because a common owl vocabulary for etymological knowledge is missing, we borrow the values of *etyLinkType* from the Lexical Mark-up Framework (as described in the normative Annex B of LMF Part 3). Specifically, *inheritance* and *borrowing* make it possible to define if we are dealing respectively with a direct hereditary relation from an ancestor or rather with a word borrowed from another genetically (un-)related language. In accordance with the Linked Data principles, the Latin cognates as well as the etymological roots may also be linked to e.g. the LiLa knowledge base, either via the *seeAlso* and *sameAs* relations, or directly. Although the system is set up for modeling different etymological hypotheses, for the time being it is up to lexicographers to choose the reconstruction that they deem most reliable. Some non standard properties are introduced to formally describe specific features, such as the data properties *stemType* to indicate which thematic class the lexical entry belongs to (e.g. *ā-* stems which are stems ending in *-*ā* < PIE *-*eh2* belonging to a specific declension type),[16] and *Uncertain* for expressing uncertainty at the level of morphology, sense and etymology. The class *Bibliography* – along with a set of properties – makes it possible to specify author, title, data, pages of the bibliographic references and to include the link to the Zotero database (see infra). Currently, it is a system-internal data structure not yet mapped to any common vocabulary. It will be rethought in the light of the new IFLA Library Reference Model (IFLA-LRM) (IFLA Functional Requirements for Bib-

[16] A similar non standard choice is done in LiLa, which defines a specific ontology for describing morphological properties of word formation, while waiting for the Ontolex morphology extension to take a definitive shape. In ItAnt it was decided that knowledge of the language systems is not yet mature for a proper modeling of this aspect, and temporarily to encode such information as a data property, although in principle its values belong to a closed class

liographic Records (FRBR) Review Group: Riva, P. et al., 2018). Examples from the Oscan lexicon will be given in §5.

4. EpiLexO: A Sketch of the Architecture

EpiLexO follows a REST architectural style, where the implementation of the client and the implementation of the servers are done independently. The server side is composed of two main back-ends, namely the LexO-server and the CASH-server, which manage lexica and text documents respectively. They expose APIs based on the HTTP protocol and exchange data in JSON format. The services conform to OpenAPI, a specification for machine-readable interface files to describe, produce, consume and display REST services.

LexO-server[17] stands for **Lex**icon and **O**ntology-server and has evolved from the experience of LexO-lite (Bellandi, 2021), a full stack tool for editing OntoLex-Lemon resources. The LexO-server allows for managing both linguistic and conceptual dimensions, and for a correct linking between each other, according to either a semasiological or an onomasiolgocal approach. Concerning the linguistic part, LexO-server heavily relies on the *OntoLex-Lemon* model, while the conceptual one is based on Simple Knowledge Organization System (SKOS). LexO-server is written in Java and uses a semantic repository called GraphDB.

CASH-server stands for **C**orpus, **A**nnotation, and Searc**H**-server[18]. It exposes a set of services for, i) managing a corpus of text documents and organize it like a file system; ii) linking corpus and lexicon, i.e., creating annotations that represent the linking of lexical elements to text portions (defined by spans of characters), with associated metadata (e.g. author, confidence, bibliography, etc.); iii) making multilevel searches involving lexicon, texts, links, and metadata. Annotations can refer to any span of characters and thus equally relate to words, subwords and multiwords. The same span can be annotated multiple times, thus allowing for the piling up of an arbitrary number of annotations, which may correspond to different descriptive layers, or concurrent alternatives. CASH is devised to be general and modular, in particular concerning the import functionalities,[19] conceived as plug-in ingestion module that may manage different file formats. At present the system supports the importing of EpiDoc-XML[20].

The EpiLexO platform also relies on external REST APIs, e.g. on Zotero[21] for associating bibliographical references to lexical items and attestations; and on KeyCloack[22] for user management, authentication and authorization.

EpiLexO GUI. The services exposed by the servers are invoked by an interface developed in Angular[23] and designed as a single-page web application made up by several components. Each component offers different functionalities for creating lexical items and (inter)linking them with other internal or external data (i.e. lexicon items, corpus texts, bibliography, vocabularies, LD resources)[24]. All interface components communicate with each other through the use of services based on RxJs technology[25], a library integrated in Angular for event-based programming and asynchronous call management.

The platform GUI, shown in Fig.2, is divided into three main vertical sections, dedicated to a set of different kinds of activities.

The left column (a) is subdivided into three panels and shows the navigation trees for the main resources: corpus, lexicon, ontology[26], each one with its peculiar structure and functionalities.

The central part (b) is the main working area devoted to the editing tasks; the lower part contains the lexicon editor, the upper part the text linker. The lexicon editor is pivotal to the whole platform, modular and contextually adaptive, i.e. it shows editing sections on the basis of the item selected in the lexical entry tree, and editing is dynamic, that is changes in the values are directly recorded and registered in the back-end. As Epilexo presently makes use only of a subset of the Ontolex model (cfr. §3.2 above), it allows for the encoding of information for lexical entries, forms, senses and etymologies.

The right column (c) contains several panels, dedicated to various kinds of "accessory information": metadata about the (edition of the) inscriptions, free textual notes, links to external resources, bibliographic references, attestations. The content of these panels is also contextual. i.e. dynamically dependent on the items selected in the left or central column.

In the following section the platform will be described into some details by means of examples based on the first bulk of the Oscan lexicon[27].

[17] https://github.com/andreabellandi/LexO-backend

[18] https://github.com/valeq/backendLexO-textAnnotations

[19] A paper focusing on the system of back-ends is in preparation, which will also discuss their potential for application in other DH scenarios.

[20] In fact, as there are several possible equally valid Epidoc-XML dialects, and given the peculiarities of the ItAnt variant, at the moment the system ingests the ItAnt Epidoc format. However, the XML importer is designed to be customizable relying on xpath syntax, and adaptation to different XML formats shall be possible. This has still to be tested.

[21] https://www.zotero.org/

[22] https://www.keycloak.org/

[23] https://angular.io/

[24] https://github.com/MicheleMallia/LexO-angular

[25] https://rxjs.dev/

[26] The services offered by the LexO-server for importing an external ontology and link its elements to lexical items, are currently not exploited in ItAnt.

[27] Encoded for ItAnt by Dott. Edoardo Middei

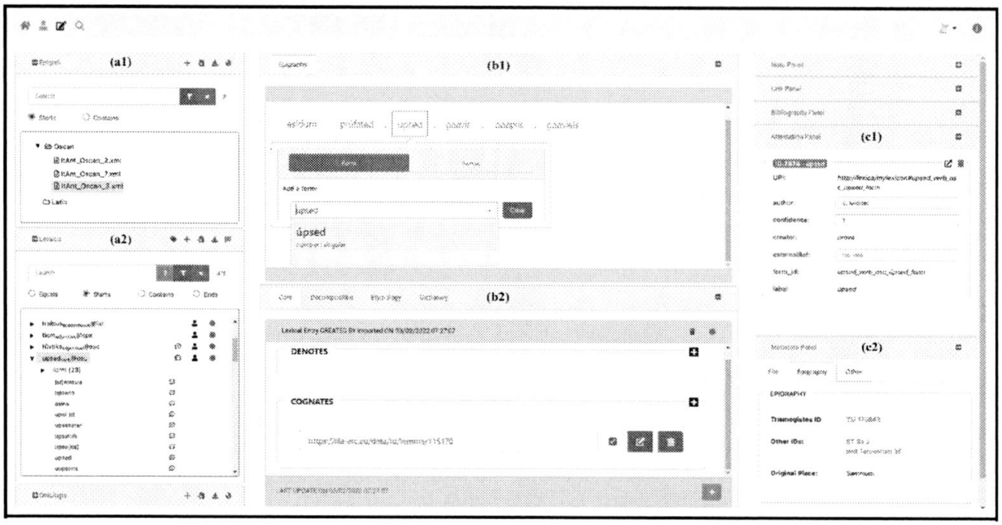

Figure 2: The EpiLexo GUI

5. Editing the Lexicon and Linking the Inscriptions

EpiLexo accommodates two possible usage workflows: 1) creation of a lexicon from scratch on the basis of (a corpus of) epigraphic texts; and 2) linking of an existing lexicon to (a corpus of) epigraphic texts in which its languages are attested. In the first scenario, a scholar imports (an EpiDoc XML corpus of) epigraphic texts into the platform and starts creating and encoding the lexical items attested in the corpus, linking them to the exact textual loci, to relevant bibliography and possibly to relevant external resources. In the second scenario the scholar starts from an existing lexicon for the language(s) of interest, imports a corpus and encodes the links to the various relevant internal and external data. Possibly (s)he can further edit and enrich the lexicon by adding e.g. new entries and forms[28].

The platform permits to perform all the required actions from a single page in a seemingly smooth way.

From within the corpus panel in the left column, the user uploads a corpus file that documents one or more lexical entries, for instance the ItAnt_Oscan_3.xml (excerpted in §3.1 above), which represents a critical edition of a Samnite inscription. The corpus panel –(a1) in Fig.2– is organized like an OS file system and allows for typical CRUD operations, based on the CASH-server APIs. Thus, the user can create folders, move files, import other Epidoc documents, add metadata tags to both files and folders. The importer automatically extracts from the EpiDoc file all metadata related to the inscription and its edition, and the platform dynamically displays them in the metadata panel in the right column, as in Fig.2 (c2). In our example, for instance one can easily check e.g. the inscription provenance (Samnium) and the other identifiers by which the inscription is also known as (i.e. TM 170843, Sa 2, Teruentum 36)[29].

The text contained in the inscription is shown in the central upper panel (Fig.2 (b1)), the Linker, which allows for linking text portions to items in the lexicon by invoking the services of the CASH-server. Because the ItAnt Epidoc corpus encodes word segmentation (cfr. §3.1), the Linker makes use of this information and displays the text into visual segments. Linking is done by selecting an entire token, a subtoken (e.g. a prefix), or a list of tokens (for linking to multiwords), and then searching for and selecting the desired form from the lexicon within a dedicated pop-up window, as shown in the figure for *úpsed*.

The act of establishing a link between a text portion and a lexical form practically corresponds to creating an Attestation for the given form, according to the model described in §3.2 above. Attestations are displayed in the dedicated panel on the right column, (c1) in the figure, from where they can be further enriched according to the model. For instance, in the case of *úpsed* we may want to set the confidence to 1 to assert certainty, attribute authorship to a different scholar, add a bibliographic reference, e.g. to Untermann (2000) where the specific attestation is discussed (see Fig.5 in the Appendix for an example of the Zotero plug-in for adding blibliographic references to the lexicon).

[28]In ItAnt, this second scenario is the actual case for the Oscan language, for which the lexicon encoding started with an ad-hoc adaptation of LexO-lite (Bellandi, 2019).

[29]Notice that the identifiers are displayed as hyperlinks pointing to the actual external resources, i.e. to the Trismegistos record and to the bibliographic records of the secondary sources in the ItAnt Zotero library[30]

Before working on the linking, (s)he might want to first check how the lexical entry for *upsed* is encoded in the lexicon. S(he) would then use the filter in the lexicon navigation tree in the left column dedicated to managing and browsing the lexicon content (cfr. Fig.2.(a2)). This panel is organized according to the key ItAnt lexical classes: Lexical Entry, Form, Senseand Etymology (cfr. §3.2), which dynamically correspond to dedicated editing views in the central part of the interface. From this panel the user can also perform some high-level lexicon editing actions, such as adding new languages and lexical entries.

Because of the theoretical and practical difficulties of lemmatization discussed in §1 and §3.2 above, forms are richly described and represent the key elements in the lexicon, acting also as the interface with the texts. In the current version, forms are all listed and grouped under a Lexical Entry, as it can be seen in Fig.3. Information about whether the lexical entry is an etymon (i.e. an etymological root), about its stem type and about its cognates is also encoded at lexical entry level, which is to be considered as a mere container for encoding those features shared by all forms (such as language and part of speech).

Cognates are encoded by linking either internally to another entry of a different language or externally to another linked data compliant lexicon. In Fig.2 (b2) we see the Latin cognate of *upsed* represented by the URI of the corresponding lemma entry, *opus*, in the LiLa knowledge base[31].

Etymological information is attached to a Lexical Entry and applies to all of its forms. Etymology has a dedicated structure which, in addition to the etymon, allows for the specification of the type of derivation and the author[32]. Although the underlying model is capable of representing derivation chains, this possibility is deliberately blocked in the current interface on theoretical basis that need further reflection and confrontations. In Fig.3 we see an example of this: here the source and target of the etymological link are default values set by the system, as they always correspond to the etymological PIE or PIT root and the current lexical entry respectively. In principle, these fields can be made editable to permit the encoding of derivation chains.

Similarly to Cognates, the PIE etymon here can link either externally to the corresponding etymon in the LiLa Etymological Dictionary, or internally to the **h3ep-* Etymon entry, as exemplified in Fig.4. In the latter case, linking to the LiLa equivalent can be encoded at lexical entry level, in the Link panel on the right column by means of a `owl:sameAs` relation, as in Fig.4.

Bibliographic references to relevant literature can be added to lexical entries, forms, senses, etymologies, as well as to Attestations, via a Zotero plug-in (see Fig.5 in the Appendix) and enriched with additional information in the Bibliography panel, in the right column.

Finally, free textual notes for describing any additional unstructured, information can be added in the Note panel on the right column to every element of the lexicon; the same applies to links to relevant external resources, which can be encoded in the Link panel as `rdf:seeAlso` or `owl:sameAs` relations for any lexical element, as in the Etymology example above.

6. Conclusion and Future Works

In this paper we have presented a newly developed editing platform for the creation of interlinked linguistic datasets for ancient fragmentary languages. While the front-end is in part tailored on the specific requirements of the project it is born to serve, the whole architecture is modular and general enough to serve other needs as well. As mentioned above, the platform is not yet complete. The 'edit mode' is about to go in production and user feedback will prove precious for bug fixing and improvements. In the immediate future efforts will be devoted to the construction of the 'view mode', which should allow multi-layer, cross-dataset queries, as well as effective presentation of the contents and search results. In this respect, plans for CASH are to experimentally support a query language based on CQL that will permit to perform complex queries mixing text content with both metadata and annotations, such as: "find all inscriptions in language *L* (metadata), containing the word *W* (content) as an attestation of the form *F* found in the lexicon (annotation), followed by a person name (content+annotation)".

Another fundamental aspect that needs to be dealt with soon is export functionalities. As one of the objectives is to produce and publish a LOD version of the results, the platform shall allow for the exporting of the data in LOD compliant formats. While the lexicon will require only minor adjustments to be fully compliant to Ontolex, we still need to make decisions on the representation of texts, bibliography, and bibliographic references or citations. For the latter, good candidates are the FRBR-aligned Bibliographic Ontology (FaBiO) or the Citation Typing Ontology (CiTO) (Peroni and Shotton, 2012), while for the bibliography the IFLA-LRM mentioned in §4 will have to be assessed. As far as texts are concerned, internal discussion is still open; one safe but sub-optimal solution might be to follow the example of the LiLa knowledge base that provides a Powla rdf representation of texts as lists of tokens. However, this is a hot research topic in the humanities

[31]The choice of whether to link externally or internally to one of the lexicon entries is left to the scholar, and mostly depends on the availability of LOD compliant lexical resource for the language(s) of interest.

[32]Given that a Lexical Entry is allowed to have many Etymology items, the possibility to state the author might be used to encode alternative hypothesis, and goes in the direction suggested in Mambrini and Passarotti (2020) of treating etymologies as scientific propositions and model them also according to CIDOC CRM-tex (Felicetti and Murano, 2021). The current implementation however leaves this under-specified and conforms to the project requirement to encode only the editors' scientific claim(s).

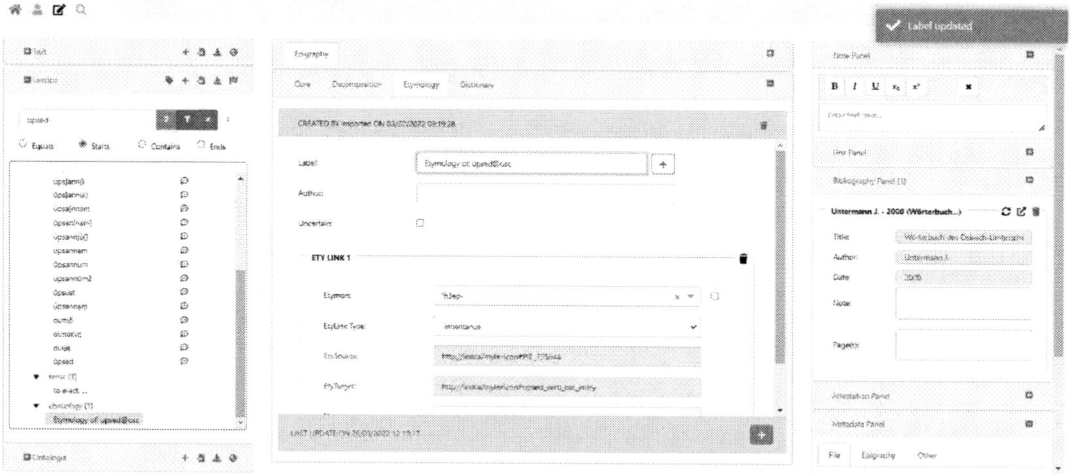

Figure 3: Etymology of *upsed*

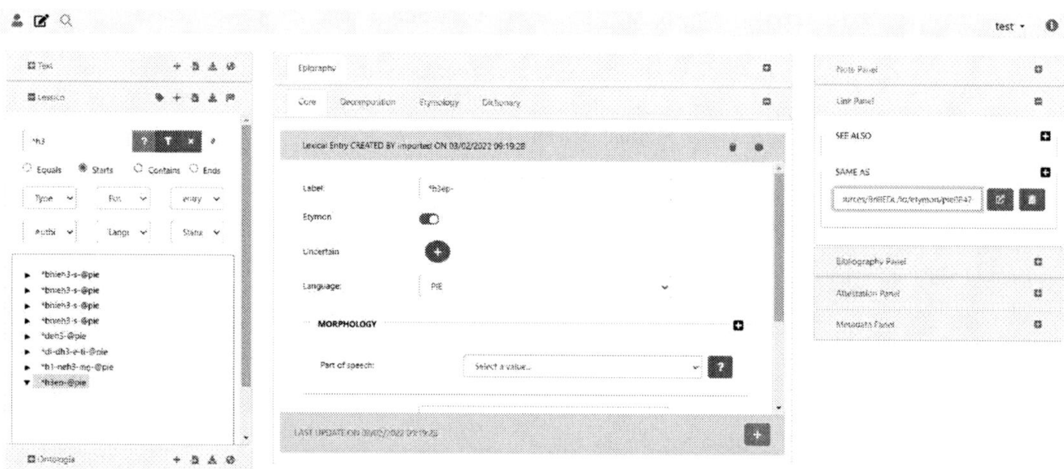

Figure 4: Linking Etymons to the LiLa Etymological Dictionary

and other options still have to be taken into account. The software is open source and, once complete, the full package will also be delivered on a docker image that can be quickly installed on any server. Finally, all results – corpus and lexical data as well the software – will be deposited in the ILC4CLARIN repository and integrated as a service into CLARIN-IT, which will guarantee long term preservation of the digital project outputs and the sustainability of the platform. To this end, work is in progress towards the integration with the CLARIN AAI and SSO services, via the Keycloak backend.

7. Acknowledgments

This work is financially supported by the Italian Ministry of University and Research under the PRIN 2017 programme and carried out within the "Languages and Cultures of Ancient Italy. Historical Linguistics and Digital Models" project (PRIN 2017XJLE8J).
It also has the support of the CLARIN-IT infrastructure.

8. Bibliographical References

Bellandi, A. (2021). LexO: an open-source system for managing ontolex-lemon resources. *Language Resources and Evaluation*, 55.4:1093–1126.

Bodard, G. and Yordanova, P. (2020). Publication, testing and visualization with EFES: A tool for all stages of the EpiDoc XML editing process. *Studia Universitatis Babeș-Bolyai Digitalia*, 65(1):17–35.

Boschetti, F. and Del Grosso, A. M. (2018). Euporia: Piattaforma digitale per l'annotazione tramite Domain Specific Languages di testi multilingui disposti in parallelo.

Chiarcos, C., Ionov, M., de Does, J., Depuydt, K., Khan, F., Stolk, S., Declerck, T., and McCrae, J. P. (2020). Modelling frequency and attestations for ontolex-lemon. In *Proceedings of the 2020 Globalex Workshop on Linked Lexicography*, pages 1–9.

Del Grosso, A. M. and Nahli, O. (2014). Towards a flexible open-source software library for multi-layered scholarly textual studies: An arabic case study dealing with semi-automatic language processing. In *Proceedings of the Third IEEE International Colloquium in Information Science and Technology (CIST)*, pages 285–290.

Del Grosso, A. M. (2015). *Designing a Library of Components for Textual Scholarship*. Ph.d. thesis in computer engineering, unpublished phd thesis, University of Pisa.

Felicetti, A. and Murano, F. (2021). Semantic modeling of textual entities: The CRMtex model and the ontological description of ancient texts. *Umanistica Digitale*, (11):163–175, Jan.

IFLA Functional Requirements for Bibliographic Records (FRBR) Review Group: Riva, P., Le Boeuf, P., and Zumer, M. (2018). IFLA library reference model: A conceptual model for bibliographic information. https://repository.ifla.org/handle/123456789/40.

Janssen, M. (2016). Teitok: Text-faithful annotated corpora. In Nicoletta Calzolari (Conference Chair), et al., editors, *Proceedings of the Tenth International Conference on Language Resources and Evaluation (LREC 2016)*, Paris, France, may. European Language Resources Association (ELRA).

Khan, A. F. (2018). Towards the representation of etymological data on the semantic web. *Information*, 9(12):304.

Mambrini, F. and Passarotti, M. (2020). Representing etymology in the LiLa knowledge base of linguistic resources for Latin. In *Proceedings of the 2020 Globalex Workshop on Linked Lexicography*, pages 20–28, Marseille, France, May. European Language Resources Association.

Mambrini, F., Cecchini, F. M., Franzini, G., Litta, E., Passarotti, M. C., and Ruffolo, P. (2020). LiLa: Linking Latin. risorse linguistiche per il latino nel semantic web. *Umanistica Digitale*, 4(8), Jan.

Peroni, S. and Shotton, D. (2012). Ontology paper: Fabio and cito: Ontologies for describing bibliographic resources and citations. *Web Semantics: Science, Services and Agents on the World Wide Web*, 17:33–43, dec.

Prag, J. R. W. and Chartrand, J. (2019). I. Sicily: Building a digital corpus of the inscriptions of ancient sicily. In Annamaria De Santis et al., editors, *Crossing Experiences in Digital Epigraphy: From Practice to Discipline*, pages 240–252. De Gruyter Open Poland.

Rix, H. (2002). *Sabellische Texte. Die Texte des Oskischen, Umbrischen und Südpikenischen*. C. Winter, Heidelberg.

Sarullo, G. (2016). The encoding challenge of the ILA project. In Antonio Felle et al., editors, *Off the Beaten Track. Epigraphy at the Borders. Proceedings of the VI EAGLE International Event (Bari, 24th-25th September 2015)*, Oxford. Archaeopress.

9. Language Resource References

Andrea Bellandi. (2019). *LexO - Lexicographic Editor for Ontolex-lemon Resources*. Istituto di Linguistica Computazionale "A.Zampolli", Consiglio Nazionale delle Ricerche, Italy, Pisa, PID http://hdl.handle.net/20.500.11752/ILC-95.

Irene Vagionakis. (2021). *Cretan Institutional Inscriptions Dataset*. Venice Centre for Digital and Public Humanities (VePDH), PID http://hdl.handle.net/20.500.11752/OPEN-548.

10. Appendix: the Zotero Plug-in

Figure 5: An example of the Zotero plug-in: searching the relevant bibliographic entry for Untermann 2000, to be linked to *upsed*.

Proceedings of the Second Workshop on Language Technologies for Historical and Ancient Languages (LT4HALA 2022), pages 68–72
Language Resources and Evaluation Conference (LREC 2022), Marseille, 25 June 2022

BERToldo, the Historical BERT for Italian

Alessio Palmero Aprosio, Stefano Menini, Sara Tonelli
Fondazione Bruno Kessler
Trento, Italy
{aprosio,menini,satonelli}@fbk.eu

Abstract

Recent works in historical language processing have shown that transformer-based models can be successfully created using historical corpora, and that using them for analysing and classifying data from the past can be beneficial compared to standard transformer models. This has led to the creation of BERT-like models for different languages trained with digital repositories from the past. In this work we introduce the Italian version of historical BERT, which we call BERToldo. We evaluate the model on the task of PoS-tagging Dante Alighieri's works, considering not only the tagger performance but also the model size and the time needed to train it. We also address the problem of duplicated data, which is rather common for languages with a limited availability of historical corpora. We show that deduplication reduces training time without affecting performance. The model and its smaller versions are all made available to the research community.

Keywords: transformer models, Italian, historical data

1. Introduction

Recent advances in language modelling have shown that fine-tuning transformer-based models (Devlin et al., 2019) represent the state-of-the-art approach for several NLP tasks. As a consequence, specific BERT-like models have been created basically for any language for which enough training data are available. More recently, transformer models have been created also starting from historical corpora, showing that their adoption can benefit classification of historical texts in different tasks such as NER, word sense disambiguation and PoS-tagging (Manjavacas and Fonteyn, 2022). Historical BERTs have been developed first for English (Manjavacas and Fonteyn, 2021; Beelen et al., 2021), being a language with a large availability of historical corpora, but have included in the last year also other languages such as Dutch and French (Gabay et al., 2022).

As for Italian, there are no historical transformer models available. For this reason, we present in this work BERToldo, an Italian BERT trained on documents extracted from different freely-available repositories of historical corpora and covering a time period between 1200 and 1900. To evaluate the model, we fine-tune and test it on a PoS-tagged dataset containing texts written by the Italian poet Dante Alighieri (1265 – 1321), in order to measure its adaptation capabilities compared to standard BERT. We also split the training data into time periods and create smaller versions of BERToldo to assess what is the impact of training size and of the temporal dimension on the accuracy of the PoS-tagger on Dante's works. All versions of BERToldo are made available to the research community at https://github.com/dhfbk/historical-bert.

2. Related Work

The development of BERT-like models trained on historical data has been investigated only recently and has concerned so far few languages. The most represented one is English, for which some historical transformer models have been created following different approaches. A first strategy has been to further train a standard BERT model using historical data (Hosseini et al., 2021; Beelen et al., 2021). A second approach, instead, relies on training BERT from scratch using only historical data, which has led to the development of MacBERTh (Manjavacas and Fonteyn, 2021). The same authors have shown that this latter approach works better on a number of NLP tasks rather than fine-tuning standard BERT (Manjavacas and Fonteyn, 2022). Beside English, a historical version of BERT has been created also for French (Gabay et al., 2022), following the same approach as MacBERTh, i.e. training a RoBERTa-like model from scratch. Since no similar model has been developed for Italian, we create BERToldo in different versions, covering different time spans and using the two different training approaches described above.

3. Corpus Collection and Cleaning

BERToldo has been collected starting from two available digital repositories containing Italian texts belonging to various centuries.

- **Liberliber.it**[1] is a collection of more than 4,000 Italian books with different types of copyright. Most of them, whose authors have died more than 70 years ago, are released under the public do-

[1] https://www.liberliber.it/benvenuto/

main license (CC0).[2] In total, Liberliber.it contains around 230M tokens.

- **Wikisource**[3] is an online digital library operated by Wikimedia. The project contains works that are either in the public domain or freely licensed. Wikisource exists in 72 languages, and the Italian version includes more than 170,000 pages of content,[4] for a total of around 140M tokens.

While Wikisource is downloadable for free from the Wikimedia Downloads website,[5] Liberliber.it is freely available for navigation, but one needs to make a donation of 9.99 euros to download the entire resource.

Within BERToldo, we want to create models of Italian texts covering different periods in the history of language. To this purpose, after downloading the texts, we need to identify at least the century in which each document was written. This can be done easily in datasets where such information is structured and included as metadata. In both Liberliber.it and Wikisource, however, any additional information (such as publication year, author, translator, etc.) is only included along with the document itself, therefore all the documents need a pre-processing phase where the additional data are collected and removed from the file that is then used to train the BERT model.

The extraction of metadata information from the two repositories is error prone, since the years are often uncertain or written in a way that a machine could not easily understand (for example, "XVI secolo circa", *around XVI century*, or "tra il 1628 e il 1650", *between 1628 and 1650*). To deal with these problems, we build a list of common patterns in order to convert as many possible date expressions as possible, leaving only some tens of remaining cases to a manual check. During the conversion, we compute the date in the middle in case of time periods. For example, "XVI secolo circa" (*around XVI century*), becomes 1550, and "tra il 1628 e il 1650" (*between 1628 and 1650*), becomes 1639.

Sometimes, no year is found or the date associated with the document corresponds to the year of publication, that is often centuries after the actual date of the composition. To deal with these cases, we searched the author's name into WikiData[6] and get their biographical information.[7] If the year extracted from the document is not compatible with the lifespan of the author, we discard it and set a new one as the average between 20 years after the author's birth date and 5 years before their death.

3.1. Removing duplicates

As a last step, we deal with a relevant problem that to our knowledge was not addressed in other existing historical transformer models, i.e. duplicated content. Indeed, the amount of digital documents that can be used to create historical BERTs is limited compared to crawled content largely used for standard, contemporary transformers. For some languages, including Italian, the availability of digitised historical documents is so limited that the few digital repositories available tend to contain a large amount of overlapping documents. In fact, the *Project Gutenberg*[8] data, which are the third large repository of digital documents in Italian, were not included in BERToldo because the majority of the documents were already present in Wikisource or Liberliber.

Even between these two repositories (and also between documents in the same collection) we observed some overlaps, which are difficult to remove given that no curated list of metadata is released with the texts. We therefore have to first identify automatically existing duplicates and then remove them using the Fuzzy-Wuzzy string matching Java library.[9] In particular, we use the token set ratio, performing a set operation that takes out the common tokens. Extra or same repeated words do not matter. Therefore, we obtain a very high value when one document is completely included in the other one (this happens often in our task, since sometimes one dataset contains a single poem, while the other one contains a collection of poems, including the first work considered).

Since fuzzy matching algorithms are often very slow, expecially on long texts, making a comparison all-versus-all is not feasible in a reasonable time. Removing duplicates makes sense since one can save time during training the language model without drop in performance (see Section 4), but if this filtering takes too much time, it becomes useless for the purpose.

For this reason, we first cluster the documents applying the fuzzy algorithm to authors' names. Documents where the author is not known or where our tool cannot extract it correctly are merged together in a single cluster. The clusterization is managed using JGraphT.[10]

[2] `https://www.liberliber.it/online/opere/libri/licenze/`

[3] `https://it.wikisource.org/`

[4] Usually longer works span on more than one page; for instance, "La Divina Commedia", written by Dante Alighieri, uses around 120 wiki pages.

[5] `https://dumps.wikimedia.org/`

[6] `https://www.wikidata.org/`

[7] In Wikisource, the author is often already linked to WikiData, resulting in a perfect match; in Liberliber.it, we searched the name into WikiData and use the information when it is not ambiguous, under the assumption that if a text is present in Liberliber.it then its author is famous enough to be present in WikiData.

[8] `https://www.gutenberg.org/browse/languages/it`

[9] `https://github.com/xdrop/fuzzywuzzy`

[10] `https://jgrapht.org/`

For each cluster, a complexity value is calculated, multiplying the number of documents considered for each dataset (Wikisource or Liberliber.it). When such complexity is very high, a sub-clustering is performed using the titles of the works.
In addition to fuzzy matching, authors and titles are also searched through WikiData, so to merge names expressed using different spellings (for example "Francesco Bacone", "Francis Bacon", and "Franciscus Baco", all referring to the same person).
The fuzzy matching between texts is then applied in an all-versus-all paradigm inside the single cluster, reducing drastically the execution time of the entire process (from tens of hours to tens of minutes).
We use the `TokenSetRatio` fuzzy algorithm, because it gives a high percentage matching on subsets: in fact, it often happens that a collection of works by a single author is considered as a single work in a dataset and a set of works in another (i.e., collection of poems). Since we want our computation to be fast, in case of very long works we restrict the comparison to the first 10,000 characters.
We consider two texts as overlapping when the similarity score between them is higher than 0.9 (1 meaning perfect match). We retain the longest text, just to avoid discarding useful data for our training.
After the filtering operation, the resulting dataset contains 304M tokens (starting from 410M, obtained after merging the two above-described resources).

4. Training BERToldo

The creation of the pre-trained model using the corpora presented in Section 3 follows as much as possible the BERT (uncased) architecture. Tokenization is performed by segmenting the input text data into subword units using the `BertWordPieceTokenizer`. As vocabulary size we keep 30,522 subword tokens. Pre-training is done with a maximum sequence length of 128 and a batch size of 64, while for the other parameters we keep the default values, following when possible the configuration adopted in MacBERTh (Manjavacas and Fonteyn, 2021).
We create eight versions of BERToldo. BERToldo$_{all}$ is the biggest one and was trained from scratch using all the documents from Wikisource and Liberliber after duplicate removal. BERToldo$_{till1500}$ was trained only on documents issued before 1500, BERToldo$_{1500\text{-}1700}$ was trained with documents from 1500 to 1700 and BERToldo$_{1700\text{-}1900}$ was created using documents published between 1700 and 1900. For each of the splits, the model is trained for 10 epochs.
Following the approach presented in (Gururangan et al., 2020) and adopted also for the creation of historical BERT for English presented in (Hosseini et al., 2021), four additional models are created starting from standard Italian BERT-base uncased and further training it with additional historical data. BERT-base is available from Hugging Face and was created starting from a recent Wikipedia dump and various texts from the OPUS and OSCAR corpora collections.[11] The additional training process is carried out considering the three time slices independently, and then all together. Also in this case, the model is trained for 10 epochs. We summarise the different configurations in Table 1.

5. Evaluation

Similar to previous works (Manjavacas and Fonteyn, 2022; Gabay et al., 2022), we evaluate our BERToldo models on a task where historical language needs to be processed. By comparing the performance obtained with a standard BERT and a historical one, we can assess to what extent historical models can be beneficial. Unfortunately, the availability of historical datasets in Italian with some kind of manual annotation is very limited. Two exceptions are the corpus of Alcide De Gasperi's documents (Tonelli et al., 2019), a subset of which has been enriched with manual annotation of named entities and events, and the D(h)ante corpus (Basile and Sangati, 2016), containing annotated PoS-tags in CoNLL-like format. Since De Gasperi's documents were issued between 1920 and 1950, their language is not much different from contemporary Italian and it is not particularly necessary to use historical transformer models. We therefore perform our evaluation on Dante's texts.
We fine-tune the different BERT versions in Table 1 using the same test, development and train split of Dante's corpus used in (Basile and Sangati, 2016). For fine-tuning we use MaChAmp,[12] an extension of AllenNLP library that supports out-of-the-box a variety of standard NLP tasks (van der Goot et al., 2021).
The classification results of the different PoS-tagging models in terms of accuracy are reported in Table 2. We include in the last row also the classification result reported in (Basile and Sangati, 2016) and obtained using the same data splits with the Max-Ent Stanford Tagger included in Stanford CoreNLP version 3.5.2 (Toutanova et al., 2003).
These results provide interesting insights into the effectiveness of transformer models trained on historical data. First, (historical) BERTs are all better than the maximum entropy tagger. Among the transformers, further training BERT-base with historical data yields (slightly) better results than training BERT from scratch. This is in contrast with the findings in (Manjavacas and Fonteyn, 2022), showing the opposite on PoS-tagging English data. We will investigate in the future possible reasons behind this difference. Our results show also that BERToldo$_{till1500}$ performs worse than the models trained with more historical data, even if they were published centuries later than Dante's works. Overall, using BERT trained with a large amount of

[11] `https://huggingface.co/dbmdz/bert-base-italian-xxl-uncased`
[12] `https://github.com/machamp-nlp/machamp`

Dataset	Continue	Time (h)	Data	Tokens
BERToldo$_{till1500}$	No	42	127 MB	1,595,768
BERToldo$_{1500\text{-}1700}$	No	48	143 MB	1,784,656
BERToldo$_{1700\text{-}1900}$	No	214	700 MB	7,176,328
BERToldo$_{all}$	No	328	970 MB	10,556,752
Hugging Face BERT			81 GB	
ContBERToldo$_{till1500}$	Yes	+36	81 GB + 127 MB	+1,595,768
ContBERToldo$_{1500\text{-}1700}$	Yes	+40	81 GB + 143 MB	+1,784,656
ContBERToldo$_{1700\text{-}1900}$	Yes	+213	81 GB + 700 MB	+7,176,328
ContBERToldo$_{all}$	Yes	+300	81 GB + 970 MB	+10,556,752

Table 1: Training and size information for each BERToldo version. The models in the upper part of the table were trained from scratch on historical data, while those below (ContBERToldo) are the outcome of continuous training starting from Hugging Face BERT-base uncased. For this reason, the training time and the amount of documents for the ContBERToldo should be added to the ones needed to train BERT-base.

Dataset	Accuracy
BERToldo$_{till1500}$	0.939
BERToldo$_{1500\text{-}1700}$	0.937
BERToldo$_{1700\text{-}1900}$	0.951
BERToldo$_{all}$	0.955
Hugging Face BERT	0.952
ContBERToldo$_{till1500}$	0.960
ContBERToldo$_{1500\text{-}1700}$	0.958
ContBERToldo$_{1700\text{-}1900}$	0.958
ContBERToldo$_{all}$	**0.961**
Stanford CoreNLP	0.92

Table 2: BERToldo evaluation of Part-of-Speech tagging task on D(h)ante.

historical data performs better than using less data which are specific to the time period of the training and test sets. Continuous training with all historical data yields the best result, but if no standard BERT is available, comparable results can be obtained by training BERT from scratch with less than 1 GB of historical data.

As a comparison, we run the same experiments training BERToldo$_{till1500}$ and BERToldo$_{1500\text{-}1700}$ without duplicate removal described in Section 3.1. While the training time to build the BERToldo models increases by 19%, the accuracy of the Part-of-Speech tagger after fine tuning remains exactly the same. This demonstrates that removing duplicates makes BERT training less computationally expensive without a performance drop. The effects of duplication removal have been recently analysed also on large language models trained on contemporary corpora, confirming that deduplication should be generally encouraged (Lee et al., 2022).

6. Dataset and Models Release

We release all the BERT models and the source code on Github.[13]. We also release the data used to train BERToldo in an aggregated format divided into time periods. The dataset contaning the documents is distributed under the CC0 (public domain) license. The models are released under the Creative Commons Attribution 4.0 International (CC BY 4.0).[14] Finally, the source code (written in Java and Python) is free to use under the Apache License 2.0.

7. Conclusions

In this work we present BERToldo the first historical BERT for Italian. The model has been trained using freely-available documents published between 1200 and 1900. We plan to improve this first version of BERToldo by adding new historical documents as soon as they are available online. Another possible improvement could be performing language identification before creating the models, since we noticed that the split of documents published before 1500 contains some texts in Latin. We also plan to make our evaluation more robust by adding new tasks. This would be possible if diverse types of annotated data are created for Italian covering different time periods.

8. Acknowledgements

This research has been supported by the European Union's Horizon 2020 program project ODEUROPA under grant agreement number 101004469.

[13] https://github.com/dhfbk/historical-bert

[14] https://creativecommons.org/licenses/by/4.0/

9. References

Beelen, K., Nanni, F., Coll Ardanuy, M., Hosseini, K., Tolfo, G., and McGillivray, B. (2021). When time makes sense: A historically-aware approach to targeted sense disambiguation. In *Findings of the Association for Computational Linguistics: ACL-IJCNLP 2021*, pages 2751–2761, Online, August. Association for Computational Linguistics.

Devlin, J., Chang, M.-W., Lee, K., and Toutanova, K. (2019). BERT: Pre-training of Deep Bidirectional Transformers for Language Understanding. In *Proceedings of the 2019 Conference of the North American Chapter of the Association for Computational Linguistics: Human Language Technologies, Volume 1 (Long and Short Papers)*, pages 4171–4186, Minneapolis, Minnesota, June. Association for Computational Linguistics.

Gabay, S., Suarez, P. O., Bartz, A., Chagué, A., Bawden, R., Gambette, P., and Sagot, B. (2022). From freem to d'alembert: a large corpus and a language model for early modern french.

Gururangan, S., Marasović, A., Swayamdipta, S., Lo, K., Beltagy, I., Downey, D., and Smith, N. A. (2020). Don't stop pretraining: Adapt language models to domains and tasks. In *Proceedings of the 58th Annual Meeting of the Association for Computational Linguistics*, pages 8342–8360, Online, July. Association for Computational Linguistics.

Hosseini, K., Beelen, K., Colavizza, G., and Ardanuy, M. C. (2021). Neural language models for nineteenth-century english. *Journal of Open Humanities Data*, 7.

Lee, K., Ippolito, D., Nystrom, A., Zhang, C., Eck, D., Callison-Burch, C., and Carlini, N. (2022). Deduplicating training data makes language models better. In *Proceedings of the 60th Annual Meeting of the Association for Computational Linguistics (Volume 1: Long Papers)*, pages 8424–8445, Dublin, Ireland, May. Association for Computational Linguistics.

Manjavacas, E. and Fonteyn, L. (2021). Macberth: Development and evaluation of a historically pre-trained language model for english (1450-1950). In *Proceedings of the Workshop on Natural Language Processing for Digital Humanities (NLP4DH)*.

Manjavacas, E. and Fonteyn, L. (2022). Adapting vs Pre-training Language Models for Historical Languages. working paper or preprint, April.

Toutanova, K., Klein, D., Manning, C. D., and Singer, Y. (2003). Feature-rich part-of-speech tagging with a cyclic dependency network. In *Proceedings of the 2003 Human Language Technology Conference of the North American Chapter of the Association for Computational Linguistics*, pages 252–259.

van der Goot, R., Üstün, A., Ramponi, A., Sharaf, I., and Plank, B. (2021). Massive choice, ample tasks (MaChAmp): A toolkit for multi-task learning in NLP. In *Proceedings of the 16th Conference of the European Chapter of the Association for Computational Linguistics: System Demonstrations*, pages 176–197, Online, April. Association for Computational Linguistics.

10. Language Resource References

Basile, Angelo and Sangati, Federico. (2016). *D(H)ante: A New Set of Tools for XIII Century Italian*. European Language Resources Association (ELRA).

Tonelli, S., Sprugnoli, R., and Moretti, G. (2019). Prendo la parola in questo consesso mondiale: A multi-genre 20th century corpus in the political domain. In *Proceedings of the Sixth Italian Conference on Computational Linguistics (CLiC-it 2019)*.

Proceedings of the Second Workshop on Language Technologies for Historical and Ancient Languages (LT4HALA 2022), pages 73–83
Language Resources and Evaluation Conference (LREC 2022), Marseille, 25 June 2022

In Search of the Flocks: How to Perform Onomasiological Queries in an Ancient Greek Corpus?

Alek Keersmaekers, Toon Van Hal
University of Leuven
Blijde-Inkomststraat 21, 3000 Leuven, Belgium
{alek.keersmaekers; toon.vanhal}@kuleuven.be

Abstract

This paper explores the possibilities of onomasiologically querying corpus data of Ancient Greek. The significance of the onomasiological approach has been highlighted in recent studies, yet the possibilities of performing 'word-finding' investigations into corpus data have not been dealt with in depth. The case study chosen focuses on collective nouns denoting animate groups (such as *flocks* of people, *herds* of cattle). By relying on a large automatically annotated corpus of Ancient Greek and on token-based vector information, a longlist of collective nouns was compiled through morpho-syntactic extraction and successive clustering procedures. After reducing this longlist to a shortlist, the results obtained are evaluated. In general, we find that πλῆθος can be considered to be the default collective noun of both humans and animals, becoming especially prominent during the Hellenistic period. In addition, specific tendencies in the use of collective nouns are discerned for specific semantic classes (e.g. gods and insects) and over time. Throughout the paper, special attention is paid to methodological issues related to onomasiologically searching.

Keywords: onomasiology, data querying, collective nouns, Ancient Greek

1. Introduction

This paper explores the possibilities of onomasiologically querying corpus data of Ancient Greek. The significance of the onomasiological approach has been highlighted in recent studies, yet the possibilities of performing 'word-finding' investigations into corpus data have not been dealt with in depth. English has a wide range of words denoting groups of animals or people, such as a "pack of dogs", "a school of fish" and "a gang of bandits". This paper aims to explore how similar collective nouns can be detected in the Ancient Greek corpus by adopting an onomasiological approach to the data.

The paper is organized as follows. A survey of the state of the field (Section 2) precedes an outline of our strategies adopted to tracing collective nouns in Greek (Section 3). Section 4 analyzes various groups of animate entities in Ancient Greek by means of corpus data and discusses onomasiological change in Ancient Greek. In the concluding part (Section 5), alternative approaches and further avenues are discussed. The case studied in this paper has identifiable morpho-syntactic characteristics (see Section 3.2), but in the future it should be also made possible to find words expressing a certain concept for which the availability of syntactical and morphological annotation is not helpful.

2. State of the field

2.1 Onomasiological searching

Corpus-based research is usually based on a (set of) predefined term(s), of which the meaning is traced. In addition to this semasiological or 'sense-finding' approach, it is also conceivable to take a certain meaning (concept or notion) as a starting point, and examine which terms are used to shape this meaning in a corpus. In recent decades, linguists have strongly emphasized the importance and relevance of such an onomasiological or 'word-finding' approach (see e.g. Grzega; 2002; Geeraerts, 2009; Fernández-Domínguez, 2019), and more recently there have been increasing advocates of the onomasiological approach among conceptual historians too (see e.g. Müller & Schmieder, 2016; Cananau, 2019). For obvious reasons, querying corpora with a semasiological, word-based approach is much easier than meaning-based onomasiological queries, because unlike a meaning a term is a tangible starting point. In a methodological survey paper published against the backdrop of a corpus-based computational historical semantics project, Bernhard Jussen and Gregor Rohmann mention the onomasiological approach, yet the case-studies they present are semasiological in nature (Jussen & Rohmann, 2015). While there has been some research on querying onomasiological dictionaries (Kipfer, 1986; Sierra, 2008; Moerdijk et al., 2008 on the development of 'semagrams'), the literature on how to onomasiologically querying corpora is limited (see McGillivray, 2020; see also Kutuzov, 2020). In general, onomasiological search strategies generally boil down to making use of annotations that approximate the concept under investigation as much as possible, the results of which are complemented through bottom-up approaches (see e.g. Goossens, 2013). Hence, this presupposes the presence of an annotated corpus, which is a demanding and time-consuming investment, if such a corpus is not yet available (see Mehl, 2016: 50; 92; Atallah et al., 2018). The type of annotations required depends on the onomasiological task at stake. For certain tasks, part-of-speech tags can be helpful, while for other tasks more detailed morphological, syntactic, semantic and/or pragmatic information is needed.

2.2 Collective nouns

Words as 'flock' and 'herd' are styled quantifying collectives and collective nouns by Biber et al. (2003: 61-62). The terms have been criticized for being too vague (see the references in Dedè, 2012). Some scholars have treated collective nouns as classifiers (or 'classifier constructions', cf. Lehrer, 1986). Aikhenvald (2000: 115-116) however argues why such terms do not meet the criteria of genuine classifiers. Zwarts (2020) distinguishes 'crowd' and 'club' words. The first type of collective nouns has its starting point in a number of *individuals*, which are spatially so closely associated to each other that a line can be drawn to establish the collective (dynamic **a** → **b** in Fig. 1). Conversely, club words have their starting point in the *whole*, which is open to individual members (dynamic **c** → **b** in Fig. 1.).

a **b** **c**

Figure 1: The distinction between crowd words (a → b) and club words (c → b) after Zwarts (2020: 539)

Collective nouns have attracted much scholarly attention for their behavior in subject agreement: in the singular, they typically refer to more than one entity, while they can be combined both with plural and singular verbs (see Birkenes & Sommer, 2014). In the Anglo-Saxon tradition, collective nouns are even defined on the basis of this concord criterium, whereas in continental research strands semantic criteria prevail (cf. Joosten et al., 2007: 88).

Many modern European languages have a proliferation of, often highly specialized or idiosyncratic, animal collective nouns (such as "a murder of crows" and "a rout of wolves" in English) — a phenomenon having its roots in middle age hunting practice and Books of Courtesy (Rhodes, 2014). To the best of our knowledge, there has been so far no systematic research into the range of collective nouns in Ancient Greek, even though the 'oldest grammar of the West' by (Pseudo-)Dionysius Thrax already defines the collective noun (περιληπτικὸν) as τὸ τῷ ἑνικῷ ἀριθμῷ πλῆθος σημαῖνον ("signifying a multitude in the singular number"), offering the examples of δῆμος, χορός and ὄχλος (see Swiggers & Wouters, 1998). In most grammars, collective nouns are mainly discussed against the background of subject agreement, with only a few examples offered (see e.g. Kühner-Gerth, 1966: §359, more extensive treatment in Viteau, 1896: 103-11). The research undertaken by Birkenes & Sommer (2014) is limited to a very small number of collective nouns in Ancient Greek. A number of contributions aim to prove that the etymology of certain Greek words suggests a past of a collective noun (see e.g. Leroy, 1956; Kaczyńska, 2019), while others examine specific terms or a limited set of collective nouns, mostly in contexts other than linguistics (see e.g. Dieckhoff, 2018). The following section explores therefore how one can computationally trace the equivalents used in Ancient Greek to express such notions.

3. Identifying collective nouns in Ancient Greek

3.1 Starting points of the research

As pointed out in 2.1, onomasiological queries highly benefit from corpus annotations. This is especially true for Ancient Greek, a language with a highly flexible word order and complex inflectional morphology, which reduces the effectiveness of strictly form-based (as opposed to lemma-, morphology- and syntax-based) queries. For Ancient Greek, the most well-known corpora are the Greek treebanks (several annotators, consisting of dependency trees with syntactic, morphological and lemma annotation: see Celano, 2019 and Keersmaekers et al., 2019), which are manually annotated but not extremely large (1.5M tokens), and the Diorisis corpus (a corpus that is annotated for lemmas and morphology, cf. Vatri and McGillivray, 2018), which is relatively sizable (10.2M tokens) but is automatically annotated and does not contain syntactic information. We therefore made use of the (so far unreleased) GLAUx corpus (Keersmaekers, 2021), a corpus containing literary (8th century BC-3th century AD) and documentary texts (3th century BC-8th century AD) automatically annotated for lemmas, morphology and syntax (28.8M tokens): see Keersmaekers (2021) for an evaluation of the quality of the annotation, which was high enough not to provide any substantial obstacles for the research described below.

Although some steps for semantic annotation of Greek have been taken (see Celano & Crane, 2015 and Keersmaekers, 2020 for semantic role annotation; Bizonni et al., 2014 and Biagetti et al., 2021 for Ancient Greek WordNet), so far no large-scale semantically annotated corpus resource for Ancient Greek with the level of granularity that is necessary for the research described in this paper has been created. We therefore made use of a bottom-up approach that has become highly popular in recent years to represent semantics computationally, the so-called 'distributional' approach to semantics, where meaning is represented by vectors of real numbers (with semantically similar words or constructions receiving mathematically similar vectors). These vectors are based on the context patterns of words in large text corpora (see Erk, 2012; Lenci, 2018 for more detail). Distributional semantic methods have been applied to Ancient Greek by Boschetti (2010), Rodda, Senaldi & Lenci (2017), Rodda, Probert & McGillivray (2019), Keersmaekers (2020), Keersmaekers & Van Hal (2021), and Perrone et al. (2021). For this paper we use the implementation of Keersmaekers & Van Hal (2021), which calculates word vectors on the basis of PPMI-scaled syntactic dependency-based co-occurrence counts in the GLAUx corpus, with an SVD-based dimension reduction to 100 latent dimensions.

3.2 Morpho-syntactic extraction

In Greek, collective nouns are syntactically well-defined, since they are usually accompanied by a so-called partitive genitive (Benvenuto, 2013). Based on the GLAUx corpus, we could extract all constructions of type 'noun + animate entity in the genitive plural, having 'attribute' as its syntactic feature'. The animacy was determined via supervised machine learning techniques, training a deep learning model[1] on data annotated for the animacy class of the lemma as the dependent variable and a 100-dimensional word vector of the lemma (as described in 3.1) as the independent variable(s) (see Keersmaekers, 2020: 103-116). Our training data was an animacy lexicon containing

[1] As implemented in R package *h2o* (LeDell et al., 2022), using a multi-layer feedforward artificial neural network trained with stochastic gradient descent using back-propagation.

486 animate and 2650 inanimate entities; animate entities yielded precision of 0.941 and recall of 0.914 – an estimation via 10-fold cross validation on the training data. On this basis, 1991 lemmas were labeled as animate, which allowed us to identify possible collective nouns.

Our approach is not infallible: in addition to possible errors in the automatically annotated data, we should note that there are a number of alternative constructions that can express collective nouns and that are not included in the extracted data. For example, the genitive can sometimes be replaced with an adjective (e.g. the LSJ dictionary of Ancient Greek, Jones et al., 1996, cites μελισσαῖος οὐλαμός "a swarm of bees", with the adjective μελισσαῖος 'consisting of bees'). Some collective nouns have no (need for) further attributive specification – especially if the animal is already lexicalized in the collective noun itself (e.g. βουκόλιον "a group of cows", συβόσιον "a group of pigs", αἰπόλιον "a group of goats"). Obviously, plural morphology might also be used to indicate a group of animate entities (e.g. simply αἶγες 'goats' instead of αἰπόλιον αἰγῶν 'a flock of goats'). Finally, constructions with a genitive in the singular are conceivable (e.g. 'a swarm of vermin' in English). Of the extracted lemmas (5488), only lemmas with a frequency of ≥ 5 (frequency of the lemma accompanied by an animate genitive plural) were retained (1266 in total). These lemmas thus count as potential collective nouns, out of which we attempted to identify the real collective nouns using several computational techniques.

3.3 Visualization and clustering techniques

The query defined in section 3.2 likely has a high recall, since we expect most collective nouns to occur in the construction defined there, even though there are some other ways to express groups of animate entities as discussed above. However, its precision is rather low, since many nouns occurring in the noun + animate genitive plural construction are not collective nouns: this construction admits many more types of nouns such as body parts (e.g. 'the legs of the horses'), possession relations (e.g. 'the money of the men') and so on. To retrieve collective nouns from this large set (1266 nouns), we used a variety of dimension reduction and clustering techniques to find structure in our dataset, as well as lexicographical data (the LSJ dictionary, Jones et al., 1996) and corpus examples from the GLAUx corpus (in case of doubt) to identify collective nouns in these structured datapoints. The dimension reduction and clustering techniques were applied to the cosine distances between the nouns in our dataset, which mathematically represent the 'semantic distances' between the nouns (see Erk, 2012: 636-637).

As a first step, we made use of t-SNE (t-distributed stochastic neighbor embedding, Van den Maaten and Hinton, 2008), a dimension reduction technique that allows us to represent high dimensional data (a 1266x1266 matrix representing the cosine distances between nouns) in a low-dimensional (in our case two-dimensional) space, with words that are similar in meaning occurring close to each other on the tsne-map.[2] This enables us to find structure in the data and identify which words are worth looking at to retrieve collective nouns. For instance, the cluster on the bottom right of Fig. 2 (in dark yellow) contains words that clearly refer to body parts (e.g. μῦς 'muscle', γαστήρ 'belly', θρίξ 'hair'). It is unlikely that a collective noun would occur in such a cluster, so these words can safely be discarded after identifying the thematic coherence of the cluster. Instead, on the bottom/center-left of the plot there are several clusters that clearly contain many collective nouns: military units (in red: e.g. ἴλη, λόχος, οὐλαμός), words referring to herding (in dark blue, with several words that mean 'a flock or herd', such as αἰπόλιον, ἀγέλη, πῶυ, but also some non-collective nouns such as νομεύς 'herdsman') and a small cluster of words referring to groups in general (in yellow: πλῆθος, ὄχλος, πληθύς, ὅμιλος, ἑσμός, σμῆνος); additionally, a little more doubtful are the clusters in pink (generally containing words related to transport such as ἅμαξα 'wagon', φορτίον 'load' and ἵππος 'horse' but also some collective nouns such as συνωρίς 'pair of horses' and κτῆνος 'beast', but also 'flock'), dark green (mainly poetic words referring to family such as φῦλον 'tribe', but maybe also 'swarm', γένεθλον 'family', but also unrelated poetic words such as σημάντωρ 'leader') and light blue (two words referring to the action of collecting or coming together but maybe also to a collection or group, viz. ἄθροισμα and συνδρομή). After identifying these clusters, we used dictionaries and corpus data to check whether each word occurring in these clusters is actually a collective noun.

Next, we used two cluster techniques that are prevalent in corpus linguistics to identify additional nouns that we may have missed with the t-SNE analysis, viz. partitioning around medoids (PAM) and hierarchical agglomerative clustering (AGNES).[3] The former technique divides the data into a predetermined number (k) of clusters. After experimenting with the values for k, in the end we settled for a small number of k=20 clusters. The latter technique hierarchically clusters all nouns into a tree, with similar words occurring in the same 'branches' of the tree – a subpart of the tree, containing many collective nouns, is shown in Fig. 3. As with the t-SNE analysis, we analyzed the thematic coherence of each cluster that was formed (in the case of PAM, simply each of the 20 clusters; in the case of AGNES, branches of the tree occurring roughly at the same height), and looked into more detail at the more 'promising' clusters containing many collective nouns. These techniques allowed us to identify some additional collective nouns that we had previously missed: these were especially words in the festive or public domain including θίασος, χορός and σύλλογος, along with some words thematically related to the words we previously found such as σύστημα (a military unit, or also a group in general) and νέφος (literally 'cloud', but also a group of people or animals).

[2] We made use of the R package *Rtsne* (Krijthe and Van der Maaten, 2018). We used a perplexity of 5, theta of 0.0 and 5 iterations.

[3] As implemented in R package *cluster* (Maechler et al., 2022). We used out-of-the-box settings.

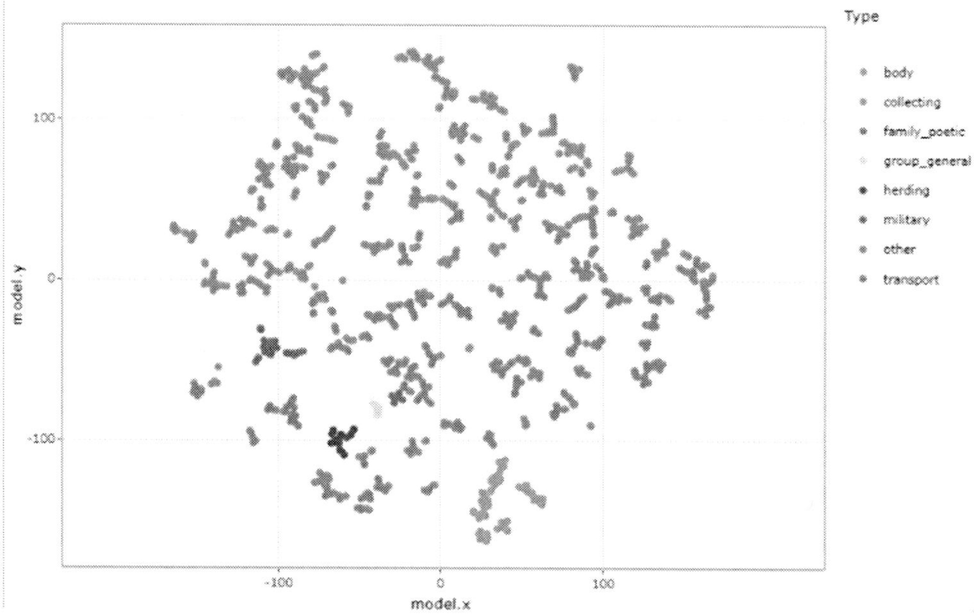

Figure 2: Visualization of the t-SNE embeddings

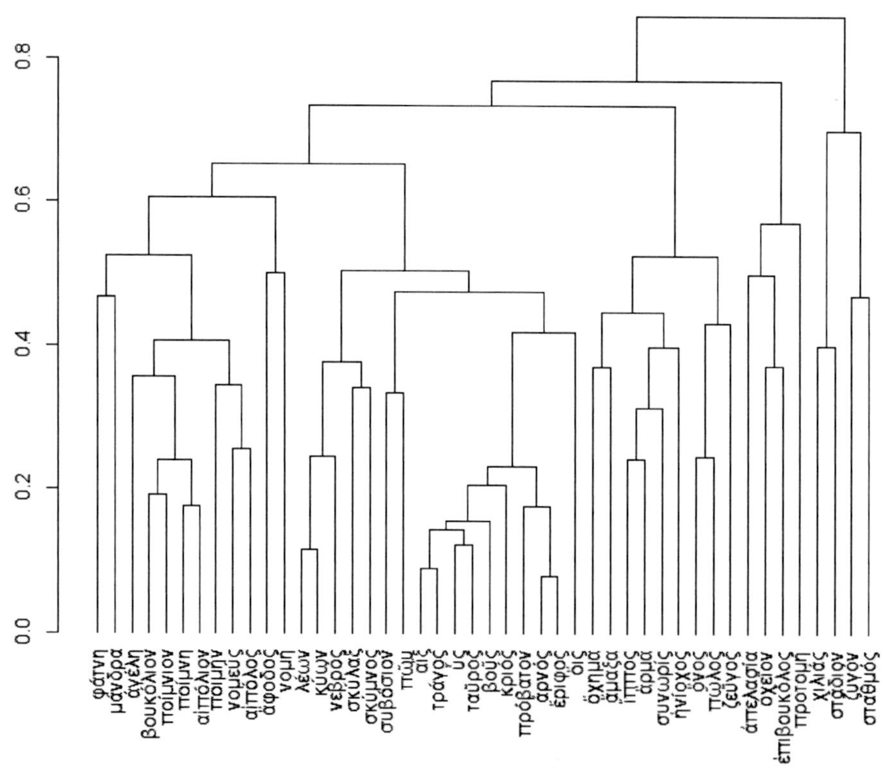

Figure 3: Subpart of the tree of hierarchical agglomerative clustering (AGNES)

4. Results and discussion

4.1 Discussion of shortlist in general

In total, we have traced 40 collective nouns (see Table 1). The dataset on which this paper is based is available through a csv-file.

5 collective nouns appeared more than 100 times in the data. At the top of the list, without a doubt, is the word πλῆθος (token frequency 998), which can be regarded as the default collective noun for animate referents. There is no semantic class in which this collective noun does not occur. In some cases, πληθύς is used too, which is according to most dictionaries merely an Ionian variant (this, however, should be checked against the data). πλῆθος is followed by ἀγέλη (215), φῦλον (129), τάξις (125) and χορός (109). Some words are exclusively used as collective nouns for animals, such as πῶυ (10), αἰπόλιον (8), βουκόλιον (7) and συβόσιον (5), while words that occur only with human referents are more numerous, viz. λόχος (37); τάγμα (34); σύνταγμα (22); σύλλογος (12); θίασος (10); οὐλαμός (10); ἄθροισμα (6).

	total		animal		human	
πλῆθος	998	40%	331	41%	667	40%
ἀγέλη	215	9%	184	23%	31	2%
φῦλον	129	5%	37	5%	92	6%
τάξις	125	5%	8	1%	117	7%
χορός	109	4%	8	1%	101	6%
ὄχλος	84	3%	1	0%	83	5%
ἴλη	74	3%	5	1%	69	4%
ὅμιλος	70	3%	4	0%	66	4%
ζεῦγος	68	3%	60	7%	8	0%
λόχος	37	1%	0	0%	37	2%
συναγωγή	37	1%	3	0%	34	2%
νομή	36	1%	31	4%	5	0%
φάλαγξ	35	1%	2	0%	33	2%
σύνοδος	34	1%	2	0%	32	2%
τάγμα	34	1%	0	0%	34	2%
σύστημα	32	1%	4	0%	28	2%
στρατιά	30	1%	1	0%	29	2%
στρατός	28	1%	2	0%	26	2%
πληθύς	27	1%	6	1%	21	1%
στῖφος	25	1%	1	0%	24	1%
σύνταγμα	22	1%	0	0%	22	1%
σμῆνος	22	1%	20	2%	2	0%
ἐκκλησία	20	1%	1	0%	19	1%
συνέδριον	20	1%	1	0%	19	1%
ἑσμός	17	1%	15	2%	2	0%
νέφος	16	1%	13	2%	3	0%
σπεῖρα	13	1%	3	0%	10	1%
ἄγημα	12	0%	2	0%	10	1%
συνωρίς	12	0%	11	1%	1	0%
σύλλογος	12	0%	0	0%	12	1%
ποίμνιον	12	0%	9	1%	3	0%
ποίμνη	11	0%	9	1%	2	0%
θίασος	10	0%	0	0%	10	1%
πῶυ	10	0%	10	1%	0	0%
οὐλαμός	10	0%	0	0%	10	1%
αἰπόλιον	8	0%	8	1%	0	0%
κτῆνος	8	0%	7	1%	1	0%
βουκόλιον	7	0%	7	1%	0	0%
ἄθροισμα	6	0%	0	0%	6	0%
συβόσιον	5	0%	5	1%	0	0%

Table 1: Collective nouns denoting animals and humans

It is important to point out which collective nouns are not included in our data, and why. The word δῆμος, also cited by Dionysius Thrax, was not clearly identified in the cluster techniques applied. Related to δῆμος are words like λεώς and ἔθνος, all of which first of all refer to a 'people' or 'tribe' rather than to a 'group'. This however implies that Homeric collocations such as ἔθνεα [...] μελισσάων ("clouds of bees", Il. 2.87-89) are not captured in the data.[4] Some words designating 'flock' or 'group', such as βοτά and κῶμος mentioned in the Woodhouse English-Greek dictionary (Woodhouse, 1987), turn out to be very infrequent in our data. In addition, we have deliberately excluded a fairly long list of words which did turn up via our methodology, but (a) where inspection of the examples showed that only a minority of cases could count as a collective noun or (b) where its status as a collective noun is more doubtful. The cases in question are the following: ἀγών; ἀποσκευή; βόσκημα; βουλή; γένεθλον; γέννα; δεκάς; διατριβή; δικαστήριον; διλοχία; ἑορτή; ἱππαρχία; κατάλογος; λεία; μόρα; ὁμιλία; πομπή; πρόβατον; συνουσία; συσσίτιον; σχολή; χιλιάς; χρῆμα. A case of (a) is συνουσία 'company, intercourse': although there are some corpus examples which may allow for a collective reading, in the vast majority of cases it rather means 'the state of being together' (or 'sexual intercourse'); a case of (b) is δικαστήριον 'court', which is a club word (like many other words in this list) referring to a group of judges. Although we included several club words in our shortlist, we excluded those where people assemble for a highly specialized purpose, in this case making a judicial decision. It should be emphasized that by eliminating these words (as well as the δῆμος and equivalents mentioned above) we have eliminated some clear examples of collective nouns. However, we felt that the inclusion of these words would give way to considerable noise in the data. Conversely, it should be noted that not all instances included in the shortlist unambiguously refer to a collective noun. This is certainly the case for a word like τάξις, which is very polysemous (e.g. also 'order', 'class', 'rank' etc.). Due to the scale of our undertaking, it was infeasible to inspect the data token-wise. We are however aware that our type-based approach is vulnerable to noise.

4.2 Classes of animals and humans

Next, we divided the lemmas of animals and people in a number of subgroups. These subgroups were semi-automatically created: through hierarchical clustering (AGNES) of the vectors of these lemmas, we first checked which of them were highly semantically related and created subgroups on this basis, but the final groups were created with a high degree of human control (e.g. if the cluster algorithm would cluster a specific fish with a bird together, we would put this fish in the group 'water animals and fish' rather than 'birds'). Fig. 4 shows the frequency of collective nouns with the most frequent groups of animals,

[4] The data in Johnston (2019) suggests that collective nouns are rare in Homeric similes.

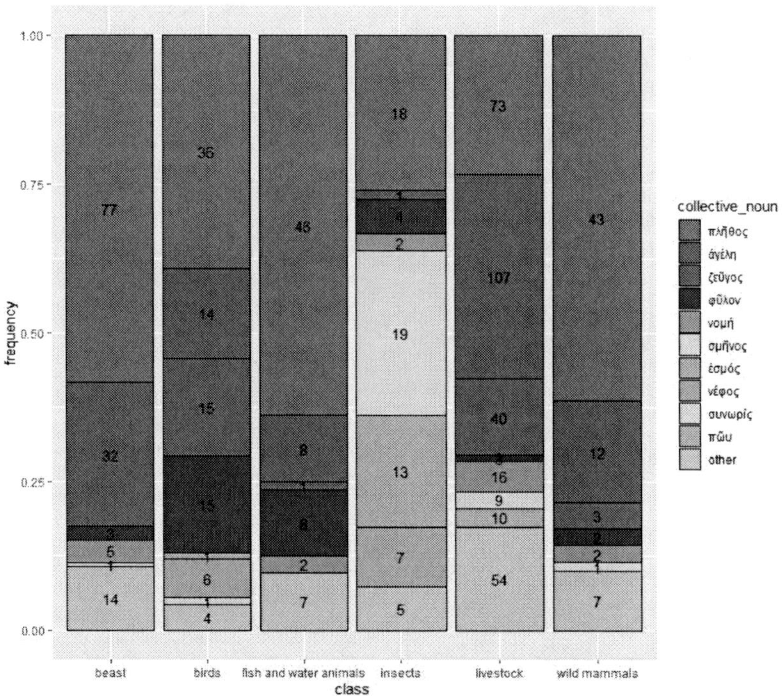

Figure 4: Variation in the presence of animal collective nouns according to semantic subgroups

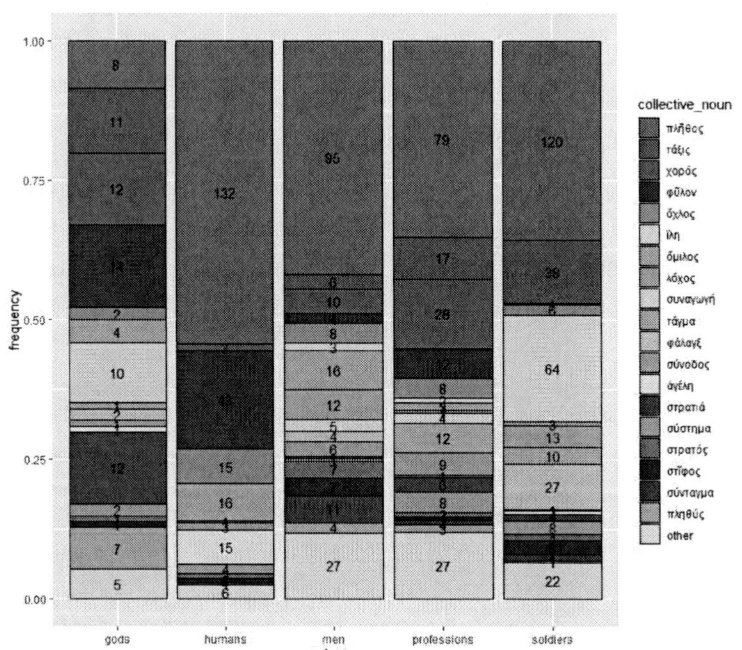

Figure 5: Variation in the presence of human collective nouns according to semantic subgroups

viz. animals in general, birds, water animals and fish, insects, livestock and wild mammals. The default word πλῆθος is used in all categories, although remarkably less frequently in the case of livestock, insects and, to a lesser extent, birds. It is also notable that ἀγέλη (often translated as 'flock') is used in every subgroup, and not exclusively for livestock. In the category of insects, the subgroup where ἀγέλη is underrepresented, one can notice the use of a number of specific collective nouns that are almost exclusively used for insects, viz. ἑσμός, σμῆνος and νέφος, the latter of which is also used for birds (see also 4.3). This specialization seems to be rather atypical: φῦλον, νομή and, to a lesser extent, ζεῦγος are animal collectives that can be used for almost any subgroup. One should also notice the high degree of 'other' with livestock: besides the 'default' options of ἀγέλη and πλῆθος, Ancient Greek has a large number of specialized words for livestock (e.g. βουκόλιον 'group of cows')."

The humans can also be divided into a number of subgroups. Fig. 5 makes a distinction between the most frequent subgroups, viz. gods, humans in general, men, professions and soldiers. The data shows that in case of the gods certain collective nouns, viz. χορός and φῦλον, outnumber the 'default' use of πλῆθος. Among the military category one finds the most specialized collective nouns, such as τάξις, ἴλη, λόχος and φάλαγξ. Strikingly, στρατιά and στρατός ('army') are hardly represented in this category. In general, it is noticeable that there are plenty combinatory possibilities.

4.3 Degree of specialization

This leads us to the question of to what extent there are exclusive combinations in Greek, showing one-to-one correspondences between a specific collective noun and a specific animate type, like the English 'murder of crows'. Table 2 shows the top results of a Pointwise Mutual Information (PMI) calculation, a measure of association showing whether two variables co-occur more frequently than expected based on their individual frequencies (see Gries 2010: 275-277 for more detail). We have only included collocational combinations that occur at least five times. The results show that in some cases there is a clear etymological connection between the collective noun and the species at stake (συβόσιον, αἰπόλιον, βουκόλιον), thus logically excluding alternative combinations (such as βουκόλιον and αἴξ). Excluding these words and the Homeric word πῶυ, which is exclusively used for ὄις 'sheep', it seems that especially specific insects (μέλισσα 'bee'; ἀκρίς 'grasshopper', the same goes for less frequent insects such as κηφήν 'drone' and σφήξ 'wasp') are combined with specific collective nouns (νέφος; ἑσμός; σμῆνος), which are rarely used for animals other than insects (except νέφος which is also often combined with birds). A group of pigeons (τρυγών or περιστερά) is mostly referred to as ζεῦγος, likely indicating a duo.

Collective		Child		Collocation	PMI
συβόσιον	5	ὗς	7	5	8.5
πῶυ	10	ὄις	12	10	7.7
αἰπόλιον	8	αἴξ	26	8	6.6
νέφος	16	ἀκρίς	12	5	6.0
τάγμα	34	λοχαγός	7	5	5.7
ἑσμός	17	μέλισσα	35	12	5.7
σμῆνος	22	μέλισσα	35	14	5.5
συναγωγή	37	υἱός	16	9	5.2
ποίμνιον	12	πρόβατον	44	8	5.2
ζεῦγος	68	τρυγών	5	5	5.2
ποίμνη	11	πρόβατον	44	7	5.2
βουκόλιον	7	βοῦς	83	7	4.9
ὅμιλος	70	μνηστήρ	6	5	4.9
φάλαγξ	35	ὁπλίτης	54	22	4.9
ὄχλος	90	οἰκότριψ	6	6	4.8

Table 2: Strongest PMI associations between collective nouns and the genitives occurring with them

Closer inspection reveals that some of the exclusive correspondences in Table 2 might be somewhat deceptive, for example, because all the attestations come from one author. This is the case for the association between ὄχλος and οἰκότριψ, which seems to be a personal style characteristic of Origenes.

4.4 Diachronic developments

In the previous sections, we mapped the onomasiology of Ancient Greek collective nouns in a static way. However, this onomasiology is obviously prone to semantic change, i.e. the terms used to express groups of animate entities change over time. This section will consider how computational methods can shed light on this onomasiological change. To this aim, we have divided the data into archaic (8th-6th century BC), classical (5th-4th century BC), Hellenistic (3rd-1st century BC) and Roman eras (1st-4th century AD) (see Fig. 6 and Fig. 7). However, caution is advised here: for instance, we have almost exclusively epic texts from the archaic period, so that developments between the archaic and the classical period may be explained in terms of genre rather than in diachronic terms. In the archaic period, the number of data points is very limited. For the classical period the data for the animals are also rather limited, so that the transition between the Hellenistic and Roman period especially lends itself for a study of diachronic developments.

The main evolution that can be traced with respect to the animal collectives (cf. Fig. 6) is the prominence of πλῆθος in the Hellenistic period, which clearly decreases in the Roman period. There is no clear challenger; rather, there seems to be a diversification in general, with, for example, a more frequent use of ἀγέλη, φῦλον and ζεῦγος (even though πλῆθος and ζεῦγος are likely not simply interchangeable). In a few cases we can also observe a tendency to specialization: it is especially in the Roman period that words for insects are associated with specific collective nouns, namely νέφος; ἑσμός; σμῆνος, whereas in the Hellenistic period πλῆθος is still predominating here (see Table 3).

Collective	Hellenistic	Roman
πλῆθος	9	8
ἀγέλη	0	1
φῦλον	0	3
νομή	0	1
σμῆνος	3	15
ἑσμός	1	10
νέφος	3	4
χορός	0	2

Table 3: Collective nouns used for insects in the Hellenistic and Roman period

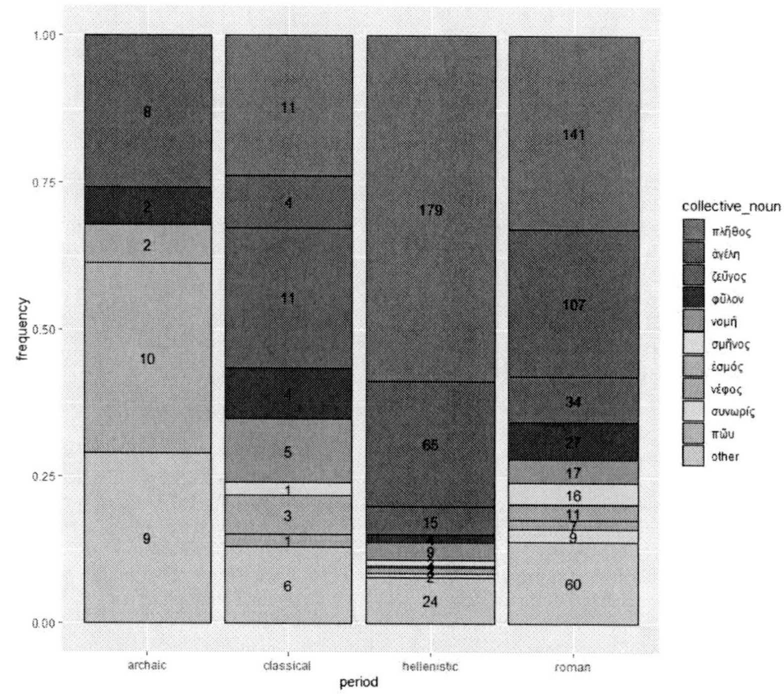

Figure 6: Evolution in the presence of animal collective nouns over time

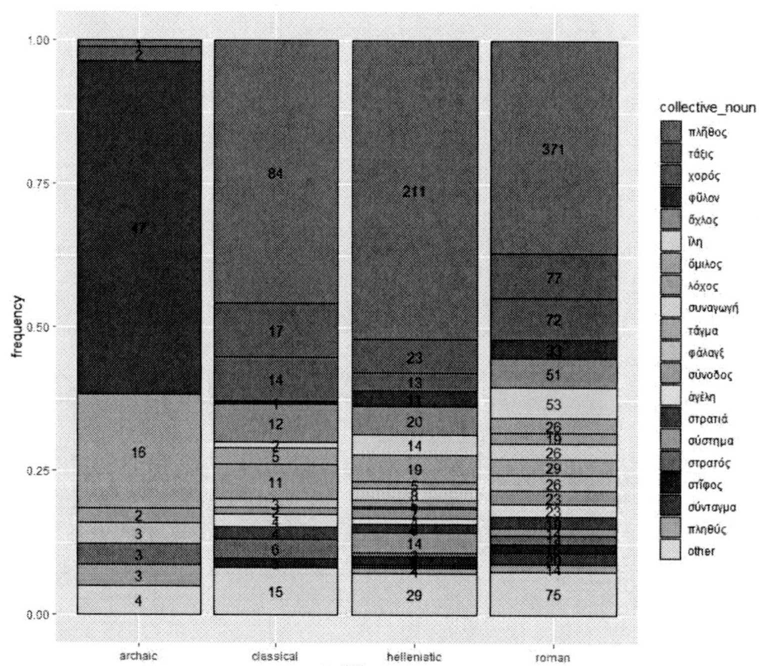

Figure 7: Evolution in the presence of human collective nouns over time

For the human collective nouns the diachronic changes are less clear (cf. Fig. 7). A number of archaic collective nouns are used much less frequently in later periods. A clear example is ὅμιλος, which in later periods is mainly taken up by a few authors (especially Philo Judaeus). Another example is φῦλον. Here again we observe the prominence of πλῆθος in the Hellenistic period, but the decline in the Roman period is less pronounced. What is particularly striking is the diachronic increase of ἴλη as a collective noun for soldiers in the Roman period (12 instances of ἴλη and 58 instances of πλῆθος in the Hellenistic period versus 52 instances of ἴλη and 53 instances of πλῆθος in the Roman period). In addition, there is a clear increase of χορός among certain 'professions' (2 instances of χορός and 19 instances of πλῆθος in the Hellenistic period versus 23 instances of χορός and 51 instances of πλῆθος in the Roman period). Inspecting the data, this is especially true when the profession has a 'didactive' or 'heralding' function, e.g. philosophers, teachers and prophets.

5. Conclusions and outlook

The syntactic/morphological-based extraction and clustering techniques have allowed us to detect a large number of collective nouns. Nevertheless, there are some important caveats. The quantitative methods used have enabled us to compile a longlist. A final manual selection, reducing the longlist to a shortlist, nevertheless remained necessary. This step involves a large degree of subjective decisions, many of which can be debated. In addition, we cannot evaluate which relevant words were not found ('recall'). Furthermore, polysemy causes any clustering technique to be problematic. The multidimensional nature of semantics implies that Ancient Greek equivalents for polysemous and idiosyncratic collocations (such as e.g. English 'murder of crows') will be difficult to identify. Some 'collective nouns' can also be frequently combined with inanimate entities (e.g. πλῆθος χρημάτων "a group or amount of money"). While these examples were filtered out during the animacy detection described in section 3.2 (i.e. we only included words with a sufficient number of animate genitive attributes in the cluster analysis in section 3.3, and similarly only analyzed words with such attributes during the corpus analysis described in 4), these contexts with inanimate entities were still included in the word vectors, and therefore might distort the results of the cluster analysis. In the future, word vectors modelling the meaning of a word in context rather than the general meaning of a word might allow for a higher degree of precision. The results could also be improved by means of an objective set of criteria whether or not a word can be considered a collective noun. Another difficulty resides in the data scarcity, which makes it very difficult to make statements about the significance of the connection between certain collective nouns and specific animals. By way of example, we see that for θύννος ('tuna'), attested thrice in the data, three different collective nouns are used: besides the generic πλῆθος, στρατός and ἴλη occur. Table 1 shows that both στρατός and ἴλη tend to be used as collective nouns of humans (especially in a military context; see 4.4). The question here is whether we are dealing with a fixed, conventional collective noun for tuna or a context-related metaphor. Obviously, close reading of the relevant passages may shed more light on the matter. For this particular case, it seems to be an occasional metaphor twice. However, if there would have been more data, it could be determined with more certainty to what extent the use of στρατός and ἴλη is rooted in context or convention. The same applies to many other lemmas, so that it is very difficult to make firm statements about which combinations were idiomatically acceptable in Greek.

There are also alternative methods possible for onomasiological queries, including searching for English translations of the concept in question through lexica (e.g. the English-Greek dictionary by Woodhouse 1987, or reverse-searching the LSJ lexicon by Jones et al. 1996) or through parallel translations, as well as using Ancient Greek WordNets – a first Ancient Greek WordNet was created by Bizzoni et al. (2014), while recently a new attempt has been undertaken by Biagetti et al. (2021). Although we could not systematically compare these approaches to the one adopted in this paper due to time and space constraints, we will briefly address the advantages and disadvantages of both through a quick exploration. Searching the Woodhouse and LSJ lexica for words such as 'flock', 'herd', 'crowd' and 'group' returned many words listed in Table 1, but also missed some (e.g. neither lexicon included νέφος under an English lemma referring to a collective noun, for example, and Woodhouse expectedly does not contain Homeric words such as πῶυ or post-classical words such as ἴλη as it is limited to the Classical Attic dialect). On the other hand, they also include words missed by our computational approach, especially low-frequent ones that we filtered out in an initial step (see 3.2), e.g. κῶμος (only 3 occurrences with an animate genitive noun). Additionally, they also reveal some alternative constructions to express a group of living beings rather than the noun + genitive construction, e.g. adjective + noun constructions such as μελισσαῖος οὐλαμός (see section 3.2) or δρακονθόμιλος συνοικία "a swarm of dragons" (Woodhouse). However, a big limitation of this approach is that it simply shifts the burden of determining which on words or constructions can express a particular concept from one language (Ancient Greek) to another one (e.g. English). For instance, the word ἄθροισμα is defined, among other definitions, as 'aggregate' in the LSJ lexicon. While 'aggregate' is certainly a collective noun in English, one must take this English term into account as one of the many possibilities to express collective nouns in order to retrieve ἄθροισμα with a lexical-based method. While the Ancient Greek WordNets seem to be less vulnerable in this respect, as they encode semantic relations between words in the target language – in this case Greek – the WordNet designed by Bizzoni et al. (2014) was in fact based on automatic linking between Greek-English lexica and therefore prone to similar problems, while the Biagetti et al. (2021) WordNet is still in active development. All these human-curated resources are also highly dependent on human judgments and the data they have considered during their developments, while the automatic approach discussed in this paper can easily take the whole Greek corpus into account (although it is fair to say that the quality of the semantic methods is highly dependent on the frequency of specific genres in the input data, see also Perrone et al. 2019).

For this first exploration of onomasiologically searching, we have deliberately chosen a case with identifiable syntactic characteristics. The challenge for future research consists in choosing less straightforward cases, where syntactic and morphological encoding is significantly less decisive. Without doubt, one of the greatest onomasiological challenges is to trace in the Ancient Greek corpus concepts that may be present but for which lexicalized words are missing (possible examples include modern concepts such as 'queer', 'fashion', etc.).

6. Acknowledgements

This research was made possible by FWO grant 3H200733: "Language and Ideas: Towards a New Computational and Corpus-Based Approach to Ancient Greek Semantics and the History of Ideas". We would like to thank three anonymous reviewers for their stimulating criticisms.

7. Bibliographical References

Aikhenvald, A.Y. (2000). Classifiers: a Typology of Noun Categorization Devices. Oxford: Oxford University Press.

Atallah, C., Bras, M., & Vieu, L. (2018). Exploring a Corpus Annotated in Causal Discourse Relations for the Study of Causal Lexical Clues. In *Final Action Conference TextLink 2018, Mar 2018, Toulouse, France*. Retrieved from https://hal.archives-ouvertes.fr/hal-02982984.

Benvenuto, M.C. (2013). Genitive. In Encyclopedia of Ancient Greek Language and Linguistics. Leiden: Brill. Retrieved from <http://referenceworks.brillonline.com/entries/encyclopedia-of-ancient-greek-language-and-linguistics/genitive-COM_00000140>.

Biagetti, E., Zanchi, C., & Short, W.M. (2021). Toward the Creation of WordNets for Ancient Indo-European Languages. In *Proceedings of the 11th Global Wordnet Conference*. University of South Africa (UNISA): Global Wordnet Association, pp. 258-266.

Biber, D., Conrad, S., & Leech, C. (2003). *Longman Student Grammar of Spoken and Written English*. Harlow: Longman.

Birkenes, M.B., & Sommer, F. (2014). The agreement of collective nouns in the history of Ancient Greek and German. In C. Gianollo, A. Jäger & D. Penka (Eds.), Language Change at the Syntax-Semantics Interface. Berlin: De Gruyter, pp. 183-221.

Bizzoni, Y., Boschetti, F., Diakoff, H., Del Gratta, R., Monachini, M., & Crane, G. (2014). The Making of Ancient Greek WordNet. In *Proceedings of the Ninth International Conference on Language Resources and Evaluation (LREC'14)*. Reykjavik: European Language Resources Association (ELRA), pp. 1140-1147.

Boschetti, F. (2010). A Corpus-based Approach to Philological Issues. Unpublished PhD Thesis. University of Trento.

Cananau, I. (2019). Toward a Comparatist Horizon in Conceptual History. History of European Ideas, 45(1), pp. 117-120. https://doi.org/10.1080/01916599.2018.1493307

Celano, G.G. (2019). The Dependency Treebanks for Ancient Greek and Latin. In M. Berti (Ed.), Digital Classical Philology. Berlin & Boston: Walter de Gruyter, pp. 279-298.

Celano, G.G. A., & Crane, G. (2015). Semantic Role Annotation in the Ancient Greek Dependency Treebank. In M. Dickinson, E. Hinrichs, A. Patejuk, & A. Przepiórkowski (Eds.), *Proceedings of the Fourteenth International Workshop on Treebanks and Linguistic Theories (TLT14)*. Warsaw, pp. 26-34.

Dedè, F. (2012). Some Remarks on the Metalinguistic Usage of the Term 'Collective'. In *Proceedings of the First Workshop on the Metalanguage of Linguistics. Models and Applications. University of Udine – Lignano, March 2-3, 2012*. Roma: Il calamo, pp. 81-94.

Deroy, L. (1956). La valeur du suffixe préhellénique *-nth-* d'après quelques noms grecs en -νθος. Glotta, 35(3/4), pp. 171-195.

Dieckhoff, A. (2019). Peuples et populisme. Annuaire international de justice constitutionnelle, 34, pp. 691-698. https://doi.org/10.3406/aijc.2019.2719

Erk, K. (2012). Vector Space Models of Word Meaning and Phrase Meaning: A survey. Language and Linguistics Compass, 6(10), pp. 635-653.

Fernández-Domínguez, J. (2019). The Onomasiological Approach. In Oxford Research Encyclopedia of Linguistics. Oxford: Oxford University Press. https://doi.org/10.1093/acrefore/9780199384655.013.579.

Geeraerts, D. (2009). Theories of Lexical Semantics. Oxford: Oxford University Press.

Goossens, D. (2013). Assessing Corpus Search Methods in Onomasiological Investigations. In H. Hasselgård, J. Ebeling, S. Oksefjell Ebeling (Eds.), Corpus Perspectives on Patterns of Lexis. Amsterdam & Philadelphia: John Benjamins, pp. 271-292.

Gries, S. Th. 2010. Useful Statistics for Corpus Linguistics. In *A Mosaic of Corpus Linguistics: Selected Approaches*, In A. Sánchez & M. Almela (Eds.), Studien zur romanischen Sprachwissenschaft und interkulturellen Kommunikation. Frankfurt am Main: Peter Lang, pp. 269-291.

Grzega, J. (2002). Some Aspects of Modern Diachronic Onomasiology. *Linguistics*, *40*(5), pp. 1021-1045. https://doi.org/10.1515/ling.2002.035

Johnston, I. (2019). A List of Homeric (Epic) Similes from the Iliad and Odyssey. Retrieved from http://johnstoniatexts.x10host.com/homer/homericsimiles.html.

Jones, H.S., Henry George Liddell, MacKenzie, R., Scott, R., & Thompson, A.A. (1996). A Greek-English Lexicon (New ed. with new supplement). Oxford: Clarendon.

Joosten, F., Sutter, G.D., Drieghe, D., Grondelaers, S., Hartsuiker, R.J., & Speelman, D. (2007). *Dutch Collective Nouns and Conceptual Profiling*. Linguistics, *45*(1), pp. 85-132.

Jussen, B., & Rohmann, G. (2015). Historical Semantics in Medieval Studies: New Means and Approaches. Contributions to the History of Concepts, 10(2), pp. 1-6. https://doi.org/10.3167/choc.2015.100201

Kaczyńska, E. (2019). Laconian βοῦα 'Band of Boys' as a collective noun. Graeco-Latina Brunensia, (1), pp. 93-103. https://doi.org/10.5817/GLB2019-1-7

Keersmaekers, A. (2020). A Computational Approach to the Greek Papyri: Developing a Corpus to Study

Variation and Change in the Post-Classical Greek Complementation System. Unpublished PhD Dissertation. KU Leuven. Retrieved from https://lirias.kuleuven.be/retrieve/590983.

Keersmaekers, A. (2021). The GLAUx corpus: methodological issues in designing a long-term, diverse, multi-layered corpus of Ancient Greek. In *Proceedings of the 2nd International Workshop on Computational Approaches to Historical Language Change 2021*, pp. 39-50.

Keersmaekers, A., Mercelis, W., Swaelens, C., & Van Hal, T. (2019). Creating, Enriching and Valorizing Treebanks of Ancient Greek. In *Proceedings of the 18th International Workshop on Treebanks and Linguistic Theories (TLT, SyntaxFest 2019)*. Association for Computational Linguistics (ACL), pp. 109-117.

Keersmaekers, A., & Van Hal, T. (2021). A Corpus-Based Approach to Conceptual History of Ancient Greek. In G. Kristiansen, K. Franco, S. De Pascale, L. Rosseel, & W. Zhang (Eds.), Cognitive Sociolinguistics Revisited. Berlin & Boston: Walter de Gruyter, pp. 213-225.

Kipfer, B.A. (1986). Investigating an Onomasiological Approach to Dictionary Material. Dictionaries: Journal of the Dictionary Society of North America, *8*, pp. 55-64.

Krijthe, J., & van der Maaten, L. (2018). Rtsne: T-Distributed Stochastic Neighbor Embedding using a Barnes-Hut Implementation (Version 0.15). Retrieved from https://CRAN.R-project.org/package=Rtsne.

Kühner, R., & Gerth, B. (1966). Ausführliche Grammatik der griechischen Sprache. München: Hueber.

Kutuzov, A. (2020). Distributional Word Embeddings in Modeling Diachronic Semantic Change. Unpublished PhD-dissertation. Oslo University.

LeDell, E., Gill, N., Aiello, S., Fu, A., Candel, A., Click, C., … H2O.ai. (2022). h2o: R Interface for the 'H2O' Scalable Machine Learning Platform (Version 3.36.0.4). Retrieved from https://CRAN.R-project.org/package=h2o.

Lehrer, A. (1986). English Classifier Constructions. Lingua, 68(2-3), pp. 109-148.

Lenci, A. (2018). Distributional models of word meaning. Annual Review of Linguistics, 4, pp. 151-171.

Maechler, M., Rousseeuw, P., Struyf, A., Hubert, M., Hornik, K., Studer, M., … Murphy, K. (2022). cluster: 'Finding Groups in Data': Cluster Analysis Extended Rousseeuw et al. (Version 2.1.3). Retrieved from https://CRAN.R-project.org/package=cluster.

McGillivray, B. (2020). Computational methods for semantic analysis of historical texts. In K. Schuster & S. Dunn (Eds.), Routledge International Handbook of Research Methods in Digital Humanities. London: Routledge, pp. 261-274.

Mehl, S. (2016). *Corpus Onomasiology: A study in World Englishes*. Unpublished PhD-dissertation: UCL London.

Meyer, P., & Tu, N.D.T. (2021). A Word Embedding Approach to Onomasiological Search in Multilingual Loanword Lexicography. In *Proceedings of eLex 2021*, pp. 78-91.

Moerdijk, F., Tiberius, C., & Niestadt, J. (2008). Accessing the ANW Dictionary. In *Coling 2008: Proceedings of the Workshop on Cognitive Aspects of the Lexicon (COGALEX 2008)*. Manchester: Coling 2008 Organizing Committee, pp. 18-24. Retrieved from https://aclanthology.org/W08-1903.

Müller, E., & Schmieder, F. (2016). Begriffsgeschichte und historische Semantik: ein kritisches Kompendium. Frankfurt am Main: Suhrkamp.

Perrone, V., Palma, M., Hengchen, S., Vatri, A., Smith, J.Q. & McGillivray, B. (2019). GASC: Genre-Aware Semantic Change for Ancient Greek. In *Proceedings of the 1st International Workshop on Computational Approaches to Historical Language Change*. Florence: Association for Computational Linguistics, pp. 56-66.

Perrone, V., Hengchen, S., Palma, M., Vatri, A., Smith, J.Q., & McGillivray, B. (2021). Lexical Semantic Change for Ancient Greek and Latin. In N. Tahmasebi, L. Borin, A. Jatowt, Y. Xu, & S. Hengchen (Eds.), Computational Approaches to Semantic Change. Berlin: Language Science Press, pp. 287–310.

Rhodes, C. (2014). An Unkindness of Ravens: A Book of Collective Nouns. London: Michael O'Mara Books.

Rodda, M.A., Probert, P., & McGillivray, B. (2019). Vector space models of Ancient Greek word meaning, and a case study on Homer. TAL Traitement Automatique Des Langues, 60(3), pp. 63-87.

Rodda, M.A., Senaldi, M.S., & Lenci, A. (2016). Panta Rei: Tracking Semantic Change with Distributional Semantics in Ancient Greek. In *CLiC-It/EVALITA*.

Sierra, G. (2008). Natural Language Searching in Onomasiological Dictionaries. In *Coling 2008: Proceedings of the Workshop on Cognitive Aspects of the Lexicon (COGALEX 2008)*. Manchester: Coling 2008 Organizing Committee, 32-38. Retrieved from https://aclanthology.org/W08-1905.

Swiggers, P., & Wouters, A. (1998). De Tékhnē grammatikē van Dionysius Thrax: de oudste spraakkunst in het Westen. Leuven: Peeters.

Vatri, A., & McGillivray, B. (2018). The Diorisis Ancient Greek Corpus. Research Data Journal for the Humanities and Social Sciences, 3(1), pp. 55-65.

Viteau, J. (1896). Étude sur le Grec du Nouveau Testament: comparé avec celui des septante. Sujet, complément et attribut. Paris: E. Bouillon.

Woodhouse, S.C. (1987). English-Greek dictionary: a vocabulary of the Attic language (Repr.). London: Routledge and Kegan Paul.

Zwarts, J. (2020). Contiguity and membership and the typology of collective nouns. In *Proceedings of Sinn Und Bedeutung, 24*(2). Osnabrück : Osnabrück University, pp. 539-554.

Proceedings of the Second Workshop on Language Technologies for Historical and Ancient Languages (LT4HALA 2022), pages 84–93
Language Resources and Evaluation Conference (LREC 2022), Marseille, 25 June 2022

Contextual Unsupervised Clustering of Signs for Ancient Writing Systems

Michele Corazza[1], Fabio Tamburini[1], Miguel Valério[2], Silvia Ferrara[1]
[1]Department of Classical Philology and Italian Studies, University of Bologna.
[2] Departament de Prehistòria, Universitat Autònoma de Barcelona
{michele.corazza2, fabio.tamburini, s.ferrara}@unibo.it
miguel.valerio@uab.cat

Abstract

The application of machine learning techniques to ancient writing systems is a relatively new idea, and it poses interesting challenges for researchers. One particularly challenging aspect is the scarcity of data for these scripts, which contrasts with the large amounts of data usually available when applying neural models to computational linguistics and other fields. For this reason, any method that attempts to work on ancient scripts needs to be *ad-hoc* and consider paleographic aspects, in addition to computational ones. Considering the peculiar characteristics of the script that we used is therefore a crucial part of our work, as any solution needs to consider the particular nature of the writing system that it is applied to. In this work we propose a preliminary evaluation of a novel unsupervised clustering method on the Cypro-Greek syllabary, a writing system from Cyprus. This evaluation shows that our method improves clustering performance using information about the attested sequences of signs in combination with an unsupervised model for images, with the future goal of applying the methodology to undeciphered writing systems from a related and typologically similar script.

Keywords: Deep Learning, ancient writing systems, clustering,inventory of signs in a script.

1. Introduction

The aim of this work is to investigate whether automatic methods can be applied to ancient undeciphered writing systems. One particularly challenging aspect for research can be the sign inventory of a script, as with certain undeciphered scripts there is no consensus among experts. Namely, it can be very difficult to distinguish what is a sign on its own right (grapheme) or a mere variant of a sign (allograph). This issue is detrimental to any attempt at decipherment and it can be further complicated in cases in which the writing system is scarcely attested and the corpus has many damaged inscriptions.

This work constitutes a preliminary investigation of a neural model that aims to learn good latent representations for signs in ancient, undeciphered writing systems. We are interested in the application of computational methods to ancient scripts from the Aegean and Cyprus, in particular to Cypro-Minoan. Cypro-Minoan is a script from the second millennium BCE, attested in Cyprus and the Syrian town of Ugarit. Since there is uncertainty regarding the inventory of signs of this script, we can only use unsupervised methods, which do not use prior information on the status of individual signs. This has the added benefit of avoiding any bias from hypotheses formulated by experts in the field.

In this work, we propose a new method for undeciphered writing systems using images as its input and no gold standard labels. The system improves upon existing methods for images in order to adapt them to this specific domain by incorporating information about the attested sequences of signs. Since no gold standard can be obtained directly from undeciphered writing systems, we describe a preliminary step consisting in the evaluation of our improvement over a baseline, using the Cypro-Greek (CG) syllabary as our ground truth for the evaluation, as CG is descendant script, thus closely related to Cypro-Minoan and it has been deciphered.

2. Related Work

In recent years, the prominence of deep neural networks in natural language processing tasks has increased, leading to improved performance on many tasks. The usage of these models for ancient writing systems however poses unique challenges: these scripts are scarcely attested and when they are undeciphered no evaluation can be performed to assess the performance of neural models. Nevertheless, some scholars have proposed various approaches that deal with ancient writing systems.

In particular, some models tackle the problem of damaged inscriptions, trying to reconstruct textual content in ancient Greek (Assael et al., 2019) and Babylonian Akkadian (Fetaya et al., 2020) using neural models. Another interesting task is the identification of scribal hands, where the goal is to investigate whether documents were inscribed by the same person or not. Computational methods for this task have been applied to the Dead Sea Scrolls (Popović et al., 2021) and to Linear B inscriptions (Srivatsan et al., 2021). Finally, a deep learning model was proposed in order to identify textual content written in the Indus Valley script (Palaniappan and Adhikari, 2017), which constitutes, to the best of our knowledge, the first application of neural networks to an undeciphered writing system.

While in recent years there have been attempts to apply machine learning methods to ancient writing systems, as far as we are aware no unsupervised model has been applied to the inventory of signs of ancient writing systems. Since we are interested in unsupervised

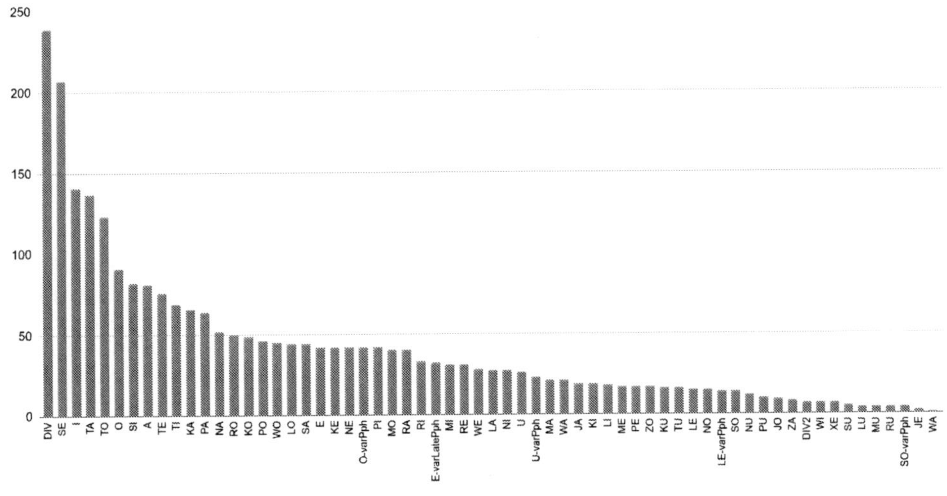

Figure 1: Number of attestations for each sign as represented in our dataset.

approaches, we will now discuss the state of the art of such systems for image classification.

Recent advancements in the application of unsupervised methods to image classification use a multitude of methods, that can be divided in different overarching approaches. Since our evaluation uses clustering as the main task for the model in a two-step approach, we are especially interested in clustering-based models. These are models that use clustering not only after having learned good quality representations for images, but also during training. Some methods using clustering for unsupervised learning on images use Convolutional Neural Networks and perform clustering on the latent representations of images. This is the case, among others, of DEC (Xie et al., 2016), DAC(Chang et al., 2017) and DeepCluster(Caron et al., 2018). Other approaches aim to maximise the mutual information between an image and augmented versions of it. This is the case for IIC (Ji et al., 2019) and IMSAT (Hu et al., 2017). SWAV (Caron et al., 2020) works similarly, by using assignments between two augmented versions of the same image, and using the swapped assignments as the labels to train the model. DeepClusterv2 (Caron et al., 2020) is a combination between SWAV and DeepCluster, using augmented versions of images, but still obtaining pseudo-labels for training from K-Means clustering. SCAN (Van Gansbeke et al., 2020) ditches clustering altogether, and uses a two-step approach: first, it minimizes the distance between an image and its augmentation as a pretext task, then the nearest neighbors of each vector are computed, and used to classify images in the same category.

3. Dataset

To assess the performance of our unsupervised model, we looked for a writing system with three characteristics:

- deciphered status, allowing us to compare our results with a known ground truth;
- a close relationship and typological similarity to Cypro-Minoan, in order to count with signs of the same type (syllabic) and sign inventory of comparable size (some dozens of syllabograms);
- a large enough corpus to provide us with a reasonable amount of data.

The obvious choice was then the Cypro-Greek syllabary, which is the only known script that meets all aforementioned criteria. The script (in use roughly between the 11th or 10th and the 4th centuries BCE) is deciphered and is known to have been adapted from Cypro-Minoan to write a well-understood ancient dialect of Greek (Arcado-Cypriot). Like Cypro-Minoan, its signs are syllabograms that represented open syllables, i.e. Vowel (V) or Consonant-Vowel (CV) syllables. In addition to 56 syllabograms, the Cypro-Greek script also comprised numerical signs and punctuation signs, namely dividers of sequences, which stood for words or groups of words (Egetmeyer, 2010).

Our dataset was obtained from drawings of Cypro-Greek inscriptions from various sources (Casabonne et al., 2002; Egetmeyer, 2010; Masson, 1983; Mitford, 1981; Karageorghis and Karageorghis, 1956; Karageorghis, 1976; Karnava, 2019; Masson and Mitford, 1986; Mitford, 1971; Masson and Olivier, 1983; Mitford, 1958; Mitford and others, 1961; Olivier, 2007; Mitford et al., 1983). The drawings were scanned, and the single signs of each inscription were manually segmented. They were also cropped to obtain square images of 100x100 pixels, retraced as clean black signs on white background. Each file was then labelled with the transcription (reading) of the sign in question. The reading assigned followed reference editions of the texts (Masson and Olivier, 1983; Egetmeyer, 2010), except for some specific cases where the updated transcription stemmed from individual publications (amongst the ones cited above).

The total number of sign images obtained was 2995 from 164 inscriptions. We then proceeded to exclude images of signs that were broken or damaged, and which therefore did not show their shape in full. Whenever a sign was damaged but the full form was still preserved and drawn, the noise (e.g., cracks or scratches on the inscription medium) was manually removed from the drawing. The number of excluded sign images was 322, so that after this filter we were left with a total of 2673 images.

Because our method considers the context (the position of signs in relation to other signs in the sequences and texts), we gave preference to larger texts written clearly in Greek language. The longest text in the dataset (ICS 217, side B) yielded 584 sign images, while the shortest provided only 2, but on average a document of the dataset provided 9 signs. To make the dataset as representative as possible of the complete corpus of the script, which surpasses 1,050 inscriptions (Egetmeyer, 2010), we deliberately included documents from various geographical areas and different time periods, even if an equal number of signs between locations was not achieved.

The number of categories of signs represented by these images is 64, which includes syllabograms, numerical and punctuation signs, and 'space', which refers to a space in the inscription probably used as a separating device. Importantly, the Cypro-Greek syllabary existed in two main varieties: one used mainly in the area of ancient Paphos, in West Cyprus ('Paphian') and another used in most of the rest of the island ('Common'). The Paphian variety features specific variants of some signs (5 in our dataset), which have different shapes but the same phonetic values as their counterparts in the Common variety. As their shape is significantly different, to the extent where it would affect the clustering method, the images pertaining to these categories received specific labels that distinguished them as Paphian. Finally, out of the 56 syllabograms that make up the sign inventory of Cypro-Greek (excluding the Paphian graphic variants), only one is not represented in our dataset. This is syllabogram XA, as it is a rare sign not found among the 164 inscriptions we compiled.

Like most linguistic features, the sign frequency follows a Zipf distribution (Figure 1), with some categories appearing fewer than 10 times in the entire corpus. This situation, while expected, makes any attempt at creating a neural model classifying signs very challenging, especially since we use an unsupervised method to cluster them. The most common grapheme is the divider denoted in the plot by "DIV". This sign is used to separate sign sequences, which in the Cypro-Greek script can stand for single words or entire phrases, such as 'the city of Idalion'.

4. Model

As the basis for our approach we use DeepClusterv2 (Caron et al., 2020), an unsupervised convolutional model for images, an improvement on the original DeepCluster (Caron et al., 2018) algorithm. DeepCluster (Figure 2) is an unsupervised model that applies K-Means to the output of a convolutional neural network, a ResNet50 (He et al., 2016), in order to learn pseudo-labels that are then, in turn, used to update the weights of the model. Before each epoch the vectors representing all of the signs are obtained from the model. These are then normalized to be unit vectors by dividing them by their L2 norm. On these, a K-means clustering algorithm is applied, obtaining pseudo-labels that can be used to train the model on a classification task.

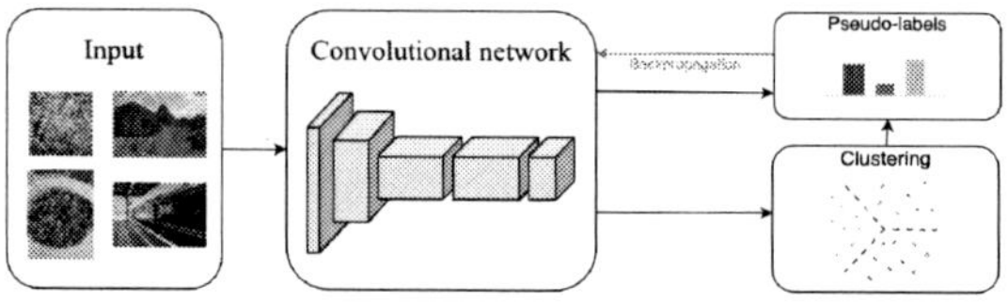

Figure 2: DeepCluster

DeepClusterv2 improves upon its predecessor in some significant ways:

- It replaces the output layer of DeepCluster with one obtained by using the centroids of the clusters from K-means. The application of this output layer to the vectors from the ResNet50 calculates the dot product between each vector and each centroid. Since both the centroids and the vectors representing images are normalized unit-norm vectors, this corresponds to the cosine similarity between vectors and centroids. With this method, the output layer does not need to be reinitialized after every epoch and the proximity of the sign to its centroid is enforced directly in the model;
- The model uses random augmentations of the images (crops, color distortion, random flips) both before clustering and when training the model;
- Other minor adjustments include cosine learning rate and the usage of a multi-layer perceptron as a projection head for the image vectors.

Our model, Sign2Vec$_c$ (Figure 3), improves upon the existing DeepClusterv2 approach by considering the role of contextual information when dealing with images representing signs. In fact, the preceding and following sign bear important information when attempting to detect allographs in writing systems, as similar sign shapes found within the same position of a sequence are more likely to be variants of the same sign. This information is often used by paleographers, as it can give precious insight into the allography of signs and it is also a crucial aspect for any attempt at decipherment.

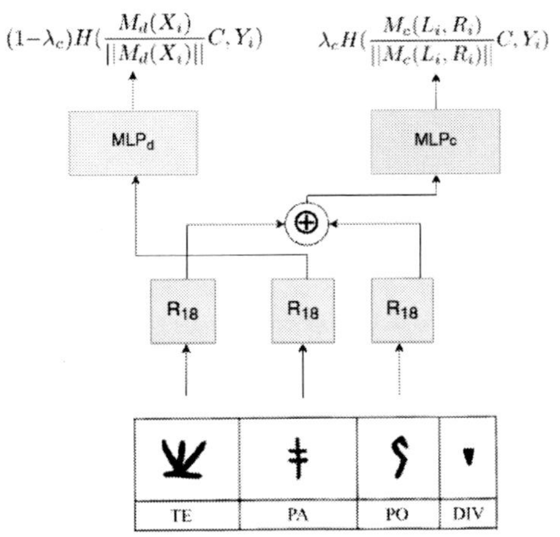

Figure 3: Sign2Vec$_c$.

Sign2Vec$_c$ is inspired by the CBOW approach (Mikolov et al., 2013) often used in computational linguistics to learn word embeddings. In this approach, a word is predicted from its left and right context. Similarly, our aim is to train a model that can predict a sign from its context. In our case, however, we have no source of supervision and cannot provide the model with a symbolic representation of signs, since images are our only input. Additionally, we do not have labels that can be used to directly train a model to predict a syllabogram from its context. Therefore, we extend the DeepClusterv2 framework by using a joint learning objective. In addition to the usual DeepClusterv2 loss, we use the signs to the left and right of the one under examination in order to predict the cluster that the central sign belongs to. The choice of such a small context window (size one) might seem low when compared to larger context windows traditionally used in computational linguistics. However, its properties fit our task well: as CG is a syllabary, by limiting the window size to one, we never cross the boundaries of syllabic sequences, as there is always a sign separating them. Also, with larger context windows, when dealing with a sign found at the end of a document, we would need to introduce extra virtual signs on the right side (and the same applies to the left side at the beginning of a text), which is problematic.

Formally, we use the following training objective:

$$\mathcal{L}(\mathrm{C}, \mathrm{X_i}, \mathrm{Y_i}) = (1-\lambda_c)\, H(\frac{M_d(X_i)}{||M_d(X_i)||}C, Y_i) + \lambda_c\, H(\frac{M_c(L_i, R_i)}{||M_c(L_i, R_i)||}C, Y_i) \quad (1)$$

Where $C \in \mathbb{R}^{v_s \times n_c}$ is a matrix representing all the centroids of the clusters obtained from K-means, and v_s is the size of the vectors obtained from the model, while n_c is the number of clusters obtained from K-Means. X_i is the central sign, while L_i, R_i represent the signs to the left and right of X_i, respectively. Y_i is the cluster that the central sign X_i belongs to according to K-means. H is the categorical cross entropy. Consider the fact that since we normalize both branches of the loss by dividing the vectors by their L2 norm, they both have unit norm. Therefore the product between the vectors obtained from the model and C corresponds to the cosine similarity of the vector with each centroid. λ_c is a constant used to determine the relative weight of the two components of the loss.

The neural model is implemented by the two functions M_d and M_c:

$$M_d(X_i) = MLP_d(R_{18}(X_i))$$
$$M_c(L_i, R_i) = MLP_c(R_{18}(L_i) \oplus R_{18}(R_i))$$

Where MLP_d and MLP_c are two multi-layer perceptrons that project the central sign and the concatenation ($\oplus$) of the left and right sign respectively to a vector of the same size. The outputs of M_d and M_c are both in $\mathbb{R}^{b_s \times v_s}$, where b_s is the batch size. Notice that, therefore, the matrix products of equation 1 between MLP_d, MLP_c respectively and C are in $\mathbb{R}^{b_s \times c_n}$, so they calculate, for each image in a mini-batch, a proximity to all centroids. As MLP_d and MLP_c operate on vectors with different sizes and perform different tasks, they do not share weights. R_{18} is the ResNet18 convolutional network that we use to replace the ResNet50 present in the original implementation of DeepClusterv2 to reduce the number of parameters. It is shared by both branches of the model.

Since Sign2Vec$_c$ uses contextual information to improve the base DeepClusterv2 model, there are some peculiar situations that arise. First, we need to consider how to provide context to the model at the beginning or end of inscriptions. For this situation, we can leverage a peculiar characteristic of the Cypro-Greek syllabary, which is also present in the Cypro-Minoan script: the system uses vertical lines or dots as sequence separators, so we can simply use a random sequence divider from the corpus to replace the beginning or the end of an inscription in the context, since the limits of a document also represent sequence boundaries. This random sequence divider is chosen at run-time and altered at every epoch for a given context, since always choosing the same separator from the dataset would be arbitrary. This also means that we implicitly provide the model with some information about separators. However, dividers are not syllabograms and do not encode phonetic information, so we can safely exclude them from any further evaluation. Additionally, since they are very frequent, specialists agree on their function even in the undeciphered Cypro-Minoan script and they can be distinguished from other signs without any uncertainty.

Another aspect that needs careful consideration is the fact that some signs are damaged and some inscriptions are broken. In this case, when we needed to represent a damaged sign or a broken portion of the inscription, we generate random black dots on a white background at run time, using Poisson disc sampling (Bridson, 2007). This choice was made in an effort to reduce the effect that a fixed image representing damage would have on the model, since this might lead the model to rely on the fixed "damage" image, while the missing signs that are damaged are variable in nature. The usage of dots matches the conventional representation of damage used by some paleographers in their drawings.

5. Experimental settings

In this section, we provide additional information on the settings and hyper-parameters we use to train all our models. The first important aspect to consider regards the parameters used in order to obtain the augmented versions of images during training. In our models, we use two sets of cropped augmentations for each image, with a relative size compared to the original image chosen randomly in the ranges $[0.6, 1.0]$, $[0.4, 0.6]$. The two sets of crops are 6 and 10 for each image, respectively.

We did not alter the rest of the augmentation steps used by DeepCluster, which include a random horizontal flip of the image and a random color distortion. It needs to be noted, though, that while it is sensible for the Cypro-Greek syllabary, the application of a random horizontal flip might not be suitable in general, as it introduces an invariance with respect to flipped images that might be problematic. Since, however, the Cypro-Greek syllabary doesn't contain distinct graphemes that are horizontally flipped, we conclude that there is no reason to drop this augmentation step. The only alteration we made to the original augmentation is the reduction of the strength of the color distortion by using a parameter of 0.1 instead of the default 1.0, considering that we worked on black and white images and that such a strong level of color distortion was making the signs barely distinguishable from the background. We provide the values for all hyper-parameters used to train the model in Table 1.

Another important aspect of our evaluation is the choice of the number of clusters provided to K-Means (number of prototypes in Table 1). Since we are interested in evaluating the performance of our model by simulating its application to an undeciphered writing system, we cannot provide the model with the exact number of signs present in the dataset. We therefore proceed by overclustering the signs, and use a very generous estimate of 100 which should be more than any kind of system based on the syllabograms it contains. The fact that 100 is repeated three times in the parameters means that we apply K-means clustering three times. Naturally, we also have three different output layers for the model, one for each K-Means application. Since the algorithm initializes centroids at random, running K-means multiple times increases the robustness of the model and reduces the impact of the random initialization of the centroids.

Hyper-parameter	Value
Architecture	Resnet18
Base Learning Rate	4.8
Batch size (b_s)	16
Crops for assign	0
Epochs	100
Feature dimensions (v_s)	128
Final learning rate	0.0048
Number iterations before freeze	300000
λ_c	0.2
Hidden MLP size	2048
Max scale crops	[1.0, 0.6]
Min scale crops	[0.6, 0.4]
Number of crops	[6, 10]
Number of prototypes (n_c)	[100,100,100]
Size of the crops	[80, 60]
Start warmup	0.3
Temperature	0.1
Warmup Epochs	10
Weight decay	1×10^{-6}

Table 1: Hyper-parameters for Sign2Vec$_c$

Since we cannot use the number of classes during training, K-Means, which needs this information to initialize its centroids, can't be used as a clustering algorithm to evaluate performance. We are also unable to use the output layer of the model directly, since it overclusters our data. We therefore use a density based clustering algorithm, DBSCAN (Ester et al., 1996), which does not require the number of clusters as an input, in order to evaluate the performance of our model. The algorithm is applied to the latent representations of single signs learned by the models, given by:

$$\frac{M_d(X_i)}{||M_d(X_i)||}$$

We use the implementation of DBSCAN from scikit-learn (Pedregosa et al., 2011).

6. Results and evaluation

To evaluate the effectiveness of Sign2Vec$_c$ on the CG dataset, we need to perform a comparison with a DeepClusterv2 model trained with the same parameters but no context. However, we also need to adapt the model so that DBSCAN can be applied. In particular, we note that using oversampling is the best way to increase the density of signs belonging to the same class, allowing the usage of DBSCAN as a clustering algorithm. However, oversampling minority classes is not possible as we have no access to the ground truth labels. For this reason, we apply oversampling by replicating the entire dataset twice. This approach allows us to obtain two objectives: on one hand, we keep the centroids fixed for a longer time, since every epoch is twice the length of a standard one. On the other, we also oversample less frequent signs when applying K-Means, thus helping the clustering algorithm to detect more rare shapes and create a cluster around them. It is worth noting that,

Model	ϵ value	Adjusted Rand Index	Adjusted Mutual Information	V-measure
DC2, no oversample	0.05	0.30 ± 0.02	0.59 ± 0.02	0.66 ± 0.03
DC2, oversample	0.06	0.47 ± 0.02	0.68 ± 0.02	0.73 ± 0.01
S2V, oversample	0.08	$\mathbf{0.51 \pm 0.04}$	$\mathbf{0.72 \pm 0.02}$	$\mathbf{0.75 \pm 0.01}$

Table 2: Means and standard deviations for all the best clustering metrics of the three models.

Models	Adjusted Rand Index	Adjusted Mutual Information	V-measure
DC2 with and without oversampling	$1.92 * 10^{-5}$	$1.21 * 10^{-4}$	$1.71 * 10^{-4}$
S2V with oversampling, DC2 with oversampling	0.01	$3.60 * 10^{-5}$	$1.17 * 10^{-4}$

Table 3: One tailed t-tests comparing the metrics obtained from the models.

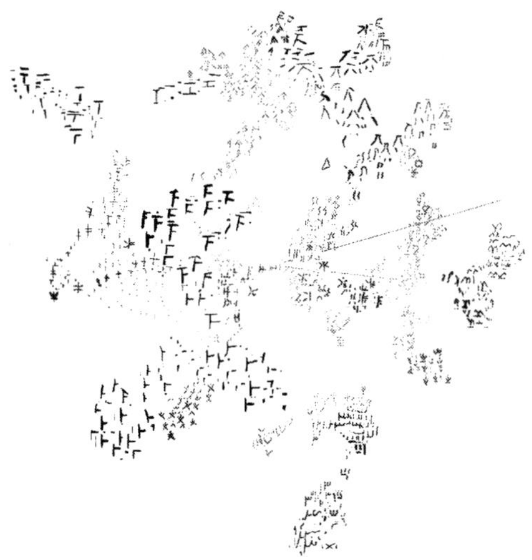

Figure 4: Three dimensional t-SNE projections for sign representations.

since every epoch and every sign is subject to random crops, the two copies of the same sign are not identical and therefore this method of oversampling has a positive effect on the application of K-means as well.

Before quantitatively evaluating performance using DBSCAN, another useful output of the model is the possibility to create three-dimensional scatter plots from the sign representations (Figure 4), in order to visualize the distance between signs. Since both DeepClusterv2 and Sign2Vec$_c$ work by minimizing distances between similar signs, the best choice for a dimensionality reduction algorithm is to use t-distributed stochastic neighbor embedding (t-SNE), which uses the Kullback-Leibler divergence between the distributions of distances in the original space and those in the reduced space (Van der Maaten and Hinton, 2008). By applying t-SNE (from scikit-learn) to the outputs of all three models we can create three visualizations[1] of the vector space which can be used by experts to spot incorrectly classified signs. To a lesser extent, we can also qualitatively assess the improvement that we obtain by applying Sign2Vec$_c$ and we see that, in general, Sign2Vec$_c$ tends to create groups of signs that are more separated from each other when compared to DeepClusterv2. This is especially evident when we compare the scatter plot from Sign2Vec$_c$ with the one obtained from DeepClusterv2 and no oversampling, as those have the largest difference in terms of performance. However, evaluating performance on the scatter plot alone is unfeasible, as the data is highly multidimensional and it is not always clear which model performs best. Scatter plots are not just useful for coarse evaluations of models. They also make for a state-of-the-art visual tool with important applications and implications for the paleographic study of ancient scripts. They can provide specialists with a method for quickly comparing large numbers of sign shapes, and, in that way, independently postulate hypotheses about the classification of graphemes or even identify misread signs.

We show the improvement in performance when using overclustering with DeepClusterv2, then we evaluate the further improvement in performance obtained by Sign2Vec$_c$. In order to compare models, we retrain each of them 10 times, in order to reduce the impact of the random initialization of the parameters as a factor and test for the statistical significance of the results.

Since we already use sequence dividers as a given to replace the end of sequences, we exclude them from the evaluation of clusters. In the same way, we exclude numerals from the evaluation, as they are not syllabograms and hence not our main focus. Moreover, the basics of the system for writing integers is largely shared by all related Aegean and Cypriot scripts (Linear A, Linear B, Cypro-Minoan, and Cypro-Greek).

When applying DBSCAN for our numerical evaluation, however, two parameters must be established. The first one is the minimum number of neighbors needed for a point to be considered a core point in the algorithm. Since we are using an unsupervised approach, we cannot assume any minimum size for these local neighborhoods, so we choose the minimum possible value of 2. Another crucial parameter required by DBSCAN is an ϵ value that controls the maximum distance

[1] `https://corpora.ficlit.unibo.it/INSCRIBE/PaperCG/`

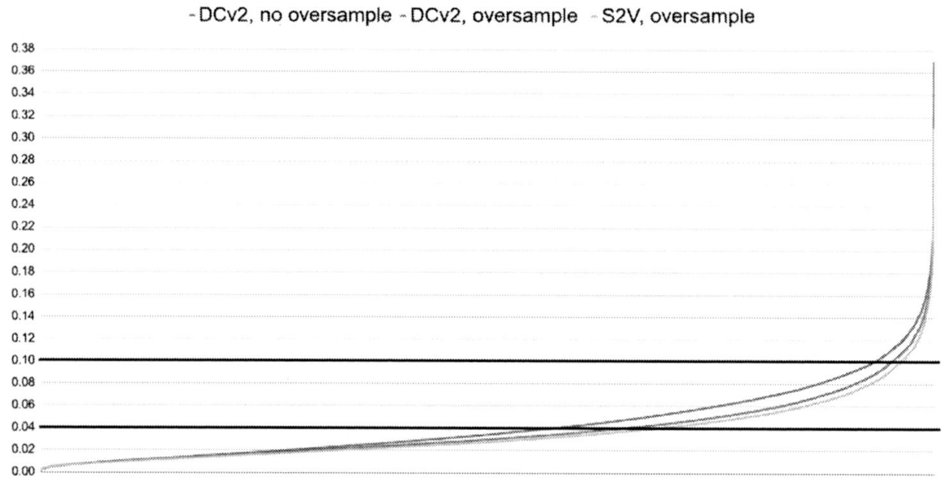

Figure 5: The elbow plots obtained from DeepClusterv2 with no oversampling, DeepClusterv2 with oversampling and Sign2Vec$_c$ with oversampling. The two horizontal lines show the range of ϵ values we used for our evaluation.

between a vector and its neighbors to initialize the algorithm. This parameter indirectly controls the number of clusters that will be created, as well as the number of signs that are deemed to be impossible to cluster by the algorithm. Lower values of ϵ result in a higher number of clusters, while higher values create fewer clusters. One of the few proposals for a heuristic to choose ϵ is the elbow criterion (Rahmah and Sitanggang, 2016). This method works on a vector space by first computing, for each vector, the farthest amongst its two nearest neighbors. Then, these values are sorted in ascending order and the elbow obtained by using this method is used to select the value of ϵ. This corresponds to finding a point of diminishing returns, where increasing ϵ does not result in many more vectors having local neighbors.

In Figure 5 we show the elbow plot obtained by sorting the maximum distance from the two nearest neighbors of each sign. While this criterion is useful, in practice we notice that when applied to approximately 27000 signs (the total number of signs x 10 models), the elbow can be ambiguous and does not always lead to an acceptable level of performance for all models. Moreover, we will show that Sign2Vec$_c$ with oversampling appears to tolerate a wider range of values for ϵ, while this is not true for the non-contextual versions of the model. While Sign2Vec$_c$ is superior to DeepClusterv2 in this aspect, we consider an arbitrary choice of ϵ as unfairly advantageous to our model. Therefore, we choose to evaluate the relative performance of the three models over a range of ϵ values, also shown with black lines in Figure 5. While it is debatable where the elbows lie in this kind of figure, we use a wide range to avoid the reliance on a single value of ϵ. Even if it can be argued that we do not include the elbow for all models, the results show that we do consider the best performing values of ϵ for all of them.

To assess the clustering performance of all three models we use some standard metrics for clustering: Adjusted Rand score, Adjusted mutual information and V-Measure, as implemented by scikit-learn (Pedregosa et al., 2011). As we use a range of values of ϵ for our evaluation, we provide two different ways to show the improvement in performance obtained from Sign2Vec$_c$: we plot all the mean values of the metrics for the different values of ϵ, then we select the best value for each model and compare them using a one tailed t-test to evaluate the statistical significance of the observed difference in performance between models.

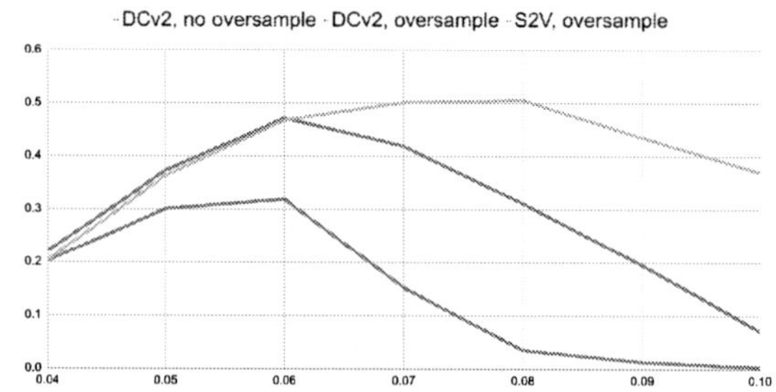

Figure 6: Adjusted Rand score of the three models for different values of ϵ.

By observing the mean of each metric obtained from the models with varying ϵ values (Figures 6,7,8), we can clearly spot some interesting trends. First, we consider a wide enough range of values for ϵ that the global maximum for all metrics is included, while at the edges of the plot we observe decreasing performance. When comparing the oversampled variant of DeepClusterv2 to the non oversampled one, we can see a marked improvement across all metrics, suggesting that over-

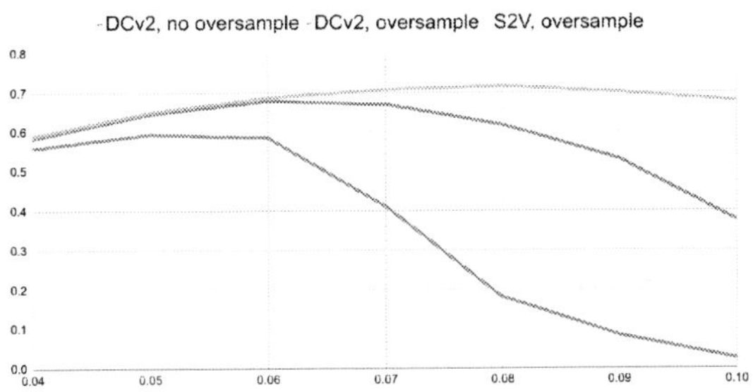

Figure 7: Adjusted mutual information of the three models for different values of ϵ

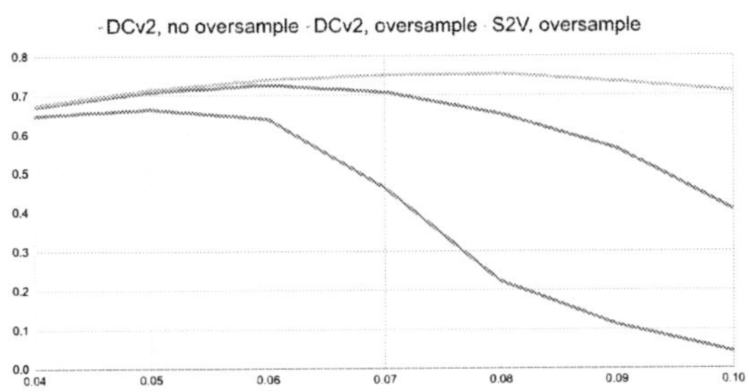

Figure 8: V-measure of the three models for different values of ϵ.

sampling leads to a measurable improvement in performance when using DBSCAN for clustering. Additionally, our Sign2Vec$_c$ model achieves the highest values. While for low values of ϵ Sign2Vec$_c$ and the oversampled version of DeepClusterv2 show similar performance, for $\epsilon > 0.06$ Sign2Vec$_c$ performance clearly improves while DeepClusterv2 shows a sharp decrease across all metrics. Also, Sign2Vec$_c$ appears to be more stable than DeepClusterv2 across a wider range of ϵ values. In practice, this means that Sign2Vec$_c$ is preferable for any attempt at automatic clustering on an undeciphered script, where the number of clusters is not known in advance and ϵ can only be chosen by using heuristics such as the elbow method or by evaluating the quality of the clusters manually.
Table 2 shows the means and standard deviations across all metrics for the best performing values of ϵ of each model. The metrics show a clear trend that reflects the improvement of the oversampled model with respect to the non oversampled variant, while the best performing model overall is Sign2Vec$_c$. Table 3 presents the results of the t-tests comparing the metrics obtained by the various models. We compare DeepClusterv2 with and without oversampling, DeepClusterv2 with oversampling and Sign2Vec$_c$, respectively. The table shows that all differences observed in the metrics are in fact statistically significant ($p < 0.05$) even with a relatively small sample size of 10 models. This, in conjunction with the aforementioned advantage of Sign2Vec$_c$ even when considering multiple values of ϵ, shows that using context in order to augment the vector representations obtained from DeepClusterv2 leads to improved clustering performance that cannot be due to random chance.

7. Conclusions

In the previous sections, we describe the peculiar challenges that are associated with the application of machine learning models to ancient writing systems, with particular attention to undeciphered scripts. In particular, we focus on syllabic systems from the Aegean and chose the Cypro-Greek syllabary as our gold standard, in order to be able to create an ad-hoc system that deals with such scripts.
We then propose an evaluation framework that can be used to assess whether performance improvements over existing methods can be obtained by tailoring the approach to ancient scripts. In particular, this approach uses DBSCAN as a clustering algorithm over the sign representations learned from neural models, since it allows us to obtain clusters without directly providing their exact number to the system, since this value might be unknown in the context of undeciphered scripts. Furthermore, we use contextual information in an unsupervised model for undeciphered scripts called Sign2Vec$_c$, and prove that this model leads to a clear improvement in performance over the baseline.
The evaluation of the different models on the Cypro-Greek syllabary shows two interesting findings. We observe that using oversampling can be useful when data is scarce, as it greatly improves performance while clustering using DBSCAN. In addition to that, we show that including contextual information leads to a further improvement in performance, suggesting that the usage of context helps the model to generalize variations in shape of the same sign, by also considering its position in sequences. This last finding matches the common approach used by experts, that evaluate the status of signs by examining their position in sequences. This work constitutes, to the best of our knowledge, the first application of unsupervised methods to the sign inventory of ancient writing systems, with the goal of a future application of a similar approach to undeciphered scripts. In addition, it is the first method integrating contextual information with an unsupervised neural model that directly uses the graphical representations of signs.

Acknowledgments

The research contained in this article is part of the ERC Project "INSCRIBE. Invention of Scripts and Their Beginnings". This project has received funding from the European Research Council (ERC) under the European Union's Horizon 2020 research and innovation program (grant agreement No 771127).

8. Bibliographical References

Assael, Y., Sommerschield, T., and Prag, J. (2019). Restoring ancient text using deep learning: a case study on greek epigraphy. In *Proceedings of the 2019 Conference on Empirical Methods in Natural Language Processing and the 9th International Joint Conference on Natural Language Processing (EMNLP-IJCNLP)*, pages 6367–6374. Association for Computational Linguistics.

Bridson, R. (2007). Fast poisson disk sampling in arbitrary dimensions. *SIGGRAPH sketches*, 10(1):1.

Caron, M., Bojanowski, P., Joulin, A., and Douze, M. (2018). Deep clustering for unsupervised learning of visual features. In *European Conference on Computer Vision*, pages 139–156.

Caron, M., Misra, I., Mairal, J., Goyal, P., Bojanowski, P., and Joulin, A. (2020). Unsupervised learning of visual features by contrasting cluster assignments. In *Proceedings of Advances in Neural Information Processing Systems (NeurIPS)*, pages 9912–9924.

Casabonne, O., , and Egetmeyer, M. (2002). À propos du sceau de diweiphilos. In *Notes ciliciennes*, volume 10 of *Anatolia Antiqua*, pages 177–181. Institut français des études anatoliennes.

Chang, J., Wang, L., Meng, G., Xiang, S., and Pan, C. (2017). Deep adaptive image clustering. In *Proceedings of the IEEE international conference on computer vision*, pages 5879–5887.

Egetmeyer, M. (2010). *Le dialecte grec ancien de Chypre. Tome I: Grammaire; Tome II: Répertoire des inscriptions en syllabaire chypro-grec.* De Gruyter.

Ester, M., Kriegel, H.-P., Sander, J., and Xu, X. (1996). A density-based algorithm for discovering clusters in large spatial databases with noise. In *Proceedings of the Second International Conference on Knowledge Discovery and Data Mining*, KDD'96, page 226–231. AAAI Press.

Fetaya, E., Lifshitz, Y., Aaron, E., and Gordin, S. (2020). Restoration of fragmentary babylonian texts using recurrent neural networks. *Proceedings of the National Academy of Sciences*, 117(37):22743–22751.

He, K., Zhang, X., Ren, S., and Sun, J. (2016). Deep residual learning for image recognition. In *Proceedings of the IEEE conference on computer vision and pattern recognition*, pages 770–778.

Hu, W., Miyato, T., Tokui, S., Matsumoto, E., and Sugiyama, M. (2017). Learning discrete representations via information maximizing self-augmented training. In *International conference on machine learning*, pages 1558–1567. PMLR.

Ji, X., Henriques, J. F., and Vedaldi, A. (2019). Invariant information clustering for unsupervised image classification and segmentation. In *Proceedings of the IEEE/CVF International Conference on Computer Vision*, pages 9865–9874.

Karageorghis, V. and Karageorghis, J. V. (1956). Some inscribed iron-age vases from cyprus. *American Journal of Archaeology*, 60(4):351–359.

Karageorghis, J. (1976). Une cruche chypriote inscrite du début du 5e siècle av. notre ère. *Studi Ciprioti e rapporti di scavo*, 2:59–68.

Karnava, A. (2019). Old inscriptions, new readings: A god for the rantidi sanctuary in south-west cyprus. *Cahiers du Centre d'Études Chypriotes*, 49:19–36.

Masson, O. and Mitford, T. B. (1986). Les inscriptions syllabiques de kouklia-paphos.

Masson, É. and Olivier, M. (1983). Appendix 4: Les objets inscrits de palaepaphos-skales. In V. Karageorghis et al., editors, *Palaepaphos-Skales: An Iron Age Cemetery in Cyprus*, Ausgrabungen in Alt-Paphos auf Cypern, pages 411–415. Universitätsverl.

Masson, O. (1983). Les inscriptions chypriotes syllabiques: recueil critique et commenté. *(Étude chypriotes 1). Réimpression augmentée.*

Mikolov, T., Chen, K., Corrado, G., and Dean, J. (2013). Efficient estimation of word representations in vector space. *arXiv preprint arXiv:1301.3781*.

Mitford, T. B. et al. (1961). Unpublished syllabic inscriptions of the cyprus museum. *Minos*, 7:15–48.

Mitford, T., Masson, O., and Institut, D. A. (1983). *The Syllabic Inscriptions of Rantidi-Paphos*. Ausgrabungen in Alt-Paphos auf Cypern. Universitätsverlag Konstanz.

Mitford, T. B. (1958). Three inscriptions of marium. *Bulletin of the Institute of Classical Studies*, 5:58–60.

Mitford, T. B. (1971). *The inscriptions of Kourion*, volume 83. American Philosophical Society.

Mitford, T. B. (1981). *The Nymphaeum of Kafizin: the inscribed pottery*, volume 2. De Gruyter.

Olivier, J.-P. (2007). *Édition holistique des textes chypro-minoens*. Fabrizio Serra Editore.

Palaniappan, S. and Adhikari, R. (2017). Deep learning the indus script.

Pedregosa, F., Varoquaux, G., Gramfort, A., Michel, V., Thirion, B., Grisel, O., Blondel, M., Prettenhofer, P., Weiss, R., Dubourg, V., Vanderplas, J., Passos, A., Cournapeau, D., Brucher, M., Perrot, M., and Duchesnay, E. (2011). Scikit-learn: Machine learning in Python. *Journal of Machine Learning Research*, 12:2825–2830.

Popović, M., Dhali, M. A., and Schomaker, L. (2021). Artificial intelligence based writer identification generates new evidence for the unknown scribes of the dead sea scrolls exemplified by the great isaiah scroll (1qisaa). *PloS one*, 16(4):e0249769.

Rahmah, N. and Sitanggang, I. S. (2016). Determination of optimal epsilon (eps) value on dbscan algorithm to clustering data on peatland hotspots in sumatra. In *IOP conference series: earth and environmental science*, volume 31, page 012012. IOP Publishing.

Srivatsan, N., Vega, J., Skelton, C., and Berg-Kirkpatrick, T. (2021). Neural representation learning for scribal hands of linear b. In *ICDAR 2021 Workshop on Computational Paleography*.

Van der Maaten, L. and Hinton, G. (2008). Visualizing data using t-sne. *Journal of machine learning research*, 9(11).

Van Gansbeke, W., Vandenhende, S., Georgoulis, S., Proesmans, M., and Van Gool, L. (2020). Scan: Learning to classify images without labels. In *European Conference on Computer Vision*, pages 268–285. Springer.

Xie, J., Girshick, R., and Farhadi, A. (2016). Unsupervised deep embedding for clustering analysis. In *International conference on machine learning*, pages 478–487. PMLR.

Proceedings of the Second Workshop on Language Technologies for Historical and Ancient Languages (LT4HALA 2022), pages 94–100
Language Resources and Evaluation Conference (LREC 2022), Marseille, 25 June 2022

Towards the Creation of a Diachronic Corpus for Italian: a Case Study on the GDLI Quotations

Manuel Favaro[§], Elisa Guadagnini[§], Eva Sassolini[§], Marco Biffi[*^], Simonetta Montemagni[§]
[§]Istituto di Linguistica Computazionale "A. Zampolli" – CNR
[*]Università di Firenze
[^]Accademia della Crusca
manuel.favaro@ilc.cnr.it, elisa.guadagnini@ilc.cnr.it, eva.sassolini@ilc.cnr.it, marco.biffi@unifi.it, simonetta.montemagni@ilc.cnr.it

Abstract
In this paper we describe some experiments related to a corpus derived from an authoritative historical Italian dictionary, namely the *Grande dizionario della lingua italiana* ('Great Dictionary of Italian Language', in short GDLI). Thanks to the digitization and structuring of this dictionary, we have been able to set up the first nucleus of a diachronic annotated corpus that selects—according to specific criteria, and distinguishing between prose and poetry—some of the quotations that within the entries illustrate the different definitions and sub-definitions. In fact, the GDLI presents a huge collection of quotations covering the entire history of the Italian language and thus ranging from the Middle Ages to the present day. The corpus was enriched with linguistic annotation and used to train and evaluate NLP models for POS tagging and lemmatization, with promising results.

Keywords: Diachronic Corpus, Adaptation of Annotation Tools, Historical Dictionaries

1. Introduction

Over the past decades, the number and variety of historical corpora available for different languages has been progressively growing. They represent an invaluable asset in the era of Digital Humanities, given the increasing interest in applying quantitative and computational methods to diachronic linguistics and historical text analysis.

For Italian, diachronic corpora are still few. Among them, covering a large timespan going from the origin of the Italian language to the present day, it is worth mentioning the *MIDIA corpus* (Gaeta et al., 2013, D'Achille and Grossmann, 2017), from which the *CODIT* was developed (Micheli, 2022), the *Letteratura italiana Zanichelli* (LIZ, later reissued as BIZ), and *BibIt*[1]. Other corpora focus on specific periods, such as the *Corpus OVI dell'Italiano antico* (Squillacioti, 2021) for Old Italian, the epistolary corpus *CEOD*[2] for 19th c. Italian, the *DiaCORIS corpus* (Onelli et al., 2006) and the reference corpus built for the construction of a *Dynamic Vocabulary of Modern Italian* (*VoDIM*, Marazzini and Maconi, 2018) for post-unitarian Italian. Many of these corpora have been enriched with linguistic annotation (typically, POS tagging and lemmatization), carried out (semi-)automatically or manually, and can be queried through advanced search tools. Yet, they are not distributed as linguistically annotated corpora: they were conceived as reference resources to be queried by scholars for the analysis of linguistic phenomena over the covered period of time and across the different varieties of language use testified (e.g. textual genres). Unfortunately, this feature makes them of limited use for the application of NLP-based methods with a specific view to the adaptation of linguistic annotation tools for the processing of historical varieties of language and for computational analyses focusing e.g. on semantics or style.

To the best of our knowledge, only two linguistically annotated corpora testifying historical varieties of language are available for Italian: the *Voci della Grande Guerra* corpus (VGG, Lenci et al., 2020) containing texts related to different varieties (both textual genres and registers) of Italian at the time of the World War I; and the corpus of the politician Alcide De Gasperi's public documents (Tonelli et al., 2019), a multi-genre corpus spanning 50 years of European history, written or transcribed between 1901 and 1954. VGG and Alcide corpora are available as multi-level annotated corpora, with both silver and gold annotations, which are compliant to internationally recognized representation standards. In Alcide, gold annotation was used to assess the accuracy of lemmatization, POS tagging and named entity annotation which was performed with tools trained on contemporary language. In VGG, gold annotation was also used to specialize the annotation tools to deal with the challenges posed by the linguistic varieties subsumed in the corpus (De Felice et al., 2018): retrained models were then used to annotate the rest of the corpus.

In the general picture depicted above, the aim of this paper is twofold. First, it illustrates the preliminary steps towards the creation of a linguistically annotated diachronic corpus for Italian, whose time span goes from old to contemporary Italian. Second, it reports the results of experiments aimed at assessing the accuracy of linguistic annotation (lemmatization and POS tagging) carried out with specialized annotation models against a diachronically representative sample of the corpus (gathering texts both in prose and poetry, going from the 13th to the 20th century).

For the composition of the corpus, we decided to use an interesting diachronic textual collection, represented by the set of quotations in a historical dictionary of Italian, namely the *Grande dizionario della lingua italiana* ('Great

[1] http://www.bibliotecaitaliana.it/

[2] http://ceod.unistrasi.it/

Dictionary of Italian Language', in short GDLI). Since quotations are seen as the "bedrock" of any historical dictionary (Hawke, 2016), we believe that they can be usefully exploited to build a wide coverage diachronic corpus. Studies carried out on quotations databases (see e.g. Hoffman, 2004; Rohdenburg, 2013) demonstrate how they can be used as a valuable information source for different typologies of studies, including quantitative ones.

The challenges of the linguistic annotation of historical texts are well known (Piotrowski, 2012). For Italian, an exploratory study on a diachronic corpus with texts (both prose and poetry) from the 13th to the 19th century focusing on morphological and morpho-syntactic annotation (Pennacchiotti and Zanzotto, 2008) highlights the specific issues (mostly, graphical, phonological, and morphological variability) connected with the automatic processing of Italian historical texts. More recently, adaptation experiments have been carried out to improve the performance of the automatic analysis tools by using manually revised sub-corpora to retrain the automatic linguistic annotation tools, with promising results. This is the case of De Felice et al. (2018) for the VGG Corpus and of Favaro et al. (2020) for a subset of the VoDIM corpus.

The paper is organized as follows. Section 2 describes the GDLI source with a specific view to the huge collection of quotations. Section 3 illustrates the selection criteria and the corpus composition of the first nucleus of the diachronic corpus. Sections 4 and 5 report the results of the annotation experiments carried out on the corpus. The final section mainly highlights current directions of research.

2. The Corpus Source: GDLI

GDLI, edited by Salvatore Battaglia and later by Giorgio Barberi Squarotti, is the most important historical dictionary of the Italian language in existence. Published by UTET in 21 volumes between 1961 and 2002 (with the addition of two update volumes, published in 2004 and 2009, for a total number of over 23,000 pages), GDLI covers the entire history of the Italian language, from the Middle Ages to the present day. Born with the aim of updating the *Dizionario della lingua italiana* known as "Tommaseo-Bellini" (1861-1879), which in turn was a sort of update of the famous *Vocabolario degli Accademici della Crusca*, GDLI—like its predecessors—bases its lexicographic description of Italian words on quotations taken from mainly literary works and authors. Within the entries, each definition and sub-definition is accompanied by a rich (often very rich) set of quotations, which attempt to cover the widest possible chronological span. Like and more than its predecessors, GDLI draws its quotations from a very wide range of authors and works: within the confines of the Italian literary or paraliterary (treatises, letters, translations, a few statutes) written tradition, not only those who are part of the canon of the major authors, but also a huge number of minor and minimal authors and works enter among the quoted. Overall, the breadth of the range of authors and works cited is impressive: GDLI quotes 6,226 authors and 13,848 sources (cf. Biffi and Guadagnini 2022).

Each quotation tends to preserve the syntactic autonomy of the textual passage, or rather to restore its overall sense (often beyond sentence boundaries): the GDLI entries are in fact conceived as a sort of small anthology of authorial citations, aimed at representing the uses of that particular word in the history of Italian writing (and specifically of Italian literature). These characteristics of the quotation cutting methods, combined with the very high number of authors and works consulted, make the corpus of quotations of GDLI an extremely rich textual set that can potentially be exploited as a resource in its own right.

Given the peculiar history of Italian, which is in fact a written and literary language until the twentieth century, a corpus that collects all the quotations present in the GDLI entries (henceforth, referred to as GDLI Quotations Corpus, in short GDLI-QC) can be considered as a "representative" diachronic corpus of Italian (Biffi, 2018). Provided, of course, that by "representativeness" we mean the ability, offered by this corpus, to extrapolate data regarding the use of words within the boundaries of the Italian literary tradition, as it is documented by the texts that have come down to us (possibly through the medium of previous dictionaries) (Burgassi and Guadagnini, 2017, p. 11; Kabatek, 2013). It must be kept in mind, of course, that GDLI-QC is particularly appropriate for lexical research, while it is far less reliable for investigations on other linguistic planes—namely spelling and phonology. Indeed, it should be remembered that GDLI draws virtually all of its quotations from printed texts, which are not always modern critical editions: e.g., medieval or otherwise pre-normative texts may be quoted from nineteenth-century printings, where the spelling and sometimes morphological features happen thus to be sometimes modified and modernized.

In this paper, we illustrate a case study aimed at creating the GDLI-QC. With this in mind, we have created a first nucleus of a linguistically annotated corpus (divided into two sub-corpora: Annotated GDLI-QC-prose and Annotated GDLI-QC-poetry) that is somewhat representative of the overall corpus. For the time being, linguistic annotation focused on POS tagging and lemmatization.

3. GDLI-QC Construction and Composition

3.1 GDLI Quotation Extraction

GDLI quotations were automatically extracted from the TEI XML version of the dictionary, obtained through a semi-automatic conversion process aimed at structuring the dictionary contents from the OCRed version of the dictionary. The goal of semi-automatically reaching an articulated structuring of GDLI entries has been organized into several iterative steps, each with the function of progressively refining and organizing the dictionary structure previously identified. The general approach to the extraction and structuring of GDLI contents, described in Sassolini et al. (2019), Biffi et al. (2020) and Sassolini et al. (2021), adopts a strategy substantially based on pattern matching. The specific identification criteria cover a wide range of features ranging from the layout of the page to structural information relating to the different parts of the lexical entry. The goal is focused on the conversion of the dictionary contents into macroareas structured and mapped in the XML TEI standard format.

Abiàtico (*abbiàtico, aviàtico*), sm. (femm. *abiàtica, abbiàtica*). Dial. Nipote (figlio del figlio o della figlia).

Comp. Antico Testamento [Tommaseo]: Seppe... come lo aveva trovato in lo bosco e comprese che questo era suo abiatico. *Vite di imperatori romani* [Tommaseo]: Tiberio voleva piuttosto che succedesse questo suo abiatico che questo Gaio. *Idem* [Tommaseo]: La figlia e le abiatiche fece usare all'esercizio della lana. *Fogazzaro*, 5-18: A poppa sotto la bandiera, v'era seduto don Franco Maironi, l'abiatico della vecchia marchesa.

2. Antenato.

Moretti, 32-116: Camere... piene di tante goffaggini, oleografie, ritratti dei padroni di casa, d'abiatici, che non sono stati neppure Reggenti.

= Lat. mediev. *abiaticus* o *aviaticus* (nella *Lex Longobardorum*, del sec. XI), dal lat. class. *avus* (attraverso l'agg. **avius*: dell'avo, nipote dell'avo). È voce dell'Italia settentrionale.

```
<entry>
  <form type="lemma">
    <orth>Abiàtico</orth>
  </form>
  <form type="variant">
    <orth>(abbiàtico, aviàtico)</orth>
  </form>
  <gramGrp>
    <gram type="partOfSpeech">sm. </gram>
    <gram type="subc">(femm. abiàtica, abbiàtica)</gram>
</gramGrp>
<sense level="1" n="1">
  <def>Dial. Nipote (figlio del figlio o della figlia).</def>
  <cit>
    <bibl> Comp. Antico Testamento [Tommaseo]:</bibl>
    <quote> Seppe... come lo aveva trovato in lo bosco e comprese che questo era suo abiatico.</quote>
    <bibl>Vite di imperatori romani [Tommaseo] :</bibl>
    <quote> Tiberio voleva piuttosto che succedesse questo suo abiatico che questo Gaio.</quote>
    <bibl>Idem [Tommaseo]:</bibl>
    <quote> La figlia e le abiatiche fece usare all'esercizio della lana.</quote>
    <bibl>Fogazzaro, 5-18:</bibl>
    <quote> A poppa sotto la bandiera, v'era seduto don Franco Maironi, l'abiatico della vecchia marchesa.</quote>
  </cit>
</sense>
<sense level="1" n="2">
  <def>2. Antenato.</def>
  <cit>
    <bibl>Moretti, 32-116:</bibl>
    <quote> Camere... piene di tante goffaggini, oleografie, ritratti dei padroni di casa, d'abiatici, che non sono stati
neppure Reggenti.</quote>
  </cit>
 </sense>
 <etym>= Lat. mediev. abiaticus o aviaticus (nella Lex Longobardorum, del sec. XI), dal lat. class. avus (attraverso l'agg.
'avius : dell'avo, nipote dell'avo). È voce dell'Italia settentrionale.</etym>
</entry>
```

Figure 1: TEI representation of the *abiàtico* GDLI entry

Quotation extraction is part of this iterative process. In what follows we briefly exemplify the TEI XML conversion of the GDLI quotation macrofield, which includes author, reference and quotation text information. Figure 1 exemplifies the source GDLI entry and the automatically generated TEI XML counterpart for the lemma *abiàtico* 'grandchild'. It can be seen that, for each sense, the set of quotations is annotated using the <cit> element which in turn contains one or more pairs of <bibl>/<quote> elements, respectively encoding a loosely-structured bibliographic citation (whose sub-components are not further structured at the moment) and the quotation text. For this case study we used only volumes I and II of GDLI, for which the manual revision of entry segmentation was completed.

3.2 GDLI-QC Composition

We developed two sub-corpora selected to be representative of the whole GDLI-QC. The most cited authors in the dictionary were considered (cf. Biffi and Guadagnini, 2022), choosing those who would allow to cover the widest chronological span. These writers are milestones in Italian literature and history of Italian language, such as Dante, Boccaccio, Petrarca, Ariosto and Manzoni. Their different linguistic features, determined by diachronic and stylistic factors, are very valuable to test and possibly retrain linguistic annotation tools, that, as we already observed, are usually trained on contemporary language varieties (typically, newswire texts). Moreover, we chose authors and works representative of different text typologies: texts belong to several genres, such as chronicle, literary prose, poetry, treatises. This is a first experiment carried out with a view to the future structuring of GDLI-QC in balanced sub-corpora both in diachrony and based on text belonging to different genres.

Author	Century	Quotes	Tokens
Dante Alighieri (*Convivio*)	XIV	100	2839
Giovanni and Matteo Villani (*Nuova Cronica*)	XIV	100	2114
Giovanni Boccaccio (*Decameron*)	XIV	100	2681
Leon Battista Alberti	XV	100	1931
Baldassarre Castiglione	XVI	100	2307
Niccolò Machiavelli	XVI	100	2102
Giorgio Vasari	XVI	100	2549
Daniello Bartoli	XVII	100	2843
Giambattista Vico	XVII-XVIII	100	2149
Giacomo Leopardi	XVIII-XIX	100	2089
Alessandro Manzoni (*I promessi sposi* [1840])	XIX	100	2327
Ippolito Nievo	XIX	100	2363
Oscar Luigi Pirandello	XIX-XX	100	1982
Alberto Moravia	XX	100	2166
Vasco Pratolini	XX	100	2294
	tot.	1500	34736

Table 1: Annotated GDLI-QC_prose composition

As a result, the first nucleus of GDLI-QC are two balanced sub-corpora, concerning works written between 14th and 20th century: one collecting 1500 prose quotes (henceforth,

Annotated GDLI-QC_prose) from 15 authors (100 each), see Table 1; one gathering 500 poetry quotes (henceforth, Annotated GDLI-QC_poetry) from 10 authors (50 each), see Table 2. Annotated GDLI-QC_prose size is about 35.000 tokens, whereas Annotated GDLI-QC_poetry is about 10.000.

Author	Century	Quotes	Tokens
Francesco Petrarca	XIV	50	1043
Matteo Maria Boiardo	XV	50	1109
Ludovico Ariosto	XVI	50	1115
Torquato Tasso	XVI	50	1152
Giovan Battista Marino	XVII	50	1111
Vittorio Alfieri	XVIII	50	1099
Ugo Foscolo	XVIII-XIX	50	947
Giosuè Carducci	XIX-XX	50	937
Giovanni Pascoli	XIX-XX	50	880
Eugenio Montale	XX	50	762
	tot.	500	10115

Table 2. Annotated GDLI-QC_poetry composition

4. Linguistic Annotation

Next step was corpus annotation. First, texts were preprocessed to reach a unified text segmentation. In fact, each quote of both sub-corpora was processed as an individual sentence; furthermore, we removed slashes, used to separate lines in poetry quotes, to focus on the underlying syntactic structure while disregarding the verse unity (which potentially pertains a distinct annotation layer). We could do that also because GDLI quotations are syntactically complete. This means that, already in the dictionary, poetry quotations are considered as "normal" sentences.

Both sub-corpora were automatically annotated through Stanza (Qi et al., 2020), a state-of-art fully neural pipeline for multilingual NLP trained on Universal Dependencies treebanks (UD, De Marneffe et al. 2021). Annotation concerned tokenization, POS tagging and lemmatization (sentence splitting was not needed here due to the overlapping with the quotation).

Automatic annotation was then manually revised and whenever needed corrected to create gold standard corpora. Regarding lemmatization, we chose a low-level lemmatization strategy; in fact, we kept the same graphical and phonological features for historical variants (e.g. *amministragione* vs *amministrazione*) and allotropes (e.g. *vizio* vs *vezzo),* which potentially cause errors in all models. The only exception regards variants with apocope (*cor* vs *core*, *fratel* vs *fratello* etc.), because this linguistic phenomenon, widespread in poetic language, is also common in contemporary Italian (*dir* vs *dire*, *buon* vs *buono* etc.). Normalization of lemma variants will be carried out as a post-processing step, in order to make it possible—in perspective—to query the corpus on different abstraction levels.

To improve the POS tagging and lemmatization accuracy on historical varieties of Italian, each gold Annotated GDLI-QC sub-corpus was split in two parts: 80% was used for retraining, and the remaining 20% for testing.

ISDT, the biggest UD treebank for contemporary Italian (Bosco et al., 2013), was used in combination with corpora representative of the historical varieties of language to be analysed, in particular: for prose annotation, the VoDIM annotated corpus (Favaro et al., 2020) and the Annotated GDLI-QC_prose sub-corpus to be used for training; for poetry annotation, the Annotated GDLI-QC_poetry sub-corpus was also used for retraining. Tables 3 and 4 show the composition of the corpora used for retraining, for prose and poetry respectively.

Training corpus	Tokens
ISDT	260173
VoDIM	16250
Annotated GDLI-QC_prose	27711
tot.	304310

Table 3. Annotated GDLI-QC_prose training corpus

Training corpus	Tokens
ISDT	260173
VoDIM	16250
Annotated GDLI-QC_prose	27711
Annotated GDLI-QC_poetry	8090
tot.	312400

Table 4. Annotated GDLI-QC_poetry training corpus

5. Evaluation of POS Tagging and Lemmatization

Tables 5 and 6 show the accuracy scores respectively obtained for POS tagging and lemmatization, with the baseline and retrained models.

	UPOS	XPOS	UFeats
Baseline Model	96%	96%	96%
GDLI-QC prose retrained Model	97%	97%	96%
Baseline Model	92%	92%	92%
GDLI-QC poetry retrained Model	94%	94%	93%

Table 5. POS tagging accuracy

	Lemma
Baseline Model	94%
GDLI-QC prose retrained Model	97%
Baseline Model	90%
GDLI-QC poetry retrained Model	94%

Table 6. Lemmatization accuracy

As a baseline, we used the Stanza "combined" model, pre-trained with a combination of available Italian UD treebanks. The retrained models for prose and poetry were obtained by using the training corpora listed in Tables 3 and 4 above. To test the performances of the different models (baseline and retrained), we used a 5-fold cross validation. So, the results in the tables are an average of 5 training iterations and 5 test set evaluations.

Let us compare now the overall results achieved with the baseline and retrained models. Contrary to our expectations, baseline POS tagging models are still effective in relation to GDLI-QC_prose, even in the case of older diachronic varieties (see below). Indeed, the accuracy of the GDLI-QC prose retrained POS tagging model increases only by 1% for both Universal POS (UPOS) and language-specific POS (XPOS). No improvement is reported for what concerns Universal Features (UFeats), showing the same value in both baseline and retrained models. Regarding GDLI-QC_poetry, the accuracy distance between the baseline POS tagging model and the GDLI-QC poetry retrained model is bigger (+2% for UPOS and XPOS, +1% for UFeats). This distance further increases if we consider lemmatization results: both retrained lemmatizers show higher accuracy values (97% for prose and 94% for poetry). Although there is still room for improvement, we believe that the strategy adopted is already able to effectively face the language variability and complexity typical of historical varieties of language.

A last remark is in order here. Namely, model retraining doesn't require a large amount of data. Performances significantly increase through just a handful of tokens concerning specific historical varieties: for prose they represent 15% of the whole training corpus and for poetry 17%.

		Baseline Model		Retrained Model	
Author	Century	POS	Lemma	POS	Lemma
Dante	XIV	95%	91%	95%	95%
Villani	XIV	98%	96%	98%	98%
Boccaccio	XIV	94%	93%	95%	97%
Alberti	XV	91%	87%	93%	93%
Castiglione	XVI	98%	93%	98%	97%
Machiavelli	XVI	96%	93%	97%	96%
Vasari	XVI	98%	96%	98%	97%
Bartoli	XVII	97%	95%	97%	97%
Vico	XVII-XVIII	96%	96%	97%	98%
Leopardi	XVIII-XIX	98%	94%	99%	98%
Manzoni	XIX	97%	96%	98%	98%
Nievo	XIX	98%	96%	98%	99%
Pirandello	XIX-XX	98%	96%	97%	98%
Moravia	XX	98%	95%	98%	98%
Pratolini	XX	98%	97%	98%	97%

Table 7. Authors accuracy (GDLI-QC prose)

We also carried out an analysis of the annotation accuracy registered for single authors, detailed in Tables 7 and 8 (note that POS accuracy values refer here to the Universal POS, UPOS).

		Baseline Model		Retrained Model	
	Century	POS	lemma	POS	lemma
Petrarca	XIV	86%	86%	91%	95%
Boiardo	XV	92%	88%	97%	93%
Ariosto	XVI	93%	90%	94%	94%
Tasso	XVI	91%	91%	96%	95%
Marino	XVII	94%	90%	93%	94%
Alfieri	XVIII	91%	87%	91%	95%
Foscolo	XVIII-XIX	91%	89%	96%	96%
Carducci	XIX-XX	95%	92%	97%	96%
Pascoli	XIX-XX	96%	90%	95%	95%
Montale	XX	96%	92%	95%	95%

Table 8. Authors accuracy (GDLI-QC poetry)

In general, POS tagging and lemmatization results achieved with retrained models show a significant improvement with respect to the baseline. The biggest difference between baseline and retrained models is recorded for Alberti (prose), Petrarca and Alfieri (poetry). Only for Petrarca this distance could be explained in terms of diachronic factors: most part of the errors involves historical variants, such as functional words with apheresis (*'l* vs *il*), words with single consonant instead of double (*abassare* vs *abbassare*), verbal polimorphy (*fuor* vs *furono*), to mention only a few. These kinds of errors are fewer in the retrained model (5 vs 18 in the baseline model), but still significant since they represent 56% of the total number of errors (in the baseline model the error percentage was 67%). For Alberti and Alfieri, annotation difficulties are more likely concerned with other features of their language use. For example, Alberti adopted an Italian language graphically near to Latin, making even functional elementary words like conjunction *e* 'and' (in Alberti *et*) difficult to process. In particular, we observe that *et* and words with similar graphical features (*adricto* vs *addiritto*, old italian form for *diritto* or *dritto*; *adviato* vs *avviato* etc.) cover 30% of the errors in the baseline model, whereas this percentage drops to 12% in the retrained model.On the other hand, Alfieri uses in his verses a solemn style, full of classical poetic forms, both phonological—many words are contracted with apocope, e.g. *cor*, *figliuol*—and lexical (*alma*, *nascoso*, *prisco* etc.) variants, that correspond to 57% of errors in the baseline model, and drop to 27% in the retrained.

Besides the individual cases reported above, it is very interesting to note that retrained models reach very good results also in relation to Middle Ages authors, especially with prose quotations. For example, Villani's (14th century) accuracy scores are very close to values reported for 19th and 20th century authors.

Stylistic features also affect POS tagging performances, due to complex and archaic syntactic constructions occurring in these texts. Consider, for example, the following Alfieri's quotation from *Rime* (Maggini F. ed., Firenze, 1933, 83):

> *«Cede ei talor, ma ai tempi rei non serve; abbonito e temuto da chi regna, non men che dalle schiave alme proterve»* (Eng. 'Sometimes he surrenders, but in guilty times (it) doesn't serve; calmed down and feared by those who reign, not less than by insolent slave souls')

where the sequence *schiave alme proterve* represents a complex syntactic structure, used mostly in poetry as a figure of speech, formed by a noun nestled between two adjectives, one on its right, one on its left. So, because of the rare syntactic construction as well as the rare used poetic words (*alme* and *proterve*), only *schiave* 'slave' was properly tagged as an adjective by the models, whereas *alme* 'souls' and *proterve* 'indolent' were erroneously annotated as verbs (instead of noun and adjective, respectively), which also lead to lemmatization errors.

These preliminary results require further investigation; however, they clearly show that diachronic factors are not the only ones contributing to the distance between the investigated authors and contemporary Italian. Underlying this distance there could be stylistic factors, or the textual genre or the linguistic register the text belongs to (see Favaro et al., 2020). The used reference editions represent another variable that will need to be carefully evaluated and managed in subsequent developments.

6. Conclusions

We presented the first steps towards the creation of a linguistically annotated diachronic corpus for Italian, including both prose and poetry and covering a wide timespan (going from the 14th to the 20th century), which is compliant with respect to the current *de facto* representation standard of Universal Dependencies. We focused on the design, preprocessing and composition of the corpus and on the adaptation of annotation tools to reliably process diachronic varieties of language use. The encouraging results achieved so far suggest that it will soon be possible to linguistically annotate the whole GDLI-QC with a high degree of accuracy, which however can be further improved. Current directions of research include: experiments aimed at identifying the most appropriate model for processing texts of a given author or specific variety of language use; the definition of an incremental strategy for lemmatizing texts characterized by a high degree of variability.

7. Acknowledgements

This work was supported by the project "Trattamento Automatico di Varietà Storiche di Italiano" ('Automatic processing of historical varieties of Italian', TrAVaSI) funded by Regione Toscana (POR FSE 2014 - 2020) with the financial support of Accademia della Crusca.

8. Bibliographical References

Biffi, M. (2018), Tra fiorentino aureo e fiorentino cinquecentesco. Per uno studio della lingua dei lessicografi. In La Crusca e i testi. Lessicografia, tecniche editoriali e collezionismo librario intorno al Vocabolario del 1612, a cura di Gino Belloni e Paolo Trovato, Padova, libreriauniversitaria.it edizioni, pp. 543-560.

Biffi, M. and Guadagnini, E. (2022), «Le citazioni riconducono il dizionario nell'ambito della letteratura e della vita»: un primo sguardo d'insieme sui citati del *GDLI*, Studi di Lessicografia Italiana, in press.

Biffi, M. and Sassolini, E. (2020), Strategie e metodi per il recupero di dizionari storici, in Marras, C., Passarotti, M., Franzini, G. & Litta, E. (Eds), La svolta inevitabile: sfide e prospettive per l'informatica umanistica. Atti del IX Convegno Annuale dell'Associazione per l'Informatica Umanistica e la Cultura Digitale (AIUCD, 15-17 gennaio 2020), Milan: Associazione per l'Informatica Umanistica e la Cultura Digitale, pp. 235-239.

Bollmann M. (2013), POS Tagging for Historical Texts with Sparse Training Data. In Proceedings of the 7th Linguistic Annotation Workshop & Interoperability with Discourse, pages 11-18, Sofia, Bulgaria, August. Association for Computation Linguistics (ACL).

Bosco, C., Montemagni, S., and Simi, M. (2013). Converting Italian Treebanks: Towards an Italian Stanford Dependency Treebank. In Proceedings of the "7th Linguistic Annotation Workshop & Interoperability with Discourse" (August 8-9, 2013), pages 61-69, Sofia, Bulgaria, August. Association for Computation Linguistics (ACL).

Burgassi C. and Guadagnini E. (2017), La tradizione delle parole. Sondaggi di lessicologia storica, Strasbourg, ÉLiPhi.

D'Achille P. and Grossmann M. (2017), Per la storia della formazione delle parole in italiano. Un nuovo corpus in rete (MIDIA) e nuove prospettive di studio, Florence, Italy: Franco Cesati.

De Felice, I., Dell'Orletta, F., Venturi, F., Lenci, A. and Montemagni S. (2018), Italian in the Trenches: Linguistic Annotation and Analysis of Text of the Great War. In Proceedings of 5th Italian Conference on Computational Linguistics (CLiC-it, 10-12 dicembre 2018), pages 160-164, Torino, Italy, December. Associazione Italiana di Linguistica Computazionale (AILC).

De Marneffe M. C., Manning C. D., Nivre J. and Zeman D., Universal Dependencies, Computational Linguistics, 47(2): 255-308.

Dereza O. (2018), Lemmatization for Ancient Languages: Rules or Neural Networks?, in Ustalov D., Filchenkov A., Pivovarova L. & Žižka J. (Eds), Artificial Intelligence and Natural Language 7th International Conference, AINL 2018 St. Petersburg, Russia, October 17–19, 2018 Proceedings, Cham, Switzerland: Springer, pp. 35-47.

Favaro M., Biffi M. and Montemagni S. (2020), Risorse e strumenti per le varietà storiche dell'italiano: il progetto TrAVaSI. In Proceedings of the Seventh Italian Conference on Computational Linguistics (CLiC-it 2020), Online, Bologna, Italy. Associazione Italiana di Linguistica Computazionale (AILC).

Hawke, A. (2016), Quotation Evidence and Definitions. In Durkin P. (Ed.), The Oxford Handbook of Lexicography, Oxford University Press, pp. 176-202.

Hämäläinen M., Partanen N. and Alnajjar K. (2021), Lemmatization of Historical Old Literary Finnish Texts in Modern Orthography. In Actes de la 28e Conférence sur le

Traitement Automatique des Langues Naturelles, pages 189-198, Lille, France, June. TANL-RECITAL.

Hoffmann, S. (2004), Using the OED quotations database as a corpus: A linguistic appraisal. “ICAME Journal”, 28, pp. 17-30.

Hupkes D. and Bod R. (2016), POS-tagging of Historical Dutch. In LREC 2016: Tenth International Conference on Language Resources and Evaluation (May 23-28), pages 77-82, Portorož, Slovenia, May. European Language Resource Association (ELRA).

Iacobini C., De Rosa A., Schirato G., Part-of-Speech tagging strategy for MIDIA: a diachronic corpus of the Italian language, in Proceedings of the First Italian Conference on Computational Linguistics CLiC-it 2014 & and of the Fourth International Workshop EVALITA 2014, 9-11 December 2014, pages 213-218, Pisa, Italy, December. Associazione Italiana di Linguistica Computazione (AILC).

Kabatek J. (2013), ¿Es posible una lingüística histórica basada en un corpus representativo?, Iberoromania, 77, pages 8-28.

Lenci, A., Montemagni, S., Boschetti, F., De Felice, I., De Rossi, F., Dell’Orletta, F., Di Giorgio, M., Miliani, M., Passaro, L. C., Puddu, A., Venturi, G., and Labanca, N. (2020), Voices of the Great War: A Richly Annotated Corpus of Italian Texts on the First World War. In Proceedings of the 12th Conference on Language Resources and Evaluation (LREC 2020, 11– 16 maggio 2020), pages 911-918, Marseille, France, May. European Language Resource Association (ELRA).

LIZ 4.0: letteratura italiana Zanichelli CD-ROM dei testi della letteratura italiana. Stoppelli, P., Picchi, E. (Eds.), Zanichelli, 2001

Marazzini, C. and Maconi L. (2018), Il Vocabolario dinamico dell’italiano moderno rispetto ai linguaggi settoriali. Proposta di voce lessicografica per il redigendo VoDIM, Italiano digitale, 7(4): 101-20.

Micheli, M.S. (2022), CODIT. A new resource for the study of Italian from a diachronic perspective: Design and applications in the morphological field, Corpus (23).

Onelli C., Proietti D., Seidenari C. and Tamburini F. (2006), The DiaCORIS project: a diachronic corpus of written Italian. In 5th Conference on Language Resources and Evaluation (LREC2006), pages 1212-1215, Genoa, Italy, May. European Language Resource Association (ELRA).

Pennacchiotti, M., Zanzotto, F.M. (2008). Natural Language Processing Across Time: An Empirical Investigation on Italian. In Proceedings of GoTAL - 6th International Conference on Natural Language Processing (25-27 August 2008), pages 371-382, Gothenburg, Sweden, August. Centre for Language Technology (CLT).

Piotrowski, M. (2012). Natural Language Processing for Historical Texts. Synthesis Lectures on Human Language Technologies, Morgan & Claypool Publishers, San Raphael, California.

Qi P., Zhang I., Zhang Y., Bolton J., Manning C. D. (2020), Stanza: A Python Natural Language Processing Toolkit for Many Human Languages. In Proceedings of the 58th Annual Meeting of the Association for Computational Linguistics: System Demonstrations, ACL 2020, July 5-10, pages 101-108, Online, July. Association for Computational Linguistics (ACL).

Rohdenburg, G. (2013), Using the OED quotations database as a diachronic corpus. In Krug M. et al. (Eds.), Research Methods in Language Variation and Change, Cambridge University Press, pp 136-157.

Sassolini, E., Fahad Khan, A., Biffi, M., Monachini, M. and Montemagni S. (2019), Converting and Structuring a Digital Historical Dictionary of Italian: A Case Study, in Kosem, I., Zingano Kuhn, T., Correia, M., Ferreria, J. P., Jansen, M., Pereira, I., Kallas, J., Jakubíček, M., Krek, S. & Tiberius, C. (Eds.), Electronic lexicography in the 21st century: Smart lexicography. Proceedings of the eLex 2019 conference (1-3 October 2019, Sintra, Portugal), Brno: Lexical Computing CZ, pp. 603-621.

Sassolini, E., Biffi, M., De Blasi, F., Guadagnini, E., and Montemagni, S. (2021), La digitalizzazione del GDLI: un approccio linguistico per la corretta acquisizione del testo?. In Boschetti, F., Del Grosso A. M. & Salvatori E. (Eds.), AIUCD 2021 - DHs for society: e-quality, participation, rights and values in the Digital Age. Book of extended abstracts of the 10th national conference, Pisa: Associazione per l’Informatica Umanistica e la Cultura Digitale, pp. 159-166.

Squillacioti, P. (2021), I progetti digitali dell’OVI. “Griseldaonline”, 20, 2, pp. 197-203.

Tonelli, S., Sprugnoli, R., Moretti, G., & Kessler, F. B. "Prendo la Parola in Questo Consesso Mondiale: A Multi-Genre 20th Century Corpus in the Political Domain". In Proceedings of CLiC-it 2019.

Yang. I., Eisenstein J. (2016), Part-of-Speech Tagging for Historical English. In Proceedings of the 2016 Conference of the North American Chapter of the Association for Computational Linguistics: Human Language Technologies, (June 2016), pages 1318-1328, San Diego, California, June. Association for Computational Linguistics (ACL).

Proceedings of the Second Workshop on Language Technologies for Historical and Ancient Languages (LT4HALA 2022), pages 101–107
Language Resources and Evaluation Conference (LREC 2022), Marseille, 25 June 2022

Automatic Translation Alignment for Ancient Greek and Latin

Tariq Yousef*, Chiara Palladino†, David J. Wright†, Monica Berti*
*University of Leipzig
Augustusplatz 10, 04109 Leipzig, Germany
{tariq.yosef, monica.berti}@uni-leipzig.de

†Furman University
3300 Poinsett Highway, 29613, Greenville SC, USA
chiara.palladino@furman.edu, djwrig85@gmail.com

Abstract

This paper presents the results of automatic translation alignment experiments on text corpus in Ancient Greek translated into Latin. We used a state-of-the-art alignment workflow based on a contextualized multilingual language model that is fine-tuned on the alignment task for Ancient Greek and Latin. The model is fine-tuned on monolingual Ancient Greek texts, bilingual parallel datasets, and manually aligned sentences. The performance of the alignment model is evaluated on an alignment gold standard dataset consisting of 100 parallel fragments aligned manually by two domain experts, with a 90.5% Inter-Annotator-Agreement (IAA). An interactive online interface is provided to enable users to explore the aligned fragments collection and examine the alignment model's output.

Keywords: Translation Alignment, Multilingual Language Models, Evaluation, Alignment Gold Standards

1. Introduction

Translation alignment is the process of finding translation equivalents between a text and its translations. It can be performed at various levels of granularity, from document or paragraph level to word level. It is an important task in Natural Language Processing and Digital Humanities: besides its key role in statistical machine translation (Brown et al., 1993), parallel text alignment has a variety of applications, including cross-lingual annotation projection (Müller, 2017; Xia et al., 2021), language learning (Palladino et al., 2021), and bilingual lexicon induction (Aker et al., 2014; Shi et al., 2021).

Brown et al. (1993) were the first to develop automatic alignment models (*IBM Models*) aiming to extract translation pairs from bilingual corpora. Later, (Och and Ney, 2000) created *Giza++*, an alignment tool based on IBM models and Hidden-Markov alignment models. The continuous efforts made in this field have led to the development of several statistical alignment tools, such as fast_align (Dyer et al., 2013) and EfLoMAl (Östling and Tiedemann, 2016) that outperformed the previous tools on many languages pairs. A new generation of automatic alignment models has emerged with the advances in neural machine translation systems and multilingual contextualized language models. The recent studies employ pre-trained multilingual contextualized word embeddings (Jalili Sabet et al., 2020; Dou and Neubig, 2021) or the attention weights between the encoder and decoder of neural machine translation models (Garg et al., 2019; Chen et al., 2020) to extract translation equivalents from two parallel texts.

1.1. The Challenge of Translation Models for Ancient Languages

In the domain of ancient and generally low-resourced languages, automatic models for translation alignment are still underdeveloped, often due to the lack of large and readily available digitized texts with parallel translations. For Ancient Greek and Latin, the language pair examined in this study, the scarcity is even more staggering, since very little of the hundreds of Latin translations of Greek literature, from the Renaissance to the 19th century, has ever been digitized. Moreover, there are very few manually aligned datasets or gold standards for ancient languages and their translations. These resources are essential to improve automatic translation models, either as training data for automatic methods, or as gold standards against which machine outputs may be tested. To facilitate the collection of alignment pairs and gold standards, various tools have been designed for modern languages (Yousef and Jänicke, 2022). In the case of ancient and low-resourced languages, there are two main web-platforms publicly available: Alpheios [1] and Ugarit [2], which was used in this study [3].

The work presented here uses one of the most extensive digitally available parallel corpora of ancient texts, the *Digital Fragmenta Historicorum Graecorum* (DFHG), which includes over 8000 fragments of Ancient Greek historiographical works and their transla-

[1] https://alpheios.net/.

[2] http://ugarit.ialigner.com/.

[3] The space of this paper does not allow for an extensive description of Ugarit. More information on the tool and its various applications for ancient languages can be found in (Palladino et al., 2021; Yousef et al., 2022)

tions into Latin. We follow the alignment workflow proposed by (Jalili Sabet et al., 2020; Dou and Neubig, 2021), which utilizes contextualized multilingual word embeddings to measure the semantic similarity among the tokens in every two parallel fragments. The contextualized embeddings are generated by a multilingual language model trained and fine-tuned for historical languages. We also created a gold standard dataset annotated manually by two domain experts with alignment guidelines, against which we tested the model's performance. The results are available in an interactive web-based user interface [4] where users can explore the aligned corpus and examine the output of the alignment model. The pre-trained language model is available on `https://huggingface.co/UGARIT/grc-alignment`.

2. The Corpus

The DFHG is the digital open version of the five volumes of the first big printed collection of ancient Greek fragmentary historians edited by Karl Müller in the 19th century[5]. The collection gathers more than eight thousand quotations and text-reuses (*fragments*) of lost works written by more than six hundred authors ranging from the 6th century BC through the 7th century CE (Berti, 2019a; Berti, 2021). Fragments are extracted from still extant source texts and are generally constituted by short passages with information about the relevant lost author and work.

Almost every Greek fragment is translated or shortened into Latin. Limits are of course represented by the fact that the Latin of the corpus is the language used by philologists in the 19th century and not the language of ancient sources. In spite of that, the alignment is very useful not only for translation studies, but also for generating data that can be used for other philological corpora. An example is represented by Named Entities (personal names, places, etc.) that are a strong component of DFHG fragments and that contribute to the creation of authority lists, which are today needed for historical, philological, and linguistic studies (Berti, 2019b). All these characteristics make the DFHG corpus a precious data set for experimenting with translation alignment techniques of ancient languages.

The work described in the following sections has been produced starting with 636 structured XML files of the entire DFHG corpus that are arranged according to volumes and authors of the printed edition and that allow to automatically extract pairs of ancient Greek fragments and their corresponding Latin translations[6].

3. Creating a Gold Standard and Alignment Guidelines

To create the gold standard, 100 fragments randomly selected from the corpus were aligned manually by two experts using Ugarit. An Annotation Style Guide to ensure consistency in the gold standard was also designed in the following way: the two experts, who had previous experience with the alignment of Ancient Greek to Latin in Ugarit, drafted a preliminary set of shared rules together, assessing the most relevant issues (for example, establishing a strategy to manage the presence of articles, which exist in Greek but not in Latin, or defining how to handle enclitics and elliptical constructions). These preliminary rules formed the backbone of the Annotation Style Guide. The experts started the alignment process with a subset of fragments, and discussed issues as they encountered them, revising the Style Guide until it was deemed satisfactory. Then, the experts completed the alignment separately minimizing further discussion, to test the efficiency of the rules defined in the Guide. The gold standard and the guidelines are available on Github[7].

In order to estimate the reliability of the alignment guidelines and the quality of the alignment gold standards, we measured the Inter-Annotator-Agreement (IAA) on the manually annotated fragments, considering the agreement between the annotators on the aligned tokens and the unaligned ones. IAA is a measure that reflects how agreeably multiple annotators can make the same alignment decision for specific tokens.

Ugarit allows annotators to create multi-word alignments (1-to-N, N-to-1, and N-to-N). Therefore, we converted the multi-word alignments to 1-to-1 pairs in order to consider the partial matching of the translation pairs. For instance, the translation pair (A, B C) is considered as two translation pairs (A, B) and (A, C). The resulting IAA is 90.50% and calculated based on equation 1:

$$IAA = 2 * I/(A_1 + A_2) \qquad (1)$$

Where A_1 and A_2 be the flattened translation pair sets created by the first and second annotators, respectively, and I is the intersection between them.

To evaluate the performance of automatic alignment systems, (Och and Ney, 2003) proposed two categories of alignments, sure and possible alignments. We followed the same categorization when combining the alignments of the two annotators. We defined sure and possible alignment sets for every sentence as follows:

$$S = A_1 \cap A_2 \quad , \quad P = A_1 \cup A_2$$

Where A_1 and A_2 are the alignment sets created by the first and second annotators, S denotes sure alignments which include all translation pairs where both annotators agree, P denotes possible alignments where the translation pairs are aligned by at least one annotator.

[4] http://ugarit.ialigner.com/dfhg/

[5] https://www.dfhg-project.org

[6] https://dfhg-project.github.io

[7] `https://github.com/UgaritAlignment/Alignment-Gold-Standards/tree/main/grc-lat`

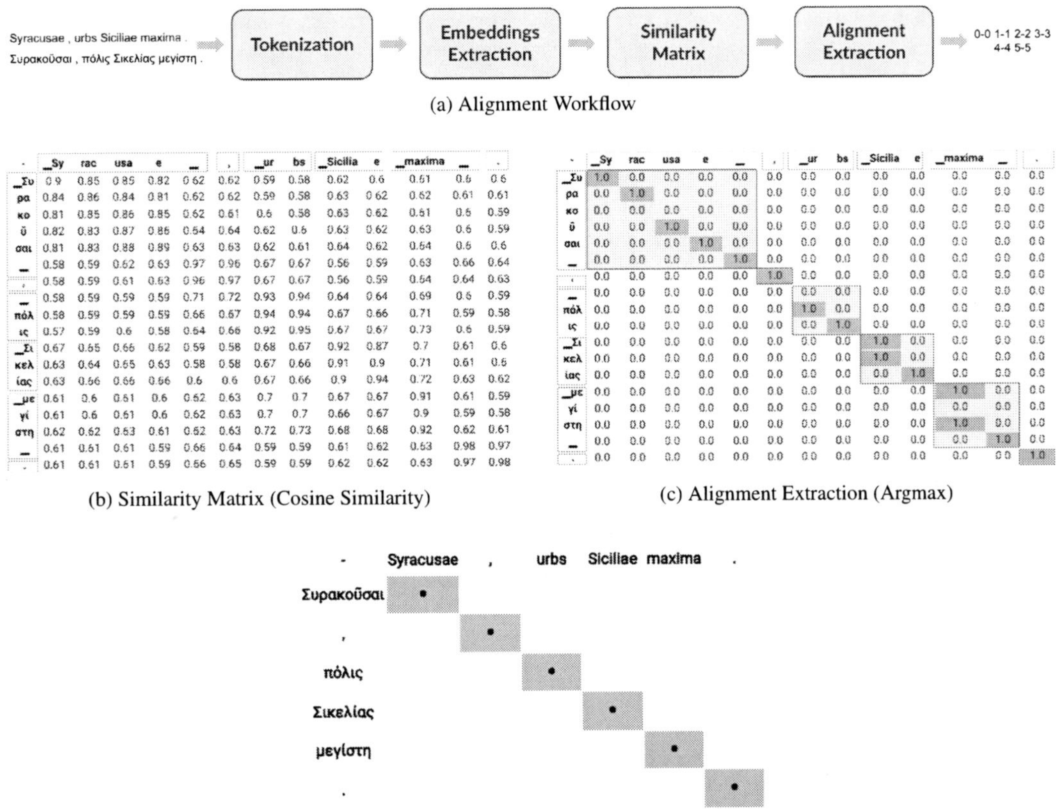

(a) Alignment Workflow

(b) Similarity Matrix (Cosine Similarity)

(c) Alignment Extraction (Argmax)

(d) Alignment Result

Figure 1: The alignment process and an example illustrates its workflow.

4. Automatic Alignment

Translation alignment process aims to map word-level equivalents between the source sentence $S = (s_1, s_2, .., s_n)$ and its translation $T = (t_1, t_2, .., t_m)$ (Brown et al., 1993). The process takes S and T as inputs, and produces the set $A = \{(s_i, t_j) : s_i \in S, t_j \in T\}$ where s_i is a translation equivalent of t_j.

Until recently, statistical translation alignment models such as *Giza++*, *fast_align*, and *EfLoMAl* were considered state-of-the-art. However, with the recent advances in language modelling and transformer models, new neural alignment models have been proposed and outperformed the statistical models.

In this paper, we use the state-of-the-art alignment workflow proposed by (Jalili Sabet et al., 2020) and (Dou and Neubig, 2021) which employs pre-trained multilingual contextualized language models to generate word alignments. Further, we fine-tune a language model that can align ancient Greek-English and ancient Greek-Latin with a novel training approach. It combines training over monolingual and bilingual datasets, in addition to supervised training over accurate word-level alignments annotated manually by experts on UGARIT.

4.1. Alignment Workflow

The alignment workflow consists of four main steps (figure 1a): The first step is tokenizing the two parallel sentences into two lists of tokens G and L. Then, extracting embeddings from pre-trained multilingual contextualized language models such as mBERT (Devlin et al., 2018) and XLM-RoBERTa (Conneau et al., 2019) or fine-tuned versions of them for each token. Both models use subword-based tokenization[8], but the tokenization method differs according to the underlying language model. For instance, mBERT uses *WordPiece Tokenizer* whereas XLM-RoBERTa uses a *byte-level BPE* tokenizer. In all experiments, the word embeddings were extracted from the 8th layer of mBERT and XLM-RoBERTa models, since it has achieved the best performance.

The next step is to generate a similarity matrix of size $m * n$ (Figure 1b) where $m = |L|, n = |G|$ and fill it

[8]A tokenization approach splits infrequent words into smaller meaningful subwords. It has shown great performance against word tokenization, especially with multilingual language models, by solving the problems of large vocabulary size and out-of-vocabulary tokens.

using the following formula:

$$\sum_{i}^{n}\sum_{j}^{m} SIM(i,j) = F_{sim}(t^{i}_{grc}, t^{j}_{lat}) \quad (2)$$

Where t^{i}_{grc} is the embedding vector of the ith token in G, t^{j}_{lat} is the embedding vector of the jth token in L, and F_{sim} is a similarity function between the two vectors such as *Cosine Similarity*, *Dot Product*, and *Euclidean distance*.
Once the similarity matrix is computed, alignments can be extracted by applying an extraction algorithm (Figure 1c). (Dou and Neubig, 2021) proposed two probability thresholding-based methods to extract alignments from the similarity matrix, namely, $Softmax$ and $Entmax$ (Peters et al., 2019). Dou and Neubig (2021) applies the extraction in two directions and then considers the intersection between them. Moreover, (Jalili Sabet et al., 2020) proposed three methods including $Argmax$, a baseline method , $Itermax$, an iterative method, and $Match$, a graph-based method.
The last step of the alignment workflow is to convert subword-level alignments to word-level alignments. For this purpose we follow the heuristic principle *"two words are aligned if any of their subwords are aligned"* as in Jalili-Sabet et al. (2020), (Zenkel et al., 2020), and Dou and Neubig (2021) (Figure 1d).

4.2. Language Models

The existing multilingual contextualized language models mBERT and XLM-RoBERTa are not trained on ancient Greek texts but on modern Greek, which is very different. Therefore, we had to train and fine-tune them with ancient Greek texts to enable them to process ancient Greek texts. To this end, we propose a training approach that consists of three main phases:
- ***Ex1***: in this initial phase, we train the models on 12 million Ancient Greek tokens with Masked Language Model (MLM) training objective. The training dataset is extracted from the Perseus Digital Library, the First1KGreek Project[9], and the PROIEL, PERSEUS[10], and Gorman [11] treebanking datasets.
- ***Ex2***: in this phase, we perform unsupervised fine-tuning of models obtained from the previous phase using 32500 Ancient Greek-English parallel sentences taken from the Perseus Digital Library[12] (*Iliad, Odyssey, Xenophon, New Testament*), in addition to 8000 Ancient Greek-Latin parallel fragments (DFHG Corpus)[13], with 4000 further parallel sentences taken from UGARIT database. The texts are in different languages, mainly Ancient Greek-English, Ancient Greek-Latin, and Ancient Greek-Georgian. The training objectives used in this phase are: Masked Language Model (MLM), Translation Language Modeling (TLM), Self-training Objective (SO), and Parallel Sentence Identification (PSI).
- ***Ex3***: in this phase, we perform supervised training with Self-training Objective (SO) to the fine-tuned models obtained after *EX2* using manually word-level aligned dataset provided by UGARIT. The alignments are accurate and clean since they are done by scholars, teachers, and experts. The dataset consists of 2265 parallel texts and almost 100k translation pairs.
The training objectives used in the experiments are proposed by (Dou and Neubig, 2021).

4.3. Evaluation

We evaluated the performance of the proposed alignment workflow based on our fine-tuned language models against the alignment gold standard by employing $Precision$, $Recall$, $F1$, and Alignment Error Rate (AER) which can be computed as in equations 3.

$$Precision = \frac{|A \cap P|}{|A|} \quad , \quad Recall = \frac{|A \cap S|}{|S|}$$
$$F1 = \frac{2 * Precision * Recall}{Precision + Recall} \quad (3)$$
$$AER = 1 - \frac{|A \cap P| + |A \cap S|}{|A| + |S|}$$

Where A indicates the alignments set predicted by the model, P and S indicate respectively the $Possible$ and $Sure$ alignment sets in the gold standards, and |.| denotes the length of the set.
As baseline models, we used *Giza++*, *fast_align*, and *EfLoMAl* with their default parameters trained on the whole DFHG dataset.
Table 1 shows poor performance for the statistical models *Giza++* and *fast_algin* since they require a vast parallel corpus, and because of the high number of unique word forms in the corpus (66% of the ancient Greek words and 59% of the Latin, Table **??**).
Further, The table shows that the baseline models outperform the zero-shot XLM-RoBERTa and mBERT with all extraction algorithms, which is understandable since both models are trained on modern Greek, which differs significantly from ancient Greek. The results also show that training the models on monolingual ancient Greek texts (Ex1) enhanced the performance of the alignment workflow and reduced the *AER* significantly. Both models at this point outperformed *Giza++* and *fast_align* but underperformed *EfLoMAl*.
Further performance enhancement is accomplished by fine-tuning the models with bilingual sentences (Ex2); the model outperforms all baseline models significantly. Moreover, the remarkable enhancement has been achieved by incorporating supervised signals by fine-tuning the models on word-level manually aligned parallel texts (Ex3) with the Self-training Objective (SO). SO encourages the aligned words to have closer

[9] https://opengreekandlatin.github.io/First1KGreek/
[10] https://universaldependencies.org
[11] https://vgorman1.github.io/
[12] https://github.com/PerseusDL/canonical-greekLit
[13] The 100 fragments used as gold standard are excluded.

		Precision		Recall		F1		AER	
Baseline	Giza++	55.03%		67.61%		60.67%		39.48%	
	fast_align	51.64%		70.51%		59.62%		40.67%	
	EfLoMAl	76.79%		78.12%		77.45%		22.57%	
		XLM-RoBERTa				mBERT			
		Precision	Recall	F1	AER	Precision	Recall	F1	AER
Zero-Shot	Softmax	49.35%	42.10%	45.44%	54.49%	55.40%	51.52%	53.39%	46.55%
	Argmax	62.10%	41.88%	50.02%	49.77%	80.25%	34.86%	48.61%	50.87%
Ex1	Softmax	63.79%	57.61%	60.54%	39.40%	65.89%	69.49%	67.64%	32.41%
	Argmax	75.15%	59.20%	66.23%	33.61%	81.20%	55.43%	65.88%	33.84%
Ex2	Softmax	80.89%	82.68%	81.78%	18.24%	82.48%	83.91%	83.19%	16.83%
	Argmax	86.71%	81.74%	84.15%	15.79%	87.94%	78.55%	82.98%	16.90%
Ex3	Softmax	88.94%	89.13%	89.03%	10.97%	85.67%	84.64%	85.15%	14.83%
	Argmax	91.49%	87.32%	89.36%	**10.60%**	90.15%	78.26%	83.79%	16.09%

Table 1: Evaluation Results, The evaluation was conducted using the five extraction approaches, but we mentioned only the top two.

contextualized representations, increasing their semantic similarity. We also noticed that supervised training had a greater impact on the performance of fine-tuned XLM-RoBERTa than fine-tuned mBERT model.

Figure 2 shows a visual evaluation (Yousef and Jänicke, 2022) of the output of two alignment extraction approaches based on the fine-tuned XML-RoBERTa language model of Ex3. The agreement is shown in green color, big and small dots denotes gold standards sure and possible alignments. As we can see, *Softmax* predicts more translation pairs than *Argmax*, and *Argmax* output is a subset of *Softmax* output, which explains why *Softmax* outperforms *Argmax* regarding the Recall and underperforms it regarding the Precision. A full comparison of different alignment models over the gold standard dataset is available under `http://vis4nlp.com/alignmenteval/`.

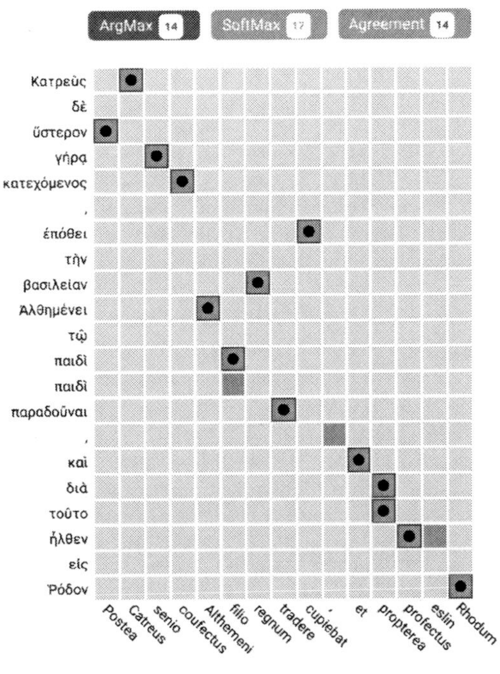

Figure 2: Alignment model (Ex3) output with two alignment extraction approaches compared to the gold standard.

4.4. Qualitative Evaluation

While quantitative evaluation provides a summarized overview of the quality of the models, it fails to provide an in-depth analysis of performance limitations, strengths, or frequent alignment errors. Therefore, we conducted a qualitative evaluation of the alignment output on 50 random fragments, performed by a domain expert.

The evaluation subset includes a total of 748 translation pairs with 40 incorrect pairs (5.35%). The model correctly aligned 54 of 54 prepositions (100%), 18 of 18 adverbs (100%), 186 of 188 Named-Entities (98.94%), 53 of 54 adjectives (98.15%), 53 of 54 conjunctions (98.15%), 40 of 41 pronouns (97.56%), 119 of 125 verbs (95.20%) and 125 of 133 substantives (93.98%).

Most recurrent errors are due to the absence of articles in Latin: Greek articles are sometimes incorrectly aligned with contextual Latin adjectives, pronouns, and substantives. Other limits are also due to elliptical constructions, where finding a certain match is more complex. Finally, Greek particles are variously aligned with Latin conjunctions and adverbs.

5. Conclusion

In this paper, we fine-tuned a multilingual language model that can align ancient Greek and Latin texts following a state-of-the-art alignment workflow. Moreover, we created a gold standard dataset to evaluate the model's performance. Both quantitative and qualitative evaluations confirmed the good performance of the model.

The main challenge we encountered was aligning long fragments. Since most of the fragments are long (over 100 tokens/fragments), there is a need to develop better text segmentation or sentence level alignment models. Further, this study was limited to the specific dataset of the DFHG, which is one of the largest digitized GRC-LAT parallel corpora available. However, in the future, we plan to include more diverse datasets, e.g. expanding towards other literary genres, such as poetry, by scouting available digital libraries and implementing our collaboration with Ugarit users who work on the alignment of these two languages. In addition, we also plan to expand the model and train it to include more language pairs such as ancient Greek-Italian, ancient Greek-French and further.

Acknowledgment

This project is developed thanks to the important contribution of our community of scholars and language learners: Gregory R. Crane, Chiara Palladino, Monica Berti, Farnoosh Shamsian, Maia Shukhoshvili, Anise D'Orange Ferreira, David J. Wright, Christopher Blackwell, Clifford Robinson, Brian Clark.

6. Bibliography

Aker, A., Paramita, M. L., Pinnis, M., and Gaizauskas, R. (2014). Bilingual dictionaries for all eu languages. In *LREC 2014 Proceedings*, pages 2839–2845. European Language Resources Association.

Berti, M. (2019a). Historical fragmentary texts in the digital age. In Monica Berti, editor, *Digital Classical Philology. Ancient Greek and Latin in the Digital Revolution*, pages 257–276. De Gruyter, Berlin.

Berti, M. (2019b). Named entity annotation for ancient greek with inception. In Kiril Simov et al., editors, *Proceedings of CLARIN Annual Conference 2019*, pages 1–4, Leipzig, Germany. CLARIN.

Berti, M. (2021). *Digital Editions of Historical Fragmentary Texts*. Digital Classics Books 5. Propylaeum, Heidelberg.

Brown, P. F., Della Pietra, S. A., Della Pietra, V. J., and Mercer, R. L. (1993). The mathematics of statistical machine translation: Parameter estimation. *Computational Linguistics*, 19(2):263–311.

Chen, Y., Liu, Y., Chen, G., Jiang, X., and Liu, Q. (2020). Accurate word alignment induction from neural machine translation. In *Proceedings of the 2020 Conference on Empirical Methods in Natural Language Processing (EMNLP)*, Online, November. Association for Computational Linguistics.

Conneau, A., Khandelwal, K., Goyal, N., Chaudhary, V., Wenzek, G., Guzmán, F., Grave, E., Ott, M., Zettlemoyer, L., and Stoyanov, V. (2019). Unsupervised cross-lingual representation learning at scale. *CoRR*, abs/1911.02116.

Devlin, J., Chang, M., Lee, K., and Toutanova, K. (2018). BERT: pre-training of deep bidirectional transformers for language understanding. *CoRR*, abs/1810.04805.

Dou, Z.-Y. and Neubig, G. (2021). Word alignment by fine-tuning embeddings on parallel corpora. In *Proceedings of the 16th Conference of the European Chapter of the Association for Computational Linguistics: Main Volume*, pages 2112–2128, Online, April. Association for Computational Linguistics.

Dyer, C., Chahuneau, V., and Smith, N. A. (2013). A simple, fast, and effective reparameterization of IBM model 2. In *Proceedings of the 2013 Conference of the North American Chapter of the Association for Computational Linguistics: Human Language Technologies*, pages 644–648, Atlanta, Georgia, June. Association for Computational Linguistics.

Garg, S., Peitz, S., Nallasamy, U., and Paulik, M. (2019). Jointly learning to align and translate with transformer models. In *Proceedings of the 2019 Conference on Empirical Methods in Natural Language Processing and the 9th International Joint Conference on Natural Language Processing (EMNLP-IJCNLP)*, pages 4453–4462, Hong Kong, China, November. Association for Computational Linguistics.

Jalili Sabet, M., Dufter, P., Yvon, F., and Schütze, H. (2020). SimAlign: High quality word alignments without parallel training data using static and contextualized embeddings. In *Findings of the Association for Computational Linguistics: EMNLP 2020*, pages 1627–1643, Online, November. Association for Computational Linguistics.

Müller, M. (2017). Treatment of markup in statistical machine translation. Association of Computational Linguistics.

Och, F. J. and Ney, H. (2000). Improved statistical alignment models. In *Proceedings of the 38th Annual Meeting on Association for Computational Linguistics*, ACL '00, page 440–447, USA. Association for Computational Linguistics.

Och, F. J. and Ney, H. (2003). A systematic comparison of various statistical alignment models. *Computational Linguistics*, 29(1):19–51.

Östling, R. and Tiedemann, J. (2016). Efficient word alignment with Markov Chain Monte Carlo. *Prague Bulletin of Mathematical Linguistics*, 106:125–146, October.

Palladino, C., Foradi, M., and Yousef, T. (2021). Translation alignment for historical language learning: a case study. *Digital Humanities Quarterly*, 15(3).

Peters, B., Niculae, V., and Martins, A. F. (2019). Sparse sequence-to-sequence models. In *Proceedings of the 57th Annual Meeting of the Association for Computational Linguistics*, pages 1504–1519.

Shi, H., Zettlemoyer, L., and Wang, S. I. (2021). Bilingual lexicon induction via unsupervised bitext construction and word alignment. *CoRR*, abs/2101.00148.

Xia, P., Qin, G., Vashishtha, S., Chen, Y., Chen, T., May, C., Harman, C., Rawlins, K., White, A. S., and Van Durme, B. (2021). Lome: Large ontology multilingual extraction. *arXiv preprint arXiv:2101.12175*.

Yousef, T. and Jänicke, S. (2022). Visual evaluation of translation alignment data. In *Proc. EuroVis*, volume 22.

Yousef, T., Palladino, C., Shamsian, F., and Foradi, M. (2022). Translation alignment with ugarit. *Information*, 13(2).

Zenkel, T., Wuebker, J., and DeNero, J. (2020). End-to-end neural word alignment outperforms GIZA++. In *Proceedings of the 58th Annual Meeting of the Association for Computational Linguistics*, pages 1605–1617, Online, July. Association for Computational Linguistics.

Proceedings of the Second Workshop on Language Technologies for Historical and Ancient Languages (LT4HALA 2022), pages 108–113
Language Resources and Evaluation Conference (LREC 2022), Marseille, 25 June 2022

Handling Stress in Finite-State Morphological Analyzers for Ancient Greek and Ancient Hebrew

Daniel G. Swanson, Francis M. Tyers
Department of Linguistics,
Indiana University,
{dangswan,ftyers}@iu.edu

Abstract

Modeling stress placement has historically been a challenge for computational morphological analysis, especially in finite-state systems because lexically conditioned stress cannot be modeled using only rewrite rules on the phonological form of a word. However, these phenomena can be modeled fairly easily if the lexicon's internal representation is allowed to contain more information than the pure phonological form. In this paper we describe the stress systems of Ancient Greek and Ancient Hebrew and we present two prototype finite-state morphological analyzers, one for each language, which successfully implement these stress systems by inserting a small number of control characters into the phonological form, thus conclusively refuting the claim that finite-state systems are not powerful enough to model such stress systems and arguing in favor of the continued relevance of finite-state systems as an appropriate tool for modeling the morphology of historical languages.

Keywords: Greek, Hebrew, finite-state

1. Introduction

Morphological analysis, the identification of lexical and morphological information for a given word form, is an important step in the study of texts, most basically for the tasks of searching and indexing, particularly in more inflected languages such as Greek and Hebrew.

Computational morphological analysis, moreover, has proved itself useful in searching and indexing (Crane, 1991), pedagogy (Packard, 1973), and translation (Forcada et al., 2011), among other tasks.

One of the most common ways to implement a morphological analyser has been to use Finite-State Transducers (FSTs), which specify a mapping between two sets of strings (in this case, surface form and morphological analysis) in a compact and efficient form.

Modeling stress, however, has historically been a challenge for FSTs, to the point of being called impossible to implement as a sequence of local rewrite rules (Smith, 2016). In this paper, we demonstrate two successful approaches to stress: a full stress-placement system for Ancient Greek and a simpler stress-shifting system for Ancient Hebrew.

Section 2 discusses prior work and the capacities of finite-state systems, Section 3 describes the relevant details of the Greek and Hebrew stress systems, Section 4 describes the implementation, Section 5 provides a quantitative evaluation of the current state of development, and Section 6 concludes.

2. Finite-State Morphology

Several morphological analyzers for Ancient Greek already exist, including the mostly finite-state Morpheus (Smith, 2016), though this system required an ad-hoc extension due to difficulties in formulating the Greek stress system as a sequence of rewrite rules.

We are not aware of any prior analyzers for Ancient Hebrew, though for Modern Hebrew, which is morphologically quite similar, there are several, such as HAMSAH (Yona and Wintner, 2008).

In both of these cases, it has been concluded that finite-state transducers are not up to the task of representing all the relevant morphological alternations in a maintainable way (Smith, 2016; Wintner, 2008). However, this is due to the assumption that the only available operations when building FSTs are appending suffixes and applying rewrite rules.

In fact, there are at least three other tools available to a grammar writer which, combined, make modeling complex morphological phenomena possible and make maintaining dictionaries as they expand much easier.

The first tool is interlacing lexical entries, which is supported by the lexicon compiler Lexd (Swanson and Howell, 2021). From the perspective of the grammar writer, they make lists of affixes and where they go in relation to the root and the compiler internally expands this into a sequence of append operations, making Hebrew's templatic morphology far easier to model. An example of how this can be used is given in Figure 1.

The second tool is constraints (Karttunen, 1991). These can be written in a format almost identical to rewrite rules, but they apply in parallel so the developer does not need to carefully sequence the operations. An example of such constraints is given in Figure 2.

The final tool is intersection. A lexicon compiler can be used to generate an FST containing all forms allowed by a language's phonotactics. This can then be composed or intersected with the analyzer, leaving only valid forms.

All of these tools have compilers available which allow the rules to be written in formats which closely resemble how the processes they model would be de-

```
LEXICON VerbRoot(3)
' m r[1']
' s p[1']
b ' {sh}[reg]
b d l[reg]
b h l[reg]

ALIAS VerbRoot C

PATTERN Pa'al
C(1) C(2) [:{~o}{*?}] C(3)[reg]
C(1) C(2) [:{~a}{*?}] C(3)[1']
```

Figure 1: A fragment of the lexicon and rules for generating Hebrew verbal stems. The `VerbRoot` lexicon contains the tri-consonantal verb roots, which each consonant in a separate column. Each root is also tagged with features that affect verb stem formation. Here the tags are `reg` for "regular" and `1'` for roots where the first consonant is the glottal stop א. The `ALIAS` line specifies an alternate name for the `VerbRoot` lexicon so that the stem patterns can be written more concisely. Finally, the last two lines specify how to insert vowels between the three consonants of the root to form the Pa'al (active) stem.

```
"schwa deletes before determiner"
@:0 <=> _ {h}: ;

"determiner before gutturals"
a:á <=> {h}: _ [ ' | {'} ] ;

"{h} deletes after vowel"
{h}:0 <=> Vowel: _ ;
```

Figure 2: The phonological rules controlling the realization of the Hebrew definite article. These can be read like rewrite rules (the second, for instance, reads "a becomes á if and only if it is preceded by some realization of {h} and followed by either ' (א) or {'} (ע)"). However, they are applied simultaneously, and thus the order they are written in has no effect.

scribed in theoretical linguistic analyses, which thus gives finite-state systems the advantage that the rules used to compile them are, in themselves, a form of linguistic documentation. Furthermore, since these rules have to be executed by a computer, they may well be more precise and complete than a purely linguistic description of the same phenomena.

3. Stress in Greek and Hebrew

In this section, we will summarize the relevant facts about stress and how it is marked in Greek and Hebrew.

3.1. Greek

Ancient Greek texts employ three accent marks: acute (ά), circumflex (ᾶ), and grave (ὰ).

The grave accent replaces the acute when it occurs on the final syllable in certain contexts. While handling this aspect of the Greek stress system within a single FST is possible, it results in a single entry spanning arbitrarily many words, which wouldn't be a problem when analyzing running text, but would cause the analyzer to sometimes fail on single forms. Thus our analyzer simply accepts both forms.

When analyzing, these alternate forms never change the identification of the form and when generating, the selection of the surface form can be handled in Apertium using a second FST which is not composed and which operates on surface forms across word boundaries.

The acute and circumflex are subject to the following restrictions:

1. The circumflex may only appear on long vowels or diphthongs.

2. The circumflex may occur on the final syllable or on the penultimate syllable if the final is short.

   Thus σκηνῆς (long-long, final stress) and σωτῆρα (long-long-short, penultimate stress) are possible, but *σκῆνης (long-long, initial stress) is not.

3. The acute may appear on either of the last two syllables or the last three if the final is short.

   Thus in the five syllables of παιδευομενος, *παίδευομενος and *παιδεύομενος are impossible, but παιδευομένος and παιδευομενός are allowed, and since ο is short, so is παιδευόμενος.

4. If the accent falls on a long penultimate syllable and the final syllable is short, the accent must be a circumflex.

   So σωτήρων with long final syllable, but σωτῆρα with short.

In general, nouns have a lexically determined accented syllable and the accent will be placed as close to that syllable as possible. For example, forms of ἄνθρωπος "human" will have the stress on the initial syllable (αν) whenever the final syllable is short and on the second syllable (θρω) otherwise, such as in the genitive ἀνθρώπου. On the other hand, θεός "god", will always have the stress on the final syllable.

Verbs, on the other hand, will place the accent on the earliest permissible syllable, so, according to the rules, παιδευομεθα "I am being taught" can have an acute accent on ο, ε, or α, so it will have it on the earliest one, giving παιδευόμεθα. Meanwhile, παιδευω "I am teaching" can have an acute on ευ or ω or a circumflex on ω, and selecting the earliest one gives παιδεύω.

Additionally, if certain vowels are adjacent, they will merge into a long vowel or diphthong. The stress, however, is placed as if they weren't merged except that an acute accent on the first vowel will become a circumflex. Thus τιμῶμαι "I am honored" has penultimate stress even though the final αι counts as short in this context because it is underlyingly τιμάομαι with antepenultimate stress (van Emde Boas et al., 2019).

3.2. Hebrew

Unlike Greek, Hebrew orthography in general does not mark the location of stress except in religious texts where diacritics called "cantillation" or "trope" are placed on stressed syllables indicating how the word is to be sung. Additionally, the different cantillation marks indicate how closely connected a word is to its neighbors, which gives some indication of the syntax (Gesenius and Kautzsch, 2006).

As a result, if identifying morphological forms is the only goal, then tracking stress is not strictly necessary. However, explicitly modeling stress makes other rules more parsimonious and allows the rules to more effectively serve as a form of documentation of the language's morphophonology.

Stress usually falls on the final syllable of a word, though some nouns have initial stress. Additionally, there are two verbal forms (one of which, the vav-consecutive construction, is the most common form in biblical narrative) which move the stress to penultimate syllable of the stem. This shift changes the final vowel and may delete the final syllable entirely, depending on the final consonant (Gesenius and Kautzsch, 2006).

4. Implementing Stress

In this section, we describe the structure of our analyzers. Both analyzers were created in the Apertium machine translation platform (Forcada et al., 2011; Khanna et al., 2021) using the lexicon compiler Lexd (Swanson and Howell, 2021) with two-level phonology (Twol) (Koskenniemi, 1983; Lindén et al., 2009) and are freely available under the GPLv3 open-source license[1].

4.1. Greek

The Greek transducer is the result of composing a lexicon transducer with five sets of rules. The process is shown in Table 1.

4.1.1. Morphophonology

The first step is the morphophonology, which takes a sequence of morphemes from the lexicon, such as φυ{'}λακ+σ, and adjusts vowels and consonant clusters as required by Greek phonology and phonotactics (in this case giving φυ{'}λαξ). The symbol {'} indicates the lexical stress location.

[1]The code can be found on Github at https://github.com/apertium/apertium-grc and https://github.com/apertium/apertium-hbo

```
Dental = T Δ Θ
         τ δ ϑ ;
Cx:0 <=> _ Mod:* .#. ;
         _ Mod:* [:σ|:ς|σ:|ς:] ;
         where Cx in Dental ;
```

This rule, for example, deletes dental stops (τ, δ) or fricatives (ϑ) when they occur at the end of a word (`.#.`) or before sigma. `Mod:*` indicates that the rule should still apply if there are any control characters between the two consonants.

4.1.2. Orthographic Transformations

The second step ensures that all initial vowels have breathing marks and that all final sigmas are ς rather than σ, since this turned out to be significantly easier to write than combining it with the first step.

```
σ:ς <=> _ .#. ;
```

This is the rule that ensures final sigmas are always ς.

4.1.3. Syllable Boundaries

The third step inserts a marker ({.}) after each syllable nucleus and also marks final αι and οι, since they are treated as short vowels rather than diphthongs for the purposes of stress placement if they occur word-finally.

```
0:%{.%} <=>
    Vowel: VowelMod* _
    [Consonant|.#.|NonSecondDiph] ;
```

This rule says to insert the syllable marker after a vowel, possibly accompanied by some control characters, if it is followed by a consonant, the end of the word (`.#.`), or a vowel which cannot be the second letter of a diphthong.

4.1.4. Stress Placement

Next the fourth step consists of a Lexd file which lists every possible combination of long and short vowels and lexical accent marks in the last three syllables of a word and which vowel should receive the stress mark.

```
Prefix LongVowel(3) Acute BD
FinalShortSyllable

LEXICON LongVowel(4)
αι:αι  αι:αί  αι:αῖ  αι:αὶ
ει:ει  ει:εί  ει:εῖ  ει:εὶ
...

PATTERN FinalShortSyllable
CC ShortVowel(1) BD CC
```

This rule matches a word consisting of arbitrarily many initial syllables (`Prefix`), a long vowel or diphthong (`LongVowel`), a stress marker (`Acute`), and a short syllable with no stress marker (`FinalShortSyllable`). The `(3)` indicates that the penultimate vowel should be modified based on the third column of the `LongVowel` lexicon (the one with circumflexes).

4.1.5. Vowel Contraction

Finally, if there are any vowels separated by the contraction sign ({+}), they are merged, adjusting the accents if necessary.

```
[ ά %{%+%} [ ε ι | ῃ | α ι | ᾳ ] ] -> ᾷ
```

This rule specifies that if an alpha with an acute accent (ά) is contracted with any of the four listed diphthongs, the acute becomes a circumflex and the resulting vowel is an alpha with an iota subscript (ᾷ).

4.2. Hebrew

The Hebrew FST is likewise a lexicon followed by a cascade of five sets of rules. All steps except the final one are currently in a Latin-alphabet transliteration because rules operating on combining diacritics being hard to read and modify. However, since this issue is primarily a matter of text editor support, it should be possible to convert the process to Hebrew script. The process is shown in Table 2.

4.2.1. Morphophonology

The first step is applying morphophonological rules to the forms generated by the lexicon.

```
"feminine plural drop -áh: á"
á:0 <=> _ h: %>: w o t ;
"feminine plural drop -áh: h"
h:0 <=> á: _ %>: w o t ;
```

These two rules together indicate that when a noun ending in `áh` (ָה is followed by the feminine plural suffix `wot` (וֹת) then the `áh` should be deleted.

4.2.2. Stress Selection

In the lexicon, stress markers are placed both on roots and on suffixes, so the next step is to remove spurious ones leaving a single stress position.

```
Stress = %{%*%} %{%*%?%} ;
%{%*%?%}:0 <=> _ :* Stress: ;
```

This rule any stress markers for which there is another stress marker later in the word.

4.2.3. Stress Movement

In the third step, if there is a prefix containing a symbol marking that stress moves earlier in the word, the stress marker is inserted in the preceding syllable and the original one is replaced by a marker that reduction should occur if possible.

```
%{%*%}:%{%-%*%} <=> %{%$<$%*%}: :* _ ;
```

This rule replaces a stress marker ({⋆}) with a former-stress marker ({−⋆}) if there is a preceding move-stress marker ({<⋆}).

4.2.4. Stress Reduction

The fourth step applies morphophonological rules to adjust certain vowels based on the position of stress and reduction marks.

```
h:0 <=> %{%-%*%}: _ ;
```

This rule deletes h (ה) if it is immediately preceded by a former-stress marker.

4.2.5. Transliteration

Finally, the resulting form is transliterated into Hebrew script.

```
CL:CH <=> _ ( Vowel: ) .#. ;
      where CL in ( k m n p c )
            CH in ( ך ם ן ף ץ )
      matched ;
```

This rule ensures that consonants which have a distinct final form are transliterated to their final form if they are the last consonant in a word.

5. Evaluation

Development of these analyzers was originally begun as part of an experiment in processing Biblical texts in the Apertium framework and, as a result, both are currently focused on the Biblical varieties of the languages. Incorporating multiple language varieties is, however, fairly straightforward and is often done in other Apertium analyzers. We have not yet attempted such an expansion and so report results on Biblical texts only.

The Greek FST provides analyses for nearly all words in the New Testament, as shown in Table 3. The development of the Hebrew FST, on the other hand, is not as far along, and it only provides analyses for a bit less than two thirds of the book of Genesis.

Both FSTs currently overgenerate somewhat. In Greek this affects about 8% of words and is largely due to partially irregular verbs not being properly labeled in the lexicon, resulting in them having both the correct irregular form as well as an incorrect regularized form in the FST.

In Hebrew, on the other hand, various morphological processes insert different vowels in different contexts, and some of these realizations have not yet been properly constrained. This primarily affects any form involving a possessive or object pronoun. In addition, work on nominal morphology is rather incomplete, which limits the usefulness of the Hebrew FST for generating anything besides the most common verb forms.

6. Conclusion and Future Work

This paper has presented the implementation of stress in morphological analyzers for Ancient Greek and Ancient Hebrew.

In addition to the issues mentioned in Section 5, there remains a significant amount of expansion to be done

Step	Output	Output
	τιμαω<v><ind><actv><impf><pres><p1><sg>	φυλαξ<n><m><sg><nom>
Lexicon	{'}τιμα{'?}{+}ο{+long}	{'}φυ{'}λαϰ{g+}{'?}ς
Morphophonology	{'}τιμα{+}ω	{'}φυ{'}λαξ
Orth. Transforms	{'}τιμα{+}ω	{'}φυ{'}λαξ
Syllable Boundaries	{'}τι{.}μα{.}{+}ω{.}	{'}φυ{'}{.}λα{.}ξ
Stress Placement	τιμά{+}ω	φύλαξ
Vowel Contraction	τιμῶ	φύλαξ

Table 1: The steps involved in generating two surface forms in the Greek transducer. Analysis follows the same process but in reverse. Since each layer is a finite-state transformation, the entire sequence can be composed to produce a single transducer, so the intermediate states are not actually present at runtime. The tags in angle brackets on the first line indicate "verb, indicative, active, imperfective, present, 1st person, singular" and "noun, masculine, singular, nominative", respectively.

Step	Output	Hebrew Script
	w<cnjcoo>+'mr<v><actv> <impf><p3><m><sg><consec>	(ו אמר)
Lexicon	w{andc}{<*}y{i}>{paal}'m{˜a}{*?}r>	(ו י אם ר)
Morphophonology	w{andc}{<*}y.o'ma{*?}r	(ו יֹאמַ ר)
Stress Selection	w{andc}{<*}y.o'ma{*}r	(ו יֹאמַ ר)
Stress Movement	w{andc}y.o{+*}'ma{-*}r	(ו יֹ אמַ ר)
Stress Reduction	way.o{*}'mér	וַיֹּ אמֶר
Transliteration	וַיֹּאמֶר	—

Table 2: The steps involved in generating a surface form in the Hebrew transducer. Analysis follows the same process but in reverse. Since each layer is a finite-state transformation, the entire sequence can be composed to produce a single transducer, so the intermediate states are not actually present at runtime. The transliteration step is also applied to the analysis side, so the final transducer contains these words as ו<cnjcoo> and אמר<v>. The tags in angle brackets on the first line indicate "coordinating conjunction" and "verb, active, imperfective, 3rd person, masculine, singular, vav-consecutive form".

	Text	Total	Known	Coverage
Greek	NT	153,665	146,265	95.2%
Hebrew	Gen	20,573	13,201	64.2%

Table 3: Naive coverage for the two analyzers. The Greek analyzer was tested on the New Testament and the Hebrew on the book of Genesis. Total is the number of tokens in the corpus and Known is the number of tokens given an analysis by the analyzer. Coverage is Known as a fraction of Total.

in the Hebrew lexicon and several morphological processes have yet to be implemented at all (adjectives and participles, for instance, currently do not appear at all). In addition, the analyzer currently only accepts text with vowels, which limits the range of texts it can be used on. Fortunately, this latter problem will be straightforward to solve once the overgeneration problem has been dealt with.

In this paper, we have shown by example that finite-state systems are sufficient to model phonological phenomena which operate on the syllable level. Given this, we commend the use of finite-state systems in building analyzers for historical languages as adequate for implementing most morphological processes and beneficial in their capacity to serve as theoretical linguistic documentation for future scholars.

7. Acknowledgements

Our thanks to Matthew Fort and Nick Howell for reading drafts of this paper.

8. Bibliographical References

Crane, G. (1991). Generating and Parsing Classical Greek. *Literary and Linguistic Computing*, 6(4):243–245, 01.

Forcada, M. L., Ginestí-Rosell, M., Nordfalk, J., O'Regan, J., Ortiz-Rojas, S., Pérez-Ortiz, J. A., Sánchez-Martínez, F., Ramírez-Sánchez, G., and Tyers, F. M. (2011). Apertium: a free/open-source platform for rule-based machine translation. *Machine translation*, 25(2):127–144.

Gesenius, W. and Kautzsch, E. (2006). *Gesenius' Hebrew Grammar*. Dover Publications.

Karttunen, L. (1991). Finite-state constraints. In *Proceedings of the International Conference on Current Issues in Computational Linguistics*.

Khanna, T., Washington, J., Tyers, F., Bayatlı, S., Swanson, D., Pirinen, T., Tang, I., and Alòs i Font, H. (2021). Recent advances in apertium, a free /

open-source rule-based machine translation platform for low-resource languages. *Machine Translation*.

Koskenniemi, K. (1983). *Two-level Morphology: A General Computational Model for Word-Form Recognition and Production*. phdthesis.

Lindén, K., Silfverberg, M., and Pirinen, T. (2009). Hfst tools for morphology–an efficient open-source package for construction of morphological analyzers. In *International Workshop on Systems and Frameworks for Computational Morphology*, pages 28–47. Springer.

Packard, D. W. (1973). Computer-assisted morphological analysis of Ancient Greek. In *COLING 1973 Volume 2: Computational And Mathematical Linguistics: Proceedings of the International Conference on Computational Linguistics*.

Smith, N. (2016). Morphological analysis of historical languages. *Bulletin of the Institute of Classical Studies*, 59(2):89–102.

Swanson, D. and Howell, N. (2021). Lexd: A finite-state lexicon compiler for non-suffixational morphologies. In Mika Hämäläinen, et al., editors, *Multilingual Facilitation*. University of Helsinki Library.

van Emde Boas, E., Rijksbaron, A., Huitink, L., and de Bakker, M. (2019). *The Cambridge Grammar of Classical Greek*. Cambridge University Press.

Wintner, S. (2008). Strengths and weaknesses of finite-state technology: a case study in morphological grammar development. 14(4):457–469.

Yona, S. and Wintner, S. (2008). A finite-state morphological grammar of hebrew. 14(2):173–190.

Proceedings of the Second Workshop on Language Technologies for Historical and Ancient Languages (LT4HALA 2022), pages 114–118
Language Resources and Evaluation Conference (LREC 2022), Marseille, 25 June 2022

From Inscription to Semi-automatic Annotation of Maya Hieroglyphic Texts

Christian M. Prager, Cristina Vertan
Rheinische Friederich-Wilhelms-Universität Bonn, Berlin-Brandenburgische Akademie der Wissenschaften
Oxfordstrasse 15, 53111 Bonn, Unter den Linden 8, 10117 Berlin
cprager@uni-bonn.de, vertan@uni-hamburg.de

Abstract

The Maya script is the only readable autochthonous writing system of the Americas and consists of more than 1000 word signs and syllables. It is only partially deciphered and is the subject of the project "Text Database and Dictionary of the Classic Maya"[1]. Texts are recorded in TEI XML and on the basis of a digital sign and graph catalog, which are stored in the TextGrid virtual repository. Due to the state of decipherment, it is not possible to record hieroglyphic texts directly in phonemically transliterated values. The texts are therefore documented numerically using numeric sign codes based on Eric Thompson's catalog of the Maya script. The workflow for converting numerical transliteration into textual form involves several steps, with variable solutions possible at each step. For this purpose, the authors have developed ALMAH "Annotator for the Linguistic Analysis of Maya Hieroglyphs". The tool is a client application and allows semi-automatic generation of phonemic transliteration from numerical transliteration and enables multi-step linguistic annotation. Alternative readings can be entered, and two or more decipherment proposals can be processed in parallel. ALMAH is implemented in JAVA, is based on a graph-data model, and has a user-friendly interface.

Keywords: Digital Epigraphy, Linguistic Annotation, Maya Hieroglyphic Writing

1. The Maya and Their Writing System

Figure 1: Detail of hieroglyphic inscription carved on Stela 2 from Dos Pilas, Guatemala. Karl Herbert Mayer, 1978 (CC BY 4.0).

This paper addresses the semi-deciphered written language of the Classic Maya, whose cultural area extended over territories of the present-day nation states of Mexico, Guatemala, Belize and Honduras. Maya hieroglyphic writing was used between between 300 BC and AD 1500. It is a mixed, morphographic and syllabic writing system comparable to Egyptian hieroglyphs or cuneiform of Mesopotamia. As a visual language, Classic Mayan survived in more than ten thousand texts (Houston and Martin, 2016). Most sources exhibit biographical information on political elites and provide written evidence for political relations between the more than sixty ruling dynasties (Martin, 2020). The inscription's focus lies on religious and political events that marked elite daily life (Stuart, 1998). Maya kings made their public claim to power through writing and iconography. In this context, written and pictorial records, especially those on stone (Figure 1), wood, ceramics, bone and fig-bark paper, not only served as vehicles for cultural memory at the time, but today form the most important material basis for reconstructing elite history and culture. Furthermore, most texts display calendar dates that record exact sequences of events, providing not only historical insights, but also unique data on the history of Maya writing and language.

The Maya writing system is considered a hieroglyphic script because of the iconic character of its more than 1,000 graphs depicting figurative and abstract objects from the natural environment, flora, fauna, material culture, human and animal body parts, or portraits of supernaturals. Typologically, it is a logographic-syllabic writing system with two basic, functional sign types: syllabic signs and logographs (Grube, 1994). The latter denote concrete words and bound morphemes, whereas the former represent vowels and open syllables and thus permit syllabic spellings of lexical and grammatical morphemes. In addition, syllabic signs were used as phonetic complements that were pre- or post-fixed to morphographs. Thus, it was possible to write words entirely with syllabic signs, by using morphographs alone or by combining the two sign types. To create hieroglyphic text, graphs were squeezed and stacked into quadratic or rectangular blocks (Figure 1). It is the basic structural unit of a Classic Mayan text that usually corresponded to the emic concept of a word. The blocks were usually arranged in double columns to be read from left to right and from top to bottom. Researchers identified a range of calligraphic principles with which not only individual graphemes, but also Classic Mayan words could be realized in a variety of ways (Zender, 1999). The high aesthetic quality of an overall work was meant to catch the eye, monotony, conformity and repetition, it seems to today's viewer of the hieroglyphs, were to be avoided by applying a common set

[1] The project is directed by Nikolai Grube. The following collaborators have contributed significantly to the contents of the project: Maximilian Behnert-Brodhun (programming) (2014-2022), Katja Diederichs (metadata and image database) (2014-2022), Franziska Diehr (metadata) (2014-2017), Sven Gronemeyer (2014-2020) (epigraphy, linguistics, ALMAH), Antje Grothe (bibliography, image database), Guido Krempel (epigraphy), Tobias Mercer (information technology), Uwe Sikora (metadata) (2017-2018), Céline Tamignaux (image database) (2016-2019), and Elisabeth Wagner (epigraphy and iconography).

of graphetic and graphemic principles described by Prager and Gronemeyer (2018)

2. The Digital Exploration of Classic Mayan

Maya writing and language forms the subject of the long term research project "Text Database and Dictionary of Classic Mayan"[2] (Prager et al., 2018). The project's goal is to compile a text database and a dictionary of Classic Mayan. Such efforts would permit a detailed and precise investigation of the Classic Mayan literary language, for instance by comparing text passages using co-text and co-occurrence analysis. Until now, such systematic and cross-linked work with text, image, and information carriers was impossible, because the necessary technology did not yet exist in this field of research. This undertaking can only be initiated using methods and technologies from the digital humanities, whereby the project is drawing upon tools and technologies that are already available in the virtual research environment TextGrid or that are being developed and implemented in the context of the project, e.g. an annotator for the linguistic analysis of the Maya hieroglyphs (Grube et al., 2014).

For this purpose, the inscribed artefacts and their illustrations are currently being researched in the literature, in archives and photo collections and are made accessible with the help of digital methods and technologies in the virtual research environment TextGrid (Prager, 2015). At the present time, about one third of the known text carriers including their metadata have been recorded, and the relevant literature has been documented. Images of the texts are continuously added to the project's online "Maya Image Archive"[3] (Diederichs et al., 2020). In the long term, research data will be published in the TextGrid repository, including persistent identifiers, and made freely available through a research portal[4]. In cooperation with the Bonn University and State Library the project is also publishing selected content from the TextGrid repository in the "Archive of Maya Hieroglyphic Texts", as part of ULB's Digital Collections[5]. In the past years the project started to transfer the hieroglyphic texts into an XML/TEI-based machine-readable format[6]. For this purpose, the project has simultaneously implemented a digital inventory for the signs in Maya script, which currently comprises almost 1000 elements (Diehr et al. 2018, 2018). Due to the vague state of decipherment of the Maya script, it is not possible to record hieroglyphic texts in phonemically transliterated values, in contrast to comparable projects in Egyptology or cuneiform research (Diehr et al., 2019). Therefore, Maya texts are numerically transcribed using sign codes adapted from Eric Thompson's catalog of Maya hieroglyphs (1962). Since the start of the project this catalog has been critically scrutinized and supplemented with signs that were not included in the original work (Prager and Gronemeyer 2018). Thompson's inventory is still regarded as the standard work for Maya epigraphers, which is why the project has been adopting his nomenclature while removing misclassifications and duplicates, merging graph variants under a common nomenclature, and adding new signs or allographs to the sign index in sequence (Diehr et al., 2018).

In order to generate linguistic documents from these numerically encoded hieroglyphic texts the project in cooperation with Cristina Vertan has developed an annotation tool for the linguistic analysis of the machine-readable texts, which takes into account the vague decipherment status of the Maya script and the current state of research on Classic Maya language (Gronemeyer, 2014; Law and Stuart, 2017). In order to generate a readable text from the text corpus encoded in TEI XML, the tool, called ALMAH "Annotator for the Linguistic Analysis of Maya Hieroglyphs", queries the linguistic transliteration values stored in the digital sign catalog and, on this basis, semi-automatically generates a phonemic transliteration of the texts, which are further processed manually. Based on this workflow, the corpus-based Dictionary of Classic Maya is generated, which digitally maps the dictionary of Classic Mayan and its use in writing and forms the prerequisites for a deeper understanding of Maya culture, history, religion and society.

The digital-based epigraphic analysis of an inscription according to digital methods begins with the topographical description of the hieroglyphic writing (Iglesia et al., 2021). Thereby the individual graphs of the inscribed monuments are classified numerically. Based on these annotations, the linguistic analysis consisting of transliteration, transcription, morphological segmentation, linguistic interpretation and translation is performed using the annotation tool ALMAH (see chapter 4), and the results are finally published in the text database.

3. Encoding of Maya Hieroglyphic Texts

To document the arrangement of signs in the hieroglyphic block, the project applies Thompson's annotation convention to the XML/TEI scheme (Iglesia et al., 2021), according to which adjacent signs are separated by a period (.), superposed ones by a colon (:). Block segments within the hieroglyphic block are enclosed with square brackets [ ]. If a sign is inserted into another sign, it is marked with a degree sign (°) and the merging of two signs is indicated with a plus sign (+) (Prager and Gronemeyer, 2018). Definitions and editorial conventions, such as annotation of text structure, reading direction, topographic text arrangement, unreadable or reconstructed text passages, and text carrier design (shape, relief depth, framing, coloring, etc.) are predefined in the TEI schema and specified in the editorial guidelines. In the TEI annotation, the signs are referenced to the sign catalog using a TextGrid URI. For this purpose, the TextGrid URI to a graph must be retrieved in order to specify it in the TEI document. This is done using a TEI parser developped by Maximilian Behnert-Brodhun, which searches for the references from a numeric transcription code and generates the corresponding TEI structure automatically. Subsequently, the TEI document is parsed from an XML file in which only information about the text-carrying surfaces is given and the text fields and the individual hieroglyphic blocks are defined with the help of alphanumeric IDs. For each

[2] Rheinische Friedrich-Wilhelms-Universittät Bonn, Abteilung für Altamerikanistik, https://mayawoerterbuch.de

[3] https://classicmayan.kor.de.dariah.eu

[4] https://classicmayan.org

[5] https://digitale-sammlungen.ulb.uni-bonn.de/

[6] https://tei-c.org/

block, the numerical transliteration of the graph entered in the digital sign catalog is entered using the conventions defined in the projects editorial guidelines, e.g. a hieroglyphic block transcribed using sign codes based on the catalog of Maya hieroglyphs : 1br.[501st:25st]. With the increasing number of encoded inscriptions, the sign catalog, which currently counts more than 1000 signs, is also being completed. With the help of the TEI parser, the XML files with the previously created numerical transliterations of the hieroglyphic texts are transformed into TEI documents and saved in TextGrid. At the same time, the TEI file is displayed online and can be viewed on screen and checked for errors.

A special feature for the quality control of our epigraphic work is the display of the original spelling. For this purpose, the parser, as well as the annotator ALMAH, retrieve the image of the graph from the digital sign catalog using the numeric character codes and displays it next to the numeric transliteration in the parser's result window. This visual validation allows the numeric transliteration to be checked and, if necessary, corrected before processing the TEI document. If the transliterations are correct, the generated TEI document can be checked and validated in TextGrid. For the annotation of unreadable and reconstructed text passages, for example, the project uses a specific TEI-P5 application profile and follows the EpiDoc Guidelines[7] to document classic or ancient texts in TEI XML. Damages, reconstructions, explanations for reconstructed text passages as well as the layout of the text carrier are not created into the XML by the parser, but have to be edited manually in the document according to our editorial guidelines. In the further course of the project, the parser will be extended to include these editorial functions so that these areas can also be created automatically in the future.

4. Annotator for the Linguistic Analysis of Maya Hieroglyphs (ALMAH)

Figure 2: Eleven annotation levels of Maya texts used in ALMAH (concept and terminologies by S. Gronemeyer, layout by Prager)

Linguistic transliterations and transcriptions of the inscriptions are generated automatically with the help of the analysis or annotation tool ALMAH in the next step. The linguistic backbone model is developed and extensively described in (Gronemeyer 2014). It processes a total of eleven epigraphic annotation levels (Figure 2), which are dynamically generated from the annotation of the previous level. The analysis and annotation typically proceeds as follows: The annotation tool is accessing the data in TextGrid or locally via an OAI-PMH interface. Once a file is selected, the TEI document is loaded and the automatic analysis process begins. Analysis levels 1 - 4 are first generated automatically: 1) and 2) Numeric transliteration 1 and 2 with graph and character numbers. 3) and 4) Graphemic transliteration 1 and 2 with possible manual rearrangement of the reading order of the signs. Here the results of automatic transliteration are displayed block by block. In addition to the numerical transliteration, the images of the individual graphemes are imported from TextGrid into ALMAH and displayed with analysis level 1-4. From the third annotation level on, manual corrections, additions and multiple analytical variants are possible, so that we can, for example, operate simultaneously with several decipherment suggestions. For example, if several linguistic readings are available for a sign, the analysis in graphemic transliteration allows selection of a particular reading or readings stored in the digital sign catalog via a selection window. If two or more readings are selected, ALMAH generates a corresponding number of graphemic transliteration variants that can be analyzed in parallel by the editors. However, if no reading is entered in the sign catalog, ALMAH takes the sign number and inserts it into the transliteration. On the level of graphemic transliteration 2, the reading order of the signs can also be rearranged as well as the morpheme boundaries can be changed with the help of a graphical interface. The conversion of the reading order becomes necessary when it does not correspond to the original writing order. From the graphemic transliteration of level 4, the phonemic transliteration of level 5 is created in the following step. Here, the morpheme boundaries between the phonemes are defined with the help of a graphical interface in order to distinguish free and bound morphemes. At level 6, the morphologically segmented transcription, the lexical and grammatical morphemes, such as inflections, derivations, proclitics or enclitics are segmented, reconstructed or superfluous sounds or sound loss are marked. For this purpose, transcriptions are dissected into phonetic chains, whereby superfluous sounds are removed, needed ones are inserted, morpheme boundaries are set, or null morphemes are used. At level 7, the morphophonemically consolidated transcription is created. At level 8, the consolidated morphosyntactic glossing is done. In this process, the brackets and special characters inserted at level 7 are removed and only the cleaned transcription is displayed, on which the interlinear morpheme glossing of the lexical and grammatical morphemes is performed. Interlinear morpheme glosses indicate the meanings and grammatical properties of individual words and parts of words. The morpheme glossing used in ALMAH is based on the Leipzig glossing rules, which have been extended and adapted by Frauke Sachse and Michael Dürr (2016) for the analysis of Mayan languages. The glosses are assigned in the tool to the lexical classes nouns, verbs, adjectives, adverbs, particles, pronouns, articles, classifiers, conjunctions, demonstratives, numerals, and prepositions, and are searchable and selectable via a matrix of language examples. If a definite assignment is not possible, several

[7] https://sourceforge.net/p/epidoc/wiki/Home/

glosses can be assigned to one morpheme. Based on these analysis steps, the consolidated transcription of the inscription (without special characters and brackets) is automatically generated on level 9. On annotation level 10, the editors can create the literal translation of the inscription, and finally, on level 11, the free translation. Free annotations of the hieroglyphic blocks also allow scholars to annotate calendrical information, nominal phrases, place names, or events and to ontologically link them to datasets from TextGrid in order to interpret the text and vocabulary of Classic Maya embedded in their historical and sociocultural context. In this way, over one hundred and fifty years of epigraphic research history and findings can be linked to our current analyses in an ontology.

5. Architecture and Functionalities

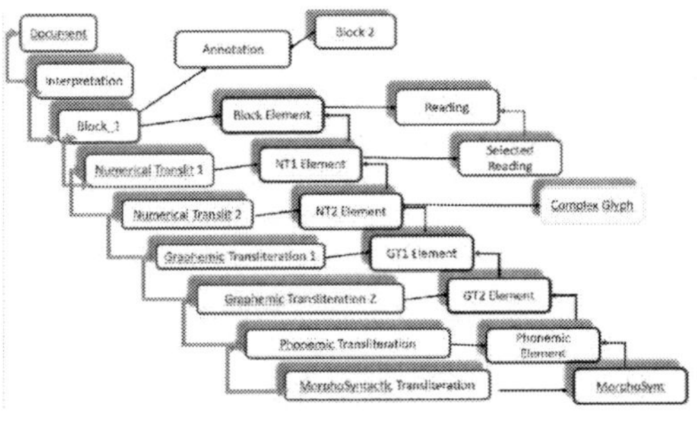

Figure 3: ALMAH Data Structure

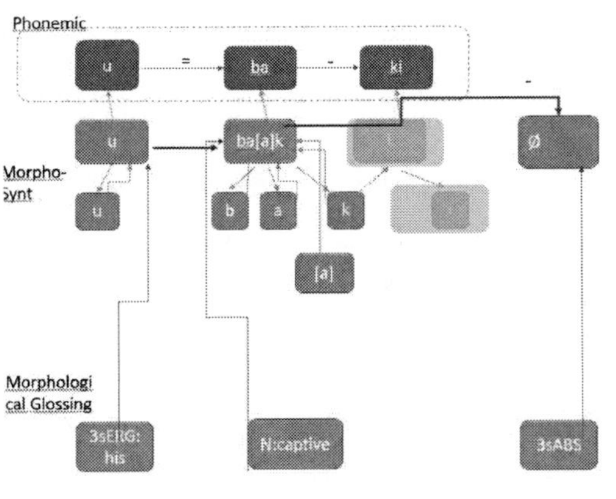

Figure 4: Data Model Example (interconnection of Elements among several transliteration levels)

This complex linguistic model is mapped on a graph-based data model. Each transcription level represents a node in a tree structure. Each node contains information about the current transliteration level (Id, label) and a nested graph representing the structure of the transliteration. A transliteration is represented by a succession of elements (nodes of the structure graph) and operators (labelled edges in the structure graph). Elements of each transliteration know their ancestors. In this way we have the possibility at every moment to reconstructs the analysis path. The data Structure is presented in Figure 3 and an example in figure 4.

The structure gives also the possibility to operate dynamically changes on the graph label. Each transliteration level can generate several variants at the next level (working hypothesis). The first for levels are automatized: readings of the elements are extracted from the RDF-Database. If an element has several readings, the user is asked to select the possible ones for the current block. If more than one alternative reading is selected, the tool generates all possible combinations. At the linguistic level we give the possibility of linking the semantic annotation with English Wordnet-Sysets (only when the meaning of the word truly corresponds with a wordnet sysnset). In Figure 5 we present an example of processing done with the ALMAH Tool:

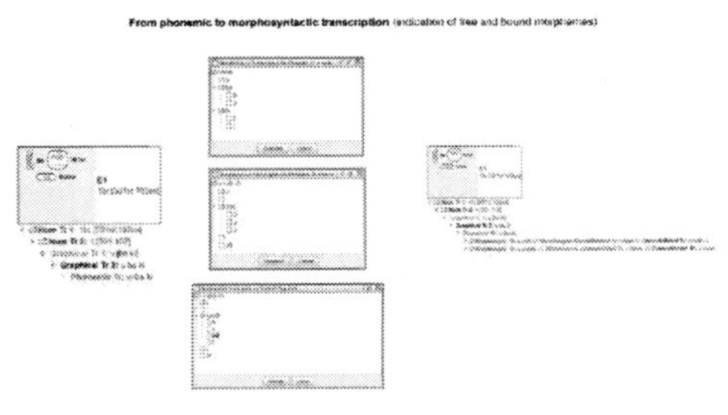

Figure 5: Interface of the ALMAH Tool

At this moment the linguistic information at phonetic and morphological level is done manually. Given the fact that the deciphering process is not completed it is quite common, that the user works at each level with more than one working hypothesis. A rule-based linguistic annotation approach, as known from the state-of-the art computational linguistics is in this case not possible. A supervised machine learning approach is in absence of a large annotated training corpus (given the number of featured to be learned) not realistic at this stage. However we are planning to use the manually annotations for building such a corpus, and introduce in a further version of the system a translation-memory –like approach. At each step, the system will search in the database for existent solution and will present the user possible annotation hypothesis, from which one or more will be manually selected. A fully unsupervised machine-learning algorithm is at this moment not appropriate, as long as the grammar of the language is not completely researched. In a third step, we envisage the possibility of exporting ALMAH –output in an ANNIS[8]-compatible format, which will allow corpus-linguistics specific queries.

6. Conclusions and further work

The newly developed tool ALMAH supports the epigraphic annotation and linguistic analysis of Maya hieroglyphic texts by standardising the decipherment process through semi-automatic processes and improving the epigraphic

[8] https://corpus-tools.org/annis/

workflow through machine learning. The tool provides the necessary flexibility to operate with alternative readings where a unique identification of characters in a block is not possible or multiple reading variations exist for a character or hieroglyph. ALMAH combines the linguistic annotation of hieroglyphs, including morphoglossification, with the creation of lemmas, which form the basis for the dictionary of Classic Mayan.

The tool is written in Java 8 as client application. An Internet connection is for the data reading and save necessary. Although it relies on a complex data-structure the interface is user friendly and transparent. The graph data structure is represented as such (through usage of graph libraries) and users can change edges, order of the graph nodes , i.e. realise permutation od elements, rename edges of the graph). Data is stored in an instance of OrientDB[9], which is the only database allowing graph and document data structures. Further work concerns the (semi) automatisation of the annotation steps (through a learning mechanism) as well as the generation of entries for a lexicon of Classic Mayan, the language of the hieroglyphs.

7. Bibliographical References

Diederichs K., Prager C.M., Brodhun M., and Tamignaux C. (2020), *„Ich brauch' mal ein Foto ... ": der Umgang mit Bildern im Projekt Textdatenbank und Wörterbuch des Klassischen Maya* [in:] "Bilddaten in den Digitalen Geisteswissenschaften.," C. Hastik, P. Hegel (eds.), Wiesbaden: Harrassowitz, pp. 175–197.

Diehr F., Brodhun M., Gronemeyer S., Diederichs K., Prager C.M., Wagner E., and Grube N. (2018), *Ein digitaler Zeichenkatalog als Organisationssystem für die noch nicht entzifferte Schrift der Klassischen Maya,* [in:] "Knowledge Organization for Digital Humanities: Proceedings of the 15th Conference on Knowledge Organization WissOrg'17 of the German Chapter of the International Society for Knowledge Organization (ISKO) [30th November - 1st December 2017, Freie Universität Berlin]," C. Wartena, M. Franke-Maier, E. de Luca (eds.), pp. 37–43, Berlin: Freie Universität Berlin.

Diehr F., Gronemeyer S., Prager C.M., Diederichs K., Grube N., and Sikora U. (2019), *Modelling Vagueness – A Criteria-based System for the Qualitative Assessment of Reading Proposals for the Deciphering of Classic Mayan Hieroglyphs* [in:] "Proceedings of the Workshop on Computational Methods in the Humanities 2018," Lausanne: Université de Lausanne, pp. 33–44.

Gronemeyer S. (2014), *The Orthographic Conventions of Maya Hieroglyphic Writing: Being a Contribution to the Phonemic Reconstruction of Classic Mayan,* Ph.D. Dissertation, Department of Archaeology, La Trobe University, Melbourne. http://hdl.handle.net/1959.9/321048

Grube N. (1994), *Mittelamerikanische Schriften* [in:] "Schrift und Schriftlichkeit: ein interdisziplinäres Handbuch internationaler Forschung = Writing and its Use: an Interdisciplinary Handbook of International Research," H. Günther, O. Ludwig (eds.), Berlin: Walter de Gruyter, Vol. 1, pp. 405–415.

[9]https://orientdb.org/

Grube N., Prager C.M., Diederichs K., Gronemeyer S., Wagner E., Brodhun M., Diehr F., Maier P. (2014), *Jahresabschlussbericht 2014* [Electronic Document]. http://mayawoerterbuch.de/?p=4477

Houston S.D. and Martin S. (2016), *Through Seeing Stones: Maya Epigraphy as a Mature Discipline,* Antiquity 90(350):443–455.

Iglesia M. de la, Diehr F., Sikora U., Gronemeyer S., Behnert-Brodhun M., Prager C.M., and Grube N. (2021), *The Code of Maya Kings and Queens: Encoding and Markup of Maya Hieroglyphic Writing,* Journal of the Text Encoding Initiative Issue 14. Retrieved from https://journals.openedition.org/jtei/3336

Law D., and Stuart D. (2017), *Classic Mayan: An Overview of Language in Ancient Hieroglyphic Script* [in:] "The Mayan Languages," J. Aissen, N.C. England, R. Zavala (eds.), London; New York: Routledge / Taylor & Francis Group, pp. 128–172.

Martin S. (2020), *Ancient Maya Politics: A Political Anthropology of the Classic Period 150–900 CE,* Cambridge: Cambridge University Press.

Prager C.M. (2015), *Das Textdatenbank- und Wörterbuchprojekt des Klassischen Maya: Möglichkeiten und Herausforderungen digitaler Epigraphik* [in:] "TextGrid: Von der Community - für die Community: Eine Virtuelle Forschungsumgebung für die Geisteswissenschaften," H. Neuroth, A. Rapp, S. Söring (eds.), Glückstadt: Werner Hülsbusch, pp. 105–124.

Prager C.M., and Gronemeyer S. (2018), *Neue Ergebnisse in der Erforschung der Graphemik und Graphetik des Klassischen Maya* [in:] "Ägyptologische 'Binsen'-Weisheiten III: Formen und Funktionen von Zeichenliste und Paläographie," S.A. Gülden, K.V.J. van der Moezel, U. Verhoeven-van Elsbergen (eds.), Stuttgart: Franz Steiner Verlag, pp. 135–181.

Prager C.M., Grube N., Brodhun M., Diederichs K., Diehr F., Gronemeyer S., and Wagner E. (2018), *The Digital Exploration of Maya Hieroglyphic Writing and Language* [in:] "Crossing Experiences in Digital Epigraphy: From Practice to Discipline," A. De Santis, I. Rossi (eds.), Berlin: De Gruyter, pp. 65–83.

Sachse F., and Dürr M. (2016), *Morphological Glossing of Mayan Languages under XML: Preliminary Results* [Electronic Document]. http://mayawoerterbuch.de/?p=2122

Stuart D. (1998), *Dynastic History and Politics of the Classic Maya* [in:] "Maya Civilization," P. Schmidt, M. de la Garza, E. Nalda (eds.), London: Thames and Hudson, pp. 320–335.

Thompson J.E.S. (1962), *A Catalog of Maya Hieroglyphs,* Norman, OK: University of Oklahoma Press.

Zender M. (1999), *Diacritical Marks and Underspelling in the Classic Maya Script: Implications for Decipherment,* M.A. Thesis, Department of Archaeology, University of Calgary, Calgary.

Proceedings of the Second Workshop on Language Technologies for Historical and Ancient Languages (LT4HALA 2022), pages 119–128
Language Resources and Evaluation Conference (LREC 2022), Marseille, 25 June 2022

Multilingual Named Entity Recognition for Medieval Charters using Stacked Embeddings and BERT-based Models

Sergio Torres Aguilar
École nationale des chartes, Centre Jean-Mabillon, Paris, France
sergio.torres@chartes.psl.eu

Abstract

In recent years the availability of medieval charter texts has increased thanks to advances in OCR and HTR techniques. But the lack of models that automatically structure the textual output continues to hinder the extraction of large-scale lectures from these historical sources that are among the most important for medieval studies. This paper presents the process of annotating and modelling a corpus to automatically detect named entities in medieval charters in Latin, French and Spanish and address the problem of multilingual writing practices in the Late Middle Ages. It introduces a new annotated multilingual corpus and presents a training pipeline using two approaches: (1) a method using contextual and static embeddings coupled to a Bi-LSTM-CRF classifier; (2) a fine-tuning method using the pre-trained multilingual BERT and RoBERTa models. The experiments described here are based on a corpus encompassing about 2.3M words (7576 charters) coming from five charter collections ranging from the 10th to the 15th centuries. The evaluation proves that both multilingual classifiers based on general purpose models and those specifically designed achieve high-performance results and do not show performance drop compared to their monolingual counterparts. This paper describes the corpus and the annotation guideline, and discusses the issues related to the linguistic of the charters, the multilingual writing practices, so as to interpret the results within a larger historical perspective.

Keywords: Latin NER, old spanish NER, old french NER, medieval NLP, NLP for historical languages

1. Introduction

Named entity recognition (NER) is one of the first steps towards information extraction aiming at locating words used as rigid designators in an unstructured text and classify them according to a set of predefined categories such as person names, locations and organizations. NER has quickly become part of the Natural Language Processing (NLP) toolboxes used to structuring and mining vast textual collections. However, its application to ancient and pre-orthographic texts still involves some challenges. In the case of medieval charters, we can mention the following:

Low-resources language varieties : Medieval charters are written in medieval versions of Latin until the 15th century and vernacular languages (e.g Old and middle French, old Spanish) from the 13th c. onwards. Annotated corpora for these languages are still rare preventing the developing of powerful and adapted NLP toolboxes. In addition to this, the written testimonies show different language states defined by more or less important linguistic changes over time and space which complicates generalization model capacities.

Multilingualism : Multilingual NER libraries are quite recent and the overall performance is usually lower compared to the monolingual systems. Charter collections dated from the mid-13th century display documents in both Latin and vernacular languages. Public powers continue to use *scripta latina*, especially for solemn documents, until the end of the Middle Ages; while vernacularization of private documents occurs since the late 12th century (Glessgen, 2004). Code-switching practices and bilingual sequences can be detected even within the same charter, as in the case of the *vidimus* : a charter for revalidating old rights that includes a verbatim copy of the original act issued in Latin; or in the case of the late use by notaries of long-established Latin formulae in the legal language of the acts. (See two bilingual charters in the annexus).

Strong topic-dependency : Charters are legal deeds whose wording was framed by well-defined documentary models using stereotyped discursive structures and a formulaic and archaizing vocabulary. Charters are not mass productions, but they use a series of more or less recurrent sequences according to their typologies and the legal actions recorded in the document. This stands for a fundamental problem when using popular classifiers since they hardly fit on this kind of documents whose syntax and semantics may be largely unknown to an out-of-the-box classifier trained on present-day discourse from news and Wikipedia.

Complex denomination : Nested entities and context ambiguity are open questions in modern NER research. Most of the NER classifiers work in a flat mode while in medieval texts, nested entities are quite common in the form of locatives, patronyms and periphrasis coupled with baptismal names as a strategy of social distinction against a high homonym ratio. On the other hand, the concept of moral person, common category in modern NER works, is relatively foreign in charters, since most organizations are presented in an ambiguous manner using the context of locations from which it is often very difficult to distinguish them.

These four aspects of charters will be explored in our experiments in the aim of creating robust multilingual named entities models to provide an indexed structure to historical collections that can potentially contain texts with nested entities as well as different languages and language states. These efficient NER models would allow the implementation of information retrieval techniques and adapt diplomatic and historical research methods to large scale corpora.

Our contribution can be summarized as follows: (1) An annotated multilingual corpus built upon five different collections of medieval charters in a range of five centuries (10th to 15th), (2) an adequate training and validation framework, to create supervised NER models able to automatically distinguish places and person names in unstructured multilingual texts; (3) A robustness protocol to evaluate the models' ability to generalize on a wide range of acts regardless of regional, typological and chronological differences.

2. Related work

NER is a classic sequence classification task. Traditionally the best neural approaches for NER were based on LSTM or Bi-LSTM approaches working with word and character-level representations. Lately, these approaches were partially replaced by the transformers architectures based on attention mechanisms as they eliminate the vanishing gradient problem providing direct connections between the encoder states and the decoder. Recently the use of pre-trained contextual language representations such as BERT (Devlin et al., 2018) and ELMO (Peters et al., 2018) have become the standard for sequence classification as they can be fine-tune on many downstream tasks in a supervised fashion.

The leveraging on these pre-trained models increases significantly the performance compared with traditional word-based approaches (Ehrmann et al., 2021) and eliminates the need to deploy methods depending on rich features engineering in favor of fine-tuning processing based on the update of word and sub-word representations from labeled data. Yet, contextualized word representations and even static embeddings require large-scale annotated corpora for training and fine-tuning, and their adaptation to ancient language versions (*«états de langue»*) or domain-specific texts has not been fully studied. An advanced version of these models such as mBERT (Devlin et al., 2018) and RoBERTa (Conneau et al., 2019) trained on multilingual big datasets has proven that it is possible to generalize across languages and get powerful models capable of handling tasks in a multilingual environment.

Despite this, some popular NER systems on ancient Western languages are still deploying ruled-based analyzers coupled with gazetteers and patronymic lists (Erdmann et al., 2016; McDonough et al., 2019) due to the lack of relevant annotated corpora which block the deploying of supervised approaches, while others are skill-dependent using the NLP tools for ancient languages that have been published in the last years. Indeed, some lemmatization and PoS tools are available for ancient languages (Clérice et al., 2019; Prévost and Stein, 2013). But there is a lack of large language models for tasks such as text classification and NER, given that PoS tools only detect, but do not classify proper names or deal with their length and composition. And in the best of our knowledge any NLP resource exists to treat medieval documents at a multilingual level.

3. Corpus description

To remedy the lack of relevant training corpora, we created a relatively large dataset for the present task, composed of ca. 2.3 millions of tokens, from four database sources ranging from 10th to the 15th century (See figure 1): *Diplomata Belgica* (de Hemptinne et al., 2015), *HOME-Alcar* (Stutzmann et al., 2021), the *CBMA* (Magnani, 2020) and the *Codea* (Borja, 2012) corpus. The first three contain Latin and French charters while the CODEA corpus concentrates on old Spanish. Furthermore, we have annotated two other single cartularies, taken here as external datasets, for testing the classifier robustness: the cartularies of the seigneury of Nesle (1217-1282) (Hélary, 2007) and of the monastery of Eslonza (912-1399) (Vignau, 1885) written in French-Latin and Spanish-Latin respectively.

3.1. The CBMA

The CBMA (*Corpus de la Bourgogne du Moyen Âge)* is a large database composed of about 29k charters coming from the Burgundy region dated between the 9th and 14th centuries. Since 2016 the CBMA project has made freely available a sub-corpus of 5300 manually annotated charters with named entities. This sub-corpus constitutes the core component of our modeling for medieval Latin. The documents it contains, coming from nearly a hundred small localities in Burgundy, are taken from ten different cartularies, i.e, volumes containing copies of charters about land exchanges, public privileges concessions, disputes, contracts, papal letters, etc. The preparation of these volumes was normally undertaken by religious or public institutions with the aim of keeping a memorial record of their history but also to serve as a source of legal proofs about rights and properties acquired by donation or purchase. Most part of annotated CBMA documents are in Latin coming from private persons and public institutions. Many French charters can be found in the corpus but they were not originally included on the annotated subset. To extend the annotations for French, we have selected and annotated the cartulary of the city of Arbois (Stouff, 1989) belonging to the same collection. This is a municipal cartulary commissioned in 1384 by the aldermens (*prud'hommes*) of the city and contains documentary types that can hardly be found in the cartularies from religious institutions : agreements about public issues such as military services and war costs, or about taxes and customs; charters declaring communal land purchases or lawsuits in court, reflecting the economic and social interactions between the community and the lords or other communities.

	LATIN		FRENCH		SPANISH	
Acts (7576)	5474		1245		857	
Tokens (2.3M)	1.36M		0.53M		0.51M	
CBMA	5282		65		-	
DIBE	-		922		-	
HOME	39		203		-	
CODEA	77		-		800	
Nesle	28		55		-	
Arlanza	48		-		57	
category/ length	PERS	LOC	PERS	LOC	PERS	LOC
1	66921 (91%)	33291 (71%)	6079 (42%)	14391 (90%)	5381 (34%)	15610 (89%)
2	3173 (4%)	9841 (21%)	2849 (19%)	1057 (7%)	7998 (50%)	883 (5%)
3	3178 (5%)	986 (2%)	4703 (33%)	245 (1%)	1068 (7%)	364 (2%)
>3	743 (1%)	2607 (6%)	812 (6%)	356 (2%)	1490 (9%)	558 (3%)
# entities	74015	46735	14443	16049	15937	17415
# tokens	85976	69435	29348	18739	30823	20855
Density	6.31%	5.10%	5.51%	3.51%	6.09%	4.12%
Flat Density	11.08%		8.17%		9.73%	

Table 1: Statistics on entities for each corpus according to their length (number of tokens). *Density* represents the percentage of tokens in the whole corpus annotated as entities. *Flat density* expresses the sum of densities without taking in account the nested LOC cases, v.g. the locative in a person name.

3.2. The Diplomata Belgica (DiBe)

The *Diplomata Belgica* are a large database published by the Belgian Royal Historical Commission in 2014. It contains almost 19,000 full transcriptions of mostly Latin and middle French charters. It is based on (Wauters and Halkin, 1866 1907; Bormans et al., 1907 1966). The edited charters range from the early 8th century to the late 13th century with a high concentration on the period from the mid-12th century (84% of the corpus). They are related to private and public business and issued by or for institutions and persons in nowadays Belgium and Northern France.

For this work, we have annotated all the French charters (922 docs) edited in the *Diplomata Belgica*. They all are dated in the 13th century, and transmit diverse legal actions (donations, privileges, concessions and confirmations, judicial sentences, sales and exchanges) concerning individuals and corporate bodies (lay or religious institutions). In this sub-corpus are also included 374 chirographs (i.e. charters produced in double or triple copy to give one to each stakeholder) from the aldermen of Ypres, concerning private affairs linked to trade and industry, e.g. sales, exchange contracts, loans, recognition of debts (Valeriola, 2019).

3.3. HOME-Alcar

The HOME-Alcar corpus (Stutzmann et al., 2021) was produced as part of the European research project *HOME History of Medieval Europe*. This corpus provides the images of medieval manuscripts aligned with their scholarly editions as well as an annotation of named entities (persons and places), in the aim to serve as a resource to train synchronously Handwritten Text Recognition (HTR) and NER models.

HOME-Alcar includes 17 cartularies dated between the 12th and 14th centuries. The corpus has 3090 acts (2760 in Latin, 330 in Old and Middle French) and almost 1M tokens. From this corpus we have selected French charters coming from four cartularies: (1) Cartulary of Charles II of Navarre : 96 acts (Lamazou-Duplan et al., 2010); (2) the Cartulary of seigneury of Nesle; 83 acts (Hélary, 2007); (3) Cartulary of Fervaques abbey : 54 acts (Schabel and Friedman, 2020); (4) the so-called «White Cartulary» of Saint-Denis Abbey : 53 acts (Guyotjeannin, 2019)

The first two are from lay families. In the case of Navarre, the transcribed acts, dated between the 1297 and 1372, contain private donations and exchanges as well as other legal categories that are uncommon in religious cartularies, e.g., treatises, successions, indemnities. In the case of the cartulary of Nesle compiled in the 1270s, it contains documents related to purchases, debts, distribution of inheritances, land disputes, which attempt to accurately describe the patrimony of Jean, lord of Nesle. The other two were produced by religious institutions, namely Norman and Ile-de-France abbeys respectively, and have mostly donations from lay people and privileges from public authorities. The French acts are dated between 1250 and 1285 for Fervaques and between 1244 and 1300 for Saint-Denis.

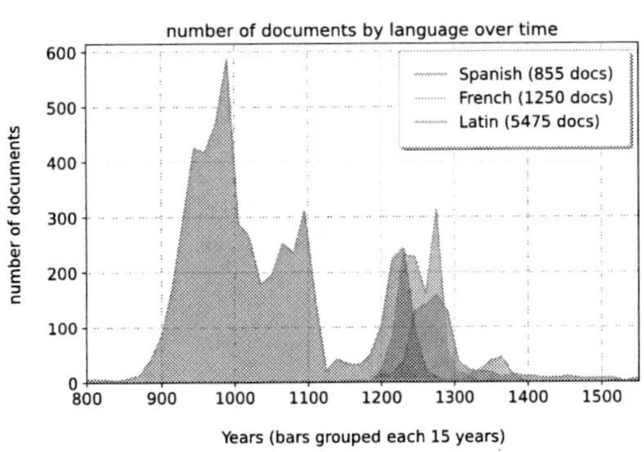

Figure 1: Number of documents over the time by languages including all the 7.6k documents

3.4. The CODEA corpus

The CODEA corpus (*Corpus of Spanish Documents Prior to 1800*) is a free available corpus made public in 2012 by the University of Alcalá. Its main objective is tracing the evolution of Spanish from the High Middle Ages to the emergence of modern Spanish (Borja, 2012). The origins of the documents are quite diverse as the CODEA team tries to generate a plural image that includes charters from different regions of the Iberian Peninsula (but mainly from the former Aragon and Castille areas), as well as from different social states and institutions : chancelleries and city offices, but also notaries and small scriptoria. These diachronic series aim to facilitate the analysis of changes in the written language and in writing practices considering the social, economic and institutional origin of the document. Consequently, the typological variety of CODEA charters is quite wide, since we have chancery documents: privileges, mandates, provisions, grants; private charters as contracts, sales, letters, wills, and normative documents : regulations, reports, inventories. Unlike the aforementioned collections, the number of charters coming from ecclesiastical institutions is small including these from the papacy that continues to write in Latin until after the Middle Ages.

Today the corpus contains 2,500 charters, ranging from the 11th to 16th centuries. To enrich our model with Spanish named entities, we have chosen and annotated a random sub-set of 877 documents of which we can say that 800 are written in Spanish, or mostly in Spanish, and 77 in Latin, or mostly in Latin, since clear linguistic separations are in some cases impossible.

3.5. The Eslonza cartulary

The scholarly edition of the cartulary of Eslonza was published in 1895 (Vignau, 1885), it contains the charters transcriptions from the cartulary of the Benedictine monastery of San Pedro de Eslonza (León, Spain) founded in 1099. The cartulary contains 227 acts (57 in medieval Spanish) dated between the 912 and the 1350. As in other cartularies from religious institutions the acts are related to land exchanges and business between the abbey and public and private persons. Some acts are dated prior to the foundation of the abbey and some other describe exchanges between two lay landowners. This is explained because when a monastery inherited a land from lay people the charters attesting the legal origin of this land were also transferred and preserved as legal guarantee. These documents defined as *munimina* by diplomatics appear together with *instrumenta*, solemn acts such as diplomas where the monastery is the author and recipient of an act that attests the receipt of a property or a right, later validated by an authority.

4. Corpus annotation

4.1. Annotation parameters

Our annotation is focused on the named entities considered as rigid designators including proper names and excluding pronouns, co-occurrences terms and complex periphrasis, which form the so-called «full-entity», because they contain words belonging to the dictionary. For example in the case of the full-entity « *don Suero Pérez , obispo de Çamora* » we annotate « *Suero Pérez* » (PERS) and « *Çamora* » (LOC) but we do not include the honorific prefix: « *don* » (Lord, dominus) and the dignity title: « *obispo* » (bishop).

In addition, we annotate the nested entities which are detected in charters since the early 11th century and whose use became the norm since the late-12th century. The composition of these nested entities, also called «by-names», varies according to the regions and times, but in general the structure is composed by either a locative or a patronym (*nomen paternum*) or both coupled to a baptism name by declension of using a nexus. These added locatives provide precious historical information as they typically correspond to micro-toponyms, whose existence is often not recorded otherwise. In these cases, a «LOC» tag is partially aligned to a «PERS» entity. For example : *Matheus Guidonis d'Attrebato; Bartolome de Moral del Payuelo.*

Furthermore, our annotation only records person and place names. The corporate bodies entities, normally annotated as organizations (ORG), where folded to «places» (LOC) as in the other corpora, because they are mostly ambiguous in medieval texts. In many cases a same entity can be a reference to an institution, a building or a land: the cathedral of «Saint-Vincent» or the lordship of «Oisy» mean a place and a corporate body at the same time. In other cases, it is unclear if a name involved in an action refers to a land, a corporal body or a moral person: as for example: a land donation to «Sanctus Petrus» is made materially to a monastery, but under the patronage of the saint to whom it is dedicated. The annotation of ORG entities needs the use of external resources for disambiguation and a LOC tag must be preferred for these cases.

4.2. Annotation process

The charters of the HOME-Alcar corpus were already annotated and corrected by two experts following a double scope: single entities (proper names and simple periphrasis) and full entities (proper names and co-occurrences). This annotation was made on the basis of an automatic annotation using a CRF-NER model, then later corrected by two expert annotators. The alpha Inter-annotator agreement was not measured.

The charters of *Diplomata Belgica*, Arbois, CODEA and Arlanza were annotated in the single-entity style in the same manner. A single expert manually corrected an automatic first hypothesis.

We use the usual BIO format to encode the annotated labels as follows: B-tag, I-tag and O-tag to represent Begin (B) of label, continuation (I) of label and absence (O), respectively. During the robustness test we also add a special «L(location)-PERS» tag to mark nested location entities in a flat-mode.

Token	Nested		Flat	Flat-nested
Magister	O	O	O	O
Iobertus	B-PERS	O	B-PERS	B-PERS
de	I-PERS	O	I-PERS	I-PERS
Ponte	I-PERS	B-LOC	I-PERS	L-PERS
curie	O	O	O	O
Senonensis	O	B-LOC	B-LOC	B-LOC
officialis	O	O	O	O
don	O	O	O	O
Pedro	B-PERS	O	B-PERS	B-PERS
de	I-PERS	O	I-PERS	I-PERS
Leorna	I-PERS	B-LOC	I-PERS	L-PERS
abat	O	O	O	O
del	O	O	O	O
monasterio	O	O	O	O
de	O	O	O	O
Santa	O	B-LOC	B-LOC	B-LOC
María	O	I-LOC	I-LOC	I-LOC
de	O	I-LOC	I-LOC	I-LOC
Valbuena	O	I-LOC	I-LOC	I-LOC

Table 2: Example of annotations for named entities in # CBMA 18296 , and # CODEA-0346

5. Training of the models

5.1. Data preparation

Our ground-truth corpus is composed of 7576 acts ($\sim$ 2,31 M tokens), divided into two sets in order to conduct two experiments: (1) training and test on a homogeneous corpus; (2) test on additional, external corpora to measure the robustness of the model. The first experiment is based on a corpus containing 7388 acts (177253 annotated entities) and encompassing the charters from the five aforementioned corpora. It is randomly split with a 0.8 - 0.2 ratio: training set (5911 acts), and validation and test sets (441 and 1036 acts). This experiment consists of two steps: in the first, we train three monolingual models (table 3); in the second, we train multilingual models in order to compare performances (table 4). The second experiment tests the generalization capacity of the models on a unseen corpus : the cartularies of Eslonza (105 charters) containing Latin and Spanish charters and Nesle (83 charters) containing Latin and French charters. The monolingual and multilingual classifiers trained on the entire first corpus were applied on the second (table 6).

5.2. Problem definition

We see our problem as a traditional sequence labeling task. The input is a defined sequence of tokens $x = (x_1, x_2...x_{n-1}, x_n)$ and the output must be defined as a sequence of tokens labels $y = (y_1, y_2...y_{n-1}, y_n)$. We have implemented three training modes following the nested nature of the entities: The first one operates in a nested mode and both steps (PERS and LOC) have independent training processes using two classifiers; the second operates in a Flat (multi-class) mode, that means PERS and LOC are recognized in a synchronous manner without overlapping; the third, introduces a «L-PERS» special tag (see table 2) in the traditional BIO-format with the aim of recognizing cases of nested entities (locatives within personal names) using a single classifier. Results are presented in table 5.

5.3. The BERT-based models : mBERT and XLM-RoBERTa

We fine-tune two multilingual BERT varieties: on the one hand, mBERT (Devlin et al., 2018) which uses a 12 multi-head attention layers like the BERT-Base model but instead of being trained on raw English texts it is trained on Wikipedia pages of 104 languages. On the other hand, XLM-RoBERTa (Conneau et al., 2019) which is a large model using 24 layers and trained on 10 times more data that mBERT.

Both BERT-based encoders learn on a massive amount of raw data a deep language representation in an unsupervised way generating an embedding contextualized vector for each input token. In contrast to classic sequence models that predict the next word, BERT tries to optimize a Masked Language Model (MLM) objective and next-sentences prediction thus performing contextual token encoding and understanding the relationship between two contiguous sequences. XLM-RoBERTa optimizes the same MLM objective but prefers a dynamic masking during the training.

In these approaches the training is done in a unsupervised fashion without any alignment between the languages. Instead of using specific language vocabularies they introduce a shared vocabulary which activate cross-lingual transfer operations during training and fine-tuning. This reduces complexity of space and helps the model learn the underlying structure of a language rather than just learning the monolingual vocabulary. Several experiments prove that both mBERT and RoBERTa perform well in cross-lingual generalization for a variety of downstream tasks. (Muller et al., 2020; Conneau et al., 2019)

Training a NER BERT-based classifier is a three-steps task: Firstly, we vectorize the sentence and label sequences using the BERT-based word-pieces tokenizer; secondly, we freeze all the layers except the last in order to keep the pre-trained weights; finally, we pass the annotated data through the final layer, thus partially retrained the model using a cross-entropy loss function.

5.3.1. Hyperparameters

We fine-tune the models to perform sub-word level classification over sentences with a max-length of 250 word-pieces. Each model was fine-tuned over 5 epochs starting in a 2.0e-5 learning rate. We ran a 16 batch and AdamW as dynamic optimizer. In addition, since BERT models relies on word-pieces tokenizations (v.g: "Garner", "##us", "Dei", "gra", "##tia", "Tre", ##cens", "epi", "##sco", "##pus") which do not match the original token-split annotation, we decide, as was done in the original BERT paper, to train the model on the tag labels for the first word piece token of each word.

5.4. The stacked embeddings model (+Bi-LSTM-CRF)

Bi-directional LSTM classifiers using a final CRF-layer are one of the most used architectures for addressing sequence tagging tasks. Used together with static

Lang / Category	Latin Pr	Rc	F1	Support	French Pr	Rc	F1	Support	Spanish Pr	Rc	F1	Support
B-PERS	99.2	99.0	99.1	10052	96.6	97.5	97.0	1811	99.1	98.9	99.0	2248
I-PERS	95.8	94.0	94.9	1808	97.8	98.7	98.3	1973	99.6	98.3	98.9	1911
micro avg	98.7	98.2	**98.5**	11860	97.2	98.2	**97.7**	3784	99.3	98.6	**99.0**	4159
B-LOC	97.2	98.1	97.6	6204	97.5	96.5	97.0	2493	98.7	99.2	99.0	2605
I-LOC	96.7	95.7	96.2	2848	92.1	93.6	92.8	359	93.1	96.7	94.9	306
micro avg	97.0	97.3	**97.2**	9052	96.8	96.1	**96.5**	2852	98.1	99.0	**98.5**	2911

Table 3: Evaluation results on test set for the monolingual models using the bi-LSTM-CRF + stacked embeddings architecture : Pr (Precision), Rc (Recall), F1 (F1 score), micro avg (micro-averaging score), Support (number of observations).

	Model / Category	Combined Pr	Rc	F1	Multi_Flair Pr	Rc	F1	Multi_BERT Pr	Rc	F1	XLM_RoBERTa Pr	Rc	F1	Support
(a)	B-PERS	98.9	98.8	98.8	98.8	98.9	98.8	98.3	98.9	98.6	98.9	98.8	**98.9**	14111
	I-PERS	97.8	97.1	97.4	97.9	96.4	97.1	97.8	96.8	97.3	97.6	97.4	**97.5**	5692
	micro avg	98.6	98.3	98.4	98.6	98.2	98.4	98.2	98.3	98.2	98.5	98.4	**98.5**	19803
	B-LOC	97.6	98.0	97.8	97.6	98.5	**98.0**	97.6	97.7	97.7	97.8	97.7	97.8	11302
	I-LOC	95.9	95.6	95.7	96.1	96.3	**96.2**	94.5	95.8	95.2	95.0	96.2	95.6	3513
	micro avg	97.2	97.4	97.3	97.3	98.0	**97.6**	96.8	97.3	97.1	97.1	97.4	97.2	14815
(b)		PERS	LOC		PERS	LOC		PERS	LOC		PERS	LOC		
	Correct (TP)	13839	11012		13841	11071		13848	10990		13842	10988		
	Incorrect	126	124		133	111		133	141		132	147		
	Missed (FN)	146	166		137	120		130	171		137	167		
	Spurius (FP)	137	213		137	219		223	213		142	174		
	Pr	98.1	97.0		98.0	97.1		97.5	96.8		98.0	97.2		
	Rc	98.0	97.4		98.1	98.0		98.1	97.2		98.1	97.2		
	F1	98.1	97.2		**98.1**	**97.5**		97.8	97.0		98.1	97.2		

Table 4: Evaluation results on test set for the multilingual models using the bi-LSTM-CRF + stacked embeddings architecture (Combined and Multi_Flair) and the fine-tuned BERT-based models (mBERT and XLM-RoBERTa) : TP (True positive), FN (False negative), FP (False positive). First table (a) indicates tag-level performance; second table (b) indicates entity-level performance.

embeddings and later with contextual embeddings became popular in recent years for NER tasks. Recent works indicate that stacking both classes of embeddings by concatenating and remapping them can significantly improve performance (Catelli et al., 2020), especially in multilingual environments when the pretraining languages have similar characteristics (Akbik et al., 2018). We think that the stacking strategy can also be effective when working with old linguistic varieties, since words and sub-words embeddings can help to deal with both the polysemy of the language and the inconsistency in spelling.

We train the Bi-LSTM-CRF classifier using Flair, one of the state-of-the-art Library in NLP tasks, based on Pytorch and natively supporting the stacking of embeddings. The contextual embeddings were trained on a concatenated trilingual corpus of 20M of words from medieval charters using the contextual embeddings Flair model that capture latent syntactic-semantic information (Akbik et al., 2018). The static embeddings were generated from this same corpus using Fasttext word-representation which is trained on subword-level information (Bojanowski et al., 2017).

5.4.1. Hyperparameters

The FastText embeddings were training with 200 dimensions using a skipgram model. The Flair embeddings were training in a bidirectional mode using a 1024 hidden-size and a maximum sequence length of 250 tokens. As for the Bi-LSTM classifier, the grid search was evaluated on three key options: batch-size {4,16,32}, starting learning rate {1.0e-2, 2.0e-2, 5.0e-3} and hidden size {256, 512}.

6. Evaluation

Table 3 shows the best results obtained for the three monolingual classifiers using the Bi-LSTM-CRF + stacked embeddings architecture. We provide the usual Precision, Recall and F1-score metrics at a token-level (B- and I- tags). We also include full-entity level metrics on strict match: strict match occurs when the hypothesis and the ground-truth match perfectly. These models were trained by choosing the charters that correspond to each language within the train, test and dev datasets (see 4.1). Table 4 shows the best results for the multilingual models using the adapted and the fine-tuned BERT methods. These models were trained on the entire datasets. The «combined» column of table 4 concatenates the inferences of the 3 monolingual models in order to compare performances of the lingual-specialized models against the cross-lingual models as they are trained and tested on the same data.

Summarizing over the results we can state that multilingual models (table 4) do not show a performance loss over their monolingual counterparts. Except in the case of I-LOC, we can state that the differences between all the models are marginal. But we must emphasize that while the multilingual models use just two classifiers (PERS and LOC) the monolingual ones use 6 (PERS and LOC x 3 languages) to reach the same result.

	Flat-nested mode									Flat mode									
	Multi_Flair			Multi_BERT			XLM-RoBERTa			Multi_Flair			Multi_BERT			XLM-RoBERTa			
	Pr	Rc	F1	Pr	Rc	F1	Pr	Rc	F1	Pr	Rc	F1	Pr	Rc	F1	Pr	Rc	F1	Support
B-PERS	99.0	98.8	**98.9**	98.6	98.9	98.7	98.7	98.9	98.8	99.0	99.0	**99.0**	97.4	97.2	97.3	98.9	98.8	98.9	14111
I-PERS	97.9	97.0	**97.4**	97.6	96.8	97.2	97.2	96.9	97.1	98.1	97.2	**97.7**	95.4	97.4	96.4	97.7	97.3	97.5	4148 / 5692
L-PERS	97.7	97.0	**97.3**	96.2	96.6	96.4	96.5	96.8	96.6	-	-	-	-	-	-	-	-	-	1544 / 0
B-LOC	97.2	98.1	**97.7**	97.2	97.4	97.3	97.1	97.7	97.4	97.1	98.2	**97.7**	94.8	94.6	94.7	97.1	97.8	97.4	9877
I-LOC	95.6	96.1	**95.9**	94.2	95.9	95.0	94.2	95.8	95.0	95.4	96.3	**95.9**	92.3	90.5	91.4	94.2	96.3	95.2	3394
micro avg	97.9	98.0	**98.0**	97.5	97.8	97.6	97.4	97.9	97.7	97.9	98.2	**98.1**	95.9	96.1	96.0	97.6	98.0	97.8	33074

Table 5: Evaluation results on test set for the multilingual Flat and Flat-nested models using the bi-LSTM-CRF + stacked embeddings architecture and the fine-tuned BERT-based models.

	Eslonza + Nesle												
Model /	Combined			Multi_Flair			Multi_BERT			XLM-RoBERTa			
category	Pr	Rc	F1	Pr	Rc	F1	Pr	Rc	F1	Pr	Rc	F1	Support
B-PERS	97.7	97.9	97.8	98.3	97.9	**98.1**	96.4	96.8	96.6	97.9	97.1	97.5	4697
I-PERS	97.0	97.6	97.3	97.4	97.2	**97.3**	95.8	95.9	95.9	97.0	96.7	96.8	3302
micro avg	97.4	97.8	97.6	98.0	97.6	**97.8**	96.1	96.4	96.3	97.5	96.9	97.2	7999
B-LOC	96.4	95.0	95.7	96.8	96.3	**96.5**	93.3	95.4	94.3	95.7	95.0	95.3	2896
I-LOC	95.7	89.8	92.6	95.2	92.5	**93.8**	92.6	87.9	90.2	95.2	89.5	92.3	1104
micro avg	96.2	93.5	94.9	96.4	95.2	**95.8**	93.1	93.3	93.2	95.6	93.4	94.5	4000
	PERS	LOC		PERS	LOC		PERS	LOC		PERS	LOC		
Correct (TP)	4537	2715		4542	2749		4490	2705		4484	2698		
Incorrect	97	54		88	58		100	97		117	91		
Missed (FN)	63	127		67	89		107	94		96	107		
Spurius (FP)	74	84		49	73		143	175		78	99		
Pr	96.3	95.1		97.0	95.4		94.9	90.9		95.8	93.4		
Rc	96.6	93.7		96.7	95.0		95.5	93.4		95.5	93.2		
F1	96.4	94.4		**96.9**	**95.2**		95.2	92.0		95.6	93.3		

Table 6: Evaluation results on external test set for the multilingual models using the bi-LSTM-CRF + stacked embeddings architecture and the fine-tuned BERT-based models.

Both monolingual and multilingual models obtain high performance results in PERS (98% in average) and LOC (97% in average) categories also showing an harmonic recall and precision along the categories. As is often seen in NER for ancient texts, the detection of I-classes is slightly lower due to ambiguities and imbalances in the corpus, since complex (multi-word) entities, especially in places, represent a low percentage of the total (see table 1). But in general, we realize that all the models can correctly detect the boundaries of the entities regardless of their length.

Furthermore, the mBERT and especially RoBERTa models achieve almost the same result as Flair-based ones by fine-tuning a general-purpose model without formally requiring external embeddings, which are generally not available for historical texts. Thus, demonstrating that an adaptation of BERT during 5 epochs (2 hours in a RTX3090) could be enough to obtain a suitable model for applications to medieval texts.

Switching to a Flat mode (table 5) does not mean an improvement in performance. Training in this mode may seem easier than a nested mode, but in the latter, there is actually a smaller number of categories to classify. Although the task seems much more complicated for BERT who is outperformed by RoBERTa and Flair.

In the same way, the Flat-nested model (table 5) shows an almost identical result to the Flat mode on a task that is slightly more complex, thus proving that a single classifier can be enough to obtain an excellent result (98%), just below the best performance (98.1%), in a multilingual, multi-class and multi-label NER task.

6.1. Evaluation on external corpora

Table 6 shows the predictions of the multilingual and monolingual models on the external test corpus (Eslonza + Nesle). The proportion of shared entity mentions between these corpus and the training corpus is of the order of 27% for personal names (mostly common baptismal names) and 25% for place names.

Again, we can state a very high precision and recall in the recognition of the personal name (97% in exact-match) and slightly lower on locations (95% in exact-match). The drop in performance with respect to the test corpus is quite low (1 to 2 points), thus confirming that all our classifiers have an acceptable generalization capacity on unknown documents.

On the other hand, the Flair model is more competent when facing unseen documents than BERT and RoBERTa, who present a much higher number of false negatives and false positives. Analyzing much more closely his inferences we can detect two kind of errors: label misclassification (v.g *Alffonso Martines alcalde del Rey* (true: B-PERS ; false: B-LOC); *Pero Breton* (true: I-PERS ; false: B-LOC) *archipreste*) and confusion between NEs and non-NEs classes (v.g : *in octabis Sancti Martini* (true: O-O ; false: B-LOC-I-LOC); *in festo beati Andree* (true: O ; false: B-PERS) *Apostoli*). The first ones correspond to contextual errors whose presence does not seem aberrant; while the second ones correspond to errors about the dates (not annotated in our corpus), since in the Middle Ages, they were written down using saints' festivities, who are sometimes recognized by the classifiers as location entities.

7. Discussion

This work clearly proves that high-performance NER classifiers for medieval charters can be modeled using neural approaches and pre-trained models. The results on the test sets being multilingual and multi-regional proves the models are robust against changes on personal denomination traditions, chronologies and language. This may be explained as follows:

1) Although personal naming strategies change according to regional traditions, they follow a recurring pattern in which the model easily fits. As we have seen, the so-called by-name does not stand for an insurmountable issue for the models that captures well the periphrases and couplings used in the formation of the by-name and is even capable of classifying the nested location entity. This has a lot to do with the fact that the stock of personal names is relatively restricted. In the case of *CODEA* charters with a chronology limited to two centuries (13th-14th) the 52% of persons take one of the top ten names: *Pedro, Fernando, Joán, Alfonso, Martín, Domingo, Sancho, Rodrigo, García, María.* While in a more diverse corpus with a longer chronology (10th-14th) like the CBMA the concentration is less dense, but still very high compared to modern standards as at least 18% of people take one of the top ten names : *Hugues, Bernardus, Rotbertus, Petrus, Stephanus, Durannus, Willelmus, Iohannes, Odon, Arnulfus*, and their variants (v.g for *Rotbertus* : *Rotbertus, Rodberto, Robertus, Rotbert*).

2) In an analogous way, the entity co-occurrences, which are crucial to calculate transition scores in a contextual way, belongs to a restricted stock. The charters use a stable and shared vocabulary that reflects the social and administrative order and tries to specify the legal action as much as possible. A broad but regular system of titles, dignities and offices is activated to specify the category of benefactors, recipients and witnesses and usually precede the personal name. For example, in *Diplomata Belgica*, five terms (*sire/messire, bourgois, signor/monsigneur, eschevin, dame/madame*) co-occur in 24% of all personal entities. Similarly, space is well delineated both in the consciousness of men and in scriptural practices, and a hierarchical order of territorial organization serves as a coordinate system to spatially locate the movable and immovable property that is the object of the exchange. This can be verified in the CBMA corpus where the six top spatial words: *uilla, pagus, terra, ecclesia, locum, ager* co-occurs with almost a third (32%) of the total locations entities since it is the most common vocabulary, before the 13th century, for spatial determination in land transfers, the most abundant legal action in this corpus.

3) The formulaic nature of the charters proposes a relatively stable discursive structure. The documents follow a model according to the type of act and the legal action and are individualized by particular information such as the named entities. The charters have parts that support a freer wording, for example those dedicated to explaining the background and the conditions of the exchange and other more constrained ones, such as naming the authors and witnesses, the dates and the validation signs. This structure facilitates the identification of the entities since it reduces the complexity of the sequences and the probability distribution for the predictions. Certainly, the charters are not mass-produced and most of the formulas are not strictly fixed, but during their drafting, a restricted vocabulary and a regulated discursive form are used, since this is one of the elements that give the charter its value as legal proof.

4) Moreover, acts with legal value follow similar writing forms throughout Western Europe based on Latin legal language and Latin formularies. The change from the Latin code to the vernacular languages does not occur drastically and supposes the coexistence of documents of similar value written in both languages over a period of several centuries. The scribes continue to use common Latin formulation, a legal vocabulary set by prestige and tradition and following a discursive format typical of the Latin legal act in their intention to communicate a legal action clearly and explicitly. Phenomena such as linguistic interference, bilingualism, literal translations and code-switching are common in late medieval written production. Languages codes appear to be interchangeable or specific to certain situations and form a «charter language» with high semantic and lexical overlapping between Latin and vernacular languages. These overlaps favor the cross-lingual generalization during modeling since the shared words and structures are mapped onto similar representations at the same time as their co-occurrences, thus spreading the generalization effect over other word pieces of the sequence. These circumstances greatly help to create multilingual models whose performances are competitive with their monolingual counterparts.

8. Conclusion

We present an annotated multilingual corpus of medieval charters to address NER tasks. We have demonstrated that fine-tuned on general-purpose models and off-the-shelf library architectures are able to capture the underlying structure of the charters' entities in a multilingual environment reaching an average of 98% in the recognition of persons and places names. Our evaluation on unseen data confirms that they can be successfully applied to other diplomatic collections despite chronological, regional and linguistic differences. Besides, we can confirm that our models are able to produce a multi-class hypothesis using a single classifier which implies a high confidence on the recognition of nested entities extensively used in medieval charters. These models and the annotated data on which they are built, which are themselves new contributions, can be easily integrated into other pipelines, thus contributing to enhance the toolbox for the automatic treatment of the medieval text regarding other supervised methods and other Latin-derived languages.

9. Model repositories

The models, source code and the annotated corpora supporting this work are available at (Torres Aguilar, 2022) and at our git repository: `https://gitlab.com/magistermilitum//ner_medieval_multilingual/`

10. Bibliographical References

Akbik, A., Blythe, D., and Vollgraf, R. (2018). Contextual string embeddings for sequence labeling. In *Proceedings of the 27th international conference on computational linguistics*, pages 1638–1649.

Bojanowski, P., Grave, E., Joulin, A., and Mikolov, T. (2017). Enriching word vectors with subword information. *Transactions of the Association for Computational Linguistics*, 5:135–146.

Borja, P. S.-P. (2012). Desarrollo y explotación del «corpus de documentos españoles anteriores a 1700»(codea). *Scriptum digital. Revista de corpus diacrònics i edició digital en Llengües iberoromàniques*, (1):5–35.

Bormans, S., Marien, F., Halkin, J., Cuvelier, J., Hoebanx, J.-J., and Wirtz, C. (1907-1966). *Table chronologique des chartes et diplômes imprimés concernant l'histoire de la Belgique*. Commission royale d'histoire, Palais des Académies, Bruxelles.

Catelli, R., Gargiulo, F., Casola, V., De Pietro, G., Fujita, H., and Esposito, M. (2020). Crosslingual named entity recognition for clinical de-identification applied to a covid-19 italian data set. *Applied Soft Computing*, 97:106779.

Conneau, A., Khandelwal, K., Goyal, N., Chaudhary, V., Wenzek, G., Guzmán, F., Grave, E., Ott, M., Zettlemoyer, L., and Stoyanov, V. (2019). Unsupervised cross-lingual representation learning at scale. *arXiv preprint arXiv:1911.02116*.

de Hemptinne, T., Deploige, J., Kupper, J.-L., and Prevenier, W. (2015). *Diplomata Belgica: les sources diplomatiques des Pays-Bas méridionaux au Moyen Âge*. Commission royale d'Histoire.

Devlin, J., Chang, M.-W., Lee, K., and Toutanova, K. (2018). Bert: Pre-training of deep bidirectional transformers for language understanding. *arXiv preprint arXiv:1810.04805*.

Ehrmann, M., Hamdi, A., Pontes, E. L., Romanello, M., and Doucet, A. (2021). Named entity recognition and classification on historical documents: A survey. *arXiv preprint arXiv:2109.11406*.

Erdmann, A., Brown, C., Joseph, B. D., Janse, M., Ajaka, P., Elsner, M., and de Marneffe, M.-C. (2016). Challenges and solutions for latin named entity recognition. In *COLING 2016: 26th International Conference on Computational Linguistics*, pages 85–93. ACL.

Glessgen, M.-D. (2004). L'écrit documentaire dans l'histoire linguistique de la france. *La langue des actes. Actes du XIe Congrès international de diplomatique*.

Guyotjeannin, O. (2019). Édition électronique des chartes de l'abbaye de Saint-Denis, 2019.

Hélary, X. (2007). L'édition électronique du cartulaire de la seigneurie de nesle. *Bulletin du centre d'études médiévales d'Auxerre| BUCEMA*, (11).

Lamazou-Duplan, V., Goulet, A., and Charon, P. (2010). *Le cartulaire dit de Charles Ii roi de Navarre*. Presses universitaires de Pau et des Pays de l'Adour.

Magnani, E. (2020). Des chartae au corpus: la plateforme des cbma-chartae/corpus burgundiae medii aevi. *Digitizing Medieval Sources. Challenges and Methodologies.*, pages 57–67.

McDonough, K., Moncla, L., and Van de Camp, M. (2019). Named entity recognition goes to old regime france: geographic text analysis for early modern french corpora. *International Journal of Geographical Information Science*, 33(12):2498–2522.

Muller, B., Anastasopoulos, A., Sagot, B., and Seddah, D. (2020). When being unseen from mbert is just the beginning: Handling new languages with multilingual language models. *arXiv preprint arXiv:2010.12858*.

Peters, M. E., Neumann, M., Iyyer, M., Gardner, M., Clark, C., Lee, K., and Zettlemoyer, L. (2018). Deep contextualized word representations. *arXiv preprint arXiv:1802.05365*.

Schabel, C. and Friedman, R. L. (2020). *The Cartulary of Fervaques Abbey, a Cistercian Nunnery*. in press.

Stouff, L. (1989). *Cartulaire de la ville d'Arbois au comté de Bourgogne*. Revue bourguignonne de l'enseignement supérieur, 8, n° 2.

Stutzmann, D., Torres Aguilar, S., and Chaffenet, P. (2021). HOME-Alcar: Aligned and Annotated Cartularies. Zenodo: https://doi.org/10.5281/zenodo.5600884.

Valeriola, S. d. (2019). Le corpus des chirographes yprois, témoin essentiel d'un réseau de crédit du xiiie siècle. *Bulletin de la Commission royale d'Histoire*, 185(1):5–74.

Vignau, V. (1885). *Cartulario del Monasterio de Eslonza*. Madrid : Imp. de la viuda de Hernando y Cª.

Wauters, A. and Halkin, J. (1866-1907). *Table chronologique des chartes et diplômes imprimés concernant l'histoire de la Belgique*. M. Hayez, Bruxelles.

11. Language Resource References

Clérice, Thibault and Camps, Jean-Baptiste and Pinche, Ariane. (2019). *Deucalion, Modèle Ancien Francais (0.2.0)*. Zenodo. https://doi.org/10.5281/zenodo.3237455.

Prévost, Sophie and Stein, Achim. (2013). *Syntactic reference corpus of Medieval French (SRCMF)*.

Torres Aguilar, Sergio. (2022). *Multilingual named entity recognition for medieval charters. Datasets and models*. Zenodo. https://doi.org/10.5281/zenodo.6463699.

12. Appendix

Two annotated examples (red for persons, blue for places) of bilingual charters in the CBMA (Charter 1) and in the CODEA (Charter 2) : Common Latin formulations in the charter protocols and the notarized act in vernacular.

Charter 1. **CBMA 18859**. Vidimus (1273), by Hugues, archdeacon of Langres, of the charter according to which Jehanz, parish priest of Châteauvillain and dean of Chaumont, makes it known that Renauz li Acuers d'Orges admitted having donated to the abbey of Vauxbons one piece of land located at village of Orges (1256). AD Haute-Marne, 1 H 84, pièce no 8. Chauvin Benoît, L'abbaye de moniales cisterciennes de Vauxbons au diocèse de Langres (... 1175 - 1394...). Étude historique et édition du chartrier, Devecey, 2004, A27.

Universis presentes litteras inspecturis, Hugo, archidiaconus Lingonensis, salutem in Domino. Noveritis quod nos litteras inferius annotatas vidimus et verbo ad verbum legimus non cancellatas, non abolitas nec in aliqua sui parte viciatas quarum tenor talis est : Nos Jehanz, curez de Chastelvilen et doien de Chaumont, fasonz savoir a tout cas qui verrunt ces presantes latres que an ma presance estaubliz Renauz li Acuers d'Orges qui fuit filz Roelim la Lemont d'Orges a requeneu qu'il a donei de dei et d'armone por l'ame de ces acesors un jornel de terre[1] a l'abaiassa de Valbaion et es dames de leaus, li quez jornez de terre siet or finaige d'Orges ce est a savoir es seillons dares la maison au palletz aupres [2] Jaquel le Graure Chapusot. Au tamonnaige de laquel chosse, a la requeste de l'une partie et de l'autre, nos avons mis notre seel en ces presantes latres. Ce fut fait an l'an de grace mil et IIC et LVI, or mois de mars lou vanredi davant lou diemange que on chante Letare Jherusalem[3]. In cuius rei testimonium presenti transscripti, sigillum nostrum apposuimus. Datum a nobis die sabbati ante festum beate Marie Magdalenes anno Domini M°CC° septuagesimo tercio, mense julio.

Charter 2. **CODEA 0231**. Charter of sale (1216) by which Ordón Pédrez de Cavia sells several real estate properties (lands, wastelands, meadows, etc.) in the locality of Cillamayor (Palencia) to Taresa Verbúdez for 50 maravedies. Archivo Histórico Nacional, Clero, Palencia, carpeta 1653, n° 16.

In Dei nomine et eius gratia. Notum sit omnibus hominibus tam presentibus quam futuris quod ego Ordon Pedrez de Cavia vendo illa hereditate quantam habeo en Cellamayor e en Alfoz de Santo Juliano e illa renta que habeo en santa Juliana de Candiola : solares, los poblados e los ermos, plados e tierras, et illa parte de la eclesia de Santa Maria de Cellamayor, esto es, la cuarta parte quod fuit de donna Urraca Ferrandez mea avola, vendo a donna Taresa Verbudez por L morabetis et sum pacati de precio e de rovla[4]. Et si aliquis homo de mea progenie vel de extranea istam cartam voluerit disrumpere sit ille maledictus e excomunicatus cum Judas traditore in inferno dampnatus et pecet in coto[5] C morabetis regi terre. Facta carta in era MCCLIIII[6] regnante rege don Anric in Toleto e in Castella. Alferaz el conde don Alvaro, mayordomus don Gonzalvo Roiz, merino mayor Ordon Martinez, episcopus en Burgos maestre Mauriz. Hec sunt testes estantes e videndentes: Gonzalvo Garciaz de Grajera, Gonzalvo Johanes de Quintana Tello, Alvar Munioz de Rebiela [...] Petrus Isidorus qui notuit.

[1] A *journal* is a unit of land measurement (corresponds approximately to the area worked by a man in a day).
[2] Translated as: «[This land is located] in the furrows behind the fence of the house of Jaquel le Graure Chapusot».
[3] The «Laetare Ierusalem» was sung the fourth Sunday in the season of Lent (Laetare Sunday).
[4] Translated as: «The price and the *robra* are agreed». The *robra* was a treat paid by the buyer to close a sale.
[5] *Pechar in coto* is a common sanction formula that orders the person who opposes the contract to pay a sum as compensation.
[6] The calculation of the data according to the Hispanic Era starts from the year 38 BC.

Proceedings of the Second Workshop on Language Technologies for Historical and Ancient Languages (LT4HALA 2022), pages 129–134
Language Resources and Evaluation Conference (LREC 2022), Marseille, 25 June 2022

Linguistic Annotation of Neo-Latin Mathematical Texts: a Pilot-Study to Improve the Automatic Parsing of the *Archimedes Latinus*

Margherita Fantoli[1], Miryam de Lhoneux[123]
[1]KU Leuven, [2]University of Copenhagen, [3]Uppsala University
[1]Oude Markt 13, 3000 Leuven,[2] Universitetsparken 1. DK-2100 Copenhagen, [3]Thunbergsvägen 3H, 752 38 Uppsala
margherita.fantoli@kuleuven.be, ml@di.ku.dk

Abstract

This paper describes the process of syntactically parsing the Latin translation by Jacopo da San Cassiano of the Greek mathematical work *The Spirals* of Archimedes. The Universal Dependencies formalism is adopted. First, we introduce the historical and linguistic importance of Jacopo da San Cassiano's translation. Subsequently, we describe the deep Biaffine parser used for this pilot study. In particular, we motivate the choice of using the technique of treebank embeddings in light of the characteristics of mathematical texts. The paper then details the process of creation of training and test data, by highlighting the most compelling linguistic features of the text and the choices implemented in the current version of the treebank. Finally, the results of the parsing are discussed in comparison to a baseline and the most prominent errors are discussed. Overall, the paper shows the added value of creating specific training data, and of using targeted strategies (as treebank embeddings) to exploit existing annotated corpora while preserving the features of one specific text when performing syntactic parsing.

Keywords: Dependency parsing, Latin mathematical language, Universal Dependencies

1. Introduction

Jacopo da San Cassiano (1395-1494) translated most of the archimedean corpus from Ancient Greek to (Neo)-Latin around 1450 probably on the orders of Pope Nicholas V (d'Alessandro and Napolitani, 2012). The works of Archimedes, alongside Euclides' *Elements*, are considered a pillar of Hellenistic, and, in general, Greek mathematics (Heath, 1921). Jacopo's translation became a crucial medium for the rediscovery of Archimedes, and thus of Greek mathematics, among Humanists (Høyrup, 2019) and was used in the *editio princeps* of the Greek texts (Thomas Gechauff Venatorius, Basel 1544): the Latin translation was considered necessary to properly understand such a difficult work. Unlike modern mathematical texts, that rely heavily on symbolic notation, Ancient Greek mathematical texts are entirely written in plane natural language. Expressions that nowadays are rendered as 'AB:CD=DE:EF' were expressed as 'the line AB has to the line CD the same proportion that DE has to EF'. This creates an extremely peculiar variety of Ancient Greek (Acerbi, 2011; Acerbi, 2012; Netz, 2003), translated to Latin by Jacopo adopting the same style. The study of the linguistic features of Jacopo's translation hasn't been undertaken until now. Nonetheless, the creation of a treebank of this corpus is promising for different reasons:

- The text features a variety of Latin rarely targeted by linguistic studies and underrepresented in linguistic resources.
- The adaptation of the Latin language for translating the Greek of mathematics poses unique challenges.
- The availability of linguistically annotated Renaissance texts is still limited.

By creating the *Archimedes Latinus* treebank we aim at investigating the syntactic peculiarities of mathematical (Neo)-Latin. Given the success of the Universal Dependencies (UD) initiative (Nivre et al., 2016), and the large treebank availability (160), the Latin Archimedes treebank adopts the UD formalism. In addition, the recently created UDante treebank (Cecchini et al., 2020a) represents a milestone for Latin UD annotation. In fact, it is the first "native" UD treebank and its creation has generated the first (not-yet complete) language-specific guidelines for Latin[1]. Regularity is one of the most striking features of mathematical language, since a handful of terms and syntactic structures, indicating mathematical objects and relations, constitute the bulk of the text. Hence, we aim at verifying whether a syntactic parser, trained on a part of Jacopo's translation, can successfully parse the rest of the corpus, or at least reach results that significantly accelerate the post-correction for the treebank creation. This paper is structured as follows: section 2 describes the syntactic parser that we have finetuned for this study and introduces the concept of treebank embedding; section 3 describes the creation of training and test data; section 4 discusses the results of the parsing.

2. Parser

Treebank (or dataset) embeddings have been developed by (Stymne et al., 2018) on the ground of (de Lhoneux

[1]Cf. for example `https://universaldependencies.org/la/dep/obl-cmpr.html`.

et al., 2017), in order to tackle the problem of training a monolingual dependency parser using heterogenous treebanks. In fact, different UD treebanks for the same language might differ on specific aspects of the UD formalism: for instance, on the choice of the PoS for non clear-cut categories such as DET and PRON (see discussion below). Such inconsistencies might cause poor performances of parsers trained on multiple treebanks (Stymne et al., 2018). Treebank embeddings are used to prioritize, when parsing a new text, the conventions of one of the treebanks used for the training. To this goal, during training, a treebank embedding is concatenated to each word and thus one representation is learned for each of the treebank used. The representation is the same for every token of one treebank and differs from one treebank to another. When parsing a new text, a treebank identifier is given and the sentences get parsed following the 'style' of the chosen treebank. This method allows to take advantage of large training sets without overlooking treebank-specific features. The same method has been exploited to use treebanks of related languages during the training of a dependency parsing model (Smith et al., 2018). By applying this method to our case, we aim at verifying whether the parser picks up the specific, 'regular', features of the mathematical text while taking advantage of other existing treebanks. Hence, we train a multitask model to predict Parts-of-Speech (POS) and parse the text. We use the deep biaffine parser (Dozat and Manning, 2017) implementation of MaChAmp (van der Goot et al., 2021) with the use of dataset embeddings in the encoder introduced in (van der Goot and de Lhoneux, 2021). The parser uses mBERT[2] (Devlin et al., 2019) as an encoder, and a dataset embedding is concatenated to the embedding of each wordpiece before it is passed to the decoder.

3. Data Creation

3.1. Text extraction and tokenization

B. Sisana, a scholar specializing on Jacopo's work[3], has shared the critical edition of the whole corpus of Jacopo's archimedean translations, as contained in the the manuscript Nouv. Acq. Lat. 1538 (Paris, Bibliothèque nationale) identified as the autograph (d'Alessandro and Napolitani, 2012). The text is edited using MauroTeX, a specific mark-up language developed for the edition of mathematical texts[4]. Via a Python script, the text of the *Spirals* (on which this pilot study focusses) was extracted from the TeX file[5]. The tokenization and an automated PoS tagging have been performed using the Pie Latin LASLA+ model 0.0.6 (Manjavacas et al., 2019), fine-tuned on ca. 1,500,000 tokens taken from the LASLA Latin corpus[6] (Clérice, 2021).

3.2. Creating training data and test data

A training and test sets of sentences of *The Spirals* have been created[7]. They both qualify as Gold Standard since they have been manually annotated by a Latin philologist. The training set consists of the first 48 sentences of the book (1307 tokens), while the test set consist of 30 sentences taken from Propositions XIX and XX of the same book (913 tokens). The automatic PoS tagging of the Pie Latin LASLA+ model 0.0.6 has been corrected using Pyrrha, a language independent post correction app for PoS and lemmatization (Clérice et al., 2019). The PoS tagset used in Pyrrha has been converted to the Universal PoS tagset (Petrov et al., 2012) adopted in the UD initiative. At this point, the annotation of mathematical letters remains an open challenge. In fact, to indicate points, lines, circumferences and other mathematical objects, Ancient Greek authors use letters, in expression such as 'the line AB', often reduced to 'the AB'. In Greek manuscripts, a line is traced on the top of the letters. Jacopo follows the same convention, adding to dots around the string of letters, as visible in Figure 1. Recent studies have argued that these (groups of) letters have the purely linguistic anaphoric value of labels, since they allow to refer unambiguously to the same mathematical object across the same proof (Acerbi, 2020). This goes against the theory according to which their primary goal is to identify specific points in a diagram. It is thus not obvious whether the string of letters can be considered as a single token and what PoS should be assigned to it. Based on the graphic evidence of the manuscripts, we decided to keep the forms as a single token, instead of considering each letter as separate token corresponding to a point. The PoS has been left undetermined at this stage (X), but will be assigned either to NOUN [8] and SYM[9] following additional discussions with UD experts. In fact, UD guidelines assign the PoS SYM to

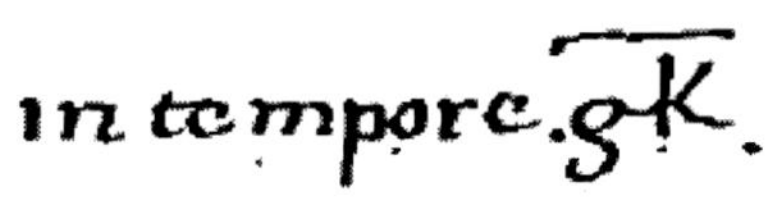

Figure 1: Snippet of the Nouv. Acq. Lat. 1538 'in tempore gk'

[2]We also experimented with latin-bert (Bamman and Burns, 2020) and used only the Latin treebanks for the training, but this led to slightly worse results so we decided to stick with mBERT and the multilingual cluster.

[3]PhD student at the Università di Roma Tre.

[4]See https://people.dm.unipi.it/maurolic/mtex/mtexen.htm

[5]The extracted text is available at https://github.com/mfantoli/Archimedes$_{L}atinus/blob/main/texts/Spirals.txt$

[6]http://web.philo.ulg.ac.be/lasla/

[7]The annotated data are available here https://github.com/mfantoli/Archimedes_Latinus.

[8]https://universaldependencies.org/u/pos/NOUN.html

[9]https://universaldependencies.org/u/pos/SYM.html

'word-like entities that differ from ordinary words by form, function, or both' and indicate that mathematical operators are SYM. Given the specific layout of these strings in the manuscripts, the choice SYM seems appealing. On the other hand, in the UDante treebank, in expressions such as *linea recta ad A*, *A* is tagged as NOUN, and indeed single letters are considered nouns in traditional lexicographical resources. The decision does not impact the syntactic parsing, but will be defined before the publication of the final version of the data. In addition, to mirror the layout of the manuscript, the mathematical letters are kept between square brackets (*linea* [AB]). In order to create gold data for the syntactic parsing, the Biaffine parser discussed in section 2 has been trained on a cluster of ancient languages described in (Smith et al., 2018): the UD version of Latin Index Thomisticus Treebank (Passarotti, 2019), of the Perseus Ancient Greek and Latin Dependency Treebanks (Bamman and Crane, 2011), of the PROIEL Old Church Slavonic, Gothic, Latin and Ancient Greek Treebanks (Eckhoff et al., 2018), of the Late Latin Charter Treebank (Cecchini et al., 2020b; Korkiakangas, 2021), and the UDante treebank. (Cecchini et al., 2020a). The sentences of the training and test sets have been parsed using the UDante embedding as treebank 'model', and manually corrected using UD Annotatrix (Tyers et al., 2017). The annotation follows the UD-style available guidelines for Latin[10] and takes into account the choices implemented in the UDante treebank (Cecchini et al., 2020a). Nonetheless, given the still limited availability of language-specific UD guidelines for Latin, and the non-literary and non-classical linguistic features of *The Spirals*, some choices have been implemented following discussions with UD experts[11]. In the UD formalism, syntactic annotation consists in identifying typed dependency relations between the words forming the sentence. Each word of a sentence - except the root- depends on one another word (head). The relation (EDGE) between a word and its head is typed based on UD dependency relations (DEPRELs[12]). The root is the head of the sentence. The DEPREL between the term indicating the mathematical object and the label (*linea AB*) has been indicated as 'flat'[13], since it is comparable to expressions such as 'President Obama'[14]. Conventionally, we indicated as head the NOUN (*'linea'*), which generally coincides, with few exceptions, with the first word of the compound[15]. However, flat relations imply that the choice of the head is arbitrary since the two words do not hold a head-modifier relation. The length of sentence represents a second challenge: the digitized text is, in fact, the direct transcription of a Renaissance manuscript. Manuscripts tend to record only minimal punctuation (Parkes, 1992), and the transcription sticks to the original layout. This entails extremely long sentences, whose clauses are rarely separated by commas: in the test set, the median length is of 21.5 words with a maximum of 104, resulting in syntactic trees with a median depth of 5.5 layers. This will be addressed for the final version of the treebank, by adding punctuation as modern editors regularly do. The lack of punctuation entails additional difficulties in analyzing the role of Latin particles in the sentence. Words such as *enim* ('namely', 'indeed'), *autem* ('however', 'on the other hand'), *rursus* ('on the contrary'), can both linking clauses belonging to the same sentence or link one sentence with the preceding one, structuring the discourse (Kroon, 1995). In very long sentences composed of a number of juxtaposed clauses, it is challenging to establish whether the tuple (verb, particle) should receive the DEPREL 'cc'[16], in case the particle functions as coordinating conjunction, or 'discourse'[17], when functioning as discourse marker.

4. Training and evaluation

Once the training data and test data have been created, the Biaffine parser is again trained on the cluster of ancient languages described above, with the addition of the newly created mathematical training data. For the prediction of the PoS tags, the mathematical training data, the treebanks, and the UD versions of the LASLA corpus[18] are used as training data. The model is trained for 80 epochs[19]. The Unlabeled Attachment Score (UAS) measures the correctness of the syntactic structure (EDGES), whereas the Labeled Attachment Score (LAS) includes also the evaluation of the label attached to the dependency (DEPRELs)[20] (Buchholz and Marsi, 2006). Table 1 reports the LAS and UAS scores computed on the test data processed with this

[10] https://universaldependencies.org/guidelines.html.

[11] In particular, Flavio M. Cecchini, CIRCSE, Università Cattolica di Milano.

[12] https://universaldependencies.org/u/dep/

[13] https://universaldependencies.org/u/dep/flat.html

[14] https://universaldependencies.org/u/dep/flat.html

[15] The UD guidelines indicate that the first of the two words linked by the 'flat' DEPREL should be used as head. The few exceptions will be corrected in the final version of the Treebank.

[16] https://universaldependencies.org/docs/en/dep/cc.html.

[17] https://universaldependencies.org/docs/en/dep/discourse.html

[18] The LASLA corpus is a morphosyntactically manually annotated corpus of Latin classical texts (Denooz, 1978), see http://web.philo.ulg.ac.be/lasla/presentation-du-laboratoire/. The LASLA data were converted to UD by Flavio M. Cecchini, CIRCSE, Università Cattolica di Milano. A sample of these data has been used in the frame of Evalatin2022, https://circse.github.io/LT4HALA/2022/EvaLatin.

[19] The model will be shared soon.

[20] For this pilot study, the LAS was computed on first-level relations only, without considering any subrelation (e. g., the DEPRELS obl, obl:cmpr and obl:arg all count as obl).

parser ('Archimedes') and with UDPipe using the UD v. 2.6 for Latin (baseline)[21].

Model	PoS	UAS	LAS
Biaffine Archimedes	91.25	72.43	59.85
IT-TB	NA	68.60	55.03
Perseus	NA	68.16	50.44

Table 1: UPOS, UAS and LAS score of different parsers

The results show a significant gain with respect to the UDPipe IT-TB model, 3.83 UAS points and 4.82 LAS points. The results can still be improved significantly: at the moment such procedure can only be effectively use as a first step to accelerate the following manual annotation. Nevertheless, it seems that a multi-task learning setup is well suited to using multiple sources of data to facilitate the annotation of a new dataset. Additionally, dataset embeddings facilitate annotating new data in the style of a specific treebank.
In order to measure the impact of the addition of mathematical texts and the use of the 'mathematical embedding' on the performance of the Biaffine parser, we also evaluated the performance of the Biaffine parser with the training described in 3.2 on a very brief portion of text (ca 400 tokens, propositions VII-VIII). The results on UAS and LAS (resp.70.56 and 58.63) outperform UDPipe, but are lower than those obtained in the final stage. However, we should mention that this test-set might not be representative, since some complex sentences had to be removed due to editorial issues. The annotation of PoS scores quite high (95.6): the result, higher than with the addition of mathematical texts, can be explained by the absence, in this portion of text, of the term *spiralis* ('spiral'), which is the main source of errors for the final test-set (see below).

5. Error analysis

To complement the scores, we performed an analysis of the errors on the POS, dependencies and labels. The confusion matrix of the PoS is shown in Figure 2. The most frequent error is due to the mislabeling of *spiralis* ('spiral') as NOUN in the expression *linea spiralis* ('spiral line'), where it is an ADJ. The second most frequent source of errors is the confusion between DET[22] and PRON[23], which is mostly due to linguistic ambiguity, given that the same words, such as *ille* ('that','that

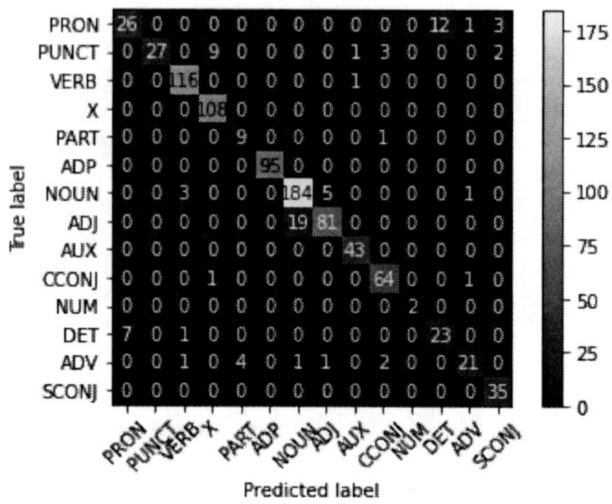

Figure 2: Confusion matrix for the PoS prediction

person') or *iste* ('this','this person'), can be used with both functions[24]. Out of the 253 cases of wrong head assignment, 57 concern mathematical labels, which is a highly specific feature of our text. In the subset of corrected predicted dependency, the most common error in DEPRELs assignment (15 times out of 127 errors) is 'nmod'[25] instead of 'flat', always between a mathematical term and its label. As it appears, most of the errors generate from the mathematical content of the text.

6. Conclusion

The linguistic annotation of non-classical, non-literary varieties of Latin poses major challenges, both because of the difficulty of adapting existing guidelines to these texts[26] and because of the lack of well-suited annotated data and tools to automate the process. In this pilot study we have shown the added value of creating specific training data, and of using targeted strategies (as treebank embeddings) to jointly exploit existing annotated corpora without losing the features of one specific text. Such strategy beats baseline results, and appears promising for the future. As next steps, the performance of the parser will be improved by assigning PoS to mathematical labels in the training data and by increasing the amount and variety of training data from Jacopo's translation of different work of Archimedes.
In a second stage, we will manually correct the output of the parser to provide a treebank of Jacopo's translation of at least one complete work of Archimedes. Finally, the completion of such project will result in the

[21]The PROIEL score is not recorded because the model splits long sentences at weak punctuation marks, and the PoS score is not reported for IT-TB and Perseus because of the 'X' PoS assigned in the gold data to the mathematical labels.

[22]see UD guidelines `https://universaldependencies.org/u/pos/DET.html`.

[23]see UD guidelines `https://universaldependencies.org/u/pos/PRON.html`.

[24]see UD guidelines `https://universaldependencies.org/u/pos/DET.html`.

[25]`https://universaldependencies.org/en/dep/nmod.html`

[26]see, for instance, (Korkiakangas and Passarotti, 2012) and (Grotto et al., 2021)

contribution to the guidelines for the UD-style annotation of Latin, in particular scientific Latin.

7. Acknowledgments

We would like to thank Flavio Cecchini for his advice on many of the annotation questions raised during this project. We would also like to thank the reviewer for their precious comments and suggestions.

8. Bibliographical References

Acerbi, F. (2011). The language of the “givens”: its forms and its use as a deductive tool in greek mathematics. *Archive for History of Exact Sciences*, 65(2):119–153, feb.

Acerbi, F. (2012). I codici stilisticidella matematica greca:dimostrazioni, procedure, algoritmi. *Quaderni Urbinati di Cultura Classica*, (101.2):167–216.

Acerbi, F. (2020). Mathematical generality, letter-labels, and all that. *Phronesis*, 65:27–75.

Bamman, D. and Burns, P. J. (2020). Latin bert: A contextual language model for classical philology. *ArXiv*, abs/2009.10053.

Bamman, D. and Crane, G., (2011). *Language Technology for Cultural Heritage*, chapter The Ancient Greek and Latin Dependency Treebanks, pages 79–98. SpingerLink.

Buchholz, S. and Marsi, E. (2006). CoNLL-X shared task on multilingual dependency parsing. In *Proceedings of the Tenth Conference on Computational Natural Language Learning (CoNLL-X)*, pages 149–164, New York City, June. Association for Computational Linguistics.

Cecchini, F. M., Sprugnoli, R., Moretti, G., and Passarotti, M. (2020a). UDante: First Steps Towards the Universal Dependencies Treebank of Dante's Latin Works. In *Seventh Italian Conference on Computational Linguistics*, pages 1–7, Bologna. CEUR-WS.org.

Cecchini, F. M., Korkiakangas, T., and Passarotti, M. (2020b). A new Latin treebank for Universal Dependencies: Charters between Ancient Latin and Romance languages. In *Proceedings of the 12th Language Resources and Evaluation Conference*, pages 933–942, Marseille, France, May. European Language Resources Association.

Clérice, T. (2021). Latin Lasla Model, Apr. DOI: 10.5281/zenodo.4661034.

Clérice, T., Pilla, J., Jean-Baptiste-Camps, and architexte. (2019). hipster-philology/pyrrha: 2.1.0, November.

Paolo d'Alessandro et al., editors. (2012). *Archimede Latino: Iacopo da San Cassiano e il Corpus archimedeo alla metà del Quattrocento con edizione della Circuli dimensio e della Quadratura parabolae*. Les Belles Lettres, Paris.

de Lhoneux, M., Shao, Y., Basirat, A., Kiperwasser, E., Stymne, S., Goldberg, Y., and Nivre, J. (2017). From raw text to Universal Dependencies - look, no tags! In *Proceedings of the CoNLL 2017 Shared Task: Multilingual Parsing from Raw Text to Universal Dependencies*, pages 207–217, Vancouver, Canada, August. Association for Computational Linguistics.

Denooz, J. (1978). L'ordinateur et le latin. techniques et méthodes. *Revue de l'organisation internationale pour l'étude des langues anciennes par ordinateur*, 4:1–36.

Devlin, J., Chang, M.-W., Lee, K., and Toutanova, K. (2019). BERT: Pre-training of deep bidirectional transformers for language understanding. In *Proceedings of the 2019 Conference of the North American Chapter of the Association for Computational Linguistics: Human Language Technologies, Volume 1 (Long and Short Papers)*, pages 4171–4186, Minneapolis, Minnesota, June. Association for Computational Linguistics.

Dozat, T. and Manning, C. (2017). Deep Biaffine Attention for Neural Dependency Parsing. In *Proceedings of the 5th International Conference on Learning Representations*.

Eckhoff, H. M., Bech, K., Bouma, G., Eide, K., Haug, D., Haugen, O. E., and Jøhndal, M. (2018). The PROIEL treebank family: a standard for early attestations of Indo-European languages. *Language Resources and Evaluation*, 52(1):29–65.

Grotto, F., Sprugnoli, R., Fantoli, M., Simi, M., Cecchini, F. M., and Passarotti, M. C. (2021). The annotation of liber abbaci, a domain-specific latin resource. In *Proceedings of the Eighth Italian Conference on Computational Linguistics (CLiC-it 2021). Milan, Italy, January 26-28, 2022, (MILANO – ITA, 26-28 January 2022)*, pages 1–8.

Thomas Heath, editor. (1921). *A History of Greek Mathematics*. Clarendon Press, Oxford.

Høyrup, J., (2019). *Archimedes: Reception in the Renaissance*, pages 1–7. Springer International Publishing, Cham.

Korkiakangas, T. and Passarotti, M. (2012). Challenges in annotating medieval latin charters. *Journal for Language Technology and Computational Linguistics*, 26(2):103–114, February.

Korkiakangas, T. (2021). Late latin charter treebank: contents and annotation. *Corpora*, 16(2):191–203.

Kroon, C. (1995). *Discourse particles in Latin : a study of nam, enim, autem, vero and at*. Gieben, Amsterdam.

Manjavacas, E., Kádár, Á., and Kestemont, M. (2019). Improving lemmatization of non-standard languages with joint learning. In *Proceedings of the 2019 Conference of the North American Chapter of the Association for Computational Linguistics: Human Language Technologies, Volume 1 (Long and Short Papers)*, pages 1493–1503, Minneapolis, Minnesota, June. Association for Computational Linguistics.

Netz, R. (2003). *The Shaping of Deduction in Greek*

Mathematics : A Study in Cognitive History. Cambridge University Press.

Nivre, J., De Marneffe, M.-C., Ginter, F., Goldberg, Y., Hajic, J., Manning, C. D., McDonald, R., Petrov, S., Pyysalo, S., Silveira, N., et al. (2016). Universal dependencies v1: A multilingual treebank collection. In *Proceedings of the Tenth International Conference on Language Resources and Evaluation (LREC'16)*, pages 1659–1666.

M.B. Parkes, editor. (1992). *Pause and Effect: An Introduction to the History of Punctuation in the West*. Routledge, Berkeley-Los Angeles.

Passarotti, M. (2019). The Project of the Index Thomisticus Treebank. In Monica Berti, editor, *Digital Classical Philology. Ancient Greek and Latin in the Digital Revolution*, pages 299–319. De Gruyter, Berlin.

Petrov, S., Das, D., and McDonald, R. (2012). A universal part-of-speech tagset. In *Proceedings of the Eighth International Conference on Language Resources and Evaluation (LREC'12)*, pages 2089–2096, Istanbul, Turkey, May. European Language Resources Association (ELRA).

Smith, A., Bohnet, B., de Lhoneux, M., Nivre, J., Shao, Y., and Stymne, S. (2018). 82 treebanks, 34 models: Universal Dependency parsing with multi-treebank models. In *Proceedings of the CoNLL 2018 Shared Task: Multilingual Parsing from Raw Text to Universal Dependencies*, pages 113–123, Brussels, Belgium, October. Association for Computational Linguistics.

Stymne, S., de Lhoneux, M., Smith, A., and Nivre, J. (2018). Parser training with heterogeneous treebanks. pages 619–625, 01.

Tyers, F. M., Sheyanova, M., and Washington, J. N. (2017). UD annotatrix: An annotation tool for Universal Dependencies. In *Proceedings of the 16th International Workshop on Treebanks and Linguistic Theories*, pages 10–17, Prague, Czech Republic.

van der Goot, R. and de Lhoneux, M. (2021). Parsing with pretrained language models, multiple datasets, and dataset embeddings. In *Proceedings of the 20th International Workshop on Treebanks and Linguistic Theories (TLT, SyntaxFest 2021)*, pages 96–104, Sofia, Bulgaria. Association for Computational Linguistics.

van der Goot, R., Üstün, A., Ramponi, A., Sharaf, I., and Plank, B. (2021). Massive choice, ample tasks (MaChAmp): A toolkit for multi-task learning in NLP. In *Proceedings of the 16th Conference of the European Chapter of the Association for Computational Linguistics: System Demonstrations*, pages 176–197, Online. Association for Computational Linguistics.

Proceedings of the Second Workshop on Language Technologies for Historical and Ancient Languages (LT4HALA 2022), pages 135–140
Language Resources and Evaluation Conference (LREC 2022), Marseille, 25 June 2022

The First International Ancient Chinese Word Segmentation and POS Tagging Bakeoff: Overview of the EvaHan 2022 Evaluation Campaign

Bin Li [1] Yiguo Yuan[1] Jingya Lu[1] Minxuan Feng[1] Chao Xu[1] Weiguang Qu[2] Dongbo Wang[3]
1. School of Chinese Language and Literature, Nanjing Normal University
2. School of Computer and Electronic Information, Nanjing Normal University
3. College of Information Management, Nanjing Agricultural University
E-mail: libin.njnu.at.gmail.com

Abstract

This paper presents the results of the First Ancient Chinese Word Segmentation and POS Tagging Bakeoff (EvaHan), which was held at the Second Workshop on Language Technologies for Historical and Ancient Languages (LT4HALA) 2022, in the context of the 13th Edition of the Language Resources and Evaluation Conference (LREC 2022). We give the motivation for having an international shared contest, as well as the data and tracks. The contest is consisted of two modalities, closed and open. In the closed modality, the participants are only allowed to use the training data, obtained the highest F1 score of 96.03% and 92.05% in word segmentation and POS tagging. In the open modality, the participants can use whatever resource they have, with the highest F1 score of 96.34% and 92.56% in word segmentation and POS tagging. The scores on the blind test dataset decrease around 3 points, which shows that the out-of-vocabulary words still are the bottleneck for lexical analyzers.

Keywords: Evaluation, Ancient Chinese, Word Segmentation, POS Tagging

1. Introduction

EvaHan2022 is the first campaign devoted to the evaluation of Natural Language Processing (NLP) systems for the Ancient Chinese. [1] Unlike English or other western languages, Chinese does not have word boundaries. Thus, word segmentation is a basic task for Chinese language processing. It has received a lot of attention in the literature (Sun and Zou, 2001; Xue et al., 2003). There are five word segmentation bakeoffs for Mandarin Chinese held by SIGHAN (Special Interest Group of Han) workshops during 2003 to 2012 (Sproat and Emerson, 2003; Emerson, 2005; Levow, 2006; Jin and Chen, 2008; Duan et al., 2012) with the highest F1 score around 98% in the open modality test.

Ancient Chinese is a dominant written language during Pre-Qin(before 221BC) and Han dynasties(202BC-220AD). This continued in later dynasties until the 1900s. It is also named as Old Chinese, or Literary Chinese (Wenyan 文言) [2]. There are huge numbers of ancient books written in this language, which requires fast and efficient automatic tools to conduct word segmentation and POS (part-of-speech) tagging. The character, lexicon and grammar of Ancient Chinese differs a lot from the Mandarin Chinese, and the existing Mandarin Chinese lexical analyzers can not run on the Ancient Chinese texts. At the same time, the ancient Chinese has many fewer lexicons and corpora for training and evaluation. Therefore, a standard shared task is needed for developing the Ancient Chinese analyzers.

EvaHan2022 aims to answer two main questions:

- How can we promote the development of resources and language technologies for the Ancient Chinese language?
- How can we foster collaboration among scholars working on Ancient Chinese and attract researchers from different disciplines?

EvaHan2022 is proposed as part of the Workshop on Language Technologies for Historical and Ancient Languages (LT4HALA), co-located with LREC 2022. [3] EvaHan is organized by the Computational Linguistics and Digital Humanities (CLDH) Group at Nanjing Normal University in Nanjing, China. Scorer and detailed guidelines are all available in a dedicated GitHub repository. [4] LT4HALA also holds the shared task for Latin lemmatization and POS tagging (EvaLatin2022), which affords an opportunity for the comparison of the two ancient languages.

2. Task

EvaHan2022 has one joint task, Word Segmentation and POS tagging:

1. Word segmentation is the process of transforming Chinese character sequence to word sequence.
2. POS tagging is the process of labelling the word sequence with its Part-of-Speech identifiers.

In this shared task, a sentence should be automatically parsed from raw text to POS tagged text shown in Table 1. The evaluation toolkit gives the scores on both word segmentation and POS tagging. EvaHan2022 does not accept running results with word segmentation only.

[1] https://circse.github.io/LT4HALA/2022/EvaHan
[2] https://en.wikipedia.org/wiki/Old_Chinese
[3] https://lrec2022.lrec-conf.org/en/
[4] https://github.com/CIRCSE/LT4HALA/blob/master/2022/data_and_doc/

Raw Text with Punctuations	亟請於武公，公弗許。
Annotated Text with word boundaries	亟 請 於 武公 ， 公 弗 許 。
Annotated Text with word boundaries and POS tags	亟/d 請/v 於/p 武公/nr ，/w 公/n 弗/d 許/v 。/w

Table 1: Examples of Word Segmentation and POS Tagging.

3. Dataset

The dataset of EvaHan 2022 is made of texts from the classic historical books *Zuozhuan* (左传), Shiji (史记) and Zizhitongjian (资治通鉴). The training and gold texts have been automatically punctuated, word segmented and POS tagged, and then manually corrected by Ancient Chinese language experts.

3.1 Data Format

The dataset consists of three parts, a Training dataset and two Test datasets. All the data is distributed following the word segmentation and POS tagging guidelines for Ancient Chinese by Nanjing Normal University (Chen et al. 2013). According to such format, annotations are encoded in UTF-8 plain text files. There are no word boundaries in Chinese texts. Thus, the raw texts contain characters and punctuation. After manual annotation, word boundaries and POS tags are added to the text. As shown in Table 1, each word is labelled with a POS tag, in the form of **Word/POS**. And each word is separated by a space. Punctuations are treated as words too.

3.2 Training Data

The training data contains punctuated, word-segmented and part-of-speech tagged text from *Zuozhuan (左传)*, an ancient Chinese work believed to date from the Warring States Period (475-221 BC). *Zuozhuan* is a commentary on the book *Chunqui (春秋)*, recording the history of the Chinese Spring and Autumn period (770-476 BC).

The files are presented in UTF-8 plain text files using traditional Chinese script. It is released via Linguistic Data Consortium (LDC)[5].

Data Sets	Sources	# Char Tokens	# Word Tokens
Train	*Zuozhuan*	194,995	166,142
Test_A	*Zuozhuan*	33,297	28,131
Test_B	*Shiji, Zizhitongjian*	62,969	55,990

Table 2: Texts distributed as training/test data in EvaHan 2022.

3.3 Test Data

Test data is provided in raw format, with Chinese characters and punctuations. The gold standard test data, which had been manually checked for the evaluation, was provided to the participants after the evaluation.
There are two test datasets. *Test_A* is designed to see how a system performs on the data from a single book. *Test_A* is extracted from *Zuozhuan*, not overlapping with *Train*. *Test_A* has been released by LDC. But the teams are not allowed to use it as training data. There have been several papers reporting their performance on this data (Shi et al., 2010; Cheng 2020 et al., 2020).

Blind *Test_B* is designed to see how a system performs on similar data, texts of similar content but from different books *Shiji (史记)* and *Zizhitongjian (资治通鉴)*. *Test_B* has not been released publicly before EVAHAN. Its size is similar to that of *Test_A*.

4. Evaluation

Each participating team initially had access only to the training data. Later, the unlabeled test data was released. After the assessment, the gold labels for the test data was also released.

4.1 Scoring

The scorer employed for EvaHan is a modified version of the one developed for the SIGHAN2008 (Jin and Chen, 2008). The evaluation aligned the system-produced words to the gold standard ones. Then, Word Segmentation (WS) and Part-of-Speech (POS) tagging were evaluated separately: precision, recall and F1 score are calculated. The final ranking will be based on F1 score.

4.2 Two Modalities

Each participant can submit runs following two modalities. In the *closed* modality, the resources each team could use are limited. Each team can only use the Training data *Train*, and the pretrained model *SIKU-Roberta*[6]. It is the word embeddings pretrained on a very large corpus of traditional Chinese collection, *Siku Quanshu* (四库全书)[7]. Other resources are not allowed in the closed modality.
In the *open* modality, there is no limit on the resources, data and models. Annotated external data, such as the components or Pinyin of the Chinese characters, word embeddings can be employed. But each team has to state all the resources, data and models they use in each system in the final report.

Limits	Closed Modality	Open Modality
Machine learning algorithm	No limit	No limit
Pretrained model	Only SIKU_Roberta	No limit
Training data	Only *Train*	No limit
Features used	Only from *Train*	No limit
Manual correction	Not allowed	Not allowed

Table 3: Limitations on the two modalities.

4.3 Procedures

Training data was released for download from Dec 20, 2021. Test data was released on March 31, 2022, and results were due on 00:00(UTC) April 7, 2022 .

[5] https://catalog.ldc.upenn.edu/LDC2017T14
[6] https://huggingface.co/SIKU-BERT/sikuroberta
[7] https://en.wikipedia.org/wiki/Siku_Quanshu

5. Participants and Results

5.1 Participants

A total of 14 teams took part in the task, submitting 55 running results. Table 4 lists the teams' basic information. Almost all the teams submitted their running results under the closed modality, while only 5 teams attended the open modality. Four files were in wrong formats (marked + in table 4), which have been corrected for evaluation. Two files were submitted overdue (marked * in table 4).

ID	Name	Affiliation	TestA		TestB	
			C	O	C	O
1	BIT1	Beijing Institute of Technology	1	0	1	0
2	BIT2	Beijing Institute of Technology	1	0	1	0
3	BLCU	Beijing Language and Culture University	2	2	2	2
4	BUPT	Beijing University of Posts and Telecommunications	1	0	1	0
5	FDU	Fudan University	2	2	2	2
6	GDUFS	Guangdong University of Foreign Studies	2	0	2	0
7	HIT	Harbin Institute of Technology	2	2	2	2
8	IMUT	Inner Mongol University of Technology	1	0	1	0
9	NJU	Nanjing University	2	0	2	0
10	NJUPT	Nanjing University of Posts and Telecommunications	1*	1^+	1*	0
11	NUAA	Nanjing University of Aeronautics and Astronautics	1	0	0	2
12	THU	Tsinghua University	1	0	1	0
13	ZNNU	Zhongbei College of Nanjing Normal University	1^+	1^+	0	1^+
14	ZYB	Zuoyebang Education Technology (Beijing) Co., Ltd	2	0	2	0
Total files		55	20	8	18	9

Table 4: Participating teams by test datasets and modalities (Closed and Open). + files with format correction * submitted overdue

5.2 Results

Table 5-8 list the performances of the teams' systems, sorted by PF (POS tagging F1-score) value (descending). The Precision, Recall and F1 score for Word Segmentation, are shortened as WP, WR and WF. The Precision, Recall and F1 score for Part-of-speech Tagging, are shortened as PP, PR and PF. We categorized the results submitted by the participants as *TestA* Closed, *TestA* Open, *TestB* Closed, and *TestB* Open. The results are ranked by the POS tagging (PF) scores. Most teams participated in closed tests. It can be seen from the four tables that there is a high correlation between word segmentation and POS tagging.

For *TestA*, the highest F1 score of POS tagging is 92.05% in the closed modality. In the open modality, it rises up to 92.56%.

The scores of word segmentation are much higher. FDU scores 96.12% and 96.34% in the closed and open modality. It is remarkble that BUPT scores 96.16% in the closed modality, with a slightly lower score 91.24% for POS Tagging.

For *TestB*, which is designed to see how the systems perform on similar data, the scores all drop down about 3 to 5 points. In the closed modality, FDU achieves 87.77%, only a little lower than 87.87% in the open modality, which means, the outter resources do not help much. The segmentation scores drops to 93.34% and 93.60% in the closed and open modality. The lower performer on *TestB* is possibly caused by the OOV(Out of Vocabulary) words.

ZNNU scores 89.47% in *TestB*, ranking the first place in the open modality. But they did not submit the running file in the closed modality, and this score is even higher than their performance on *TestA*. The outer resources may help them achieve this high score.

Team	WP	WR	WF	PP	PR	PF
FDU	95.39	96.68	**96.03**	91.43	92.67	**92.05**
	95.57	96.67	**96.12**	91.50	92.55	**92.02**
BIT	95.18	96.49	95.83	90.96	92.22	**91.59**
BUPT	95.81	96.52	**96.16**	90.90	91.57	91.24
NUAA	95.63	96.33	95.98	90.88	91.54	91.21
GDUFS	94.85	96.52	95.68	90.34	91.93	91.13
THU	94.70	95.72	95.20	89.59	90.55	90.07
NJU	94.15	95.46	94.80	89.29	90.53	89.90
	94.18	95.44	94.81	89.28	90.47	89.87
GDUFS	92.27	95.46	93.84	88.14	91.18	89.63
BIT2	94.48	94.99	94.74	88.95	89.43	89.19
IMUT	94.67	93.10	93.88	89.73	88.24	88.98
ZYB	94.90	95.07	94.99	88.30	88.46	88.38
ZNNU	92.76	91.45	92.10	88.80	87.54	88.16
ZYB	94.86	94.95	94.90	87.49	87.58	87.53
HIT	90.78	93.03	91.89	84.70	86.80	85.74
	90.81	92.99	91.89	84.72	86.77	85.73
BLCU	91.39	93.22	92.29	84.39	86.09	85.23
	91.39	93.27	92.32	84.20	85.93	85.05
NJUPT*	78.13	86.32	82.03	58.48	64.61	61.39

Table 5 *TestA* closed modality (%)

Team	WP	WR	WF	PP	PR	PF
FDU	95.81	96.88	**96.34**	92.05	93.07	**92.56**
	95.73	96.84	**96.28**	91.88	92.94	**92.41**
ZNNU	92.78	90.18	91.46	88.97	86.48	**87.71**
HIT	91.20	93.49	**92.33**	85.41	87.56	86.47
	91.09	93.41	92.24	85.27	87.45	86.35

BLCU	90.91	92.40	91.65	83.55	84.92	84.23
	90.56	92.29	91.41	83.13	84.72	83.92
NJUPT	78.14	86.31	82.02	57.35	63.35	60.20

Table 6 *TestA* open modality (%)

Team	WP	WR	WF	PP	PR	PF
FDU	94.72	91.99	**93.34**	89.07	86.50	**87.77**
	94.65	91.68	**93.14**	88.98	86.19	**87.57**
BIT	94.48	91.70	93.07	88.40	85.80	**87.08**
GDUFS	94.59	92.70	**93.64**	87.87	86.12	86.99
	92.81	93.20	93.01	86.58	86.94	86.76
BUPT	94.04	90.59	92.28	86.86	83.67	85.24
THU	93.51	90.35	91.90	86.38	83.32	84.82
IMUT	93.65	86.43	89.89	87.05	80.33	83.56
BIT2	93.07	88.90	90.94	85.45	81.61	83.49
ZYB	93.59	89.89	91.70	84.69	81.34	82.98
	93.61	89.97	91.75	84.00	80.74	82.33
NJU	90.00	87.94	88.96	80.89	79.03	79.95
	89.56	87.31	88.42	80.56	78.53	79.53
BLCU	87.72	84.50	86.08	75.32	72.55	73.91
	87.65	84.61	86.10	75.21	72.60	73.88
HIT	82.79	78.82	80.75	71.37	67.95	69.62
	82.19	77.82	79.94	70.21	66.45	68.27
NJUPT*	81.24	85.13	83.14	58.25	61.04	59.62

Table 7 TestB closed modality (%)

Team	WP	WR	WF	PP	PR	PF
ZNNU	95.26	94.79	**95.03**	89.70	89.25	**89.47**
FDU	94.97	92.26	**93.60**	89.16	86.62	**87.87**
	94.81	91.94	**93.35**	88.85	86.16	**87.48**
NUAA	94.50	91.69	93.07	87.79	85.18	86.47
	94.49	91.69	93.07	87.79	85.18	86.46
BLCU	87.09	83.43	85.22	73.99	70.88	72.40
	87.03	83.38	85.16	73.48	70.40	71.91
HIT	83.27	79.30	81.24	71.81	68.38	70.05
	82.23	78.31	80.22	70.77	67.40	69.04

Table 8 *TestB* open modality (%)

5.3 Baselines and Toplines

To provide a basis for comparison, we computed the baseline and possible topline scores for each of the test sets according to the scores in Fourth International Chinese Language Processing Bakeoff (Jin and Chen, 2008).

5.3.1 Word Segmentation

The baseline for ancient Chinese word segmentation is constructed by left-to-right maximal match algorithm using the training set vocabulary. The topline employs the same procedure, but instead uses the test set vocabulary.

Test Set	WP	WR	WF
TestA	84.98	89.20	87.04
TestB	80.43	85.28	82.78

Table 9. Word segmentation baselines (%)

Test Set	WP	WR	WF
TestA	99.04	98.20	98.62
TestB	98.48	97.11	97.79

Table 10. Word segmentation toplines (%)

The word segmentation scores of most teams exceed the baselines in *TestA* and *TestB*. The best scores outperform the baselines by around 10 points as shown in Table 11.

Test set	WP	WR	WF
TestA	+10.83	+7.68	+9.30
TestB	+14.83	+9.51	+12.25

Table 11. The promotion to the baselines of word segmentation (%)

5.3.2 POS tagging

The baseline for ancient Chinese POS tagging is constructed on the test set, word-segmented by the baseline for word segmentation and calculated by generating a list of words and POS tags from the training set. The tagging process is: (1) Tag those words which have only one POS tag in the list; (2) For those words that have not only one tag, the unique most frequent tag in the training set is assigned to them; (3) For each word that does not have a unique most frequent tag, its tag which is the most frequent in the overall training set is assigned to it; (4) Those words that are not in the list are assigned with the most frequent tag in the overall training set. The topline for ancient Chinese POS tagging is constructed on the test sets word-segmented by the topline for word segmentation and calculated by generating a list of words and POS tags from each test set.

The scores of most teams exceed the baselines in *TestA* and *TestB*, as shown in Table 14. And the best POS tagging score exceeds the topline, shown in Table 15.

Test Set	PP	PR	PF
TestA	75.93	79.70	77.77
TestB	66.83	70.87	68.79

Table 12. POS tagging baselines

Test Set	PP	PR	PF
TestA	91.76	90.99	91.37
TestB	89.77	88.51	89.14

Table 13. POS tagging toplines

Test Set	PP	PR	PF
TestA	+16.12	+13.37	+14.79
TestB	+22.87	+18.37	+20.68

Table 14. The promotion to the baselines of POS tagging

Test Set	PP	PR	PF
TestA	+0.29	+2.08	+1.19
TestB	-0.07	+0.74	+0.33

Table 15. The promotion to the topline of POS tagging

5.4 Comparison with EVALATIN

EvaHan2022 is co-held with EvaLatin2022. As an evaluation of the same type, EvaHan2022 has its own features. EvaLatin2022 mainly evaluates the NLP tools for Latin about Lemmatization and Part-of-Speech tagging. These 2 tasks are each with 3 sub-tasks (i.e. Classical, Cross-Genre and Cross-Time). Articles by five representative Latin authors were selected as Training data and Test data. Each team conducts a closed modality and then chooses whether to conduct an open modality. A total of five teams submitted test results in EvaLatin2022 (Sprugnoli et al., 2022), choosing the different methods and all the results exceed the baseline.

The best results in the lemmatization task for the three subtasks in terms of F1 score are 97.26% (Classical), 96.03% (Cross-genre) and 92.15% (Cross-time). And the best results in the POS tagging task for the three subtasks in terms of F1 score are 97.99% (Classical), 96.78% (Cross-genre) and 92.97% (Cross-time), as shown in Table 16. Also, we can see that the best results are almost all in open modality. Differently, EvaHan2022 divides the results of evaluation into four categories as *TestA* Closed modality, *TestA* Open modality, *TestB* Closed modality and *TestB* Open modality. The best results for these four types of tasks are 92.05% (FDU), 92.56% (FDU), 87.77% (FDU) and 89.47% (ZNNU).

Test	LF	PF
Classical Closed	96.45	97.61
Classical Open	97.26	97.99
Cross-Genre Closed	93.05	94.78
Cross-Genre Open	96.03	96.78
Cross-Time Closed	91.68	92.97
Cross-Time Open	92.15	92.70

Table 16. The best F1 scores on Lemmatization(LF) and POS tagging(PF) in EvaLatin2022 (%)

The shared tasks of EvaLatin2022 and EvaHan2022 both achieved good results. The POS tagging results of Latin are 4-5 points higher than that of Ancient Chinese. From the linguistic perspective, the inflections are the markers of the words' grammatical functions, thus the POS tagging of Latin is easier than Ancient Chinese. On the other hand, the best score of lemmatization of Latin is similar to that of word segmentation of Ancient Chinese, which is around 96%.

Comparing with the Mandarin Chinese's word segmentation and POS tagging scores in SIGHAN bakeoffs, the Ancient Chinese is around 1 point lower in word segmentation, while about 3 points lower in POS tagging.

6. Conclusion

EVAHan2022 is the first bakeoff for Ancient Chinese word segmentation and POS tagging. The best system from Fudan University outperforms almost all the other systems. Deep learning models raise up the scores for the Ancient Chinese, as it does on other languages like Latin. However, performance on single-source (ie. one book) dataset is better than on multiple-source datasets. It is caused by out-of-vocabulary (OOV) words in the new dataset. OOV is always a challenge for any lexical analyzers. So, there should be more attention paid to it.

In the future, the next EvaHan bakeoff should be extended to more genres and cross-time corpora, in order to improve the performance on more data.

7. Acknowledgements

Thank the reviewers for their advices. Thank Tongzheheng Zheng, Xue Yu, Min Shi, Lili Yu, Qingqing Wang, Yaxin Li, Qian Yang, Lu Wang, for their data annotation of the datasets. This work is supported in part by National Social Science Funds of China (18BYY127, 21&ZD331), Project of Social Science Foundation of Jiangsu Province (20JYB004).

8. Bibliographical References

Hongmei Zhao and Qun Liu. (2010). The CIPS-SIGHAN CLP2010 Chinese Word Segmentation Backoff. In *Proceedings of The First CIPS-SIGHAN Joint Conference on Chinese Language Processing*. pp. 199-209.

Huiming Duan., Zhifang Sui., Ye Tian and Wenjie Li. (2012). The CIPS-SIGHAN CLP 2012 ChineseWord Segmentation on MicroBlog Corpora Bakeoff. In *CIPS-SIGHAN*. pp.35-40.

Guangjin Jin and Xiao Chen. (2008). The Fourth International Chinese Language Processing Bakeoff: Chinese Word Segmentation, Named Entity Recognition and Chinese POS Tagging. In *Proceedings of the Sixth SIGHAN Workshop on Chinese Language Processing*.

Gina-Anne Levow. (2006). The Third International Chinese Language Processing Bakeoff: Word Segmentation and Named Entity Recognition. In *Proceedings of the Fifth SIGHAN Workshop on Chinese Language Processing*, pp.108–117, Sydney, Australia. Association for Computational Linguistics.

Ning Cheng, Bin Li, Liming Xiao, Changwei Xu, Sijia Ge, Xingyue Hao, Minxuan Feng. Integration of Automatic Sentence Segmentation and Lexical Analysis of Ancient Chinese based on BiLSTM-CRF Model. In *First Workshop on Language Technologies for Historical and Ancient Languages, (LT4HALA 2020)*, pp 52-58. Marseille, 11–16 May 2020.

Nianwen Xue. (2003). Chinese Word Segmentation as Character Tagging. *International Journal of Computational Linguistics & Chinese Language Processing*, Volume 8, Number 1, February 2003: Special Issue on Word Formation and Chinese Language Processing, pages 29–48.

Richard Sproat and Thomas Emerson. (2003). The first international Chinese word segmentation Bakeoff. In *Proceedings of the second SIGHAN workshop on Chinese language processing - Volume 17 (SIGHAN '03)*. Association for Computational Linguistics, USA, 133–143.

Sprugnoli, Rachele and Passarotti, Marco and Cecchini, Flavio Massimiliano and Fantoli, Margherita and Moretti, Giovanni. (2022). Overview of the EvaLatin 2022 evaluation campaign. In *Proceedings of LT4HALA*

2022-2st Workshop on Language Technologies for Historical and Ancient Languages.

Maosong Sun, Jiayan Zou.(2001). A Critical Appraisal of the research on Chinese Word Segmentation. China : *Contemporary Linguistics*, 2001, 3(1), 22-32+77.

Min Shi, Bin Li and Xiaohe Chen. (2010). CRF Based Research on a Unified Approach to Word Segmentation and POS Tagging for Pre-Qin Chinese. China: *Journal of Chinese Information Processing*. pp. 39-46.

Thomas Emerson. (2005). The Second International Chinese Word Segmentation Bakeoff. In *Proceedings of the Fourth SIGHAN Workshop on Chinese Language Processing*.

Xiaohe Chen, Minxuan Feng, Runhua Xu. (2013). *Information Processing of Pre-Qin Chinese*. Beijing : World Publishing Corporation.

9. Language Resource References

Xiaohe Chen, Bin Li, Minxuan Feng, et al. (2017). Ancient Chinese Corpus, distributed via LDC, Text resources, 1.0, ISLRN 924-985-704-453-5.

Proceedings of the Second Workshop on Language Technologies for Historical and Ancient Languages (LT4HALA 2022), pages 141–145
Language Resources and Evaluation Conference (LREC 2022), Marseille, 25 June 2022

Automatic Word Segmentation and Part-of-Speech Tagging of Ancient Chinese based on BERT Model

CHANG Yu[1], ZHU Peng[1], WANG Chaoping[2], WANG Chaofan[3]
1.School of Data Science and Application, Inner Mongolia University of Technology, Hohehot Municipality, Inner Mongolia, China
2. Institute of Sinology, Nanchang University, Nanchang, Jiangxi, China
3. College of Acupuncture & Tuina and Rehabilitation, Hunan University of Traditional Chinese Medicine, Changsha, Hunan, China
20211100482@imut.edu.cn, 20211800690@imut.edu.cn, 2273718186@qq.com, 2272592717@qq.com

Abstract

In recent years, new deep learning methods and pre-training language models have been emerging in the field of natural language processing (NLP). These methods and models can greatly improve the accuracy of automatic word segmentation and part-of-speech tagging in the field of ancient Chinese research. In these models, the BERT model has made amazing achievements in the top-level test of machine reading comprehension SQuAD-1.1. In addition, it also showed better results than other models in 11 different NLP tests. In this paper, *SIKU-RoBERTa* pre-training language model based on the high-quality full-text corpus of *SiKuQuanShu* have been adopted, and part corpus of *ZuoZhuan* that has been word segmented and part-of-speech tagged is used as training sets to build a deep network model based on BERT for word segmentation and POS tagging experiments. In addition, we also use other classical NLP network models for comparative experiments. The results show that using *SIKU-RoBERTa* pre-training language model, the overall prediction accuracy of word segmentation and part-of-speech tagging of this model can reach 93.87% and 88.97%, with excellent overall performance.

Keywords: natural language processing, deep learning, BERT model, automatic part-of-speech tagging

1. Introduction

At present, the automatic lexical analysis technology for modern Chinese (including automatic word segmentation, part of speech tagging, named entity recognition, etc.) has been basically mature. People try to use the existing modern Chinese analysis model to deal with ancient Chinese. However, due to the use of traditional characters in ancient Chinese, it first needs to spend a lot of resources and time to convert traditional characters into simplified characters. Secondly, there are significant differences between ancient Chinese and modern Chinese in font, vocabulary and grammar. Finally, more ancient Chinese texts lack sentence breaks and punctuation, which brings great difficulties to further data analysis, knowledge mining and the development of related intelligent applications.

The research on automatic word segmentation of ancient Chinese has also experienced three stages: rule-based system, statistics-based method and deep-learning-based network model.

Huang et al. designed the automatic word segmentation algorithm of agricultural ancient books through *N-ary* grammar and dictionary word segmentation technology. After testing, it has a good word recognition rate on 13 agricultural ancient books. Xu et al. proposed a rule-based word segmentation method for *ZuoZhuan*, and the F1 value of this method reached 89.46%.

Fang et al. proposed a word segmentation algorithm based on likelihood ratio statistical method, and realized the automatic word segmentation of tea classic through tree pruning algorithm. Chen et al. constructed an improved statistical model of ancient Chinese text based on Kalman filter. Compared with the baseline model, the accuracy of word segmentation in *ShiJi* and *Song History* increased by 30%.

Wang et al. determined the combined feature template through conditional random field model and statistical method, and finally obtained the part of speech automatic annotation algorithm model for Pre-Qin classics. The harmonic average value f of the model reaches 94.79%. Cheng et al. proposed an integrated annotation method of sentence segmentation and lexical analysis based on BiLSTM-CRF neural network model. The F1 value of word segmentation task and part-of-speech tagging task on the comprehensive test set of the model reached 85.73% and 72.65%.

SIKU-RoBERTa is a natural language pre-training model based on BERT model and trained with *SiKuQuanShu*. This experiment will use part of the *ZuoZhuan* as the training set, fine-tune on the basis of *SIKU-RoBERTa*, and complete the tasks of word segmentation and part-of-speech tagging. In addition, some classical natural language processing models will be used as comparative experiments.

2. Model Introduction

BERT model is a pre-training language model proposed by Google, which breaks through the limitation that text representation methods such as one-hot and word2vec can only generate a word vector for each word in the thesaurus, and solves the thorny problem of polysemy. In addition, based on the self-attention mechanism, BERT model can contain deeper context information, which plays a decisive role in the effect of natural language processing tasks. It is a milestone in the research of natural language processing. It has set a new record in 11 natural language processing tasks and has become the focus of current research.

The basic BERT model is composed of 12 layers of transformer encoder units, each layer has 12 Attention, and the hidden layer size H is 768, that is, the word vector dimension. Its structure is shown in Figure 1.

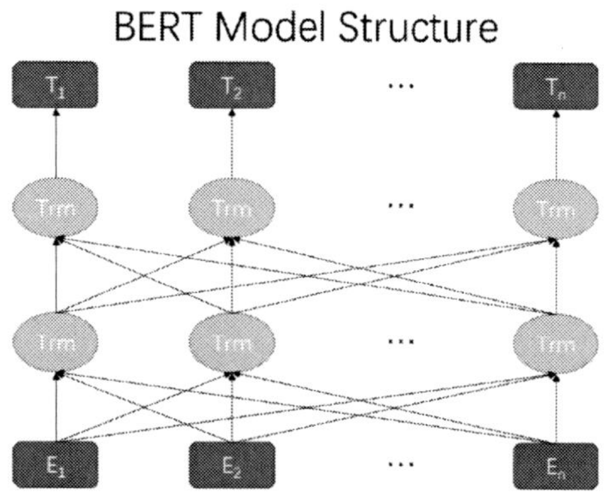

Figure 1: BERT model structure

The intermediate feature extraction adopts the structure of the encoder part of the transformer, but uses a new activation function GeLU (Gaussian error linear unit) instead of the original activation function ReLU of the transformer.

The embedding layer of BERT model is shown in Figure 2, which is obtained by the superposition of *Token Embedding*, *Segment Embedding* and *Position Embedding*. The *Segment Embedding* can be used for sentence classification tasks, such as judging whether the two sentences are semantically similar and whether the two sentences are context, etc.

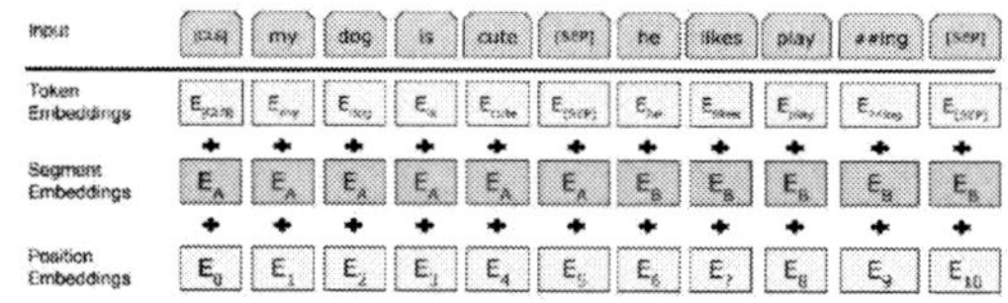

Figure 2: Embedding layer of BERT model

According to the output structure of the BERT model, inputting the output of the BERT model into a Full Connection Layer, each token of the input sentence can be labeled to complete the sequence labeling task, and then complete the tasks such as word segmentation, part-of-speech tagging, named entity recognition and so on. Its structure is shown in Figure 3.

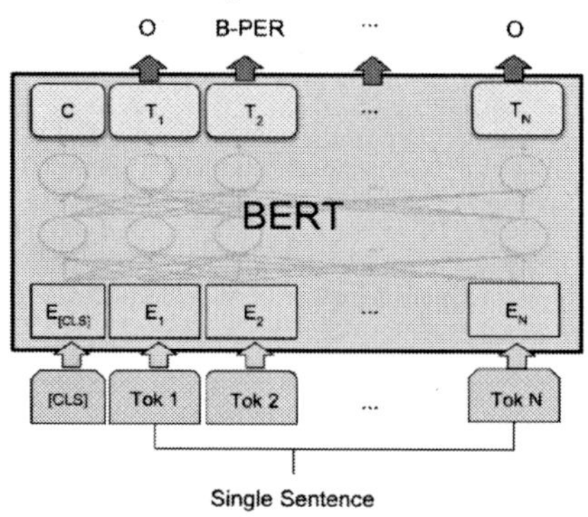

Figure 3: The structure of sequence annotation

The Data Set	Characters Quantity	Words Quantity	POS Distribution(Top 5)
Training Set	186282	157441	Verb(24.4%), Punctuation(21.3%) Noun(16.3%), Person(6.7%), Pronoun(6.4%)
Test Set A	33297	28131	Punctuation(26.1%), Verb(23.7%) Noun(12.9%), Person(7.2%), Pronoun(6.1%)
Test Set B	62969	53835	Verb(23.5%), Pronoun(21.7) Noun(13.8%), Person(7.9%), Location(6.2%)

Table 1: overview of experimental data set

3. Data Set Introduction

3.1 Datasets with Labels

The training set used in this experiment is from *ZuoZhuan(左传)*, which has been segmentation and marked with part-of-speech. The sentence segmentation is realized by the end of the sentence in the corpus, such as period, question mark, exclamation mark and other symbols. The source language in the final training corpus, i.e. the marked ancient Chinese sample (from *ZuoZhuan*), is as follows:

二十一年/t ，/w 春/n ，/w 天王/n 將/d 鑄/v 無射/n

This experiment uses two test sets, test set A and test set B. The corpus in test set A is also from *ZuoZhuan*, but it does not intersect with the corpus in training set. Test set B is a collection of corpora from different ancient books. The word statistics and part-of-speech distribution of the data set are shown in Table 1.

3.2 Datasets without labels

In order to further study the effect of the model in the field of ancient Chinese analysis, we selected some corpora from ancient Chinese and ancient traditional medical books that are quite different from Zuozhuan in sentence pattern and content, such as *ZhaoMingWenXuan* «昭明文选» (anthology of literature), *ShangHanLun* «伤寒论» (treatise on febrile diseases caused by cold) and *ShuoWenJieZiZhu* «说文解字注» (Collected commentaries on the *ShuoWenJieZi*).The corpus selected from *ZhaoMingWenXuan* is mainly fragments of Ci and Fu, such as *LuoShenFu*, *ShangLinFu* and so on. The corpus selected from *ShangHanLun* is mainly the disease conclusion and prescription of ancient Chinese medicine. The corpus selected from *ShuoWenJieZiZhu* is mainly explanatory articles. The specific format and contents are shown in Table 2.

Book	Corpus
ZhaoMingWenXuan	髣髴兮若輕雲之蔽月，飄颻兮若流風之回雪。遠而望之，皎若太陽升朝霞；迫而察之，灼若芙蕖出淥波。
	As obscure as a light cloud covering the moon, as drift as a gust of wind blowing up the snow. From afar, it's shining like the soleil and the glory of the dawn,and upon closer inspection, it looks like hibiscus in the green water.
ShangHanLun	太阳病，得之八九日，如疟状，发热恶寒，热多寒少，其人不呕，清便欲自可，一日二三度发。脉微缓者，为欲愈也。
	Disease of Taiyang, got it for eight or nine days, like malaria, have fever and dread cold, fever is more serious than dreading cold, that one won't vomit and still able to defecate normally, symptoms two or three times a day. If the pulse becomes slightly softer, it's about to heal.
ShuoWenJieZiZhu	除，開也。从阜。取以漸而高之意。余聲，直魚切，五部。
	Chu(除) means open. Fu(阜) as the radicals. It to the effect that higher and higher. Yu(余) as the phonetic indictors. *ZhiYu Qie*. It's located at the fifth part of the Rhyme categories of Old Chinese.

Table 2: Format and content of some corpus

4. Experimental Design

4.1 Integrated Label Design

The commonly used annotation method for word segmentation is {B, I, E, S}, where B represents the first character of word, E represents the last character word, I represents the middle characters of word when the word length is greater than 3, and S represents the word formation of a single character, for example:

*二**B** 十**I** 一**I** 年**E** 春**S***

The actual labels used in this experiment are obtained by the combination of the tagging method mentioned and part-of-speech. The label examples of training corpus are shown in Table 3.

Character	Label
天	*B-n*
王	*E-n*
將	*S-d*
鑄	*S-n*
無	*B-n*
射	*E-n*
，	*S-w*

Table 3: Training corpus label examples

4.2 Network Model Parameters

In this experiment, four network models were used to, which are *BiLSTM*, *BiLSTM_CRF*, *SIKU-RoBERTa* and *SIKU-RoBERTa_CRF*. All models are tested in the same hardware and software environment. The experimental tool and environment selected for this experiment is *pytorch-1.10.0*, *python-3.8* and *cuda-11.3*. The hardware configuration is GPU: *12G RTX3060*, CPU: *20G 7-core Intel(R) Xeon(R) CPU E5-2680 V4 @ 2.40GHz*.

Super Parameter	Value
embedding_size	128
hidden_size	256
num_layers	2
train_batch_size	32
eval_batch_size	8
learning_rate	0.005
num_train_epochs	20
drop_out	0.5

Table 4: Main super parameters of BiLSTM

The super parameters of both BiLSTM network models are shown in Table 4. And The network models super parameters of RoBERTa is shown in Table 5.

Super Parameter	Value
num_attention_heads	12
hidden_size	768
train_batch_size	64
val_batch_size	8
learning_rate	2.0E-5
num_train_epochs	10
drop_out	0.1

Table 5: Main super parameters of RoBERTa

5. Results Analysis

5.1 Evaluation Indexes

In this experiment, due to the small amount of training data, the training data is randomly divided into training set and Validation set according to 9:1, and the 10 fold cross verification method is used to increase the amount of data, enhance the accuracy of the experiment and reduce the error. The confusion matrix between the predicted value and the real value is shown in Table 6.

Confusion Matrix		Actuality	
		Positive	Negative
Prediction	Positive	True Positive (TP)	False Positive (FP)
	Negative	False Negative (FN)	True Negative (TN)

Table 6: Confusion Matrix

The commonly used evaluation indexes of deep learning model include *P*(Precision), *R*(Recall) and *F1-score*(harmonic mean). *P* reflects the accuracy of the model prediction, *R* reflects the comprehensiveness of the model prediction, and *F1-score* combines the advantages of the two, which can more objectively evaluate the prediction results of the model. The calculation method of the three evaluation indexes is as follows:

$$P = \frac{TP}{TP + FP} \times 100\%$$

$$R = \frac{TP}{TP + FN} \times 100\%$$

$$F1 = \frac{2 \times P \times R}{P + R} \times 100\%$$

5.2 Cross Verification

In order to more accurately evaluate the performance of *SIKU-Roberta* model, we use the 10 fold cross verification method to evaluate the model. The results of the *Precision*, *Recall* and *F1-score* of each group are shown in Table 7.

Group	Precision	Recall	F1-score	support
1	87.26	87.50	86.99	12260
2	90.32	89.22	89.30	15319
3	91.92	92.66	92.20	14978
4	91.69	92.24	91.68	14003
5	89.89	90.42	89.95	15405
6	90.42	90.60	90.27	16203
7	90.61	93.01	91.72	14809
8	90.16	92.47	91.21	18198
9	89.98	91.91	90.81	17496
10	91.78	93.04	92.30	16793
Mean	90.403	91.307	90.643	15546

Table 7: The result of cross verification with *SIKU-RoBERTa*

Through the comparative analysis of 10 groups of evaluation indexes of models using different pre-training models, it can be seen that the overall *Precision* of part-of-speech tags using *SIKU-RoBERTa* achieves 90.40%, *Recall* achieves 91.31%, and *F1-score* achieves 90.64%.

5.3 Prediction Results

This experiment uses the three network models mentioned in Chapter 4 to test the sequence label prediction task on the *Test Set A* and *B* mentioned in Chapter 3. The results of the final word segmentation and part-of-speech tagging experiment are shown in Table 8 and Table 9.

Test Set	Model	P	R	F1
Test A	*BiLSTM*	92.31	92.88	92.60
	BiLSTM_CRF	92.99	93.42	93.20
	SIKU-RoBERTa	93.09	94.66	93.87
	SIKU-RoBERTa_CRF	95.47	93.48	94.46
Test B	*BiLSTM*	88.38	86.59	87.48
	BiLSTM_CRF	87.98	84.82	86.37
	SIKU-RoBERTa	86.42	93.64	89.89
	SIKU-RoBERTa_CRF	94.39	86.78	90.43

Table 8: Word segmentation experiment results

5.4 Exploratory Experiment Results

The exploratory experiment used the unlabeled test set mentioned in Chapter 3 to evaluate the *SIKU-RoBERTa* model. Since the test set has no label, we can't show our evaluation results digitally. However, with reference to the opinions of relevant professionals, the experimental results of word segmentation and part-of-speech tagging in the above corpus are not as good as those in *Test Set A* or *Test Set B*. Through the analysis and comparison of the corpus, we believe that there are the following reasons:

- Differences in sentence structure: for example, there are great differences in sentence structure between *ZuoZhuan* and *ShuoWenJieZiZhu*.
- Existence of professional terms: there are a large number of disease names in ancient medical texts, such as "太阳病". And the ancients used the inverted phonetic notation, such as "直魚切".
- Difficulty in tagging function words: function words in ancient Chinese are different from those in modern Chinese and English in function and meaning.
- Particularity of poetry: ancient poetry and ancient prose are also different in grammar and semantics.

Test Set	Model	P	R	F
Test A	*BiLSTM*	85.71	86.23	85.97
	BiLSTM_CRF	87.03	87.75	87.39
	SIKU-RoBERTa	88.24	89.73	88.97
	SIKU-RoBERTa_CRF	91.02	89.12	90.06
Test B	*BiLSTM*	73.60	72.11	72.84
	BiLSTM_CRF	75.87	73.14	74.48
	SIKU-RoBERTa	80.33	87.04	83.55
	SIKU-RoBERTa_CRF	88.17	81.06	84.46

Table 9: POS tagging experiment results

6. Conclusion and Discussion

The comparative experiments of four natural language models *BiLSTM*, *BiLSTM_CRF*, *SIKU-RoBERTa* and *SIKU-RoBERTa_CRF* verify that the pre-training model *SIKU-RoBERTa* can improve the accuracy of word segmentation and part-of-speech tagging in ancient Chinese, perform more prominently in the non-specific corpus, and have better generalization ability.

Inspired by the exploratory experiment, there are two thoughts on how to improve the prediction accuracy of the model :

- Expand the training set: increase the diversity of sentence patterns in the training set corpus, so that the model can learn more sentence structures.
- Increase the number of labels: identify some proper nouns through labels.

7. Acknowledgements

Inner Mongolia Autonomous Region university network security and Education Management Information Engineering Research Center construction support project.

8. Bibliographical References

Chang, L., Dongbo, W., Tian, H. H., Qin, Z. Y., & Bin, L.(2021). Research on automatic word Segmentation of Classic Books with external features for digital humanities: A case study of sikuBERT pre-training model. *Library Tribune*, 1-13.

Dongbo, W., & Chang, L. (2021). SikuBERT and SikuRoBERTa: Research on the construction and application of pre-training model of *SiKuQuanShu* for Digital Humanities. *Library Tribune*, 1-14.

RunHua, X., & Xiaohe, C. (2021). A Method of Segmentation on "Zuo Zhuan" by Using Commentaries. *Journal of Chinese Information Processing, 26*(02), 13-17+45.

Yundong, G., Yiqin, Z., Huan, L., & Dongbo, W. (2021).

Automatic part-of-speech tagging of Chinese ancient classics in the context of digital humanities research:A case study of SIKU-BERT pre-training model. *Library Tribune* 1-11.

Zhiting, Y., & Hanjie, M. (2021). Automatic—annotation me thod for e me rge ncy te xt corpus based on BE R T. *Intelligent Computer and Applications.*

Ning, C., Bin, L., Sijia, G., Xingyue, H., & Minxuan, F. (2020). A Joint Model of Automatic Sentence Segmentation and Lexical Analysis for Ancient Chinese Based on BiLSTM-CRF Model. *Journal of Chinese Information Processing, 34*(04), 1-9.

Devlin, J., Chang, M.-W., Lee, K., & Toutanova, K. (2019, jun). *BERT: Pre-training of Deep Bidirectional Transformers for Language Understanding*, Minneapolis, Minnesota.

Dongbo, W., Shuiqing, H., & lin, H. (2017). Researches of Automatic Part-of-speech Tagging for Pre-Qin Literature Based on Multi-feature Knowledge. *Library and Information Service, 61*(12), 64-70. doi:10.13266/j.issn.0252-3116.2017.12.008

TONG FEI C，WEI MENG Z，XUE QIANG L，et al.A kalman filter based human-computer interactive word segmentation system for ancient chinese texts[M]. Chinese computational linguistics and natural language processing based on naturally annotated big data.Berlin，Heidelberg：Springer，2013：25-35.

FANG M，JIANG Y，ZHAO Q，et al.Automatic word segmentation for Chinese classics of tea based on tree-pruning[C]//2009 Second International Symposium on Knowledge Acquisition and Modeling. IEEE, 2009，（01）：438-441.

Jiannian, H. (2009). *Research on Automation of Sentence Segmentation, Punctuation and Word Segmentation of Agricultural Ancient Books.* (D). Nanjing Agricultural University, Available from CNKI.

9. Language Resource References

Ancient Chinese Corpus. (2017). Linguistic Data Consortium. Chen, Xiaohe, et al., 1.0, ISLRN 924-985-704-453-5.

Proceedings of the Second Workshop on Language Technologies for Historical and Ancient Languages (LT4HALA 2022), pages 146–149
Language Resources and Evaluation Conference (LREC 2022), Marseille, 25 June 2022

Ancient Chinese Word Segmentation and Part-of-Speech Tagging Using Data Augmentation

Yanzhi Tian, Yuhang Guo*
School of Computer Science, Beijing Institute of Technology, Beijing 100081, China
{tianyanzhi, guoyuhang}@bit.edu.cn

Abstract

We attended the EvaHan2022 ancient Chinese word segmentation and Part-of-Speech (POS) tagging evaluation. We regard the Chinese word segmentation and POS tagging as sequence tagging tasks. Our system is based on a BERT-BiLSTM-CRF model which is trained on the data provided by the EvaHan2022 evaluation. Besides, we also employ data augmentation techniques to enhance the performance of our model. On the Test A and Test B of the evaluation, the F_1 scores of our system achieve 94.73% and 90.93% for the word segmentation, 89.19% and 83.48% for the POS tagging.

Keywords: ancient Chinese, word segmentation, POS tagging, data augmentation

1. Introduction

Ancient Chinese (a.k.a. classical Chinese) is a written language of Chinese used widely around 1000 BC to 221 BC. Most of the ancient Chinese records are written in classical Chinese. The classical Chinese is different from modern Chinese in several aspects, including wording and syntax. In order to study ancient Chinese automatically, classical Chinese word segmentation and Part-of-Speech (POS) tagging are of high research values.

Compared with the research on word segmentation and POS tagging of modern Chinese, the corpus of ancient Chinese with label is insufficient. The evaluation of EvaHan2022 provides a set of labeled corpus selected from the Zuozhuan corpus (Chen, Xiaohe, et al., 2017) and a pre-trained model called SikuBERT (Wang et al., 2021) which is trained based on ancient Chinese corpus.

We build an end-to-end ancient Chinese word segmentation and POS tagging system based on SikuBERT and attended the EvaHan2022 evaluation. We train our model on the given corpus. To ease the shortage of the labeled corpus, we employ data augmentation techniques. On the Test A and Test B of the evaluation, the F_1 scores of our system achieves 94.73% and 90.93% on the word segmentation, 89.19% and 83.48% on the POS tagging.

Our codes and results are available at `https://github.com/YanzhiTian/EvaHan-2022`.

2. Method

2.1. Model

We regard the word segmentation and POS tagging as sequence tagging tasks. BiLSTM-CRF is a well known sequence tagging model, in which the BiLSTM layers utilize both past and future input features efficiently, and the CRF layer reduces the possibility of the appearance of the illogical output tagging sequence (Huang et al., 2015). BERT(Devlin et al., 2018) is a pre-trained model and it is proved that the fine-tuning BERT-CRF model performances well on NER which is also a sequence tagging task (Souza et al., 2019). Here we apply the BERT-BiLSTM-CRF model.

In our system, we use the final output of SikuBERT as the input of the BiLSTM layer. We use dropout (Srivastava et al., 2014) to avoid overfitting and a linear layer to project the BiLSTM features to a lower dimension which corresponds to the input of CRF layer. The architecture of our model is shown in Figure 1.

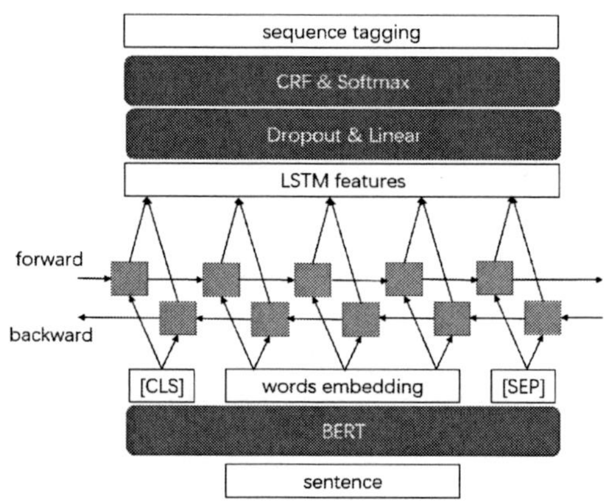

Figure 1: The architecture of our model.

2.2. Data

Our end-to-end model jointly handles the word segmentation and POS tagging which avoids the error propagation in the cascade model. We design a series of taggings including both word segmentation information and POS information. For example, the tagging

* Corresponding author.

"b-n" refers to the beginning of a word segment and noun POS, the tagging "i-n" refers to the middle or end of a word segment and noun POS. We have 47 kinds of tagging (including [PAD], [CLS] and [SEP]) in total. An example of tagging is shown in Figure 2, the first row is the raw sentence, the second row is the tagging sequence in raw training set and the third row is the tagging sequence after processing.

宋	武	公	生	仲	子	。
/nr			/v	/nr		/w
/b-nr	/i-nr	/i-nr	/b-v	/b-nr	/i-nr	/b-w

Figure 2: An example of tagging.

2.3. Data Augmentation

We use data augmentation to ease the shortage of the labeled data and to enhance the performance of the model. Our strategy of data augmentation is to mask several words with a special token [MASK] dynamically. Before the sequence is input into the model, our system will generate a boolean array randomly to mask the words in the sequence.

Our motivation is that the model predicts tagging sequence harder compared with modern Chinese because a specific word in ancient Chinese are more variation of semantics corresponding to different kinds of POS tagging. Using our data augmentation method, the model can inference taggings from other taggings in the context instead of its word token which means the model can learn information from the sentence structure such as the sequence of POS tagging.

The mask rate should be chosen carefully. An appropriate mask rate will make the model has better performance. However a larger mask rate will reduce the performance of the model.

3. Experiments

We only use Zuozhuan_Train dataset which is provided by the EvaHan2022 evaluation to train our model. To evaluate the performance of our model, we shuffle the dataset and sample 900 sentences randomly to construct a validation set, the rest of the data to construct training set. The hyper-parameters of our model are shown in Table 1.

Hyper-parameter	Value
Learning rate	0.01
Batch size	64
Hidden dimension	2×512
LSTM layers	2
Dropout rate	0.5
Mask rate	0.2

Table 1: The hyper-parameters of our model.

The max sequence length of SikuBERT is 512(including [CLS] and [SEP]). We truncated the sentence by punctuation and kept the length of the sentence smaller than 512.

3.1. Training

In our system, the optimizer is Adam and the loss function is negative log likelihood calculated in the CRF layer. In the training step, we froze the parameters of BERT to make sure the error will not pass to the BERT layer in backpropagation because the size of our training set is much smaller compared with the size of the data used in the pre-training. This method can accelerate the convergence of model and make the training easier.

3.2. Ablation Study

We trained 4 models with different settings including BERT-Linear, BERT-CRF, BERT-BiLSTM-CRF and the Deeper Model. We also tested the mask rate of 0.2 and 0.3 on the BERT-BiLSTM-CRF model respectively. The results of these models on the validation set are shown in Table 2.

Compared with the BiLSTM-CRF model(Cheng et al., 2020), our BERT-BiLSTM-CRF model uses SikuBERT which is pre-trained on large scaled ancient Chinese corpus. We freeze the parameters of SikuBERT and use the final output as word embedding. The SikuBERT eases the shortage of the labeled corpus. Using data augmentation can introduce noises into data which is helpful to enhance the performance of the model and avoid overfitting.

The Deeper Model is a BERT-BiLSTM-Transformer Encoder-BiLSTM-CRF model. We evaluated the performance of the Deeper Model on the validation set in each epoch. The F_1 scores of the Deeper Model (solid lines) and BERT-BiLSTM-CRF model (dashed lines) of word segmentation and POS tagging in each training epoch are shown in Figure 3. The final F_1 scores of the Deeper Model are shown in Table 2.

It can be found that the F_1 scores of the Deeper Model get close to the final F_1 scores of BERT-BiLSTM-CRF model after about 50 epochs. However the BERT-BiLSTM-CRF model reaches the final F_1 score only after about 10 epochs which means the convergence of the Deeper Model is slower than BERT-BiLSTM-CRF model.

We evaluated the mask rate parameter with 0.2 and 0.3 on the validation set. As illustrated in Table 2, the evaluation results show that the mask rate with 0.2 performs better than 0.3. We use 0.2 as the mask rate parameter in our system.

4. Results

We evaluated our system on Test A and Test B closed modality tests of EvaHan2022 using BERT-BiLSTM-CRF model with data augmentation. The size and source of testing sets are shown in Table 3.

Model	WS			POS Tagging		
	P	R	F_1	P	R	F_1
BERT-Linear	93.08	92.97	93.04	84.97	84.87	84.92
BERT-CRF	93.13	93.02	93.08(+0.04)	85.27	85.17	85.22(+0.3)
BERT-BiLSTM-CRF (w/o DA)	94.24	94.49	94.37(+1.33)	88.42	88.65	**88.53(+3.61)**
BERT-BiLSTM-CRF (MR=0.2)	94.43	94.35	**94.39(+1.35)**	88.28	88.20	88.24(+3.32)
BERT-BiLSTM-CRF (MR=0.3)	93.60	94.36	93.98(+0.94)	87.12	87.84	87.48(+2.56)
The Deeper Model (MR=0.2)	94.40	94.30	94.35(+1.31)	87.52	87.42	87.47(+2.55)

Table 2: The precision(P), recall(R) and F_1 scores (%) of different models with different settings (without Data Augmentation (DA) and with different Mask Rates(MR)) on our validation set.

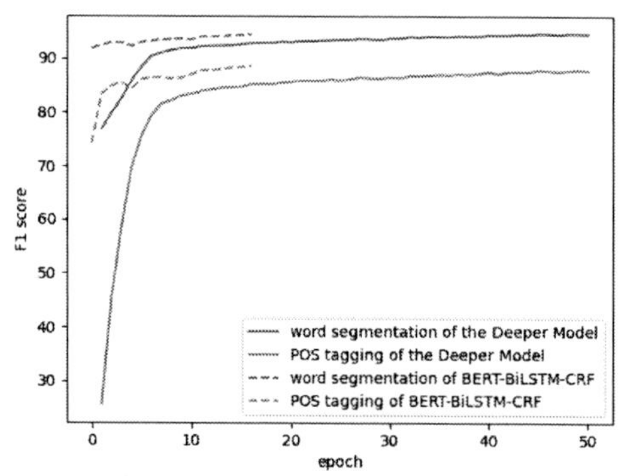

Figure 3: The F_1 scores (%) of BERT-BiLSTM-CRF model and the Deeper Model on validation set in each epochs.

Datasets	Sources	Word Tokens	Char Tokens
Test A	ZuoZhuan	28K	33K
Blind Test B	Other similar ancient Chinese Book	40K	50K

Table 3: The size and sources of test sets.

To verify the impact of data augmentation, we evaluated the performance of BERT-BiLSTM-CRF model without data augmentation. We also evaluated the performance of the Deeper Model to check the difference with other models. The results are shown in Table 4 and Table 5.

As shown in Table 4 and Table 5, the system with data augmentation achieves better performance on the POS tagging task: the F_1 scores are higher than the system without data augmentation by 1.79%, 2.41% on Test A and Test B respectively. However the effect of data augmentation for word segmentation is not significant. The system F_1 score is 1.05% higher than the system without data augmentation on Test A but is lower on Test B by 0.50%.

Compared with the widely used datasets on modern Chinese word segmentation and POS tagging, the size of the Zuozhuan(1.7M) dataset is similar to the size of PKU(1.1M) and MSRA(2.4M) dataset(Emerson, 2005) on word segmentation, however it is much smaller than the size of CTB5(4.9M) dataset(Xue et al., 2005) on POS tagging. So the improvement of data augmentation on POS tagging is more obviously than word segmentation.

Our detailed analysis shows that the most error of our system in the POS tagging comes from that our model can not distinguish the noun category including n, nr and ns representing common noun, person entity and location entity respectively.

The results also show that all the F_1 scores of the Deeper Model are lower than our system.

5. Conclusion and Future Work

In this paper, we implement an end-to-end ancient Chinese word segmentation and POS tagging system. We also propose a data augmentation method by masking words in the data using a special [MASK] token in this task. The results show that using data augmentation enhances the performance of BERT-BiLSTM-CRF model on ancient Chinese word segmentation and POS tagging. On Test A and Test B of testing data, our system achieves 94.73% and 90.93% F_1 scores on word segmentation, 89.19% and 83.48% F_1 scores on POS tagging.

In the future we plan to import an entity recognition module to improve hard POS taggings like n, nr and ns.

6. Bibliographical References

Cheng, N., Li, B., Xiao, L., Xu, C., Ge, S., Hao, X., and Feng, M. (2020). Integration of automatic sentence segmentation and lexical analysis of Ancient Chinese based on BiLSTM-CRF model. In *Proceedings of LT4HALA 2020 - 1st Workshop on Language Technologies for Historical and Ancient Languages*, pages 52–58, Marseille, France, May. European Language Resources Association (ELRA).

Devlin, J., Chang, M.-W., Lee, K., and Toutanova, K. (2018). Bert: Pre-training of deep bidirectional

Model	Word Segmentation			POS Tagging		
	P	R	F_1	P	R	F_1
BERT-BiLSTM-CRF (w/o DA)	92.92	94.46	93.68	86.69	88.13	87.40
BERT-BiLSTM-CRF (**Our system**)	94.48	94.99	**94.73(+1.05)**	88.95	89.43	**89.19(+1.79)**
The Deeper Model	94.10	94.61	94.36(+0.68)	88.44	88.92	88.68(+1.28)

Table 4: The precision(P), recall(R) and F_1 scores (%) of our models on **Test A**.

Model	Word Segmentation			POS Tagging		
	P	R	F_1	P	R	F_1
BERT-BiLSTM-CRF (w/o DA)	92.79	90.13	**91.43**	82.27	79.91	81.07
BERT-BiLSTM-CRF (**Our system**)	93.07	88.89	90.93(-0.5)	85.45	81.61	**83.48(+2.41)**
The Deeper Model	88.49	89.60	89.03(-2.4)	80.36	81.38	80.86(-0.21)

Table 5: The precision(P), recall(R) and F_1 scores (%) of our models on **Test B**.

transformers for language understanding. *arXiv preprint arXiv:1810.04805.*

Emerson, T. (2005). The second international Chinese word segmentation bakeoff. In *Proceedings of the Fourth SIGHAN Workshop on Chinese Language Processing.*

Huang, Z., Xu, W., and Yu, K. (2015). Bidirectional lstm-crf models for sequence tagging. *arXiv preprint arXiv:1508.01991.*

Souza, F., Nogueira, R., and Lotufo, R. (2019). Portuguese named entity recognition using bert-crf. *arXiv preprint arXiv:1909.10649.*

Srivastava, N., Hinton, G., Krizhevsky, A., Sutskever, I., and Salakhutdinov, R. (2014). Dropout: a simple way to prevent neural networks from overfitting. *The journal of machine learning research*, 15(1):1929–1958.

Wang, D., Liu, C., Zhu, Z., Jiang, Feng, Hu, H., Shen, S., and Li, B.-S. (2021). Construction and application of pre-training model of "siku quanshu" oriented to digital humanities.

Xue, N., Xia, F., Chiou, F.-D., and Palmer, M. (2005). The penn chinese treebank: Phrase structure annotation of a large corpus. *Natural language engineering*, 11(2):207–238.

7. Language Resource References

Chen, Xiaohe, et al. (2017). *Ancient Chinese Corpus LDC2017T14.* Philadelphia: Linguistic Data Consortium, 1.0, ISLRN 924-985-704-453-5.

Proceedings of the Second Workshop on Language Technologies for Historical and Ancient Languages (LT4HALA 2022), pages 150–154
Language Resources and Evaluation Conference (LREC 2022), Marseille, 25 June 2022

BERT 4EVER@EvaHan 2022: Ancient Chinese Word Segmentation and Part-of-Speech Tagging based on Adversarial Learning and Continual Pre-training

Hailin Zhang[1†], Ziyu Yang[1†], Yingwen Fu[1], Ruoyao Ding[2*]
Guangdong University of Foreign Studies, Guangzhou, China
[1]{20201010014, 20201002958, 20201010002}@gdufs.edu.cn,
[2]ruoyaoding@outlook.com

Abstract

With the development of artificial intelligence (AI) and digital humanities, ancient Chinese resources and language technology have also developed and grown, which have become an increasingly important part to the study of historiography and traditional Chinese culture. In order to promote the research on automatic analysis technology of ancient Chinese, we conduct various experiments on ancient Chinese word segmentation and part-of-speech (POS) tagging tasks for the EvaHan 2022 shared task. We model the word segmentation and POS tagging tasks jointly as a sequence tagging problem. In addition, we perform a series of training strategies based on the provided ancient Chinese pre-trained model to enhance the model performance. Concretely, we employ several augmentation strategies, including continual pre-training, adversarial training, and ensemble learning to alleviate the limited amount of training data and the imbalance between POS labels. Extensive experiments demonstrate that our proposed models achieve considerable performance on ancient Chinese word segmentation and POS tagging tasks.

Keywords: ancient Chinese, word segmentation, part-of-speech tagging, adversarial learning, continuing pre-training

1. Introduction

The Chinese nation has thousands of years of glorious history and culture with excellent cultural heritage mainly recorded through the ancient Chinese written language. It is a good choice to start with ancient classics if one wants to understand Chinese civilization and know about ancient Chinese literature, history, politics, economy, medicine, and other cultures. Classics can be said to be the inheritance carrier of Chinese civilization. Applying technologies such as big data and artificial intelligence (AI) to ancient books, digitizing them, and making them public can rejuvenate all dusty ancient books and make the words written in ancient books come alive, which can help more people know about the Chinese civilization. Research in the field of ancient Chinese is becoming more and more popular and important. For example, the national ancient book protection and digitization project has been listed as a key project in the inheritance and development of Chinese excellent traditional culture. This project not only speeds up the compilation and publication of ancient books but also facilitates knowledge extraction and information integration of ancient books and documents, providing a new method for the inheritance and protection of ancient books and injecting new vitality.

Although the automatic analysis of modern Chinese has achieved promising results, the automatic analysis of ancient Chinese is relatively struggling, making it difficult to meet the actual needs of Chinese historical studies and research. To promote the development of ancient Chinese resources and automatic analysis research, the Workshop on Language Technologies for Historical and Ancient languages (LT4HALA) of the International Language Resources and Evaluation Conference (LREC2022) aims at the task of word segmentation and part-of-speech (POS) tagging in Pre-Qin Chinese. The evaluation attempts to promote cooperation among scholars in related fields of ancient Chinese. This paper mainly conducts a series of research on word segmentation and part-of-speech tagging in ancient Chinese for this evaluation task.

Nowadays, research of the modern Chinese word segmentation and POS tagging tasks have achieved remarkable performance. Although the ancient Chinese word segmentation and POS tagging tasks are defined in the same way as the modern Chinese, they face many grammatical, lexical, and syntactic differences. In the fact of these differences, general modern Chinese word segmentation and POS tagging tools cannot accurately and effectively label ancient Chinese texts. In addition, previous methods proposed for modern Chinese have insufficient generalization ability for ancient Chinese due to the lack of annotated corpus. Fortunately, with the rapid development of deep learning technology, especially the emergence of pre-trained language models (PLMs) based on massive texts, the performance of deep learning models on many natural language processing (NLP) tasks in the ancient Chinese field has been greatly improved. Therefore, this paper jointly regards the ancient Chinese word segmentation and POS tasks as a joint sequence tagging task. Based on the PLM called SikuRoBERTa[1] provided by LREC2022, we add a layer of Conditional Random Field (CRF) to obtain more accurate label classification results. Besides, considering the limited amount of the provided ancient Chinese training data and the imbalance between various labels in POS tagging, we also employ various data augmentation techniques to improve the performance, including continual pre-training (Gururangan et al., 2020), adversarial training (Miyato et al., 2017), and ensemble learning. Extensive experiments conducted on the given

* Corresponding author.
† Equal contribution.
[1] https://huggingface.co/SIKU-BERT/sikuroberta

dataset demonstrate that our proposed models achieve comparable results, which reach the best F1-score of 0.9568 and 0.9114 on the online test set respectively.

2. Related Work

The task of word segmentation and POS tagging in the ancient Chinese field is not rare in NLP. Previous works on these tasks are mainly divided into the following two paradigms: (1) the step-by-step paradigm that firstly conducts word segmentation and then performs POS tagging and (2) the joint paradigm that deals with word segmentation and POS tagging at the same time. Unlike English sentences in which words are separated by spaces, Chinese sentences lack delimiter between words. Therefore, word segmentation is a fundamental step for the downstream tasks of Chinese NLP. However, when directly applying the modern Chinese word segmentation methods to ancient Chinese, it is hard to obtain an ideal effect due to the particularity of ancient texts. Hence, a more suitable word segmentation method must be proposed for ancient Chinese. For example, Gao and Zhao (2021) used a new word discovery method combining rules and statistics to discover new words from a large amount of classical literature and build an ancient Chinese word segmentation dictionary. Then the built dictionary is leveraged to segment the ancient texts. Traditional machine learning methods such as CRF combined with feature templates and professional dictionaries are employed to automatically segment ancient Chinese (Yang et al., 2017; Wang and Li, 2017). With the rapid progress of neural network (NN) technology, the Long Short-Term Memory (LSTM) and BERT models are also widely applied to the ancient Chinese word segmentation task (Gao, 2020; Gao, 2021). As for the ancient Chinese POS tagging task, researchers mainly employed rule-based methods (Liu and Dan, 2014) and traditional machine learning methods such as Hidden Markov Model (HMM) (Yang and Hu, 2020; Liang et al., 2002) and CRF model (Chiu et al., 2015).

The correctness of the POS tagging task somehow depends on the performance of word segmentation. However, the step-by-step paradigm would introduce multi-level diffusion of errors. Therefore, the joint paradigm of word segmentation and POS tagging tasks tend to bring more ideal results. Due to the particularity of ancient Chinese structure and semantics, expert knowledge would greatly affect the results of word segmentation and POS tagging. Hence, the method of leveraging rules and dictionaries is still commonly used in ancient texts (Li and Wei, 2013; Xing and Zhu, 2021). In addition, the performance of machine learning methods such as the maximum interval Markov network model (M3N) and CRF have been significantly improved (Qiao and Sun, 2010; Shi et al., 2010). In recent years, neural network models have been widely employed in ancient Chinese word segmentation and POS tagging tasks. Through integrating contextual and lexical information, the performance of POS tagging has been effectively improved (Cheng et al., 2020; Cui et al., 2020). In particular, Zhang et al. (2021) proposed a POS tagging model for ancient books based on the pre-trained language model BERT, which recently achieved the state-of-the-art performance for ancient Chinese POS tagging.

PLMs have become increasingly important in NLP. Extensive research has shown that PTMs trained on large corpora can learn general language representations, which can effectively improve the performance of downstream NLP tasks and avoid training new models from scratch. Undoubtedly, a suitable language model can greatly improve the model performance. Chinese is a language with unique features in syntax, vocabulary, and phonetics. Therefore, the Chinese PTMs should be in line with their unique characteristics. At present, scholars have proposed several PTMs for Chinese, including ERNIE (Li et al., 2019), CPM (Zhang et al., 2020), pre-trained Chinese language model using a whole-word masking strategy (Cui et al., 2021), and the fusion of glyph and pinyin information to Chinese BERT model (Sun et al., 2021).

3. Method

In this paper, we jointly model the ancient Chinese word segmentation and POS tagging tasks as a sequence labeling task. We adapt BERT-CRF as our base model and introduce four training methods to enhance the model performance, namely adversarial training (AT), continual pre-training, data augmentation[2] (DA), and ensemble learning.

3.1 Base Model

Our base model consists of two modules: the BERT encoder and the CRF output layer.

BERT. BERT is a transformer-based (Vaswani et al., 2017) pre-trained language model (PLM) that is designed to pre-train on a large unsupervised dataset to learn deep bidirectional representations. It consists of two subtasks, namely Mask Language Model (MLM) and Next Sentence Prediction (NSP). Being a variant of BERT, RoBERTa (Liu et al., 2019) aims to make full use of BERT architecture and training methods. There are three improvements in RoBERTa compared with BERT: (1) More training data; (2) Abondance of NSP task; and (3) Dynamic word masking.

We leverage the provided SikuRoBERTa to extract the representation for each token. After that, we leverage a softmax layer to produce the label scores for the tokens.

$$\boldsymbol{H} = SikuRoBERTa(\boldsymbol{X}) \quad (1)$$

$$\boldsymbol{P} = Softmax(W(\boldsymbol{H}) + b) \quad (2)$$

where W and b are parameters of the fully connected layer.

CRF. In the sequence labeling tasks, PLMs are hard to handle the dependency relationship between neighboring labels. In contrast, CRF can obtain an optimal prediction sequence by the relationship of neighboring labels, which can compensate for the shortcomings of PLMs. Thus, we further add a CRF layer to output the optimal label sequence $\boldsymbol{Y}^*$ for the input sequence.

$$\boldsymbol{Y}^* = CRF(\boldsymbol{P}) \quad (3)$$

3.2 Training Methods

Adversarial Training. AT is a training method that introduces adversarial perturbations to the original input to

[2] https://github.com/425776024/nlpcda

regularize the parameters and improve the robustness and generalization of the model. In this paper, we extend the fast gradient method (FGM) (which is originally proposed for text classification (Miyato et al., 2017)) to the ancient Chinese word segmentation and POS tagging tasks by adding the adversarial perturbations to the input token embedding of PLMs. The perturbations are calculated as follows:

$$r_{adv} = -\epsilon \frac{g}{||g||_2} \quad (4)$$

Where $\boldsymbol{g} = \nabla_x L(\theta, X, Y)$ is the model gradient.

Continual Pre-training. As stated in (Gururangan et al., 2020), it is helpful to tailor a PLM to the domain of a target task which can effectively enhance the performance of the target task. Therefore, we use the unsupervised data of the training set to continually pre-train the SikuRoBERTa to adapt the PLM to the *Zuo Zhuan* (the target domain of the given tasks) domain.

Data Augmentation. DA is a method of increasing the training data by adding small changes to the existing training data or creating new synthetic data from them. It can greatly alleviate the scenarios of insufficient data in deep learning. Given that the target task is typically a low-resource task with limited training data, we use a simple data augmentation approach with **identical label replacement** on the given training set. For example, given a sample of "*春秋左傳隱公*", we replace "*隱公*" with the identically labeled word "*惠公*" to produce a new sample "*春秋左傳惠公*". Through this method, we double the amount of training data.

Ensemble Learning. To further improve the generalization capability of the model, we use an ensemble learning approach to further fuse the results of multiple models. Specifically, using a voting mechanism, we vote on the results of multiple predictions for each word on a word-by-word basis. Then the label with the most votes is leveraged as the final output.

4. Experiment

4.1 Dataset

In this paper, the ancient Chinese annotation dataset from Zuozhuan (Li et al., 2013) provided by LT4HALA is used as the training set. After automatically segmented and tagged, the training set is then manually corrected by ancient Chinese experts. Finally, Chinese words are separated by spaces, and each token is tagged as "word/tag" format like "*隱公/nr*". We perform a statistical analysis of the POS labels in the training set, and the results are shown in Figure 1. Results show that punctuation marks (w), verbs (v), and nouns (n) appear most frequently, of which punctuation marks appear 42,315 times. However, rare categories such as rn, nn, nsr, and rr appear very few times, resulting in an imbalance between POS categories on the training set, which has also become an important improvement direction we consider when optimizing the model. In the testing phase, we used two test sets, Test A and Test B. Test A is extracted from the same book named *Zuozhuan* as the training set, which is used to evaluate the model's ability to recognize the same source but non-overlapping data. Test B is extracted from other ancient Chinese books to evaluate the generalization ability of the model in a similar ancient Chinese corpus. The dataset statistics are shown in Table 1.

Datasets	Word Tokens	Char Tokens
Train	166,142	194,995
Test A	28,131	33,298
Test B	Around 40,000	Around 50,000

Table 1: The dataset statistics.

4.2 Experimental Settings

Our models are all implemented based on the PyTorch[3] framework. As mentioned above, PTMs are proven to achieve considerable performance on ancient Chinese word segmentation and POS tagging tasks. Therefore, we first conduct a series of base experiments on different Chinese PTMs, including guwenbert-base[4], chinese-roberta-wwm-ext[5], roberta-classical-chinese-base-char[6], and the provided SikuRoBERTa. Through experimental comparison, we choose SikuRoBERTa to optimize in subsequent work because SikuRoBERTa performs better than other PTMs.

Next, we carry out extensive experiments on optimizing model parameters to fine-tune the model. Specifically, we set epoch to {2, 3, 4}; learning rate as {1e-4, 2e-5, 5e-5, 10e-6}; loss function as {CrossEntropy, Focal Loss}; batch size as {16, 24}. Since there exist several long sentences, we always set the maximum sequence length as 128 in training and 512 in inference.

As for the evaluation, we use the average F1-score over five cross-validation folds on dev data as the offline test set to represent the performance during our training phase and the official F1-score for the final online evaluation on both word segmentation and POS tagging tasks.

4.3 Results and Analysis

The results of our models on both word segmentation and part-of-speech tagging task are illustrated in Table 2. As shown in the table, all models achieve better results on word segmentation than POS tagging, among which CP_SikuRoBERTa_CRF_ADV achieves the best F1-score on Test A of 0.9568. As for the POS tagging task, the introduced continual pre-training, the added CRF layer, and adversarial training strategies all yield better performance when compared to the baseline model SikuRoBERTa-softmax. Among them, CP_SikuRoBERTa_CRF_ADV model achieves the best F1-score on Test A of 0.9114. In addition, the models perform better on Test A than Test B since Test B is extracted from a different ancient Chinese book than the training set, but also achieves an F1-score of 0.8699.

[3] https://pytorch.org/

[4] https://huggingface.co/ethanyt/guwenbert-base

[5] https://huggingface.co/hfl/chinese-roberta-wwm-ext

[6] https://huggingface.co/KoichiYasuoka/roberta-classical-chinese-base-char

Num.	Model	Evaluation Type	Test Set	Word Segmentation	Pos Tagging
1	guwenbert-base	Offline	test	0.9433	0.8595
2	chinese-roberta-wwm-ext		test	0.9468	0.8773
3	roberta-classical-chinese-base-char		test	0.9519	0.8823
4	CP_SikuRoBERTa_CRF		test	0.9520	0.8845
5	DA_SikuRoBERTa-softmax		test	0.9508	0.8840
6	SikuRoBERTa-softmax	Online	Test A	0.9363	0.8932
			Test B	0.9308	0.8667
7	CP_SikuRoBERTa-softmax		Test A	0.9365	0.8937
			Test B	0.9248	0.8588
8	CP_SikuRoBERTa_CRF_ADV		**Test A**	**0.9568**	**0.9114**
			Test B	**0.9364**	**0.8699**
9	ensemble（6+7+8）		Test A	0.9384	0.8964
			Test B	0.9301	0.8676

Table 2: The results of our models on the EvaHan shared task. In this table, CP indicates continual pre-training, DA indicates data augmentation, and ADV indicates adversarial training.

Surprisingly, it seems that the DA strategy can not improve the model performance. One possible reason might be that the augmentation method is somehow simple and often unavoidably generates many meaningless duplicate data. Considering that the training data size is small and thus this simple DA strategy does not work well.

In addition, as demonstrated in the table, we perform an ensemble learning strategy on the three models with the best performance. Although the final result is better than the single SikuRoBERTa-softmax and CP_SikuRoBERTa softmax models but is worse than the single CP_SikuRoBERTa_CRF_ADV model. We speculate the possible reason is that the difference between the three models is not obvious, and they both cannot handle well with some rare categories, resulting in unsatisfactory results in the final integration.

Figure 1: The frequency distribution of part-of-speech tags

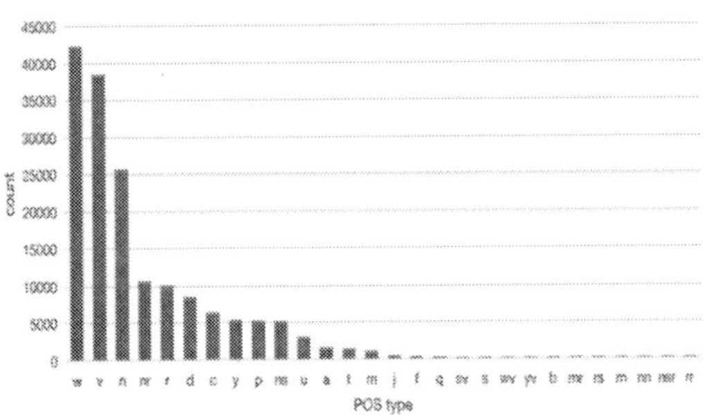

in the training data.

5. Conclusion

We present our results for the EvaHan 2022 shared task at International Language Resources and Evaluation Conference (LREC2022). We model the ancient Chinese word segmentation and POS tagging tasks as a joint sequence tagging problem and employ augmentation methods such as continuous pre-training, adversarial training, and ensemble learning after analyzing the training set. Overall, our model performs well on both word segmentation and POS tagging on the official test set, with the best F1-scores of 0.9568 and 0.9114 respectively. However, the ensemble learning strategy seems not to improve the performance as we expected. Additionally, the methods we tried are all implemented under a closed modality that only trained on the official training set, and do not consider the importance of other external data resources that might bring improvement. In future work, on the one hand, we plan to explore more efficient ensembles to improve the model performance. On the other hand, we will investigate the use of external ancient Chinese resources to further improve the model performance.

6. Acknowledgment

The work is supported by the Humanity and Social Science Youth Foundation of Ministry of Education of China (18YJCZH024) and Guangdong University of Foreign Studies (299-X5219112, 299-X5218168).

7. References

Cheng, N., Li, B., Ge, S. J., Hao, X. Y., and Feng, M. Y. (2010). A joint model of automatic sentence segmentation and lexical analysis for ancient Chinese based on BiLSTM-CRF model. *Journal of Chinese Information Processing*, (4):1-9.

Chiu, T. S., Lu, Q., Xu, J., Xiong, D., and Lo, F. (2015). PoS tagging for classical Chinese text. *CLSW*.

Cui, D. D., Liu, X. L., Chen, R. Y., Liu, X. H., Li, Z., and Qi, L. (2020). Named entity recognition in field of ancient Chinese based on Lattice LSTM. *Computer Science*, 47(S02):18-22.

Cui, Y. M., Che, W. X., Liu, T., Qin, B., Yang, Z. Q., Wang, S. J., and Hu, G. P. (2021). Pre-training with whole word masking for Chinese BERT. *IEEE/ACM Transactions on Audio, Speech, and Language Processing*, 29:3504-3514.

Gao, J. C. and Zhao, Q. C. (2021). Study on word segmentation method of classical literature based on new word discovery. *Computer Technology and Development*, 31(09):178-181+207.

Gao, Y. (2020). Ancient Chinese word segmentation system based on long and short time neural network. *Automation and Instrumentation*, (2):128-131.

Gao, Y. (2021). Research on automatic word segmentation method of ancient Chinese based on BERT prediction training model. *Electronic Design Engineering*, (22):28-32.

Gururangan, S., Marasović, A., Swayamdipta, S., Lo, K., Beltagy, I., Downey, D., and Smith, N. A. (2020). Don't stop pretraining: Adapt language models to domains and tasks. In *Proceedings of the 58th Annual Meeting of the Association for Computational Linguistics,* pages 8342–8360, Online. Association for Computational Linguistics.

Huang, L., Peng, Y. N., Wang, H., and Wu, Z. Y. (2002). Statistical part-of-speech tagging for classical Chinese. In *Text, Speech and Dialogue, 5th International Conference, TSD 2002, Brno, Czech Republic September 9-12, 2002, Proceedings. DBLP, 2002*. pp.115-122.

Li, B., Feng, M. X., and Chen, X. H. (2013). Corpus Based Lexical Statistics of Pre-Qin Chinese. *Lecture Notes in Computer Science*, 7717:145-153.

Li, X. Y., Meng, Y. X., Sun, X. F., Han, Q. H., Yuan, A., and Li, J. W. (2019). Is word segmentation necessary for deep learning of Chinese representations? In *Proceedings of the 57th Annual Meeting of the Association for Computational Linguistics*, pages 3242–3252.

Liu, Y. and Long, D. (2014). A rule-based method for identifying patterns in old Chinese sentences. CLSW.

Liu, Y. H., Ott, M., Goyal, N., Du, J. F., Joshi, M., Chen, D. Q., Levy, O., Lewis, M., Zettlemoyer, L., and Stoyanov, V. (2019). RoBERTa: A robustly optimized BERT pretraining approach. *ArXiv*, abs/1907.11692.

Miyato, T., Dai, A. M., and Goodfellow, I. J. (2017). Adversarial training methods for semi-supervised text classification. In *Proceedings of the 2017 International Conference on Learning Representations (ICLR)*, pp. 1-11.

Qiao, W. and Sun, M. S. (2010). Joint Chinese word segmentation and named entity recognition based on max-margin Markov networks. Journal of Tsinghua University(Science and Technology), 50(5):758-762,767.

Qin, L. and Wei, W. (2013). Research on the system of jointing Chinese word segmentation with part-of-speech tagging. *2013 Sixth International Symposium on Computational Intelligence and Design*, 1:387-390.

Shi, M., Li, B., and Chen, X. H. (2010). CRF based research on a unified approach to word segmentation and POS tagging for Pre-Qin Chinese. *Journal of Chinese Information Processing*, 24(2):39-45.

Sun, Z. J., Li, X. Y., Sun, X. F., Meng, Y. X., Ao, X., He, Q., Wu, F., and Li, J. W. (2021). ChineseBERT: Chinese pre-training enhanced by glyph and pinyin information. In *Proceedings of the 59th Annual Meeting of the Association for Computational Linguistics and the 11th International Joint Conference on Natural Language Processing (Volume 1: Long Papers)*, pages 2065–2075, Online. Association for Computational Linguistics.

Wang, X. Y. and Li, B. (2017). Automatically segmenting middle ancient Chinese words with CRFs. *Data Analysis and Knowledge Discovery*, 1(5): 62-70.

Yang, S. C., Ji, Y., and Zhao, L. P. (2017). Study of ancient Chinese word segmentation based on Conditional Random Field. *Computer Knowledge and Technology*, (22):183-184.

Yang, X. S. and Hu, L. S. (2020). Part-of-speech tagging of classical Chinese based on Hidden Markovian Model. *Microcomputer Applications*, 36(5):130-133.

Xing, F. G. and Zhu, T. S. (2021). Large-scale online corpus based classical integrated Chinese dictionary construction and word segmentation. *Journal of Chinese Information Processing*, 35(7):41-46.

Zhang, Q., Jiang, C., Ji, Y.S., Feng, M. X., Li, B., Xu, C., and Liu, L. (2021). Unified model for word segmentation and POS tagging of multi-domain Pre-Qin literature. *Data Analysis and Knowledge Discovery*, 5(3):2-11.

Zhang, Z. Y., Han, X., Zhou, H., Ke, P., Gu, Y. X., Ye, D. M., Qin, Y. J., Su, Y. S., Ji, H. Z., Guan, J., Qi, F. C., Wang, X. Z., Zheng, Y. A., Zeng, G. Y., Cao, H. Q., Chen, S., Li, D. X., Sun, Z. B., Liu, Z. Y., Huang, M. L., Han, W. T., Tang, J., Li, J. Z., Zhu, X. Y., and Sun, M. S. (2020). CPM: A large-scale generative Chinese pre-trained language model. *ArXiv*, abs/2012.00413.

Proceedings of the Second Workshop on Language Technologies for Historical and Ancient Languages (LT4HALA 2022), pages 155–158
Language Resources and Evaluation Conference (LREC 2022), Marseille, 25 June 2022

Construction of Segmentation and Part of Speech Annotation Model in Ancient Chinese

Longjie Jiang, Qinyu Chang, Huyin Xie, Zhuying Xia
NANJING NORMAL UNIVERSITY ZHONGBEI COLLEGE
Zhenjiang, Jiangsu, China
wppwlp010820@163.com, {1225048113, 1963912428, 2900997927}@qq.com

Abstract

Of the four ancient civilizations, China is the only one whose history has never been interrupted over the past 5000 years. An important factor is that the Chinese nation has the fine tradition of sorting out classics, recording history with words, inheriting culture through continuous collation of indigenous accounts, and maintaining the spread of Chinese civilization. In this research, the siku-roberta model is introduced into the part-of-speech tagging task of ancient Chinese by using the data set of Zuozhuan, and good prediction results are obtained.

Keywords: Natural Language Processing, Old Chinese, Word Segmentation, POS Tagging

1. Introduction

Chinese classics are vast and profound. From ancient oracle bone inscriptions to books written on paper, they have a long history of more than 3,000 years. They are numerous, diverse in form and rich in content. These classics are important civilization achievements created by the Chinese nation in the long history, and reflect the Chinese people's thought, literature, art, science and technology.

However, due to the grammatical characteristics of ancient Chinese, the use of words and other words differs greatly from modern Chinese. Digging out the essence of information from the ancient Chinese treasure house has become a huge problem. In recent years, researches on word segmentation and part-of-speech tagging of modern Chinese have achieved fruitful results, while those on ancient Chinese are still insufficient.

The usage of words in ancient Chinese is flexible, with many concurrent words and flexible parts of speech, i.e. most sequences have different segme.

2. Correlation Study

2.1 Study on Part of Speech Labeling in Ancient Chinese

Such system of ancient Chinese has experienced thousands of years of development. A word has unique significance in different times and contexts. According to different historical periods, ancient Chinese can be divided into ancient Chinese, medieval Chinese and modern Chinese. Therefore, it is not feasible to train the ancient Chinese model that is similar to the prediction of modern Chinese. Due to the different standards of part-of-speech tagging, it is also infeasible to train the ancient Chinese word segmentation model and the ancient Chinese part-of-speech tagging model with ancient Chinese corpus in different periods, which will cause trouble in the process of training supervised learning model based on corpus.

Part-of-Speech Tagging refers to assigning unique part-of-speech tags to each word's segmentation in the text according to certain marking rules, such as adjectives, nouns, verbs, etc. The labeling method is as follows:

Table 1: Gender of word m2arkers

Number	Tagging	POS	Number	Tagging	POS
1	n	普通名词	11	p	介词
2	nr	人名	12	c	连词
3	ns	地名	13	u	助词
4	t	时间名词	14	d	副词
5	v	动词	15	y	语气词
6	gv	古代动词	16	s	拟声词
7	a	形容词	17	j	兼词
8	m	数词	18	w	标点
9	q	量词	19	i	词缀
10	r	代词			

Specific annotation samples are as follows:

未/d 王命/n ，/w 故/c 不/d 書/v 爵/n ，/w 曰/v ：/w "/w 儀父/nr "/w ，/w 貴/sv 之/r 也/y 。/w

In this study, the punctuation of *Zuozhuan*, word segmentation and word class label text are used as training data packets. *Zuozhuan* is an ancient Chinese masterpiece in the Spring and Autumn Period (770－476 BC), which is believed to be dated back to the Warring States Period (475–221 BC). *Zuozhuan* is a comment on the history of Spring and Autumn Period (770–476 BC).

The training data were distributed according to Nanjing Normal University's Ancient Chinese Word Segmentation and Corpus Guide. According to this format, annotations are encoded in UTF-8 plain text files. There is no word boundary in Chinese text. Therefore, the original text contains characters and punctuation marks. After manual annotation, text boundaries and part-of-speech tags are added to the text. As shown in Table 1, each word has a POS tag in the form of Word / POS. Each word is separated by a space, and punctuations are also treated as words.

Test data is provided in original format and only Chinese characters and punctuation are provided. There are two test data sets. Test A is designed to see how the system runs the data in the same name book. Zuozhuan_Test is extracted from *Zuozhuan* and has no overlap with the Zuozhuan_Train. Zuozhuan_Test does not allow the team to use it as training data. Test B aims to explore how the system processes similar data (texts with similar contents but from different books), the size of which is similar to Zuozhuan Test.

2.2 Sequence Annotation Studies Based on Deep Learning

Deep learning is a kind of machine learning, which simulates the mechanism of human brain to explain and analyze the data of image, speech and text by establishing deep neural network. Different from the traditional statistical-based machine learning model, deep learning attempts to automatically complete feature extraction. In recent years, it has received extensive attention in the field of natural language processing and has achieved remarkable progresses in application research. Since part-of-speech tagging of word segmentation can be regarded as one of the sequence tagging tasks, the following reviews the related research based on the models involved in sequence tagging.

3. Construction of Model

3.1 Model Introduction

(1) FLAT + Sikuroberta

1. Using Lattice framework. FLAT proposed by Fudan University are adopted as the subject of lexical enhancement.

2. Switching of pre-training model. The bert-wwm originally used by FLAT is replaced with the Sikuroberta 2.0 pre-training model of closed test.

3. Training of word vectors. 50-dimensional unigram, bigram and word-level word vectors are trained based on word segmentation data from the ' Sikuquanshu ' History Department.

FLAT + Sikuroberta model is constructed based on the above three steps.

(2) FLAT

In ACL 2020, the research team of Xipeng Qiu in Fudan University proposed FLAT: Chinese NER Using Flat-Lattice Transformer. FLAT has two innovations. First, it designs a position encoding based on Transformer to fuse Lattice structure, which can introduce lexical information losslessly. Second, it integrates the dynamic structure of lexical information based on Transformer, supports parallel computing, and greatly improves inference speed. FLAT reconstructs the original Lattice, and cleverly designs position encoding to fuse Lattice structure. Each character and vocabulary is constructed two head position encoding and tail position encoding, so that FLAT can directly model the interaction between characters and all matching vocabulary information. FLAT uses relative position coding to make Transformer suitable for NER tasks.

$$A_{i,j}^{*} = W_q^T E_{x_i}^T E_{x_i} W_{K,E} + W_q^T E_{x_i}^T R_{i,j} W_{K,R} + u^T E_{x_i} W_{k,E} + u^T R_{ij} W_{k,R}$$

Four relative distances are proposed to represent the relationship between xi and xj, including the relationship between characters and words.

$$d_{ij}^{(hh)} = head[i] - head[j]$$

$$d_{ij}^{(ht)} = head[i] - tail[j]$$

$$d_{ij}^{(th)} = tail[i] - head[j]$$

$$d_{ij}^{(tt)} = tail[i] - tail[j]$$

$d_{ij}^{(hh)}$ represents the head distance from head of xi to xj, which is similar to that of xi.The relative position encoding is expressed as :

$$R_{ij} = ReLU\left(W_r\left(P_{d_{ij}^{(hh)}} \oplus P_{d_{ij}^{(ht)}} \oplus P_{d_{ij}^{(th)}} \oplus P_{d_{ij}^{(tt)}}\right)\right)$$

$d_{ij}^{(hh)}$ calculation method is the same as vanilla Transformer :

$$P_d^{(2k)} = \sin\left(d/10000^{2k/d_{model}}\right)$$

FLAT vocabulary enhancement uses transformer to design a positionencoding to fuse the Lattice structure, efficiently introduce vocabulary information, and fuse the dynamic structure of vocabulary information, which can capture long-distance dependence and greatly improve inference efficiency.

(3) Sikuroberta

The figure below illustrates the training process of the Sikuroberta model

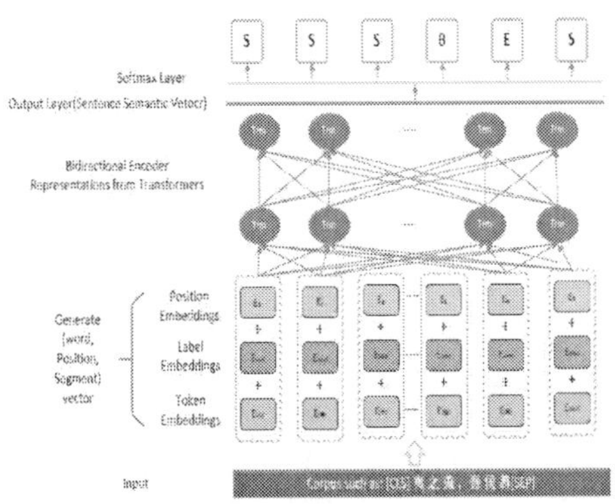

Figure 1: Training process of Sikuroberta

As shown in the above figure, at the Embedding layer, the BERT model divides the input Chinese sequences in words and maps the characters into numerical sequences using its own Chinese dictionary. For example, when the model reads into the sequence of "夷之蒐，晉侯將", this sentence is first divided by BERT model into characters with sequence start mark [CLS] and termination mark [SEP], and converted into input sequence[CLS]，夷，之，蒐，，，晉，侯，將，[SEP].Then it automatically combines the corresponding index value of each word to generate the word vector, the position of the word in the sentence, and the segment vector representing the sentence category, together generate a combined vector. Through the stacked multi-layer bidirectional transformer encoder, the final result through a softmax layer can obtain the maximum probability of each character, and the sequence annotation can be realized by exporting this series of labels. It is fairly suitable for discriminative tasks such as text classification and sequence annotation, and it is one of the most popular models in the NLP industry. In this experiment, we selected the Sikuroberta model provided by EvaHan2022. This model has completed the pre-training on the punctuation-free ‘ Four Library Encyclopedia ’ which removes the annotation information, and has remarkable effect on the Chinese natural language processing task.

3.2 Corpus Processing and Experiment

Combined with lexical information, the tag carries the dual information of word segmentation and part of speech. The experiment uses five-word tagging set, namely { B, M, E, S, O }, B represents the first word in the beginning, M represents the middle word, E represents the end word, S represents the word, O represents non-entity. After combining part-of-speech information, the labeled samples are shown in Figure 2.

魏 B-nr
子 E-nr
蒞 S-v
政 S-n
。 S-w
衛 B-nr
彪 E-nr

Figure 2: Examples of corpus preprocessing

In the above graph, it can be seen that ' 魏 ' is the first word in the beginning of this word segmentation, and the part of speech is nr; ' 子 ' is the end word of this word segmentation, and the part of speech is nr. ' 蒞 ', ' 政 'and ' . 'are single words.

3.3 Experimental Environment

The model is built based on Pytorch and FastNLP framework. The NVIDIA card is configured as follows :

Table 2:NVID card configuration

CUDA Version	GPU	Memory
10.2	NVIDIA Tesla P100	32GB

The table above shows the equipment used in this model construction.

3.4 Parameter Regulation

The following is the hyperparameter setting for the various models to reach the optimal state.

Table 3: The hyperparameters of the model

Module	Parameters
word2vec	sg=1,size=50,min_count=1, workers=15,sample=1e-3
Sikuroberta	epoch=30,batch-64, learning-rate=2e-5
Sikuroberta +CRF	epoch=30,batch=64, learning-rate=15e-5
FLAT +Sikuroberta	bert_lr_rate=0.0.5, embed_lr_rate,batch=25, epoch=50,fix_bert_epoch=20, max_seq_length=61

3.5 Model effect comparison and analysis

The study used three models for pos tagging of data, and compared their accuracy, recall rate and F score to select the best model. The three models are Sikuroberta, Sikuroberta + CRF and FLAT + Sikuroberta. We divided the training data by 9:1 and showed the results of pos tagging obtained by the three models.

Table 4: POS tagging results of the three models

	Precision	Recall	F score
Sikuroberta	90.21	90.56	90.37
Sikuroberta +CRF	85.97	85.77	85.87
FLAT +Sikuroberta	91.32	91.20	91.26

The figure shows the pos tagging results of the three models. The F score of Sikuroberta model can reach 90.37 %, and the F score of Sikuroberta + CRF model is only 85.87 %. The performance of Sikuroberta is higher than that of Sikuroberta + CRF. After adding CRF layer to BERT, the F score is not improved. In order to further improve the performance of the model, the present research used FLAT + BERT proposed by Qiu Xipeng team of Fudan University. In order to make FLAT adapt to ancient Chinese, the study replaced the bert-wwn model used in modern Chinese in FLAT with Sikuroberta in closed test. Using word2vec to train the 50-dimensional word vector.The F score of FLAT + Sikuroberta model can reach 91.26 %, which is 0.89 % higher than that of Sikuroberta, and the recall rate is 0.64 % higher, which further improves the overall performance of the model.

3.6 Data test results

Through the research, we selected the FLAT+ Sikuroberta model as the final model to obtain the prediction data of it. Based on the prediction data testa and testb released by EvaHan2022, we used FLAT+Sikuroberta model to predict data and got a best result. As for the test data testa and testb released by EvaHan2022, testa and training data are from the same book, while testb and training data are not in the same book but similar in content.We also used the FINAL script as a scorer to obtain scores. The final test data format and results are shown as follows:

孟懿子/nr 會/v 城/v 成周/ns ，/w 庚寅/t ，/w 栽/v 。/w

Table 5: Results of pos tagging

	Precision	Recall	F score
Testa_closed	88.79	87.54	88.16
Testa_open	88.97	86.48	87.70
Testb_open	89.69	89.25	89.47

Table 6: Results of word segmentation

	Precision	Recall	F score
Testa_closed	92.75	91.44	92.09
Testa_open	92.77	90.17	91.45
Testb_open	95.26	94.78	95.02

From Table 5 and Table 6, in testa of the closed mode, the score of word segmention F1 is 92.09%, and pos tagging F1 is 88.16%. In testa of open mode, the the score of word segmention F1 is 91.45%, and pos tagging F1 is 87.70%. In testb of open mode, the score of word segmentation F1 is 95.02%, and pos tagging F1 is 89.47%.

4. Conclusion

Under the development prospect of artificial intelligence and digital humanities, the research on ancient Chinese is relatively weak. Therefore, the result of pos tagging of ancient books is of great help to the subsequent research, such as the study of Ancient Chinese Literature Search, historiography, philology and Chinese history. Based on the learning model FLAT + Sikuroberta, this paper constructed the pos tagging pattern of ancient Chinese. In tasta under the same book, the score of pos tagging F can reach 87.70%, the score of word segmentation F can reach 91.45%. In testb with similar contents under different books, the score of pos tagging F can reach 89.47%, the score of word segmentation F can reach 95.02%. It can be successfully applied to pos tagging and word segmentation, has achieved the practical goal.

5. References

[1]Liu Chang, Wang Dongbo, Hu Haotian, Zhang Yiqin, Li Bin. Dictionary of integrating external characteristics for digital humanities .Research on automatic word segmentation - Taking sikuBERT pre-training model as an example [J / OL].Library forum.

[2]Zhang Qi, Jiang Chuan, Ji Youshu,et al. Unified Model for Word Segmentation and POS Tagging of Multi-Domain Pre-Qin Literature[J]. Data Analysis and Knowledge Discovery, 2021, 5(3): 2-11.

[3]Xiaonan Li, Hang Yan, Xipeng Qiu , Xuanjing Huang.FLAT: Chinese NER Using Flat-Lattice TransformerFLAT: Chinese NER Using Flat-Lattice Transformer[C].ACL2020, 2020.

[4]Hu Jie, Hu Yan, Liu Mengchi, Zhang Yan.Chinese named entity recognition based on knowledge base and entity enhanced BERT model[J/OL].Journal of Computer Applications.2021.

[5]Yue Zhang,Jie Yang.Chinese NER Using LatticeLSTM[J].arXiv:1805.02023 [cs.CL].2018.

Proceedings of the Second Workshop on Language Technologies for Historical and Ancient Languages (LT4HALA 2022), pages 159–163
Language Resources and Evaluation Conference (LREC 2022), Marseille, 25 June 2022

Simple Tagging System with RoBERTa for Ancient Chinese

Binghao Tang, Boda Lin, Si Li*
School of Artificial Intelligence
Beijing University of Post and Telecommunication, China
{tangbinghao, linboda, lisi}@bupt.edu.cn

Abstract

This paper describes the system submitted for the EvaHan 2022 Shared Task on word segmentation and part-of-speech tagging for Ancient Chinese. Our system is based on the pre-trained language model SIKU-RoBERTa and the simple tagging layers. Our system significantly outperforms the official baselines in the released test sets and shows the effectiveness.
Keywords: EvaHan 2022, Word Segmentation, POS tagging

1. Introduction

Chinese Word Segmentation (CWS) is a fundamental task in Natural Language Processing (NLP). Generally speaking, word is the basic unit containing complete semantic information. Thus CWS is widely used for difference NLP tasks, such as machine translation (Yang et al., 2018), text classification (Zeng et al., 2018), and question answering (Liu et al., 2018). Comparing with CWS, Part-of-speech (POS) tagging is a more general task for many languages, which aims to assign pre-defined syntactical property for each token in the sentence. Some research (Ng and Low, 2004) validates combining them into a joint task can provide better performance than separately conducting these two tasks in a sequence. Thus the CWS is usually implemented with the prediction of POS tagging jointly in the recent years (Tian et al., 2020a).

Previous studies about this joint task are usually deemed as sequence labeling task (Zhang et al., 2016; Higashiyama et al., 2019; Qiu et al., 2020). These models achieve excellent performance in this task, especially with the wide usage of pre-trained language model (PLM) (Tian et al., 2020b). However, most Chinese versions of PLMs are pre-trained on the multilingual corpus (Devlin et al., 2019; Liu et al., 2020; Xue et al., 2021). Even if there are few PLMs pre-trained on pure Chinese corpus, most of them use the Morden Chinese (Sun et al., 2019). Recently there are some work release PLMs pre-trained on ancient Chinese corpus to withdraw this lacking in CWS, e.g., *SIKU-BERT* (Wang et al., 2021) and *SIKU-RoBERTa* (Wang et al., 2021). Based on these two models, the first NLP tool evaluation competition in the field of ancient Chinese, i.e, EvaHan 2022 is released. EvaHan 2022 aims to exploit an efficient way to handle the joint task of CWS and POS tagging on ancient Chinese language.

In this paper, we describe our submitted system for the EvaHan 2022. Our system is based on the released ancient Chinese version of RoBERTa (Wang et al., 2021). We utilize extra knowledge from ancient Chinese via the pre-trained RoBERTa, and further encode features by concrete context information with Bi-LSTMs.

The experimental results on the two test sets demonstrate the effectiveness of our method. Our method significantly outperforms the official baselines to a large margin in the in-domain test set.

2. Related Work

2.1. Chinese Word Segmentation & POS tagging

Chinese Word Segmentation (CWS) has been studied for a long time, as one of the most fundamental NLP tasks for Chinese language processing (Higashiyama et al., 2019; Qiu et al., 2020). And part-of-speech (POS) tagging is also a basic task for natural language processing. Some research (Ng and Low, 2004) demonstrates that combining CWS and POS tagging tasks together as a joint task can improve both of them. So many researchers dedicate to CWS and POS tagging and obtain many amazing achievements (Tian et al., 2020a). However, most research is based on modern Chinese while few works pay attention to ancient Chinese. Considering this situation, EvaHan 2022 release a competition for the joint task on ancient Chinese.

2.2. Pre-trained Language Model

BERT (Devlin et al., 2019) is widely used PLM for CWS (Tian et al., 2020a). Besides, (Wang et al., 2021) apply RoBERTa to implement CWS task. while there are many differences between modern Chinese and ancient Chinese. So straightly using the PLMs in the area of ancient Chinese usually gets unsatisfactory performances. Thus *SIKU-RoBERTa* (Wang et al., 2021), which continues to train on ancient Chinese corpus based on vallina Chinese RoBERTa (Liu et al., 2019), seems to be a good choice.

3. Method

We introduce the overall procedure of our system for this evaluation task, which includes the pre-processing, model architecture and the solution for the long sentence.

*Corresponding author

`https://circse.github.io/LT4HALA/2022/EvaHan`

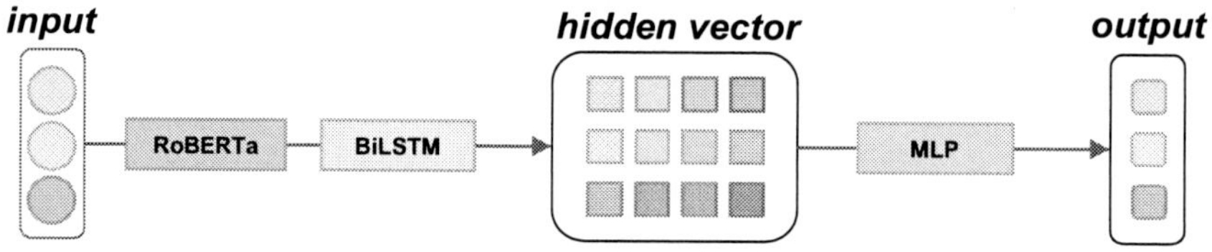

Figure 1: Overall Architecture

Set	Domain	Number of Word Tokens	Number of Character Tokens
Train	Zuozhuan	$166,142$	$194,955$
Test A	Zuozhuan	$28,131$	$33,298$
Blind Test B	Other ancient Chinese Book	Around $40,000$	Around $50,000$

Table 1: The statistics data of the datasets.

3.1. Pre-processing

We firstly pre-process raw data. For example, the input sentence is "春秋/n 左/n 定公/n". To start with, we split sentence into single tokens and use notation to distinguish each token's position in origin word, i.e., B short for Begin, M short for Mid, E short for End, and combine it with its POS label. So the processed sentence should be like: "春 b-n 秋 e-n 左 b-n e-n 定 b-nr 公 e-nr".

3.2. Model

The architecture of our model is shown in Figure 1. We define the input sequence is $S = \{c_1, c_2, ..., c_n\}$, where c_i is the i-th character of the input sentence. The input S is sent into the RoBERTa, a multi-layer Transformer (Vaswani et al., 2017) structure model. In the l-th layer of Transformer, the hidden representation H_l is calculated as following:

$$\hat{H}_l = LayerNorm(H_{l-1} + Attention(H_{l-1})) \quad (1)$$

$$H_l = LayerNorm(\hat{H}_l + FFN(\hat{H}_l)) \quad (2)$$

where the H_0 is S, $LayerNorm$ is the layer-wise normalization layer, and the $Attention$ is the multi-head attention layer. Please refer to the original paper (Devlin et al., 2018; Liu et al., 2019) for more details.

After obtaining the encoding representation H from RoBERTa, a bidirectional LSTM is applied to further encoding the context representation :

$$R = BiLSTM(H) \quad (3)$$

Finally, we use a Multi-layer Proc (MLP) to predict the labeling sequence :

$$Y = MLP(R) \quad (4)$$

3.3. Solution for Long Sentences

The dataset contains some long length sentences, which are beyond the maximum length processed by the proposed model. Considering this situation, we split these long sentences into some short sub-sentences. We try to keep all sub-sentences semantically complete thus we split the long sentence according to punctuation instead of the maximum length. Then we revert sentences from the output file of system and obtain our final submit file.

Hypermeter	Value
learning rate	$2 \times e^{-3}$
layer of BiLSTM	3
dimension of embedding	300
hidden dimension of BiLSTM	400
dimension of MLP	500
dropout ratio	0.33

Table 2: hypermeters

4. Experiments

4.1. dataset

We use the datasets released by the host of EvaHan 2022, which include one training set and two test sets. All the sentences are collected from the ancient Chinese texts like Zuozhuan (Li et al., 2012). The details about the statistics of the dataset are shown in Table 1. The training data contains punctuated, word-segmented and part-of-speech tagged text from zuozhuan, an ancient Chinese work. There are two test data sets. Test A contains different data from the same book of training data. And test A also have annotated version in the form of training data, so test A can be used as validation sets while training. Test B contains texts which have similar content from different books and only Chinese characters and punctuation. Thus test B is designed as out-of-domain sets to test the generalization of system.

4.2. Implementation Details

We use the RoBERTa as the backbone for all experiments. The PLM is implemented with Huggingface

Task (Test A)	CWS			POS		
	Precision	Recall	F1	Precision	Recall	F1
Baseline	90.64	92.08	91.35	89.06	89.54	89.30
*SIKU-BERT	–	–	88.84	–	–	90.10
*SIKU-RoBERTa	–	–	88.88	–	–	90.06
Our System	**95.81**	**96.52**	**96.16**	**90.90**	**91.57**	**91.24**
Task (Test B)	CWS			POS		
	Precision	Recall	F1	Precision	Recall	F1
Our System	94.04	90.59	92.28	86.86	83.67	85.24

Table 3: Experimental results on two tests in terms of F1 Score. The host of EvaHan 2022 do not report the results of official baseline and results of SIKU-BERT, and SIKU-RoBERTa on Test B. * means the results about POS tagging of these two models are different from joint task of CWS and POS tagging.

Transformers . We use different learning rates for PLM and non-PLM layers in the model. The learning rate for PLM is $5 \times 10e^{-5}$, and the learning rate for non-PLM layers is $2 \times 10e^{-3}$. The optimizer is Adam (Kingma and Ba, 2014). We implement all experiments on Nvidia GTX1080Ti. Our system consumes about 7GiB GPU memory and it takes about 4 hours to achieve the best performance.

The other important hyperparameters are listed in Table 2.

Instead of performing a hyperparameter search, we directly chose the values of the parameters empirically.

4.3. Metric

Following the convention of CWS and POS tagging, we use Precision (P), Recall (R), and F1 Score as the evaluation metrics for all experiments. All the results are presented in percentages (%).

4.4. Baselines

We compare our system with the official baselines, which obtains on *Zuozhuan_test* using Conditional Random Fields (CRF) training on *Zuozhuan_train* without additional resources (Xiao-he, 2010). Besides, we also choose the BERT and RoBERTa pre-trained on the SIKU, which are noted as *SIKU-BERT* and *SIKU-RoBERTa* in Table 3.

4.5. Results

The results are shown in Table 3. Our system outperforms all the baselines in all metrics on both the CWS task and the POS tagging task, which demonstrate the effectiveness of our system. Besides, our system also obtain better performance comparing with the vanilla SIKU-RoBERTa. This comparison also can be regard as a ablation study, which validate the effectiveness of the additional layers we designed.

https://huggingface.co/SIKU-BERT/sikuroberta

Algorithm 1: post-process

```
input tokens: w1/y1, w2/y − 2, w3/y3, w4/y4
output      : w1w2w3   w4
for i ← 1 to N do
    if yi = b and yi+1 = b then
        └ wi   wi+1
    if yi = b and yi+1 = s then
        └ wi   wi+1
    if yi = m and yi+1 = b then
        └ wi−1wi   wi+1
    if yi = m and yi+1 = s then
        └ wi−1wi   wi+1
    if yi = e and yi+1 = e then
        └ wi−1wiwi+1
    if yi = e and yi+1 = m then
        └ wi−1wi   wi+1
```

4.6. The Legality

The legality is an important issue for CWS task. The neural network may predicts some illegal labeling tokens such as "$w_1/b \quad w_2/b$". A traditional approach to dealing with this problem is using CRF to constrain the output sequence (Xiao-he, 2010). We do not apply CRF in our system for brevity, and the statistics results show only the 0.6% tokens in the test set are illegal.

For those illegal tokens, we correct them by post-processing which is shown in Algorithm 1. This low illegal ratio demonstrates that the great learning ability of RoBERTa can enables the model to learn implicit constraints between output labels (Liu et al., 2019).

5. Conclusion

In this paper, we describe the simple tagging system submitted for the EvaHan2022. The proposed system apply a pre-trained RoBERTa and the BiLSTM layers to encoding context information. The experimental results on the official test sets demonstrate the effectiveness of our system, especially the comparison between our system and the original official RoBERTa validate the effectiveness of the additional tagging layers. Besides, we also discuss the legality issue for CWS.

6. References

Devlin, J., Chang, M.-W., Lee, K., and Toutanova, K. (2018). Bert: Pre-training of deep bidirectional transformers for language understanding. *arXiv preprint arXiv:1810.04805.*

Devlin, J., Chang, M.-W., Lee, K., and Toutanova, K. (2019). BERT: Pre-training of deep bidirectional transformers for language understanding. In *Proceedings of the 2019 Conference of the North American Chapter of the Association for Computational Linguistics: Human Language Technologies, Volume 1 (Long and Short Papers)*, pages 4171–4186, Minneapolis, Minnesota, June. Association for Computational Linguistics.

Higashiyama, S., Utiyama, M., Sumita, E., Ideuchi, M., Oida, Y., Sakamoto, Y., and Okada, I. (2019). Incorporating word attention into character-based word segmentation. In *Proceedings of the 2019 Conference of the North American Chapter of the Association for Computational Linguistics: Human Language Technologies, Volume 1 (Long and Short Papers)*, pages 2699–2709, Minneapolis, Minnesota, June. Association for Computational Linguistics.

Kingma, D. P. and Ba, J. (2014). Adam: A method for stochastic optimization. *arXiv preprint arXiv:1412.6980.*

Li, B., Xi, N., Feng, M., and Chen, X. (2012). Corpus-based statistics of pre-qin chinese. pages 145–153, 07.

Liu, Z., Peng, E., Yan, S., Li, G., and Hao, T. (2018). T-know: a knowledge graph-based question answering and infor-mation retrieval system for traditional Chinese medicine. In *Proceedings of the 27th International Conference on Computational Linguistics: System Demonstrations*, pages 15–19, Santa Fe, New Mexico, August. Association for Computational Linguistics.

Liu, Y., Ott, M., Goyal, N., Du, J., Joshi, M., Chen, D., Levy, O., Lewis, M., Zettlemoyer, L., and Stoyanov, V. (2019). Roberta: A robustly optimized bert pretraining approach. *arXiv preprint arXiv:1907.11692.*

Liu, Y., Gu, J., Goyal, N., Li, X., Edunov, S., Ghazvininejad, M., Lewis, M., and Zettlemoyer, L. (2020). Multilingual denoising pre-training for neural machine translation. *Transactions of the Association for Computational Linguistics*, 8:726–742.

Ng, H. T. and Low, J. K. (2004). Chinese part-of-speech tagging: One-at-a-time or all-at-once? word-based or character-based? In *Proceedings of the 2004 Conference on Empirical Methods in Natural Language Processing*, pages 277–284, Barcelona, Spain, July. Association for Computational Linguistics.

Qiu, X., Pei, H., Yan, H., and Huang, X. (2020). A concise model for multi-criteria Chinese word segmentation with transformer encoder. In *Findings of the Association for Computational Linguistics: EMNLP 2020*, pages 2887–2897, Online, November. Association for Computational Linguistics.

Sun, Y., Wang, S., Li, Y., Feng, S., Chen, X., Zhang, H., Tian, X., Zhu, D., Tian, H., and Wu, H. (2019). Ernie: Enhanced representation through knowledge integration. *arXiv preprint arXiv:1904.09223.*

Tian, Y., Song, Y., Ao, X., Xia, F., Quan, X., Zhang, T., and Wang, Y. (2020a). Joint Chinese word segmentation and part-of-speech tagging via two-way attentions of auto-analyzed knowledge. In *Proceedings of the 58th Annual Meeting of the Association for Computational Linguistics*, pages 8286–8296, Online, July. Association for Computational Linguistics.

Tian, Y., Song, Y., Xia, F., Zhang, T., and Wang, Y. (2020b). Improving Chinese word segmentation with wordhood memory networks. In *Proceedings of the 58th Annual Meeting of the Association for Computational Linguistics*, pages 8274–8285, Online, July. Association for Computational Linguistics.

Vaswani, A., Shazeer, N., Parmar, N., Uszkoreit, J., Jones, L., Gomez, A. N., Kaiser, Ł., and Polosukhin, I. (2017). Attention is all you need. *Advances in neural information processing systems*, 30.

Wang, D., Liu, C., Zhu, Z., Jiang, Feng, Hu, H., Shen, S., and Li, B.-S. (2021). Construction and application of pre-training model of "siku quanshu" oriented to digital humanities.

Xiao-he, C. (2010). Crf based research on a unified approach to word segmentation and pos tagging for pre-qin chinese. *Journal of Chinese information processing.*

Xue, L., Constant, N., Roberts, A., Kale, M., Al-Rfou, R., Siddhant, A., Barua, A., and Raffel, C. (2021). mT5: A massively multilingual pre-trained text-to-text transformer. In *Proceedings of the 2021 Conference of the North American Chapter of the Association for Computational Linguistics: Human Language Technologies*, pages 483–498, Online, June. Association for Computational Linguistics.

Yang, Z., Chen, W., Wang, F., and Xu, B. (2018). Improving neural machine translation with conditional sequence generative adversarial nets. In *Proceedings of the 2018 Conference of the North American Chapter of the Association for Computational Linguistics: Human Language Technologies, Volume 1 (Long Papers)*, pages 1346–1355, New Orleans, Louisiana, June. Association for Computational Linguistics.

Zeng, J., Li, J., Song, Y., Gao, C., Lyu, M. R., and King, I. (2018). Topic memory networks for short text classification. In *Proceedings of the 2018 Conference on Empirical Methods in Natural Language*

Processing, pages 3120–3131, Brussels, Belgium, October-November. Association for Computational Linguistics.

Zhang, M., Zhang, Y., and Fu, G. (2016). Transition-based neural word segmentation. In *Proceedings of the 54th Annual Meeting of the Association for Computational Linguistics (Volume 1: Long Papers)*, pages 421–431, Berlin, Germany, August. Association for Computational Linguistics.

Proceedings of the Second Workshop on Language Technologies for Historical and Ancient Languages (LT4HALA 2022), pages 164–168
Language Resources and Evaluation Conference (LREC 2022), Marseille, 25 June 2022

The Uncertainty-based Retrieval Framework for Ancient Chinese CWS and POS

Pengyu Wang, Zhichen Ren
Fudan University, Tongji University
220 Handan Road Shanghai, China
4800 Caoan Highway, Shanghai, China
wpyjihuai@gmail.com, 1850091@tongji.edu.cn

Abstract

Automatic analysis for modern Chinese has greatly improved the accuracy of text mining in related fields, but the study of ancient Chinese is still relatively rare. Ancient text division and lexical annotation are important parts of classical literature comprehension, and previous studies have tried to construct auxiliary dictionary and other fused knowledge to improve the performance. In this paper, we propose a framework for ancient Chinese Word Segmentation and Part-of-Speech Tagging that makes a twofold effort: on the one hand, we try to capture the wordhood semantics; on the other hand, we re-predict the uncertain samples of baseline model by introducing external knowledge. The performance of our architecture outperforms pre-trained BERT with CRF and existing tools such as Jiayan.

Keywords: Bigram Features, Uncertainty Sampling, Knowledge Retrieval

1. Introduction

Chinese Word Segmentation (CWS) and Part-of-Speech (POS) Tagging are two important tasks of natural language processing. With the rapid development of deep learning and pre-trained models, the performance of CWS and POS Tagging increased significantly. A simple model using pre-trained BERT and conditional random field (CRF) can reach a high accuracy. Since words are the most common components in a Chinese sentence and words can cause ambiguity, structures that can capture word information have been used in these tasks to get better performance.

Lexicon-based methods have been widely used in CWS, Chinese POS tagging and NER tasks to capture wordhood information (Yang et al., 2018; Li et al., 2020). These methods can leverage semantic information of words and improve model performance. However, lexicon-based methods have several drawbacks. One of the most severe problems is that they depend heavily on the quality of lexicons. Unfortunately, building an ancient Chinese lexicon is more difficult than building a modern Chinese lexicon, since there are few ancient Chinese corpus, and words from different corpus are different.

Further, sentences in ancient Chinese are always shorter than sentences in Chinese, which means words in ancient Chinese have a richer meaning and can cause misunderstanding or wrong classification.

The two problems mentioned above make ancient Chinese CWS and POS Tagging a harder problem. In our model, we combine bigram features with BERT to capture wordhood information in sentences. The semantic information of bigram plays a similar role to the lexicon, while it is unnecessary to build a large lexicon for ancient Chinese corpus. To deal with the ambiguity, or uncertainty in sentences, we use MC-dropout method to find uncertain parts of sentences. Next we use a Knowledge Fusion Model to retrieve auxillary knowledge and re-predict the uncentain parts. Our experiments show that our model outperforms pre-trained BERT model `https://huggingface.co/SIKU-BERT/sikuroberta` with CRF and Jiayan `https://github.com/jiaeyan/Jiayan` in our dataset *Zuozhuan*.

2. Background and Related Work

2.1. CWS and POS Tagging

Chinese Word Segmentation (CWS) is the fundamental of Chinese natural language understanding. It splits a sentence into several words, which are basic components of a Chinese sentence. CWS is necessary because there is no natural segmentation between Chinese words. Part-of-Speech Tagging (POS Tagging) further assigns POS tags for each word in a sentence.

2.2. Knowledge Retrieval

Knowledge retrieval is a method used to enhance the performance of language models, and they are most commonly used in NER tasks. Knowledge databases (Qiu et al., 2014; Gu et al., 2018) and search engines (Geng et al., 2022) are used to retrieve knowledge, and the knowledge retrieved is used to argument the input sentences.

3. Approach

As previous work (Qiu et al., 2019; Ke et al., 2020), the CWS and POS Tagging task is viewed as a character-based sequence labeling problem. Specifically, given input sequence $X = [c_1, c_2, ..., c_n]$ composed of continuous characters, the model should output a label sequence $Y = [y_1, y_2, ...y_n]$ with $y_i \in TagSet$.

In this section, we will introduce the improvement proposed for local semantic information capture, followed by the uncertainty sampling method. Finally, we will introduce our overall framework utilizing the uncertainty sampling method.

3.1. Local Semantic Enhancement

BERT (Devlin et al., 2018) is a Transformer based bidirectional language model, which solves the problem of long-term dependence in RNN models. However, this also makes BERT lose the ability to capture local semantic features. Therefore, we integrated the bigram features to introduce local semantic information. The overall architecture of our baseline model is displayed in Figure 1, and we call it *Semantic Enhancement BERT*.

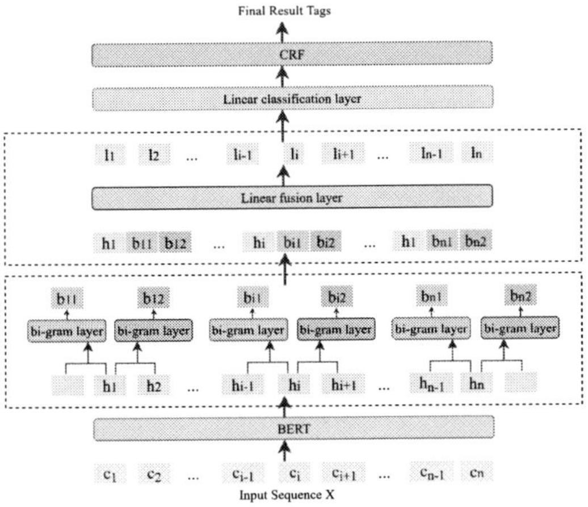

Figure 1: Architecture of baseline model.

3.1.1. Encoder

Given input sequence $X = [c_1, c_2, ..., c_n], X \in \mathbb{R}^n$. We employ BERT as our basic encoder, converting X to hidden character representations as follows,

$$H = BERT(X), \tag{1}$$

where $H \in \mathbb{R}^{n \times d_h}$.

3.1.2. Linear Bigram Layer

The vocabulary of ancient Chinese is short, consise and meaningful, and the bigram features have proved beneficial for CWS (Chen et al., 2017; Ke et al., 2020). Therefore, we construct the bigram concatenated vectors for every character c_i by concatenating it's hidden character representations with the previous character's and the latter character's. Then we convert the concatenated vectors to bigram feature vectors b_{i1}, b_{i2} by two Linear bigram layer as follows,

$$b_{i1} = LinearLayer_1(h_{i-1} \oplus h_i), \tag{2}$$
$$b_{i2} = LinearLayer_2(h_i \oplus h_{i+1}), \tag{3}$$

where $b_{i1}, b_{i2} \in \mathbb{R}^{d_b}$.

3.1.3. Linear Fusion Layer

We construct Composite feature vector h_i for character c_i by concatenating h_i, b_{i1} and b_{i2} as follows,

$$h_i^{'} = h_i \oplus b_{i1} \oplus b_{i2}, \tag{4}$$

where $h_i^{'} \in \mathbb{R}^{(d_h + 2 \times d_b)}$.
$H^{'}$ is defined as follows,

$$H^{'} = [h_1^{'}, h_2^{'}, ..., h_n^{'}]. \tag{5}$$

Then, we use a simple fusion mechanism to convert the Composite feature vectors to Fusion feature vectors by a Linear Layer,

$$L = LinearLayer_3(H^{'}), \tag{6}$$

where $H^{'} \in \mathbb{R}^{n \times (d_h + 2 \times d_b)}$, $L \in \mathbb{R}^{n \times d_l}$.

3.1.4. Decoder

The Fusion feature representations are converted into the probabilities over the POS labels by an MLP layer,

$$P^T = Softmax(WL^T + b), \tag{7}$$

where $P \in \mathbb{R}^{n \times d_t}$. d_t is the number of POS tags. P_{ik} represents the probability that the label of c_i is tag_k. Finally, we decode P using **Viterbi algorithm** to obtain the final tag sequence $T = [t_1, t_2, ..., t_n], T \in \mathbb{R}^n$.

3.2. Uncertainty Sampling

BERT is already very powerful. Under the condition that the annotated dataset is very limited, simply increasing the complexity of the model structure will not make performance better. So we introduce uncertainty sampling and knowledge retrieving.

3.2.1. Uncertainty Sampling Method

MC Dropout (Gal and Ghahramani, 2016) is a general approach to obtain the uncertain components. Formally, given input sequence X, we first obtain the provisional label sequence T_p utilizing trained baseline model. Then, we utilize MC dropout to keep dropout active and generate k candidate label sequences $T_1, T_2, ..., T_k$ with Viterbi decoding. The difference between each candidate-predicted word set and the provisional-predicted word set can be considered uncertain words. Then we obtain uncertain components by merging all overlapping uncertain words.

3.2.2. Preliminary Statistics

Similar to Geng et al. (2022)'s evaluation approach, we conduct an investigation on test set of two Ancient Chinese datasets to verify the importance of the uncertainty component. We use *Semantic Enhancement BERT* as baseline model and generate 8 candidate label sequences using MC dropout. The results are displayed in Table 3.

	Zuozhuan	*Shiji*
CWS F1 Score	95.606%	93.465%
CWS Oracle F1 Score	97.777%	96.780%
POS F1 Score	91.229%	87.618%
POS Oracle F1 Score	95.602%	93.417%
$\text{ACC}_{uncertain}$	57.190%	55.951%
$\text{ACC}_{certain}$	94.560%	91.704%

Table 1: The statistics of the uncertain components. **F1 Score** denotes the F1 score of the baseline model on the test dataset. **Oracle F1 Score** denotes the F1 score obtained by the baseline model if the labels of the uncertain components are corrected. $\textbf{ACC}_{uncertain}$ and $\textbf{ACC}_{certain}$ denote the label accuracy of the provisional results for the uncertain components and the confident components, respectively.

The significant gap between certain components and uncertain components indicates that the uncertain components are real hard components and become bottlenecks for performance. Therefore, by querying about uncertain components, the ancient corpus with the same structure can be retrieved.

3.2.3. Retrieving

Different from the retrieval idea in the NER task (Geng et al., 2022), we first collect several Pre-Qin ancient texts to form our knowledge corpus. For word w corresponding to each uncertain component, we query the sentences containing w. In particular, if the uncertain component contains only one character, we construct bigram words w_1 and w_2 for the character w by concatenating it with the previous character and the latter character. Then we look for sentences containing w_1 or w_2 instead of w.

We rank sentences by similarities in order to obtain sentences with grammatical structures similar to X. Generally, the similarity between two sentences P and Q is defined as follows,

$$\mathrm{s} = \frac{\mathrm{union(P, Q)}}{\|\mathrm{P}\| + \|\mathrm{Q}\|}, \tag{8}$$

where $union(P, Q)$ is the total number of the same characters in P and Q, $\|\mathrm{P}\|$ and $\|\mathrm{Q}\|$ is the length of P and Q, respectively. Finally, we choose the most similar sentences as auxiliary knowledge.

3.3. Framework

In this part, we will present our overall framework, which is displayed in Figure 2.

3.3.1. Stage One: Provisional Results and Uncertainty Sampling

Given input sequence $X = [c_1, c_2, ..., c_n]$, we employ baseline model to obtain the provisional label sequence T_p and candidate label sequences. Then we obtain the uncertain component $U = [c_i, c_{i+1}, ...c_{i+o}]$ using the method in Section 3.2.

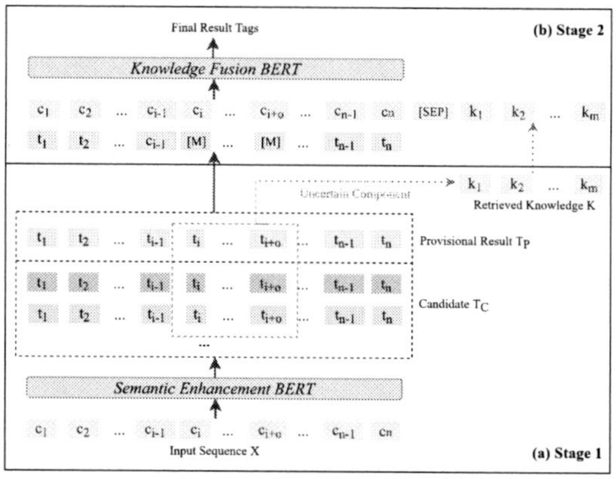

Figure 2: The overall framework.

If X has no uncertain component, T_p will be taken as the final prediction label sequence T. Otherwise, we use U to retrieve the auxiliary knowledge K. If there are multiple uncertain components, we retrieve them separately and process them independently using the method in Stage Two.

3.3.2. Stage Two: Knowledge Fusion Prediction

In the second stage, we re-predict the label sequence of input sequence X by combining the auxiliary knowledge K and the provisional label sequence T_p obtained in Stage One.

Similar to Geng et al. (2022), we concatenate X and K to obtain the knowledge-enhanced input sequence $X' = [c_1, c_2, ..., c_n, [SEP], k_1, k_2, ..., k_m]$ and construct the auxilary label sequence as follows,

$$t_i' = \begin{cases} t_i & \text{if } i \leq n \text{ and } c_i \notin U \\ [MASK] & \text{if } c_i \in U \\ [PAD] & \text{if } i > n \end{cases}, \tag{9}$$

$$T' = [t_1', t_2', ..., t_n', t_{n+1}', ..., t_{n+m+1}']. \tag{10}$$

Finally, we combine X' and T' as the input of Bert-based *Knowledge Fusion BERT* (KF-BERT) to obtain the probability distribution D,

$$E_{T'} = LabelEmbedding(T'), \tag{11}$$

$$E_{X'} = CharacterEmbedding(X'), \tag{12}$$

$$D = KF\text{-}BERT(E_{T'} + E_{X'}), \tag{13}$$

where $D = [d_1, d_2, ...d_n]$ and d_i is the probability distribution of c_i, and d_{ij} is the probability of c_i being predicted to tag_j.

Label Embedding and *Character Embedding* are parameters need to be trained. Finally, we get the final label sequence by **Viterbi algorithm**. In particular, if there are multiple uncertain components in X, we process them separately in the second stage and average all obtained D before Viterbi decoding.

Model	Test-*Zuozhuan*		Test-*Shiji*	
	CWS-F1(%)	POS-F1(%)	CWS-F1(%)	POS-F1(%)
Jiayan	82.022	/	83.141	/
Siku-RoBERTa + CRF	96.073	91.998	92.937	87.466
SE-BERT	96.018	92.019	93.092	87.594
SE-BERT^{+}	96.148	92.292	93.914	86.691
SE-BERT^{+}+KF-BERT	**96.284**	**92.410**	**93.596**	**87.873**
BERT-Bigram	96.009	91.853	93.015	87.574

Table 2: Jiayan is an NLP toolkit focusing on ancient Chinese processing. SE-BERT denotes *Semantic Enhancement BERT* using Siku-RoBERTa, SE-BERT^{+} denotes *Semantic Enhancement BERT* using Siku-RoBERTa^{+} as pre-trained BERT, and KF-BERT means *Knowledge Fusion BERT* using Siku-RoBERTa. BERT-Bigram denotes Siku-RoBERTa incorporating pre-trained bigram embedding. To utilize the entire training set, we use cross-validation and average the prediction results of K models, where K = 5.

4. Experiment

We conducted a series of experiments to validate the effectiveness of our framework. We follow the competition EvaHan2022 `https://circse.github.io/LT4HALA/2022/EvaHan`, using a tag set containing 22 POS tags and a tag set {B, M, E, S} to denote the beginning, middle, and end of a word as well as single words. Thus we have a total of 88 tags for joint CWS and POS Tagging classification. We used the standard F1-Score as evaluation metric. All experiments were conducted on a server with 8 GeForce RTX 3090.

4.1. Overall Performance

Table 2 shows the over all performance and some ablation experiments.

From Table 2, the performance of our model is much higher than the ancient Chinese processing toolkit Jiayan. our efforts in both semantic enhancement (siku-roBERTa+CRF and SE-BERT) and knowledge fusion (SE-BERT^{+} and SE-BERT^{+}+KF-BERT) show that large improvements were achieved. Also, further-pretrain of BERT on relevant domain datasets can further improve the performance (as seen for SE-BERT^{+}). Our final model combines all the advantages and achieves good results.

5. Discussion

Regarding the combination of bigram features, we did not introduce new knowledge or more complex structures in our framework. Ke et al. (2020) incorporated pre-trained bigram embedding into their model. Referring to the work of Ke et al. (2020), we conducted another experiment.

The experiment result in Table 2 shows that *Semantic Enhancement BERT* works better than $BERT\text{-}Bigram$. However, the idea still shows a good direction for future research. The ancient vocabulary is short and rich in meaning, and the performance may be further improved if well pre-trained N-gram embedding can be properly introduced.

6. Conclusion

In this paper, we propose a framework for ancient Chinese CWS and POS Tagging that implements semantic enhancement and knowledge fusion. By utilizing bigram features and re-predicting the uncertain samples by fusing knowledge, our framework makes good predictions.

7. References

Chen, X., Shi, Z., Qiu, X., and Huang, X. (2017). Adversarial multi-criteria learning for chinese word segmentation. *arXiv preprint arXiv:1704.07556*.

Devlin, J., Chang, M.-W., Lee, K., and Toutanova, K. (2018). Bert: Pre-training of deep bidirectional transformers for language understanding. *arXiv preprint arXiv:1810.04805*.

Gal, Y. and Ghahramani, Z. (2016). Dropout as a bayesian approximation: Representing model uncertainty in deep learning. In *international conference on machine learning*, pages 1050–1059. PMLR.

Geng, Z., Yan, H., Yin, Z., An, C., and Qiu, X. (2022). Turner: The uncertainty-based retrieval framework for chinese ner. *arXiv preprint arXiv:2202.09022*.

Gu, J., Wang, Y., Cho, K., and Li, V. O. (2018). Search engine guided neural machine translation. In *Proceedings of the AAAI Conference on Artificial Intelligence*, volume 32.

Ke, Z., Shi, L., Meng, E., Wang, B., Qiu, X., and Huang, X. (2020). Unified multi-criteria chinese word segmentation with bert. *arXiv preprint arXiv:2004.05808*.

Li, X., Yan, H., Qiu, X., and Huang, X. (2020). Flat: Chinese ner using flat-lattice transformer. *arXiv preprint arXiv:2004.11795*.

Qiu, X., Huang, C., and Huang, X.-J. (2014). Automatic corpus expansion for chinese word segmentation by exploiting the redundancy of web information. In *Proceedings of COLING 2014, the 25th International Conference on Computational Linguistics: Technical Papers*, pages 1154–1164.

Qiu, X., Pei, H., Yan, H., and Huang, X. (2019). Multi-criteria chinese word segmentation with transformer. *arXiv preprint arXiv:1906.12035*.

Yang, J., Zhang, Y., and Liang, S. (2018). Subword encoding in lattice lstm for chinese word segmentation. *arXiv preprint arXiv:1810.12594*.

Appendix: Datasets and Hyperparameters

The training and test datasets for this experiment are from the competition EvaHan2022 `https://circse.github.io/LT4HALA/2022/EvaHan`. The training and testa were excerpted from *Zuozhuan* and the testb was excerpted from the *Shiji*. The statistical information of the datasets is shown in Table 3

	Size	Length_{avg}
Train-*Zuozhuan*	1083K	22.415
Test-*Zuozhuan*	185K	20.902
Test-*Shiji*	352K	29.302

Table 3: Dataset statistics.

	SE-Bert	KF-Bert
Epochs	20	20
Batch Size	32	32
Weight Decay	0.1	0.1
Dropout	0.1	0.1
Learning Rate	1e-5	1e-5
Optimizer	AdamW	AdamW
Warm Up Ratio	0.1	0.1
Max $\text{Seq}_{L}en$	128	128
α	-	{0.1,1}

Table 4: Hyper parameters for *Semantic Enhancement Bert* and *Knowledge Fusion BERT*.

The hyper parameters are listed in table 4.
To enhance the learning of uncertain component, we introduce weight coefficient ω_i to set different weights for uncertain components and certain components so that the model pays more attention to the prediction of uncertain parts. The loss function L is defined as Eq. (14),

$$L = \frac{\sum_{\mathrm{i}}^{1\leq \mathrm{i}\leq \mathrm{n}} \omega_{\mathrm{i}} \cdot \mathrm{loss}_{\mathrm{i}}}{\sum_{\mathrm{i}}^{1\leq \mathrm{i}\leq \mathrm{n}} \omega_{\mathrm{i}}}, \tag{14}$$

$$\omega_{\mathrm{i}} = \begin{cases} 1 & \text{if } c_i \in U \\ \alpha & \text{if } c_i \notin U \end{cases}, \tag{15}$$

where ω_i is the weight coefficient at position i. $loss_i$ is the cross-entropy loss at position i. α is a hyper parameter ranges in $[0, 1]$. In particular, we do not make predictions for auxiliary knowledge, nor do we calculate the loss of this part.

Proceedings of the Second Workshop on Language Technologies for Historical and Ancient Languages (LT4HALA 2022), pages 169–173
Language Resources and Evaluation Conference (LREC 2022), Marseille, 25 June 2022

Data Augmentation for Low-resource Word Segmentation and POS Tagging of Ancient Chinese Texts

Yutong Shen*†, Jiahuan Li*†, Shujian Huang*†, Yi Zhou†, Xiaopeng Xie†, Qinxin Zhao†
* National Key Laboratory for Novel Software Technology, †Nanjing University, China
{shenyt, lijh, yizhou, xiaopengxie, QXZhao}@smail.nju.edu.cn,
huangsj@nju.edu.cn

Abstract

Automatic word segmentation and part-of-speech tagging of ancient books can help relevant researchers to study ancient texts. In recent years, pre-trained language models have achieved significant improvements on text processing tasks. *SikuRoberta* is a pre-trained language model specially designed for automatic analysis of ancient Chinese texts. Although *SikuRoberta* significantly boosts performance on WSG and POS tasks on ancient Chinese texts, the lack of labeled data still limits the performance of the model. In this paper, to alleviate the problem of insufficient training data, We define hybrid tags to integrate WSG and POS tasks and design Roberta-CRF model to predict tags for each Chinese characters. Moreover, We generate synthetic labeled data based on the LSTM language model. To further mine knowledge in *SikuRoberta*, we generate the synthetic unlabeled data based on the Masked LM. Experiments show that the performance of the model is improved with the synthetic data, indicating that the effectiveness of the data augmentation methods.

Keywords: Ancient texts, Word segmentation and POS tagging , Data augmentation

1. Introduction

Ancient Chinese books are precious cultural heritage, and of extremely high research value. In recent years, the protection and research of ancient Chinese books have attracted much attention, and the research is imminent. Some automatic analysis work of ancient Chinese books, such as word segmentation(WSG) and part-of-speech tagging(POS), can help relevant researchers to study ancient books.

Natural language processing technology is becoming more and more mature in recent years, among which, pre-trained language models(PLM) have achieved remarkable improvements in a lot of tasks, including word segmentation and part-of-speech tagging (Devlin et al., 2018; Liu et al., 2019). In order to better carry out the research of ancient books, Wang et al. (2022) proposed *SikuRoberta*, a masked language model trained on the large scale high-quality *Siku Quanshu* full text corpus. *SikuRoberta* significantly boosts performance on WSG and POS tasks on ancient Chinese texts.

However, the scarcity of training data and the expensive cost of manual annotation still limit the improvement of the model performance on WSG and POS tasks. Thus, how to obtain better model performance based on the existing *SikuRoberta* in the case of low resources is a problem that needs to be solved.

In this paper, we adopt a joint-tagging framework, designing hybrid tags to integrate WSG and POS tasks, to train an end-to-end network for WSG-POS task. We combine *SikuRoberta* and conditional random field(CRF) to predict tags for each Chinese characters. In addition, we use data augmentation methods to alleviate the problem of insufficient training data. We leverage DAGA (Ding et al., 2020) to generate synthetic labeled data(lstm-data) based on the LSTM autoregressive language model. To further mine knowledge in *SikuRoberta*, we generate the synthetic unlabeled data(unlabeled-data) based on the Masked LM. Then, we use the tagger model which is trained on real-data and lstm-data to label the unlabeled-data for generating mlm-data. Finally, based on real-data, lstm-data and mlm-data, we use dynamic weight sampling to balance various types of data to train the final model.

The experimental results show that the performance of the model is improved with synthetic data, which verifies the effectiveness of the data augmentation methods.

The paper is organized into 7 sections. We describe the structure of Roberta-CRF model in Section 2. Two data augmentation methods are elaborated in Section 3. Section 4 describes the flow of our entire system. Section 5 presents the experiments and some analysis of the results. We also report our final submitted results in Section 6. Finally, some conclusions are drawn in Section 7.

2. Roberta-CRF Model

Compared with the traditional pipeline method, jointly conducting WSG and POS can improve performance in both two tasks (Shi et al., 2010). Thus, We define hybrid tags and build an end-to-end network.

2.1. Hybrid Tags

There are 4 kinds of word segmentation labels 'B', 'M', 'E' and 'S', which represent the beginning of a word, the middle of a word, the end of a word and the single-character word, respectively. There are 22 kinds of parts-of-speech labels, including verbs(v), nouns(n), location(ns), person(nr), and so on.

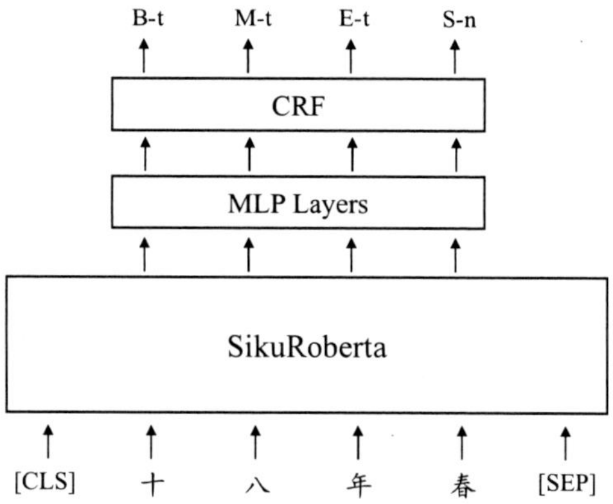

Figure 1: The structure of Roberta-CRF model

Each hybrid tag is composed of a word segmentation label and a part-of-speech label, and the two labels are connected by a connector '-'. For example, the two Chinese characters in the ancient Chinese word "春秋/n" will be marked as 'B-n' and ' E-n' respectively.

2.2. Model Structure

Formally, an ancient Chinese sentence S is sliced into n Chinese characters, denoted as $\{x_0, x_1, x_2, ..., x_{n-1}\}$, where n is the length of S. Our task is to get the corresponding tag sequence, denoted as $\{y_0, y_1, y_2, ..., y_{n-1}\}$.

We combine *SikuRoberta* and a CRF layer to form a Roberta-CRF model, whose structure is shown in Figure 1. *SikuRoberta* can produce the hidden states $H \in R^{n \times d}$ for the ancient Chinese sentence S, where d is the hidden layer size of the *SikuRoberta*. The hidden states H are fed into the two MLP layers to compute the emission scores for the CRF layer. The emission scores can be denoted as $Scores \in R^{n \times t}$.

$$Scores = W_2(W_1 H + b_1) + b_2 \tag{1}$$

where $W_1 \in R^{d \times d}$, $W_2 \in R^{d \times t}$, $b_1 \in R^d$, $b_2 \in R^t$ are the weight matrices and biases of the MLP layers respectively, and t is the number of hybrid tags.

CRF (Lafferty et al., 2001) has been widely recognized to be effective in sequence labeling tasks (Huang et al., 2015). As Eq. (2) shows, based on the emission scores, CRF calculates the tag sequence Y that maximizes the conditional probability using the Viterbi algorithm.

$$Y = \text{argmax}_y P(y|X) \tag{2}$$

where y is one of the all tag sequences of the same length as X. We update parameters of the entire network to minimize the loss function of CRF.

3. Data Augmentation

Data augmentation is one of the widely used methods in low-resource scenarios. To improve the performance of the Roberta-CRF model, we use two data augmentation methods, generating synthetic labeled and unlabeled data, respectively.

3.1. Labeled Data Generation

Ding et al. (2020) proposed a pseudo-data generation method for the sequence labeling task. We improve their method to generate pseudo label data for the WSG-POS task.

3.1.1. Modeling Text-Tag Hybrid Sequence

The model used to generate pseudo data is the LSTM (Shi et al., 2015) language model. Training dataset for this LM is the linearized labeled sentence. Linearizing the sentence is to insert the tag before the corresponding Chinese character. For example, our sentence is "十八年/t 春/n ，/w 白狄/nr 始/d /v 。/w", after linearization it is "B-t 十 M-t 八 E-t 年 S-n 春 S-w ，B-nr 白 E-nr 狄 S-d 始 S-v S-w 。"

We use the language model with the same structure as Ding et al. (2020). The only difference is that we set two independent embedding layers in our language model, one is tag embedding and another one is Chinese character embedding. The model structure can be seen in Figure 2

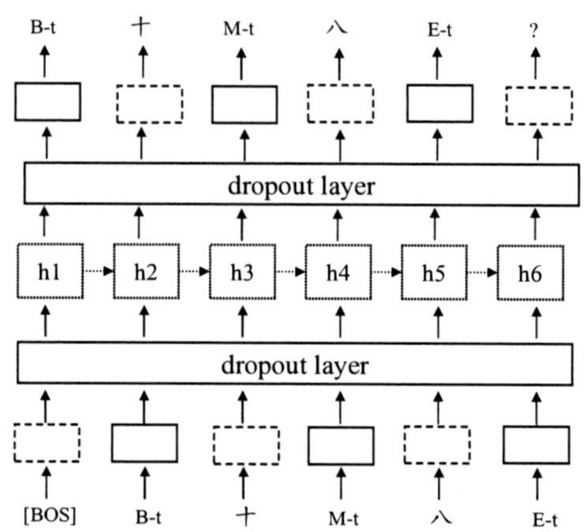

Figure 2: The structure of LSTM language model for linearized sentence.

We first feed the linearized sequence of characters $\{y_0, x_0, y_1, x_1, ..., y_{n-1}, x_{n-1}\}$ into the embedding layer to lookup the token embeddings $E = \{e_{t_0}, e_{c_0}, e_{t_1}, e_{c_1}, ..., e_{c_{n-1}}\}$.

$$e_{t_i} = \text{Embed}_t(y_i), \;\; e_{c_i} = \text{Embed}_c(x_i) \tag{3}$$

where Embed_t and Embed_c are the embedding layers of tags and characters respectively. A dropout layer is applied to token embedding E to generate $D = dropout(E)$. Then, feed D into the single layer LSTM to produce hidden states $H = LSTM(D)$. Another dropout layer is applied to H to get $D' = dropout(H)$.

For the output layer, a linear and softmax layer are used to predict the next token in the sequence. Corresponding to the dictionary settings, there are two output layers, one is to generate the probability distribution P_t on the tags, and another one is to output the probability distribution P_c on the Chinese characters.

$$P_{t_i} = \text{Softmax}(W_c d^{'}_{t_i} + b_c) \quad (4)$$

$$P_{c_i} = \text{Softmax}(W_t d^{'}_{c_i} + b_t) \quad (5)$$

Where W_t and W_c are the weight matrices of tags and characters respectively.

Data Generation After training the LM, we can use it to generate synthetic labeled data for our task. During generation, only the '[BOS]' token is fed into LM, and the following tokens are sampled based on the probabilities computed by Eq. (4). and Eq. (5).

3.2. Unlabeled Data Generation

In our preliminary error analysis, we find most errors arises from words with POS tags of verbs, nouns, and rare words such as person name and locations. However, the language model in Section 3.1 can only generates sentences similar to the given training data, and may not generate novel aforementioned words. In contrast, *Sikuroberta*, trained on a lot of ancient Chinese texts, contains some ancient Chinese knowledge which can not be acquire from the given training data. To further mine knowledge in *SikuRoberta*, we generate new words or new characters using Masked LM based on *SikuRoberta*.

We randomly mask verbs, nouns, location and person in the training sentence with 20% probability, and ask SikuRoberta to fill the masked positions. When the masked positions are consecutive spans, we fill the span iteratively from left to right. This prevents the model to generate illegal words due the independent generation of each positions. For example, given a sentence "白狄始來", the process of generating masked words is shown in Figure 3

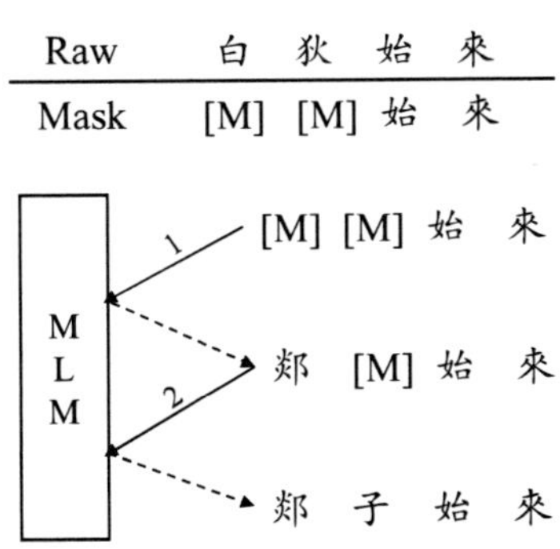

Figure 3: An illustration of the process of generating masked words iteratively

4. Implementation

We first train a tagger model based on the training data and labeled data generated by LSTM LM. Then, we use the tagger model to label the label unlabeled data generated by Masked LM. Finally, the final model is trained based on the three kinds of data.

4.1. Tagger Model

Based on LSTM LM, we generate 700k synthetic labeled data, denoted as D_{lstm}. Since the number of synthetic data is much larger than the training data, we adopt the method of dynamic weight sampling. The weights linearly changes according to the following equations:

$$W_{train_i} = \frac{i}{\text{N}} \times |D_{lstm}|$$

$$W_{lstm_i} = (1 - W_{r_i}) \times |D_{train}|$$

Where W_{train_i} and W_{lstm_i} are sampling weights of training and synthetic data, $|D_{train}|$ and $|D_{lstm}|$ are the number of training and synthetic data, $i = 0, 1, ...N - 1$, N is the number of maximum epochs. It can be seen that the weight of sampling training data at the beginning is 0. With the epoch increasing, the weight of sampling training data becomes larger.

We save the 5 model checkpoints with the smallest loss during the training process and average their checkpoints as the tagger model.

4.2. Final Model

We generate 150k unlabeled data based on Masked LM. Then, we use the tagger model to label the unlabeled data, denoted these data as D_{mlm}.

Similarly, we train the final model based on the three kinds of data and adopt the method of dynamic weight sampling.

$$W_{train_i} = \frac{i}{N} \times |D_{mlm}| \times |D_{lstm}|$$

$$W_{mlm_i} = p \times (1 - W_{r_i}) \times |D_{train}| \times |D_{lstm}|$$

$$W_{lstm_i} = (1 - p) \times (1 - W_{r_i}) \times |D_{train}| \times |D_{mlm}|$$

where W_{mlm_i} and $|D_{mlm}|$ are the sampling weight and the number of D_{mlm}, and $i = 0, 1, ...N - 1$. In our experiments, we set $p = 0.3$.

We also save the 5 model checkpoints with the smallest loss during the training process and average their checkpoints as the tagger model.

5. Experiments and Discussions

We randomly selected 1k data from the given training data as the in-domain test set and the rest as the training set. And we directly use Testb as the out-domain test set. Follow the settings in Section 4 to perform the experiments.

Model	In-domain	Out-domain
Roberta-CRF	92.14 / 84.49	86.94 / 75.09
Tagger	93.44 / 87.24	86.99 / 77.29
Final	**93.92 / 88.12**	**87.53 / 78.31**

Table 1: F1 scores of WSG and POS tasks

5.1. Results

We evaluate the model results using the F1 scores of the WSG and POS tasks. The results of the model on the test set are shown in Table 1.

It can be seen that the results of the Final model achieve the best performance for both in-domain and out-domain test sets.

Compared with the Roberta-CRF model, the F1 scores of final model results on the WSG and POS tasks are improved by 1.78 and 3.63 respectively for in-domain, and improved by 0.59 and 3.25 respectively for out-domain. It shows that data augmentation methods can enhance model performance.

For both in-domain and out-domain, the F1 scores of the Final model are also higher than Tagger model, indicating that the unlabeled data generated based on MLM can improve the model performance.

5.2. WSG: Analysis on Words of Different Frequencies

We divide the words appearing in the test set into frequent words, rare words and unknown words. Words that do not appear in the training set are unknown words. If a word appears less than 10 times in the training set, it is a rare word, otherwise it is a frequent word. We compute the accuracy rates of the three models on WSG task for different words.

		Roberta-CRF	Tagger	Final
In	fren(87.8%)	**0.969**	0.964	0.968
	rare(12.2%)	0.728	0.791	**0.807**
Out	fren(76.9%)	**0.919**	0.902	0.912
	rare(10.0%)	0.740	**0.752**	0.751
	unk(13.1%)	0.673	**0.717**	0.715

Table 2: The WSG correct rates of different words. Note that in-domian test set has no unknown words.

As shown in Table 2, for both in-domain and out-domain, the accuracy rates of the three models on frequent words are comparable. But for rare and unknown words, Roberta-CRF is the worst, its accuracy rates are 8% and 4.2% less than Final model respectively. This shows that rare and unknown words do affect performance of models, and adding pseudo data can significantly ease this problem.

5.3. POS: Analysis on Error Types

We also further analyze the results of the POS task. Since the part-of-speech tagging depends on the correct word segmentation, we only do the following statistics based on correctly segmented words. We count the types of POS errors as shown in Figure 4.

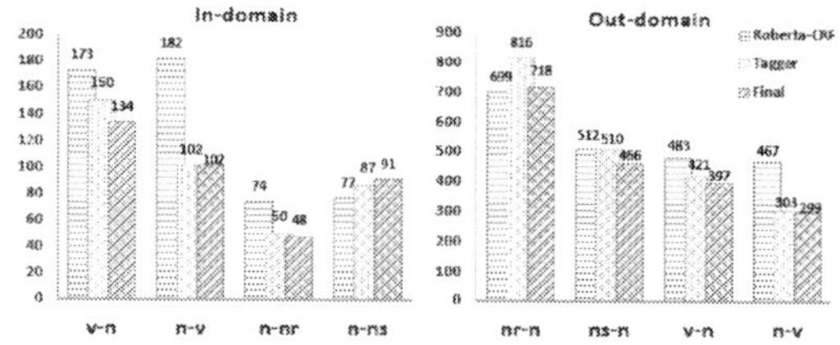

Figure 4: The types of POS errors. 'v-n' means that target label is 'v' but the output of model is 'n'.

in-domain It can be seen that the mutual misjudgment of nouns and verbs is the most common mistake. This is because a word in ancient Chinese often acts as both a verb and a noun, making it difficult for the model to distinguish between them.

out-domain However, for out-domain, there are many mistakes in labeling person as nouns. After using the data augmentation method, this error problems have not been effectively alleviated. But for other types of errors, pseudo data helps a lot.

6. Submitted System Results

For the final submitted results, we used ensemble learning to further improve the model performance. We randomly generate 10 sets of pseudo data, and then train 10 Final models respectively. Based on the 10 models, the results are obtained by voting.

on TestA with closed modality, our best F1 score of WSG is 94.81% and our F1 score of POS tagging is 89.87%. On TestB with closed modality, our best F1 score of WSG is 88.42% and our F1 score of POS tagging is 79.53%.

7. Conclusion

In this paper, we use the one-step approach, designing hybrid tags to integrate WSG and POS tasks, to train an end-to-end network for WSG-POS task. We combine *SikuRoberta* and conditional random field to predict tags for each Chinese characters.

Due to the limited training data, we use two data augmentation methods, generating synthetic labeled and unlabeled data, respectively. We refer to the DAGA to generate synthetic labeled data based on the LSTM language model. To further mine knowledge in *SikuRoberta*, we generate the synthetic unlabeled data based on the Masked LM. Finally we train the three kinds of data to obtain the final model.

The experimental results show that the performance of the model is improved after using data augmentation, which verifies the effectiveness of the data augmentation methods.

Appendix: Instances of Pseudo Data

An example of the pseudo sentences are shown in Figure 5.

Labeled data
Short 十八年/t 春/n ，/w 齊侯/nr 視/v 王/n 于/p 輔賨/ns 。/w
Long 王/n 奉/v 以/p 朝/v ，/w 曰/v ：/w “/w 同王/n 不/d 能/v 久/a 先大夫/n ，/w 不/d 可/v 慎/v 也/y 。/w 若/c 問/v 諸/j 之 /r ，/w 不/d 可/v 處/v 。/w ‘/w 君子/n 無/v 精/n ，/w 不/d 可用/v 喪/v ，/w 守/v 備/n 而/c 興/v ，/w 不/d 賜/v 臣/n 以/p 定/v 之/r 。/w ”/w

Unlabeled data	
Raw	十八年，春，**白狄**始**來**。
Pseudo1	十八年，春，鄭子始來。
Pseudo2	十八年，春，孫武始來。
Pseudo3	十八年，春，白狄始興。
Pseudo4	十八年，春，白狄始擾。

Figure 5: Some instances of pseudo data

It can be seen that we can generate reasonable labeled sentences of varying lengths. In unlabeled sentence examples, the nouns and verbs in the original sentence are be randomly replaced with other nouns and verbs.

8. Bibliographical References

Devlin, J., Chang, M.-W., Lee, K., and Toutanova, K. (2018). Bert: Pre-training of deep bidirectional transformers for language understanding. *arXiv preprint arXiv:1810.04805.*

Ding, B., Liu, L., Bing, L., Kruengkrai, C., Nguyen, T. H., Joty, S., Si, L., and Miao, C. (2020). Daga: Data augmentation with a generation approach for low-resource tagging tasks. *arXiv preprint arXiv:2011.01549.*

Huang, Z., Xu, W., and Yu, K. (2015). Bidirectional lstm-crf models for sequence tagging. *arXiv preprint arXiv:1508.01991.*

Lafferty, J., McCallum, A., and Pereira, F. C. (2001). Conditional random fields: Probabilistic models for segmenting and labeling sequence data.

Liu, Y., Ott, M., Goyal, N., Du, J., Joshi, M., Chen, D., Levy, O., Lewis, M., Zettlemoyer, L., and Stoyanov, V. (2019). Roberta: A robustly optimized bert pretraining approach. *arXiv preprint arXiv:1907.11692.*

Shi, M., Li, B., and Chen, X. (2010). Crf based research on a unified approach to word segmentation and pos tagging for pre-qin chinese. *Journal of Chinese Information Processing*, 2(24):39–45.

Shi, X., Chen, Z., Wang, H., Yeung, D.-Y., Wong, W.-K., and Woo, W.-c. (2015). Convolutional lstm network: A machine learning approach for precipitation nowcasting. *Advances in neural information processing systems*, 28.

Wang, C., Liu, Z., Zhu, J., Liu, H., Hu, Meditation, B., and Li. (2022). Sikubert and sikuroberta: Research on the construction and application of pre-trained model of “siku quanshu” for digital humanities. *http://kns.cnki.net/kcms/detail/44.1306.G2.20210819.2052.008.html.*

Proceedings of the Second Workshop on Language Technologies for Historical and Ancient Languages (LT4HALA 2022), pages 174–177
Language Resources and Evaluation Conference (LREC 2022), Marseille, 25 June 2022

A Joint Framework for Ancient Chinese WS and POS Tagging based on Adversarial Ensemble Learning

Shuxun Yang
School of Computer Science, Beijing Institute of Technology, Beijing, China
sheryl_xun@163.com

Abstract

Ancient Chinese word segmentation and part-of-speech tagging tasks are crucial to facilitate the study of ancient Chinese and the dissemination of traditional Chinese culture. Current methods face problems such as lack of large-scale labeled data, individual task error propagation, and lack of robustness and generalization of models. Therefore, we propose a joint framework for ancient Chinese WS and POS tagging based on adversarial ensemble learning, called AENet. On the basis of pre-training and fine-tuning, AENet uses a joint tagging approach of WS and POS tagging and treats it as a joint sequence tagging task. Meanwhile, AENet incorporates adversarial training and ensemble learning, which effectively improves the model recognition efficiency while enhancing the robustness and generalization of the model. Our experiments demonstrate that AENet improves the F1 score of word segmentation by 4.48% and the score of part-of-speech tagging by 2.29% on test dataset compared with the baseline, which shows high performance and strong generalization.

Keywords: Adversarial Ensemble Learning, Word Segmentation, POS Tagging

1. Introduction

Recently, researchers have gradually paid more attention to traditional culture, and the understanding and study of ancient Chinese is an important parts. However, there are many obstacles in understanding ancient Chinese due to the features of the separation of language and text, archaic and incomprehensible, and unclear segmentation. In order to better help researchers understand ancient Chinese and promote the inheritance of Chinese traditional culture, applying some basic tasks of natural language processing (NLP), such as word segmentation (WS), part-of-speech (POS) tagging, and named entity recognition (NER), to ancient Chinese has become an urgent need.

Chinese word segmentation, refers to the partitioning of a sequence of consecutive words in units of words into word-based sequences by word segmentation algorithms with the help of computer technology. Part-of-speech tagging refers to tagging the words in a sentence by part-of-speech tagging algorithms, that is, predicting the lexicality of words. These two tasks are the basis of many downstream tasks of natural language processing and play an indispensable role in various fields.

In fact, both the WS and POS tagging tasks can generally be regarded as sequence labeling tasks. Defining a suitable labeling scheme provides ideas to solve these problems. Due to the large differences between ancient Chinese and modern texts, the difficulty of understanding and the lack of obvious segmentation symbols, early ancient Chinese WS and POS tagging tasks would often be solved by taking a manual construction approach. These methods tend to have a high accuracy rate, with unacceptable cost. After that, methods based on lexical, dictionaries, and manual rules emerged. Researchers find strings that match those rules with the help of priority rules constructed manually by experts in various fields. However, these methods rely on the construction of dictionaries and knowledge bases, and system constructed tend to be less portable and scalable, and probably require experts in specific domain to spend a lot of time on construction and maintenance.

With the development of computer technology, the demand for automatic WS and POS tagging of ancient Chinese has increased, and algorithms based on machine learning and deep learning have emerged. Conditional Random Fields (CRF), Support Vector machines (SVM), Hidden Markov Models (HMM), Maximum Entropy Models (MEM), Long Short-Term Memory Networks (LSTM), Recurrent Neural Networks (RNN), Convolutional Neural Networks (CNN) and so on are widely used in WS and POS tagging task of ancient Chinese. However, supervised learning methods above usually require large-scale labeled datasets, and the field of ancient Chinese often faces the problem of sparse labeled data. Therefore, pre-trained language models (PLM) with fine-tuning have come into the forefront of researchers' attention. This approach essentially uses transfer learning to train a word vector model with rich semantic information using a large amount of unlabeled text, and then fine-tune it using labeled data, which can well solve the problem of lacking high-quality, large-scale labeled data in a specific domain.

However, WS and POS tagging models in modern standard Chinese often do not work well for ancient Chinese, and the trained models are often sensitive to noisy data and do not have good portability and transferability. Adversarial training (AT) and ensemble learning (EL) can help us solve these problems well. Adversarial training is an important way to enhance the robustness of neural networks. The essential idea of AT is adding some small but potentially misclassifying perturbations to the samples during training process will make the model adapt to such changes and thus be robust to the adversarial samples. Ensemble learning, on the other hand, as a common approach for supervised machine learning tasks, aims to improve the prediction results by the integration of multiple learning algorithms. Combing adversarial training with ensemble learning can enhance the portability and robustness of the model while improving the accuracy of ancient Chinese WS and POS tagging tasks.

In summary, we propose a joint framework based on adversarial ensemble learning for ancient Chinese WS and POS tagging tasks, called AENet, to address the problems of lack of large-scale annotation data, low model portability and robustness for joint tasks of ancient Chinese WS and POS tagging. The main innovations of this paper are as follows.

- We propose a joint framework for ancient Chinese WS and POS tagging to reduce the noise caused by individual task training process and improve recognition efficiency of the model, with the idea of pre-training and fine-tuning.
- We incorporate the ideas of adversarial training and ensemble learning into the joint framework to improve the robustness and generalization of our model effectively.
- Compared with baseline, the proposed framework achieves better performance on two ancient Chinese datasets provided.

2. Related Work

With the deepening on ancient Chinese mining research, researchers are in full swing on the study of ancient Chinese WS and POS tagging tasks. For example, Yu et al. (2020) proposed an automatic WS model for ancient Chinese based on a nonparametric Bayesian model and deep learning. This method adopts an unsupervised multi-stage iterative training, aiming to mine valuable ancient Chinese WS models by jointly using Bayesian model and BERT, and training them repeatedly in large-scale unlabeled data. Cheng et al. (2020) designed an ancient Chinese WS and POS tagging model based on BiLSTM-CRF model, and by designing appropriate WS and POS labels, these two tasks were fused, which is similar to the method of task fusion in this paper. Stoeckel et al. (2020) proposed an ensemble classifier, namely LSTMVote, for the POS tagging task of Latin languages, which integrates multiple pre-trained classifiers to obtain the optimal model.

To solve the problem of lack of ancient Chinese annotated corpus, pre-trained language models have been introduced to the study. Based on the ancient literature corpus of Daizhige [1], GuwenBERT [2] model was proposed. This method combines the weight of modern Chinese RoBERTa model and a large number of ancient Chinese corpus on the basis of the continuation training technique, and transfers some linguistic features of modern Chinese to ancient Chinese, which substantially improves the performance of the model. After that, Wang et al. (2021) constructed SikuBERT and SikuRoBERTa pre-trained language models for ancient Chinese intelligent processing tasks based on the BERT, using the calibrated high-quality full-text corpus of *Siku Quanshu* as an unsupervised training set, which provided support for researchers in ancient Chinese.

Numerous studies have proved that adversarial training can effectively improve the robustness and generalization of language models. FGSM and FGM adversarial training methods (Goodfellow et al., 2014; Miyato et al., 2017) were proposed, the core idea of which is to let the direction of perturbation follow the direction of gradient boosting. In these methods, authors assume that the loss function is linear or locally linear, and therefore the direction of gradient boosting is the optimal direction. The difference between FGSM and FGM is the normalization method, with FGSM taking max normalization of the gradient through the sign function and FGM using L2 normalization. In order to solve the linear assumption problem in FGSM and FGM, Projected Gradient Descent method (PGD) (Madry et al., 2017) was proposed, which can be used to solve the internal maximum problem. The core idea of PGD is to reach the optimum by multiple iterations and each iteration will project the perturbation to a specified range. However, this method can only utilize the gradient of the parameters and the gradient of the input alone. In order to utilize two gradients simultaneously and efficiently, FreeLB (Zhu et al., 2019) was proposed, which makes use of the gradient accumulated from multiple iterations to make updates and estimate the gradient more accurately.

Meanwhile, as an effective way of supervised learning, ensemble learning can obtain better prediction performance than using any individual learning algorithm alone by integrating multiple learning algorithms. At present, ensemble learning algorithms are mainly classified into three categories: Bagging, Boosting and Stacking, which correspond to parallel training, serial training and hierarchical training, respectively. With the help of the idea of ensemble learning, Izmailov et al. (2018) proposed a stochastic weight averaging (SWA) algorithm, whose core idea is that the average of multiple weights in the training process of a single model is closer to the optimal solution. A lot of practices have proved that SWA is superior to other optimization algorithms, such as SGD.

3. Model

In this section, we first introduce the task definition, and then present the overall framework of the joint model for ancient Chinese WS and POS tagging tasks. After that, we detail how to jointly use adversarial training and ensemble learning to improve model performance.

3.1 Task Definition

Given an input sentence of ancient Chinese with *n* tokens $X=\{x_1,x_2\cdots x_n\}$, the target sentence can be $Y=\{y_1,y_2\cdots y_n\}$, where $y_i='ws_p-pos_q'$, for example, $y_1='B-NR'$. In the formula above, $ws_p=\{B,I,E,S\}$. *B* means the current token is the beginning of a multi-token word, *I* means the current token is in the middle of a multi-token word, *E* means the current token is the end of a multi-token word, and *S* means the current token is an single word. Through this tagging method, the task of WS for ancient Chinese can be solved automatically. And then, $pos_q=\{A,C,D,J,M,N,NR,NS\cdots\}$, which refers to common parts of speech in texts. The task in this paper can be defined in the form of Equation 1, that is, given a sequence *X*, find the optimal sequence *Y* that maximizes the probability of $p(Y|X)$. According to the above tagging methods, the joint task of WS and POS tagging of ancient Chinese can be realized easily, thus reducing the noise impact and error propagation that may be brought by separate task training.

$$Y^*=\arg\max p(Y|X) \quad (1)$$

3.2 Model Framework

The overall joint framework for ancient Chinese WS and POS tagging based on adversarial ensemble learning, that is, AENet, is shown in Figure 1. The overall framework of AENet is carried out with the idea of pre-training and fine-

[1] http://www.daizhige.org/

[2] https://github.com/ethan-yt/guwenbert

tuning. Namely, given an ancient Chinese sequence, it is cut into token sequences firstly. Then, the token sequence is input into the pre-trained language model for fine-tuning, and word embeddings with rich semantic information can be obtained. The final predicted label sequences are obtained by feeding word embeddings into the CRF layer. The specific process is shown in Equation 2.

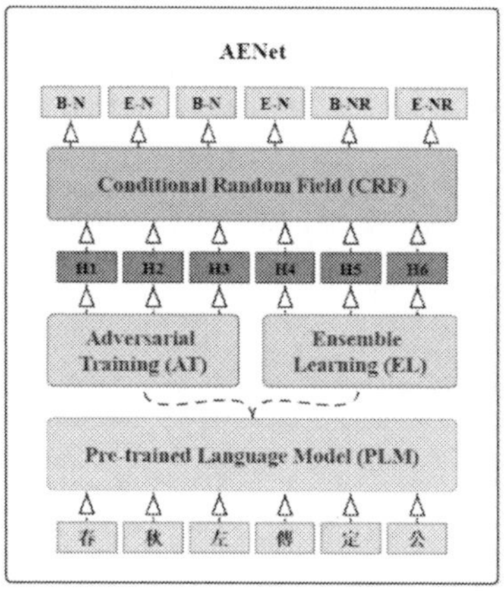

Figure 1: Framework of AENet

Throughout the entire model training process, AENet will be optimized according to the adversarial training and ensemble learning, thereby enhancing the robustness and generalization of the model. See Section 3.3 for details. The loss function of AENet is the log-likelihood function, as shown in Equation 3.

$$\begin{aligned} Embedding &= PLM(X) \\ Y &= CRF(Embedding) \end{aligned} \tag{2}$$

$$Loss = -\log P(Y \mid X) \tag{3}$$

3.3 Adversarial Ensemble Learning

The idea of adversarial training is to add some small but potentially misclassifying perturbations to the samples during the training process of the model, making the model adapt to such changes and thus increasing the robustness and the transferability of the model. The process of adversarial training is shown in Equation 4, where δ represents the perturbation, ε is a parameter set in advance to constrain the range of the perturbation and w is the model weight with parameters θ. Equation 4 means the whole process of model optimization, that is, finding the perturbation that maximizes the loss function and training the neural network model to minimize its loss on the training data after superimposing the perturbation.

$$\begin{aligned} \delta &= \underset{\|\delta\| \le \varepsilon}{\arg\max}\, Loss(f_\theta(X+\delta), Y) \\ X &= X + \delta \\ w(\theta) &= \arg\min Loss(X, Y) \end{aligned} \tag{4}$$

In this paper, we select FGM adversarial training method (Miyato et al., 2017), and the perturbation parameters are calculated as shown in Equation 5, where g represents the gradient of the loss function. During each training of the model, we calculate the perturbation and add it to the training samples, so that the trained model is sufficient to cope with the perturbation and increase the robustness.

$$\begin{aligned} \delta &= \varepsilon \cdot (g / \|g\|_2) \\ g &= \nabla_X (Loss(f_\theta(X), Y)) \end{aligned} \tag{5}$$

Meanwhile, during the overall training process of AENet, we optimize the model weights with the help of ensemble learning ideas and SWA model (Izmailov et al., 2018). The final weights of the model are calculated by Equation 6, where n, m are the parameters set in advance.

$$\bar{w}(\theta) = 1/(n-m+1)\sum_{i=m}^{n} w_i(\theta) \tag{6}$$

After incorporating adversarial training and ensemble learning into the joint framework, the whole model of ancient Chinese WS and POS tagging based on adversarial ensemble learning, namely AENet, is constructed in this paper.

4. Experiment

4.1 Experimental Setup

The experiments in this paper are conducted on a server with Ubuntu 20.04 Linux and eight 1080Ti GPUs. The code is written in Python 3.8.5 environment using PyTorch. We carry out these experiments for the EvaHan 2022 competition. This contest is divided into two modalities: closed and open. In the closed modality, only the provided training dataset and the SikuRoBERTa pretrained model are allowed to be used. In this paper, the closed modality is selected for the experiments. Therefore, the SikuRoBERTa is used for the pre-trained language model in the AENet model framework. The parameter ε in the adversarial training is set to 1, and n in the ensemble learning is set to 5 while m is set to 1. Precision, recall, and F1 score metrics are used to evaluate the results of ancient Chinese WS and POS tagging, respectively.

4.2 Dataset Description

The training data and test data involved in the experimental part of this paper are provided by the organizer of EvaHan 2022 competition. The training data is selected from *Zuozhuan*, an ancient Chinese work believed to date from the Warring States Period, which contains punctuation and ancient Chinese texts after WS and POS tagging, and is presented in the form of utf-8 plain text files. The training data has a total of 166142 word tokens and 194995 char tokens.

The test dataset is divided into test A and B. Test A is still extracted from *Zuozhuan*, which does not overlap with the training data, mainly to observe the performance of the model in the text data of the same book. Test A mainly consists of 28131 word tokens and 33298 char tokens. Test B dataset is extracted from other books, mainly to observe the performance of the model in similar text data. Its size is similar to the test A dataset.

4.3 Experimental Results

In this section, CRF and SikuRoBERTa + BiLSTM + CRF models are selected as baselines, to compare with AENet model we proposed. The running results of CRF model are provided by EvaHan 2022 organizers. The experimental results for test A dataset are shown in Table 1, and the experimental results for test B dataset are shown in Table 2.

Metric(%)	Precision	Recall	F1 score
CRF (WS)	90.64	92.08	91.35
CRF (POS)	89.06	89.54	89.30
PLM+BiLSTM+CRF (WS)	95.15	96.07	95.61
PLM+BiLSTM+CRF (POS)	90.69	91.56	91.12
AENet (WS)	**95.18**	**96.49**	**95.83**
AENet (POS)	**90.96**	**92.22**	**91.59**

Table 1: Results for test A

Metric(%)	Precision	Recall	F1 score
PLM+BiLSTM+CRF (WS)	93.49	90.39	91.91
PLM+BiLSTM+CRF (POS)	87.02	84.14	85.56
AENet (WS)	**94.48**	**91.70**	**93.07**
AENet (POS)	**88.40**	**85.80**	**87.08**

Table 2: Results for test B

The experimental results show that the use of the model framework of pre-training and fine-tuning substantially improved the performance of the model. In the test A dataset, compared with the baseline CRF model, AENet improves the F1 score of WS by 4.48% and the score of POS tagging by 2.29%.

In addition, we find that although the WS task of the AENet model is 0.22% higher than the SikuRoBERTa + BiLSTM + CRF model and the POS tagging task improves 0.47% in the test A, the WS task of the AENet model is 1.16% higher than the SikuRoBERTa + BiLSTM + CRF model in the test B and the POS tagging task improves by 1.52%. This is sufficient to demonstrate that the robustness and generalization of our AENet model are substantially improved by introducing adversarial ensemble learning.

4.4 Ablation Study

This section focuses on the ablation analysis of the AENet model and observes the degree of influence of adversarial training and ensemble learning on the robustness and generalization of the model. Therefore, we compare the model using only adversarial training, that is, $AENet_{AT}$ and only ensemble learning, that is, $AENet_{EL}$ with the original AENet model, and the experimental results for test B dataset are shown in Table 3.

Metric(%)	Precision	Recall	F1 score
PLM+BiLSTM+CRF (WS)	93.49	90.39	91.91
PLM+BiLSTM+CRF (POS)	87.02	84.14	85.56
$AENet_{AT}$ (WS)	93.93	90.66	92.26
$AENet_{AT}$ (POS)	87.91	84.85	86.35
$AENet_{EL}$ (WS)	94.39	91.58	92.96
$AENet_{EL}$ (POS)	87.83	85.21	86.50
AENet (WS)	**94.48**	**91.70**	**93.07**
AENet (POS)	**88.40**	**85.80**	**87.08**

Table3: Ablation study results for test B

It is experimentally demonstrated that compared to baseline, both adversarial training and ensemble learning improve the performance of our model for WS and POS tagging in similar ancient Chinese texts, and AENet achieves the best performance by integrating AT and EL. There is no doubt that adversarial ensemble learning in AENet improves the robustness and generalization of the model.

5. Conclusion

We introduce a joint framework based on adversarial ensemble learning in this paper, namely AENet, for the task of ancient Chinese WS and POS tagging. On the basis of pre-training and fine-tuning, AENet treats WS and POS tagging as a joint sequence tagging task, and we design a joint tagging approach to reduce the error propagation and noise impact caused by individual task training. Then, AENet incorporates adversarial training and ensemble learning, which effectively enhances the robustness and generalization of the model we proposed while improving the recognition efficiency of the model. The experimental results demonstrate that AENet has better performance in handling the ancient Chinese WS and POS tagging tasks, compared with baselines.

6. Bibliographical References

Cheng, N., Li, B., Xiao, L., Xu, C., Ge, S., Hao, X., and Feng, M. (2020). Integration of Automatic Sentence Segmentation and Lexical Analysis of Ancient Chinese based on BiLSTM-CRF Model. In *Proceedings of LT4HALA 2020-1st Workshop on Language Technologies for Historical and Ancient Languages*, pp. 52-58.

Goodfellow, I.J., Shlens, J. and Szegedy, C. (2015). Explaining and Harnessing Adversarial Examples. *Stat*, 1050, p.20.

Izmailov, P., Wilson, A.G., Podoprikhin, D., Vetrov, D., and Garipov, T. (2018). Averaging weights leads to wider optima and better generalization. In *34th Conference on Uncertainty in Artificial Intelligence (UAI 2018)*, pp. 876-885.

Madry, A., Makelov, A., Schmidt, L., Tsipras, D., and Vladu, A. (2018). Towards Deep Learning Models Resistant to Adversarial Attacks. In *International Conference on Learning Representations*.

Miayto, T., Dai, A.M. and Goodfellow, I. (2016). Virtual Adversarial Training for Semi-Supervised Text Classification.

Stoeckel, M., Henlein, A., Hemati, W., and Mehler, A. (2020). Voting for POS tagging of Latin texts: Using the flair of FLAIR to better ensemble classifiers by example of Latin. In *Proceedings of LT4HALA 2020-1st Workshop on Language Technologies for Historical and Ancient Languages*, pp. 130-135.

Wang, D., Liu, C., Zhu, Z., Liu, J., Hu, H., Shen, S., and Li, B. (2021). Construction and Application of Pre-training Model of "Siku Quanshu" Oriented to Digital Humanities. *Library Tribune*.

Yu, J., Wei, Y., Zhang, Y., and Yang, H. (2020). Word Segmentation for Ancient Chinese Texts Based on Nonparametric Bayesian Models and Deep Learning. *Journal of Chinese Information Processing*, 34(6): 1-8.

Zhu, C., Cheng, Y., Gan, Z., Sun, S., Goldstein, T., and Liu, J. (2019). FreeLB: Enhanced Adversarial Training for Natural Language Understanding. In *International Conference on Learning Representations*.

Proceedings of the Second Workshop on Language Technologies for Historical and Ancient Languages (LT4HALA 2022), pages 178–182
Language Resources and Evaluation Conference (LREC 2022), Marseille, 25 June 2022

Glyph Features Matter: a Multimodal Solution for EvaHan in LT4HALA2022

Xinyuan Wei*, Weihao Liu*, Qing Zong*, Shaoqing Zhang*, Baotian Hu†
Harbin Institute of Technology (Shenzhen)
{21S151175, 200110921, 200110513, 1190200721}@stu.hit.edu.cn
hubaotian@hit.edu.cn

Abstract

We participate in the LT4HALA2022 shared task EvaHan. There are two subtasks in this task. Subtask 1 is word segmentation, and subtask 2 is part-of-speech tagging. Each subtask consists of two tracks, a close track that can only use the data and models provided by the organizer, and an open track without restrictions. We employ three pre-trained models, two of which are open-source pre-trained models for ancient Chinese (Siku-Roberta and roberta-classical-chinese), and one is our pre-trained GlyphBERT combined with glyph features. Our methods include data augmentation, data pre-processing, model pretraining, downstream fine-tuning, k-fold cross validation and model ensemble. We achieve competitive P, R, and F1 scores on both our own validation set and the final public test set. For the word segmentation task and the part-of-speech tagging task, respectively, on F1 on the close track, we achieved 91.89 and 85.74 on test A, and 80.75 and 69.62 on test B; similarly, on the open track, we achieved 92.33 and 86.47 for test A, and 81.24 and 70.05 for test B.

Keywords: ancient Chinese, glyph features, pre-trained language model

1. Introduction

Our team HITszTMG participates in the LT4HALA shared task EvaHan 2022. This task contains two subtasks: Chinese word segmentation and part-of-speech tagging. Chinese word segmentation and part-of-speech tagging tasks are two basic tasks in natural language processing. Chinese word segmentation aims to divide the continuous word sequence into word units. The input is a continuous word sequence (a sentence), and the output is a segmented word unit sequence. The part-of-speech tagging task is to tag each word with a separate label that represents usage and its syntactic effect, such as noun, verb, adjective, etc. The input is a sequence of consecutive words (a sentence), and the output is the sequence of parts of speech corresponding to each word.

Each subtask consists of two tracks, a close track that can only use the data and models provided by the organizer, and an open track without restrictions. For close tracks, we employ Siku-Roberta model [王东波 et al.] , utilize some data post-processing methods, and try some downstream fine-tuning tricks to improve performance. For the open track, we obtain some ancient text data and use the jiayan[1] toolkit for data augmentation; we also use multiple pretraining models: GlyphBERT (pre-trained by us) [Li et al.2021], Siku-Roberta and roberta-classical-chinese, [2] for downstream fine-tuning, and use some fine-tuning tricks; finally, we employ model ensemble. We achieve competitive scores on P, R, and F1 in our test set.

* equal contribution

† corresponding author

[1]Jiayan: ancient Chinese toolkit `https://github.com/jiaeyan/Jiayan`

[2]roberta-classical-chinese `https://huggingface.co/KoichiYasuoka/roberta-classical-chinese-large-char`

2. Related Work

2.1. Chinese Word Segmentation (CWS)

Chinese Word Segentation is a fundamental task in Chinese language processing. There is extensive research ([Sproat and Shih1990], [Xue and Shen2003], [Huang et al.2007], [Liu et al.2014]). In recent years, deep neural networks have also been widely used to solve the CWS problem with great success. ([Zhou et al.2017], [Yang et al.2017], [Ma et al.2018], [Yang et al.2019]). They can better perform word segmentation through contextual information and knowledge learned in the pre-training process.

2.2. Part-of-speech Tagging

Part-of-speech (POS) tagging is a fundamental task in NLP as well. It's one of the first stages in natural language processing, as an initial stage of information extraction, summarization, retrieval, machine tranlation and speech conversion. [Patil et al.2014]One of classical approaches is generally done with a maximum entroph Markov model(MEMM) [Ratnaparkhi1996]. Recently, deep models are employed to achieve a better performance for this task ([Józefowicz et al.2016], [Choi2016]).

2.3. Pre-trained Language Model (PLM)

The classic word embedding technology, such as Word2Vec [Mikolov et al.2013] and GloVe [Pennington et al.2014] is static. These methods learn the word embeddings with fixed dimensions and meaning rather than contextual information through training on large-scale corpora. To address this problem, researchers study how to learn word embeddings that can contain more comprehensive contextual information. ELMo [Peters et al.2018] is proposed to capture contextual features. BERT [Devlin et al.2018] employs masking language model (MLM) and Next Sentence Prediction (NSP) as pre-train tasks, and then the neural network can learn the context information very well. Based on BERT's architecture and idea, some studies have proposed different pre-training methods to enhance the effect of BERT. Roberta [Liu et al.2019] improves the performance of BERT by employing the MLM by dynamically masking computation while abandoning the NSP task. Roberta optimizes its pre-training process to make the language representation learned by the model more robust, showing better performance than BERT in many tasks.

In addition, researchers are concerned that pre-trained models do not generalize to all problems in all domains, so they start training models that fit for unique domains. In the field of ancient Chinese, roberta-classical-chinese and Siku-Roberta both show excellent performance in the field of ancient Chinese by adopting different training corpora. We also pre-train Glyph-BERT, a pre-train BERT model that can capture glyph information to train a better ability of representation.

2.4. Glyph Vector

Compared with English words, Chinese characters consist of more complex symbolic results. Chinese characters often have unique structures and radicals, and these radicals are often related to the meaning of the word, so obtaining glyph information can help models better understand contextual semantics.There have also been many researches ([Su and Lee2017], [Meng et al.2019], [Chen et al.2020]) that demonstrate the effectiveness of incorporating glyph information into pre-trained models. The typical method is to use a deep convolutional neural network to extract glyph features of Chinese characters from images. Then combining glyph information and word embeddings can enhance the representation of Chinese characters. We use HanGlyph module as a feature extraction module, and pre-train our own glyph pre-training model Glyph-BERT, which also gets competitive results in this competition.

3. Our Methods

Our methods include data augmentation, data pre-processing, model pre-training, downstream fine-tuning, K-fold cross validation and model ensemble. We achieve competitive P, R, and F1 scores on both our own validation set and the final public test set.

3.1. Data Augmentation

This part focuses on the open track. Some research has shown that the larger corpus and the more distribution, the better the generalization performance and robustness of the trained model. Since this, we decide to expand a part of the pseudo-corpus as data augmentation first.

We have expanded Modern Chinese and Ancient Chinese respectively. For modern Chinese, we use the named entity datasets MSRA and People, which are two NER datasets commonly used in the field of Chinese natural language processing. And then we preprocess their test set according to our BIOE labeling way, to be consistent with our training set. The size of this corpus is about 20k. For ancient Chinese, we find a collected open source project that includes the twenty-four histories. After randomly shuffling these ancient Chinese texts, we randomly select a part of them using another open-source project Jiayan for part-of-speech tagging. The size of this corpus is about 20k.

In addition, after the test set is open, we observe the results of the model and find that the models have insufficient labeling ability for some special symbols (such as ", ", [,], etc.). We analyze that it is due to the lack of corpus of special symbols in the training set. So we collect the part of the training set that contains special symbols and perform a fine-tuning as the augmented data.

3.2. Preprocessing

In this task, we combine Chinese word segmentation and part-of-speech tagging into a sequence tagging task. After tagging the part-of-speech of each word with the BIOE tagging method, we then segmented the words according to the tags.

First, we mark all parts of speech involved in this task through the BIOE tagging method, with a total of 88 kinds.

At the same time, since there was no public test set in the early stage of the competition, we divide 1-7000 into the training set, 7001-7700 as the validation set, and the rest into the test set.

3.3. Pre-training Models and GlyphBERT

Since most of the pre-trained models are trained on modern texts, it is also important to select suitable pre-trained models. On the close track, we use the Siku-Roberta provided by the organizer. On the open track, in addition to Siku-Roberta, we also select roberta-classical-chinese and our own pre-trained GlyphBERT. Although GlyphBERT is trained through modern Chinese corpus, experiments show that GlyphBERT also has an excellent performance in this task. This may benefit from the good learning and application of glyph features by GlyphBERT, which make this model has a great ability of transfer.

3.4. Downstream Fine-tuning

Downstream fine-tuning has always been an important step that affects model performance. In this task, we add a CRF layer to the output results before the fully connected layer in the downstream, and set a different learning rate for the CRF layer. The experimental results show that the CRF layer has an excellent effect on

Models	Segmentation P	Segmentation R	Segmentation F1	Pos tagging P	Pos tagging R	Pos tagging F1
Siku-Roberta	88.2762	88.2762	89.3116	80.0600	81.9605	80.9991
+CRF	88.4167	92.0458	90.1948	80.3061	83.6022	81.9210
+Data augmentation	90.4368	91.1646	90.7993	82.6507	83.3158	82.9819
+Change Lr	91.7447	92.3494	92.0460	84.4133	84.9697	84.6906
+K-fold	**92.7101**	**94.8314**	**93.7588**	**87.4430**	**89.4438**	**88.4321**

Table 1: The experimental results of Siku-Roberta on our dividing test set. The methods we take have effectively improved the model performance.

Models	Segmentation P	Segmentation R	Segmentation F1	Pos tagging P	Pos tagging R	Pos tagging F1
roberta-classical-chinese	95.6615	95.6692	95.6654	90.4941	90.5014	90.4978
+CRF	**95.7000**	**95.7541**	**95.7270**	**90.4664**	**90.5176**	**90.4920**
+Data augmentation	95.5804	95.4953	95.5378	90.2623	90.1820	90.2221
+Change Lr	95.6294	95.2002	95.4143	90.5764	90.1698	90.3727

Table 2: The experimental results of roberta-classical-chinese on our delineated test set. Despite our use of these methods, the results are not much different from the original. So, we choose the roberta-classical-chinese model with CRF when doing model ensemble.

Models	Segmentation P	Segmentation R	Segmentation F1	Pos tagging P	Pos tagging R	Pos tagging F1
GlyphBERT	**93.9186**	**93.5467**	**93.7323**	**87.3382**	**86.9924**	**87.1650**
+CRF	92.6289	92.3450	93.3370	86.1587	86.5049	85.7965
+Data augmentation	92.6731	92.2838	92.4780	85.3341	84.9756	85.1544
+Change Lr	92.4743	92.6058	92.5400	85.5207	85.6423	85.5815

Table 3: The experimental results of GlyphBERT on our dividing test set. The methods we take are not very effective on GlyphBERT, so we choose to use GlyphBERT baseline when doing model ensemble.

the sequence labeling task, and setting learning rates for the CRF layer different from the base model is also very effective.

3.5. K-fold Cross Validation

We divide the original data into K groups (K-Fold), use each subset data as a validation set, and use the remaining K-1 sets of subset data as a training set, so that we obtain K models accordingly. The K models evaluate the results in the validation set respectively, then make predictions in the test set, and finally combine the prediction results of the K models to obtain the prediction labels of the test set. Cross-validation effectively utilizes limited data, and the evaluation results can be as close as possible to the performance of the model on the test set, which can be used as an indicator for model optimization.

3.6. Model Ensemble

Ensemble of multiple models is a common method used in competitions. The ensemble of models often requires certain differences between several models, such as using different corpora for training, or using different architectures. In this task we use 4 different models for ensemble: Siku-Roberta, roberta-classical-chinese-base-char, roberta-classical-chinese-large-char, GlyphBERT. Among them, Siku-Roberta and roberta-classical-chinese have similar architectures, but their training corpora are quite different. GlyphBERT is unique in its architecture, training corpus, and feature extraction method. So we think they will have a great effect in ensemble.

4. Experiments and Analysis

4.1. Experimental Settings

Our implementations of Siku-Roberta, roberta-classical-chinese-char, GlyphBERT are based on the public pytorch implementation from Transformers. Siku-Roberta is in large size, while roberta-classical-chinese-char models of both large and base versions are used. GlyphBERT is implemented base on Pytorch and Transformers library. During pre-training, we follow the hyper-parameters setting of the original implementation. During fine-tuning, We set the maximum length of the sentence to 512. We use a single Tesla v100s GPU with 32gb memory, and fine-tuning time varies from 6 to 12 hours for each model.

	Segmentation			Pos tagging		
	P	**R**	**F1**	**P**	**R**	**F1**
test A close1	90.8050	92.9935	91.8862	84.7235	86.7655	85.7323
test A close2	**90.7833**	**93.0326**	**91.8942**	**84.7024**	**86.8010**	**85.7389**
test A open1	91.0912	93.4130	92.2375	85.2745	87.4480	86.3476
test A open2	**91.1994**	**93.4947**	**92.3328**	**85.4086**	**87.5582**	**86.4701**
test B close1	82.1870	77.8193	79.9435	70.2067	66.4456	68.2744
test B close2	**82.7873**	**78.8168**	**80.7533**	**71.3723**	**67.9465**	**69.6173**
test B open1	**83.2716**	**79.2979**	**81.2361**	**71.8098**	**68.3830**	**70.0545**
test B open2	82.2262	78.3115	80.2211	70.7657	67.3967	69.0401

Table 4: The results of our eight submitted texts using the official final release evaluation script. On test B, the performance degradation of our model is more obvious. We think this is mainly due to the large differences in language habits in test B due to dynasties or other factors.

4.2. Experimental Results and Analysis

In the early stage of the competition, We intercept the last 1100 records of the dataset as the test set. Table 1 shows the experimental results of the baseline on this test set after using different tricks. The baseline is a Siku-Roberta model used on the close track. We set the learning rate to 1e-4, the batch size to 2, and the epoch to 5, and then obtained 89.3116 and 80.9991 points on the F1 score of word segmentation and part-of-speech tagging, respectively. After adding a CRF layer to get the prediction results, the F1 value of both tasks improved by 1 point. Then we add additional corpus besides CRF, and the scores of the two tasks also increased steadily. Finally, we set the learning rate of the CRF layer to 10 times that of the base model, and get 93.7588 and 88.4321 points in the two tasks, respectively. Table 2 and Table 3 show the cases of roberta-classical-chinese-large-char model and Glyph-BERT model, respectively. If only using the roberta-classical-chinese-large-char model, we will get scores of 95.6654 and 90.4978 on the F1 score of the two tasks, which already exceeds the performance of the Siku-Roberta model. Although the GlyphBERT model basically exceeds the Siku-Robera in all indicators, it is not as good as the roberta-classical-chinese-large-char model. Before the release of the official test data, we finally use several models to predict the original 1100 pieces of test set with various tricks. These models include roberta-classical-chinese-char (both base and large), Siku-Roberta and GlyphBERT. After the ensemble at the logits, we achieve F1 scores of 95.9438 and 90.9540 on the two tasks respectively.

In the latter stage of the competition, each team has two submission opportunities for each of the two test sets in each track. Table 4 shows the final results of our model on the competition test set. For the close track of test A, We seperately submit the Siku-Roberta model with 10-fold cross-validation, and the combined results of 5-fold and 10-fold cross-validation at a logits ratio of 1:2. For the open track of test A, based on the close track, we add the results of roberta-classical-chinese-char and Siku-Roberta training on the expanded data set, as well as results of roberta-classical-chinese-char (including both base and large versions) using 5-fold cross validation.

The model usage on test B is the same as that on test A. However, results of test B are much worse than results of test A. We argue that the results of test B may come from other dynasties, and the usage of some words is slightly different from that of Siku Quanshu, resulting in a decline in the model prediction effect.

5. Conclusion

We introduce our submission for LT4HALA shared task EvaHan2022. For the close track, we propose some simple but efficient data augmentation methods and fine-tune methods. For the open track, we propose methods including data augmentation, data pre-processing, model pretraining, downstream fine-tuning, K-fold cross validation and model ensemble. We find that our model GlyphBERT performs well on transfer learning in this task. For the word segmentation task and the part-of-speech tagging task, respectively, on F1 on the close track, we achieved 91.89 and 85.74 on test A, and 80.75 and 69.62 on test B; similarly, on the open track, we achieved 92.33 and 86.47 for test A, and 81.24 and 70.05 for test B.

6. Bibliographical References

Chen, H.-Y., Yu, S.-H., and Lin, S.-d. (2020). Glyph2Vec: Learning Chinese out-of-vocabulary word embedding from glyphs. In *Proceedings of the 58th Annual Meeting of the Association for Computational Linguistics*, pages 2865–2871, Online, July. Association for Computational Linguistics.

Choi, J. D. (2016). Dynamic feature induction: The last gist to the state-of-the-art. In *Proceedings of the 2016 Conference of the North American Chapter of the Association for Computational Linguistics: Human Language Technologies*, pages 271–281, San Diego, California, June. Association for Computational Linguistics.

Devlin, J., Chang, M., Lee, K., and Toutanova, K. (2018). BERT: pre-training of deep bidirectional transformers for language understanding. *CoRR*, abs/1810.04805.

Huang, C.-R., Šimon, P., Hsieh, S.-K., and Prévot, L. (2007). Rethinking Chinese word segmentation: Tokenization, character classification, or word-break identification. In *Proceedings of the 45th Annual Meeting of the Association for Computational Linguistics Companion Volume Proceedings of the Demo and Poster Sessions*, pages 69–72, Prague, Czech Republic, June. Association for Computational Linguistics.

Józefowicz, R., Vinyals, O., Schuster, M., Shazeer, N., and Wu, Y. (2016). Exploring the limits of language modeling. *CoRR*, abs/1602.02410.

Li, Y., Zhao, Y., Hu, B., Chen, Q., Xiang, Y., Wang, X., Ding, Y., and Ma, L. (2021). Glyphcrm: Bidirectional encoder representation for chinese character with its glyph. *CoRR*, abs/2107.00395.

Liu, Y., Zhang, Y., Che, W., Liu, T., and Wu, F. (2014). Domain adaptation for CRF-based Chinese word segmentation using free annotations. In *Proceedings of the 2014 Conference on Empirical Methods in Natural Language Processing (EMNLP)*, pages 864–874, Doha, Qatar, October. Association for Computational Linguistics.

Liu, Y., Ott, M., Goyal, N., Du, J., Joshi, M., Chen, D., Levy, O., Lewis, M., Zettlemoyer, L., and Stoyanov, V. (2019). Roberta: A robustly optimized BERT pretraining approach. *CoRR*, abs/1907.11692.

Ma, J., Ganchev, K., and Weiss, D. (2018). State-of-the-art Chinese word segmentation with Bi-LSTMs. In *Proceedings of the 2018 Conference on Empirical Methods in Natural Language Processing*, pages 4902–4908, Brussels, Belgium, October-November. Association for Computational Linguistics.

Meng, Y., Wu, W., Wang, F., Li, X., Nie, P., Yin, F., Li, M., Han, Q., Sun, X., and Li, J. (2019). Glyce: Glyph-vectors for chinese character representations. *CoRR*, abs/1901.10125.

Mikolov, T., Sutskever, I., Chen, K., Corrado, G., and Dean, J. (2013). Distributed representations of words and phrases and their compositionality. *Advances in Neural Information Processing Systems*, 26, 10.

Patil, H. B., Patil, A. S., and Pawar, B. V. (2014). Article: Part-of-speech tagger for marathi language using limited training corpora. *IJCA Proceedings on National Conference on Recent Advances in Information Technology*, NCRAIT(4):33–37, February. Full text available.

Pennington, J., Socher, R., and Manning, C. (2014). GloVe: Global vectors for word representation. In *Proceedings of the 2014 Conference on Empirical Methods in Natural Language Processing (EMNLP)*, pages 1532–1543, Doha, Qatar, October. Association for Computational Linguistics.

Peters, M. E., Neumann, M., Iyyer, M., Gardner, M., Clark, C., Lee, K., and Zettlemoyer, L. (2018). Deep contextualized word representations. *CoRR*, abs/1802.05365.

Ratnaparkhi, A. (1996). A maximum entropy model for part-of-speech tagging. In *Conference on Empirical Methods in Natural Language Processing*.

Sproat, R. and Shih, C. (1990). A statistical method for finding word boundaries in chinese text. *Computer Processing of Chinese Oriental Languages*, 4(4):336–351, March.

Su, T.-R. and Lee, H.-Y. (2017). Learning Chinese word representations from glyphs of characters. In *Proceedings of the 2017 Conference on Empirical Methods in Natural Language Processing*, pages 264–273, Copenhagen, Denmark, September. Association for Computational Linguistics.

Xue, N. and Shen, L. (2003). Chinese word segmentation as lmr tagging. 07.

Yang, J., Zhang, Y., and Dong, F. (2017). Neural word segmentation with rich pretraining. In *Proceedings of the 55th Annual Meeting of the Association for Computational Linguistics (Volume 1: Long Papers)*, pages 839–849, Vancouver, Canada, July. Association for Computational Linguistics.

Yang, J., Zhang, Y., and Liang, S. (2019). Subword encoding in lattice LSTM for Chinese word segmentation. In *Proceedings of the 2019 Conference of the North American Chapter of the Association for Computational Linguistics: Human Language Technologies, Volume 1 (Long and Short Papers)*, pages 2720–2725, Minneapolis, Minnesota, June. Association for Computational Linguistics.

Zhou, H., Yu, Z., Zhang, Y., Huang, S., Dai, X., and Chen, J. (2017). Word-context character embeddings for Chinese word segmentation. In *Proceedings of the 2017 Conference on Empirical Methods in Natural Language Processing*, pages 760–766, Copenhagen, Denmark, September. Association for Computational Linguistics.

王东波, 刘畅, 朱子赫, 刘江峰, 胡昊天, 沈思, and 李斌.). Sikubert与sikuroberta:面向数字人文的《四库全书》预训练模型构建及应用研究.

Proceedings of the Second Workshop on Language Technologies for Historical and Ancient Languages (LT4HALA 2022), pages 183–188
Language Resources and Evaluation Conference (LREC 2022), Marseille, 25 June 2022

Overview of the EvaLatin 2022 Evaluation Campaign

Rachele Sprugnoli[1], Marco Passarotti[2], Flavio M. Cecchini[2], Margherita Fantoli[3], Giovanni Moretti[2]
[1]Università di Parma, [2]CIRCSE Research Centre, Università Cattolica del Sacro Cuore, [3]KU Leuven
rachele.sprugnoli@unipr.it, marco.passarotti@unicatt.it, flavio.cecchini@unicatt.it
margherita.fantoli@kuleuven.be giovanni.moretti@unicatt.it

Abstract

This paper describes the organization and the results of the second edition of EvaLatin, the campaign for the evaluation of Natural Language Processing tools for Latin. The three shared tasks proposed in EvaLatin 2022, i. e. Lemmatization, Part-of-Speech Tagging and Features Identification, are aimed to foster research in the field of language technologies for Classical languages. The shared dataset consists of texts mainly taken from the LASLA corpus. More specifically, the training set includes only prose texts of the Classical period, whereas the test set is organized in three sub-tasks: a *Classical* sub-task on a prose text of an author not included in the training data, a *Cross-genre* sub-task on poetic and scientific texts, and a *Cross-time* sub-task on a text of the 15th century. The results obtained by the participants for each task and sub-task are presented and discussed.

Keywords: Latin, evaluation, NLP

1. Introduction

EvaLatin 2022 is the second edition of the campaign devoted to the evaluation of Natural Language Processing (NLP) tools for the Latin language. Like in 2020, EvaLatin is proposed as part of the *Workshop on Language Technologies for Historical and Ancient Languages* (LT4HALA 2022), co-located with LREC 2022.[1] Similar to what happens in other international evaluation campaigns, participants have been provided with training and test data that are made freely available for research purposes to encourage further improvement of language technologies for Latin. Participants also had the chance to evaluate their systems using a shared script. Data, scorer and detailed guidelines are all available in a dedicated GitHub repository.[2]
EvaLatin is an initiative organized by the CIRCSE research centre[3] at the Università Cattolica del Sacro Cuore in Milan, Italy, with the support of the *LiLa: Linking Latin* ERC project.[4] An agreement has been established with the Laboratoire d'Analyse Statistique des Langues Anciennes (LASLA) of the University of Liège, Belgium, for the use of the homonymous corpus, and a collaboration has been set up with the Katholieke Universiteit Leuven, Belgium.

2. Tasks and Sub-tasks

EvaLatin 2022 has three tasks:

1. **Lemmatization**, i. e. the process of transforming each word form into a corresponding conventional "base form", according to its part of speech (i. e. morphosyntactic properties) and etymology, which usually coincides with an entry found in the dictionary (i. e. lemma);
2. **Part-of-Speech tagging**, for which systems are required to assign each token a lexical category, i. e. a Part-of-Speech (PoS) tag, according to the Universal Dependencies (UD) PoS tagset (de Marneffe et al., 2021, §2.2.2), originally inspired by that of (Petrov et al., 2011).[5]
3. **Features Identification**, for which systems have both to correctly identify the UD morphological features (de Marneffe et al., 2021, §2.2.3) pertaining to the token's word form among the specific subset used in the EvaLatin 2022 dataset (see §3.), and to select correct values for them.[6]

Each task has three sub-tasks:

1. **Classical**: the test data belong to the same genres and time period of the training data;
2. **Cross-genre**: the test data belong to two different genres, namely mythological poem and scientific treatise, but roughly to the same time period compared to the ones included in the training data;
3. **Cross-time**: the test data belong to a different time period, namely the Renaissance era, compared to the ones included in the training data.

Through these sub-tasks, we aim to enhance the study of the portability of NLP tools for Latin across different genres and time periods by analyzing the impact of genre-specific and diachronic features.
Shared data and a scorer are provided to the participants, who can choose to take part in either a single task, or in all tasks and sub-tasks.

[1]https://lrec2022.lrec-conf.org/en/
[2]https://github.com/CIRCSE/LT4HALA/tree/master/2022/data_and_doc
[3]https://centridiricerca.unicatt.it/circse_index.html
[4]https://lila-erc.eu/
[5]https://universaldependencies.org/u/pos/index.html
[6]An overview is at https://universaldependencies.org/u/feat/index.html.

3. Data

The dataset of EvaLatin 2022 consists of texts mainly taken from the LASLA corpus (Denooz, 2004), a resource manually annotated since 1961 by the Laboratoire d'Analyse Statistique des Langues Anciennes (LASLA) at the University of Liège,[7] Belgium. The texts are then converted into the annotation formalism of the UD project[8] (de Marneffe et al., 2021), which is the one used by this evaluation campaign.

The LASLA corpus contains approximately 1,700,000 words (punctuation is not present in the corpus), corresponding to 133,886 unique tokens and 24,339 unique lemmas. Each token is annotated by a trained classicist, and usually the same annotator consistently takes care of a set of associated texts. The annotation takes place through a web-based interface where the annotator chooses between a set of possible analyses or adds a new analysis when necessary. To minimize human errors, a sentence cannot be validated until any token has been processed. At the end of such procedure, an index of forms and associated morphological analyses is generated and subsequently corrected by the annotator. Finally, a second philologist verifies and corrects the final version, and the most complicated cases are discussed within the LASLA team. The annotation guidelines are provided by the manual (Philippart de Foy, 2014).

Besides these texts from the LASLA corpus, the test data also include a text by Sabellicus, a Renaissance historian of the 15th century, annotated by members of the CIRCSE research center.

The conversion from the original fixed-length format of LASLA to the CoNLL-U format[9] and the UD formalism has also been developed at the CIRCSE research center and is based on Python[10] scripts complemented by the access to the LiLa lexical knowledge base (Passarotti et al., 2020). The conversion is then followed by a further step of uniformization to make all annotated texts, including those not taken from the LASLA corpus, as coherent as possible between themselves and with respect to the the UD formalism and our specific choices concerning the morphological annotation. In particular, for this campaign just a subset of UD morpholexical features is retained, thus considering only the following features: `Abbr`, `Aspect`, `Case`, `Degree`, `InflClass`, `InflClass[nominal]`, `Mood`, `Number`, `Person`, `Tense`, `VerbForm`, `Voice`. The guiding principle here is to stick only to purely morphological features which can be tracked down in the word form, and at the same time to avoid features which are annotated inconsistently among texts. The former criterion leaves aside more lexically oriented features like `PronType` (the "pronominal type"), which hinge more on semantic arguments rather than on inflectional and syntactic behaviour; on a similar note, we also discard the `Gender` feature[11] (which is lexically determined) in favor of `InflClass` (which is readable from the word form).[12] The consistency criterion excludes a feature like `Polarity` which, though morphologic, is not systematically annotated in the texts at our disposal.

Overall, the accomplished conversion and uniformization are not only a transcription into a different annotation system, but also an adjustment to the annotation principles that in the last years have been under constant development for Latin treebanks in the framework of the UD project, and which might differ in some point from the those of the LASLA corpus, or extend them. One fundamental example is the `AUX`/`VERB` split of UD, whereby the functional verb *sum* 'to be' is annotated as `AUX` (and not `VERB`, or `B` in LASLA) also in its occurrences as a copula, and not only as part of a periphrastic form. On the morphological level, another example is the separation of the notions represented in UD by the features `Mood` and `VerbForm`, which in LASLA, following the most common grammatical tradition, are conflated under the label of *mode* 'mood': so, in our dataset the *mode indicatif* corresponds to `Mood=Ind` (with `VerbForm=Fin`), while the *mode infinitif* to `VerbForm=Inf` (with no value for `Mood`). At the same time, *temps* 'tenses' are represented by different combinations of values for `Tense`, but also for `Aspect`, which is not directly indicated in LASLA.

For more details about morphological features, we point to the EvaLatin 2022 guidelines on the official website.[13]

3.1. Training Data

Texts provided as training data are the same ones adopted as training and test data for EvaLatin 2020; however, the annotation may slightly differ from that seen in the previous edition of the evalutation campaign. In fact, in 2020 we did not use the LASLA corpus directly, but instead worked with a manually revised version of the automatic annotation performed by UDPipe (Straka et al., 2016) based on the model trained on the Perseus UD Latin Treebank[14] (Bamman and Crane, 2011).

Texts are by five Classical authors for a total of more than 300,000 tokens: Caesar, Cicero, Seneca, Pliny the Younger and Tacitus. All texts are in prose but different genres are included: treatises by Caesar, Seneca and Tacitus, public speeches by Cicero, and letters by Pliny the Younger. Table 1 presents details about the training dataset of EvaLatin 2022, while Figure 1 shows an example of the format.

3.2. Test Data

Test data contain only the tokenized words but not the correct tags, which have to be added by the participant systems

[7] http://web.philo.ulg.ac.be/lasla/textes-latins-traites/

[8] www.universaldependencies.org

[9] https://universaldependencies.org/format.html

[10] https://www.python.org/

[11] We further note that the annotation of grammatical gender in LASLA drastically deviates in its logic from that of UD, making automated conversion problematic.

[12] https://universaldependencies.org/la/feat/InflClass.html

[13] https://circse.github.io/LT4HALA/2022/EvaLatin.html

[14] https://github.com/UniversalDependencies/UD_Latin-Perseus/

```
# sent_id = CaesBG4-A-01-607
# text = neque multum frumento sed maximam partem lacte atque pecore uiuunt multumque sunt in uenationibus
1   neque   neque   CCONJ   _   _   _   _   _   _
2   multum  multum  ADV _   _   _   _   _   _
3   frumento    frumentum   NOUN    _   Case=Abl|InflClass=IndEurO|Number=Sing  _   _   _   _
4   sed sed CCONJ   _   _   _   _   _   _
5   maximam magnus  ADJ _   Case=Acc|Degree=Abs|InflClass=IndEurA|Number=Sing   _   _   _   _
6   partem  pars    NOUN    _   Case=Acc|InflClass=IndEurI|Number=Sing  _   _   _   _
7   lacte   lac NOUN    _   Case=Abl|InflClass=IndEurI|Number=Sing  _   _   _   _
8   atque   atque   CCONJ   _   _   _   _   _   _
9   pecore  pecus   NOUN    _   Case=Abl|InflClass=IndEurX|Number=Sing  _   _   _   _
10  uiuunt  uiuo    VERB    _   Aspect=Imp|InflClass=LatX|Mood=Ind|Number=Plur|Person=3|Tense=Pres|VerbForm=Fin|Voice=Act   _   _   _   _
11-12   multumque   _   _   _   _   _   _   _   _
11  multum  multum  ADV _   _   _   _   _   _
12  que que CCONJ   _   _   _   _   _   _
13  sunt    sum AUX _   Aspect=Imp|InflClass=LatAnom|Mood=Ind|Number=Plur|Person=3|Tense=Pres|VerbForm=Fin  _   _   _   _
14  in  in  ADP _   _   _   _   _   _
15  uenationibus    uenatio NOUN    _   Case=Abl|InflClass=IndEurX|Number=Plur  _   _   _   _
```

Figure 1: Example of the format of training data.

AUTHORS	TEXTS	# TOKENS
Caesar	De Bello Gallico	44,818
Caesar	De Bello Civili (I, II)	17,287
Cicero	Philippicae (I–XIV)	52,563
Cicero	In Catilinam	12,564
Pliny the Younger	Epistulae (I-VIII, X)	60,695
Seneca	De Beneficiis	45,457
Seneca	De Clementia	8,172
Seneca	De Vita Beata	7,270
Seneca	De Providentia	4,077
Tacitus	Historiae	51,420
Tacitus	Agricola	6,737
Tacitus	Germania	5,513
TOTAL	TEXTS	316,573

Table 1: Training data of EvaLatin 2022, books in parentheses.

to be submitted for the evaluation. Tokenization is a central issue in evaluation and comparison, because each system could apply different tokenization rules leading to different outputs. In order to avoid this problem, test data has already been provided in tokenized format, one token per line, and with a blank line separating each sentence. The gold standard test data, i. e. the annotation used for the evaluation, was provided to the participants after the evaluation. The composition of the test dataset for the *Classical* sub-task is given in Table 2. Details for the data distributed in the *Cross-Genre* and *Cross-Time* sub-tasks are reported in Tables 3 and 4 respectively, while an example of the format of test data is given in Figure 2.

AUTHOR	TEXT	# TOKENS
Livius	Ab Urbe Condita (VIII)	13,572

Table 2: Test data for *Classical* sub-task, books in parentheses.

AUTHORS	TEXTS	# TOKENS
Pliny the Elder	Naturalis Historia (XXXVII)	11,371
Ovidius	Metamorphoseon libri (IX–X)	11,325
TOTAL	TEXTS	22,696

Table 3: Test data for *Cross-genre* sub-task, books in parentheses.

AUTHOR	TEXT	# TOKENS
Sabellicus	De Latinae Linguae Reparatione	9,278

Table 4: Test data for *Cross-time* sub-task, books in parentheses.

```
# sent_id = OvMETAM0910-M-ET-402
# text = dummodo pugnando superem tu uince loquendo congrediturque ferox
1   dummodo _   _   _   _   _   _   _   _
2   pugnando    _   _   _   _   _   _   _   _
3   superem _   _   _   _   _   _   _   _
4   tu  _   _   _   _   _   _   _   _
5   uince   _   _   _   _   _   _   _   _
6   loquendo    _   _   _   _   _   _   _   _
7-8 congrediturque  _   _   _   _   _   _   _   _
7   congreditur _   _   _   _   _   _   _   _
8   que _   _   _   _   _   _   _   _
9   ferox   _   _   _   _   _   _   _   _
```

Figure 2: Example of the format of test data.

4. Evaluation

The scorer employed for EvaLatin 2022 is a modified version of that developed for the *CoNLL 2018 Shared Task on Multilingual Parsing from Raw Text to Universal Dependencies* (Zeman et al., 2018).[15] The evaluation starts by aligning the outputs of the participating systems to the gold standard: given that our test data are already tokenized and split by sentences, the alignment at the token and sentence levels is always perfect (i. e. 100.00%). Then, POS tags, lemmas and features are evaluated and the final ranking is based on accuracy.

Each participant was permitted to submit runs for either one or all tasks and sub-tasks. It was mandatory to produce one run according to the so-called "closed modality", according to which the only annotated resources that could be used to train and tune the system are those distributed by the organizers. Also external non-annotated resources, like word embeddings, were allowed. The second run could be produced according to the "open modality", for which the use of additional annotated external data is allowed.

As for the baseline, we provided the participants with the scores obtained on our test data by UDPipe, using the model trained on the Perseus UD Latin Treebank[16] (Bamman and Crane, 2011), the same available in the tool's web

[15] https://universaldependencies.org/conll18/evaluation.html

[16] https://github.com/UniversalDependencies/UD_Latin-Perseus/

interface.[17]

5. Participants and Results

Two teams took part in EvaLatin 2022 submitting runs for all tasks and sub-tasks. Only one team (namely, Kraków) submitted one run following the open modality for each task and sub-task, whereas the other submitted runs in the closed modality only. Details on the participating teams and their systems are given below:

- Kraków, Jagiellonian University, Institute of Polish Language, Enelpol (Poland) (Wróbel and Nowak, 2022). This team employs transformer models for their runs: in particular, they use XLM-RoBERTa large (Conneau et al., 2020) for both PoS tagging and features identification, and a ByT5 model (Xue et al., 2022) for lemmatization. The runs developed following the open modality are trained adding annotated texts taken from the UD Latin treebanks and the whole LASLA corpus to the official dataset.
- KU-Leuven, KU Leuven, Brepols Publishers (Belgium) (Mercelis and Keersmaekers, 2022). The runs of this team are based on a pre-trained ELECTRA-model (Clark et al., 2020). The *Huggingface Transformers ElectraForTokenClassification* model is used for the PoS tagging task while handcrafted rules are added to handle lemmatization. For the Feature Identification task, a separate classifier is trained for each feature: the predicted labels are then joined at a later time.

Tables 5, 6 and 7 report the final rankings, showing the results in terms of accuracy, including our baseline. For each run, the team name and the modality are specified. Please note that for the *Cross-genre* sub-task the score corresponds to the macro-average accuracy.

6. Discussion

As shown in Tables 5, 6 and 7, all systems largely outperform the baseline: please note that the accuracy rate on Features Identification task is very low because there are several differences between the morphological features used to train the Perseus model of UDPipe and those in our data. For example, we adopt the feature InflClass, not attested in the training data of the Perseus model.

The open-run experiment by the Kraków team yields the best results in each of the tasks and sub-tasks: in particular, an improvement in accuracy is registered in the *Cross-genre* sub-task of the Lemmatization and PoS tasks (respectively +3.46% points and +1.44% points with respect to the run made following the closed modality). This shows that using additional annotated data (e. g. a broader portion of the LASLA corpus and UD treebanks) improves the results, despite the possible inconsistencies in the annotation styles.

Each sub-task contains only one text, with the exception of the *Cross-Genre* sub-task: the standard deviation among the texts of this sub-task (*Metamorphoseon libri* and *Naturalis Historia*) fluctuates between 1.04 and 2.02 (Lemmatization task), 0.22 and 1.75 (PoS task), 0.88 and 3.55 (Features). For the Lemmatization and PoS tagging tasks, the *Metamorphoseon libri* obtain better results than the *Naturalis Historia*, whereas for the Features Identification task, the three systems perform better on the *Naturalis Historia* than on the *Metamorphoseon libri*. This can be explained by the fact that the *Naturalis Historia* starkly differs from the training data because it deals with a very peculiar topic, i. e. precious stones, and thus features a highly specific vocabulary, which impacts the results of the Lemmatization and PoS tasks. For instance, the form *acaustoe* (also a Greek variant) of the ADJ *acaustos* 'incombustible' is wrongly lemmatized by all systems and assigned the PoS NOUN or PROPN. On the contrary, the *Metamorphoseon libri* differ from the training set because they are poetry and not prose, which entails a very different word order and syntax: such variations are likely to strongly impact the Features Identification task.

Taking a more in-depth look at the results on the test set as a whole, the easiest text to tackle with regard to Lemmatization for the KU Leuven model are the *Metamorphoseon libri* (*Cross-Genre*, accuracy of 87.22%), whereas the two Kraków models perform better on the *Ab Urbe Condita* (*Classical*, accuracy of 96.45% and 97.26%). The hardest text to tackle for all the systems appears to be the *De Latinae Linguae Reparatione* (with an accuracy ranging from 84.6% to 92.15%). This result might be surprising if one considers that this text has a significantly lower percentage of out-of-vocabulary lemmata and a lower lemma/token ratio than the *Naturalis Historia* (respectively 21.67% vs. 33.67%, and 20.2% vs. 25.6%). The results might be due to the fact that, whereas the *Naturalis Historia* is annotated following LASLA conventions, the *De Latinae Linguae Reparatione* is annotated in the frame of a different project; but probably the decisive factor is that, the *De Latinae Linguae Reparatione* being a significantly later text, orthographic variations (such as systematic *e* instead of *ae*, or spellings like *ocium* for *otium* 'leisure', or *phama* for *fama* 'reputation') have a stronger impact than expected on any task and/or system highly relying on word forms. In fact, Features Identification is more heavily impacted (losses in accuracy of up to -9.92% with respect to the *Classical* sub-task) than Lemmatization or PoS tagging (losses of up to -5.11%), which abstract more towards a lexical or syntactic level.

For the PoS tagging task, all systems perform best on the *Ab Urbe Condita*, with very similar results (accuracy ranges from 96.33% to 97.99%). The most difficult text is once again the *De Latinae Linguae Reparatione* (accuracy from 92.11% to 92.70% points). The most frequent errors occur in the categories ADJ, NOUN and PROPN. This is mostly due to the nominal use (i. e. as heads of noun phrases) of adjectival forms, like the adjective (ADJ) *Romanus* 'Roman', that can appear annotated as PROPN in the sense of 'the Roman citizen', or the presumed NOUN *malum* '(an) evil', which is nothing else than the neuter form of the ADJ *malus* 'bad'. Especially the first case is due to a general inconsistency in the annotation of the

[17] http://lindat.mff.cuni.cz/services/udpipe/

Classical	
Kraków-open	97.26
Kraków-closed	96.45
KU-Leuven	85.44
Baseline	80.36

Cross-Genre	
Kraków-open	95.08 (1.34)
Kraków-closed	91.62 (2.02)
KU-Leuven	86.48 (1.04)
Baseline	79.03 (1.52)

Cross-time	
Kraków-open	92.15
Kraków-closed	91.68
KU-Leuven	84.60
Baseline	81.92

Table 5: Results of the Lemmatization task for the three sub-tasks in terms of accuracy. The number in brackets indicates standard deviation calculated among the two documents of the test set for the *Cross-Genre* sub-task.

Classical	
Kraków-open	97.99
Kraków-closed	97.61
KU-Leuven	96.33
Baseline	78.23

Cross-Genre	
Kraków-open	96.06 (1.01)
Kraków-closed	94.62 (0.22)
KU-Leuven	92.31 (3.32)
Baseline	76.58 (1.75)

Cross-time	
Kraków-closed	92.97
Kraków-open	92.70
KU-Leuven	92.11
Baseline	74.26

Table 6: Results of the PoS task for the three sub-tasks in terms of accuracy. The number in brackets indicates standard deviation calculated among the two documents of the test set for the *Cross-Genre* sub-task.

Classical	
Kraków-open	95.46
Kraków-closed	95.42
KU-Leuven	69.91
Baseline	24.98

Cross-Genre	
Kraków-open	89.43 (0.88)
Kraków-closed	89.32 (0.88)
KU-Leuven	60.55 (3.55)
Baseline	23.34 (1.16)

Cross-time	
Kraków-closed	86.50
Kraków-open	86.50
KU-Leuven	60.09
Baseline	27.84

Table 7: Results of the Feature Identification task for the three sub-tasks in terms of accuracy. The number in brackets indicates standard deviation calculated among the two documents of the test set for the *Cross-Genre* sub-task.

datasets not solved with the conversion and uniformization process described in §3.. Moreover, in Latin, adjectives and (proper) nouns almost completely overlap on their inflectional paradigms, so that a distinction based on formal criteria can incur in difficulties. Also, the difference between `NOUN` and `PROPN` is of a purely semantic rather than morphosyntactic or functional-vs.-lexically grounded nature; this makes `PROPN` anomalous in the UD PoS scheme, and explains why a system like `KU Leuven` can drop as low as 59.8% in accuracy for this PoS, and `Kraków`'s reach some of its lowest scores.

Among verb forms, participial forms in particular are also liable to oscillate, in this case between an annotation as `VERB` on the one hand, and as `ADJ` or `NOUN` on the other hand, depending on the propension for a more morphological or syntactic analysis. Examples from the *Cross-Time* sub-task (i. e. Sabellicus's work) are i) the form *scriptis*, annotated as a `NOUN` with lemma *scriptum* 'written work' in the test data, but traced back to the `VERB` *scribo* 'to write' by one of the systems for being originally a participial form; ii) the form *occulto* (occurring in the expression *in occulto* 'secretely'), analyzed as a (participial) form of the `VERB` *occulo* 'to cover' in the test data, but labeled as a `NOUN` *occultum* 'secrecy' by one of the systems for being in a nominal context (here, an oblique argument introduced by a preposition). In fact, we see some inconsistencies in this sense between training and test data, and sometimes internally to the training data, too. In particular, the LASLA annotation seems to favor a more "functional" approach whereby e. g. a lexical adjective in a nominal context becomes tagged as a noun, while the tendency in the natively UD-annotated *De Latinae Linguae Reparatione* is to keep it annotated as an `ADJ`, delegating the representation of its more noun-like behaviour to the layer of syntactic dependency relations.

Similarly, the assignment of the label `ADV` proves to be particularly difficult with terms such as *uerum* 'certainly', *nunc* 'now' or *quippe* 'of course, by all means', which all lie in the syntactic grey area of sentence connectors and discourse particles, where the border between `ADV` and `CCONJ` (and also `PART`) can be blurred, and sometimes annotation in the data accordingly shows inconsistencies, too.

For the Features Identification task, the easiest text is again the *Ab Urbe Condita* and the hardest *De Latinae Linguae Reparatione*. The gap between the worst and best performing model is significantly larger than in the other tasks: the accuracy ranges from 69.91% to 95.46% on the *Ab Urbe Condita*, and from 60.09% to 86.53% on the *De Latinae Linguae Reparatione*. In general, `Case` is the most poorly identified feature (followed by `InflClass` and `InflClass[nominal]`), with an F1 score ranging from 53% (*Naturalis Historia*) to 95% (*Ab Urbe Condita*). The number of ambiguous forms (e. g. dative and ablative singular of the second declension, plural of second and first declensions; nominative, vocative and accusative of neuter names) and the role of the context for the disambiguation might explain this result.

7. Conclusion

This paper describes the second edition of EvaLatin, the evaluation campaign dedicated to NLP tools for the Latin language. Following the good results in terms of participation and performances obtained in 2020, this edition of EvaLatin has been organized around three tasks: in particular, the Features Identification task has been added to the

Lemmatization and PoS tasks, already proposed in 2020. Although there has been a drop in the number of participants (from 5 to 2), we are satisfied with the achieved results: new annotated data were released and new systems were tested using a common framework. Interestingly, the participating systems are both based on transformer models.

As for the future, we plan to keep organizing a new edition of EvaLatin every two years. Indeed, there are several variables still to address in the campaign, including (a) the authors and genres represented in the texts chosen for the training and test sets, and (b) the shared tasks to perform. With regard to the former, we plan to include Early Medieval documentary texts in the shared data, most likely by relying on the data provided by the Latin Text Archive.[18] For what concerns the latter, a challenge to address in the near future of EvaLatin is syntactic analysis, also in light of the results and the experience of the UD initiative.

8. Acknowledgements

This work is supported by the European Research Council (ERC) under the European Union's Horizon 2020 research and innovation programme via the *LiLa: Linking Latin* project - Grant Agreement No. 769994. The authors want to thank the LASLA, which provided newly lemmatized texts to be included in the test set. They also want to thank Federica Gamba (Charles University, Prague, Czech Republic) for the complete annotation of the *De Latinae Linguae Reparatione*, and Timo Korkiakangas (University of Helsinki, Finland) for having made it possible and permitted its distribution.

9. Bibliographical References

Bamman, D. and Crane, G. (2011). The Ancient Greek and Latin Dependency Treebanks. In Caroline Sporleder, et al., editors, *Language technology for cultural heritage*, Theory and Applications of Natural Language Processing, pages 79–98. Springer, Berlin - Heidelberg, Germany.

Clark, K., Luong, M.-T., Le, Q. V., and Manning, C. D. (2020). Electra: Pre-training text encoders as discriminators rather than generators. In *Proceedings of the International Conference on Learning Representations 2020 (ICLR)*.

Conneau, A., Khandelwal, K., Goyal, N., Chaudhary, V., Wenzek, G., Guzmán, F., Grave, É., Ott, M., Zettlemoyer, L., and Stoyanov, V. (2020). Unsupervised cross-lingual representation learning at scale. In *Proceedings of the 58th Annual Meeting of the Association for Computational Linguistics*, pages 8440–8451.

de Marneffe, M.-C., Manning, C. D., Nivre, J., and Zeman, D. (2021). Universal Dependencies. *Computational Linguistics*, 47(2):255–308, 07.

Denooz, J. (2004). Opera Latina: une base de données sur internet. *Euphrosyne*, 32:79–88.

Mercelis, W. and Keersmaekers, A. (2022). An electra model for latin token tagging tasks. In *Proceedings of LT4HALA 2022-2st Workshop on Language Technologies for Historical and Ancient Languages*.

Passarotti, M., Mambrini, F., Franzini, G., Cecchini, F. M., Litta, E., Moretti, G., Ruffolo, P., and Sprugnoli, R. (2020). Interlinking through lemmas. the lexical collection of the lila knowledge base of linguistic resources for latin. *Studi e Saggi Linguistici*, LVIII(1):177–212.

Petrov, S., Das, D., and McDonald, R. (2011). A Universal Part-of-Speech Tagset. *ArXiv e-prints*. arXiv:1104.2086 at https://arxiv.org/abs/1104.2086.

Philippart de Foy, C., (2014). LASLA – *Nouveau manuel de lemmatisation du latin*. LASLA, Liège, Belgium.

Straka, M., Hajic, J., and Straková, J. (2016). UDPipe: trainable pipeline for processing CoNLL-U files performing tokenization, morphological analysis, PoS tagging and parsing. In *Proceedings of the Tenth International Conference on Language Resources and Evaluation (LREC'16)*, pages 4290–4297.

Wróbel, K. and Nowak, K. (2022). Transformer-based part-of-speech tagging and lemmatization for latin. In *Proceedings of LT4HALA 2022-2st Workshop on Language Technologies for Historical and Ancient Languages*.

Xue, L., Barua, A., Constant, N., Al-Rfou, R., Narang, S., Kale, M., Roberts, A., and Raffel, C. (2022). Byt5: Towards a token-free future with pre-trained byte-to-byte models. *Transactions of the Association for Computational Linguistics*, 10:291–306.

Zeman, D., Hajič, J., Popel, M., Potthast, M., Straka, M., Ginter, F., Nivre, J., and Petrov, S. (2018). CoNLL 2018 shared task: Multilingual parsing from raw text to Universal Dependencies. In *Proceedings of the CoNLL 2018 Shared Task: Multilingual Parsing from Raw Text to Universal Dependencies*, pages 1–21, Brussels, Belgium, October. Association for Computational Linguistics.

[18] https://lta.bbaw.de

Proceedings of the Second Workshop on Language Technologies for Historical and Ancient Languages (LT4HALA 2022), pages 189–192
Language Resources and Evaluation Conference (LREC 2022), Marseille, 25 June 2022

An ELECTRA Model for Latin Token Tagging Tasks

Wouter Mercelis, Alek Keersmaekers
KU Leuven / Brepols Publishers - CTLO, KU Leuven
KU Leuven: Blijde-Inkomststraat 21, B-3000 Leuven, Belgium
Brepols Publishers - CTLO: Begijnhof 39, B-2300 Turnhout, Belgium
{wouter.mercelis, alek.keersmaekers}@kuleuven.be

Abstract

This report describes the KU Leuven / Brepols-CTLO submission to EvaLatin 2022. We present the results of our current small Latin ELECTRA model, which will be expanded to a larger model in the future. For the lemmatization task, we combine a neural token-tagging approach with the in-house rule-based lemma lists from Brepols' ReFlex software. The results are decent, but suffer from inconsistencies between Brepols' and EvaLatin's definitions of a lemma. For POS-tagging, the results come up just short from the first place in this competition, mainly struggling with proper nouns. For morphological tagging, there is much more room for improvement. Here, the constraints added to our Multiclass Multilabel model were often not tight enough, causing missing morphological features. We will further investigate why the combination of the different morphological features, which perform fine on their own, leads to issues.

Keywords: ELECTRA, lemmatization, POS-tagging, morphological tagging, morphological features, token tagging

1. Introduction

This short report describes the systems developed by the KU Leuven / Brepols-CTLO team for the EvaLatin 2022 Evaluation Campaign. The first section will describe the language model that is used in all three tasks. Subsequently, the three tasks (lemmatization, POS-tagging and morphological tagging) are discussed, each divided in subsections concerning the followed methodology, the results and a discussion of these results.

2. Language Model

We pretrained a custom Latin ELECTRA-model[1] (Clark et al., 2020), using Brepols' Library of Latin Texts[2] as training data (160M tokens). ELECTRA models maintain the same basic computational architecture as BERT models (Devlin et al., 2018). While they are computationally less expensive, they nevertheless achieve better results, due to a more efficient training approach. This makes them particularly suited to training models with comparatively less amounts of data. In the future, we will train a larger Latin ELECTRA model with more training data, continuing the pioneering work of Bamman and Burns' Latin-BERT (Bamman and Burns, 2020).

3. Lemmatization

3.1. Methodology

For the lemmatization task, we combined a rule-based gazetteer approach (in which handcrafted rules provide lists of possible word forms for each lemma) with a neural token tagging task. Using a rule-based approach, Brepols provided a system (ReFlex) that generates all possible forms for each lemma in their database. As a first step in our lemmatization system, ReFlex returns for each token in the lemmatization task the corresponding lemmata. If there is only one possibility, no further action is needed. Otherwise, we predict the POS-tag of the token as described in the next section, and use this POS-tag to resolve the existing ambiguity, returning the lemma with the matching POS-tag. For the remaining ambiguous tokens, we had to make a pragmatic decision, as it is not feasible to train a separate classifier for each of the remaining tokens. Therefore, we trained one classifier on choosing the right lemma out of the list of possible lemmata that ReFlex returned, using the Huggingface Transformers implementation of ElectraForTokenClassification[3]. For example, if ReFlex returned 3 possible lemmata for a token, e.g. two nouns and a verb, we would assign them the labels n1, n2 and v1 respectively. The task of the classifier consists of predicting which label is needed in the current context, and thus returning the right lemma. This is not an optimal solution, as there is no linguistic reason why a certain lemma would be first or second in the ReFlex list. However, this approach is needed to make a decision between, for example, two or three nouns, as the disambiguation based on the POS-tag is impossible in this scenario. Based on the validation data, our approach was successful concerning nouns, but fails when faced with multiple verbs as possible lemmata. Lastly, a few manual rules were written based on a run on validation data, for example converting abbreviated praenomina to their spelled out counterparts.

[1] In the future, our pretrained Latin ELECTRA-model will be uploaded to Huggingface Transformers.

[2] See Brepols' Library of Latin Texts.

[3] For this specific implementation, see ElectraForTokenClassification on Huggingface Transformers

In the same vein, ReFlex returned the original adjective when processing an adjectival adverb, while the EvaLatin dataset expects the adjectival adverb itself as the predicted lemma. We adopted the following rule to circumvent this problem: if the POS-tag is ADV, ReFlex does not return its normal lemma, but the associated adverb.

3.2. Results

The results of the lemmatization task are described in Table 1.

KU Leuven / Brepols-CTLO closed	LEMMATIZATION
Ab Urbe Condita (classical)	85.44
Metamorphoseon (cross-genre)	87.22
Naturalis Historia (cross-genre)	85.75
De Latinae Linguae Reparatione (cross-time)	84.60

Table 1: Results of the lemmatization task

3.3. Discussion

While it is clear that our system performs worse than our competitors (Sprugnoli et al., 2022), this can be at least partly attributed to differences in defining a lemma. As mentioned in the previous section, we had to implement manual rules to make sure that the ReFlex lemmata were consistent with EvaLatin lemmata. This was done based on frequent mistakes while tagging a validation dataset (20% of the provided training dataset). However, due to time constraints, it was not feasible to remove all these inconsistencies. It comes apparent, for example, that EvaLatin prefers the plural form as a lemma for demonyms such as *Allobroges*, *Samnites*, *Romani*, while ReFlex resorts to the singular *Allobrox*, *Samnis* and *Romanus*. A second problem are the so-called deponent verbs, where EvaLatin prefers the passive form as a lemma, while ReFlex returns the active form, even if this form is only attested once (otherwise, ReFlex also gives the passive form). Likewise, EvaLatin takes *fio* ("I become") as a separate lemma, while ReFlex considers it the passive form of *facio* ("I make"). Thirdly, ReFlex will always return the original verb when faced with adjectival participles such as *iratus* ("angered"), *tutus* ("guarded") and *excellens* ("towering"), while EvaLatin chooses the adjective in these cases. Finally, the relative pronoun *quis* was consistently tagged as *qui*, while the ablative *quo* (with lemma *qui* in EvaLatin) was tagged as *quo* by ReFlex as if it were an adverb ("where"). These relative pronoun errors make up 6,3 % of the lemmatization errors, which is a significant amount. In the future, we will take the frequency of a lemma into account, to avoid situations in which a very common word such as *cum* ("with", "when") is lemmatized as an infrequent lemma *Cous* ("of Cos", "Coan").

4. POS-tagging

4.1. Methodology

Our POS-tagging system is very straightforward: we trained a Huggingface Transformers ElectraForTokenClassification model on the provided datasets. Based on our own previous experiments with inflectional languages, we decided to make one modification. As most modern language models do, ELECTRA models make use of a subword tokenizer, which processes frequent forms as one token and splits less common forms into smaller subwords, e.g. *amat* ("he/she loves") is tokenized as *amat*, while *amabamini* ("you were loved") becomes *ama #bam #ini*. Thus, an important step consists of determining on which subword of the complete word the actual token tagging will take place. Usually, a tagger uses the embedding of the first subword, or the average of all the subwords. Our system uses the last subword of a token, as crucial morphological information is stored in the last part of the word, because Latin is an inflectional language (Ács et al., 2021). In the future, we will further experiment with other, more advanced subword pooling techniques, as discussed in Ács et al. Ács et al. (2021).

4.2. Results

The results of the POS-tagging task are described in Table 2.

KU Leuven / Brepols-CTLO closed	POS-TAGGING
Ab Urbe Condita (classical)	96.33
Metamorphoseon (cross-genre)	94.66
Naturalis Historia (cross-genre)	89.96
De Latinae Linguae Reparatione (cross-time)	92.11

Table 2: Results of the POS-tagging task

4.3. Discussion

The results show that our system performs well, coming just short of the results of our competitors in the EvaLatin campaign. In 52,7 % of the mistakes on the test set, PROPN is either the gold label that gets a different tag, or PROPN is wrongly predicted instead of the correct tag. Many of the latter are geographical adjectives such as *Romanus* that can also be used as nouns. Furthermore, less frequent words with non-Latin roots such as *psitthachoras* (a certain kind of tree) are often tagged as PROPN as well, probably because of the similarity with Greek personal names. This type of words is especially frequent in Pliny, describing various plants etc. Secondly, the aforementioned problem concerning the distinction between adjectives and participles (and thus, verbs) explains some mistakes in this task as well.

5. Morphological tagging

5.1. Methodology

Rather than predicting all the features at once, which causes issues of data sparsity on the one hand, and a large amount of labels on the other hand, we trained a separate classifier for each of the morphological features defined in the dataset. Next, we calculated the probability of the full morphological tag as the product of the probabilities of the individual features: e.g. P(Case=Gen—InflClass=IndEurO—Number=Sing) is defined as P(Case=Gen) * P(InflClass=IndEurO) * P(Number=Sing). This is similar to the approach used by RFTagger (Schmid and Laws, 2008) and is defined by Tkachenko and Sirts Tkachenko and Sirts (2018) as the Multiclass Multilabel model. For this, we used the same architecture as discussed before in the POS-tagging section. Afterwards, we combine the predicted labels into one tag. Rather than taking a naive approach (taking the highest-scoring prediction for each feature and combining them, without constraints), which can lead to impossible combinations (such as adjectives receiving a mood feature), we predefine a set of possible combinations of tags, which act as constraints on the output of our system. These tag combinations are mostly based on POS-tags (e.g. interjections do not have any morphological features), but are sometimes more fine-grained, particularly for verbs as there are different rules needed to distinguish, for example, finite verbs and participles. Combining this approach with a lexicon of tags that occur in the training data ensures that no impossible predictions are formed.

5.2. Results

The results of the morphological tagging task are described in Table 3.

KU Leuven / Brepols-CTLO closed	MORPHOLOGICAL TAGGING
Ab Urbe Condita (classical)	69.91
Metamorphoseon (cross-genre)	63.06
Naturalis Historia (cross-genre)	58.04
De Latinae Linguae Reparatione (cross-time)	60.09

Table 3: Results of the morphological tagging task

5.3. Discussion

The results of this task are rather disappointing. A big part in this is played by exceptions, which we will illustrate with an example. In the test data, we find instances of the word *opus*, with only InflClass=IndEurInd as a morphological feature. This is an exception to the usual morphological features of a noun, which involve an InflClass, a Case and a Number. However, to accommodate our ruleset in such a way that the exceptions are handled as well, we have to allow nouns to only have a IndEurInd feature. As such, our constraint-based system is weakened by these few exceptions, leading to mistakes where the Number feature for example, is mistakenly omitted. Furthermore, morphologically identical features, such as the nominative and accusative for neuter words, have considerably more errors than features that are morphologically different. This is already apparent while training the data: on the validation data we see that there are 317 nominatives falsely tagged as accusatives, compared to only 17 falsely tagged datives and 34 genitives (8786 nominatives received the right tag). Currently, we are looking into better ways of combining the different tags, as our separate morphological feature classifiers are performing considerably better than the sum of their parts.

6. Conclusion

In this report, we described the first steps in using an ELECTRA model for Latin token tagging tasks. In the future, we will train a larger model on the one hand, and refine our system on the other hand, especially with regards to the morphological tagging task.

7. Acknowledgements

Our work has been funded by grant no. HBC.2021.0210 of Flanders Innovation and Entrepreneurship.

8. Bibliographical References

Ács, J., Kádár, Á., and Kornai, A. (2021). Subword pooling makes a difference. *CoRR*, abs/2102.10864.

Schmid, H. and Laws, F. (2008). Estimation of conditional probabilities with decision trees and an application to fine-grained POS tagging. In *Proceedings of the 22nd International Conference on Computational Linguistics (Coling 2008)*, pages 777–784, Manchester, UK, August. Coling 2008 Organizing Committee.

Sprugnoli, R., Passarotti, M., Cecchini, F. M., Fantoli, M., and Moretti, G. (2022). Overview of the evalatin 2022 evaluation campaign. In Rachele Sprugnoli et al., editors, *Proceedings of the LT4HALA 2022 Workshop - 2nd Workshop on Language Technologies for Historical and Ancient Languages, satellite event to the Twelfth International Conference on Language Resources and Evaluation (LREC 2022)*, Paris, France, June. European Language Resources Association (ELRA).

Tkachenko, A. and Sirts, K. (2018). Modeling composite labels for neural morphological tagging. In *Proceedings of the 22nd Conference on Computational Natural Language Learning*, pages 368–379, Brussels, Belgium, October. Association for Computational Linguistics.

9. Language Resource References

Bamman, D. and Burns, P. J. (2020). Latin BERT: A contextual language model for classical philology. *CoRR*, abs/2009.10053.

Kevin Clark and Minh-Thang Luong and Quoc V. Le and Christopher D. Manning. (2020). *ELECTRA: Pre-training Text Encoders as Discriminators Rather Than Generators.*

Devlin, J., Chang, M., Lee, K., and Toutanova, K. (2018). BERT: pre-training of deep bidirectional transformers for language understanding. *CoRR*, abs/1810.04805.

Proceedings of the Second Workshop on Language Technologies for Historical and Ancient Languages (LT4HALA 2022), pages 193–197
Language Resources and Evaluation Conference (LREC 2022), Marseille, 25 June 2022

Transformer-based Part-of-Speech Tagging and Lemmatization for Latin

Krzysztof Wróbel[1,2], Krzysztof Nowak[3]
[1]Jagiellonian University, , [2]Enelpol, [3]Institute of Polish Language (Polish Academy of Sciences)
krzysztof@wrobel.pro, krzysztof.nowak@ijp.pan.pl

Abstract

The paper presents a submission to the EvaLatin 2022 shared task. Our system places first for lemmatization, part-of-speech and morphological tagging in both closed and open modalities. The results for cross-genre and cross-time sub-tasks show that the system handles the diachronic and diastratic variation of Latin. The architecture employs state-of-the-art transformer models. For part-of-speech and morphological tagging, we use XLM-RoBERTa large, while for lemmatization a ByT5 small model was employed. The paper features a thorough discussion of part-of-speech and lemmatization errors which shows how the system performance may be improved for Classical, Medieval and Neo-Latin texts.

Keywords: part-of-speech tagging, lemmatization, morphosyntactic tagging, Latin, transformers

1. Introduction

The performance of lemmatization and part-of-speech tagging tools is essential for Latin as it is for all historical languages. Due to relative scarcity of annotated data, newly developed tools may be expected to be effective or at least adaptable to handle Classical, Medieval, and Neo-Latin, despite the fact that their use spans over more than 15 centuries. The recent advancements in NLP technology along with increasing availability of large language models have opened new venues for computational Latin linguistics.

Corpus		Tokens	Sentences	Avg
EVALATIN 2022				
TRAIN		320 355	15 785	20.29
TEST	Classical	13 248	385	34.41
TEST	Cross-genre	22 086	1 329	16.62
TEST	Cross-time	9 174	246	37.29
EVALATIN 2020				
TEST	Cross-genre	13 290	597	22.26
TEST	Cross-time	11 556	883	13.09
UD LATIN[1]		977 722	58 405	16.74
LASLA[2]		1 728 933	92 170	18.76

Table 1: Corpora used in the study

In this paper, we present our submission to the EvaLatin 2022 shared task (Sprugnoli et al., 2022). First, we briefly characterize the task, focusing on specific challenges the texts included in the test dataset posed. Next, we provide a detailed description of our system and describe its two modalities. Additionally, we show what data were used to enhance the performance of the open variant of the model and provide a thorough analysis of lemmatization and part-of-speech errors. We believe that the present system may be further adapted to address challenges of linguistic annotation of the Medieval and Neo-Latin texts.

2. Training and Test Data

The training dataset of the EvaLatin 2022 shared task contains prosaic texts of five authors composed between the 1st century BC and the beginning of the 2nd century AD. The test dataset includes works which represent various genres and periods of the Latin literature history. The CLASSICAL subtask consists of the VIIIth book of Livy's *Ab urbe condita*, a work which is arguably closest to the training data. Two texts in the CROSS-GENRE sub-task differ from the training data in their literary form and subject domain. The VIIIth and IXth books of the Ovid's epic poem contain narratives of Greek mythology. Pliny the Elder's *Naturalis Historia*, on the other hand, is an encyclopedic work in prose whose XXXVIIth book discusses properties of gemstones. Both texts contain a significant number of words of Greek origin: person and place names in case of *Metamorphoses* and rare terms regarding mineralogy in case of Pliny. The only text included in the CROSS-TIME sub-task dataset is the *De Latinae Linguae Reparatione*, a Renaissance dialogue on history by Marcus Antonius Coccius Sabellicus (†1504). The major challenge seems to be its non-Classical orthography and a number of post-Classical proper names.

3. System Description

Our architecture is based on transformer models, as they are state-of-the-art in part-of-speech tagging and lemmatization. It builds on a morphosyntactic tagger KFTT (Wróbel, 2020) which won the PolEval 2020 task 1 competition (*Morphosyntactic tagging of Middle, New and Modern Polish*) and uses a transformer model contrary to its RNN-based predecessor KRNNT (Wróbel, 2017).

[2]UD corpora include 5 Latin treebanks in the Universal Dependencies format (Zeman, 2022).

[2]The LASLA corpus (Denooz, 2007) linked to the LiLa LemmaBank (Fantoli et al., 2022).

Task	Phase	UD Latin	LASLA	EvaLatin '22 Train	EvaLatin '20 X-Genre	EvaLatin '20 X-Time
POS	1	+	+		+	+
	2			+		
Feats	1	+				
	2			+		
Lemmatization	1	+	+		+	+
	2			+	+	+

Table 2: Corpora used in the *open modality* system

Part-of-speech and morphologic tagging are addressed with a transformer encoder model with a token classification head on top. The transformer, first, returns contextual embeddings of each token; next, a linear layer with softmax activation returns normalized scores for each tag seen in training.

In the lemmatization task, the system uses information about predicted parts of speech, but it does not use context of a word. It is solved with sequence to sequence model with input constructed as a word form and predicted part of speech.

In the *open modality* variant of the system, in which external resources can be employed (see Table 2), our models are first trained on a set of corpora that were annotated following different guidelines than the ones adopted in the present competition. In the next phase, the models are re-trained on the EvaLatin 2022 training dataset. Detailed information on each corpus can be consulted in the Table 1. The performance of the system in each task was evaluated using micro-averaged accuracy. 5% of the EvaLatin 2022 training data were used for validation.

For the POS and Feats tasks we used XLM-RoBERTa large (Conneau et al., 2020) – a multilingual encoder. Model training parameters were:

- batch size: 12
- epochs: 10,
- learning rate: 2e-5,
- sequence length: 256.

Lemmatization was performed with ByT5 small model (Xue et al., 2022) whose input are separate bytes of text. Initial experiments with subword models (e.g. mT5 (Xue et al., 2021)) showed worse accuracy. Model training parameters were the following:

- batch size: 128,
- epochs: 5,
- input sequence length: 48,
- output sequence length: 24,
- learning rate: 0.001.

In the *open modality* for the PoS and Feats tasks first training is performed for 2 epochs without early stopping.

All models here described are publicly available.[3]

[3]`https://huggingface.co/enelpol/`

4. Results

Our system performed best in every task in the competition. In the *closed modality* variant, it was ahead of the second best architecture by 0.9%-4.5% in the PoS task, by 25.5%-31.9% in the Feats task, and by 4.4%-11.0% in the Lemmatization task (Table 3).

Since the system is expected to be employed in Medieval and Neo-Latin corpus projects, it was essential to examine its performance in qualitative terms as well (Nowak et al., 2016). Therefore, we carefully analyzed tagging errors (1) to assess the impact of additional training data on the performance in the *open modality* and (2) to get insight into major challenges that language variation poses to the system. Due to space limitations, however, we only briefly discuss the results of the Lemmatization and PoS task.

4.1. Part-of-Speech Tagging

All texts combined, the PoS tagging errors affect in particular nominal categories, with `ADJ`s misclassified as `NOUN`s or `PROPN`s, `NOUN`s as `ADJ`s, and `VERB`s as `ADJ`s (see Figure 1). The error distribution varies slightly between sub-tasks and modalities.

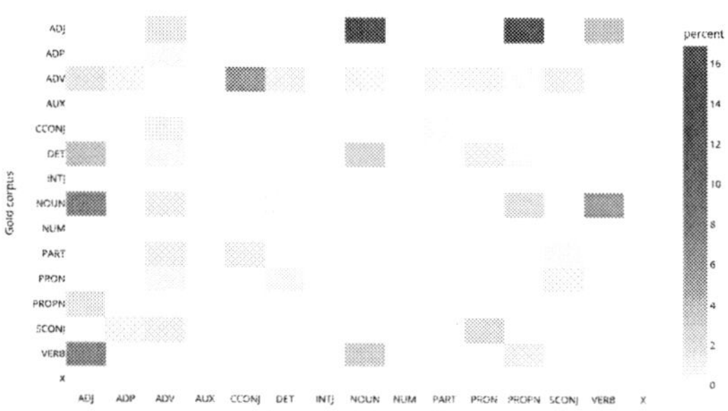

Figure 1: PoS Tagging: Confusion Matrix (*closed* and *open modalities*)

Generally, in the open version of our system, the quality of the PoS tagging improves significantly. The analysis shows (see Figure 2) that the use of annotated resources helps to distinguish `NOUN`s, `PROPN`s, `VERB`s from `ADJ`s. We discuss major improvements below.

ADJ ↔ NOUN In both CLASSICAL and CROSS-GENRE sub-tasks, using supplementary

			KU-Leuven	Cracovia	
			closed	closed	open
CLASSICAL	Livy	POS	96.33	97.61	**97.99**
		Lemma	85.44	96.45	**97.26**
		Feats	69.91	95.42	**95.46**
CROSS-GENRE	Ovid	POS	94.66	94.78	**96.78**
		Lemma	87.22	93.05	**96.03**
		Feats	63.06	88.70	**88.81**
	Pliny	POS	89.96	94.47	**95.35**
		Lemma	85.75	90.19	**94.13**
		Feats	58.04	89.95	**90.06**
CROSS-TIME	Sabellicus	POS	92.11	**92.97**	92.70
		Lemma	84.60	91.68	**92.15**
		Feats	60.09	**86.53**	86.50

Table 3: Performance of the Cracovia system for POS, Lemmatization, and Feats tagging task

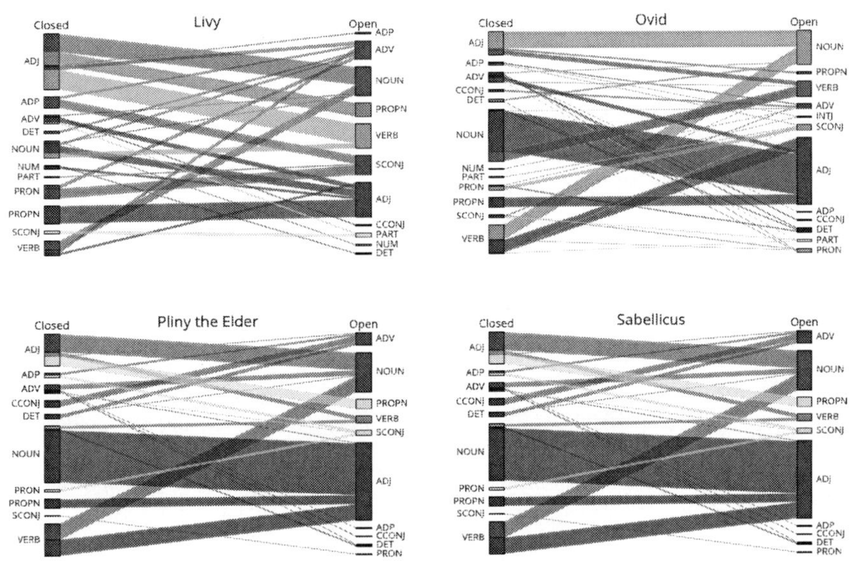

Figure 2: POS Tagging: Closed v. Open Modality

annotated resources leads to better discrimination between homonymous forms of nouns and adjectives, such as *iuuenis* 'young' : 'a young person', *securus*.ADJ 'safe' : *securis*.NOUN 'an axe' or *sacer*.ADJ 'sacred' : *sacrum*.NOUN 'a holy thing'. In the open modality, correct lemmas are assigned, for instance, to Greek-origin terms such as †*synechitus*.ADJ → *synechitis*.NOUN 'a kind of gemstone' or †*iaspidus*.ADJ → *iaspidis*.NOUN 'jasper'.

The improvement is noticeable the other way around, too. Part-of-speech labels are amended for words which were assigned either correct (†*edax*.NOUN → *edax*.ADJ 'edacious') or incorrect lemmas (†*femineum*.NOUN → *femineus*.ADJ 'feminine') in the closed modality.

PROPN ↔ ADJ Additional training data in the *open* variant of our system improves considerably the distinction between homonymous PROPN and ADJ in all but the CROSS-TIME sub-tasks. The improvement concerns both frequent lexical units, such as *Romanus*.PROPN : *Romanus*.ADJ 'Roman', and less frequent words, such as *Phlaegreus*.PROPN → *Phlaegreus*.ADJ 'of Phlegra'. Likewise, ethnonyms are usually better distinguished from homonymous adjectives: *Persus*.ADJ 'Persian' → *Persae*.PROPN 'Persians' or *Campanus*.ADJ 'of Campania' → *Campani*.PROPN 'Campanians'.

VERB ↔ NOUN, ADJ The open variant of the system reduces considerably the number of incorrect idiosyncratic annotations, such as *supero*.VERB 'surmount' instead of *superi*.NOUN for *superi* 'the gods', †*uitro*.VERB instead of *uitrum* 'glass'.NOUN for *uitri*,

or †*sideo*.VERB instead of *siderita*.NOUN 'a kind of gemstone' for *sideritis*. It also leads to improved annotation of deverbal nouns, such as *sectura* 'a cut', *partus* 'a birth', which in the closed version were misclassified as VERB forms of *resp. seco* 'to cut' and *pario* 'to bring forth,'.
For Livy's and Ovid's works, the open variant performs better in labelling participles as VERBs rather than NOUNs. It also improves recognition of verb forms in the *Metamorphoses*: *sileo*.VERB 'to keep silence' for *sileam* or *auguror*.VERB 'to augur' for *auguror*. In the closed modality, these first-person forms, untypical of prosaic discourse, are misclassified as †*auguror*.NOUN and †*silea*.NOUN.

4.2. Lemmatization

It comes of no surprise that the open variant of our system improves lemmatization results, as both lemmatization and part-of-speech tagging are closely related tasks and depend one on another.
In the CLASSICAL sub-task, for example, a number of proper nouns unseen in the training dataset are correctly lemmatized, such as *Samnites*, *Samnium*, *Samnis*, *Priuernum*, *Latium*, *Antium*, *Antiati etc.* In the CROSS-GENRE sub-task, on the other hand, the open variant of the system assigns correct lemmas to words of Greek origin related to mythology (Ovid: *heros*, *nympha*, *thalamus*) and mineralogy (Pliny: *smaragdus*, *crystallus*, *sardonyx*), as well as to proper names (Ovid: *Alcmene*, *Iphis*, *Byblis*, *Dryope*).
Correct lemmas are also reached for a number of words which occur frequently in the test data, but (1) are rare or absent from the training dataset (Ovid: *lilium* or Pliny: *gutta*); (2) present phonetic assimilation unseen in the training dataset (*traluceo* : *transluceo*); or (3) have alternative spellings (*etiam nunc* : *etiamnunc*).
In the CROSS-TIME sub-task, the open variant of our system improves significantly the lemmatization of words which display post-classical or non-standard orthography that is not accounted for in the training dataset. Correct lemmas are assigned to word forms such as:

- qu-/c-: *quum* → *cum*
- -n-/-m-: *tanquam* → *tamquam*
- -ae-/-e-: *pene* → *paene*

Likewise, a number of proper nouns, both attested and not attested in Classical texts, are correctly lemmatized in the open modality (for instance *Laurentius*, *Lactantius*, *Strabo*, *Plato etc.*).
Despite using supplementary annotated data in the open modality, a number of lemmatization errors persist (4). They include among others:

- *sui* 'their *etc.* (*sc.* friends, followers)' is frequently misclassified as *suus*.DET;
- ethnonyms, which are either assigned lemmas in singular rather than plural (e.g. *uolscus* instead of *uolsci*) or are confused with adjectives (e.g. *carchedonii*.PROPN instead of *carchedonius*.ADJ);
- homonymous forms of low-frequency words, such as *pedum*.PROPN 'a town in Latium' (incorrectly lemmatized as *pes*.NOUN 'a foot') or almost full homonym pairs, such as *aer* 'the air' : *aes* '(any) base metal'.

Classical	Cross-genre		Cross-time
	Ovid	Pliny	
quis	quis	indicus	maior
sui	aer	indi	multus
priuernates	amans	quis	minus
pedum	refero	crystallus	fama
uolsci	quo	sarda	latinus
latini	carus	sestertius	melior
triarius	lotos	margarita	adsum
apuli	ora	uisus	maxime
philo	ausum	carchedonius	epistula
comitia	superus	quod	aliqui

Table 4: 10 most confused lemmas for each task

Some lemmatization choices may also be considered arbitrary and thus should not be expected to be correctly predicted by the tagger. This is the case, for instance, of *hyacinthos* instead of *hyacinthus* or *myrrha* instead of *murra*.
Finally, the last group of tagging errors results from the non-classical orthography employed in Sabellicus' work. However, poor results of the system in the closed modality might have been expected, since the training dataset does not account for spelling variation of Medieval or Neo-Latin texts:

- -o-/-u-: *epistola* → *epistula*
- -ph-/-f-: *phama* → *fama*
- -ci-/-ti-: *ocium* → *otium*
- -oe-/-e-: *foelix* → *felix*

5. Conclusions

The system presented in this paper outperforms competing architecture in lemmatization, part-of-speech and morphological tagging of Latin texts. It handles well the diachronic and diastratic variation of the language whose range of uses and coverage may be compared only to contemporary English. The open variant of the architecture improves significantly the results of both lemmatization and PoS tagging, leaving only small group of specific issues to persist in the resulting data.
Future work can focus on training language models on unlabeled Latin texts instead of using multilingual models, using context for lemmatization, and combining models into one for all tasks. The error analysis shows that careful selection of training data should help in addressing most if not all problems related to

spelling variation, unseen proper names and domain-specific terminology. The use of curated lexical resources should permit to reach preferred lemma labels for the convenience of the linguistic community. The system may be, then, hoped to perform well in a large-scale annotation of Medieval and Neo-Latin texts (Nowak, 2022).

6. Acknowledgments

This work was supported by the PLGrid Infrastructure and by the grant of the Polish Ministry of Science *eFontes. The Electronic Corpus of Polish Medieval Latin* (11H 17 0116 85).

7. Bibliographical References

Conneau, A., Khandelwal, K., Goyal, N., Chaudhary, V., Wenzek, G., Guzmán, F., Grave, E., Ott, M., Zettlemoyer, L., and Stoyanov, V. (2020). Unsupervised Cross-lingual Representation Learning at Scale. In *Proceedings of the 58th Annual Meeting of the Association for Computational Linguistics*, pages 8440–8451, Online, July. Association for Computational Linguistics.

Denooz, J. (2007). Opera latina: le nouveau site internet du LASLA. *Journal of Latin Linguistics*, 9(3), jan.

Nowak, K., Bon, B., and Alexandre, R. (2016). Medialatinitas. Pour une intégration superficielle de ressources textuelles et lexicales en latin. In Damon Mayaffre, et al., editors, *JADT 2016. Journées Internationales d'Analyse Statistique Des Données Textuelles*, Nice, France. Presses de FacImprimeur.

Sprugnoli, R., Passarotti, M., Cecchini, F. M., Fantoli, M., and Moretti, G. (2022). Overview of the EvaLatin 2022 Evaluation Campaign. In Rachele Sprugnoli et al., editors, *Proceedings of the LT4HALA 2022 Workshop - 2nd Workshop on Language Technologies for Historical and Ancient Languages, satellite event to the Twelfth International Conference on Language Resources and Evaluation (LREC 2022)*, Paris, France, June. European Language Resources Association (ELRA).

Wróbel, K. (2017). KRNNT : Polish recurrent neural network tagger. In Zygmunt Vetulani et al., editors, *Human language technologies as a challenge for computer science and linguistics : 8th language & technology conference : November 17-19, 2017, Poznań, Poland : proceedings*, pages 386–391. Fundacja Uniwersytetu im. Adama Mickiewicza, Poznań.

Wróbel, K. (2020). Kftt : Polish full neural morphosyntactic tagger. In Maciej Ogrodniczuk et al., editors, *Proceedings of the PolEval 2020 Workshop*, pages 47–53. Institute of Computer Sciences, Polish Academy of Sciences, Warszawa.

Xue, L., Constant, N., Roberts, A., Kale, M., Al-Rfou, R., Siddhant, A., Barua, A., and Raffel, C. (2021). mT5: A massively multilingual pre-trained text-to-text transformer. In *Proceedings of the 2021 Conference of the North American Chapter of the Association for Computational Linguistics: Human Language Technologies*, pages 483–498, Online, June. Association for Computational Linguistics.

Xue, L., Barua, A., Constant, N., Al-Rfou, R., Narang, S., Kale, M., Roberts, A., and Raffel, C. (2022). ByT5: Towards a Token-Free Future with Pre-trained Byte-to-Byte Models. *Transactions of the Association for Computational Linguistics*, 10:291–306, March.

8. Language Resource References

Margherita Fantoli and Marco Carlo Passarotti and Eleonora Maria Litta and Paolo Ruffolo and Giovanni Moretti. (2022). *Linking LASLA corpus - LiLa LemmaBank.*

Nowak, Krzysztof. (2022). *eFontes. The Electronic Corpus of Polish Medieval Latin.*

Zeman, Daniel et al. (2022). *Universal Dependencies 2.10.*

Author Index

Asahara, Masayuki, 31

Bellandi, Andrea, 59
Berti, Monica, 101
Biagetti, Erica, 26
Biffi, Marco, 94
Brigada Villa, Luca, 26

Cecchini, Flavio Massimiliano, 51, 183
Chang, Qinyu C., 155
Chang, Yu, 141
Corazza, Michele, 84

de Lhoneux, Miryam, 129
Dehouck, Mathieu, 38
Ding, Ruoyao, 150

Fantoli, Margherita, 129, 183
Favaro, Manuel, 94
Feng, Minxuan, 135
Ferrara, Silvia, 84
Fischer, Lukas, 43
Fu, Yingwen, 150

Gambardella, Maria-Elena, 1
Guadagnini, Elisa, 94
Guo, Yuhang, 146

Hellwig, Oliver, 10, 20
Hu, Baotian, 178
Huang, Shujian, 169

Ichimura, Taro, 31
Ikegami, Nao, 31

Jiang, Longjie, 155

Kato, Sachi, 31
Keersmaekers, Alek, 73, 189
Khan, Fahad, 59
Kondo, Asuko, 31

Li, Bin, 135
Li, Jiahuan, 169
Li, Si, 159
Lin, Boda, 159

Lu, Jingya, 135

Mallia, Michele, 59
Megyesi, Beata, 1
Menini, Stefano, 68
Mercelis, Wouter, 189
Montemagni, Simonetta, 94
Moretti, Giovanni, 183
Murano, Francesca, 59

Nehrdich, Sebastian, 20
Nowak, Krzysztof, 193

Palladino, Chiara, 101
Palmero Aprosio, Alessio, 68
Passarotti, Marco, 183
Pedonese, Giulia, 51
Pettersson, Eva, 1
Piccini, Silvia, 59
Prager, Christian, 114

QU, Weiguang, 135
Quochi, Valeria, 59

Ren, Zhichen, 164
Rigobianco, Luca, 59

Sassolini, Eva, 94
Scheurer, Patricia, 43
Schwitter, Raphael, 43
Sellmer, Sven, 10
Shaoqing, Zhang, 178
Shen, Yutong, 169
Sprugnoli, Rachele, 183
Suzuki, Tai, 31
Swanson, Daniel, 108

Tamburini, Fabio, 84
Tang, Binghao, 159
Tian, Yanzhi, 146
Tommasi, Alessandro, 59
Tonelli, Sara, 68
Torres Aguilar, Sergio, 119
Tyers, Francis, 108

Valério, Miguel, 84

Van Hal, Toon, 73
Vertan, Cristina, 114
Volk, Martin, 43

Wang, Chaofan, 141
Wang, Chaoping, 141
Wang, Dongbo, 135
Wang, Pengyu, 164
Weihao, liu, 178
Wright, David J., 101
Wróbel, Krzysztof, 193

Xia, Zhuying Z., 155
Xie, Huyin H., 155
Xie, Xiaopeng, 169
Xinyuan, Wei, 178
Xu, Chao, 135

Yamazaki, Makoto, 31
Yang, Shuxun, 174
Yang, Ziyu, 150
Yousef, Tariq, 101
Yuan, Yiguo, 135

Zanchi, Chiara, 26
Zavattari, Cesare, 59
Zhang, Hailin, 150
Zhao, Qinxin, 169
Zhou, Yi, 169
Zhu, Peng, 141
Zong, Qing, 178

Association for Computational Linguistics
209 N. Eighth Street
Stroudsburg, Pennsylvania 18360

ISBN 978-1-7138-6127-0

CURRAN ASSOCIATES INC. proceedings.com